B4A

Ultra-fast Android App Development using BASIC

By Wyken Seagrave

B4A: Ultra-fast Android App Development using BASIC

by Wyken Seagrave
Published by Penny Press Ltd
176 Greendale Road, Coventry
CV5 8AY, United Kingdom
sales@pennypress.co.uk

Edition History

December 2015   First Edition for Version 5-5

ISBN

9781871281309 (ebook)
9781871281316 (paperback)
9781871281323 (hardback)

Table of Contents

Foreword by Erel Uziel

I started developing Basic4ppc, a development tool for Pocket PC devices (later renamed to Windows Mobile) in 2005. It was a real challenge for me to build a new programming language and development environment. Five years later, when Microsoft decided to stop developing Windows Mobile in favor of a different platform, and with the first signs of the new Android operating system, I decided that it was time to change direction and B4A was born. I had a rare opportunity to go back to the drawing board and then, with the many lessons learnt from the previous project, build a powerful and simple development tool for native Android applications.

In the last three years, since the first release, B4A has improved dramatically. Today, B4A supports 99% of the advanced features of Android. Features such as NFC, Wifi-Direct, serial ports, graphics and many more are supported, and all of the features are designed to be simple to use yet powerful enough to meet your real-world requirements.

B4A is used by companies, organizations, educational institutes and individuals from all over the world. I honestly believe that B4A is the best development tool for native Android applications available today. B4A together with B4i and B4J allows developers to easily build native cross platform solutions.

Over the years, a very active on-line community has evolved around B4A. This community is the heart of B4A. In our forums, there are almost 200 thousand messages with questions, answers, examples, bugs, tutorials, classes and libraries. The ecosystem around B4A is huge.

Many customers have asked for a full, comprehensive book to help them with their own development. I was thrilled to hear that Wyken has taken on himself the challenging task of mapping this ecosystem. I'm happy to say that Wyken, an experienced software developer and author, has done a great job.

I'm sure that this book will help you to quickly get started with development of your own Android apps.

I'm looking forward to see you becoming part of our community!

Erel Uziel
CEO, Anywhere Software

Preface

Introduction

This book describes the features of and how to develop Android apps using B4A Version 5.5.

B4A is widely recognized as the simplest and most powerful Rapid App Development tool available for Android. It is used by tens of thousands of enthusiastic developers. A complete list of its features and benefits can be found here (http://bit.ly/1IjKiZB).

Who this Book is For

This book serves two audiences:

For the Beginner

For those new to B4A, new to BASIC, or even new to programming, this book contains step-by-step tutorials for the complete beginner. It explains everything you need to know to use this exciting and easy application development environment design to create and sell your app on Android devices in the shortest possible time without having to climb the steep learning curve of learning Java.

For the Professional

For experienced B4A developers, this book brings together a huge range of reference material never previously assembled in one place and organizes it into an easily accessible form. It contains all the key terms used by the core language and its official libraries. It includes examples to show how the code is used and links to further on-line information.

How this Book is Organized

Part 1 (page 43) – **Basics**
We begin with a tutorial which walks you gently through the process of installing the free Trial Version of B4A, connecting it to your device, then writing, running, designing and debugging your very first Android app.
We explain every feature of the Integrated Development Environment and show you how to upgrade to the Full Version of B4A. This will give you access to the Libraries discussed in Part 4.

Part 2 (page 109) – **Creating Your App**
Here we go in detail through the process of creating a real app, including the principles of design, how your app can communicate with the user, how you can use Designer Scripts or Anchors to automatically modify the layout of your app to suit different devices, and how to compile, debug and test your app using either real or virtual devices.
We discuss creating graphics and databases. We examine how processes, services and activities live and die in Android. We look at the various types of modules you can create, examine ways you can make money from your app and finally explore ways you can get more help in using B4A.

Part 3 (page 272) – **Language and Core Objects**
Parts 3 and 4 form the reference sections of this book.

Part 3 includes two chapters of reference material which cover every part of B4A's language
and core objects (that is, objects accessible from every app).

We also compare B4A's language with Microsoft's Visual Basic.

Part 4 (page 450) – **Libraries**
In this reference section we discuss libraries (only available if you have upgraded to the Full
Version of B4A), and explain how to create your own libraries and share them with others
(should you wish to).
We give full details of the Standard Libraries included in the Full Version installation. We
also discuss some of the many Additional Libraries and Modules, including all the "Official"
ones created by Anywhere Software, which you can download from the B4A website.

Conventions Used in this Book

Code
Examples of B4A code are shown indented, like this:

```
Sub Activity_Create(FirstTime As Boolean)
 Msgbox("Welcome to B4A!", "")
End Sub
```
Code within other text is usually shown with this font: `Sub Activity_Create`. However,
this is not always possible, since the electronic versions of this book include many links (to
make it easy to find related parts of the book), which overlap code and have a different font.
We also use the same font to highlight options in on-screen dialog boxes.

Specifying Menus
We specify menus within B4A by surrounded by [square brackets] and separating the parts
by a greater than symbol ">" and. So the following would be shown as [Edit > Copy]:

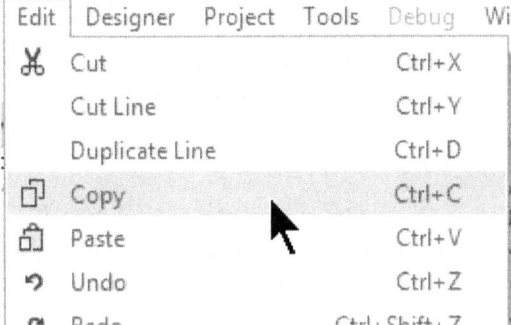

Specifying Functional Arguments
When we specify the types of the arguments which are used to call functions, we adopt a
different convention than that used in the B4A on-line documentation. On-line they include
the full path to the argument types, for example:

DrawBitmap (Bitmap1 As android.graphics.Bitmap, SrcRect As android.graphics.Rect, DestRect As android.graphics.Rect)

We find this difficult to read, so in this book we simply write:

DrawBitmap (Bitmap1 As Bitmap, SrcRect As Rect, DestRect As Rect)

The reason that the full paths are specified on-line is that B4A types, such as Bitmap, are actually "wrappers" for the full Java class. This allows for greater flexibility in extending the B4A language in the future. But in most cases you do not need to worry about this when developing your apps.

Acronyms

We use the following acronyms in this book:

ADB   Android Debug Bridge
AES-256   Advanced Encryption Standard
ANSI   American National Standards Institute
API   Application Program Interface
APK   Filename extension for Android Package
.APK   Android Package (filename extension)
ARGB   Alpha,Red,Green,Blue (Color Specification)
ASCII   American Standard Code for Information Interchange
AVD   Android Virtual Device
BA   A B4A object which library developers can use to raise events and to get access to the user activity, application context and other resources.
.BAS   Filename extension for BASic files
BASIC   Beginner's All-Purpose Symbolic Instruction Code
BOM   Byte Order Mark
C2DM   Cloud To Device Messaging
CPU   Central Processing Unit
CSV   Comma-Separated Values
DBMS   DataBase Management System
dip   density independent pixel
DOS   Disk Operating System
dp   density independent pixel (same as dip)
dpi   dots per inch
dps   density independent pixels (same as dip)
DSA   Digital Signature Algorithm
DTMF   Dual-tone multi-frequency
EAS   Embedded Audio Synthesizer
.EXE   Filename extension for an EXEcutable file
FTP   File Transfer Protocol
GMT   Greenwich Mean Time
GPS   Global Positioning System
GPU   Graphics Processing Unit
HD   High Definition
HDPI   High-density Dots Per Inch
HSV   Hue, Saturation and Value (Color Specification)
HTML   HyperText Markup Language

HTTP	HyperText Transfer Protocol
IDE	Integrated Development Environment
IME	Input Method Editor
IP	Internet Protocol (as in "IP address")
.JAR	File extension for Java ARchive
JDK	Java Development Kit
JET	The SONiVOX interactive music engine.
JSON (page 492)	JavaScript Object Notation
LDPI	Low-density Dots Per Inch
MAC	Media Access Control address of a device
MDPI	Medium-density Dots Per Inch
MIDI	Musical Instrument Digital Interface
MIME	Multi-Purpose Internet Mail Extensions
NDEF	NFC Data Exchange Format
NFC	Near-Field Communication
NMEA	National Marine Electronics Association
OEM	Original Equipment Manufacturer
OS	Operating System
PC	Personal Computer
.PNG	Filename extension for a Portable Network Graphic
POP3	Post Office Protocol 3
PPC	Pocket Personal Computer
PRN	Pseudo-Random Number
px	pixels (page 162)
RAM	Random Access Memory
RFCOMM	Radio Frequency COMMunication
RGB	Red,Green,Blue (Color Specification)
SAX	Simple API for XML
SD	Secure Digital
SDK	Software Development Kit
SFTP	SSH File Transfer Protocol or Secured File Transfer Protocol
SIM	Subscriber Identity Module
SIP	Session Initiation Protocol
SKU	Stock Keeping Unit
SMS	Short Message Service
SQL	Structured Query Language
SSH	Secure Shell Protocol
SSL	Secure Sockets Layer
TCP/IP	Transmission Control Protocol/Internet Protocol
TTS	Text to Speech
TTS	Text-To-Speech
UDP	User Datagram Protocol
UI	User Interface: the images, sounds, keyboards and other objects which allow the user to communicate with the device.
URI	Uniform Resource Identifier
URL	Uniform Resource Locator
USB	Universal Serial Bus

UTC	Coordinated Universal Time (equivalent to Greenwich Mean Time).
UTF-16	16-bit Universal Character Set Transformation Format
UTF-8	8-bit Universal Character Set Transformation Format
UUID	Universal Unique Identifier
VB6	Visual Basic 6.0
VM	Virtual Memory
VOIP	Voice Over Internet Protocol
WYSIWYG	What You See Is What You Get
XHDPI	Extra-High-density Dots Per Inch
XLS	Microsoft Excel Spreadsheet (File Extension)
XML	eXtensible Markup Language

Resources

Resources to support this book can be found here (http://bit.ly/1IjLiwC).
The main source of support is the active community of enthusiastic developers around the world who already use B4A and are very happy to support others who have problems.
See the Getting More Help Chapter (page 270) for details.

Free Upgrades

Customers who purchase an electronic version of this book from the Penny Press store are entitled to free upgrades when we introduce new editions to match changes in B4A. Sadly we cannot provide free upgrades to the paperback version. The upgrade website is here (http://bit.ly/1d5XjHo).

Newsletter

To receive notices about these upgrades to the electronic version and other news about this book, please subscribe (http://bit.ly/1IBc9lF) to the newsletter.

We'd Like to Hear from You

We hope you will enjoy this book and find it useful. Despite our best efforts, there may still be errors in this book. The publisher would be grateful if readers would send reports of them, together with any suggestions for improvements to future editions, to

b4a@pennypress.co.uk

Thank you.

We would also be very grateful if you would take the time to rate it on the main Amazon website: USA Amazon site (http://amzn.to/1Fm50Qr)

About the Author

Wyken Seagrave is a professional developer of applications and websites using Visual Basic, Visual Basic for Applications, PHP and MySQL, among other languages. He has taught computer programming at college and university, and written many user manuals for the applications he has developed.

His great passion in life is to bring knowledge of the history of the universe to a wider public. To this end he has written books and websites dealing with the subject both as fact and fiction, including the History of the Universe website (http://bit.ly/Qfdt36) (also available as an eBook on Amazon (http://amzn.to/1446HTw)) and the Time Crystal (http://bit.ly/OGsSuC) series.

Acknowledgements

Thanks to Erel Uziel and Anywhere Software for creating and supporting B4A, to Klaus Christl for his excellent documentation, to Bob Paehr for proof-reading the entire first edition and making many valuable suggestions, to Dave and Paul Holthuizen for pointing out a number of typos, and to the entire B4A user community for creating libraries and many other invaluable assets.

Wyken Seagrave

Part 1: Basics

We begin with a tutorial which walks you gently through the process of installing the free Trial Version of B4A, connecting it to your device, then writing, running, designing and debugging your very first Android app.

We explain every feature of the Integrated Development Environment.

Then we show you how to upgrade to the Full Version of B4A. This will give you access to the Libraries discussed in Part 4.

1.1 Getting Started

Note: B4A runs on PCs with Windows 2000 and above, including Windows 8. Both 32-bit and 64-bit systems are supported.

Versions

Version of B4A

This book covers the functionality of Version 5.50 of B4A.

Version of Android

The above version of B4A supports most features of all versions of Android up to and including 5.0 Lollipop. It also supports the file structures of the latest version of the Android SDK. See this section (page 182) for actions required to ensure your app is compatible with Android 5.0.

Two Versions

There are two versions of B4A: the Trial Version and the Full Version (page 102). The main differences are in brief:

Price: the trial version is FREE! The price of the full version depends upon which flavor you purchase.

Remote Compilation Mode (page 54): this feature, which makes compiling your apps simple and painless, only runs under the free trial. This means that if you are running the free version, you do not need to install the Java JDK and Android SDK packages (which are both required for local compilation), although you may if you wish. The full version only supports local compilation. This has the advantage of enabling features such as using an emulator, USB debugging and others. Note that B4A includes a Rapid Debugger (page 176) which can greatly shorten development times. You can use this feature with both the trial and full versions, but in both cases it requires that you install the Java JDK, even when you use Remote Compilation with the trial version.

Project Size: this is limited for the free version.

Duration: the free version only works for 30 days. The full version works indefinitely, although the time during which you receive free upgrades depends upon which licence you have purchased.

Advanced features: the full version supports libraries (page 451) and other advanced features missing from the trial.

What You Need to Run B4A

You will need a PC running Windows with at least 512 Mb of RAM.

You can test your app on either an emulator (page 188) (a virtual device running on your PC) or a real device. We recommend you have a real device available as it usually takes less time to install your app there than on an emulator and apps running there usually execute faster. If you use a real device it should be running Android 1.6 or above (that is Android 2.x, 3.x etc.).

Installing the Trial Version

In the tutorials, we assume you will be using the free trial version of B4A. We also assume you will not want to install the Java JDK to begin with, so we will postpone explanation of the Rapid Debugger (page 176) until Chapter 2.

Download B4A Trial

Download the latest version of the B4A Trial version from here (http://bit.ly/1IjMa4t).

Install and Run the Trial

Installing .NET Framework

B4A requires .Net Framework 4.5.2 on Windows Vista, or .Net Framework 4.0. on Windows XP. If the required Framework is not present on your machine, you will be prompted to download and install it.

After you run the Trial, you will see a welcome screen. Click **Close**

What you see

B4A presents you with a window consisting of several areas:

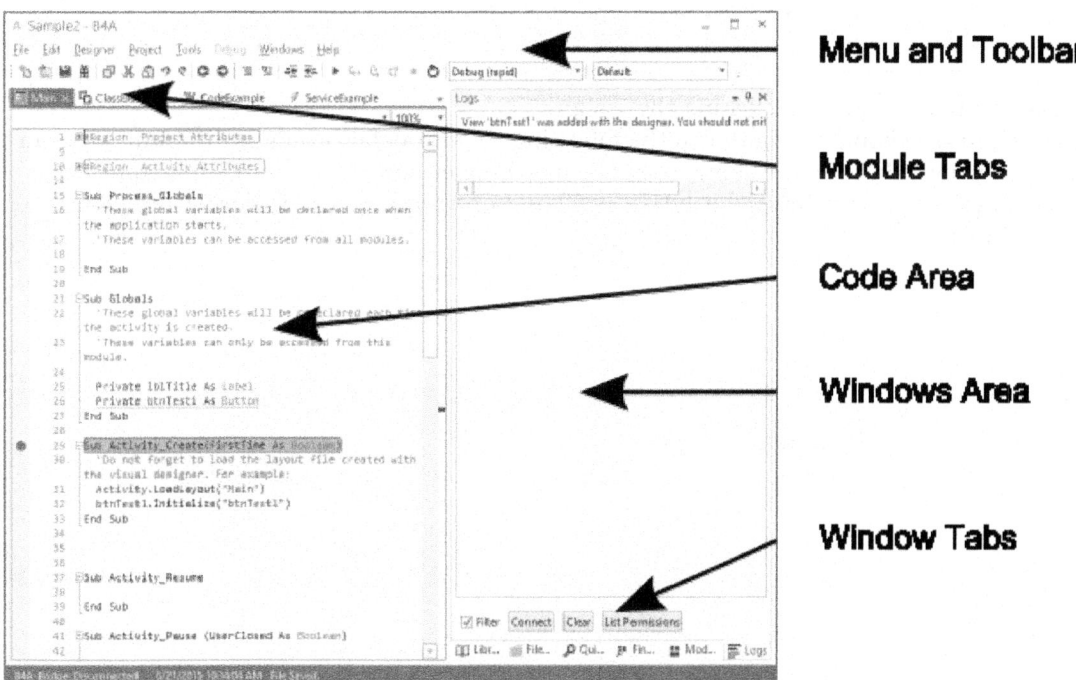

This is where you create, test and compile your apps. To begin, you will be editing code in the Code Area. We deal with all the other areas in more detail below, in the Integrated Development Environment (page 67) (IDE) section.

Note that normally apps are developed within projects (page 110) and projects are stored in folders.

Your First App

When you create a new B4A app, a sample project is already loaded into the Code Area, allowing you to create a simple app with very little additional code.

The sample project consists of two pieces of code or Modules (page 232): an Activity (page 337) module called Main and a Service (page 394) module called Starter. These are indicated by two Module Tabs (page 79) near the top of the IDE:

We will discuss the Starter (page 110) service later, and in these tutorials we can ignore it and concentrate upon the Main activity.

All types of B4A code is divided into blocks called Regions (page 80). A Region is an area of your code which you can rapidly expand or collapse, and by default the first two regions are collapsed:

```
 1   ⊞#Region   Project Attributes

 9

10   ⊞#Region   Activity Attributes
```

You can expand a Region by clicking the + sign.

The code you see should be similar to the following. If your default code is different, you can either edit your code to be the same, copy the following or download "Your First App" from this book's resource page (http://bit.ly/1IjLiwC) and unzip it to a new folder within your projects folder.

```
#Region  Project Attributes
 #ApplicationLabel: B4A Example
 #VersionCode: 1
 #VersionName:
 'SupportedOrientations possible values: unspecified, landscape or
portrait.
 #SupportedOrientations: unspecified
 #CanInstallToExternalStorage: False
#End Region

#Region  Activity Attributes
 #FullScreen: False
 #IncludeTitle: True
#End Region

Sub Process_Globals
 'These global variables will be declared once when the application
starts.
 'These variables can be accessed from all modules.
End Sub

Sub Globals
 'These global variables will be redeclared each time the activity is
created.
 'These variables can only be accessed from this module.
End Sub

Sub Activity_Create(FirstTime As Boolean)
 'Do not forget to load the layout file created with the visual
designer. For example:
 Msgbox("Welcome to B4A!", "")
End Sub

Sub Activity_Resume

End Sub

Sub Activity_Pause (UserClosed As Boolean)

End Sub
```

This is just about the minimum code required to create an app.

Debugging

Debugging is the process of removing errors (bugs) in your code. We are going to use this
simple app to learn a little about how to debug in B4A.

Legacy vs Rapid Debugger

To learn about how to debug an app, we are going to look at setting breakpoints and logging events. Note that B4A has an amazing feature called the Rapid Debugger (page 176), but to use it with Remote Compilation, you would need to install the Java JDK. For the purposes of keeping things simple during this introduction, we will use the legacy debugger, and introduce the Rapid Debugger later (page 176).

To use legacy debugging, you must first enable it using

[Tools > IDE Options > Use Legacy Debugger]

Breakpoints

An important way of debugging is to set a point where execution of your app will pause, so that you can examine the values of variables.

Note also that the default project has a single breakpoint already added:

 29 ⊟Sub Activity_Create(FirstTime As Boolean)

We deal with breakpoints (page 178) in more detail later. For now you can add or remove breakpoints by clicking the red dot, but you will need this breakpoint if you want to follow this tutorial

Save the program

Before you can run the app, first you must save the code into a project folder.

We recommend you create a single folder to hold all your B4A projects, and within this folder, create separate folders, one for each project. When you create a new program, B4A will create sub-folders called **Files** and **Objects** in the selected folder. For this reason you must put every program in a separate sub-folder of your projects folder.

Use the [File > Save] menu option to save the program, or type Ctrl+S.

B4A-Bridge

Before you can run the program, you need to connect B4A to a device or an emulator (page 188). There are several options (see Testing Options (page 184)), but as a first step we recommend using B4A-Bridge to connect to your device. B4A-Bridge is a free app which runs on an Android mobile phone or tablet. It was built using B4A! The source code is available here (http://bit.ly/141A2MC).

B4A-Bridge is made of two components. One component runs on the device and allows the second component (which is part of the IDE) to connect and communicate with the device. The connection is done over the local wireless network. (See the note below about Bluetooth.) Once connected, B4A-Bridge supports all of the IDE features which include: installing applications, viewing the logs, debugging and the visual designer (taking screenshots is not supported).

Android doesn't allow applications to quietly install other applications. Therefore, when you run your application using B4A-Bridge, you will see a dialog asking you to approve the installation.

Install the B4A-Bridge app on your device

B4A-Bridge is available free in Google Play and Amazon Market. Search for: B4A Bridge. Install the app on your device (Android mobile phone or tablet).

Run B4A-Bridge on your device

It will display a screen similar to:

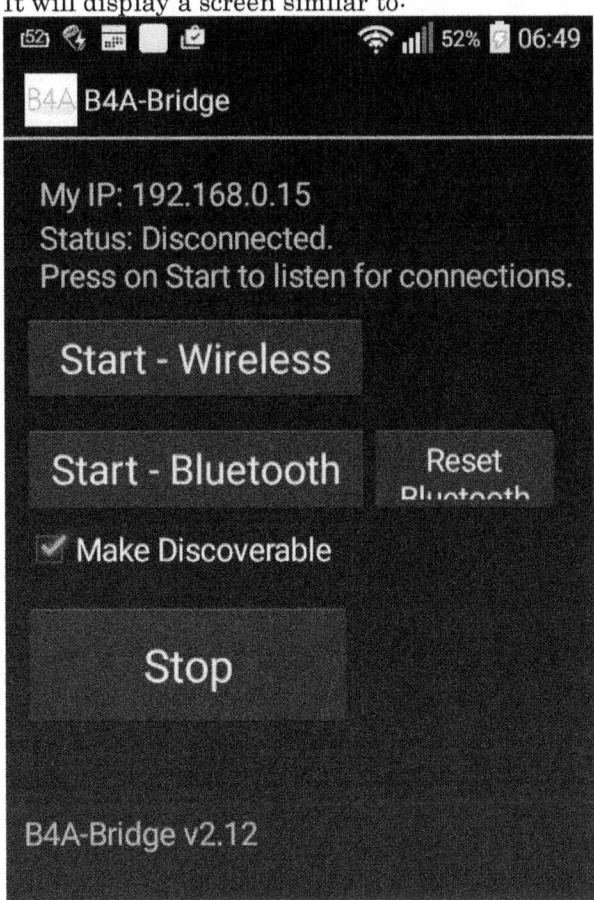

Note: the reference to Bluetooth is not applicable to version 5.0 of B4A. It was available for an earlier version and might become available for version 5 at some future date.

Note the **My IP:** address at the top of the app. This is what you will need in the next step. Click **Start – Wireless**.

Notes on Wireless Connection

In order to connect via WiFi, your development machine and your mobile device must both be connected to the same hub.

In some cases, the IP address displayed on B4A-Bridge may be the mobile network address. In that case you can find the local wireless address in the wireless advanced settings page.

Connect the IDE to the device

Go back to the B4A IDE running on your PC and select the menu option [Tools > B4A-Bridge]. If you are connecting by wireless, you can create a New IP device using the IP address noted above or, if you have connected to this device before, select its IP address from the list.

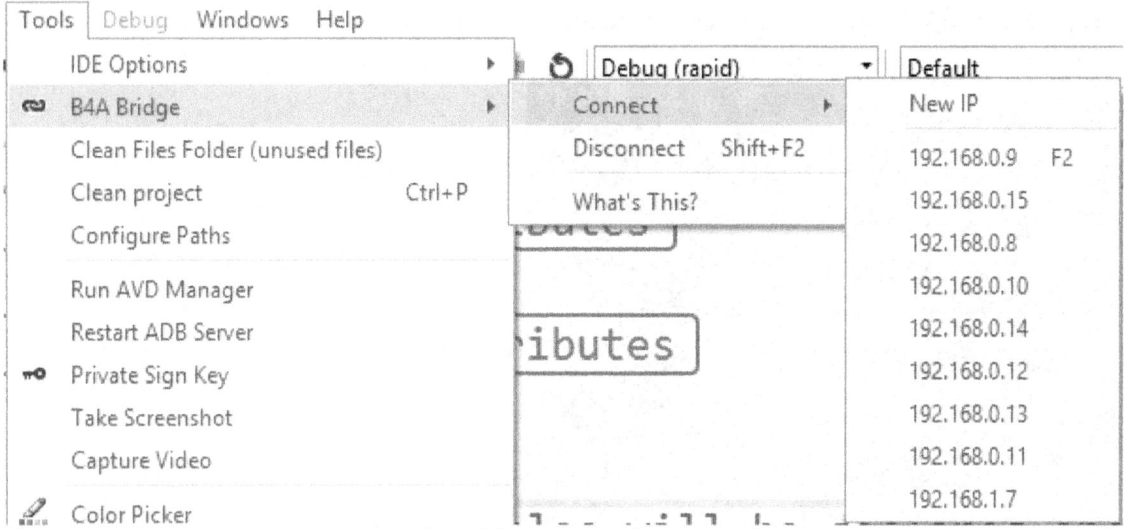

You can quickly connect to the last IP address using F2.

The B4A-Bridge: status bar at the bottom of the IDE screen will change from : Disconnected to : Trying to connect and then to : Connected

Remote Compilation Mode

When using the trial version, checking the **Remote Compilation Mode** option will allow remote compilation (page 54) without installing any further software.

B4A Designer

When B4A-Bridge gets connected, it first checks if another App, B4A Designer, needs to be updated. B4A Designer allows you to design your app directly on your device. If B4A Designer has not been installed, B4A-Bridge will ask whether to install it. You might see a screen something like this:

Select **Verify and install**, so Google can check the app for viruses. You will then see the following:

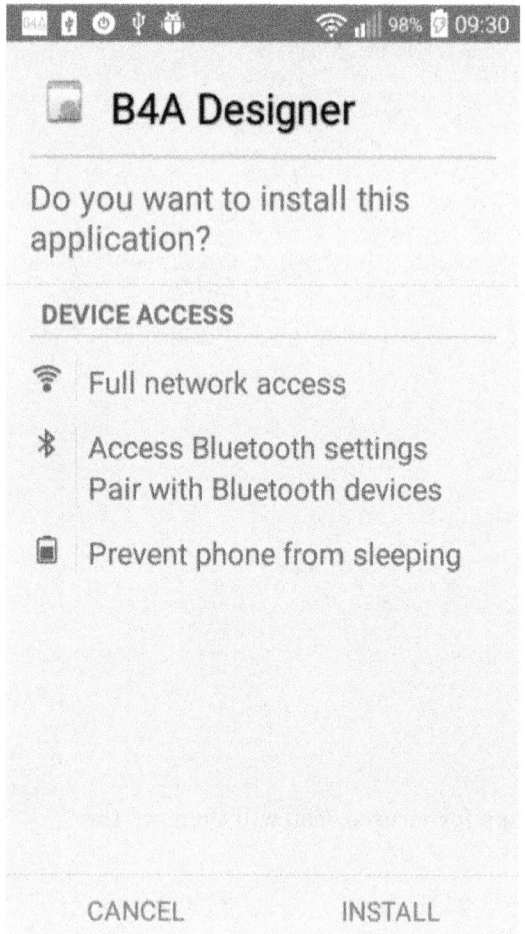

Click on **Install**. The app will be installed and you will see a confirmation page telling you so.

At this point, you do not need to open the designer, but you can do so as it will be useful soon.

Stopping B4A-Bridge

B4A-Bridge keeps running as a service (page 394) until you press on the Stop button. You can always reach it by pulling down the notifications screen from the notification bar at the top of the device's screen.

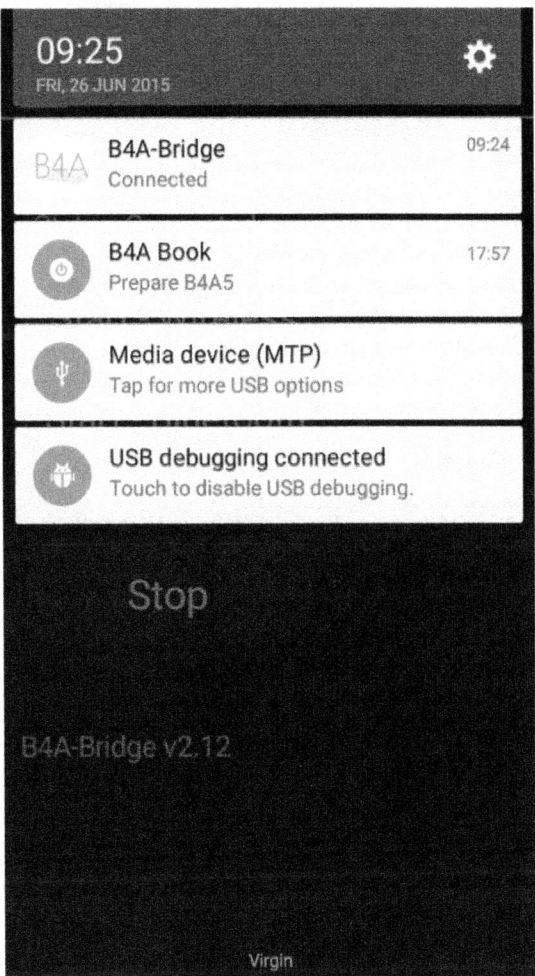

Pressing on the B4A-Bridge notification will open the main screen.

Compiling your new app

Now you can compile your app (that is, convert it into Java) and run it on your device. There are a number of ways to do this. In the toolbar of the IDE on your PC, first ensure that **Debug (legacy)** is selected in the compile options dropdown list (as shown below). Then either select [Project > Compile & Run] or press F5 or click on the black triangle in the toolbar:

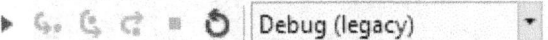

(If you have not yet saved your project, you will be prompted to do so now. See above for details.)

Note: B4A includes a Rapid Debugger (page 176) feature, but to use it you need to install the Java JDK. To keep things simple for this introduction, we explain the older form of the debugger. Note also that the Rapid Debugger significantly reduces the number of steps shown below, and hence reduces the time needed to install on the device.

During compilation you'll see a dialog box:

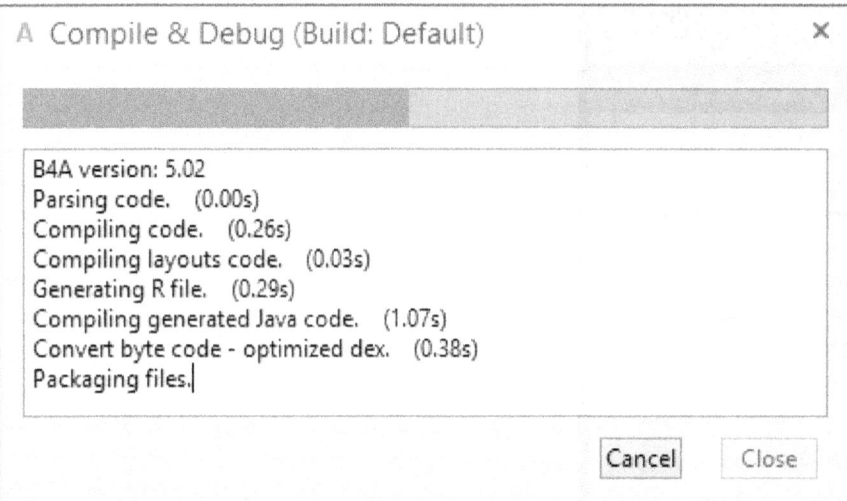

This is for information only. It will automatically close if your code compiles and installs without error.

Remote Compilation

The Trial Version of B4A includes a facility called Remote Compilation. This works by compiling your code over the web using B4A servers. This means that you can compile your app without installing the Java JDK or Android SDK.

However, Remote Compilation has limits to the size of code it will compile. If you get an error message saying the limit has been reached, you can install the Java JDK and the Android SDK (as described in Upgrade to Full Version (page 102)) and compile locally. You do **NOT** need to buy the full version to do this.

Also note that, with Remote Compilation, you cannot use the Rapid Debugger unless you install the Java JDK on your PC. For the purpose of this tutorial, therefore, we will use the legacy debugger and introduce the Rapid Debugger later (page 176).

Approve the app on your device

You might be required to approve the installation of the app, in which case you should approve it, install and open it.

Breakpoint

Assuming you left the breakpoint in your app at line 27 and you will see an alert on your device:

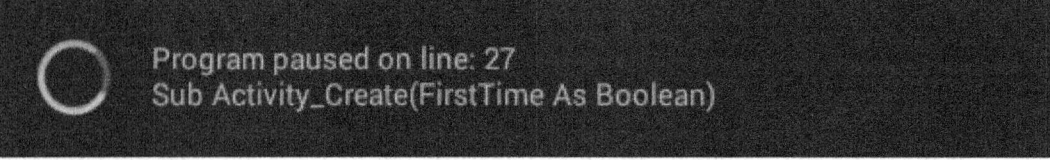

Within the IDE, the program will be paused, and the line with the breakpoint will be highlighted in yellow:

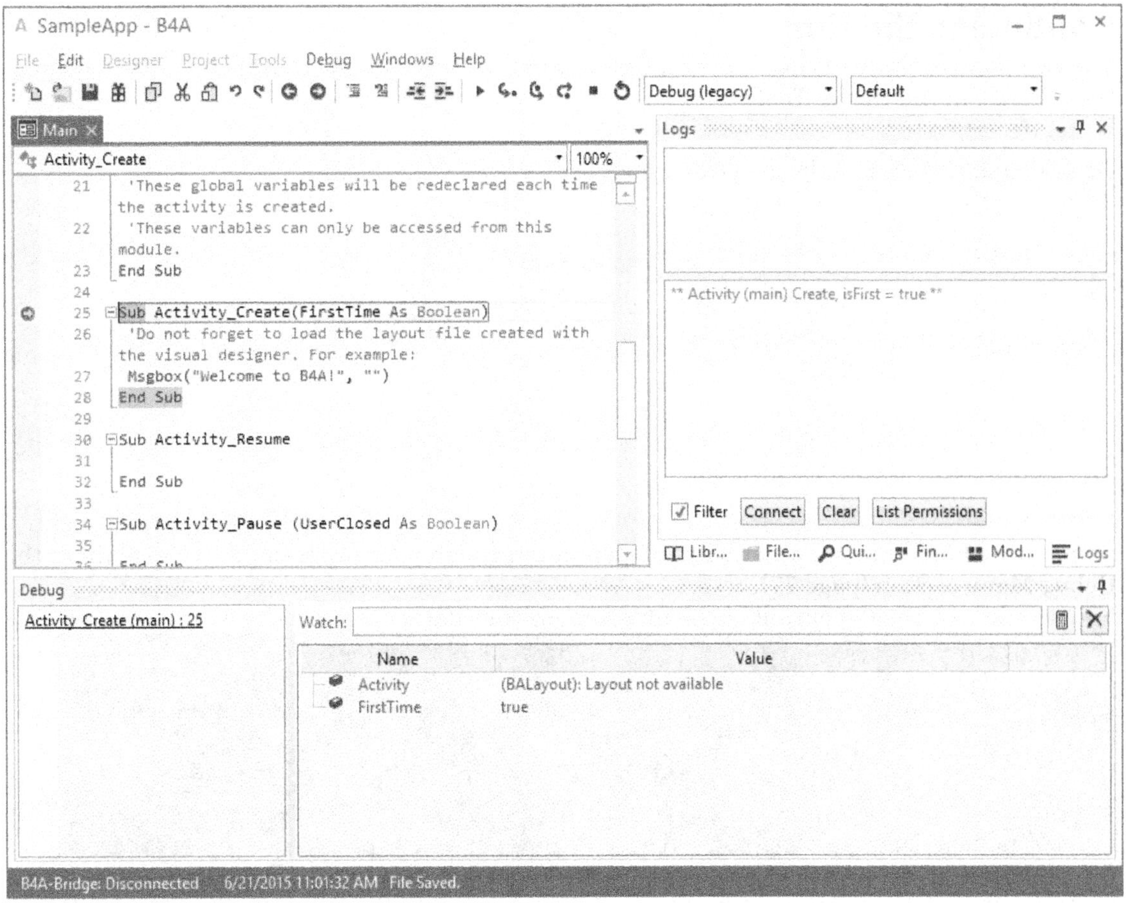

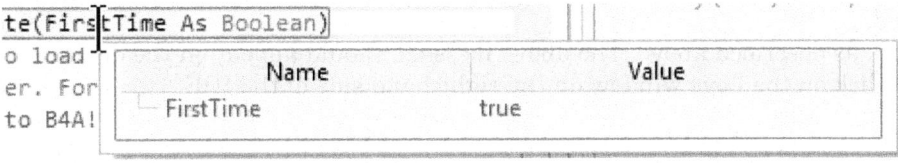

Debug Window

Another useful feature for debugging your program is shown in the lower half of the IDE (its default position). This is the Debug window. On the left is shown the location of the breakpoint (at line 27 in the Activity_Create sub of the Main activity).

On the right is a list of the variables defined by your code. The only meaningful one is FirstTime, which is the parameter of the Activity_Create sub. It has the value **true**.

Popup Variable Evaluation

You can also see the value of variables by hovering the cursor over a variable name or expression, when a window will pop up showing the value of the item, for example FirstTime:

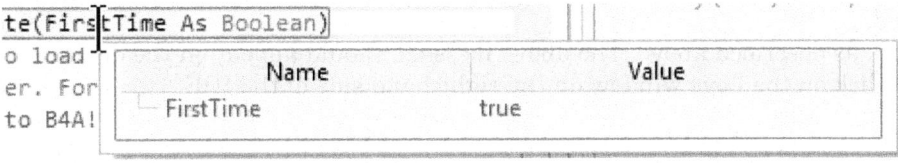

Continuing the Run

You can now continue to run your program beyond the breakpoint. Do this by either clicking the triangle in the Debug Toolbar:

▶ ↻. ↻ ↻   ■

Or selecting Continue from the Debug menu:

Debug	Windows	Help
▶	Continue	F5
↻.	Step In	F8
↻	Step Over	F9
↻	Step Out	F10
‖	Pause	
↻	Restart	F11
■	Stop	

Or pressing F5. There are other ways of stepping through your program, as we explain in the Debug Menu section (page 77).

You should now see the output of the program on your device:

If you wish, you can restart the program by clicking the Restart Icon ↻ in the toolbar, or use [Debug > Restart] or pressing F11.

Logging Events

Another useful debugging feature is to write data into the IDE Log. Let's try it. To do that we need to add some code. Stop the debugger by clicking on the **Stop** icon ■ or by using [Debug > Stop] or by pressing **F11**.

Scroll down to the line

```
Msgbox("Welcome to B4A!", "")
```

Remove the breakpoint and add a line so the code now reads:

```
Log ("Height = " & Activity.Height)
Msgbox("Welcome to B4A!", "")
```

You will see a yellow bar appear on the left side of the code, indicating areas which have recently been edited.

Now restart the app, as described above. The above message should appear on the device. Now (if necessary) click on the Logs window on the right-hand side of the IDE

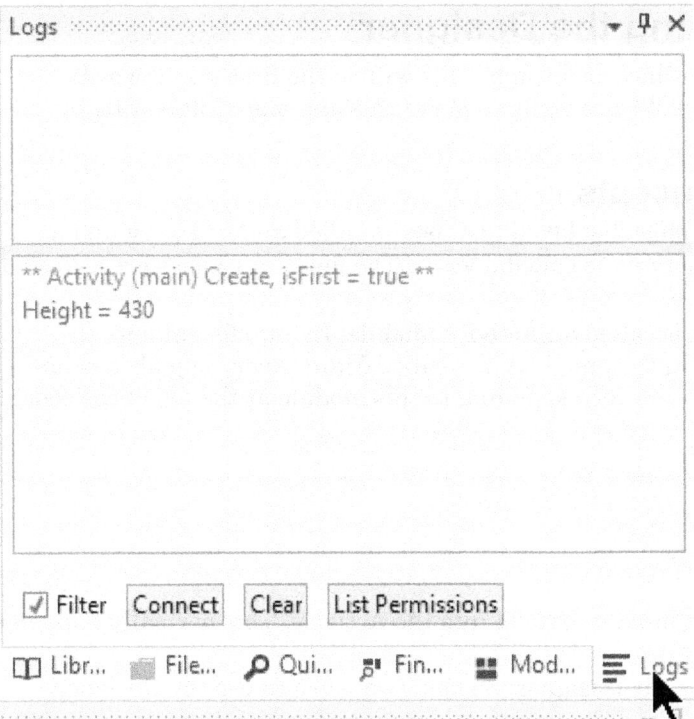

Warning

If the logs window is empty, click on the **Connect** button to connect the log to the debugger. You should see several lines of text followed by the log you want, a line like:

```
Height = nnn
```

This tells you the height of your screen in pixels.

Rotating the Device

Now, while the app is still running, rotate the device. You should see more lines appear in the **Logs** area of in the IDE, something like this:

```
** Activity (main) Pause, UserClosed = false **
** Activity (main) Create, isFirst = false **
Height = 1151
```

The IDE is logging more information than just the height of your device.

It is also telling you that the Activity_Pause and Activity_Create subs have automatically been run when you rotated the device. You will learn about when these and other subs are automatically run in the Activity Concept (page 239) section.

So you see that the log is a very useful way of tracking data while the app is running and so helping you to debug your app.

More about Debugging

For more information about the features offered by B4A see the Debugging (page 176) section.

Your Second App: Using the Designer

We will now try changing the appearance of the app. This will be the first step towards designing an effective user interface. We are going to make this app more interesting by adding a button.

The View and Layout Concepts

First a few key concepts. In B4A, a page displayed to a user is called an **Activity** and a control which can be added to the Activity is called a **View**. The details of Views are collected in a file called a **Layout**.

The code which controls the Layout is called an **Activity Module**. In our current app, the Activity Module is the only module in the app, and it is called Main. Every app always has a Main activity module. You can see a tab corresponding to this module at the top of the code area, just below the toolbar:

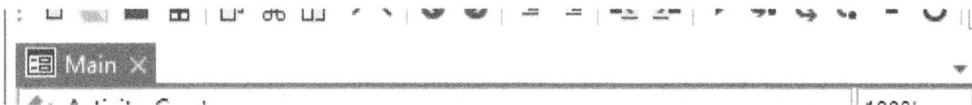

To be visible to the user, the Layout must be loaded into the Activity. This normally happens within the **Activity_Create** sub.

The tool we use to create a Layout is the **Designer**. So next, we learn to use the Designer.

Running the Designer

If your app is still running, first stop it, then select [Designer > Open Designer] in the main menu. The Visual Designer window appears:

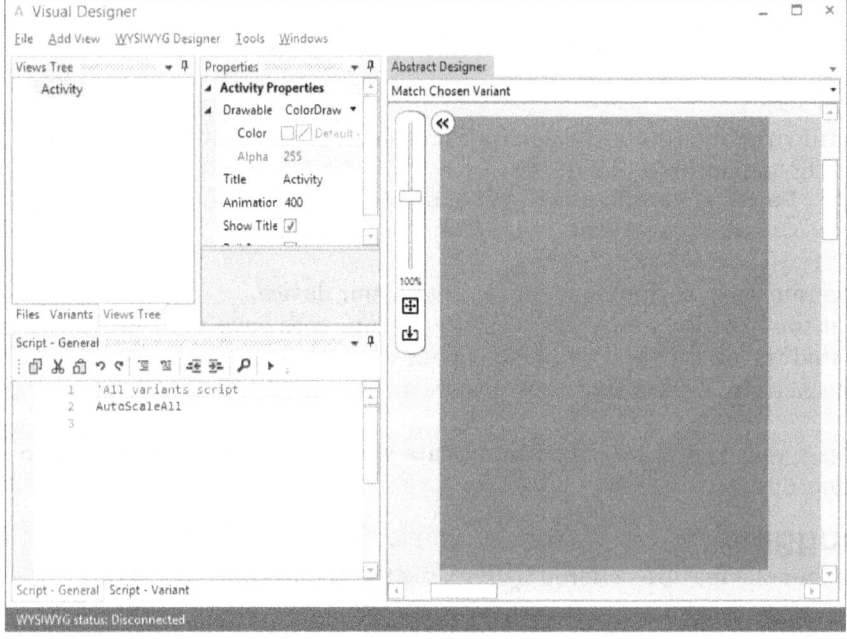

On the right is the Abstract Designer. This is where you add views (controls) and configure their properties.

Here you will see the Views of the Layout, but note the Abstract Designer (page 157) is NOT "What you see is what you get" (WYSIWYG). So how do you know how your user will see your Layout?

Connect the Designer to your device.

To see the Layout in WYSIWYG, you need to connect B4A to either a device or an emulator (page 188). In this tutorial, we will use your device and B4A-Bridge. (We describe how to use the emulator in Testing Your App (page 184).)

If it is not already running, start B4A-Bridge on your device. Then if it is not already connected, connect B4A to your device from the IDE as described above (page 49).

Now connect the Visual Designer to your device within the Designer menu:

[WYSIWYG > Connect] or by pressing F2.

The B4A Designer app will start on your device and the heading **Activity** appears on your device with a blank screen below it, since the layout has no views so far.

Add a button

In the Designer Window click [Add View > Button]

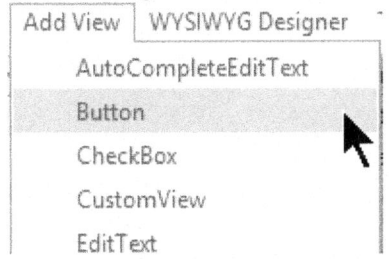

The following things will happen:

A button is added to the Views Tree:

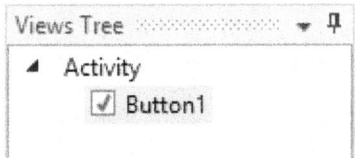

You will see some of the parameters of your button in the Designer:

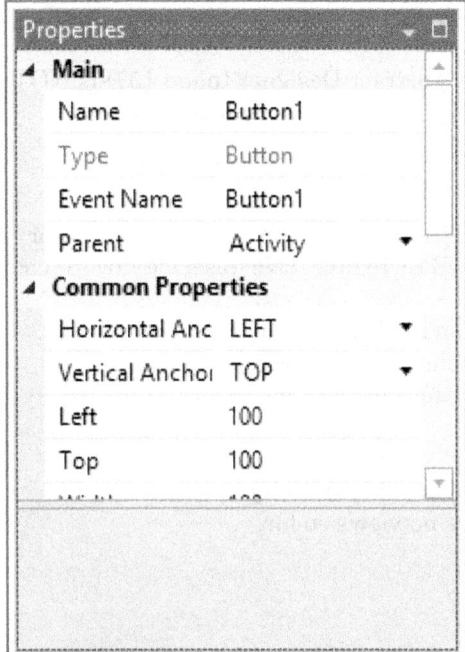

You will see the button in the Abstract Designer

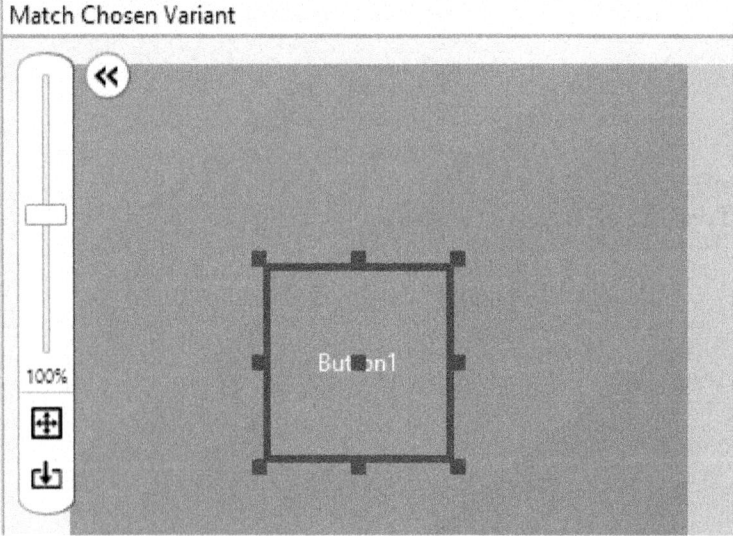

And you will see it on your device as WYSIWYG (What You See Is What You Get).

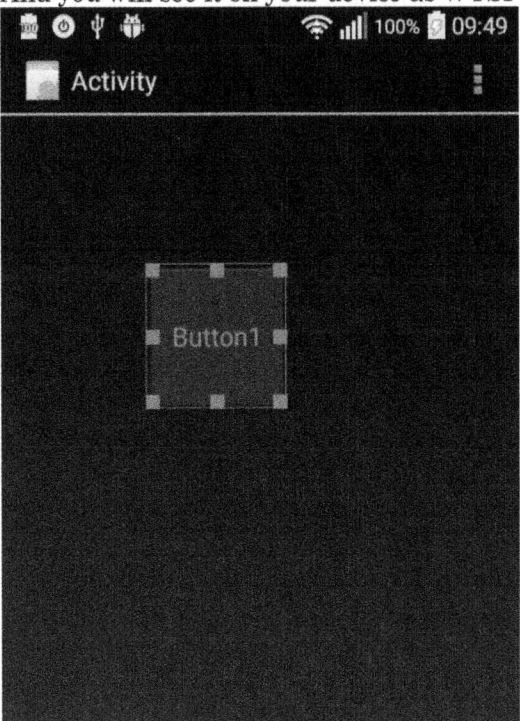

Configure your button

You will probably want to change the color and text of your button.

You can resize and reposition it either in the Abstract designer or on your device. You can also set its position in the **Common Properties**: **Left**, **Top**, **Width** and **Height** of the Visual Designer.

You can also set a relationship between the edges of your button and the edges of its container, in this case the whole screen, using Horizontal and Vertical Anchors, which we describe in detail elsewhere (page 147).

Note: B4A offers another powerful way of controlling the position of Views using Designer Scripts. We describe this in a separate chapter (page 162).

We recommend you change the name of the button (in the Properties window) to something like `btnTest`. (This type of name uses the so-called Hungarian naming convention (page 281).)

Use the Designer to change the **Text** field to "Click Me!". This is what will be displayed to the user.

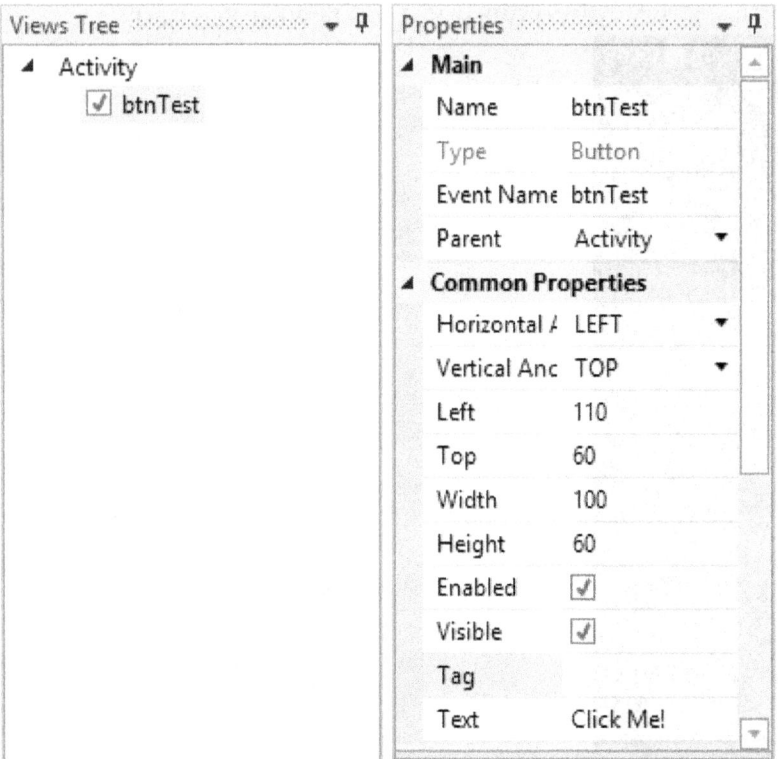

Save your layout by clicking [File > Save] or typing Ctrl+S in the Designer. You can choose any name, but it makes sense to use the same name as the **Activity Module**, in this case "Main".

Note: This creates a file called "main.bal" within the Files folder of your project.

Generate Members

In order to control the button in code, we need to declare it in the relevant **Activity Module**. The best way to make sure you do this correctly is to ask Visual Designer to generate this code for you.

First make sure the correct **Activity** module is selected in the code area, since any code you generate will be added to the currently selected activity. In this project we have only one activity.

There are two ways of generating the code: using the Designer Tool menu or using a popup window.

Using the Designer Tools Menu

Select your new button and use the Designer's [Tools > Generate Members] option. This will display the following (you might need to expand the **btnTest** list by clicking the triangle:

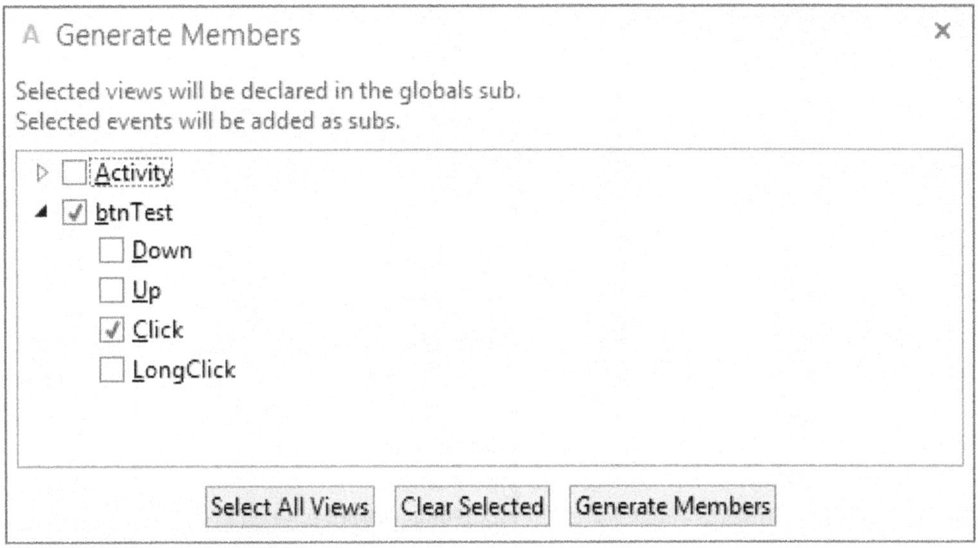

A Generate Members   ✕

Selected views will be declared in the globals sub.
Selected events will be added as subs.

▷ ☐ <u>A</u>ctivity
◢ ☑ <u>b</u>tnTest
    ☐ <u>D</u>own
    ☐ <u>U</u>p
    ☑ <u>C</u>lick
    ☐ <u>L</u>ongClick

| Select All Views | Clear Selected | Generate Members |

Check **btnTest** and **Click**, as shown.

Click **Generate members** then close the dialog box.

Using a Popup Menu

Alternatively, you can generate code by right-clicking a view in the Abstract Designer (shown below) or in the Views Tree. A menu pops up which allows you to add items to your code, but only one at a time.

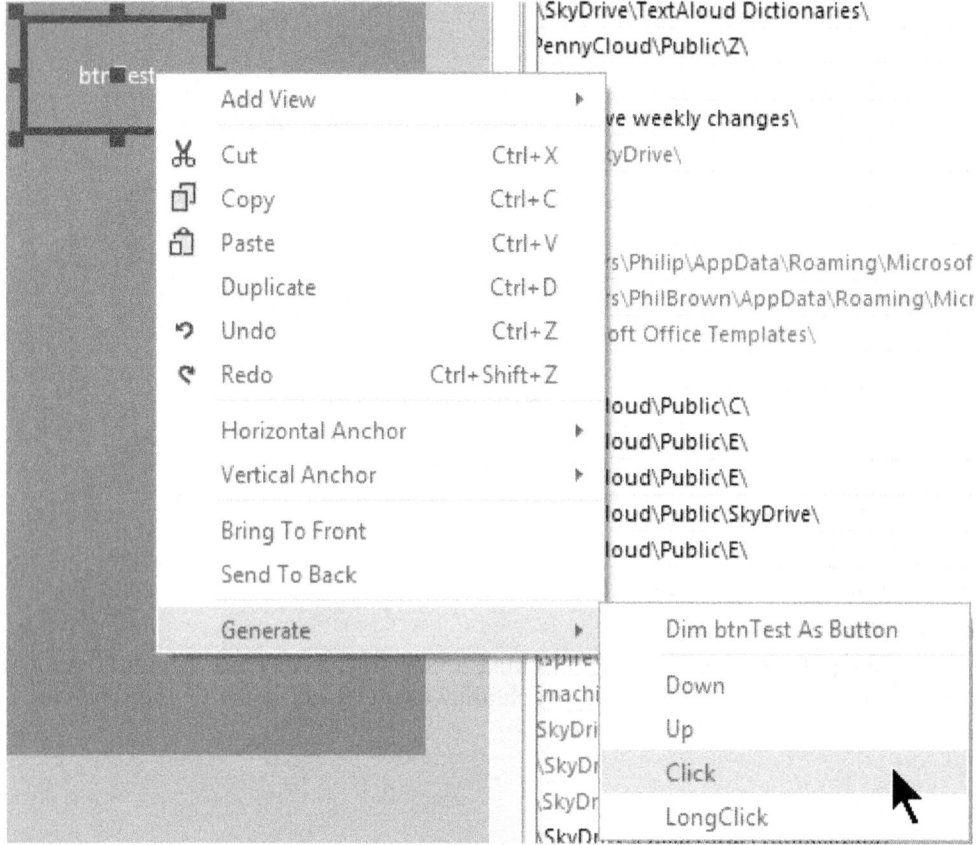

First, select [Dim btnTest as Button], then repeat the process and select [Click]. This will achieve the same result as before, although it will take longer.

Note: there is no danger about asking the Designer or Abstract Designer to generate the code twice. If the code already exists in your Activity, the request will be ignored.

You can now save your work if necessary and close the Visual Designer.

Adding Code for the Button

Two entries have been generated within your code. The first is a new line within `Sub Globals`:

```
Sub Globals
  'These global variables will be re-declared each time the activity is
created.
  'These variables can only be accessed from this module.
  Private btnTest As Button
End Sub
```

This tells your code what type of object btnTest is. The reason why view variables **must** be declared in `Sub Globals` and not in `Sub Process_Globals` is explained here (page 237).

In addition, the **Generate Members** dialog will also generate a new empty Sub:

```
Sub btnTest_click
End Sub
```

Explanation of Sub's name

You might wonder why this sub has to be called **btnTest_Click**. This code is an example of an **event handler**. We explain how events work here (page 297). Essentially, some objects can generate events, for example when a user does something, and your code has to handle that event. The first part of the event handler name "**btnTest**" tells B4A which object generated the event. The "**Click**" part of the name specifies which event we are responding to. These two parts have to be joined by an underscore to create the name of the event handler sub.

Add code to button

Now we are going to write the code to handle this event. Move the existing **Msgbox** code from the **Sub Activity_Create** into the new sub. It should now read

```
Sub btnTest_Click
 Msgbox("Welcome to B4A!", "")
End Sub
```

Load the Layout

To make this work we need to load this new layout when the app starts.

```
Remove the comment mark (a single quote) from the line
Activity.LoadLayout within the Sub Activity_Create and edit it to
read:
Sub Activity_Create(FirstTime As Boolean)
 Activity.LoadLayout("Main")
End Sub
```

Note: you must use the same name which was used to save the Layout in the Designer.

Run your app

This time you should see your button Click Me! and when you click it you should see the Welcome to B4A message:

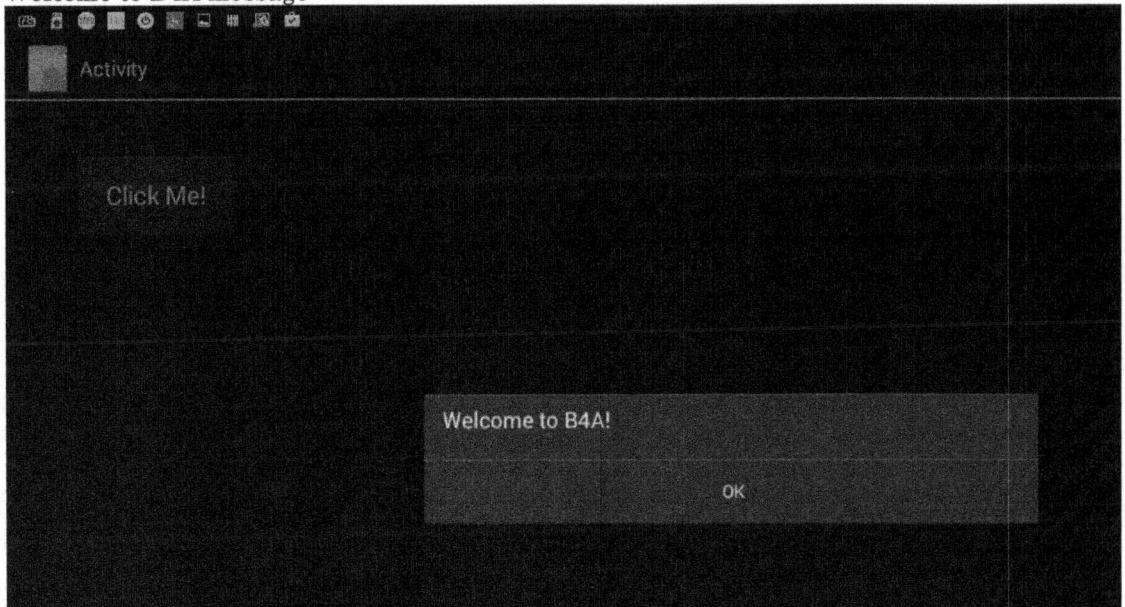

Your Third App

Now let's see if you can create an app on your own! You are going to create an app which will show the time when the user clicks a button. To do this, you need to add a label to your layout. A label is an object (a "view" in Android jargon) which can display text. Call it `Label1`.

Use the designer to generate code for the label (that is, add a `Dim` statement to your code). Now change your app so that your `btnText` will run the following code when the user clicks it:

```
Label1.Text = "The time now is " & DateTime.Time(DateTime.Now)
```

This defines the message which `Label1` will show. `DateTime` is a B4A object which provides a wide range of time-related and date-related functions. For example: `DateTime.Now` returns the number of milliseconds since 1-1-70, and `DateTime.Time` converts this number into the current time.

It may sound a bit complex but you do not need to understand the details at this stage. It's just to give an example program, so see if you can make it work. If you get stuck, you can download the solution (Your Third App) from this book's resource page (http://bit.ly/1IjLiwC).

Stopping B4A-Bridge

After you have finished developing, you should select [Tools > B4A Bridge > Disconnect] in the IDE and on your device navigate to B4A-Bridge and press on the **Stop** button, in order to save its battery.

More about Designer

For more details about the Designer see the Designer Chapter (page 139).

1.2 The Integrated Development Environment

Now we will look more closely at the parts of the Integrated Development Environment (IDE). This is what you use to develop your app. The IDE consists of the following areas:

Menu and Toolbar (page 78)
Module Tabs (page 79)
Code Area (page 80)
Windows Area (page 87)
Window Tabs (page 87)

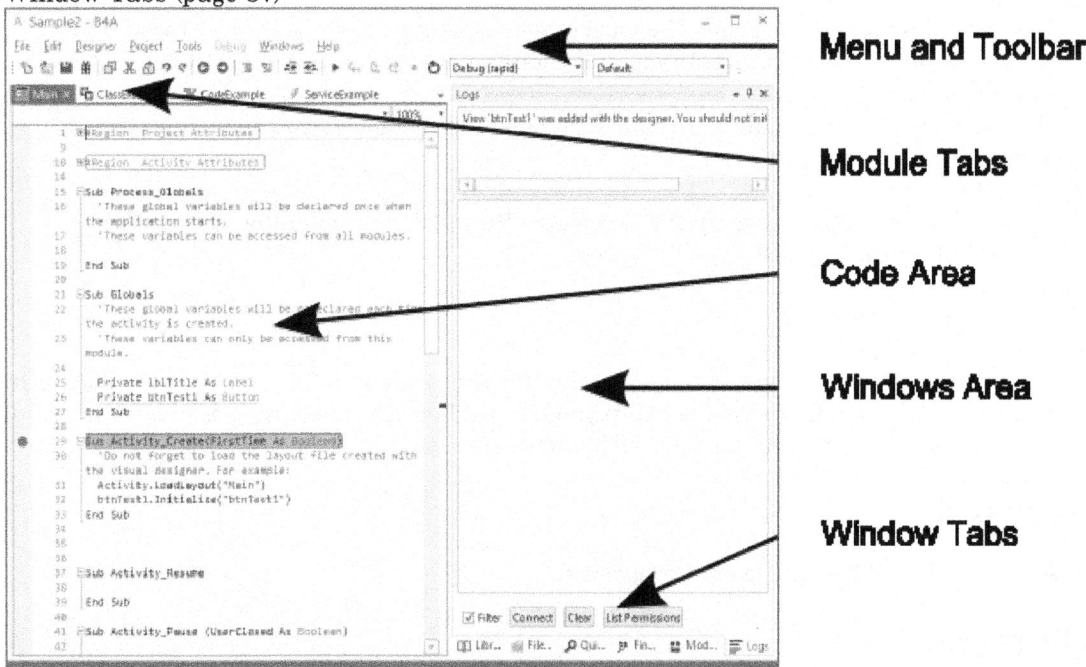

We deal with these areas below.

Icons

The following icons are used extensively in the IDE:

 Methods
 Fields and variables
 Subroutines defined in your code
 Properties
 Keywords
 Core objects
 Activity Module
 Class Module
 Code Module
 Service Module

In addition, other icons used by the Toolbar (page 78).

File Menu

New
> Generate a new empty project (page 110).

Open Source
> Load a project.

Save (Ctrl+S)
> Save the current project. Note there is no "Save As" menu. If you wish to create a new project based on an existing one, the easiest way is to copy and paste the project folder. Note you could also use Export As Zip and then import the zip into a new folder after renaming it's folder name.
> **Note**: We recommend you always rename the b4a file whenever you clone a project, to avoid confusion later.

Export As Zip
> Export the whole project in a zip file. You have the option of including or excluding Shared Modules (page 233).

Print Preview
> Show a print preview.

Print
> Print the code. Note that you can open and print your code with any text editor. The Main activity is stored in a file with the extension b4a in the root of the project folder, and code for other modules are stored in files with a bas extension.

Exit
> Leave the IDE.

Below this is a list of the last loaded programs.

Edit Menu

Cut (Ctrl+X)
> Cut the selected text and copy it to the clipboard.

Cut Line (Ctrl+Y)
> Cut the line at the cursor position. **Note**: in other programs, Ctrl+Y often redoes the previous action, which is Ctrl+Shift+Z in B4A. Note also that if word wrap is operating, the text which has been wrapped will not be cut.

Duplicate Line (Ctrl+D)
> Duplicates the line where the cursor is.

Copy (Ctrl+C)
> Copy the selected text to the clipboard.

Paste (Ctrl+V)
> Paste the text in the clipboard at the cursor position.

Undo (Ctrl+Z)
> Undo the last operation, and sequentially undo previous operations.

Redo (Ctrl+Shift+Z)
> Redo the previous operation, and sequentially redo previous operations.

Move Line(s) Up (Alt+Up)

Move the line where the cursor is or the selected lines up above the previous line

Move Line(s) Down (Alt+Down)

Move the line where the cursor is or the selected lines down below the next line

Find/ Replace (F3)

Activate the **Find and Replace** function.

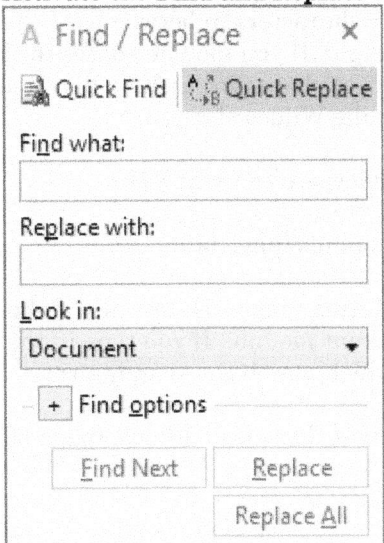

You can Look in the whole document or the selected code.

Find options are:

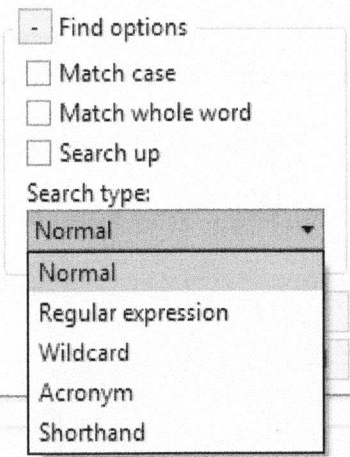

Regular expressions are explained here (page 288).

Wildcard You can use the following special characters in your search:

* matches zero or more instances of any character except a line feed. Note that * searches are "greedy", that is, they find as long a match as possible. Thus "a*b" will match the whole of abcdeb, not just the first two letters.

? matches any single character except a line feed

matches an single digit

[abcde] matches any one character in the set

[!abcde] matches any character except those in the set or the line feed

Note that Wildcard searches never find matches on more than one line.

Acronym starts the match by searching for the first character in the search string which is at the beginning of a word, then matches subsequent characters in the search string with capital letters. Thus for example "so" would match with **SupportedO**rientations.

Shorthand matches the search characters and any other characters in between.

So "be" will match a**b**cd**e**fghi and "beg" will match a**b**cd**e**f**g**hi. If you include spaces in the search string, Shorthand will match it with any whitespace character, include lien feeds. Thus Shorthand matches across more than one line (unlike Wildcards).

Quick Search (Ctrl+F)

Brings the Quick Search window to the front in the Windows Area (page 87).

Find All References (F7)

Activates the Find All References window. See here for details (page 90).

Find Sub (Ctrl+E)

Brings the Modules window to the front of the Windows Area (page 87). Initially it shows a list of Modules followed by a list of the Subs in the current module. If you type in the search field it shows Subs and Regions in all modules which match the search term.

Block Comment / Uncomment (Ctrl+Q)

Set the selected lines as comments (page 82) or uncomment the selected lines. (page 82)

Remove All Breakpoints

Breakpoints (page 178).

Outlining

Open a sub-menu containing three functions to expand or collapse code:

- **Toggle All** (Ctrl-Shift-O) - Expand collapsed code and collapse extended code.
- **Expand All** - Expand all code.
- **Collapse All** - Collapse all code.

Note that the IDE remembers (page 93) the state of outlining when you save the project.

Designer

This menu has one option which opens the Visual Designer (page 139).

Project Menu

Modules

The first four options deal with Modules (page 232):

Add New Module

lets you choose which type of module to create:

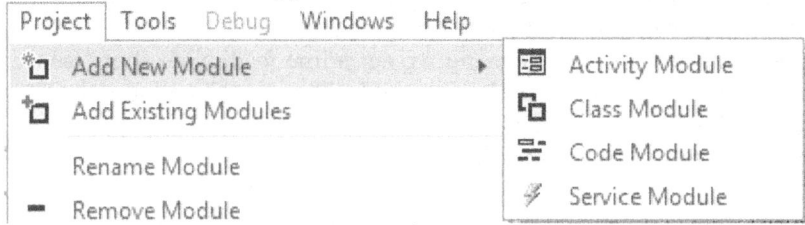

We describe these in the Modules (page 232) chapter.

Add Existing Modules

lets you select a module (either from another project or from the Shared Modules (page 233) folder) which will then be copied into this project. It will be added to the list of modules in the Modules Window and shown as the active module.

Rename Module

Change the name used in the IDE. Only possible if a module other than Main is active.

Remove Module

This will not delete the module, merely remove it from the list of active modules in the Modules Window (page 89). This will only work if a module other than Main is active.

Package Options

The next 3 options in the Project menu deal with the overall program:

Choose Icon

Choose an icon (page 259) for the program,

Build Configurations (Ctrl+B)

This is explained in more detail here (page 171) in chapter 2. Among other things, it allows you to change the package name (page 114)

Manifest Editor

Run the Manifest Editor (page 115).

Compile Options

The last 3 options in the Project Menu deal with the different compiling options.

Compile & Run (F5)

has the same effect as pressing the run icon ▶ . If more than one device is connected, you will be able to select which one you want to connect to:

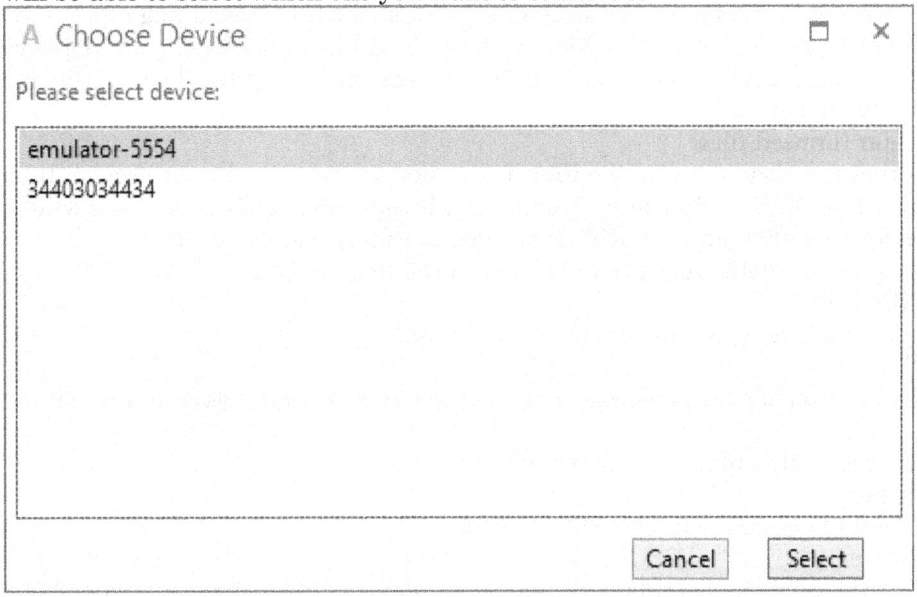

The result of the Compile & Run will depend upon which compile mode (page 172) is selected in the IDE.

For example, it will produce these files in the Objects folder if one of the Debug modes is selected:

- bin
- gen
- res
- src
- AndroidManifest.xml
- classes.dex
- Sample2_DEBUG.apk

If you want to create an apk but not to run it, select this option without having a device or emulator attached. The apk is placed in the Objects folder.

Note that the name of the apk will be the same as the name of the b4a file unless the b4a file name contains spaces, in which case the apk will be called **result.apk**

Compile & Run (background) (Alt+3)

The same as Compile & Run except no progress dialog box is shown.

Compile to Library (Alt+5)

Compile your project into a library which you can use in other projects and share with other users. More details can be found at How to Compile a Library (page 454).

Tools Menu

IDE Options

These are explained below (page 75).

B4A Bridge

See the B4A-Bridge section (page 48) for details of this method of designing and debugging your app on a real Android device. B4A-Bridge must be running on the device before you can connect. You can connect via Wireless or disconnect the device. (Bluetooth is not currently supported.)

Clean Files Folder (unused files)

Delete files that are located under the **Files** folder but are not used by the project. It will not delete any file referenced by any of the project layouts. A list of unused files will be displayed before deletion, and you will be allowed to cancel the operation.

Be careful: copies of deleted files are NOT kept in the Recycle Bin!

Clean Project (Ctrl+P)

Delete all files that are generated during compilation.

Configure Paths

Tell B4A the location of your javac.exe, android.jar and (optionally) your additional libraries.

See the Configure Paths (page 107) section for details

Run AVD Manager

See Using the AVD Manager (page 188) for details.

Restart ADB Server

In some cases the connected emulator (page 188) or device fails to respond and you might need to end the link and restart it. The link is managed by the ADB (Android Debug

Bridge) server process, hence the name of this menu option. See here
(http://bit.ly/1C6khq8) for details about the ADB server from the Android Developer site.

Private Sign Key

Allows you to create and sign your app to make it ready for publication. See the
Publishing Your App chapter (page 259) for details.

Take Screenshot

You can capture screens from the emulator (page 188) and from devices connected via
USB, but not from devices connected via B4A-Bridge. For USB connections to devices, see
USB Debugging (page 185).

The Take Screenshot function can be called either from:
– Tools menu when the IDE is in edit mode
– Debug menu when the IDE is in debug mode
These options open the following window:

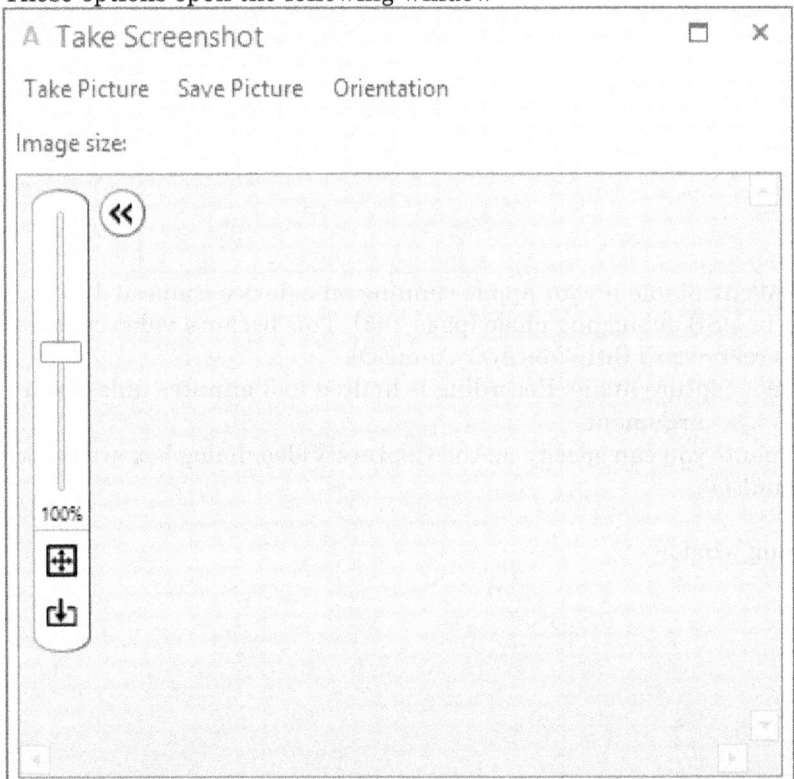

Click on **Take Picture** to take the screenshot from the device or the emulator. If several
devices are connected, you will be asked to select which one to use for the screenshot.

You can use the slider to resize the image, zoom to fit the image to the viewer, use the
Orientation menu to rotate the picture, save it as a PNG file or copy it to the clipboard by
right-clicking on the image. A **Copy to clipboard** button will pop up.

Note: You can also take screenshots on many devices, although the procedure varies.
Either press and hold the Power and Volume-down buttons simultaneously, or if that does
not work, press and hold the Power button alone for several seconds, and use the "Take

Screen Shot" option. If that does not work, your device probably does not support screenshots, but search the web to make sure.

Capture Video

This option (which is also available in the Debug Menu) allows you to record a video of the device's screen in mp4 format. This can be very useful for demonstrating your app. It shows the following:

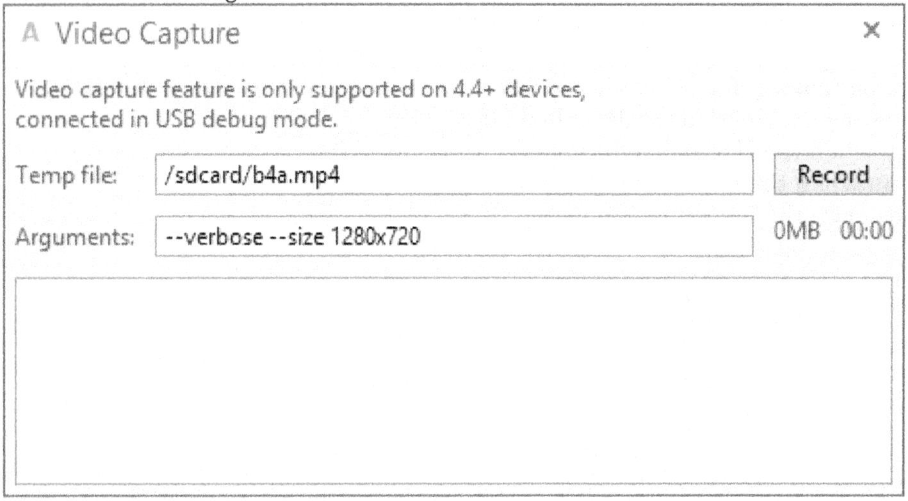

Note that capture is only available if your app is running on a device connected to your development machine in USB debugging mode (page 185). This because video capture works by calling adb screenrecord (http://bit.ly/1zAamEO).

Note also that it does not capture audio. Recording is limited to 3 minutes unless you change the `--time-limit` argument

Arguments: The arguments you can specify on the Capture Video dialog box are described here (http://bit.ly/1zAamEO).

Color Picker

This shows the following window:

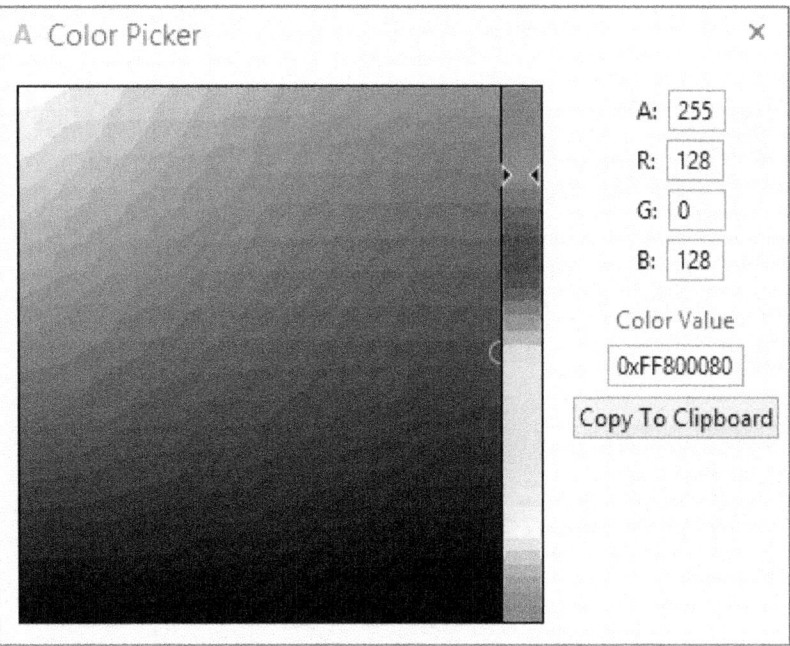

This allows you to select a color and copy its value to the clipboard as a hexadecimal quadruplet, that is, a hex literal (page 275) with four bytes or eight digits. The format is the same as given by the Colors.ARGB (page 345) function, that is, Alpha channel, Red, Green and Blue values. For example:

0xFFFFFFFF = fully opaque white
0xFF000000 = fully opaque black
0xFFFF0000 = fully opaque red

IDE Options Sub-Menu

[Tools > IDE Options] opens the following sub-menu:

Themes (Ctrl+T)

This shows the Themes Manager window:

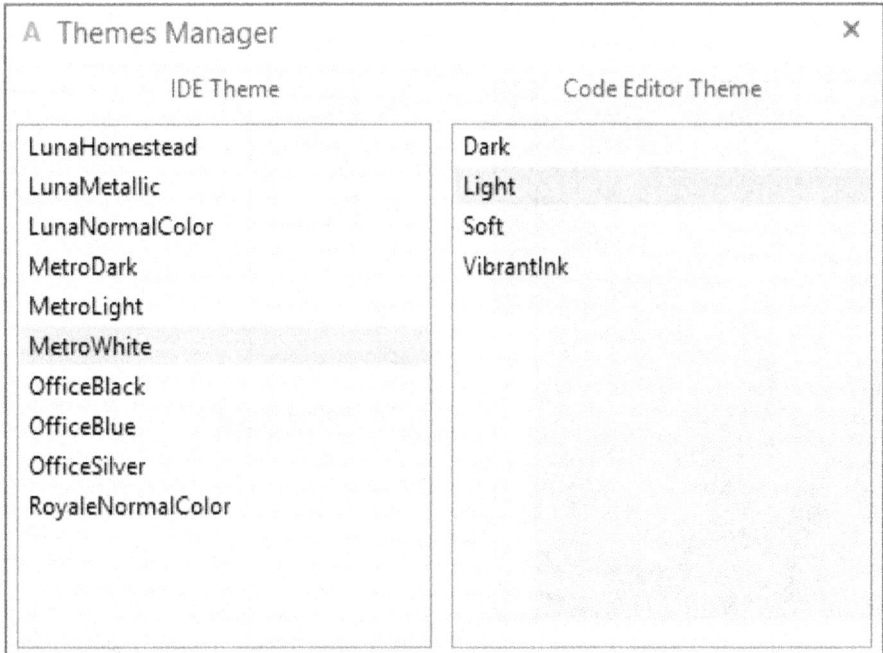

This allows you to set the color options of the IDE.

Fonts Picker

Shows the following dialog box:

Target

Lets you choose between Code Editor and Logs.

Word wrap

Without word wrap, long lines may extend beyond the visible window.

With word wrap, such lines are wrapped to the next line.

Tab Size

Sets the size of the indent when you press the tab key in the editor. The default is 4 (although 2 is probably a better value).

Auto Save

Saves the program and the layout in the Designer whenever you run the app on a connected device or emulator.

Configure Process Timeout

Specify how many seconds the IDE should wait as it tries to connect to the emulator. After this number of seconds, the IDE will show an error message in the **Compile & Debug** dialog box. This is called a Process Timeout.

Clear Logs When Deploying

If you check this option then every time you install the app on a device in debug mode, the Logs window will be automatically cleared.

Disable Implicit Auto Completion

Autocompletion and Implicit autocompletion are explained here (page 83).

Use Legacy Debugger

The Legacy Debugger is explained here (page 177).

Debug Menu

The Debug menu is only available when running your app in debug mode.
Note that most of these options are also available in the debug toolbar. This menu also offers the Pause option.

Continue (F5)

Makes the app continue to run until the next breakpoint.

Step In (F8)

Steps to the next line of code. If the current line calls a sub, the first line of the sub will be executed.

Step Over (F9)

This will step over a sub. So, if the current line calls a sub, the whole sub will be executed without stepping through each line, and the code will stop at the line after the sub call. If the current line does not call a sub, the result will be the same as Step (F8).

Step Out (F10)

This steps out of the current sub. The code will run until execution has left the current sub.

Pause

Pause the code as soon as possible.

Restart (F11)

Recompile and run the app again.

Stop

Stop the current program . Also stops the program in the Emulator. **Note**: stopping the program in the Emulator or on a device does not stop it in the IDE.

Take Screenshot

This calls the Screenshots (page 73) dialog box.

Capture Video

This calls the Video Capture (page 74) dialog box.

Windows Menu

This lists all the windows available, with their shortcuts.

Files Manager
    See here for details (page 88)
Find All References (F7)
    See here for details (page 90)
Libraries Manager
    See here for details (page 87)
Logs (F6)
    See here for details (page 90)
Modules (Ctrl+E)
    See here for details (page 89)
Quick Search (Ctrl+F)
    See here for details (page 91).
Reset
    This will move windows back to their original tab group, but will not affect modules.

Help Menu

This contains a link to the on-line help and tutorials (http://bit.ly/1CMZ6xz), and an **About** option which shows the version number, copyright and other information about Anywhere Software.

Toolbar

⁕ (Ctrl+N) Generates a new empty project (page 110).

⤴ Loads a project.

💾 (Ctrl+S) Saves the current project.

⊞ Export the project as a zip file.

⎀ (Ctrl+C) Copies the selected text to the clipboard.

✄ (Ctrl+X) Cuts the selected text and copies it to the clipboard.

⎀ (Ctrl+V) Pastes the text in the clipboard at the cursor position.

↺ (Ctrl+Z) Undoes the last edit.

↻ (Ctrl+Shift+Z) Redoes the previous "Undo".

◷ (Alt+Left) Navigate backwards to the previous code line you visited.

▾ (Alt+N) Navigation History – shows list of previous code lines visited

◶ (Alt+Right) Navigate forwards to the next code line you have visited.

≣ (Ctrl+Q) Sets the selected lines as comments (page 82).

≣ (Ctrl+W) Unsets the selected lines as comments (page 82).

⇤ (Shift+Tab) Decrease the indentation of the selected lines (page 82).

⇥ (Tab) Increase the indentation of the selected lines (page 82).

▶ (F5) Runs the compiler using the mode selected in the compiler options list

↳. (F8) Step into the next line or subroutine. Only available in break mode.

↷ (F9) Step over the next line or subroutine. Only available in break mode.

↶ (F10) Step out of the current subroutine. Only available in break mode.

■ Stop running the code Only available in break mode.

↻ (F11) Recompile the app (if necessary) and re-run.

| Debug (legacy) ▾ | Compiler options list. See Compilation Modes (page 172).

| Default ▾ | Select the required Build Configuration (page 171).

Module Tabs

Below the Toolbar is a row of tabs, one for each module (page 232) in the project, for example:

⊞ Main ✕   ⌦ ClassExample   ☰ CodeExample   ⚡ ServiceExample

The icons used are:

⊞ Activity Module

⌦ Class Module

☰ Code Module

⚡ Service Module

Clicking a tab brings the corresponding module to the front.

You can re-order these tabs by dragging them to the left and right. You can also drag the tab to undock (page 94) the module.

Note that the IDE remembers (page 93) the order of the tabs when you save the project, except for the Main module, whose tab is always placed on the left.

Closing a Module

Every module tab has an X which allows you to "close" that tab, that is, remove it from the list. You also get this option by right-clicking the tab (see below).

Note that the module is still part of the project, and is still listed in the Modules window on the right of the IDE. It can be re-opened by clicking its name in that list.

Popup Module Tab Menu

Right-clicking on a module tab at the top of the code area reveals a popup menu.

Close

  See Closing a Module above.

Close Others

  Close all other Modules except this one. See Closing a Module above.

Float

  Floating is removing a window from the IDE. See Floating (page 94).

Dock

  Fix the module within the IDE. See Docking (page 94). Only available if module is floating.

New Horizontal Tab Group

  See Horizontal Tab Group (page 95)

New Vertical Tab Group

  See Vertical Tab Group (page 96)

Code area

Subroutine Dropdown List

At the top of the code area is a dropdown list box which allows you to quickly move to a subroutine in the current module.

🐜 Activity_Create   ▾

The list it displays is the same as the list in the Modules window (page 89).

Zoom Control

Next to this is a zoom control which lets you zoom the code larger or smaller.

100%   ▾
20%
50%
70%
100%
150%
200%

Code

Below these come the actual code. Each Module Tab is linked to the area where you can edit the module's code. This is where you edit your code. Code consists of some header information, such as **Project Attributes** and **Activity Attributes**. It then contains a series of **Subroutines** (abbreviated to Sub). This is typical of BASIC programs.

Each Sub has a name, for example Sub **Globals**, and the name is shown in bold type.

Revision Color Coding

When you edit your code, the latest edits are marked with a yellow bar in the left margin:

```
32    btnTest1.Initialize("btnTest1")
33
34    Dim myAge, yourAge As Int
35    myAge = 16
36
```

When you save or compile and run the code, the yellow bar will turn green.

When you close the project, the colored bars will not be saved.

Regions

For your convenience while editing, your code is divided into blocks called Regions. A Region is an area of your code which you can rapidly expand or collapse. You can do the same with Subroutines. You can expand or collapse regions and subs by clicking on the "+" and "−" signs on the left of the Code area:

```
10  ⊞#Region  Activity Attributes
14
15  ⊞Sub Process_Globals
20
21  ⊟Sub Globals
22       'These global variables will be redeclared each time the activity is
```

You can define your own regions using **#Region** and **#End Region** and embed several subroutines within them. The benefit is that by collapsing the code, you make it easier to navigate to the required section.

Controlling Outlining

The [Edit > Outlining] menu contains three functions to expand or collapse code:

Toggle All (Ctrl-Shift-O)- Expands collapsed code and simultaneously collapses extended code.

Expand All - Expands the whole code

Collapse All - Collapses the whole code.

You can also control outlining by clicking on the + and – controls at the head of each Sub or Region. You can collapse or expand a single sub or region by right-clicking within it and selecting **Toggle Outling** from the pop-up menu.

Note that the IDE remembers (page 93) the state of collapse of each portion when you save and exit the project.

Hovering over Collapsed Code

Hovering with the mouse over a collapsed Region or subroutine shows the beginning of its content.

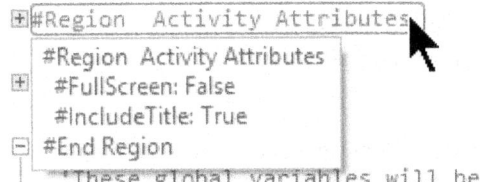

Code header

There are two pre-defined Regions in the Main Module: **Project Attributes** and **Activity Attributes**, which we describe next. Remember that Regions are purely for convenience, and Attributes can in fact be defined anywhere.

Project Attributes Region

This Region normally contains attributes valid for the whole project. These can only be defined in the Main module.

```
#Region   Project Attributes
  #ApplicationLabel: B4A Example
  #VersionCode: 1
  #VersionName:
  'SupportedOrientations possible values: unspecified, landscape or
portrait.
  #SupportedOrientations: unspecified
  #CanInstallToExternalStorage: False
#End Region
```
For details see the Project Attributes section (page 111).

Activity Attributes Region
This Region normally contains attributes which determine features of the current activity.
```
#Region   Activity Attributes
  #FullScreen: False
  #IncludeTitle: True
#End Region
```
See Activity Attributes (page 240) for details.

Service Attributes
When you add a new Service, you'll find the **Service Attributes** header:
```
#Region   Service Attributes
  #StartAtBoot: False
#End Region
```
See Service Attributes (page 255) for details.

Commenting and uncommenting code

A selected part of the code can be set to comment lines using the Block Comment icon ⬛ on the Tool Bar, or set to normal using the Block Uncomment icon ⬛.

Indentation

It is good practice to indent your code and so make its structure (of subroutines, loops etc.) more obvious and easier to verify. For example consider the following:
```
Sub getSystemDirectory As String
Dim systemDirectory As String
If File.ExternalWritable Then
systemDirectory = File.DirDefaultExternal
Else
' have to use internal folder
systemDirectory = File.DirInternal
End If
Log ("systemDirectory = " & systemDirectory)
Return systemDirectory
End Sub
```
This is clearer if the text is indented to reveal its logical structure:

```
Sub getSystemDirectory As String
 Dim systemDirectory As String
 If File.ExternalWritable Then
  systemDirectory = File.DirDefaultExternal
 Else
  ' have to use internal folder
  systemDirectory = File.DirInternal
 End If
 Log ("systemDirectory = " & systemDirectory)
 Return systemDirectory
End Sub
```

Whole blocks of code can be indented forth and back at once by selecting the code block and clicking ⇥ or ⇤ , or by selecting the block and pressing the Tab key to indent or Shift+Tab to un-indent.
Once you have indented a line of code, subsequent lines will also be indented by the same amount until you change the indentation.
You can set the size of the indentation by selecting [Tools > IDE Options > Fonts Picker > Tab Size]

Autocomplete

The autocomplete function helps you write your code. When you type into the code area, a list of matching keywords will be displayed. The display is either automatic or manual depending on the state of [Tools > IDE Options > Disable Implicit Auto Completion].
Manual display requires you to press Ctrl+Space.

For example, if you type "b", autocomplete shows:

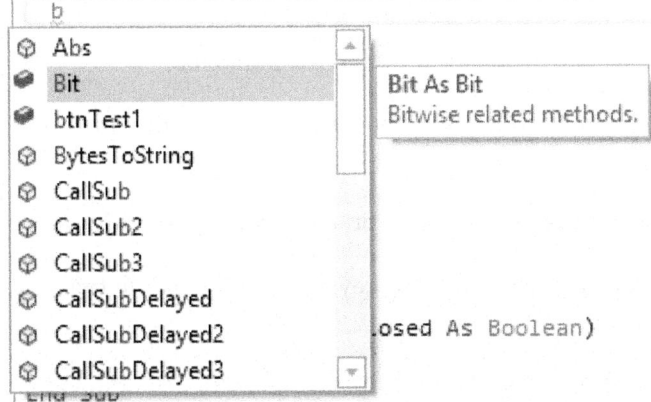

The popup menu shows all variables, views and property names plus on-line help for the highlighted word.
Note: If Implicit Auto Completion is enabled then the list only shows keywords which contain the letters you typed, as shown above.
If Implicit Auto Completion is disenabled, then manual autocomplete (summoned by typing and pressing Ctrl+Space) shows the complete list of keywords.

Select the required word by using the mouse or the arrow keys, then press Enter or Return.

Autocomplete Properties and Methods

Once a variable or object name has been selected, type a dot. All properties and methods are displayed in a popup menu:

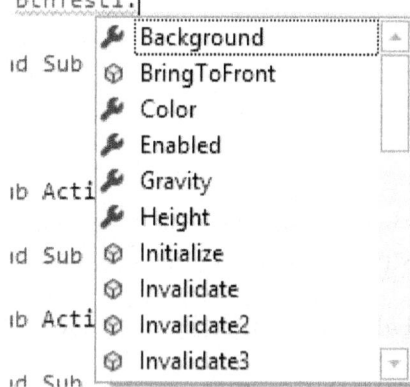

Properties have a 🔧 icon and methods have 🎯.

Autocomplete event subroutines

Before a view can raise events, it has to be initialized, and an eventname must be specified. Typically the event name is the same as the name of the view. If you are creating the view in code then you need to initialize it:

```
btnTest1.Initialize("btnTest1")
```

Note: any views created within the Visual Designer will be automatically initialized when you load the layout, and must not be initialized again. Their eventname will be the same as the view's name.

You need a Sub to define the handler for a click event. It must have a name like

```
Sub bntTest1_Click
```

where **bntTest1** is the eventname defined above. **Click** is the name of the event which is handled by the sub.

In B4A there is an Autocomplete function which allows you to create Event (page 297) subroutines **with the correct arguments**.
Enter the Sub word plus a blank character and press the Tab key. A list of available types is displayed:

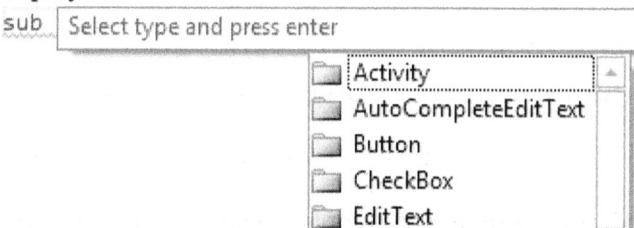

Select the type of the object which raises the event and press Enter.
A list of possible events is then displayed. For example for a Button:

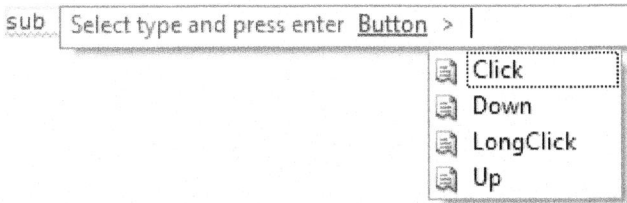

Select the event type and press Enter. The Sub name is automatically created together with its arguments:

```
⊟sub EventName_Click

End Sub
```

Now edit the EventName to match the event name which was specified when the source object was Initialized.

Comments as Documentation

The documentation feature built into B4A is very useful. Comments (page 273) above subs, such as:

```
' Split strCurrent into substrings using strDelimiter
'  and return a list
' strCurrent - the string to split
' strDelimiter - the character(s) to use to split strCurrent
' Example: <code>
' lst = splitString("Abcdefcghi", "c")
' </code>
Sub splitString(strCurrent As String, strDelimiter As String) As List
     Dim splitResult As List
```

Note: tags such <code></code>, <i></i> or <b></b> do not currently format correctly.

Now if autocomplete is active and type **sp**, the comment will automatically appear in the popup window:

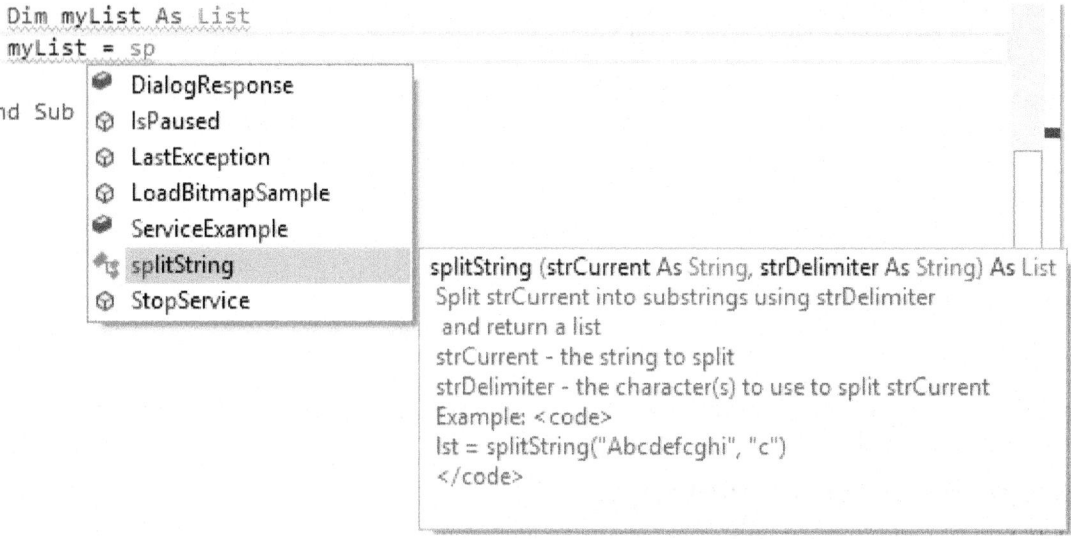

Any comment immediately before **Sub Process_Globals** is treated as the main module comment.

Block Completion

When you type a line of code which requires another line to complete a block, B4A will automatically generate the second line for you and also add an indented intervening line where you can add your code

The following keywords will automatically generate a block:

```
Sub, For...To, If...Then, For Each, Do While, Do Until, Select, Try
```

Context Menu

Right-clicking in the Code Area produces the Context Menu.

Most of these are described in the Edit menu (page 68).

Note: Cut and Copy apply to any text which is selected and beneath the cursor when you right-click. If no text is selected, the while line at the cursor will be cut or copied, but if word wrap is in operation, any wrapped text will not be cut or copied.

Other items in the Context Menu are:

Add Watch Expression

This is only available when program execution is paused at a break point.

Toggle Outlining (Ctrl+O)

Expand or collapse the current sub or region

Block Comment (Ctrl+Q)

Add comment marks to the currently selected line or block.

Block Uncomment (Ctrl+W)

Remove comment marks from the currently selected line or block.

Goto Identifier (Ctrl+Click or F12)

Jump to the definition of a subroutine or the declaration of a variable.

Color Picker

Selecting this option from the Context Menu shows the same dialog as [Tools > Color Picker (page 74)]

Highlighting occurrences of words

When selecting a word, the word is highlighted in blue (A in the following diagram) and all other occurrences in the code are highlighted in a lighter blue (B) while the scrollview on the right side indicates other occurences of the word in the document (C) in light blue.

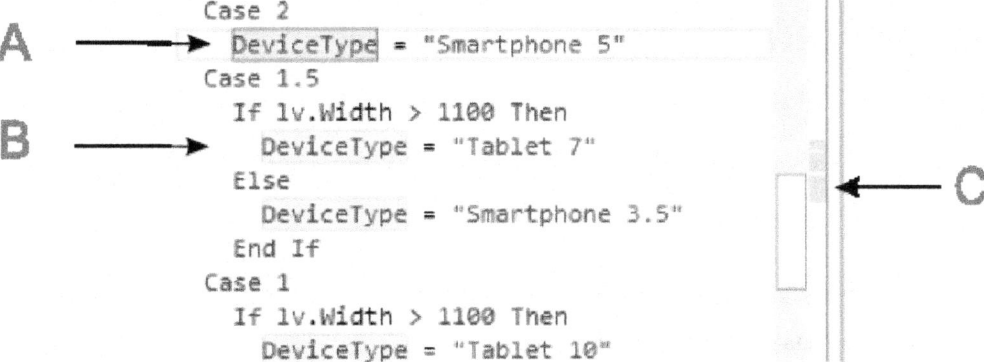

Structure Matching

When a key word is selected which defines a structure such Sub or If or Select, the editor automatically highlights the other key words which complete the structure:

```
Case 1
    If lv.Width > 1100 Then
        DeviceType = "Tablet 10"
    Else If lv.Width < 600 Then
        DeviceType = "Smartphone 3.5"
    Else
        DeviceType = "Tablet 7"
    End If
End Select
```

Windows Area

The content of the Windows Area (on the right of the IDE by default) depends upon which of the Window Tabs has been selected.

Window Tabs

There are up to 6 tabs at the bottom of the Windows Area which display the following windows.

📖 Libraries Manager
This option is only available in the Full version of B4A.
Clicking on the Libraries Manager tab brings the Libraries Manager into the Windows Area. This shows a list of the available libraries (page 451) that can be used in the project.

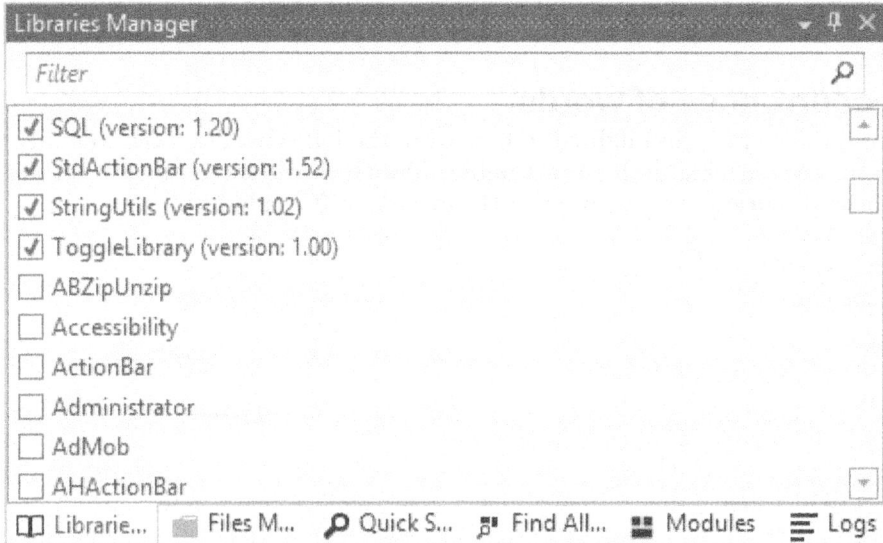

The Filter allows you to search for a specific library.

Check the libraries you need to reference in your project. They are shown at the top of the list. All projects reference the Core Library (page 336). Some other libraries (the Standard Libraries (page 456)) are included with the installation. Others are Additional Libraries (page 562), generated both by Anywhere Software (the makers of B4A) and by users.

If you need to download an Additional Library, you will find a partial list of them here (http://bit.ly/16H9C7s), although it does not include them all. More information about libraries can be found here (page 451).

Files Manager

The Files Manager lists of the files that have been added to the project.

Files Manager	▼ ⃞ ✕
Filter	🔎
☐ bluetoothOff.png	▲
☐ bluetoothOn.png	
☐ Chart.bal	
☐ ConnectDevice.bal	
☐ help.bal	
☐ history.bal	
☐ ic_action_edit.png	
☐ ic_action_new.png	▼
[Add Files] [Remove] [Sync]	
📖 Librarie... 📂 Files M... 🔎 Quick S... ⌨ Find All... ▦ Modules ☰ Logs	

Add Files

To add files to the list, either drag and drop files from Windows File Explorer or click on **Add Files**. These can be any kind of files: layouts, images, texts, etc. On your PC, the selected files will be copied to the **Files** folder of your project. On the device, these files will be saved in the Files.DirAssets (page 371) folder.

Remove

Checking one or more files in the list enables the **Remove** button.
Clicking on the **Remove** button shows the following dialog:

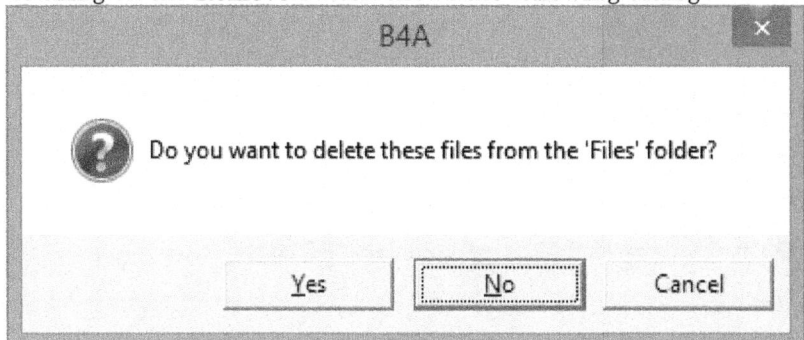

Yes: removes the selected file(s) from the list and from the **Files** folder of the project. **Make sure to have a copy of the files you remove, because they are removed from the Files folder, but not transferred to the recycle bin. This means they are definitively lost if you don't have a copy.**
No: removes the selected files from the list but does not delete them from the project's **Files** folder.
See Files (page 365) for file handling.

Sync

Clicking on **Sync** will update the list of files to reflect the actual files in the project's file folder.

⸬ Modules Window

An app can contain several modules (page 232). Clicking on the Modules tab shows a list of all the modules in the top of the Windows Area, and a list of Subroutines below it.

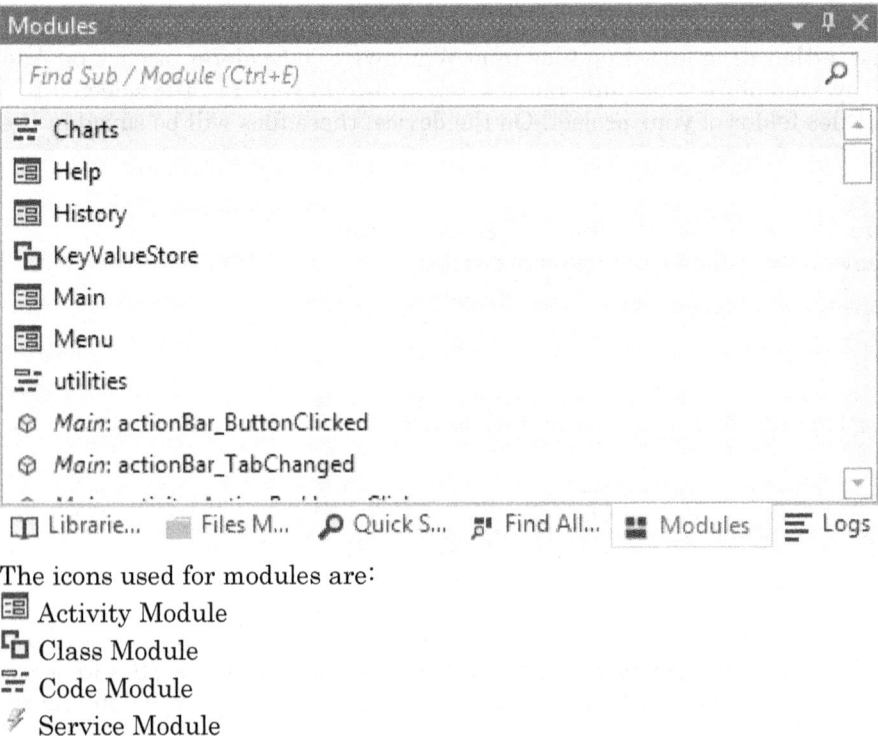

The icons used for modules are:

📇 Activity Module

🖧 Class Module

☲ Code Module

⚡ Service Module

Clicking on one of the module names brings that module to the top in the Code Area and lists all of its subroutines. Clicking on one of the subroutines in the list moves the cursor directly to the selected routine. You can type into the Find Sub/Module (Ctrl+E) area to quickly locate the sub you want.

☲ Logs Window

Clicking on the Logs window tab displays at the top a list of compiler errors and warnings, and at the bottom shows the log (page 181) generated by the program the last time it ran in the current session. Note that logs are not preserved when B4A closes.

⅋ Find All References (F7)

Contains a list of all references in all modules to the variable or sub currently selected in the code. (Searching for keywords will return an empty result.) You **must** press F7 to execute the search. The selected variable or sub is highlighted in the search results.

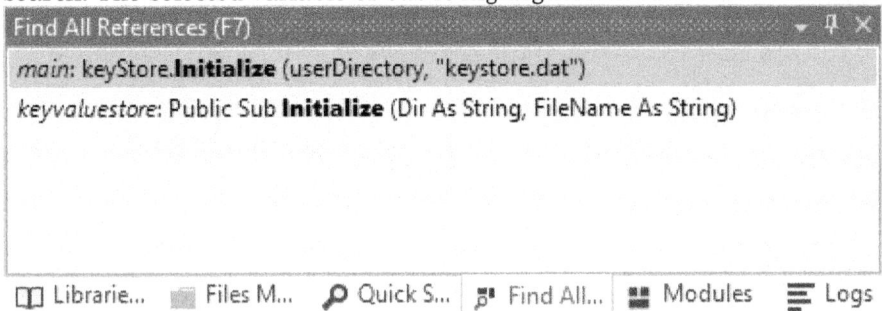

You can click a reference to quickly go to that line of code.

🔎 Quick Search

This allows you to find all instances of the given text in all modules, and move to them by clicking the line in the search result list.

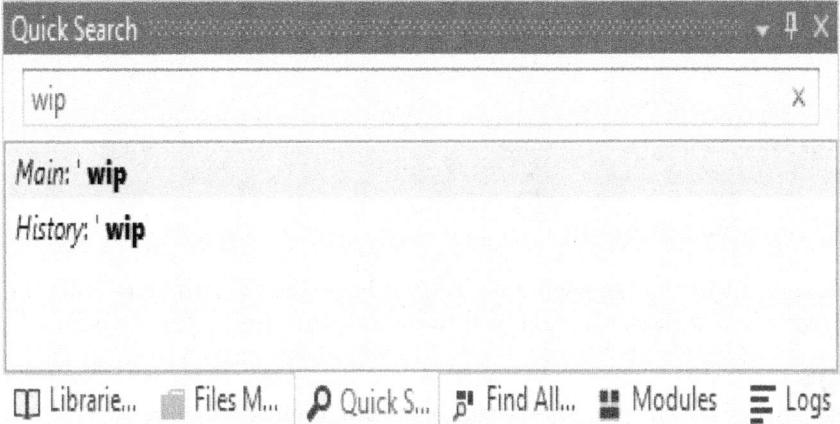

Bookmark Substitute

Note that (unlike previous versions) version 5.0 of B4A does not allow you to create **Bookmarks** in your code; however you can simulate them by adding special comments such as

```
' wip keystore variables and constants
```

where wip means Work In Progress and then doing a Quick Search for wip (or whatever text you chose to mark your work), such as shown above.

Navigate Backward / Forward ⊖ ⊖

Note another way of moving quickly through your code is to use the Navigate icons in the toolbar, which move to the previous and next code lines you have visited recently.

The Warning Engine

The Warning Engine runs when you compile or save your project, and also as you type, warning you immediately of errors in your code. When you open a project it remembers the warnings.

The offending lines of code are underlined (A in the following diagram) and they are listed at the top of the Logs Window (B), errors in red, warnings in purple. If you hover your mouse above an error or warning in the code area, you see its details (C). Their position is marked on the scrollbar (D) with the same color code.

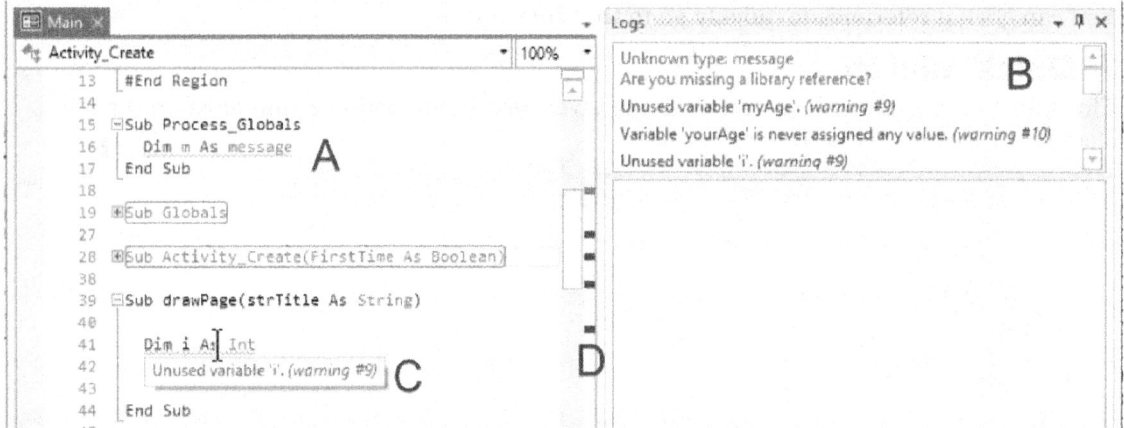

Warnings might be too long to fit in the Logs window (B), but hovering over them reveals the full text. Clicking on a Logs window item will take you to the relevant line in the source code.

Ignoring Warnings

You can disable warnings, either for specific lines or for a specific type of warning in a module. To ignore warnings for a line, add a comment with the word "ignore":

```
Sub Activity_KeyPress(KeyCode As Int) As Boolean 'ignore
```

To disable specific types of warnings in a module, add the **#IgnoreWarning** attribute. For example, to disable warnings #10 and #12 in an **Activity module**:

```
#Region Activity Attributes
  #FullScreen: False
  #IncludeTitle: True
  ' add the following line
  #IgnoreWarnings: 10, 12
#End Region
```

For modules which have no Attributes Region, add the line near the top of the code, for example:

```
'Class Person module
  IgnoreWarnings: 12
```

The warnings

1: Unreachable code detected.
2: Not all code paths return a value.
3: Return type (in Sub signature) should be set explicitly.
4: Return value is missing. Default value will be used instead.
5: Variable declaration type is missing. String type will be used.
6: The following value misses screen units ('dip' or %x / %y): {1}.
7: Object converted to String. This is probably a programming mistake.
8: Undeclared variable '{1}'.
9: Unused variable '{1}'.
10: Variable '{1}' is never assigned any value.
11: Variable '{1}' was not initialized.
12: Sub '{1}' is not used.
13: Variable '{1}' should be declared in **Sub Process_Globals**.

14: File '{1}' in Files folder was not added to the **Files** tab. You should either delete it or add it to the project. You can choose Tools - Clean unused files.

15: File '{1}' is not used.

16: Layout file '{1}' is not used. Are you missing a call to `Activity.LoadLayout`?

17: File '{1}' is missing from the **Files** tab.

18: TextSize value should not be scaled as it is scaled internally.

19: Empty Catch block. You should at least add Log(LastException.Message).

20: View '{1}' was added with the designer. You should not initialize it.

21: Cannot access view's dimension before it is added to its parent.

22: Types do not match.

23: Modal dialogs are not allowed in `Sub Activity_Pause`. It will be ignored.

24: Accessing fields from other modules in `Sub Process_Globals` can be dangerous as the initialization order is not deterministic.

In addition, B4A gives the following **runtime warnings:**

1001: `Panel.LoadLayout` should only be called after the panel was added to its parent.

1002: The same object was added to the list. You should call `Dim` again to create a new object.

1003: Object was already initialized.

1004: `FullScreen` or `IncludeTitle` properties in layout file do not match the activity attributes settings.

The IDE Meta File

When you save your project, B4A saves a file with the same name as the .b4a file but with the .meta extension. This stores details about the current breakpoints, the state of outlining, which modules are shown and in what order (except the Main tab, which is always placed on the left), and the build last used.

If you are using a source control system you should exclude the meta file. Note also that the project will load correctly without a meta file. Also note that if you add a breakpoint and then close the project without saving it, the meta file will not be saved.

1.3 Docking

Docking is a way of organising your working environment in a way which suits yourself by positioning windows such as modules or windows within the IDE or the Visual Designer.

Window Menus

Both modules and windows in the IDE have menus which can be used to control their docking.

Module Menu

If you right-click a module's tab, you will see a menu with these options:

Close

Close the current module.

Closed modules can be re-opened by double-clicking them from the Modules window.

Close Others

Close all other Modules except this one.

Float

Let this window float separate from the IDE. See Floating.

Dock

Fix the module within the IDE. Only available if floating. See Docking.

New Horizontal Tab Group

See Horizontal Tab Group

New Vertical Tab Group

See Vertical Tab Group

Window Menu

If you click on the window's down arrow, you will see an options list:

Float

Let this window float separate from the IDE. See Floating.

Dock

Move the window back into the IDE. Only available if floating. See Docking.

Dock as Document

This option is only available in the Visual Designer, as discussed below.

Auto Hide

Selecting this option will make the window or group of windows automatically close. See Auto Hide below for details.

Close

Close the current window.

Closed windows can be re-opened by selecting them from the [Windows] menu.

Floating

A module or window can be completely removed from the IDE so it floats in a window of its own.

To float a Module: right-click a module's tab (shown above) and select Float.

To float a Window: click on the window's down arrow to reveal its options list (shown above) and select Float.

Note that you do not need to float modules or windows if you merely wish to move them to a new docking position. You can instead click and drag, as explained below.

Tab Groups

A tab group is a region of the screen which includes several windows on top of each other, and which have a set of tabs to allow you to select which window is uppermost.

Horizontal Tab Group

If you right-click on a module tab you will see an option to create a New Horizontal Tab Group. A horizontal tab group is one in which the new group lies below the original, and stretches horizontally across the same space. So here are two horizontal tab groups:

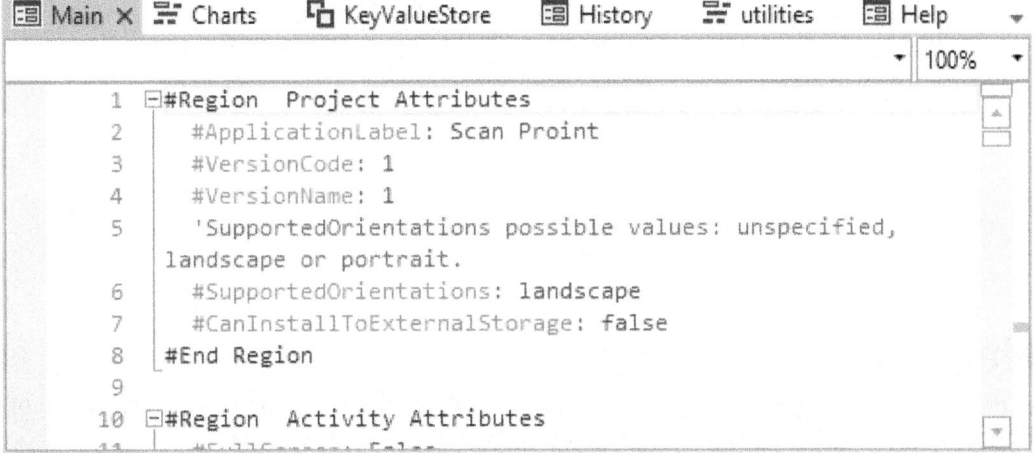

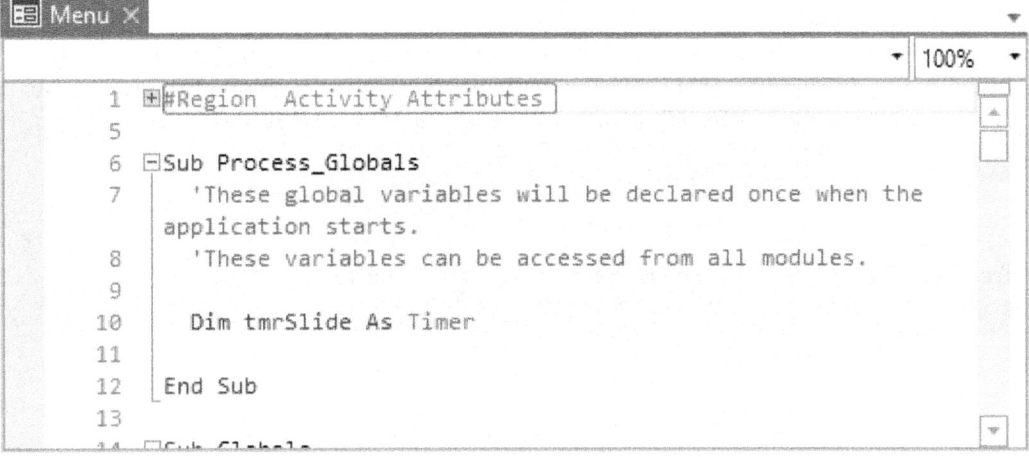

Vertical Tab Group

A vertical tab group, on the other hand, sits to the right of the original, and fills the same vertical space:

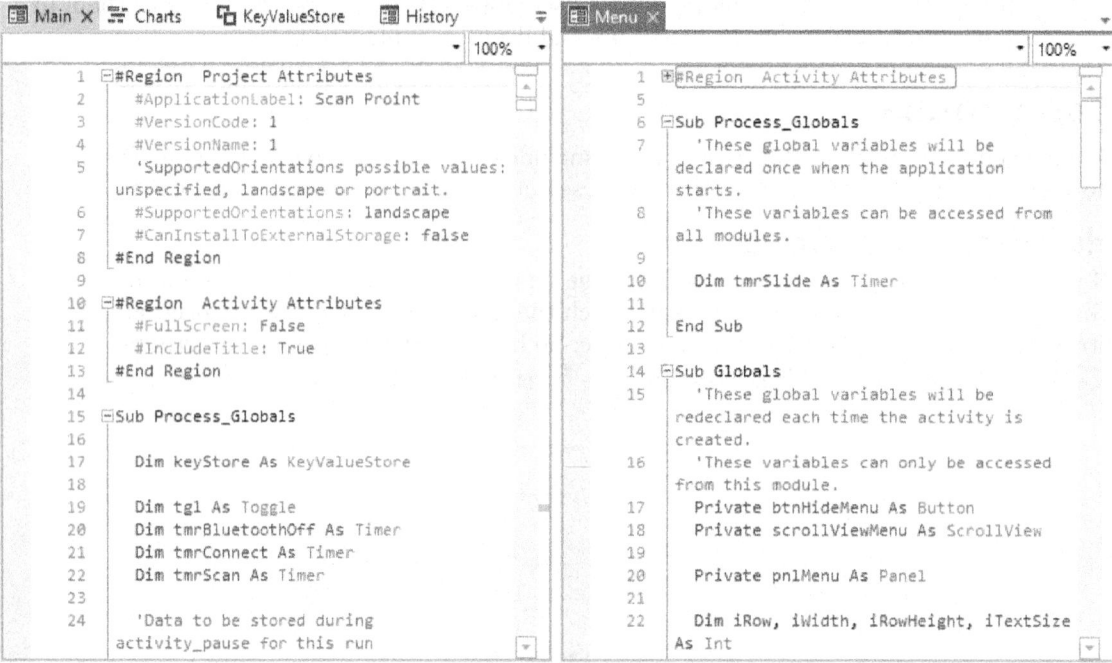

Docking

Docking is the process of fixing a window within the IDE. It might be attached to the edge of the IDE, or it might occupy a place alongside other windows in a tab group.

Dragging Windows

If the window is part of a tab group, you can move it to a different docking position by clicking on its tab and dragging. If the window is floating, or is not part of a tab group, you can click and drag its header. A free-floating module's header is a solid bar:

While a free-floating tool-window's header has a crosshatch pattern:

Docking a Module

When you drag a module over the IDE, you will see a guide:

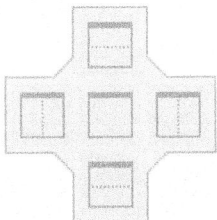

If you position the mouse pointer over one of the boxes in the guide, a colored area will show where the dragged window can be docked:

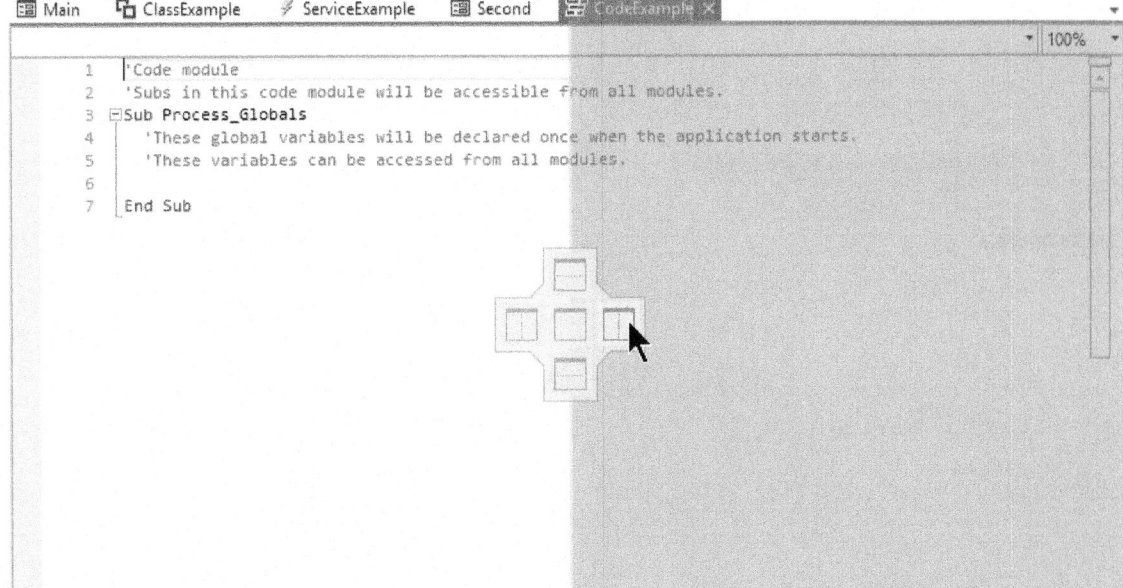

It can be docked to left, right, top or bottom of the current tab area, or in the group of tabs if you select the central box. For example, if you accept the docking shown above, the module will occupy a separate tab group to the right of the current one.

This allows you to see and edit two or more modules at the same time. You can drag and drop modules between these tab groups. You can even open more tab groups:

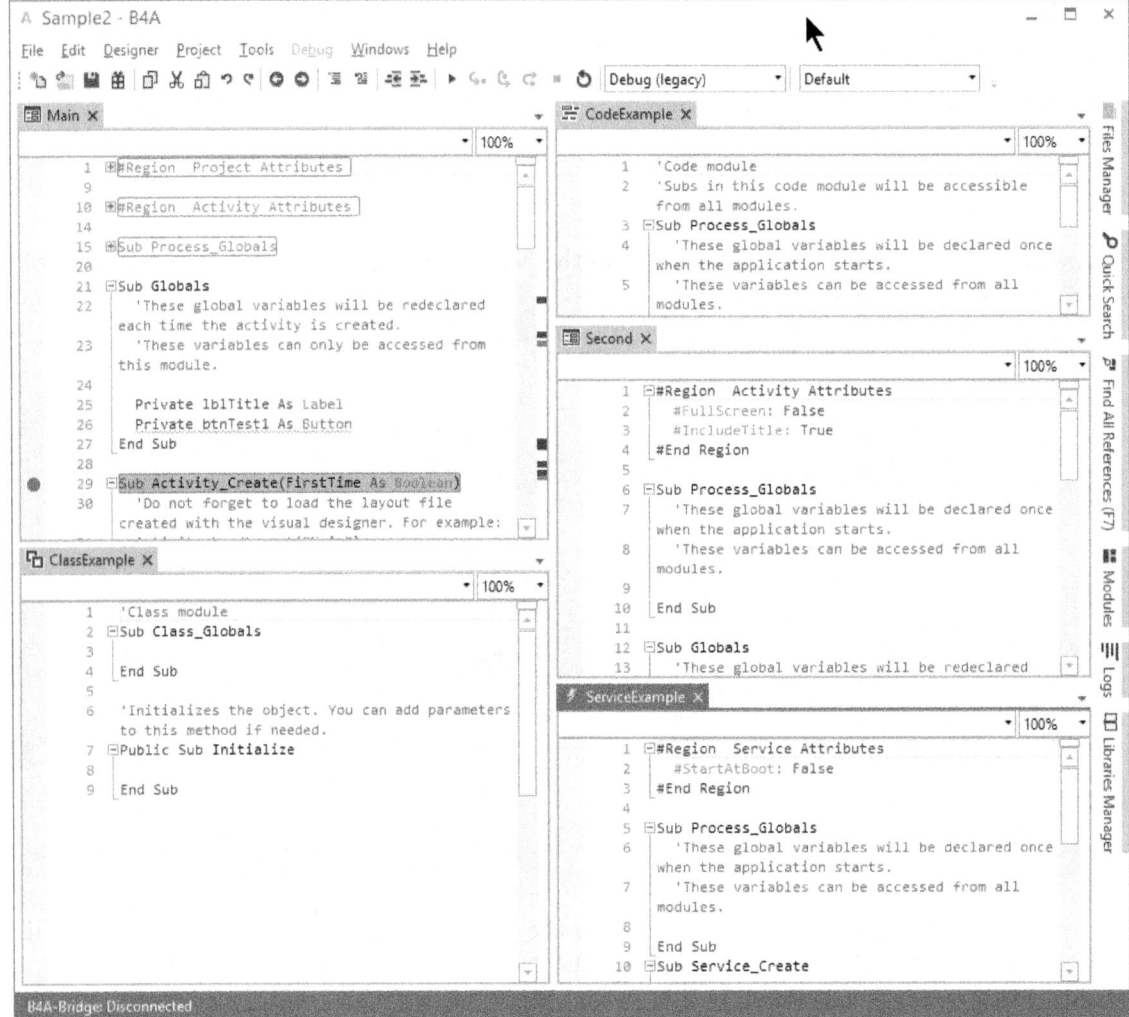

Docking Windows

If you drag a tool window which is normally shown in a tab group on the right of the IDE, the guide you see looks different from when you drag a module.

As you drag the window within the IDE, you will see a guide with a set of sub-guides:

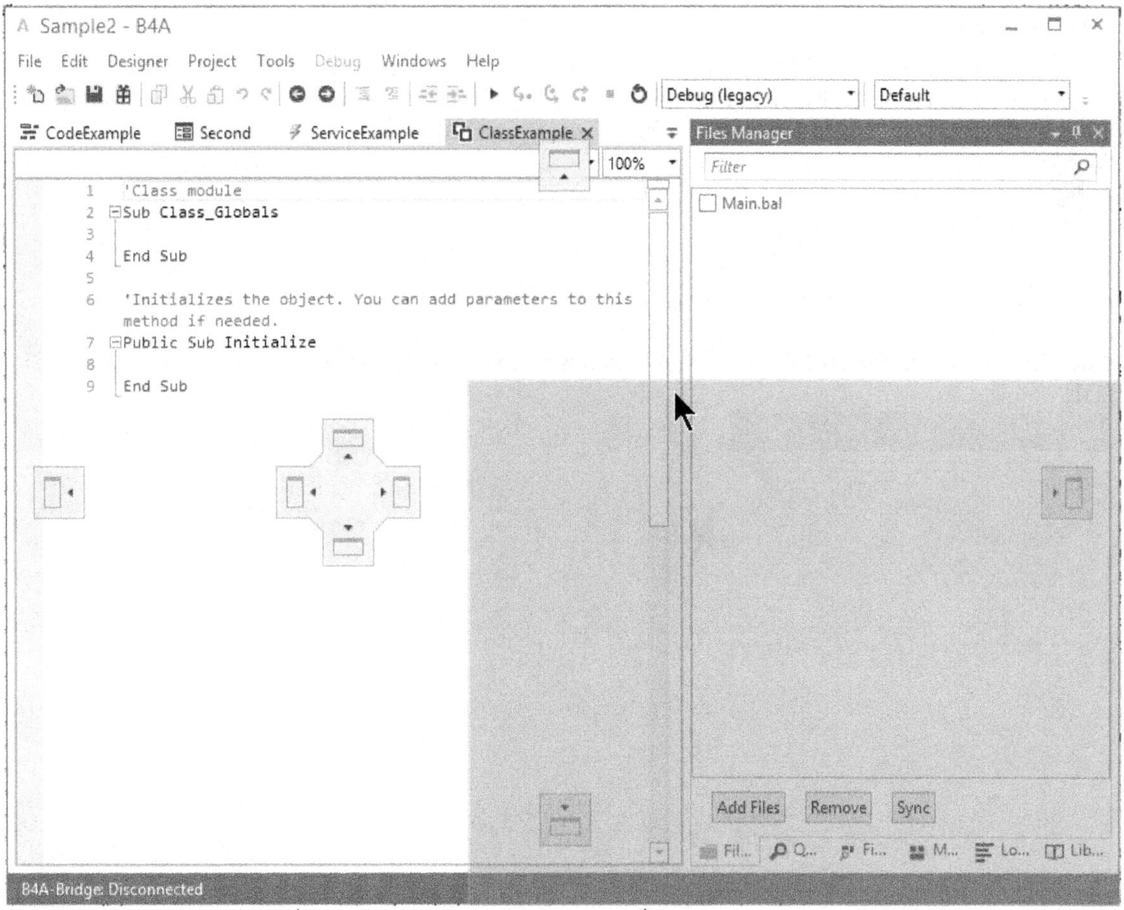

The single outer guides (such as the one shown below) allow you to dock the window to the IDE's outer window,

wheras the four inner guides allow docking within a selected tab group.

Note that tool-windows and modules cannot occupy the same tab group, so the central guide only has 4 options, not 5 as was the previous case.

Moving a Tab Group

If you drag the header of a window which is part of a tab group, this will move all the windows in that tab group, not just the one on top.

Docking Windows

If you have undocked a window, or a group of windows, you can dock them by dragging them back into the IDE.

You can also dock a window at a new position within the IDE by dragging its tab or header, as shown above.

Auto Hide

Windows can be made to automatically close into a vertical menu on the side of the IDE. Auto hiding is achieved by either clicking on the pushpin in the window header to change it from a vertical pin (not hidden) into a horizontal pin (hidden).

Alternatively you can select Auto Hide from the windows header options drop-down list.

Auto-hidden windows will reveal themselves when you click on the menu at the side of the IDE:

The window will close again when you click somewhere else within the IDE.

Visual Designer

You can dock the windows within the Visual Designer in a similar way to that shown above. The main difference is that the Abstract Designer is a "document". Other windows can be docked in the same tab group by selecting "Dock as Document" from their options. Or they can be dragged and dropped following the guides in the way described above.

Your arrangement of docked windows will be remembered the next time you open the Visual Designer. You could, for example, organise all the windows in a tab group on the right, in a similar way to those in the IDE:

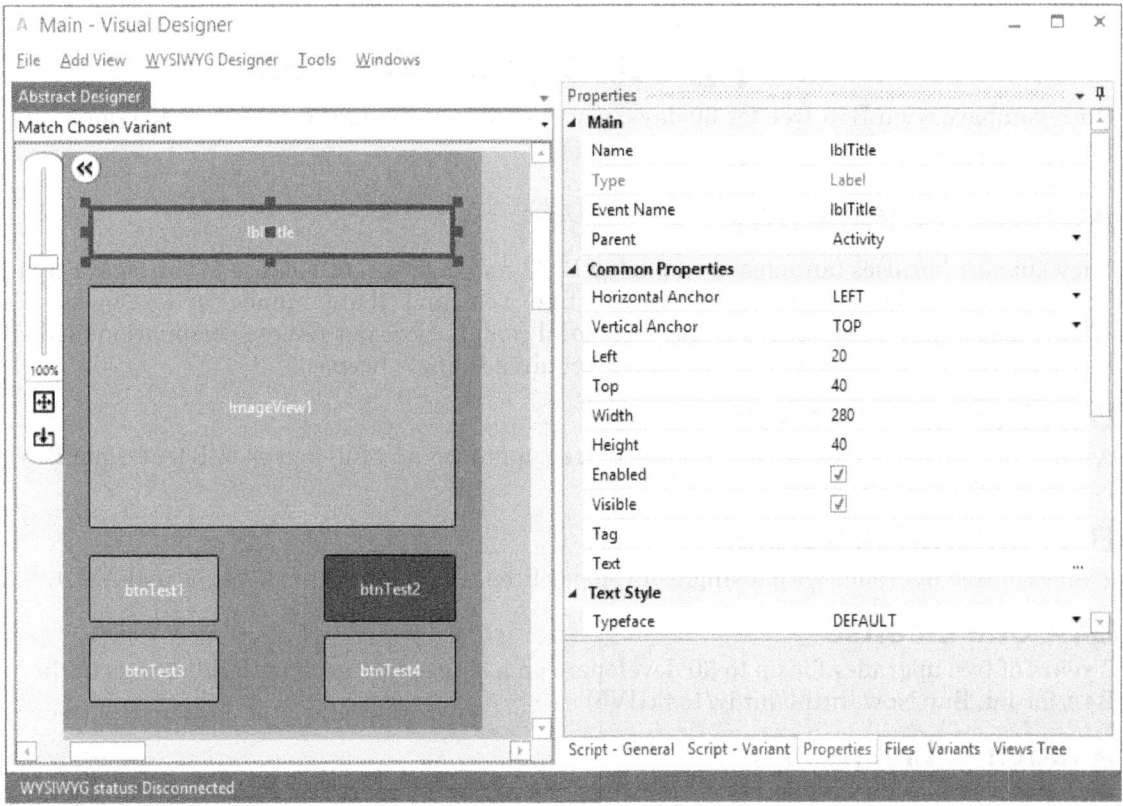

Restoring All Windows

To restore windows to their original docking positions within the IDE or the Visual Designer, use [Windows > Reset]. Note that within the IDE, this will only restore windows to their original position with the tab group on the right of the IDE. Modules which have been positioned will remain in the place you put them.

1.4 Upgrade to Full Version

Once you have tried B4A free for 30 days, you might want to upgrade to a Full Version. There are several of these:

About Full Versions

They support libraries (an important part of B4A) and give you full access to the B4A forum. Applications developed with B4A are royalty free. You can sell any number of developed applications. The full version only supports local compilation, not remote compilation mode. Licenses are per developer. Each developer requires a single license.

B4A Standard Version

A single developer license with 2 months of free upgrades and full access to B4A forum. Buy Now (http://bit.ly/14uTuGS)

B4A Enterprise Version

2 years of free upgrades with a single developer license. Buy Now (http://bit.ly/1e4kAZD)

B4A Site License

2 years of free upgrades for up to 30 developers on a single site, each with full access to the B4A forum. Buy Now (http://bit.ly/1e4kHV5)

Academic Licenses

Academic licenses (for students, teachers and researchers) are available for half the price. Please contact support@basic4ppc.com and include your academic details.

Purchase

You can use Paypal to purchase any of the above versions from here (http://bit.ly/1IjMUqn). After purchasing, you will receive an email with an attached licence file and a link to download the program. **Make a note of which email address received this email**. You will need it to register the program.

Registering B4A

When you install the full version you will be asked to enter the email address you used when purchasing B4A. This is the email address to which the above email was sent.
You will then be asked to locate the licence file, which is called b4a-license.txt.

Java JDK and Android SDK Installation

The full version does not support remote compilation, only local compilation, so you must install Java JDK and Android SDK. (These are optional with the trial version.) So we must now visit the murky world of Java. Luckily you have chosen B4A so our visit will be brief!

Check if the Java JDK is already installed

You might want to verify whether the Java JDK is already installed on your PC.
Open [Control Panel > Programs and Features] and search for the JDK. Confusingly, this will be called "Java SE Development Kit N Update X" where N and X are numbers.

If you already have JDK 64 Bit

In some cases, the Android SDK installer fails to find JDK 64bit. Therefore, it is recommended to install the 32bit version of the JDK. However, if the SDK is already installed, then it should work. Skip the next step and proceed to install the Android SDK. If it finds the JDK then it's fine. If it fails, then come back to the step below and install the 32bit version.

Install the 32 bit Java JDK

For all machines, even 64 bit, it is recommended to select 32bit **"Windows x86"** in the platforms list. This is because in some cases the Android SDK installer fails to find JDK 64bit. See the note above if you already have the 64bit JDK.

Installation

The first step should be to install the Java JDK, also known as the Java SE Development Kit. **Note**: there is no problem with having several versions of Java installed on the same computer. The steps are:
- Goto the Java SE Development Kit download web page here (http://bit.ly/1IjN1lE).
- Find the latest version of the Java Platform (usually at the top of the page)
- Click the link to download the JDK
- Check the **Accept License Agreement** radio button.
- Find the Java SE Development Kit NuNN section (N will vary depending on the latest version available).
Note: Demos and Samples are not needed.
- Download the relevant exe (X86 recommended, see above) and run it.
- **Note the folder in which you install the JDK**. You will need this information later.

Install the Android SDK and a platform

The Android software development kit (SDK) is a comprehensive set of development tools including a debugger, libraries, a device emulator (page 188), documentation, sample code, and tutorials. It provides the API libraries and developer tools to build, test, and debug apps for Android, and is required in order to use the full version of B4A. With the trial version it is optional.

You need to install the SDK but do not need the ADT Bundle (which includes a version of the Eclipse (http://www.eclipse.org/) IDE, since you will be using the (far superior) B4A!).

Install the SDK

Goto the SDK page (http://bit.ly/1IjN94N).
Click the link to DOWNLOAD the stand-alone SDK Tools. This will take you to a page where you can download the SDK Tools Only.
Note: Since you will be using B4A as your IDE, you do not need the Android SDK bundle for Android Studio or the Android Studio Packages.

Select the appropriate version, if necessary agree to the terms and conditions and download and run the installer.
If asked whether to "install for anyone using this computer" or "just for me", select whichever seems more appropriate.

The SDK doesn't always behave properly when it is installed in a path with spaces (like "Program Files"). It is recommended to install it to a custom folder similar to C:\android-sdks.

Note the folder where you install it. You will need this information later.

You now need to download the required packages. You should automatically see the Android SDK Manager, as shown below. (You can also run this from the SDK folder).

You need the Android SDK Tools and SDK Platform-tools. In the following example, an update to the Android SDK Tools is available for installation.

On a new installation, the platform tools and the latest platform image (API) are selected for installation by default.

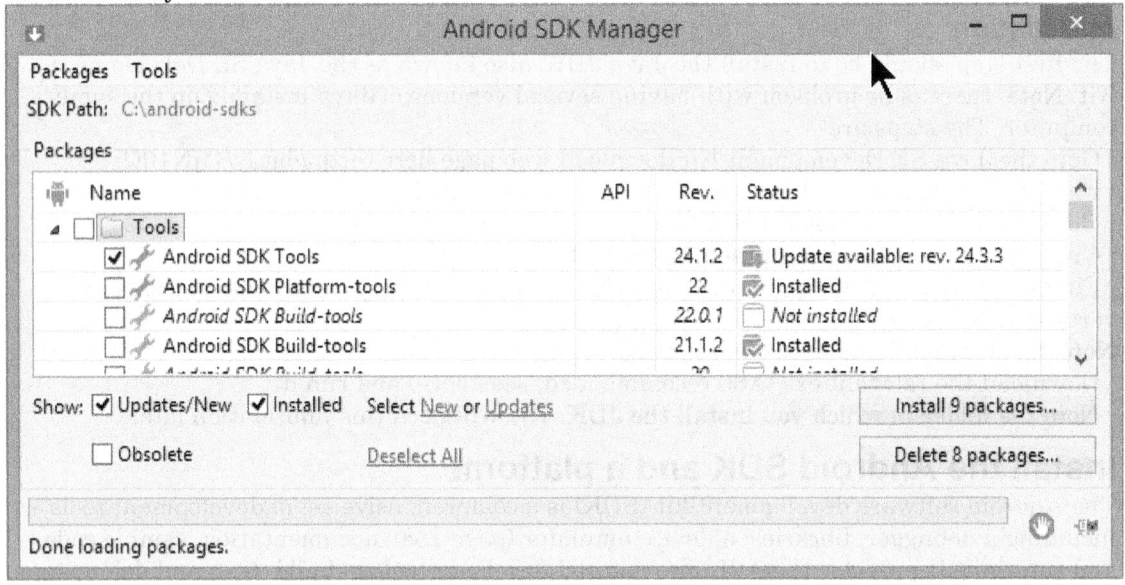

You also need at least one API. Platform images are named "Android VVV (API NN)" where VVV is the version and NN is the API number. The latest one is selected by default. You may select any older ones you need, depending on the hardware you wish to emulate. In the example, API 14 has been chosen.

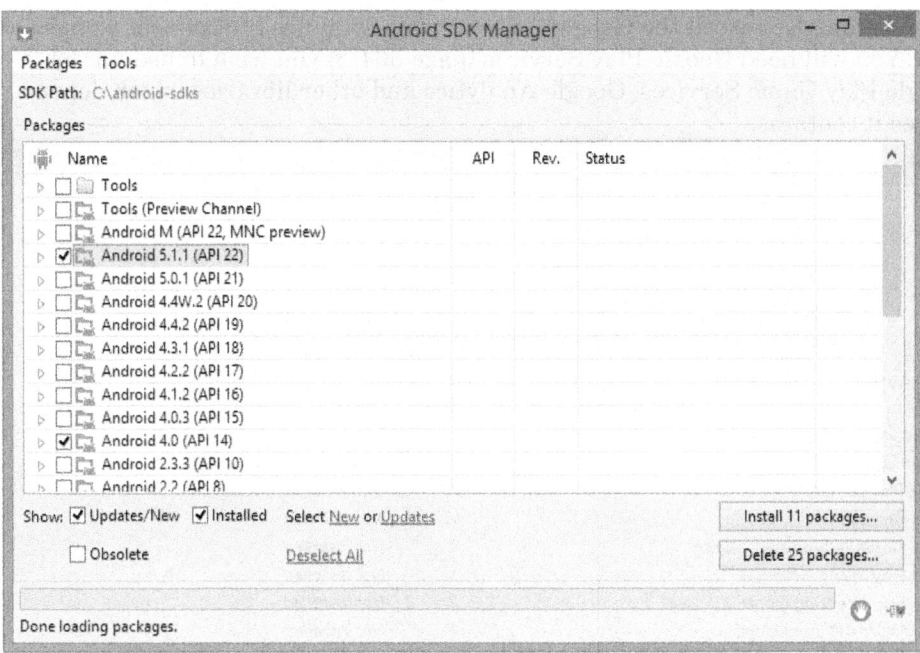

By default, all options within an API are selected. For each API, the SDK Platform is needed. The ARM, Intel and MIPS System Images will be used by the emulator (page 188).

The Google APIs are needed, but Documentation, Samples and Sources are not required, although they may be downloaded if preferred.

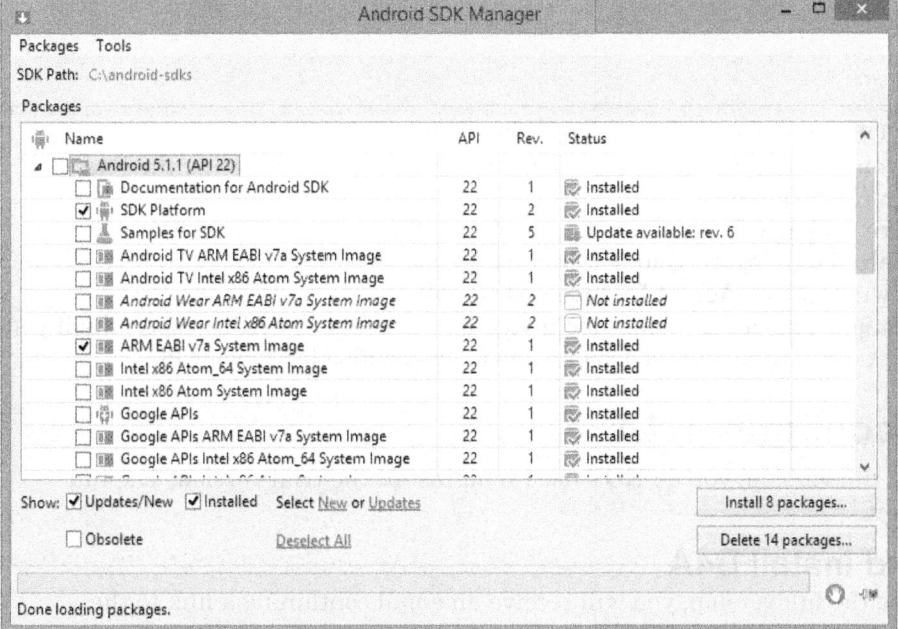

Under "Extras", you can also install the Google USB Driver, if you need to connect a physical device with USB. You will need Google Play Services (page 564) if you wish to use AdMob, GoogleMap, Google Play Game Services, Google Analytics and other libraries which depend upon the resources it contains.

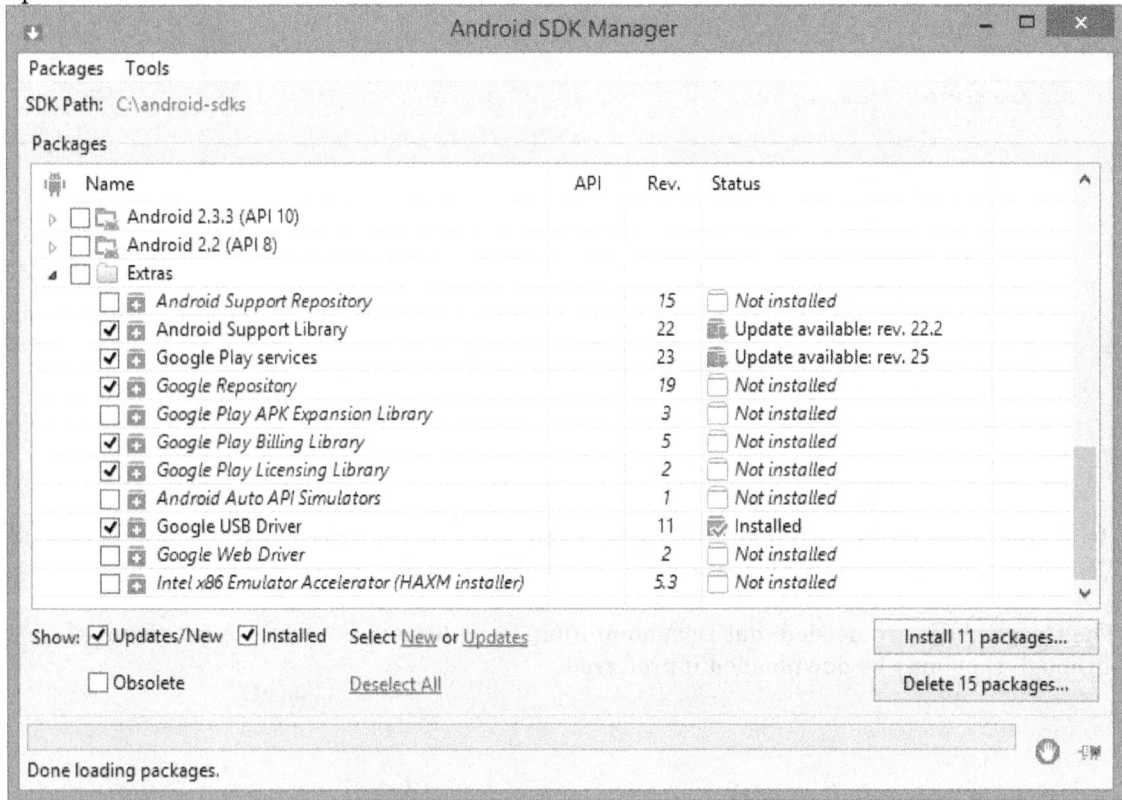

Information about OEM drivers is available here (http://bit.ly/1IjNbte).

Note: B4A allows you to connect to any device over the local network by using the B4A-Bridge (http://bit.ly/1MoNsLe) tool.

You can install more packages later.

Click **Install NN Selected** to install your selected packages.

A dialog box is shown. Click on **Accept License** and **Install**.

Note: installation might take a very long time if you have select many APIs, especially if you have a slow Internet connection, since each one has to be downloaded to your PC.

Install and configure B4A

When you install a full version, you do **NOT** need to uninstall the trial version. The full version overwrites it.

Download and install B4A

When you purchase the full version, you will receive an email containing a link to the download, with a username and password, plus a text file containing your license.

Open B4A

The first time you run B4A, it will check to see if .Net Framework is installed and if not, it will show a dialog box shown previously (page 45). You must download and install .Net Framework or B4A will not run.

License

The email you receive contains a license file (b4a-license.txt) which you should store on your computer. On the first run, B4A will ask you to first locate the license file and afterwards it will ask you for the email address you have used when you purchased B4A.

Notes

The license is not a text file, so you should not open it with a text editor.

It is a good idea to save a copy in a different folder, since the license will be deleted after it is authenticated. The copy will allow you to re-install if you move to a different version of Windows, for example.

Configure Paths

Once B4A has installed and is running, you need to configure several path options for the system to work correctly.

Select menu [Tools > Configure Paths]. The following dialog appears:

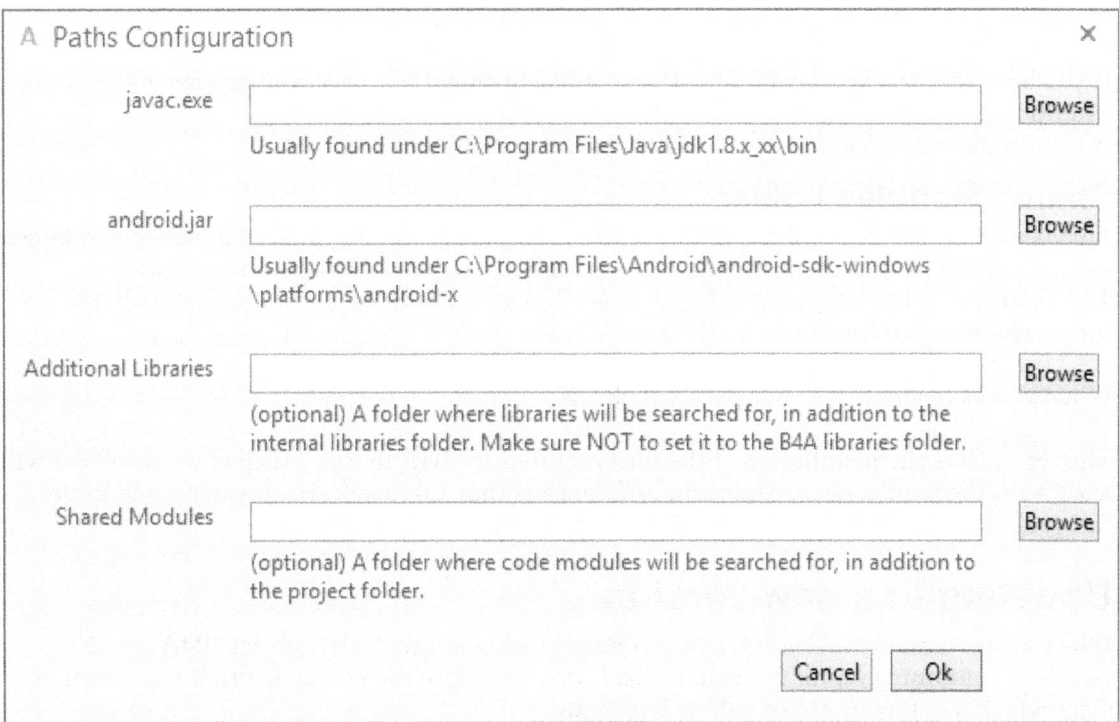

To complete this, you will need the paths which you noted during the installation process.

Javac.exe

This is typically C:\Program Files\Java\jdkN.N.N_NN\bin\javac.exe where N will vary.
- Use the browse buttons to locate "javac.exe" and "android.jar"
javac is located under <java folder>\bin.

Android.jar

This file is located under <android-sdk-windows>\platforms\android-NN where <android-sdk-windows> depends on where you installed the Android SDKs. You should have recorded this location when you installed the SDK. If not, you will need to find it. The NN depends on the Android version.
You might have installed different version of the Android SDKs, and by selecting different folders in the Paths Configuration dialog, you can compile your app to suit different environments, for example:
D:\android-sdks\platforms\android-10
D:\android-sdks\platforms\android-17

Additional Libraries

The Full Version of B4A allows you to download Additional Libraries which provide extra functionality. For example, there are libraries for OpenGL, Camera access, Barcode Readers, FTP and HTTP functions, to name but a few. More details in Additional libraries Chapter (page 562).
You use the "Additional Libraries" option to tell B4A where those downloaded library files are stored on your computer.
If you have the trial version or do not have any additional libraries, you can leave the "Additional Libraries" option blank for initial testing.
It is recommended to use a specific folder for Additional libraries.

Shared Modules Folder

This is a folder where you keep modules which are shared among various projects, and hence are not kept in your main project folder. See Shared Modules (page 233) for details.
This field can be left blank but it is recommended you create a separate folder ready for future shared modules.

When you have identified your paths, click **OK**.

That completes the installation of the files required for B4A to run. Much of what follows will work with the trial version. The main difference is that Libraries are only available in the full version.

Updating to a new version

When a new version is released, you will receive an email with the subject "B4A vNNN is released" containing a link to the download. It is therefore recommended that you create a filter which will flag up this email as important.

Part 2: Creating Your App

Here we go through the process of creating a real app, including the principles of design, how your app can communicate with the user, how you can use Designer Scripts to automatically modify your app to suit different devices, and how to compile, debug and test your app using either real or virtual devices.

We discuss creating graphics and databases. We examine how processes, services and activities live and die in Android. We look at the various types of modules you can create, examine ways you can make money from your app and finally explore ways you can get more help in using B4A.

2.1 The Project

A project is a piece of work which defines an app or library (page 451). You create a project by creating a folder in which you save your B4A code and other files as required.

Modules

Every project consists of one or more pieces of code called **modules**.
More details about Modules can be found here (page 232).

Default Modules

When you create a new project, B4A will create the skeletons of two modules: the Main activity module and a Starter service module.

Main Module

Every project has an **Activity Module** called "Main" which is stored within a file with the extension b4a. It may also contain other modules which are stored in separate files with the extension bas.

Starter Service

By default, all new projects also contain a service module called Starter. If this service exists, it is the first module to be executed when your app begins.

Process_Globals

Starter Service is designed as a safe place to declare and initialize your Process_Globals. The reason it is better to declare Process_Globals here than within an activity is that, if the activity is terminated either by the user or by the system, your global variables will be lost. By declaring them in a service, you can ensure that they will be available when your app is next run.

This is especially important if you have other service modules which are scheduled to run at a later time, using either the StartServiceAt (page 325) or StartServiceAtExact (page 325). Your app would crash if the service referred to globals within an activity which had been closed.

If you do not use the Starter service and you have several activities which hold Process_Globals, your app can also crash when you refer to a variable stored in one of these activies which has been closed, for example by the Android system.

We strongly recommend that SQL objects, data read from files and bitmaps used by multiple activities should all be declared in the Starter service, and be initialized in its Service_Create sub.

Uncaught Runtime Exceptions

The Starter Service also enables improved handling of uncaught runtime exceptions (page 302), as described below (page 303).

Notes on Starter Service

The Starter service is identified by its name. You can add a new service named Starter to an existing project and it will be the program entry point. It is created in new projects.

Note that you can delete the Starter service module if you wish, in which case the Main activity will be the first code to be executed. However, it is recommended that you retain the Starter service and use it to declare your Process_Globals.

Note too that the Starter service only starts once, when your app is first started, and is retained in memory until the device is powered off.

You can call StopService(Me) in Service_Start if you do not want the service to keep running. However this means that the service will not be able to handle events for objects declared here. For example, you will not be able to use asynchronous SQL methods.

The Starter service should be excluded from compiled libraries. Its #ExcludeFromLibrary attribute is therefore set to True by default.

You should not start an activity from the Starter service. When the Starter service ends, the Main activity will automatically be run.

Note also that the Starter service does not consume any CPU cycles unless one of your other services or activities calls it, so it is not a large drain on the device's resources.

Attributes

B4A defines values called attributes which are identified within the code with a # prefix, for example #VersionCode. Attributes can be classified as Project Attributes (discussed next), Module Attributes (page 233) Activity Attributes (page 240), Conditional Attributes (page 172) or Library Attributes (page 454).

Project Attributes

Project Attributes are valid for the whole project. By convention they are grouped with the Project Attributes Region at the top of the Main Activity module.

```
#Region  Project Attributes
 #ApplicationLabel: B4A Example
 #VersionCode: 1
 #VersionName:
 'SupportedOrientations possible values: unspecified, landscape or
portrait
 #SupportedOrientations: unspecified
 #CanInstallToExternalStorage: False
#End Region
```

These attributes will be added automatically to existing projects when they are first loaded with the latest version of B4A.

In addition to Project Attributes, Activity Attributes (page 240) specify parameters for a specific activity, and Library Attributes (page 454) are relevant when compiling a library.

Available project attributes are:

#ApplicationLabel:

The application label, a string which will appear in lists of applications on the device, for example in [Settings > Apps] and beneath the app icon.

#CanInstallToExternalStorage:

Whether the application can be installed to external storage. Values: `True` or `False`

#CustomBuildAction: Step, Command, Arguments

The build process is made of a number of steps. You can add additional steps that will run as part of the build process. For example, you can run a batch file that will copy the latest resource files from some folder before the files are packed.

Note: you can add any number of build actions.

CustomBuildAction should be added to the main activity.

The current folder is set to the Objects folder within the project folder.

Step : can be one of the following:

1 - Before the compiler cleans the objects folder (it happens after the code is parsed).

2 - Before the R.java file is generated.

3 - Before the package is signed (the APK file at this point is: bin\temp.ap_).

4 - Before the APK is installed.

5 - After the APK is installed.

Command: the Windows program to be executed

Arguments: the arguments to pass to **Command**

Examples

- Copy the logo file (could be part of a conditional compilation (page 172)):

```
#CustomBuildAction: 1, c:\windows\system32\cmd.exe, /c copy
    D:\B4A\IconFull.png res\drawable\icon.png
```

- To mark all files under the **res** folder as read-only before the compiler tries to clean the Objects folder:

```
#CustomBuildAction: 1, c:\windows\system32\attrib.exe, +r res\*.* /s
```

- Convert the res folder files to be writable again after the compiler has finished:

```
#CustomBuildAction: 4, c:\windows\system32\attrib.exe, -r res\*.* /s
```

#DebuggerDisableOptimizations: Value

By default this value is False and the debugger is optimized for speed. However, this can lead to certain problems when debugging with breakpoints. For example, suppose you put a breakpoint on the line below labelled 'put a breakpoint here

```
Sub Timer1_Tick
    S1
    Log("After S1")
End Sub

Sub S1
    Log("abc")  'put a breakpoint here
    Log("def")  'this line will be paused
End Sub
```

Now suppose you run the program in debug mode until it hits the breakpoint.

If you press F8 (Step) twice, it will step out of Sub S1 but will not pause at the line Log("After S1"). This is the sort of problem which the #DebuggerDisableOptimizations attribute can overcome.

Setting Value to **True** will disable optimization, meaning your code would pause on every line, but it would execute much more slowly.

#SupportedOrientations: Value

Sets the orientations supported by this app. Value can be (case is important): unspecified, portrait or landscape

#VersionCode: Value

Value must be an integer

#VersionName: Name

Name is a string

#AdditionalRes: Location, Package (optional)

Location specifies a folder containing resource files. This folder must be placed in your Additional libraries folder (page 562). Typically, the resources would be written in Java and generated by Eclipse (https://eclipse.org/) or some other IDE. These resource files will be added to the Android Package (APK) file. The optional Package parameter specifies the package name of an Android library project. This is required when wrapping a library that includes resource files. Example code:

```
#AdditionalRes: C:\AdditionalB4ALibraries\Sample\res,
com.abc.sample.lib
```

An example is available here (http://bit.ly/1IjNgNy).

To use it, click Download ZIP, save and unzip to your Additional libraries folder. Add the following code to your project, using the appropriate folder location:

```
#AdditionalRes: C:\AdditionalB4ALibraries\SlidingMenu-
master\library\res, com.jeremyfeinstein.slidingmenu.lib
```

You can use #AdditionalRes multiple times.

$AdditionalLibs$

You can use **$AdditionalLibs$** as a shortcut for the path to your Additional Library Folder (page 562). Thus, for example, you could write:

```
#AdditionalRes: $AdditionalLibs$\SlidingMenu-master\library\res,
com.jeremyfeinstein.slidingmenu.lib
```

$AndroidSDK$

You can use **$AndroidSDK$** as a shortcut to the Android SDK folder which you specified in the android.jar field of [Tools > Configure Paths]. Thus, for example, you could write:

```
#AdditionalRes: $AdditionalLibs$\Sample\res, com.abc.sample.lib
```

#DebuggerForceFullDeployment:

Forces the rapid debugger to redeploy the complete project every compilation. This can be useful if you get slow performance after modifing the code. It will disable the quick redeployment feature of the rapid debugger.

Values: True or False.

#DebuggerForceStandardAssets:

Disables the virtual assets feature of the rapid debugger. By default, the rapid debugger doesn't use the standard assets folder. This allows the debugger to only redeploy updated files.

Values: True or False.

#SignKeyFile:

Specifies the name of the file which holds the certificate used to sign the app.

#SignKeyPassword:

Specifies the password of the file specified by the #SignKeyFile attribute.

Example of usage:

```
#if DEBUG
  #SignKeyFile: ""
  #SignKeyPassword: ""
#Else
  #SignKeyFile: "path to my keystore file"
  #SignKeyPassword: "password of my keystore file"
#End If
```

Library compilation attributes

In addition to the project attributes mentioned above, there exist Library compilation attributes which are covered in the library compilation (page 454) section.

Project Icon

This icon (called the Launcher Icon in Android documentation) can be set with the menu [Project > Choose Icon]. More details in the Launcher Icon (page 260) section.

Package name

Every app needs a unique Package Name. The package name is a unique identifier for the application and the default name for the application process. In B4A, it can be set with the menu
[Project > Build Configurations (page 171)].

Unique name

The package name must be unique. To avoid conflicts with other developers, you should use an Internet domain which you own as the basis for your package names, written in reverse, for example:
uk.co.pennypress.B4A_book
You can register a domain name with a Domain Name Registrar.
You can release multiple versions of a single app, for example a free one and one which is paid, by using slightly different names for each package.

Allowed Characters

The name may contain dots, lower case letters ('a' through 'z' but see Note below), numbers, and underscores ('_'). Individual package name parts (between dots) may only start with letters. Package names should contain at least two components separated with "." (a dot).
Note: the use of lower case is a convention. Upper case letters A through Z are also accepted but can occasionally lead to problems, so it is safer to use only lower case.
The name you enter will be validated before it is accepted.

Google Play URL

The Package Name will be used by Google Play to determine the URL of your app. So if the package name is uk.co.pennypress.abc, it will appear on Google Play as: https://play.google.com/store/apps/details?id=uk.co.pennypress.abc

Caution: Name cannot be changed

Once you publish your application, you cannot change the package name. The package name defines your application's identity, so if you change it, then it is considered to be a different application and users of the previous version cannot update to the new version.

The Manifest

Every app running on an Android device requires a file named AndroidManifest.xml. B4A compiler generates this file from data stored within the project's b4a file. In most cases, there is no need to change anything.

However, in some cases, especially when using third-party libraries (ads for example), the developer is required to add some elements to the manifest file. This can be achieved with the Manifest Editor.

Manifest Editor

B4A includes a Manifest Editor (available from the menu [Project > Manifest Editor]) which allows you to add or modify elements in the manifest while also allowing the compiler to add the standard elements.

If you open the Manifest Editor (which is a modal dialog, so you will not be able to use the IDE or Designer while it is open), you will see something like:

```
'This code will be applied to the manifest file during compilation.
'You do not need to modify it in most cases.
'See this link for for more information:
http://www.basic4ppc.com/forum/showthread.php?p=78136
AddManifestText(
<uses-sdk android:minSdkVersion="4" android:targetSdkVersion="14"/>
<supports-screens android:largeScreens="true"
  android:normalScreens="true"
  android:smallScreens="true"
  android:anyDensity="true"/>)
SetApplicationAttribute(android:icon, "@drawable/icon")
SetApplicationAttribute(android:label, "$LABEL$")
'End of default text.
```

The meaning of these parameters is explained below.

You can modify these elements or add other elements as needed. To make it easier to add multiline strings and strings that contain quote characters, the manifest editor treats all characters between the open parenthesis and the closing parenthesis or comma (for commands with multiple parameters) as a single string.

Escaping end of string characters

If you need to write a string containing a comma, you should write two commas: ,, The same thing is true for strings with closing parenthesis:))

Manifest commands

You can add the following commands at the bottom of the manifest. There are several types of commands: commands that add an additional text inside an element, commands that set the value of an attribute (replacing the old value if it already exists) and two other commands which will be discussed later.

Note: you can call 'add text' commands multiple times.

AddActivityText(Activity, Text)

Adds the given text to the given activity. Example:

```
addactivitytext(Main, <intent-filter>
<action android:name="uk.co.pennypress.myview.rest" />
</intent-filter>)
```

AddApplicationText (Text)

Adds Text to the Application element. Can be used to add permissions, although this is normally achieved with **AddPermission**.

AddManifestText(Text)

Add given text to the manifest element.

AddPermission (Permission)

Adds a permission if it doesn't already exist. You can also add permissions using AddApplicationText. The advantage of AddPermission is that it makes sure to only add each permission once. Example:

```
AddPermission (android.permission.INTERNET)
```

AddReceiverText(Service, Text)

Appends Text to the given Service element. For example, to use C2DM push framework you should add some text to the receiver. **Note:** a Service module in B4A is actually made of a native service and a native receiver. The name of the receiver is the same as the service module.

Example:

```
AddReceiverText(PushService,
<intent-filter>
<action android:name="com.google.android.c2dm.intent.RECEIVE" />
<category android:name="anywheresoftware.b4a.samples.push" />
</intent-filter>
<intent-filter>
<action android:name="com.google.android.c2dm.intent.REGISTRATION" />
<category android:name="anywheresoftware.b4a.samples.push" />
</intent-filter>)
```

AddReplacement(OldValue, NewValue)

Replaces all occurrences of OldValue with NewValue. The compiler automatically adds the following declarations: $PACKAGE$ (replaced with the package name), $LABEL$ (replaced with the application label) and $ORIENTATION$ (replaced with the orientation value).

The string replacement happens as the last step. You can use it to delete other strings by replacing them with an empty string.

AddServiceText(Service, Text)

Appends given text to the given service element.

RemovePermission(Permission)

Removes given permission from the manifest.

SetActivityAttribute(Activity, Attribute Name, Attribute Value)

Set attribute with given Name of given Activity to given Value. For example, the following command can be used to set the orientation of a specific activity:

```
SetActivityAttribute(Main, android:screenOrientation, "portrait")
```

SetApplicationAttribute (Attribute Name, Attribute Value)

Set the application's attribute with the given Name to the given Value. For example if you wish to use accelerated hardware, you would add the line:

```
SetApplicationAttribute(android:hardwareAccelerated, "true")
```

Note: the attribute name is case sensitive.

SetManifestAttribute (Attribute Name, Attribute Value)

Set the manifest attribute with the given Name to the given Value.

SetReceiverAttribute (Service, Attribute Name, Attribute Value)

Sets a receiver attribute with the given Name for the given Service to the given Value. Example:

```
SetReceiverAttribute(HttpUtilsService, android:exported, "true")
```

SetServiceAttribute (Service, Attribute Name, Attribute Value)

Sets an attribute with the given Name for the given Service to the given Value.

Notes

- Attributes names are case sensitive.
- Deleting the whole text will restore the default text (after you reopen the manifest editor).
- As stated above, in most cases you do not need to add anything to the manifest editor.
- Open AndroidManifest.xml to better understand how it is built.

Conditional Manifest Commands

You can use conditional commands (page 172) #If and #End If to exclude parts of the Manifest depending on words in the Conditional Symbols field of a Build Configuration (page 171). For example:

```
#if tablet
SetActivityAttribute(Main, android:screenOrientation, "landscape")
#end if
```

More information

For more about the Android Manifest see here (http://bit.ly/1IjNmon).

2.2. Designing Your App

Fulfilling Wants and Needs

Any successful product has to fulfill the wants and needs of a specific audience. Before you begin to design your app, therefore, it is wise to think about these questions and talk to potential customers to understand what they really need and want.

You should also look at other similar apps on the market and identify where there is a gap, evaluate their strengths and weaknesses and decide how your app will be better.

Android Versions

One of the main problems about creating Android apps is that the operating system is rapidly changing. New versions of the Android API appear on a regular basis, introducing new features, while there are still many devices which have old versions. You must decide whether you want to use the new features or design your app for one of the old versions. Note that Android 5 (API version 21) introduced a new design concept called "Material Design". See here (page 182) for more details.

See here (http://bit.ly/1OcxCT3) for a complete list of Android versions and their API numbers.

Popularity of Android Versions

You can see which versions of Android are currently running on devices which visited the Google Play Store in the past seven days here (http://bit.ly/19gY7I5). The information is displayed as follows. Visit the page to see the latest information.

Version	Codename	API	Distribution
2.2	Froyo	8	0.3%
2.3.3 - 2.3.7	Gingerbread	10	5.6%
4.0.3 - 4.0.4	Ice Cream Sandwich	15	5.1%
4.1.x	Jelly Bean	16	14.7%
4.2.x		17	17.5%
4.3		18	5.2%
4.4	KitKat	19	39.2%
5.0	Lollipop	21	11.6%
5.1		22	0.8%

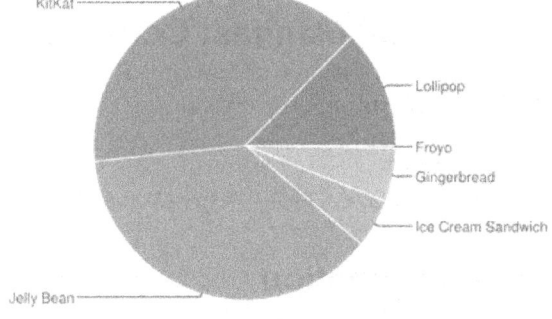

However, note that these data do not accurately reflect the devices which are in use, since users with older devices might be less likely to add new apps. Nevertheless, since you are interested in users who install apps, it is probably a good indication of what Android versions you need to target.

Editing the Manifest

You need to specify the lowest API version your app will run on by using the Manifest Editor (page 115) to change the `minSdkVersion` parameter in the Manifest (page 115). You also need to specify the version which is ideal for your app (`targetSdkVersion`). The relevant line in the Manifest is something like:

```
<uses-sdk android:minSdkVersion="4" android:targetSdkVersion="14"/>
```

The numbers refer to the API version. See the links above for a list of popular Android versions and their API numbers.

Note: B4A will not support versions below 2.0.

Compiler Warning

If you do not include `targetSdkVersion` in the Manifest, the compiler will issue a warning:

```
Add android:targetSdkVersion="14" to the manifest editor (Warning #26)
```

If targetSdkVersion is less than 20 and you do not set a theme, the compiler will warn you:

```
Add SetApplicationAttribute(android:theme,
"@android:style/Theme.Holo")
```

Note that it is a good idea to set this attribute even if you are using version 20 or above. See here (page 182) for more details.

Nevertheless, despite these warnings, the app will compile and install.

Backward Compatible

Android is backward compatible. You can use the latest API to compile your code (specified by [Tools > Configure Paths (page 107)] dialog **android.jar** field) and it will still work on devices with an earlier version. **But your app will have problems if your users try to use new features not available in the API of their old device**. See the next section.

Checking Version-Dependent Compatibility

Every version of Android introduces new features. You need to be aware which version is required to run the features you are using. You then need to set the Manifest `minSdkVersion` to reflect the lowest SDK level on which your app will run.

To ensure your app is compatible with older versions, you should install it on a device using the selected lowest SDK version or, if you do not have one, using an emulator (page 188) with the minimum version of Android.

If the app is incompatible, installation or execution will fail. It is not always obvious that the SDK is the problem. B4A's Compile window might show the message:

Failure [INSTALL_FAILED_OLDER_SDK]

Or the app might compile and install but fail to run without any error showing in the Log. You could try removing the Log filter, but the information is not very helpful.

Play Store Compatibility Check

To ensure compatibility, Play Store checks the version of the user's device and will not allow downloads of apps whose `minSDKversion` is less than the level of the device.

Installing from the APK

You might want to allow users to download the APK and install it themselves, for example while getting feedback from reviewers. In that case, if you app uses more advanced features the user will see a message

Parse error: There is a problem parsing the package

Discovering the API of the current device

You could use the Phone library SdkVersion (page 511) to discover the API level of the user's device. You could then use features appropriate to that type of device. But be aware of the comment above regarding Play Store's compatibility check. You would have to set `minSdkVersion` to match the lowest permissible value within your app.

The Android Screen

The appearance of the screen within which your app runs will vary depending not just on the size of the device but the version of Android.

We discuss how to cope with different screen sizes in the Designer Scripts Reference (page 162).

The parts of the screen surrounding your app will normally consist of the Status Bar at the top of the screen and, for Android 4.x, a Navigation Bar at the bottom.

Status Bar

The Status Bar at the top of the screen shows pending Notifications (page 389) on the left and status information (such as time, battery level, and signal strength) on the right.

You should not hide the Status Bar (by using Activity Attribute (page 240) `#FullScreen:True`) unless absolutely necessary.

Navigation Bar

For devices running Android 4.x, a Navigation Bar is shown at the bottom of the screen (if the device does not have the traditional hardware keys). It houses the device navigation controls Back, Home, and Recents, and also displays a menu for apps written for Android 2.3 or earlier.

Notifications

The user can swipe down from the status bar to show notification details.

Consider whether your app needs to give Notifications (page 389) to the user.

App Design Step by Step

You want your app to be appealing and useful, so you need to think about the user interface early in the design process.

Basic Design Principles

Make your app **visually appealing**. Where possible, use graphics instead of words, and if you must use words, keep them brief.

Always offer your user a **consistent experience**, for example, when moving between screens. Be faithful to the Android experience, for example, by swiping to navigate.

Break your app into **logical chunks** and offer each on a separate screen. Organize your screens logically and let your users know where they are and how to get somewhere else.

Title Bar

If the #IncludeTitle Activity Attribute (page 240) is set to **True**, an activity will display a Title Bar below the Status Bar at the top of the screen. On later versions of Android, it also includes the Launcher Icon (page 260):

Action Bar

You might want an **Action Bar** at the top of your app to let your user select the page to view or the action to take.

The Android Action Bar was introduced with Android 3.0 (API level 11). Read more about this here (http://bit.ly/1OcxRgS). Read about how to design your action bar here (http://bit.ly/1IrN1hW).

With Material Design (page 182), Google recommends you use a toolbar instead of an Action Bar. Further, if you continue to use an Action Bar, the appearance changed. For example, there is no Application Icon in Material Design. They also changed its name to "App Bar (http://bit.ly/1eibfz1)" which is a special kind of toolbar.

The StdActionBar (page 566) library supports tabs and dropdown lists on the action bar on devices running Android 4 or above. It also responds when the user clicks the action bar icon, on the left of the action bar. Add an action bar to your project by including the library and using

```
Sub Globals
  Private actionBar As StdActionBar

Sub Activity_Create(FirstTime As Boolean)
  actionBar.Initialize("actionBar")
```

The AHActionBar Library available here (http://bit.ly/176cKvc) lets you create an Action Bar on older devices.

Action Bar in Holo Theme

The parts of the ActionBar as they appear if you are using the Holo Theme (page 182) are shown below. Some of the differences when using Material Design (page 182) are indicated in the discussion.

Navigation Tree

This is the name we give to the relationship between the various pages seen by the user. These correspond to the Activites in your app, or the different Layouts loaded into an Activity.

For the user to make sense of your app, there should be one main page (the root of the tree). In addition, there may be vaious branches, which might have sub-branches.

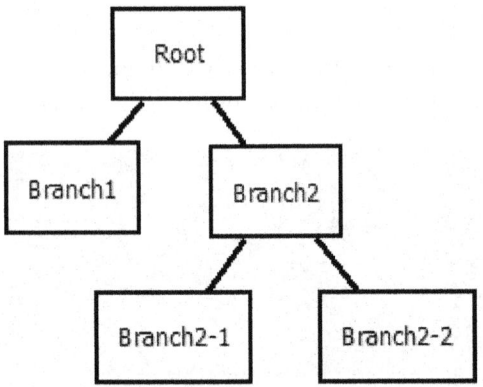

Note: the tree is considered as having its root at the top!
The Action Bar is divided into the following parts:

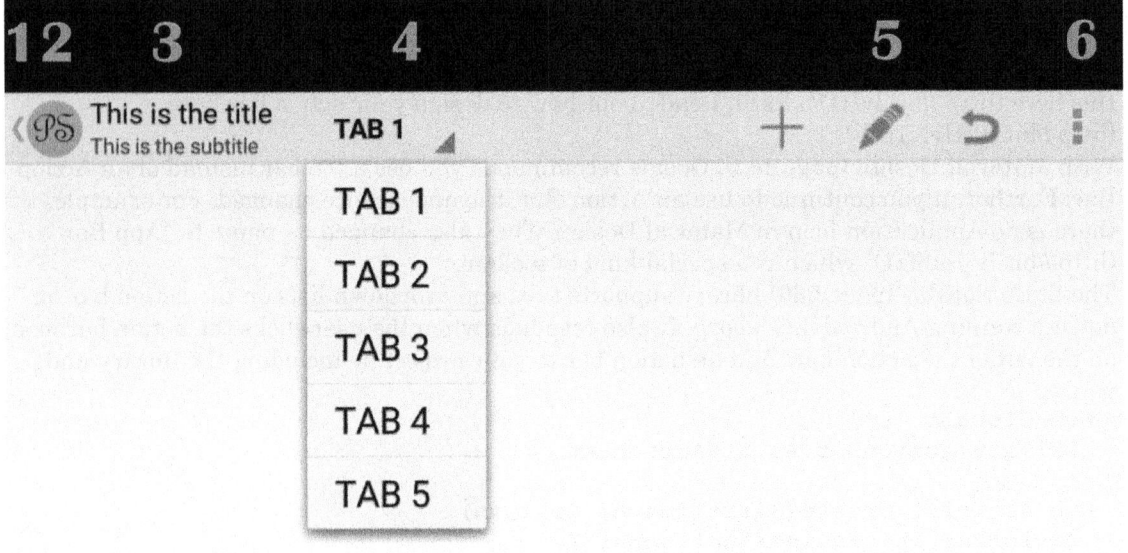

1 Up Button

According to Android user interface specifications (http://bit.ly/1IjNogf), the Up Button (which actually points to the left!) should not be shown if the user is at the top (the root) of the navigation tree. To hide it, call:

```
actionBar.ShowUpIndicator = False
```

The Up Button should only be shown if the user has navigated down to a branch of the tree, and should return the user to the next highest level of the tree. To show it, call:

```
actionBar.ShowUpIndicator = True
```

On devices running Android API 20 or less, you handle clicks of the Up Button by processing the Action Bar's **ButtonClicked** event. In Android 5 (API 21) and later, the **ButtonClicked** event no longer works and instead you should use the activity_ActionBarHomeClick (page 338) event. This fires when the user clicks the Up Button, the Action Bar Icon or the Title.

Note: in Material Design (page 182), the Up Button is no longer supported. However the App Bar's Nav Icon ▤ can be used to navigate upward through the hierarchy, exactly like the Up Button. It can also be used to open a "Navigation Drawer on the left of the screen". You might therefore decide that in your app, the Up Button (which points to the left) will open this type of navigation menu.

See here (http://bit.ly/1eibfz1) for more details about the Nav Icon.

2 Action Bar Icon

You can show an icon on the Action Bar by calling
```
actionBar.Icon = LoadBitmap(File.DirAssets, "myIcon.png")
```
Note: there is no Application Icon in apps using Material Design (page 182).

3 Action Bar Title

The title shown on the Action Bar is defined by
```
Activity.Title = "My title"
```
In addition, you can add a subtitle by using
```
actionBar.Subtitle = "This is the subtitle"
```

4 Tabs

You can add tabs to your Action Bar by calling
```
actionBar.AddTab("Title")
```
If there is enough room, all tabs will be shown side by side.

If not, they will be shown as a dropdown list box, as illustrated above. It is worth checking whether the tab names are wrapped correctly within the dropdown list.

5 Icons

You can add icons to the Action Bar. These normally indicate common actions the user might want to take. Use the `Activity.AddMenuItem3 (page 340)` command to add icons.

6 Overflow

The overflow icon (3 dots) is shown if either
- if there is not enough room to show all items in the Action Bar (after tabs have been converted to a dropdown list) or
- if `Activity.AddMenuItem` has been called.

Action Bar Split

If the screen is too narrow to show all the items in the Action Bar, some of them may be shown at the bottom of the screen. Typically tabs will be shown at the top and icons (added with `Activity.AddMenuItem3 (page 340)`) at the bottom:

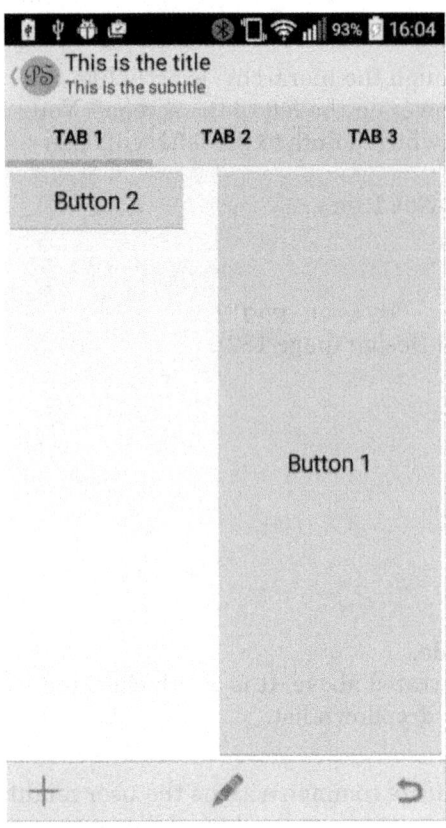

Menu

An easy way of allowing your user to make selections is by adding a menu. The menu is shown if the user presses the Menu button (on older devices) or selects the overflow symbol (3 vertical dots) on the Action Bar, as in the previous image.

The Activity.AddMenuItem (page 339) commands (with 3 variants) allow you to do this easily.

If you use AddMenuItem3 (page 340) (which tries to install an entry directly in the Action Bar), it will still work when run on Android 2.x, but will appear in the Menu instead, revealed by the device's Menu button.

Tabbed Views

TabHost (page 438) is a View which allows you to create a row of tabs which call different pages.

TabHostExtras Library (page 585) is a user-generated extension of this view which gives you more power over its appearance.

Sliding Pages

Many users are used to apps which allow them to flip between activities by sliding pages horizontally. As well as tabs and dropdown lists on the action bar, the StdActionBar (page 566) library supports sliding pages on devices running Android 4 or above, as shown on this tutorial (http://bit.ly/1Ij0VU6).

The AHViewPager library allows the user to slide pages sideways on devices with Android 2.x and allows you to use tabs to activate the pages. The library and sample project are available here (http://bit.ly/1bAV9Iu). You can use both AHViewPager and AHActionBar libraries in a single app which uses the action bar to select a page. A sample app can be downloaded from this book's resource page (http://bit.ly/1IjLiwC).

Navigation Drawer

The navigation drawer was introduced with Google's Material Design (page 182) model. It is a panel that slides in from the left edge of the screen and displays the app's main navigation options. The user can bring the navigation drawer onto the screen by swiping from the left edge of the screen or by touching the application icon on the action bar.
See here (http://bit.ly/1eicDBP) for more details.
You can create a menu which slides in and out using this user-generated SlidingMenu library (http://bit.ly/1IRBAMk). Or you could create your own menu using an overlay, although you would probably want to animate it sliding in and out using a timer.
At present, there is no navigation drawer which is backward compatible with early versions of Android, but you might consider using Sliding Pages, Tabbed Views or simply use a ListView as a popup menu (page 420).

Animating your App

Animating your app can make it more appealing for your users. There are several ways you can do this:
- animating views (page 443) (on devices with Android 3 or later) by using their methods
- animating views by using the Animation Library (page 459)
- animating activities (page 146) (on devices with Android 3 or later)
- using a HorizontalScrollView (page 414) or ScrollView (page 431) with animated scrolling

Advertising

If you are going to include advertising in your app, you need to plan the screen layout to allow space for them. See here (page 266) for more about advertising plans.

Android Themes

Themes are Android's mechanism for applying a consistent style to an app or activity. The style specifies the visual properties of the elements that make up your user interface, such as color, height, padding and font size. For more about Themes, see here (http://bit.ly/1gvrvtm). For a B4A tutorial which shows you how to select an android theme based on what version of Android the device is using, and how to create a custom theme, see here (http://bit.ly/17j7KOL).

Android 5 Device Compatibility

With Android 5.0, a new design concept was introduced called "Material Design". See here (page 182) for more details.

More Advice

The Android Developer website has a lot of advice on how to design an effective app. Start from here (http://bit.ly/1IjNynQ).

Managing Settings

Editing Settings

Your app will almost certainly need to have settings, that is, user preferences and details.
You will need to allow the user to change them. There is an easy way to do this in B4A: the
Preference Activity Library (page 528). There is a tutorial here (http://bit.ly/11jIyFd) about
how to use it.

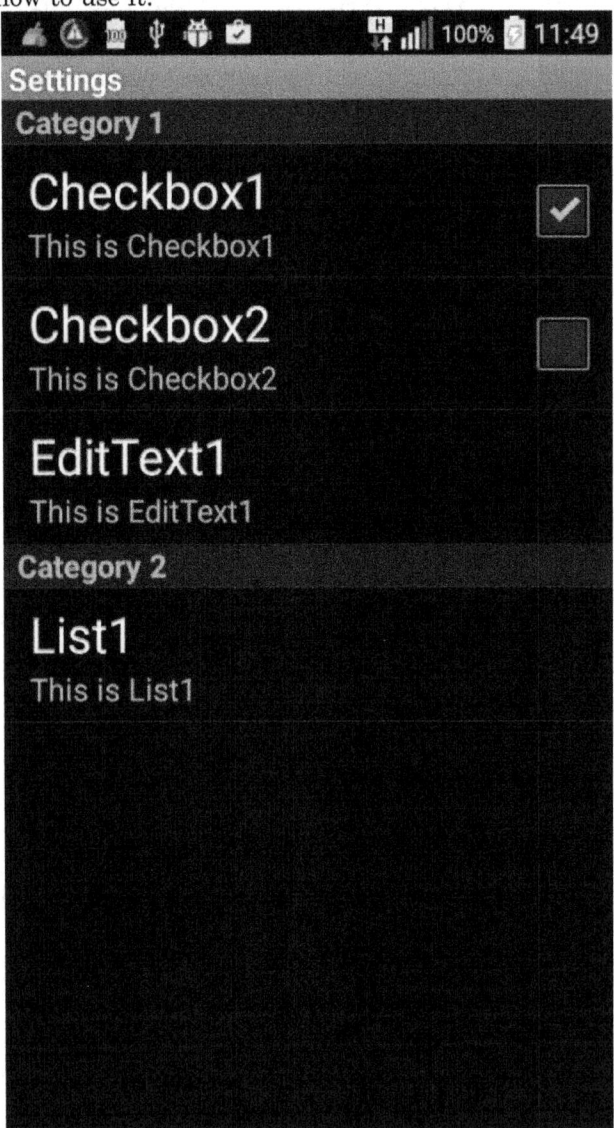

Saving and Retrieving Settings

StateManager (page 566) is a code module you can add to your projects to handle saving user
settings to persistent storage and retrieving them when needed.

Screens and Layouts

With the large and increasing number of devices available on the market, all with different screen sizes and resolutions (page 162), it becomes increasingly difficult to design an app that looks good on all of them.

There is no universal rule to manage this problem. It depends on:

- What kind of project you are designing
- What devices and screen sizes you are targeting
- What you want to show on the different screens

For example, it might be enough to show the same layout simply stretched according to the different screen sizes. Or you might need different layout variants for the different sizes. A layout which looks good on a small screen seldom appeals on a big one, where increased space means that more views (such as both the View Control and the Content Area) can be displayed at the same time.

The same layout might not look good in both portrait and landscape orientations, although your work will be simpler if you can design one which does.

The Designer

The most common way to create a layout is to use the Designer. We describe this in detail in a later chapter (page 139).

Multiple activities

If you have complex coding for each page then it would be better to have separate activity modules. You would normally create a separate layout for each activity.

In order to call the second activity from the first, use `StartActivity(OtherActivity)`. The second activity automatically runs `Sub Activity_Create` which will load the relevant Layout by calling `Activity.LoadLayout("OtherLayout")`

Returning from an Activity

To return to the first activity, the second would typically:

- Save any data to return in a `Process_Globals` variable
- Close the current activity with `Activity.Finish`

In the original activity you could use `Sub Activity_Resume` to check the value of the saved data.

Overlays

Menu Overlay

You might want to have a menu popup over an Activity. The simplest way to do this is to use a `ListView`, as we describe here (page 420).

Layout as Overlay

You can also call a second layout from within the first Activity, using `Activity.LoadLayout("Layout2")`. In this case the second layout will be seen floating above the first. To hide parts of the first, the second must have opaque panels (Alpha set to 255). This might be used to show a menu floating over the main layout.

How to Detect the Display Size

LayoutValues

Use **LayoutValues** to get information about the screen including the resolution. This object holds values related to the display. For more details, see the LayoutValues main entry (page 379).

You can get the values of the current display by calling GetDeviceLayoutValues
For example:

```
Dim lv As LayoutValues
lv = GetDeviceLayoutValues
Log(lv)
```

This will print the following line to the log:

320 x 480, scale = 1.0 (160 dpi)

The first value (320) is the screen width, the second value its height.

Thus the above result is for a screen in portrait mode.

Note: **Activity.LoadLayout** and **Panel.LoadLayout** return a **LayoutValues** object with the values of the chosen layout variant.

You can use **LayoutValues.scale** to check the device type. This returns the scale (page 163), where 1 is a screen with 160 dpi.

For example, you could then use **TextSizeRatio** to scale text on the screen:

```
Dim TextSizeRatio As Float
Dim LayoutVals As LayoutValues

LayoutVals = GetDeviceLayoutValues
TextSizeRatio = GetDeviceLayoutValues.Scale
lblSample.TextSize = lblSample.TextSize * TextSizeRatio
```

Detecting Device Orientation

You may need to know whether the screen is portrait or landscape.

You could use either:

```
If Activity.Width > Activity.Height Then
```

Or the equivalent but longer:

```
Dim lv As LayoutValues
lv = GetDeviceLayoutValues
If lv.Width > lv.Height Then
  . . .
```

Allowed Screen Orientation

The screen orientation values which an app can support can be defined by the #SupportedOrientations attribute in the Project Attributes (page 111). It can have the values portrait, landscape or unspecified (meaning both portrait and landscape).

```
#Region  Project Attributes
  #ApplicationLabel: MyFirstProgram
  #VersionCode: 1
  #VersionName:
  #SupportedOrientations: unspecified
  #CanInstallToExternalStorage: False
#End Region
```

Note you can use the Phone Library (page 502) to set the current screen orientation:

```
Dim Phone1 As Phone
Phone1.SetScreenOrientation (-1)
```

Possible values are 0 (Landscape only), 1 (Portrait only) or -1 (Both)

Adding views by code

Layouts are most commonly defined using the Designer (page 139), but it is also possible to create and modify views directly in your Activity code.

Advantage: you have full control of the view.

Disadvantage: you have to define almost everything. For example, you must initialize any view added in code, as shown in the following:

Example

The source code for an example project, AddViewsByCode, is in this book's resources page (http://bit.ly/1IjLiwC). This is part of it:

```
Sub Globals
 Dim lblTitle As Label
End Sub

Sub Activity_Create(FirstTime As Boolean)
 lblTitle.Initialize("")
 lblTitle.Color = Colors.Red
 lblTitle.TextSize = 20
 lblTitle.TextColor = Colors.Blue
 lblTitle.Gravity = Gravity.CENTER_HORIZONTAL +
Gravity.CENTER_VERTICAL
 lblTitle.Text = "Title"
 Activity.AddView(lblTitle, 20%x, 10dip, 60%x, 30dip)
End Sub
```

dips

To write code, you need to be aware of **D**ensity **I**ndependent **P**ixels (dips (page 163)). Dips are a way of solving the uncertainty caused by the variety of screen resolutions available on different devices. Dips are defined so that, on all devices

160dip = 1 inch

Thus, if you want a button to be 2 inches wide on any device, you would write:

```
btnStop.Width = 320dip
```
Any number followed by the string dip will be converted. **Note**: no spaces are allowed between the number and the word **dip**. Read more about dips here (page 163).

DipToCurrent(Length as Int)

You can also set the size of a view using **DipToCurrent**. This function converts Length, given in dips, into a value for the current screen. For example, the following code will set the width value of this button to be 1 inch wide on all devices.

```
EditText1.Width = DipToCurrent(160)
```
You might consider that simply saying 160dip is easier!

Percentage of Activity

As well as specifying the absolute size of an object, you can set the size as a percentage of the screen (actually of the current **Activity**).

PerXToCurrent (Percentage As Float) As Int

Returns the given percentage of the activity width, converted to dip (page 163).
Example: set the width of Button1 to 50% of the width of the current activity:

```
EditText1.Width = PerXToCurrent(50)
```
A shorthand syntax for this method is available. See below.
PerYToCurrent performs a similar function for the height.

%x and %y

These are shorthand ways of achieving the same result. 50%x means 50% of the width of the current activity, converted to dip (page 163). So the previous code is equivalent to:

```
EditText1.Width = 50%x
```
Note: there is no space between the number and the %.
To specify 5% of the height of the screen: `EditText1.Height = 5%y`

Does the device have a keyboard?

You can find out with the following code. This requires the Reflection Library (page 579).

```
Dim r As Reflector
r.Target = r.GetContext
r.Target = r.RunMethod("getResources")
r.Target = r.RunMethod("getConfiguration")
Dim keyboard As Int = r.GetField("keyboard")
Log ("keyboard=" & keyboard)
```
The possible values of keyboard are:
1 = KEYBOARD_NOKEYS
2 = KEYBOARD_QWERTY
3 = KEYBOARD_12KEY

App or Widget ?

B4A supports the creation of miniature application views called App Widgets that can be embedded in other applications (such as the Home screen) and receive periodic updates. These views are referred to as Widgets in the user interface.
An application component that is able to hold other App Widgets is called an App Widget host, which is typically the home screen.

Because another application is hosting your widget, it is not possible to directly access the widget's views. Instead, you must use a special object called RemoteViews (page 393) which gives you indirect access to the widget's views.

You create a RemoteViews object based on the layout file using ConfigureHomeWidget (page 309).

```
Sub Process_Globals
 Dim rv As RemoteViews
End Sub


Sub Service_Create
  rv = ConfigureHomeWidget("LayoutFile", "rv", 0, "Widget Name")
End Sub
```

Each widget is tied to a Service module (page 254). The widget is created and updated through this module.

Widgets do not support all view types. The following views are supported:

Button (default drawable)

Label (`ColorDrawable` or `GradientDrawable`)

Panel (`ColorDrawable` or `GradientDrawable`)

ImageView

ProgressBar (both modes)

All views support the `Click` event and **no other event**.

The widget layout and configuration must be defined with XML files. During compilation, B4A reads the layout file created with the designer and generates the required XML files.

For a tutorial on creating widgets with B4A, see here (http://bit.ly/14Lm40H) for part 1 and an example program. For part 2 of the tutorial, building a more extensive example, see here (http://bit.ly/16TSq09).

Managing Permissions

When an Android app is installed, it must tell the user what resources and data it needs to access on the device, and the user has the opportunity to cancel the installation. This is achieved by your app including a list of the required permissions in the Manifest (page 115) file.

Normally, B4A will create this Manifest for you, automatically detecting the required permissions. We list these required permissions in this book, within the documentation for objects which need them.

However, it might be that you need to manually add permissions to the Manifest. You achieve this by using the AddPermission (page 116) command in the Manifest editor.

2.3 Communicating with your User

As your program runs, you will need to send messages to your user from time to time. We deal here with the methods of doing this. Of course, there are many Views (such as buttons) which allow the user to take actions during an `Activity`, but here we are thinking about how you can take specific actions to gain your user's attention.

Modal Dialogs

There are several ways to show your user a message in a dialog box which remains visible until the user clicks (sometimes called "modal" or "blocking" dialogs). The program will not continue and timers will be suspended until the user responds. See the section below about how to handle modal dialogs (page 136) if Android interrupts your app, for example when the user rotates the device.

Msgbox

Use the Msgbox (page 320) keyword to show a simple message without any options. You can specify the message and the box title:

```
Msgbox ("Please select a route first", "Error")
```

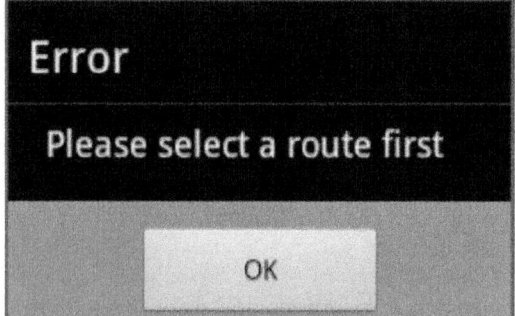

Note the exact appearance varies, depending on the version of Android running on the device.

Msgbox2

If you want to show more options, Msgbox2 (page 320) allows you to include any combination of the following: a positive button, a negative button, a cancel button and an icon. It will return one of the DialogResponse (page 346) constants, and you can detect the user's response and act accordingly:

```
Dim bmp As Bitmap
Dim choice As Int
bmp.Initialize(File.DirAssets, "question.png")
choice = Msgbox2("Would you like to select a route?", "Please specify
your choice", "Yes please", "", "No thank you", bmp)
If choice = DialogResponse.POSITIVE Then ...
```

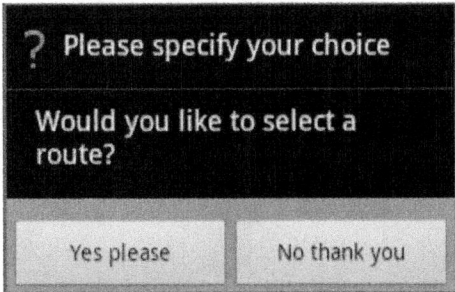

Important Note: the icon will not show on devices running Lollipop (Android 5.0, API version 21). And the exact appearance of the buttons also depends on the version of Android running on the device.

InputList

InputList (page 314) shows the user a modal dialog with a list of options. It ends when the user clicks on an option and returns either the index of the selected item, or `DialogResponse.Cancel` if the user presses the back key.

```
Dim choice As Int
Dim lst As List
lst.Initialize2(Array As String("1", "More than 10", "I don't care"))
choice = InputList(lst, "How many friends do you want?", 1)
```

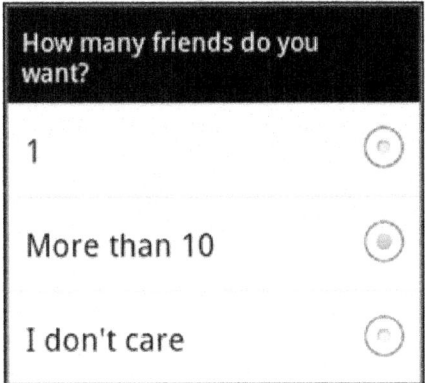

InputMultiList

InputMultiList (page 315) lets you show a list from which the user can select multiple items before returning.

```
Dim choice As Int
Dim lstInput, lstOutput As List
lstInput.Initialize2(Array As String("Apples", "Bananas", "Mangos",
"Oranges"))
lstOutput = InputMultiList (lstInput, "Select all the fruits you
want")
For Each index As Int In lstOutput
  Log (index)
Next
```

If Bananas and Oranges are selected, the numbers 1 and 3 will be logged.

InputMap

This looks and acts much like an **InputMultiList**, but items in the list can be pre-selected and the result is returned in a different way.

```
Dim m As Map
m.Initialize
m.Put("Apples", True)
m.Put("Bananas", False)
m.Put("Mangos", False)
m.Put("Oranges", True)
InputMap(m, "Select all the fruits you want")
```

This will show an input list with the **True** items pre-selected:

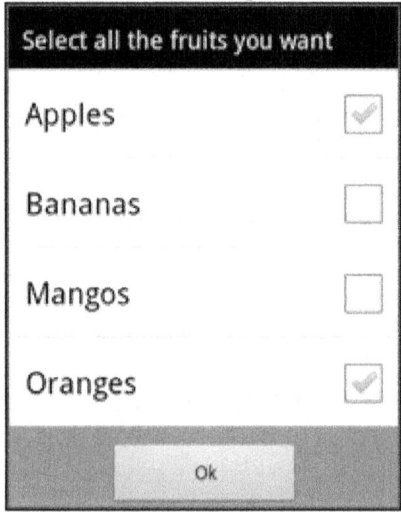

To process the result, check the map:

```
For Each fruit As String In m.Keys
 If m.Get( fruit ) Then
 Log( fruit )
 End If
Next
```

Handling Long Lists

`InputList`, `InputMultiList` and `InputMap` can all display long lists, but if the list is too long to fit on the screen, parts of it will be hidden so that not all the items will be visible. Although the user can drag the list to reveal hidden items, there is no visual indication of this to the user. This is normal with Android. It might be wise to add a message indicating this to the user:

```
Dim choice As Int
Dim lst As List
lst.Initialize
For i = 0 To 9
 lst.Add ( "Item " & i)
Next
choice = InputList (lst, "Select all the items you want (drag up/down
for more)", 1)
```

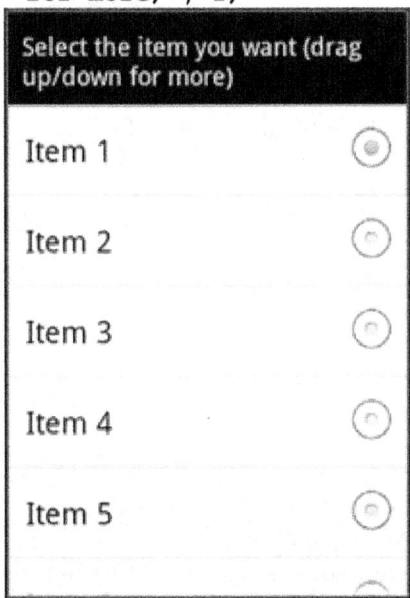

Notice also the list has already scrolled down to show the selected item.

Dialogs Library

This library, written by Andrew Graham, contains several modal dialogs (meaning they remain visible until the user takes some action). They are useful if you need your user to enter data. At present, they are an InputDialog for text, a TimeDialog for times, a DateDialog for dates, both a ColorDialog and a ColorPickerDialog for colors, a NumberDialog for numbers, a FileDialog for folders and file names, and a CustomDialog. We describe them in the Dialogs Library (page 568) section.

Handling Modal Dialogs when your App Pauses

Android does not provide modal dialogs, but a special mechanism in B4A permits them. The Android Activity lifetime system makes this support complicated because Activities can be created and destroyed at will by Android. To avoid stack runaway on the GUI thread when an Activity is destroyed, the stack must be unwound to the lowest level. The B4A modal mechanism does this by closing any modal dialog being shown and exiting the Sub that called the dialog, and any Sub that called that Sub and so on, in order to return the main thread to the message loop.

This means that the application does not necessarily receive a return value from the dialog and has its expected flow of execution interrupted. This will probably most often happen if the device is rotated while a modal dialog is displayed, so the Activity is destroyed and rebuilt with a new layout.

Because this may happen unexpectedly, applications (depending upon their logical structure) may need code in the **Pause** and **Resume** Subs to deal with the fact that modal dialog closure may not always be detected. Setting a variable defined in **Sub Process_Globals** when a modal dialog is shown, and clearing it when it returns with some checking code in the Resume Sub, is one way of dealing with this possibility.

The above discussion applies to Dialogs Library objects as well as the B4A modal dialogs **InputList**, **InputMultiList**, **Msgbox** and **Msgbox2**.

ToastMessageShow

ToastMessageShow (page 326) shows a message to the user which lasts for only a few seconds.

```
ToastMessageShow ("No messages received", False)
```

You can make it last a bit longer by setting the last parameter to **True**.

Alarms

You can create a Service module (page 254) which will sound an alarm and perhaps show a notification at a certain time. You can use the StartServiceAt (page 325) or StartServiceAtExact (page 325) methods to schedule when your service will start. See Simple Alarm (http://bit.ly/14yNI4n) for an example of how to implement this type of alarm. You could also use a Timer (page 401) to do something similar, but a service will continue to run even when your app is not running.

Notifications

Both activities and services can display status bar notifications. For services, it is their main way of interacting with the user.

The notification displays an icon in the status bar.

When the user swipes the bar down, she or he sees the notification. The user can press on the message, which will open an activity as configured by the Notification object (page 389).

ProgressDialog

You can use ProgressDialogShow (page 321) to show a dialog with a circular spinning disc and the specified text, telling the user that a long-running task it in progress.

```
ProgressDialogShow("Please wait while we fetch your information")
```

Unlike Msgbox (page 320) and InputList (page 314) methods, the code will not be blocked; so the activity can continue to run until the task is completed.

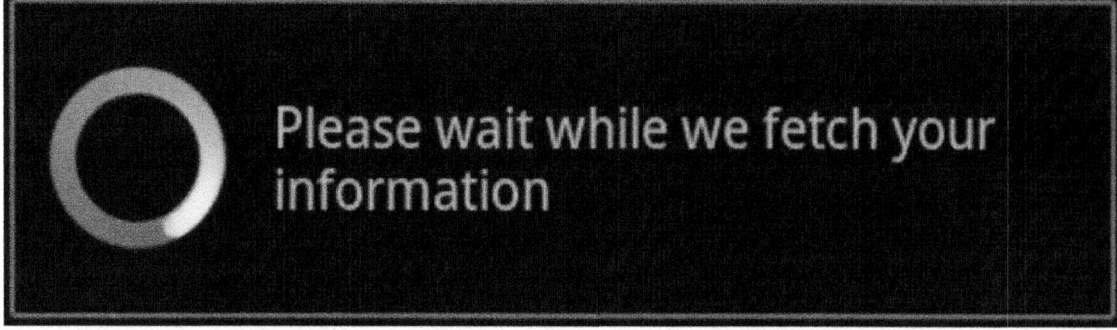

You should call **ProgressDialogHide** to remove the dialog. The dialog will also be removed if the user presses on the Back key. However by using **ProgressDialogShow2** you can prevent this.

```
ProgressDialogShow2("Please wait while we fetch your information",
False)
```

The second argument specifies whether the user can dismiss the dialog by pressing on the Back key.

ProgressBar

Unlike a **ProgressDialog**, which floats above an activity, a **ProgressBar** belongs to the **Activity**. It gives your user information about how far a long-running process has progressed, or how far they are through a series of steps. The exact nature of the visible bar depends upon the device. Here is one example

Example code:

```
Sub Activity_Create(FirstTime As Boolean)
  Activity.LoadLayout("Main")
  ProgressBar1.Progress = 0
  Timer1.Initialize("Timer1", 1000)
  Timer1.Enabled = True
End Sub

Sub timer1_Tick
  'Handle tick events
  ProgressBar1.Progress = ProgressBar1.Progress + 10
  If ProgressBar1.Progress = 100 Then
  Timer1.Enabled = False
  End If
End Sub
```

See ProgressBar (page 427) for more details.

2.4 The Visual Designer

We introduced the Designer in an earlier tutorial (page 58). It allows you to organize views (page 403) (component on a page) into layouts and see how they look on either an emulator (page 188) or a real device.

Start the Designer using the B4A [Designer > Open Designer] menu.
Initially, the Designer looks like this:

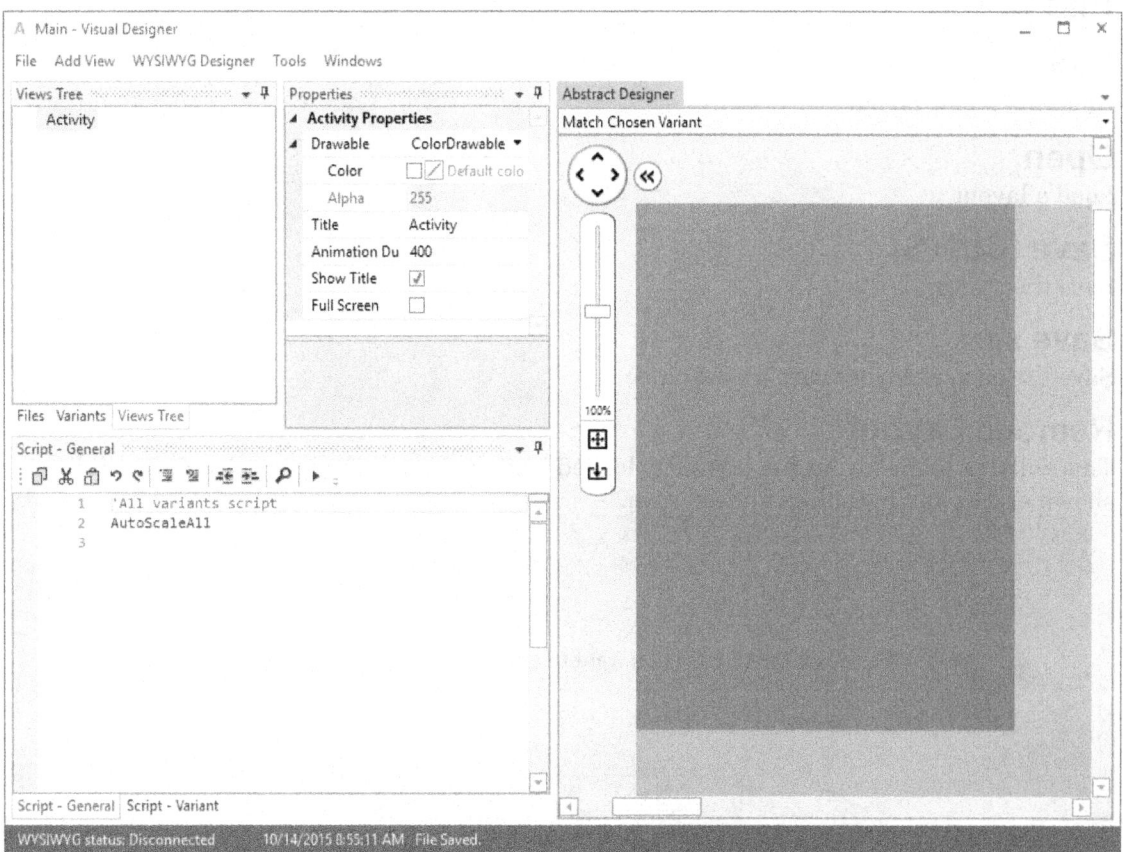

Layouts

The purpose of the Visual Designer is to create a "layout", which is a file with a .bal extension specifying the views shown on the user's screen. When you run your app, you can load a layout so the user can see it using code such as

```
Activity.LoadLayout("Main")
Panel.LoadLayout("Help")
```

Docking Windows

You can dock parts of the Visual Designer in the same way you dock windows in the IDE, as described here (page 94). Any changes you make will be remembered the next time you open the Visual Designer.

File Menu

New
Generate a new layout.

Open
Load a layout.

Save (Ctrl+S)
Save the current layout.

Save As
Save the current layout with a new name.

Remove Layout
This will delete the layout file currently loaded into the Visual Designer. An alert will be shown asking you to confirm the deletion.

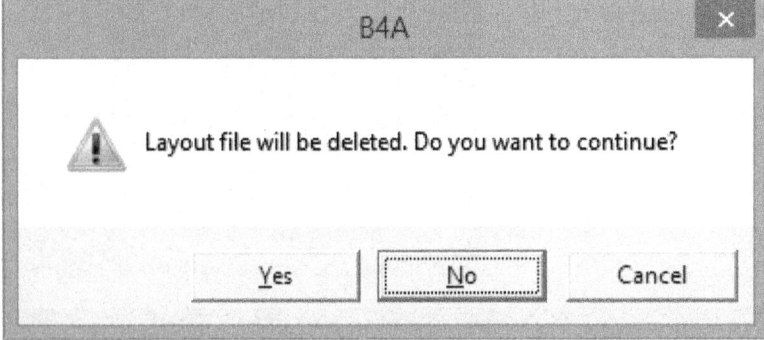

No and **Cancel** have the same effect.
Note: The file will not be moved to the Recycle Bin, so this deletion cannot be undone.

Below this is a list of the layout files in the current project (page 110).

AddView Menu

This menu allows you to select the view (object) you want to add on the current layout on the device or the Emulator. The views you can add are: AutoCompleteEditText (page 403), Button (page 407), CheckBox (page 409), CustomView (page 410), EditText (page 411), HorizontalScrollView (page 414), ImageView (page 416), Label (page 418), ListView (page 420), Panel (page 425) , ProgressBar (page 427), RadioButton (page 429), ScrollView (page

431), SeekBar (page 433), Spinner (page 435), TabHost (page 438), ToggleButton (page 441), WebView (page 445)

WYSIWYG Designer Menu

The view of a layout given in the Abstract Designer (page 157) is not WYSIWYG (What You See Is What You Get). It is an abstract representation of views. In order to get a WYSIWYG view, you need to connect the Visual Designer to a device or emulator. That is what this menu allows you to do.

Note that the WYSIWYG Designer also allows you to preview (page 182) your activity using different Material Themes (page 182).

Connect (F2)

This will connect the Designer to a device or emulator if any are available and start the B4A Designer on the connected device.

If no device is available for connection, an error message will be shown. We describe how to connect to a device or to an emulator in Testing Your App (page 184).

If several devices are available you will be able to chose which one you want to connect with. We recommend that for designing, the emulator is the preferred option since the screen on a real device will normally blank out after a minute or two to save battery.

Connection Status

Once connected, the Connection Status (at the bottom of the Designer Window) will show details about the device to which it is connected, for example:

Disconnect (Shift+F2)

Disconnect from the device or emulator previously connected.

Tools Menu

Generate Members

This allows you to quickly generate `Dim` statements and skeleton Subs within the Activity currently selected in the code editor.

Note: You should first select the Module where you want the declarations to appear before using this option.

Note also that this option does not work if you are running the app in debug mode.

When selected, this option shows a menu of all views and a tree of their possible Subs:

Select the Views for which you wish the Dim statements to be created (in `Sub Globals`).
Expand the tree and select the Events for which you want to generate a skeleton Sub.

Click **Generate members**.

This will add the following to the **Activity module**:
```
Sub Globals
  Dim btnChangePeriod As Button
End Sub
```
And
```
Sub btnChangePeriod_Click

End Sub
```
Note that you also get the option to generate code declarations if you right-click views within
the Abstract Designer (page 157), although that only allows one declaration to be declared at
a time.

Warning: If the code is executing then Generate members options have no effect, although
they do not show an error message.

Change grid

The (invisible) grid determines the minimum distance (in pixels) which a View moves when
you drag it in the Abstract Designer or in a connected device or emulator. This option lets
you change the grid size. The default is 10 pixels. When you specify the grid, the value is
stored in the Layout file, so different layouts can have different grids.

Send To UI Cloud (F6)

The Visual Designer menu [Tools > Send To UI Cloud F6] allows you to see how layouts look on different devices. The layout file will be sent to the B4A site and, after a delay of no more than 10 seconds, a page will be opened in your default web-browser showing your layout on different devices with different screen resolutions and densities. It's a very convenient tool to check the layout look without needing to have physical devices.

Example of a UI Cloud screen

The top of a typical web page looks like this:

B4A UI Cloud

Useful links:

- Supporting Multiple Screens - tips and best practices
- Designer Scripts Tutorial
- Designer Scripts & AutoScale Tutorial

Build a robust layout in 3 steps:

- **Scale** - Call AutoScaleAll keyword to scale the views based on the device physical size
- **Adjust** - Adjust the views position (for example views that need to be docked to the bottom, right or center)
- **Fill** - Use SetLeftAndRight and SetTopAndBottom methods to resize the views that should fill the available space

This is a temporary link. It will expire in several minutes.

Number of connected devices: 9
Total process time: 7.83 seconds

Galaxy Note (5.3" phone)

Process time: 2.56 seconds

Note: in the web-browser, you can click on an image to show it full-size, and you can scroll down to see the layout on many other devices.

Windows Menu

Properties Window
This selects the Properties window.

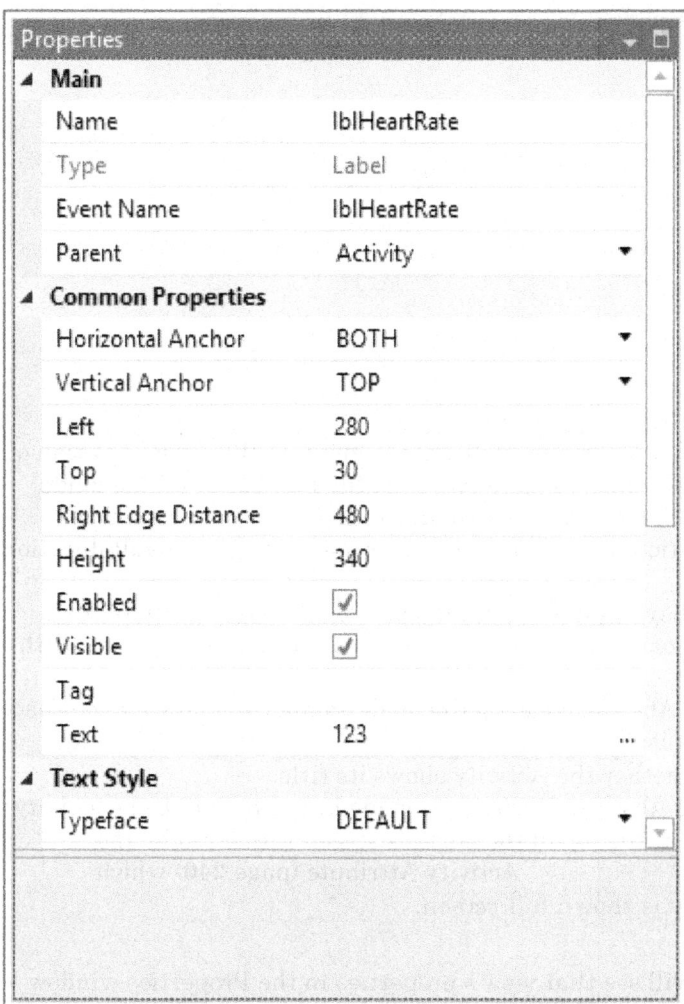

Note in version 5.00 this menu option was called "Grid" because it showed the Properties Grid.

Properties list

The upper part of the Properties Window lists all the properties of the selected view (or the Activity, if selected) organized in groups, and allows you to modify them.

Activity Properties

If you select the Activity in the tree, you will see the Activity properties and attributes:

Properties	▼ 및
◢ **Activity Properties**	
◢ Drawable	ColorDrawable ▼
Color	☐ ⊘ Default color
Alpha	255
Title	Activity
Animation Duration (ms)	400
Show Title	✓
Full Screen	☐

For an explanation of Drawable, see below (page 149).

The **Activity Animation Duration** field determines whether to animate the initial position of the views within the activity. Set to 0 to disable, otherwise set the number of milliseconds the animation should take. If Animation Duration is greater than 0, views move in from outside the activity, their initial position depending upon their anchors. The default duration is 400ms.

Note that if you add views in code, they are not animated. Note also that animations will only work on devices with Android 3 or higher. On earlier devices, the activity appears with the views already in place.

Show Title: If this is set to True, the Abstract Designer is made smaller to allow for the space occupied by the title. But note that it is actually the #IncludeTitle Activity Attribute (page 240) which actually controls whether the Activity shows its title.

Full Screen: If this is set to True, the Abstract Designer is made larger to match the activity size when the Status Bar (page 120) at the top of the device's screen is covered by the activity. But note that it is the the #FullScreen Activity Attribute (page 240) which actually controls whether the activity is shown full-screen.

View Properties

If you select a view in the tree, you will see that view's properties in the Properties window (as shown above).

View properties are grouped under the headings of Main Properties, Common Properties and other groups depending on what type of view has been selected. Groups can be expanded or collapsed for convenience. We discuss these groups next.

Main Properties

These properties can be changed by entering data or selecting items from drop-down lists in the column on the right.

Name: Name of the view. It is good practice to give meaningful names. Common usage is to give a 3 character prefix and add the purpose of the view. In the example shown above, the view is of type Label and its purpose is to enter a result. So we give it the name "lblHeartRate", "lbl" for Label and "HeartRate" for the purpose. This does not take much time during the design of the layout but saves a lot time during coding and maintenance of the program.

Type: Type of the view, not editable. It is not possible to change the type of a view. If you need to, you must remove the view and add a new one.

Event Name: Prefix for the subroutines which manage this view's events. By default the Event Name is the same as the view's name. Thus, for a label called lblHeartRate, the Designer menu [Tools > Generate Members] would generate a sub such as

```
Sub lblHeartRate_Click
```

The Events of several Views can be redirected to a single subroutine. In that case, you must enter the name of that routine in the Event Name field.

Parent: Name of the parent view as shown in the tree (Activity in the example below). The parent view can be changed by selecting a new one from the pull-down list:

◢ **Main**		
Name	btnPause	
Type	Button	
Event Name	btnPause	
Parent	Activity	▼
◢ **Common Properties**	Activity	
Horizontal Anchor	pnlGraph	

Common Properties

The next properties are grouped together as Common Properties, and the first few of these deal with anchors.

Anchors

◢ **Common Properties**		
Horizontal Anchor	RIGHT	▼
Vertical Anchor	TOP	▼
Right Edge Distance	10	
Top	550	
Width	120	
Height	50	

You can also select anchor types directly in the Abstract Designer by right-clicking a view and using its context menu (page 160).

Anchors are a powerful feature of the Visual Designer which allow you to specify how a view will position itself relative to the containing object, which could be a panel or the Activity (the screen).

Horizontal anchors can be set to LEFT, RIGHT or both.

Vertical anchors can be TOP, BOTTOM or BOTH.

You can set the distances between the view and its parent either by entering numbers (dips) in the Properties window or by dragging the view in the Abstract Designer.

If a view belongs to a panel then the distances are relative to the corresponding edge of the panel.

When you set the anchors to anything other than LEFT and TOP, small white dots are shown in the Abstract Designer to indicate which sides are anchored:

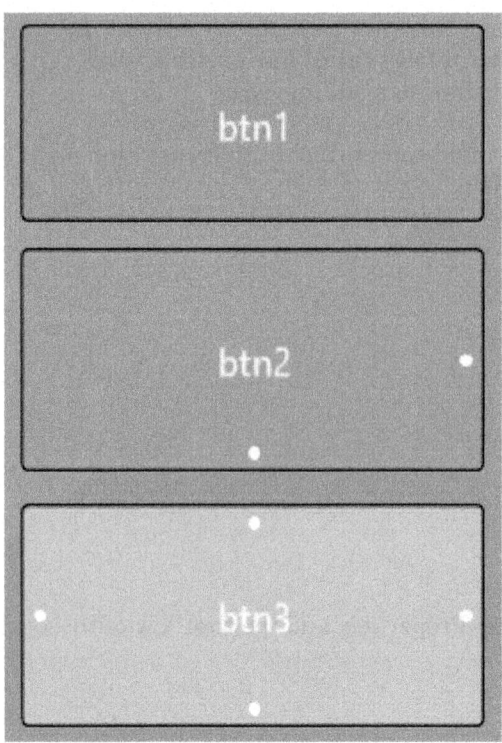

btn1 is anchored TOP and LEFT. Note that in this case no dots are shown, as this is considered the default anchorage.

btn2 is anchored RIGHT and BOTTOM. btn3 is anchored BOTH and BOTH.

On a device or emulator, each view will automatically position itself to the distance from the corresponding edge(s) of its containing object as specified in the Designer.

Anchors can be of great benefit, although sometimes you may need to fine-tune the layout by using Designer Scripts (page 162).

Horizontal and Vertical Anchor: Allows you to select the anchor mode for this view. Depending on what you select, you will some some of the following fields.

Left: X coordinate of the left edge of the View from the left edge of its parent View, in dips (page 163).

Top: Y coordinate of the upper edge of the View from the upper edge of its parent View, in dips (page 163).

Width: This option specifies the width of the View in dips (page 163).

Right Edge Distance: This option specifies the gap in dips (page 163) between the right edge of the View and the right edge of its parent.

Height: This option specifies the height of the View in dips (page 163).

Bottom Edge Distance: This option specifies the gap in dips (page 163) between the bottom edge of the view and the bottom edge of its parent.

Enabled: Enables or disables the use of the View

Visible: Determines if the View is visible to the user or not.

Tag: This is a place holder which can be used to store additional data. Tag can simply be text but can also be any other kind of object when accessed in code.

Text: The text to be shown on the View. Only relevant for certain types of View.

Multiline Editor: If the View is an EditText then the Text field includes a menu button

Clicking this will call up the Multiline Editor which allows you to enter multiple lines into the EditText:

Text Style

If you can enter the Text for a View then you can also configure the style in which the text is shown. Parameters you can set include the Typeface, Style, Horizontal and Vertical Alignments, Size and Color.

Note: Text Color can be copied and pasted from one View to another, or from one Color parameter to another within the same View.

Drawable

This property is available for some types of View. The Drawable properties refer to the background upon which the View is drawn. We discuss Drawables in more detail in the View Drawables (page 200) section.

The options you see within the Drawable property depends upon which type of view is currently selected. The options are:

DefaultDrawable: This is set by default and uses default colors.

StatelistDrawable: Allows you to chose drawable parameters for each of the three button states: Enabled, Disabled and Pressed. See StateListDrawable (page 203) in the Graphics and Drawing chapter.

Color: can be copied and pasted from one View to another, or from one Color parameter to another within the same View.

Alpha: A value from 0 to 255, where 0 is fully transparent and 255 is fully opaque.

Other Drawable parameters include Corner radius, Border Color and Border Width.

Properties Help area

When a property is selected, a gray box at the foot of the Properties Window shows help information about what the property does. For example, if the "Tag" property is selected, the following appears in the help area:

> **Tag**
> A string value that you can later retrieve.

Note that the Help Area can be expanded or contracted by clicking and dragging on the space between the Help Area and the overall properties box area. If you only see the word "Tag", you can click and drag the top of the Help Area upward to see the rest of the Help information.

Variants Window

One of the most common issues that Android developers face is the need to adapt the user interface to devices with different screen sizes and orientations.

Using B4A, it is possible to create multiple layout variants, one to match every different device, and to adapt to changes in device orientation.

But creating many layout variants is neither feasible nor recommended.

A better solution is to use the minimum number of variants, perhaps just four: a portrait and a landscape for each of a phone and a tablet. You can then make them adapt themselves automatically to the user's device by using the features which B4A offers, such as Anchors (page 147) in the Abstract Designer or the AutoScale function (page 166) in Designer Scripts.

Standard Variant

The default or standard variant or standard screen (page 163) used by B4A is 320 x 480 pixels with a scale of 1.

Multiple Variants

Multiple variants can all be managed in a single layout file.

The Variants window shows the different screen sizes for which you have created a variant.

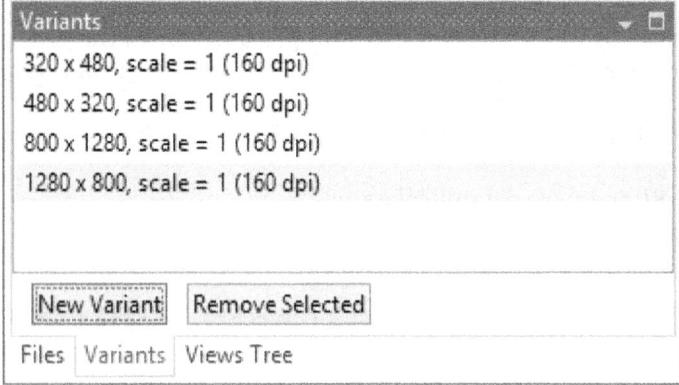

New Variant

If you click New Variant you will see a dialog box where you can specify the dimensions of the variant you wish to add:

A Create New Layout Variant   ✕

Standard values:

○ Phone (portrait): 320x480, scale=1   ○ Other: Width   [   ]

○ Phone (landscape): 480x320, scale=1   Height [   ]

○ Tablet (portrait): 800x1280, scale=1   Scale   [1.0   ]

○ Tablet (landscape): 1280x800, scale=1

                                                                    [Cancel]   [Ok]

You can select a pre-defined standard value or define a new one. (Note: The dimensions of the Standard value Tablet referred to are suitable for a 10" tablet.)
The new variant will be added to the Variants list.

Adding Other Variants

It is possible to select Other and add the Width and Height (in pixels) and the Scale (page 163). The new variant will be added to the Layout Variants list.

Normalized Variants

Normalized variants are variants with scales (page 163) of 1.0. The layout you create with the Visual Designer is scaled (not stretched or resized) automatically. This means that the layout will look exactly the same on two phones with the same physical size. The scale doesn't matter.

Do not add too many variants

Note that in most cases it is not recommended to add variants other than these recommended ones. It is all too easy to create many variants, but they are very difficult to maintain. Instead, you should use Anchors (page 147) or the designer script feature to adjust (or fine tune) your layout.

Add Only Normalized Variants

It is highly recommended to design your layout with normalized variants only. For example, a variant of 480x800, scale=1.5, matches the normalized variant: 320x533, scale=1.0 (divide each value by the scale value). Now it is easy to see that this device is slightly longer than the "standard" variant: 320x480, scale=1.0.

Why this recommendation?

Consider a device (such as the Samsung Galaxy Nexus phone) whose screen data is 720x1184 at 320 dpi (scale 2). It may seem completely different from the default phone which is 320x480 at 160 dpi (scale 1), but if you calculate the normalized values of the Galaxy Nexus to scale 1, its layout actually matches: 360x592 at 160 dpi. This means that it is only slightly wider and longer than the default phone size. It should be easy to handle these differences using anchors or designer scripts.

How variants are shown in Abstract Designer

If you want the Abstract Designer to show the variant with the gray background automatically resized to match the layout, then you must select **Match Chosen Variant** from the drop down list box (page 159) at the top of the Abstract Designer.

In this case, when you select a variant in the Variants window, the views which you have added to the Abstract Designer will automatically move to the positions and with the anchors set for that variant. For example portrait...

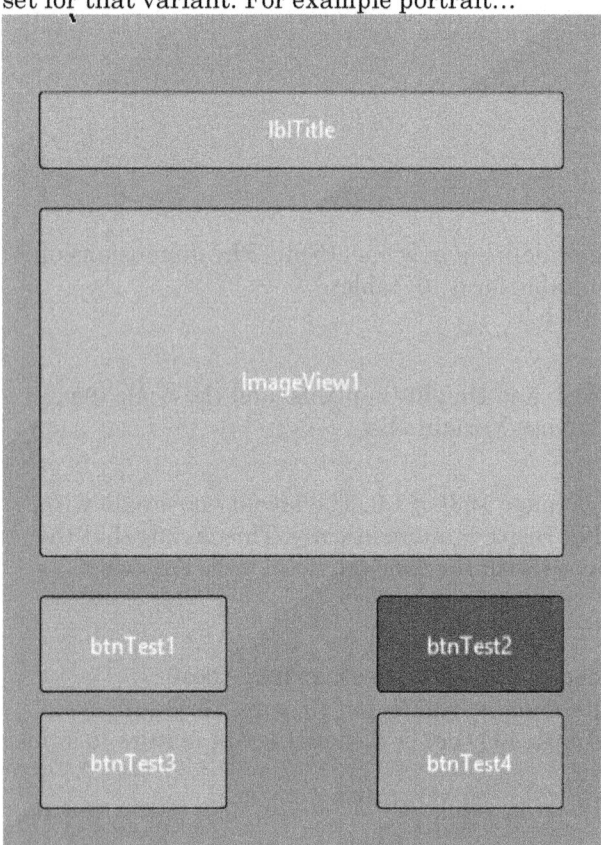

...and landscape...

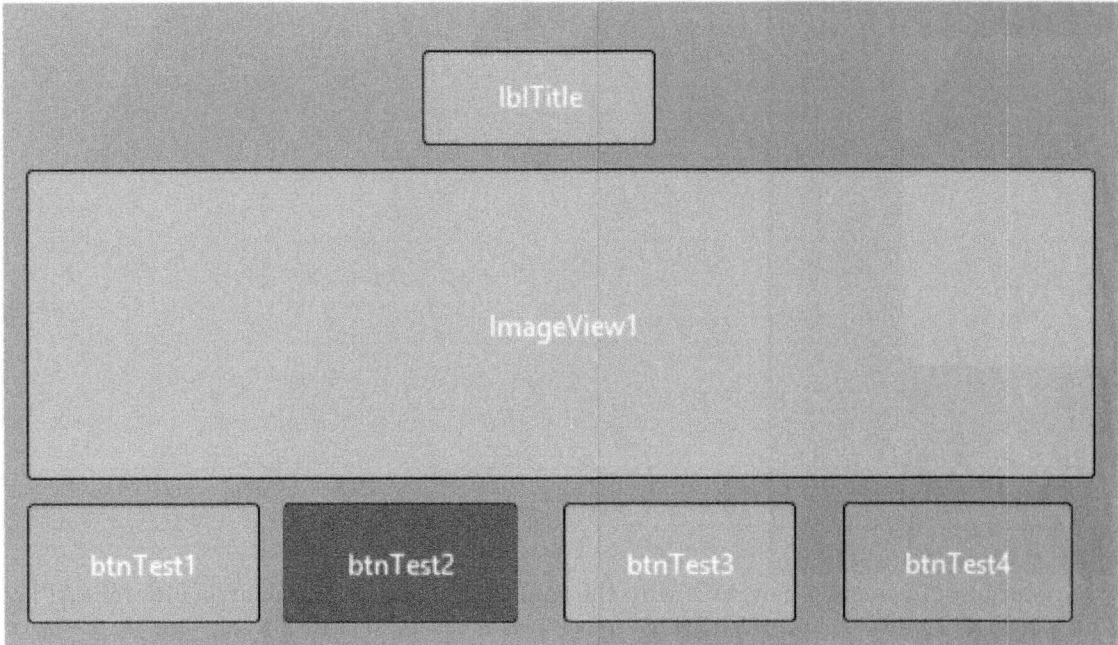

Rotating the Emulator

If the layout selected is in landscape and you want to see the WYSIWYG on an emulator, you will need to change your Emulator to the same mode. Select the Emulator and press Ctrl + F11 to change its orientation.

Warning: Bug in Emulator

There is a bug in the Emulator using Android 2.3.x (API 9 or 10) for the AVD. It can get stuck in a certain orientation so that pressing Ctrl + F11 repeatedly can cause the Emulator to become confused, rotating the text on its screen but not resizing correctly:

One solution is to create a new AVD with the same specifications but using a different API level (such as 7 or 8). Or use B4A-Bridge to connect to a real device.

Files Window

This window allows you to add (or remove) images to be shown on the layout:

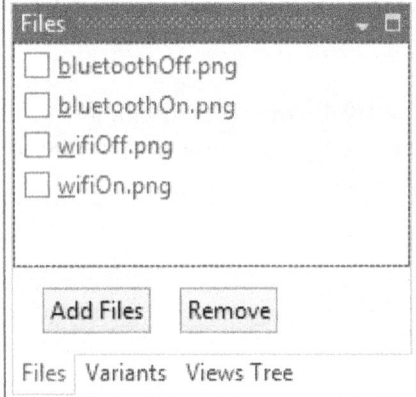

Add Images: Allows you to select an image anywhere on your development computer. The selected files will be copied to the Files folder of the current project. Once added, you can add an `ImageView` to your layout and select the required image in the Image file property.

Selecting Files: Either click the checkboxes or right-click and select all or none.

Remove Selected: shows the following dialog:

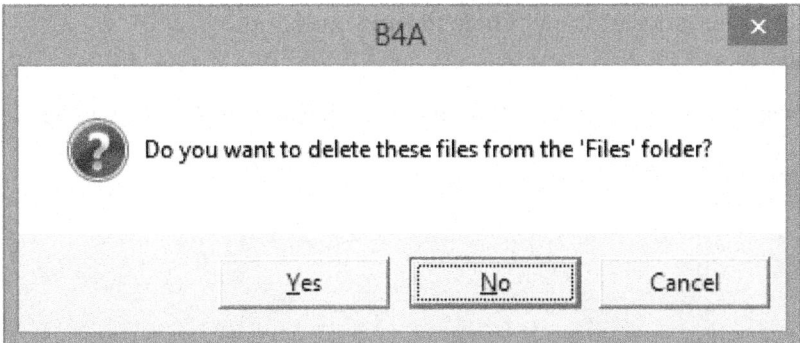

Yes: removes the selected files from the list and from the **Files** folder of the project. **Make sure to have a copy of the files you remove, because they are removed from the Files folder, but not transferred to the recycle bin. This means they are definitively lost if you don't have a copy.**

No: removes the selected files from the list but does not delete them from the project's **Files** folder.

Script Windows

The Windows menu includes links to the two scripting windows: Script-General and Script-Variant which by default are part of a single tab group:

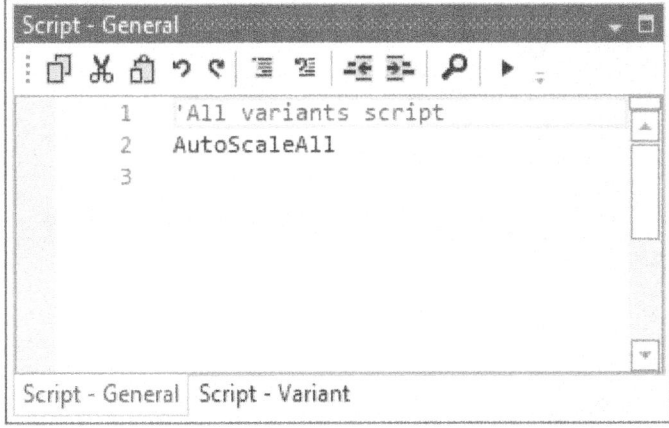

We describe creating and running scripts in detail in the Designer Scripts Reference (page 162) chapter.

Script General

The script written here will be applied to all variants.

Script Variant

Designer Scripts written here will only apply to the Current Variant (page 164).

Script Toolbar

Several tools are provided in the scripting toolbars to facilitate editing. These are a subset of the tools in the IDE toolbar (page 78).

See Running Scripts (page 162) for a description of how to run your script.

Views Tree

The Views Tree shows a hierarchy of views within the layout, including the Activity which holds them all:

Note that the items at the bottom of the list are at the front of the display, as shown by their names in the above image. This order may seen illogical was probably chosen because they are consequently nearest to the viewer. Thus in the Abstract Designer, the above tree of views appear as:

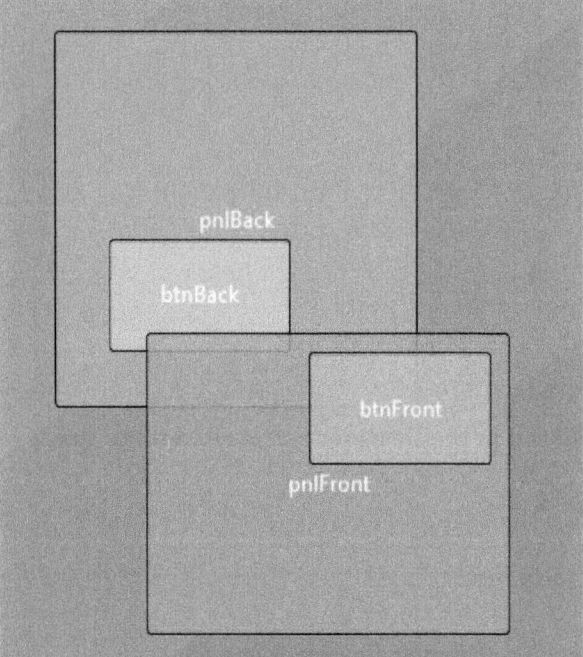

The tree is convenient for selecting a view and seeing how they are nested. If you select a view in the Abstract Designer or a connected device or emulator (page 188), the same view is automatically selected here.

You can drag items up and down the tree to a limited extent to re-order them or assign them to panels.

However the tree does NOT allow you to: drag items into a panel unless it already has at least one daughter; drag a view to the bottom of the tree so it is a daughter of the Activity if there is a panel with children already at the bottom of the tree.

In these cases, you will need to assign a view's parent using the Properties Parent field, or cut and paste views within the Abstract Designer.

Reset

This option will move all the windows back to their default positions.

The Abstract Designer

The Abstract Designer shows the layout you are creating in the Designer.

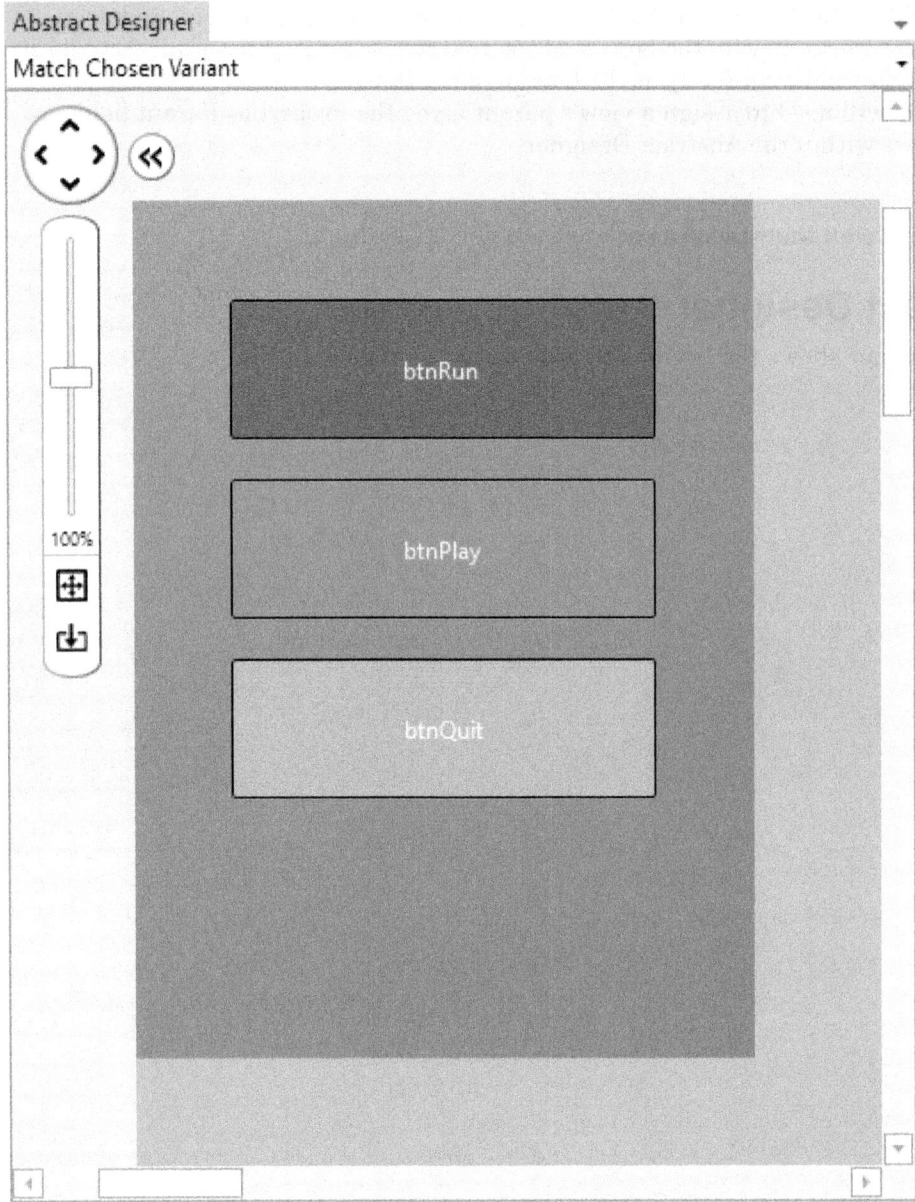

Its main purpose is to help you create and position your layout and its variants. The different views are **not** shown with their actual appearance but only as colored rectangles—hence the name Abstract Designer. However, if you connect the designer (page 141) to a device or an emulator, that will show you a WYSIWYG (What You See Is What You Get) display of your layout.

Clicking on a view in the Abstract Designer or a connected emulator or device shows its properties in the Properties window and selects it in the Views Tree.

Match Chosen Variant

At the top of the Abstract Designer is a dropdown list box which allows you to select from a wide range of pre-determined variants:

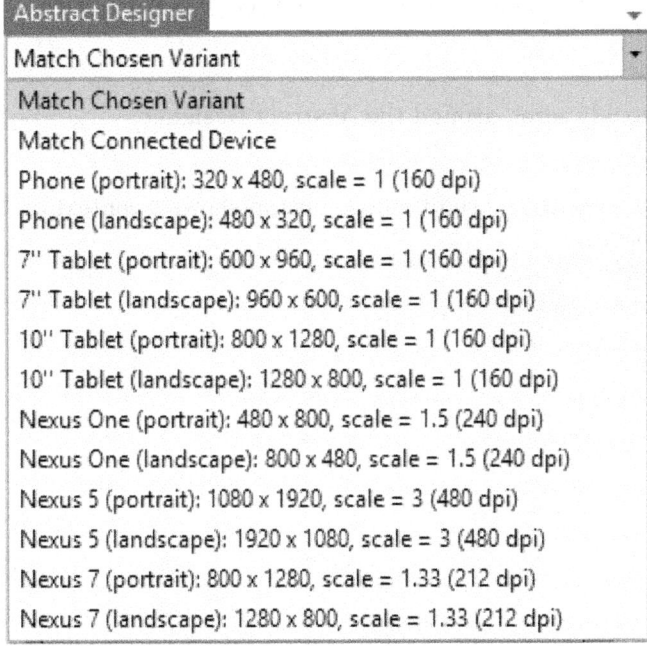

This is useful for checking your layout in a wide range of variants.

Note that another way to do this is with the [Tools > Send to UI Cloud (F6)] option.

View Controls

There are various ways to control the appearance of the Abstract Designer window. The Zoom tool can resize your view of your layout:

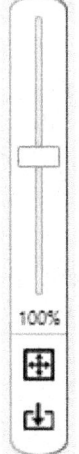

The slide bar allows you to zoom from 10% to 300%.

Note that you can also use the mouse wheel to zoom, if you have one.

The Zoom to Fit button ⊞ automatically zooms the layout to fit the Abstract Designer.
The Reset View button ⬇ resets the zoom to 100%.

The Minimize button ⪡ hides the zoom control and changes into a Maximize button.

The Navigation Pad ⬥ lets you quickly scroll around the Abstract Designer.

Context menus

Clicking on a view in the Abstract Designer with the right mouse button shows a context or popup menu which has the following options:

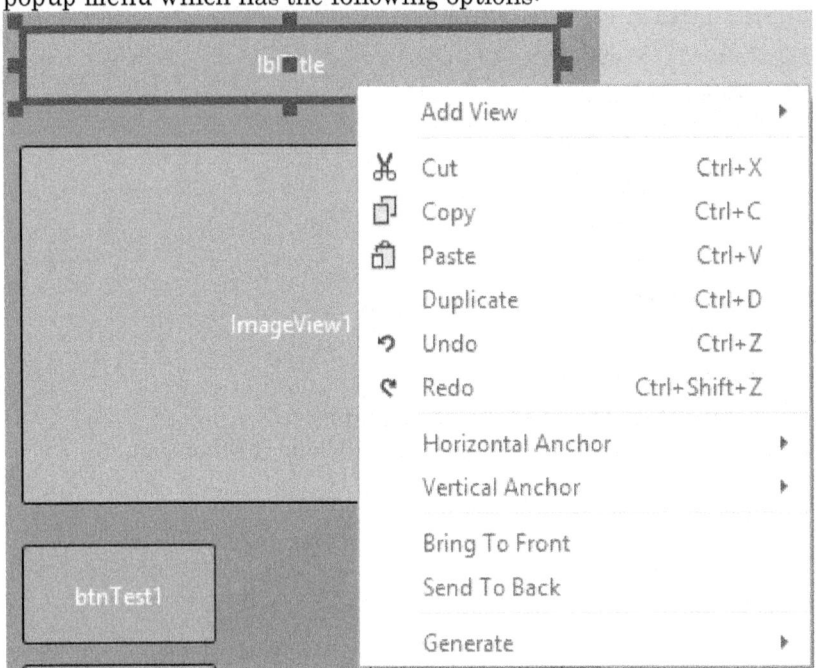

Note that if only one view is selected, the Generate option lets you generates a single Dim statement or an event routine for the selected View. If several views are selected, Generate becomes Generate Dialog and it opens the same dialog as Designer [Tools > Generate Members (page 141)] option.

Selecting views

The selected views have a red border. You can select a single view by clicking on the view. Select several views by clicking on the first view, holding the Ctrl key and selecting more views or by dragging the cursor around them in the Abstract Designer.
After making a selection you can:
- Move the selected views by
  - using the arrow keys of the keyboard in the four directions
  - dragging one of the selected views with the mouse
- Use the Context menu (as described above)
- Modify the view with the Properties window.

Note: With several views selected in the Abstract Designer, you can change those properties they hold in common in the Properties window.

Designer Scripts

The Designer includes two Scripts windows. These are explained in the Designer Scripts chapter.

Adding views in code

Instead of using the Designer, it is also possible to create and modify views directly in your Activity code. See Adding Views by Code (page 129) for details.

2.5 Designer Scripts Reference

Background

One of the most common issues that Android developers face is the need to adapt the user interface to devices with different screen sizes. As described in the Variants Window (page 150) section, you can create multiple layout variants to match different devices. However, it is neither feasible nor recommended to create and maintain a lot of layout variants.

To solve this problem, B4A supports designer scripts which help you fine-tune your layout and easily adjust it to different screens and resolutions. The idea is to combine the usefulness of the visual designer with the flexibility and power of programming code.

You can write a simple script to adjust the layout based on the dimensions of the current device and immediately see the results on a connected device or emulator (page 188). There is no need to compile and install the full program each time. You can also immediately see the results in the Abstract Designer (page 157). This allows you to quickly test your layout on many different screen sizes.

We described the two Scripts windows (page 155) in the Visual Designer chapter.

Designer Scripts and Activity Code

Note: a designer script runs before the code in your activity. If, for example, you have designer scripts for different orientation variants, when the user rotates the screen, the designer script will run first, then your activity code will be run as explained in Process and Activity (page 241).

Running Scripts

A script will automatically run when a Script window is selected in the Visual Designer, and the Abstract Designer will show the message:

```
Script mode (read-only).
Click on the properties grid to exit this mode.
```

Click the Properties window to go back to the Abstract Designer edit mode.

If you edit a script, it will not automatically run. If you want to run your new script and update the Abstract Designer (page 157), you need to press F5 or click the Run icon ▶ in the Script window toolbar. This will also show the result in any connected device / emulator (page 188).

Key Concepts

First, we define some key concepts for working with layouts and devices.

Pixel

A pixel (or picture element) is the smallest addressable physical element on a screen. It corresponds to a glowing dot of light. Its size varies from one device to another. This could be a problem, but this is resolved using "dips" (see below).

Resolution

The number of pixels on the device's screen, for example, 320 x 480

dpi : dots per inch

Dots per inch (also called dpi or pixels per inch or ppi or density) is a measure of the physical number of pixels in one inch of a device. A pixel is the smallest addressable element of the display. dpi will vary from one device to another, and vertical and horizontal dpi may differ on a single device. Things can get pretty complicated!

B4A developers do not need to worry about this, however! See **dip** below.

Screen Size

Typically the diagonal dimension of a screen is quoted in inches.

dip

We now come to a key concept. Suppose you want a button in your app to always be ½ inch wide. If you know the device's resolution is 160 dpi then you can work out the button should be 80 pixels wide. Your code might be:

```
Button1.Width = 80 'This is pixels and can cause a problem
```

But what if your app runs on a device with a screen resolution of 240 dpi? Your button will only be 1/3 inch wide! This is the problem which dips were created to solve.

"dips" are **D**ensity **I**ndependent **P**ixels (sometimes called **device** independent pixels, dips, dps or dp). They are abstract units that are independent of the dpi of the device. One dip is defined as equal to 1/160 inch. It is equal in size to one pixel on a 160 dpi screen. 160 dips will measure very close to one inch, no matter what the density of the device.

80 dips are always close to half an inch. Magic!

Note that sizes are not always exact. Experiments[1] on a small sample of devices show that a label designated as 160dip wide can in fact be anything from 1.04 to 1.19 inches wide. Nevertheless, dips give you far better control than pixels, so the above code should say:

```
Button1.Width = 80dip    'About 1/2 inch wide!
```

Use dip units for all specified sizes (except TextSize - see below).

By using dip units, the values will be sized close to what you want on devices with higher or lower resolution. You should always use dips when specifying the size or position of a view (control). This way the view's *physical* position and size will be the same on any device. This is true for both B4A code and designer script.

Text Size

Text size is measured in physical units, that is, in pixels; you should **not** use dips with text size values. However, you can automatically change the text size using `AutoScale` (page 167).

Standard Screen

The Standard Screen is assumed to have a density of 160 dpi and a resolution of 320 x 480 pixels. This is the same as the Designer's Standard Variant (page 150).

---

[1] Thanks to Bob Paehr for this information.

Scale

The standard screen resolution is 160 dpi. This is said to have a scale of 1. To calculate the scale of a specific device, divide the dpi by 160. So, a phone with 320 dpi has a scale of 320/160 = 2 and a screen with 240 dpi has a scale of 240/160 = 1.5.

Typical scale values are: 0.75, 1.0, 1.5 and 2. Most phones today have 240 dpi, so their scale is 1.5. Most tablets have a scale of 1.0.

Should you want to, you can convert dips to physical pixels by multiplying by the scale. So, 80dip on a device with scale 2 would be 160 pixels.

You can find the scale value for the current device by using the Scale property (page 380) of a LayoutValues object.

Dock and Fill Strategy

A common way of designing a layout is to dock some views to the edges of the screen, then use the other views to fill in the space between them. You can dock a view with an anchor (page 147) or with the Designer Script, for example:

```
button1.Right = 100%x
```

It is often useful to dock a panel and then fill it with views, such as buttons in a ToolBox Panel.

Designer Scripting Basics

We described the Script windows (page 155) and how to run scripts in the Visual Designer chapter.

Scripts are also run after the layout is loaded when the app is running. The general script is first executed followed by the variant script specific to the device and orientation. The system will automatically decide which variant to apply.

Selecting Variants

If you have added more than one variant in the Visual Designer's Variants (page 150) window, then when you select that variant in the Variants Window (page 150), the corresponding script is automatically loaded into the Variant Specific Script area (page 155) and run. It will also update the Abstract Designer to show the effect of the script on the selected variant.

Script Language

The script language is simple and is optimized for managing layouts.

Variables

You can use variables in Designer Scripts. You do not need to declare the variables before using them. There is no **Dim** keyword in the script.

```
gap = 3dip
cmd0.Left = gap
```

Note that the script editor has an autocomplete (page 83) facility, the same as the IDE code editor.

%x and %y

50%x means 50% of the maximum width available.

100%y means 100% of the height available.

So to set view EditText1 at the bottom of the space available, you would use:

```
EditText1.bottom = 100%y
```

These values are relative to the view that loads the layout. Usually it will be the activity. However, if you use **Panel.LoadLayout**, then it will be relative to this panel.

Note: **ScrollView** inner panel width is set to **-1**. This is a special value that causes the panel to fill its parent's available size.

If you want to load a layout file (with a script) to the inner panel then you will need to first set the panel width:

```
ScrollView1.Panel.Width = ScrollView1.Width
```

Properties Within Scripts

You can get or set a view's position using the properties **Width**, **Height**, **Left**, **Right**, **Top**, **Bottom**, **HorizontalCenter**, **VerticalCenter**.

For example:

```
EditText1.Left = 0
EditText1.Top = 0
lblTitle.Right = 100%x
lblTitle.Bottom = 100%y
```

Warning: Set Internal Properties before External

It is important that you set internal properties (Width or Height) BEFORE you set the external properties (**Left**, **Right**, **Top**, **Bottom**, **HorizontalCenter**, **VerticalCenter**). If you set the external properties first, then the view will be positioned wrongly. For example, suppose you want a button positioned at the bottom of the screen. You might think the following are equivalent:

```
btnTest1.Bottom = 100%y
btnTest1.Height = 20%y

btnTest2.Height = 20%y
btnTest2.Bottom = 100%y
```

But in fact the buttons will be positioned differently:

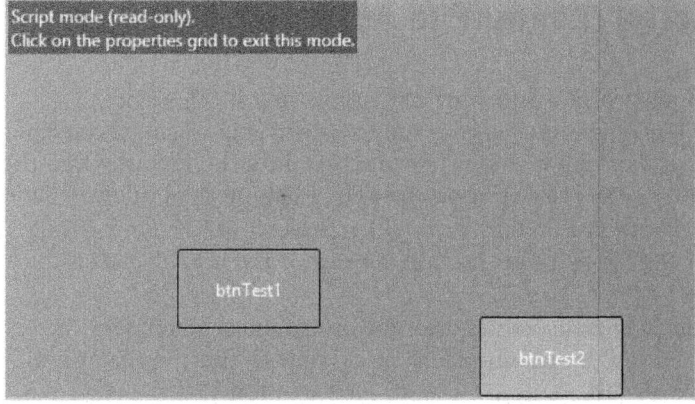

btnTest2 is positioned as you would expect, so remember to set internal before external properties. The letters "IE" might help to remind you of this. Alternatively, you could use `SetLeftAndRight` or `SetTopAndBottom`. See below for details.

Text Properties

You can get or set the text size and textual content of views such as labels and buttons which show text:

- **TextSize** - Gets or sets the text size (page 163) in pixels.
You should not use 'dip' units with this value as it is already measured in physical units.
- **Text** - Gets or sets the view's text size in pixels.

Other Properties

- **Image** - Sets the image file (write-only). Only supported by ImageView.
- **Visible** - Gets or sets the view's visible property.

Methods

- **SetLeftAndRight** (Left, Right) - Sets the view's left and right properties. This method changes the width of the view based on the two values.
- **SetTopAndBottom** (Top, Bottom) - Sets the view's top and bottom properties. This method changes the height of the view based on the two values.

Other Keywords

- **Min / Max** - Same as the standard Min / Max keywords.
- **ActivitySize** - Returns the approximate diagonal size of the activity, measured in inches.
- **Autoscale** - see below.
- **If ... Then...Else If...Else...End If** condition blocks
Both single line and multiline statements are supported. The syntax is the same as for regular If blocks.
- **Landscape** - Returns True if the current orientation is landscape.
- **Portrait** - Returns True if the current orientation is portrait.

Activity Methods

Activity.RerunDesignerScript (LayoutFile As String, Width As Int, Height As Int)

A Designer Script will be called automatically when your app starts and if the device orientation changes (see Note below), but in some cases it may be desirable to run the script again while your app is executing. For example, you may want to update the layout when the soft keyboard becomes visible. The `Activity.RerunDesignerScript` method allows you to run the script again and specify the width and height that will represent 100%x and 100%y. In order for this method to work, all the views referenced in the script must be declared in `Sub Globals`.

Note: this method should **not** be used to handle screen orientation changes. When the device's orientation changes, the activity will automatically be recreated and the script will run during the `Activity.LoadLayout` call.

AutoScale: Layouts for Different Sized Devices

Larger devices offer a lot more available space. The result is that, if the physical size of a view is the same, it looks smaller. Some developers use %x and %y to specify the view's size. However, the result is far from perfect. The layout will just be stretched. The solution is to combine the dock and fill strategy (page 164) with a smart algorithm that increases the view's size and text size (page 163) based on the running device's physical size.
Note: `AutoScale` is the only way to automatically change the `TextSize`.

How AutoScale works

B4A internally calculates the values given below. You do not need to understand these calculations, but we include them here for reference:
Delta: a measure of the ratio of the current screen compared to the standard variant, calculated by the formula
```
delta = ((100%x + 100%y) / (320dip + 480dip) - 1)
```
Rate: How much we want to stretch the views. It is a value between 0 (no scaling) and 1 (scaling is proportional to your device's physical size). The default is 0.3, but this can be changed with the `AutoScaleRate()` function.
Scale: The multiplication factor applied to individual views, calculated by
```
scale = 1 + rate * delta
```
These values have no effect until either `AutoScale` or `AutoScaleAll` are called by the Designer Script.

How to See the Effect of AutoScale

AutoScale bases its calculations upon the standard variant: resolution 320 x 480, 160 dpi, scale = 1. Therefore, when used with this variant, `AutoScale` will have no effect. To see the effect of `AutoScale`, you need to add a different sized variant. Go to the Variants window in the Visual Designer and do the following:
1) add a New Variant, such as 960 x 600
2) select the variant in the Variants window
Now you can use the `AutoScale` commands, as described next, and see their effect.

How to See the Effect of AutoScale on Text Size

Note: because the Abstract Designer is not WYSIWYG, you will not see the effect of `AutoScale` on text size (page 163). You must connect (page 141) the Visual Designer to an emulator or a real device to see the actual results. **Note also**: select Match Connected Device from the drop down list box at the top of the Abstract Designer if you want to see the size of the device shown as a gray box.
If you are designing for a specific size of device then you might want to add this variant to your layout. But in general it is better to restrict the number of variants you design for, as discussed above (page 150).

How to Use AutoScale

Often your script will select the `AutoScaleRate` and then you will `AutoScaleAll` so that all views are scaled. So your script might be something like this:

```
AutoScaleRate(0.5)
AutoScaleAll
```

By changing the value for **AutoScaleRate**, you can find the best value for different variants. Occasionally you might need to scale individual views, in which case you would use the **AutoScale** function. We describe these functions next:

AutoScaleRate(rate)

As mentioned above, rate is how much we want to stretch the views. It is a value between 0 and 1.

0 means no change at all.

1 is almost similar to using %x and %y

The rate determines the change amount in relation to the device physical size. If the physical size is twice the size of the standard phone, then the size will be twice the original size. Values between 0.2 to 0.5 seem to give good results. **AutoScaleRate** sets the rate value for above scale calculation. If this is not called, **rate** defaults to 0.3. Example:
```
AutoScaleRate(0.5)
```
If a view has a **Text** property, its **TextSize** is also multiplied by the scale value.

Note: **AutoScaleRate** cannot be called by B4A code, only by a Designer Script.

AutoScaleAll

Scales all the views in the selected layout using the algorithm shown above. Normally you call it after **AutoScaleRate**.

AutoScale(View)

AutoScale multiplies the **Left**, **Top**, **Width**, **Height** and **TextSize** properties of the specified view by the scale value calculated as explained above.

Example: `AutoScale(btnTest1)`

This is equivalent to:
```
btnTest1.Left = btnTest1.Left * scale
btnTest1.Top = btnTest1.Top * scale
btnTest1.Width = btnTest1.Width * scale
btnTest1.Height = btnTest1.Height * scale
btnTest1.TextSize = btnTest1.TextSize * scale
```
Note: "scale" is not a keyword so it cannot be used in your scripts.

Different Layouts for Portrait and Landscape

A layout rarely looks good in both portrait and landscape mode. For example, a row of buttons might look better along the bottom in portrait but down the side in landscape. Therefore, it can be a good idea to create different layouts, one for each orientation. Suppose we have already created a Designer Script for portrait mode. To make it work for both portrait and landscape, the Designer Script code must be changed.

For the portrait variant, we keep only the most general code in the `All variants script` area of the Main layout file. For example:
```
'All variants script
AutoScaleRate(0.5)
AutoScaleAll
```
All the other code is moved to the `Variant specific script` areas.

Scaling strategy

You should decide what will happen with your layout when it runs on a larger device. Usually some views will be docked to the edges. This can be done easily with anchors (page 147) or a designer script. For example, to dock a button to the right side:

```
Button1.Right = 100%x
```

Some views should fill the available area.

Again this can be done with anchors or in a script with the **SetTopAndButtom** and **SetLeftAndRight** methods:

```
'Make an EditText fill the available height between two buttons:
EditText1.SetTopAndBottom(Button1.Bottom, Button2.Top)

'Make a Button fill the entire PARENT panel:
Button1.SetLeftAndRight(0, Parent1.Width)
Button1.SetTopAndBottom(0, Parent1.Height)
```

Editing Views in a program

As well as using the Designer to create a Layout, you can create or modify Views in code.

Example

Here is some code which will produce the following screen:

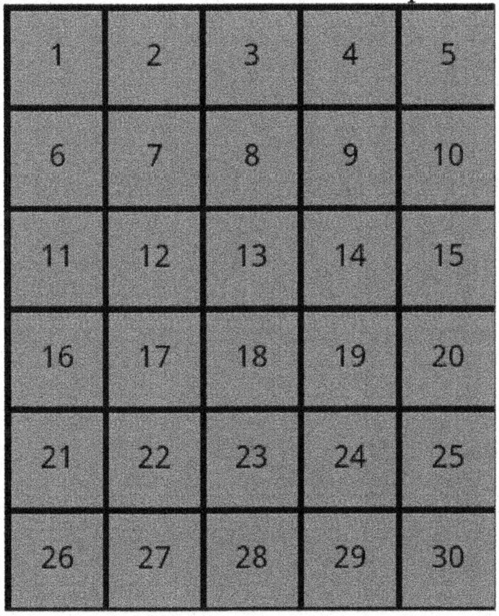

1	2	3	4	5
6	7	8	9	10
11	12	13	14	15
16	17	18	19	20
21	22	23	24	25
26	27	28	29	30

```
Sub Activity_Create(FirstTime As Boolean)
 Dim i, j, k, nx, ny, x0, x1, x2 As Int

  x0 = 4dip
  x1 = 60dip
  x2 = x0 + x1

  nx = Floor(Activity.Width / x2) - 1
  ny = Floor(Activity.Height / x2) - 1
  k = 0
  For j = 0 To ny
   For i = 0 To nx
    k = k + 1
    Dim btn As Button
    btn.Initialize("btn")
    btn.Color = Colors.Red
    Activity.AddView(btn, x0 + i * x2, x0 + j * x2, x1, x1)
    btn.Text = k
    btn.TextSize = 20
   Next
  Next
End Sub
```

2.6 Compiling, Debugging & Testing

Compiling

To test and later distribute your project, you must compile it (that is, convert it into java files) and create a Manifest (page 115) file and an APK (page 263) file which are stored in the Objects folder of the project.

You compile it using either one of the compile options (page 71) in the [Project] menu or their shortcuts or the ▶ Run icon in the toolbar or the Command Line Compiler (page 174).

The result of a compile is specified by the current Build Configuration, described below.

Android Version

You specify the lowest version of Android (page 118) your app will run on by selecting the appropriate android.jar file in the [Tools > Configure Paths (page 107)] dialog.

Build Configuration

A Build Configuration specifies the type of build to be executed when you run or compile your project. B4A contains some built-in configurations and also allows you to define your own Build Configurations.

Defining a Build Configuration

Select [Project > Build Configurations (Ctrl+B)].

```
A  Build Configurations                              ×

Configuration:       Default                    ▼      Create New

Configuration Name:  Default
                                                       Delete
Package:             b4a.example

Conditional Symbols:

                     Example: Full, NoAds

                                          Cancel    OK
```

Configuration: If you select `Default` then the configuration will automatically be set to one of the pre-defined build configurations, DEBUG or RELEASE, depending on the current compilation mode.

If you wish to define some Conditional Symbols, click Create New to add a new Configuration.

Note that a new configuration is given a name automatically, such as New_1, but you can change the name using the Configuration Name field. But note also that the name is not actually changed until you save the configuration.

When you click OK, the new configuration will be added to the Build Configuration list shown below.

Configuration Name: The name of the configuration.

Package: The name of the package. For details see Package Name (page 114). You can produce APKs with different package names from the same project, one for each configuration, or multiple configurations can share the same package name.

Conditional Symbols: one or more words, separated by commas which determine Conditional Compilation, as explained below. These are not case-sensitive. Note that the build configurations DEBUG and RELEASE include conditional symbols with the same names.

Build Configuration List

Having created your own build configuration, you need to make it active by selecting it from the Build Configuration list near the top of the IDE:

Conditional Compilation

You can use conditional attributes #If, #Else, #Else If, AND, OR, #End If in conjunction with Conditional Symbols to include or exclude parts of your B4A code, Manifest (page 115) or Designer scripts (page 162). You can create your own Conditional Symbols, as described above. In addition, you can test for one of the two Compilation Modes DEBUG and RELEASE. These are always defined, irrespective of what conditional symbols you have added.

For example, suppose you create a build configuration which has the defined Conditional Symbol firstInstall. Then the following code would be valid:

```
#If DEBUG OR FIRSTINSTALL
    lblTitle.Text = "Debug"
#Else If RELEASE
    lblTitle.Text = "Release"
#Else
    lblTitle.Text = "Some Other Condition"
#End If
```

Note that the symbols are not case-sensitive

Note that conditional attributes are also used to define inline Java code (page 449).

Compilation Modes

There are four compilation modes which are selected by a drop-down list box at the top of the IDE:

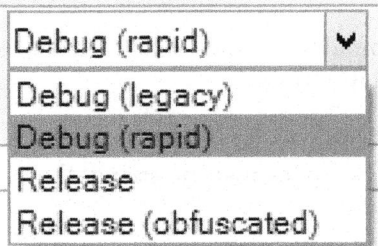

Debug Legacy Mode

This mode requires a device or emulator (page 188) to be attached to the IDE. This option will sign the package file with a debug key (page 263), ready for debugging, and produce a file **projectname_DEBUG.apk** in the **project\Objects** folder. If no device is attached, it will still compile the code, but produce an error message. See Legacy Debugging (page 177) for details.

Debug Rapid Mode

This mode requires a device or emulator (page 188) to be attached to the IDE. This option will sign the package file with a debug key (page 263), ready for debugging, and produce a file **projectname_RAPID_DEBUG.apk** in the **project\Objects** folder. If no device is attached, it will still compile the code, but produce an error message. See Rapid Debugging (page 176) for details.

Release Mode

In this mode, the debugger code will not be added to the apk file. For more details about creating an apk for distribution, see Generating Your APK (page 263).

Release (obfuscated)

B4A includes a code obfuscation feature. During compilation, B4A generates Java code which is then compiled with the Java compiler and converted to Dalvik (Android byte code format). There are tools that people can use to decompile the Dalvik byte code back into Java code. The purpose of obfuscation is to make the decompiled code less readable, harder to understand and make it more difficult to extract strings like developer account keys. For more details about creating an apk for distribution, see Generating Your APK (page 263).

It is important to understand how the obfuscator works.
When compiled in this mode, the debugger code will not be added to the apk file, but the program file will be modified, as follows:

Strings obfuscation

Any string written in **Sub Process_Globals** (and only in this sub) will be obfuscated, making it much harder to extract important keys. The strings are deobfuscated at runtime. **Note**: several keys are used during obfuscation including the package name, version name and version code. Modifying these values with the manifest editor will break the deobfuscation process, so your code will not run.

Renaming of Variables

The names of global variables and subs are converted to meaningless strings. Local variables are not affected as their names are lost anyway during the compilation.

The following identifiers are **not** renamed:

- Identifiers that contain an underscore (which is required for handlers of events).
- Subs that appear in `CallSub` statements. If the sub name appears as a static string, the identifier will not be renamed.
- Names of Designer views.

Tip: If, for some reason, you need to prevent the obfuscator from renaming an identifier, you should add an underscore in the identifier name.

A file named `ObfuscatorMap.txt` will be created under the Objects folder. This file maps the original names of identifiers to their obfuscated names. This mapping can be helpful to analyze crash reports.

Conditional Compilation

You can use Compilation Modes to control conditional compilation.

Command Line Compiler

You can compile your app from the command line using a program called B4ABuilder.exe, located in your B4A installation folder. To run this you can either

- use the Command Prompt program
- use a batch file to run B4ABuilder.exe

We strongly recommend you use batch files, but we next document the Command Prompt method for completeness.

To run B4ABuilder you need to provide parameters. The parameters available are:

– Task: What you want to do. Possible values:
   Build - Similar to Release compilation (default value)
   BuildLibrary - Similar to Library compilation.
– BaseFolder: The project folder. Default value is the current folder.
– Project: Main project file. Can be omitted if there is only one b4a file in the base folder.
– NoSign: If True then the APK is not signed. Similar to Compile without signing option.
– Obfuscate: If True then the compiled APK will be obfuscated.
– ShowWarnings: Whether to list the compilation warnings.
– Configuration : Build configuration.
– Optimize : Whether to include an optimization step during the byte conversion (dexer).
– NoClean : Whether to skip the project cleaning step.
– Output : Compiled APK name (does not affect libraries builds).

Usage example: B4ABuilder -task=Build -obfuscate=False

Editing the command line is not easy, and for this reason, we recommend using batch files.

Running from Batch Files

A batch file is a text file with the extension .bat which contains a series of Windows operating system commands. You can edit it with any text editor such as Notepad.
You can add remarks to document your code using the letters REM. You can redirect output from the batch file by using the redirection operator > to create a file or >> to append to the file.

You can have one batch file in each project (in which case you do not need to use the -BaseFolder or -Project parameters), or you could collect them together into a single folder.

The following batch file will find all projects in folders contained within the folder where the batch file is situated and try to compile them. A summary of the results will be written to a text file called result.txt, and the details of each compilation to detail.txt.

```
REM Compile projects in all folders below this one

REM B4ABuilder.exe Parameters:
REM -Task: What you want to do. Possible values:
REM   Build - Similar to Release compilation (default value)
REM   BuildLibrary - Similar to Library compilation.
REM -BaseFolder: The project folder. Default value is the current
folder.
REM -Project: Main project file. Can be omitted if there is only one
b4a file in the base folder.
REM -NoSign: If True then the APK is not signed. Similar to Compile
without signing option.
REM -Obfuscate: If True then the compiled APK will be obfuscated.
REM -ShowWarnings: Whether to list the compilation warnings.
REM -Configuration : Build configuration.
REM -Optimize : Whether to include an optimization step during the
byte conversion (dexer).
REM -NoClean : Whether to skip the project cleaning step.
REM -Output : Compiled APK name (does not affect libraries builds).

SET b4abuilder="C:\Program Files (x86)\Anywhere
Software\Basic4android\B4ABuilder.exe"

REM Initialize output files
ECHO Starting New Run %time% %date% > detail.txt
ECHO Starting New Run %time% %date% > result.txt

FOR /D %%i IN (*) DO (
  ECHO === Compiling %%i === >> detail.txt
  REM ECHO %b4abuilder% -Task=build -BaseFolder=%%i -Output=%%i.apk >>
outputb4a.txt
  %b4abuilder% -Task=build -BaseFolder=%%i -Output=%%i.apk >>
detail.txt
```

```
IF ERRORLEVEL 1 (
  echo %%i Failed >> result.txt
  ) ELSE (
  echo %%i Succeeded >> result.txt
  )
)
```

Save this code in a file with a .bat extension. If necessary, edit the line beginning SET
b4abuilder so it points at the location of your B4ABuilder.exe file.
Double-click to run the batch file.

Note that if the -Output parameter is not specified then no APK file will be produced.

Debugging

Debugging is the process of finding "bugs" or faults in your code.
The two major methods for debugging are setting Breakpoints and Logging (page 181). There
are two debugging modes in B4A: Rapid Debugging and Legacy Debugging. We describe
these next.
Select the required mode from the toolbar:

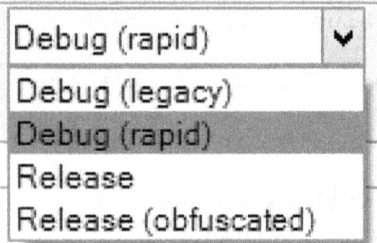

Then either select [Project > Compile & Run] or press F5 or click on ▶ in the toolbar, to
compile and run the app.

Restart (F11)

B4A gives you the ability to edit your code and restart to run it in either of the two debugging
modes (discussed next). You achieve this by clicking the ↻ icon, pressing F11 or using the
[Debug > Restart] option. The program will normally restart quicker in Rapid Debug mode.

Debugging

There are two debugging modes, Legacy Debugging and Rapid Debugging, which we discuss
here. By default, B4A will use the Rapid Debugger. There might be times when you want to
use the Legacy debugger. To use the Rapid Debugger, you must first disable the Legacy
Debugger by unsetting the option [Tools > IDE Options > Use Legacy Debugger].

To debug your app, you must activate the **Debug** compilation mode at the top of the IDE.
The Rapid Debugger is a very powerful tool which provides features not available in any
other native Android development tool. Using this feature, you can compile and install your
app on your device very quickly, usually within a few seconds. You can modify your code

while your app is running and re-deploy it to your device immediately; you will not need to reinstall it. Similarly, the next time you start B4A, you will not need to re-install the app to the device. The Rapid Debugger also only re-deploys those files you have modified after an edit, making deployments of large projects much quicker.

Limitations of the Rapid Debugger

- If you are using the free Trial Version of B4A, then you will need to install Java JDK version 6 or 7 on your PC before the Rapid Debugger option will work. See here (page 103) for how to install the JDK.
- Execution of apps using the Rapid Debugger is slower than using any of the other compile options. It is not recommended to use the Rapid Debugger for any apps which require a lot of computation or graphics manipulation such as games.
- If you add or remove Globals variables, you will need to restart the Rapid Debugger.
- You cannot run the app on a device if it is not connected to the IDE. The reason is that the app actually runs in a Debugger Engine within the IDE, as explained below.
- You cannot use the #ExcludeFromDebugger attribute when using the Rapid Debugger.
- You cannot use the Rapid Debugger if you have connected to the device via Bluetooth.

How the Rapid Debugger Works

The Rapid Debugger sends a simple "Shell App" to the device. This handles the user interface but provides no other functionality. Your app actually runs in a "Debugger Engine" which is a virtual device running on your PC, as shown in the following diagram:

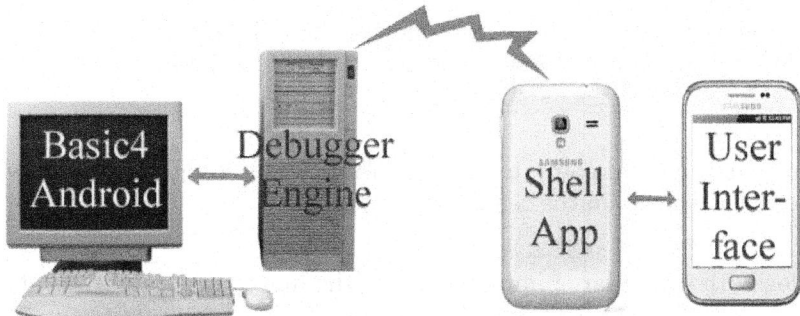

Thus, when you modify your app, only the code within the Debugger Engine needs to be changed. This is why deployment is so incredibly quick.

Note that if you add files to your app or modify the manifest, then a new Shell App will need to be uploaded to the device, but you will not need to re-approve the installation on the device, so this upload will be rapid.

Note also that, if you are using the Trial Version of B4A and using remote compilation, the remote server will only need to be accessed in those rare circumstances when the Shell App needs to be changed. So modifying your app will usually be extremely rapid, as you normally only change the code in the Debugger Engine. See the limitations section above for more about using the Rapid Debugger with the Trial Version.

Editing Code using the Rapid Debugger

The benefit that the Rapid Debugger offers over the Legacy Debugger is speed of compilation.

Legacy Debugging

As well as Rapid Debugging, B4A also supports on older form of debugging called Legacy
Debugging. This has the benefit that you do not need to install the Java JDK. To use legacy
debugging, you must enable first enable [Tools > IDE Options > Use Legacy Debugger]. If
this option is selected, then the compiled code will contain debugging code.

The debugging code allows the IDE to connect to the program and inspect it while it runs.
The name of the compiled APK file will end with `_DEBUG.apk`. You should not distribute this
apk file as it contains the debugging code which adds a significant overhead, and is
furthermore signed with a debugging key (page 263). To distribute files, you **must** select
either the **Release** or the **Release (obfuscated)** compilation mode.

#ExcludeFromDebugger Attribute

If you do not want some modules to be included in the legacy debugger, you can use the
#ExcludeFromDebugger: True attribute near the top of the excluded module.
This does not have any effect if using the Rapid Debugger.

Both Rapid and Legacy Debugging will open the Debug Window within the IDE.

Breakpoints

You can can mark lines of code as "breakpoints". When the program runs, it pauses when it
meets a breakpoint.

Create breakpoints by clicking on the grey margin at the left of the IDE. The breakpoint is
shown as a red dot in the left margin, and the line of code is highlighted in red:

    ●   29 ⊟Sub Activity_Create(FirstTime As Boolean)

When the program has stopped at a breakpoint, the breakpoint line is highlighted in yellow
in the IDE, and a yellow arrow is shown on the red dot:

    ◉   29 ⊟Sub Activity_Create(FirstTime As Boolean)

In the app, a blocking dialog with a circular spinning disc and the line number and code at
the breakpoint is shown:

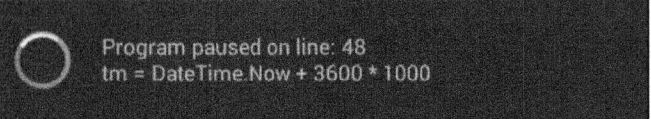

Note the IDE remembers (page 93) breakpoints (storing them in the metadata file) when you
save the project.

You can remove breakpoints by clicking their red dots or by using [Edit > Remove All
Breakpoints].

Breakpoint Limitations

– Breakpoints in the following subs will be ignored: `Globals, Process_Globals` and
`Activity_Pause`.

– Services - Breakpoints that appear after a call to StartService will be ignored.

– Breakpoints set in `Service_Create` and `Service_Start` will pause the program for up
to a specific time (about 12 seconds). This is to avoid Android from killing the Service.

– If the program is already paused at a breakpoint, events that fire will nevertheless be executed. Breakpoints in the code which process the event will be ignored.

Debugger Control

When in either of the debug modes, buttons and options in the [Debug] menu (page 77) are available to control the execution of your program while debugging:

▶ (F5) Continue code execution.

⤷• Step (F8). Step into a sub if one exists, or step to the next line. This is very useful to see the real program flow and the evolution of variable values.

⤷ Step Over (F9). Step to the next line without entering any subroutine called on the current line.

⟳ Step Out (F10). Run the program until it leaves the current sub, then pause.

■ Stop the current program. **Note**: stopping the program in the Emulator or on a device does not stop it in the IDE.

⟳ Restart (F11) Recompile and execute from the beginning.

Debug Menu Offers More Control

Once the debugger is running, the [Debug] menu (page 77) will be available, which also offers the **Pause** command, pausing the code as soon as possible.

Debug Window

When the program is run in either Rapid or Legacy mode, a Debug Window opens within the IDE:

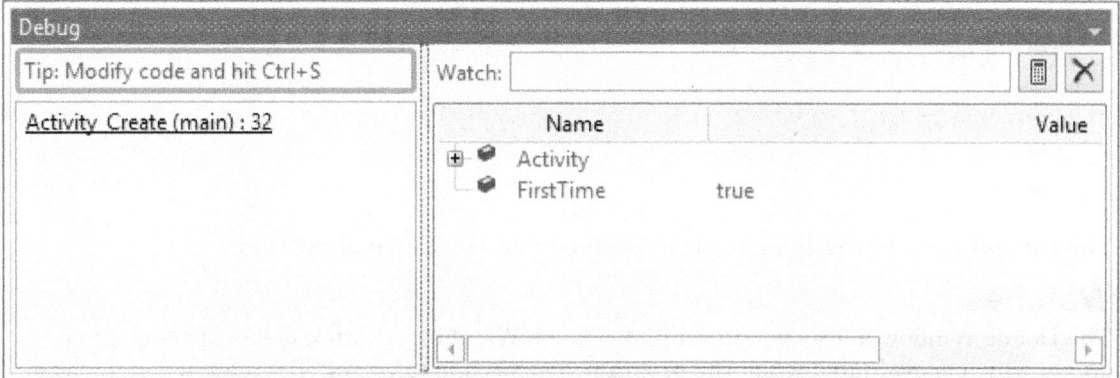

Note: The tip "Modify code and hit Ctrl+S" is only shown when running in Rapid Debug mode.

Call Stack

When the program reaches a breakpoint it pauses and the left panel of the Debug Window shows a list of currently active subroutines, usually known as the call stack, execution stack, control stack run-time stack, or machine stack, showing the sub name, the line number where the sub called the next sub in the stack and giving a link to jump to that line:

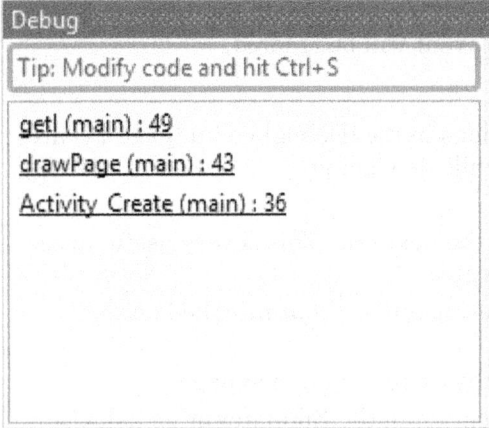

Variables List

When the program reaches a breakpoint, information about current variables is displayed in a list in the right panel of the Debug window:

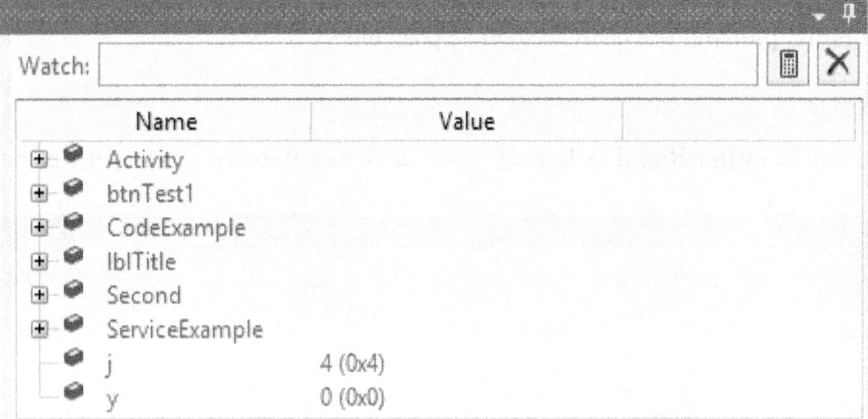

The values of integers is shown in both decimal and hexadecimal notation.

Watches

The Debug Window allows you to set and remove Watches. A watch is an expression you create which is evaluated when the program reaches a breakpoint. To create a watch, type your expression into the Add Watch field. Press the return key or click the Add Watch Expression button 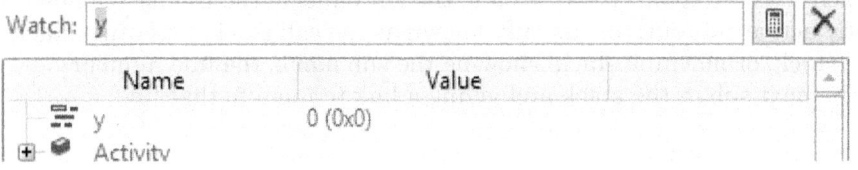 to create the watch.

When the program meets a breakpoint, the evaluated values of all watch expressions are shown at the top of Information Area:

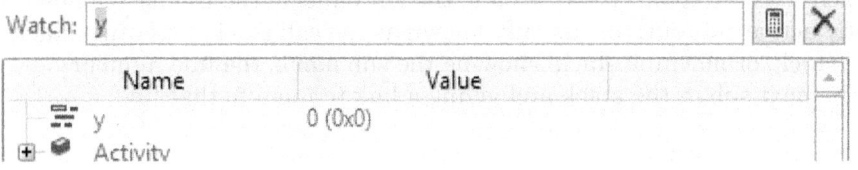

Tip: Typing expressions in the Watch input box is not easy as there is no auto-complete function. An easier way to create watches might be to use the hover function, as discussed below.

Deleting Watches

Clicking on the delete button ✘ to the right of the Watch input area will delete ALL watches.

Warning: there is no way to restore watches once deleted, and at present individual watches cannot be deleted.

Hovering

You can see the value of variables by hovering the mouse over a variable within the code:

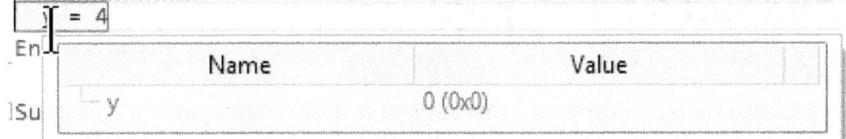

You can create a watch by selecting some text in the code and right-clicking. This will pop up the Context menu (page 86) which includes **Add Watch Expression**.

Logging

The other useful way of debugging your app is to use logging. For example
```
Log("Y = " & y)
```
This produces messages in the bottom half of the Logs (page 90) window:

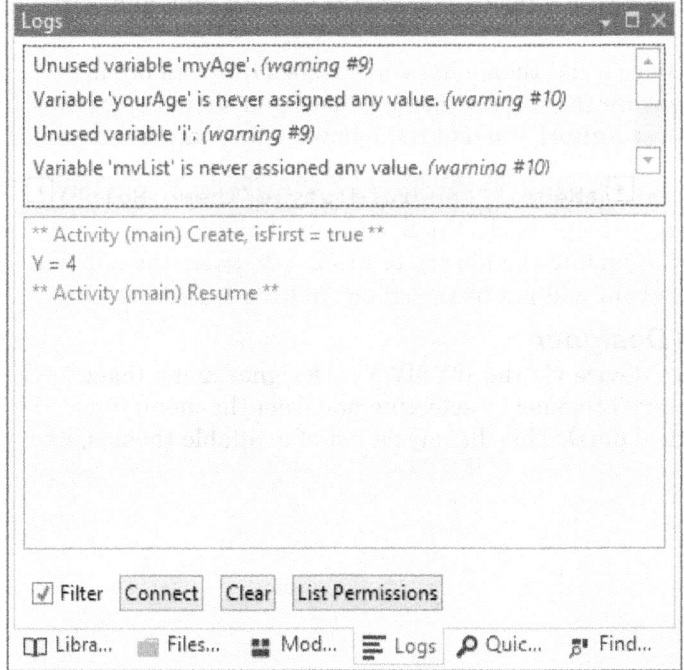

The log also shows messages related to the components life cycle, for example when the **Sub Activity_Create** runs.

When **Filter** is checked in the Log window, you will only see messages related to your program. When it is unchecked, you will see all the messages running in the system. If you are encountering an error and do not see any relevant message in the log, it is worth unchecking the filter option and looking for an error message.

Click **Clear** to delete the data in the Logs window. **Note**: the log is maintained by the device. When you connect to a device, you will also see previous messages.

Right-clicking on the log allows you to copy either all the log or the selected line (if any) to the clipboard.

Compiling for Android 5.0 Lollipop

Material Design

Android 5.0 (API version 21, also called "Lollipop") introduced a new design concept for apps called "Material Design". If you want to create apps which will run on devices with either 5.0 or older version of Android, it would be ideal to understand Material Design, although you can still use B4A without detailed knowledge.

See here (http://bit.ly/1McQH7R) for Google's introduction to the concept and here (http://bit.ly/1ei6khA) for a developer's guide.

You use Material Design to create a Theme. See here (http://bit.ly/1Dj3Aby) for a tutorial on Material Design using B4A and here (http://bit.ly/1KaGeIF) for a tutorial on using the AppCompat library which brings similar features to older Android releases. In B4A, you can change the material theme at runtime. See here (http://bit.ly/1Qu3y8E) for an online tutorial.

Holo Theme

At the time of writing, the Android 5.0 material theme has some issues that can break layouts written for older devices. To ensure the correct theme is used you should open the Manifest Editor with [Project > Manifest Editor] and add the following (assuming that you didn't set a different theme):

```
SetApplicationAttribute(android:theme, "@android:style/Theme.Holo")
```

If you are using the StdActionBar library (http://bit.ly/1McS4DG) and handling the **ButtonClicked** event then you need to update the library to v1.52, otherwise the app will crash. Note that the **ButtonClicked** event will not be raised on Android 5 devices.

Material Themes in WYSIWYG Designer

If you connect the Visual Designer to a device via the WYSIWYG Designer menu (page 141), you will be able preview different material themes by selecting one from the menu (for example by clicking on the three vertical dots). This displays a list of available themes, like this:

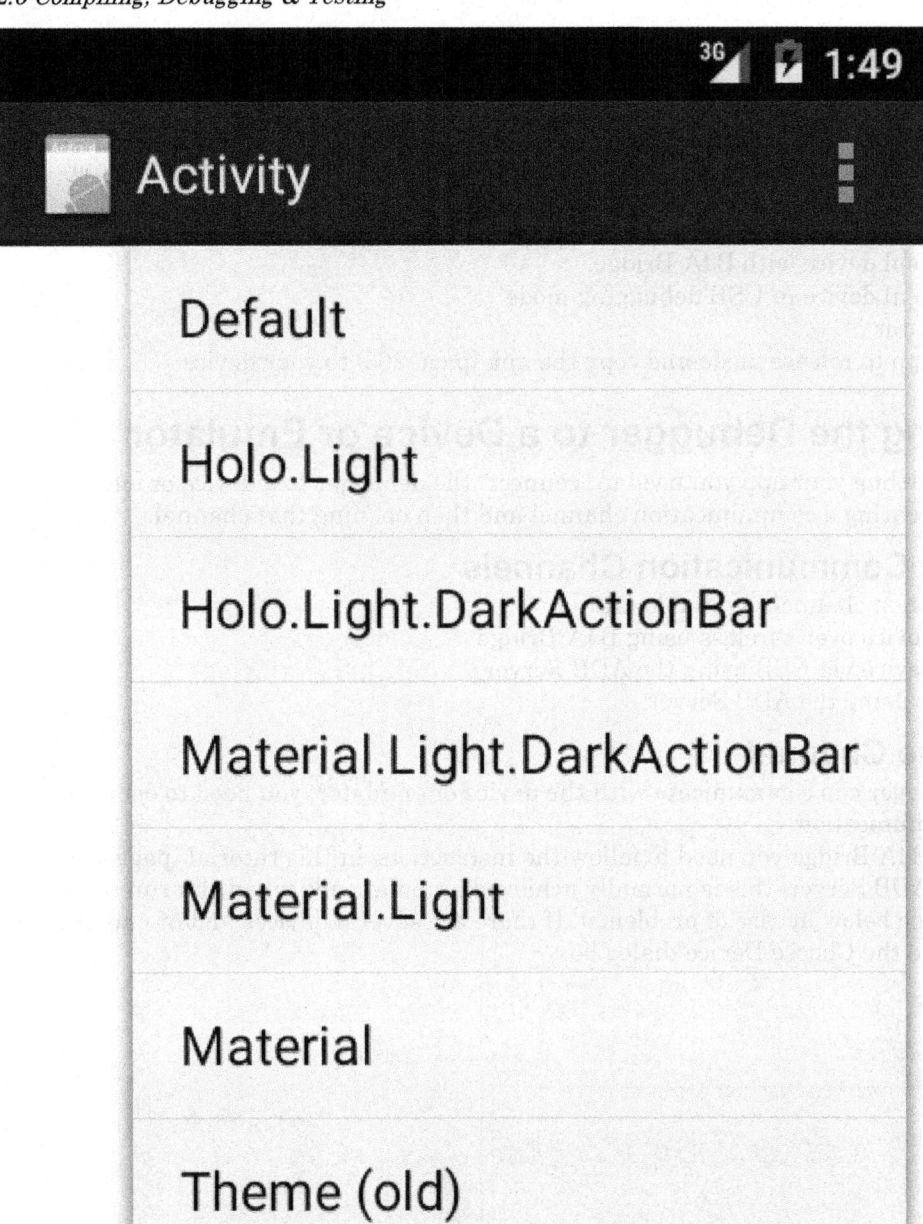

To implement the selected theme in your app, you will need to edit the Manifest as described above.

Testing your App

Before publishing your app, you should always test and debug it on one or more real devices, using one of the first two of the following options. You can also use the third option, the emulator, to test it on other types of device. If you have trouble connecting B4A to your device, you could use the fourth option.

The options are:

– Connect to a real device with B4A-Bridge.
– Connect to a real device in USB debugging mode
– Android emulator
– Compile the app in release mode and copy the apk (page 263) to your device

Connecting the Debugger to a Device or Emulator

Before you can debug your app you need to "connect" the debugger to a device or emulator. This requires creating a communication channel and then opening that channel.

Debugging Communication Channels

The communication channels available are:

- to a physical device over wireless using B4A-Bridge
- to a physical device via USB using the ADB Server
- to an emulator using the ADB Server.

Opening the Channel

Before the debugger can communicate with the device or emulator, you need to open the channel of communication.

To connect via B4A-Bridge you need to follow the instructions in this tutorial (page 48).

To connect via ADB Server, this is normally achieved automatically when you run the debugger (but see below in case of problems). If there are several devices and/or emulators then you will see the Choose Device dialog box:

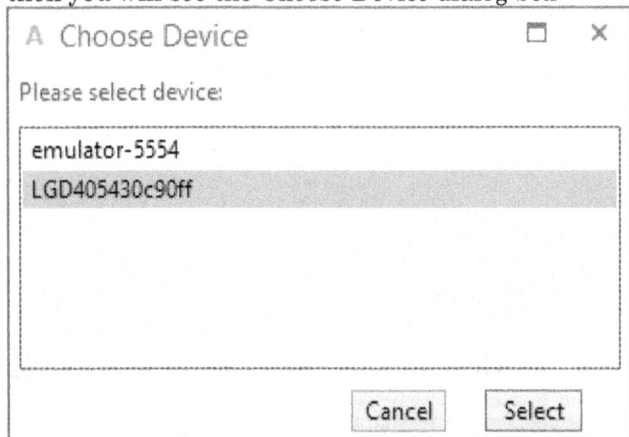

This dialog remembers the last device to which you connected.

Problems Opening the Channel

If you disconnect and reconnect a USB connection, or if you start a new emulator, then the debugger might loose the connection. In this case, you can restart the connect by selecting [Tools > Restart ADB Server] and clicking the **Connect** button at the foot of the Logs window.

B4A-Bridge

B4A-Bridge is an easy way to debug your app on a real device. You need to connect your PC to the device via wireless connections over the local network. This is the recommended option. It is easier than USB connection and faster than an emulator. We explain the details in this tutorial (page 48).

Note: in earlier releases, you used to be able to connect to B4A-Bridge via a Bluetooth connection, but this is not currently available (despite being an option shown in the the B4A-Bridge app) because, according to the developer, "There were many problems with this feature". It might become available in the future.

USB Debugging

In theory you should be able to debug your app by connecting your device via a USB cable to your development machine. In order to make this work, you need to have the correct USB driver installed on your PC. It can be difficult to find the right USB driver for all devices, and in that case you would have to use B4A-Bridge, unless you are obliged to use USB for some reason (such a video capture (page 74)).

The benefits of USB debugging are:
- Connection does not require you start B4A-Bridge
- Able to take screenshots and make video capture (page 74)

However, in practice it can be somewhat difficult to get the two machines to talk to each other. See the details below for what is required.

I recommend that you use USB debugging if you are able to make them talk. If that is not possible then use B4A-Bridge. Here we describe some of the elements of the Android Debug Bridge (ADB) system and the mechanism for connecting the machines together, but this explanation is far from complete.

Connecting the Device via USB

If you want to test your apps by connecting B4A to an Android-powered device, then you need to configure your device and install the appropriate USB driver on your development machine.

Configure the Device

To use USB debugging, you will need to first configure your device to support USB debugging.

Starting from Android 4.2, the developer menu is hidden. In order to reveal it you need to:
- Choose [Settings > About Phone] or [Settings > About Tablet] or similar.
- Find the Build Number entry and click on it 7 times

You should see a message saying "You are now a developer" or something similar.

Once the developer menu is visible, you need to open it to enable USB debugging. You might find this option in one of the following places, or somewhere similar, depending how menus are configured on your device:

[Settings > Development > USB debugging]
[Settings > Developer Options > USB debugging]
[Settings > Applications > Development > USB debugging]
[Settings > {} Developer options > USB debugging]
When you enable this option, you will see a dialog asking you to confirm you want to allow USB debugging.

The USB Driver

You also need to install the USB driver on your development machine. This is not the same as the driver which allows you to use Windows Explorer to see files on the machine. You need the driver which allows you to debug over USB.

Checking to see if the driver is already installed

You can tell if the driver is installed by simply connecting the device to your computer via a USB cable. If the computer has the driver installed, a window may pop-up on the device such as

Once you have clicked OK (not necessary if you have previously checked the box "Always allow from this computer") you will see a Notification (page 389) such as:

USB debugging connected
Touch to disable USB debugging.

Install the USB Driver

If you do not see the above notification it means you have not installed the USB driver for your device on your development machine. You should download the Google USB Driver in the Android SDK Manager (page 103). If this driver doesn't work, you need to find, download and install the specific driver for your device. You can find links to the web sites for several original equipment manufacturers (OEMs) (although not all) here (http://bit.ly/1IjNbte). The Galaxy Nexus driver is distributed by Samsung, where the driver can be found by searching for model SCH-I515.

However, if your device is one of the Android Developer Phones (ADP), a Nexus One, or a Nexus S, then you need the Google USB Driver instead of an OEM driver.

There are more details about connecting your device via USB here (http://bit.ly/141xVIP) and here (http://bit.ly/141zLJG) and here (http://bit.ly/1C6k6Li).

Install from APK

If you have trouble connecting B4A to your device via USB, you can compile (page 171) the app in release mode and copy the resulting apk (page 263) to your device in order to test it. You will find the apk in <Project>\Objects.

Copy the file to your device, open a file manager on the device and click on the apk. You will see an option to Install the app. You might need first to set the Security Options on your device to allow apps to be installed from Unknown Sources by selecting

either: [Settings > Applications > Unknown sources]

or: [Settings > Security > Unknown sources]

or: [Settings > Privacy > Security > Unknown sources]

Debugging over a USB Connection

Once you have installed the correct driver, when you connect a USB cable to your device you should see the pop-up and notification shown above. Now you need to ensure that the ADB software is running, as we describe next.

To ensure that B4A can find the device, you might need to restart the ADB Server, as described below.

Android Debug Bridge

The way a development machine connects to a real device or an emulator is by using Android Debug Bridge (ADB). You can find more details about ADB here (http://bit.ly/1C6khq8) and here (http://bit.ly/1C6klGg).

ADB consists of 3 parts:

The ADB Client

This runs on your development machine. The ADB client (adb.exe) can be found either in <android-sdks>\tools or in <android-sdks>\platform-tools, where <android-sdks> is the first part of the folder which you specified in the **android jar** field of the Paths Configuration dialog, available from [Tools > Configure Paths]. It is a command-line program, so you need to have a Command Prompt program running on the development machine. From here you can type in commands.

When you enter an adb command, the client checks whether an adb server is running, and if not it will start one. One useful command is **adb.exe devices**, which will show a list of all attached devices:

```
C:\android-sdks\platform-tools>adb.exe devices
List of devices attached
34403034434      device
```

However this does not mean that B4A will be able to successfully install and debug your app on the device.

The ADB Server

This runs on your development machine. It can be started by B4A by using the [Tools > Restart ADB Server] option.

The ADB Daemon

This runs on the attached device or emulator.

If you have problems connecting B4A with your device using USB, you could check on the B4A On-line Community Forum. For example there is a discussion of the failure to connect here (http://bit.ly/1zsrEna).

Debugging with USB

Once the ADB Server and Daemon are running, you should be able to debug your app, for example using rapid debugging, by simply clicking on the Run icon ▶ .

The Emulator or Android Virtual Device (AVD) Manager

Another way to run your app is by using an emulator. These are created and managed by the AVD Manager. **Note**: an emulator can be quite memory-hungry.

Introduction

The AVD (Android Virtual Device) Manager is a utility provided by Google as part of the Android SDK which allows you to create emulated Android devices. You can run the AVD from the IDE by clicking on [Tools > Run AVD Manager].

You can create as many devices as you require, with different hardware specifications and with different screen resolutions. You are not restricted to running just one emulated device at a time. You can start as many devices as you need (dependent upon the memory on your computer of course) and you can keep those devices running as you edit and compile your code within B4A. But note that emulators can consume a lot of memory.

How B4A interacts with Emulated Devices

On successful code compilation, B4A will look for any active Device Emulators, or real devices which have been connected to your computer and will provide a list of those devices. You can then choose which device - real or emulated - from that list upon which to run the compiled code.

Since you can have multiple emulated devices running at one time, this means that you can test your code against several different devices in a reasonably fast manner - you just run your code against each device in the list.

Using the Android Virtual Device Manager

In the IDE, select [Tools > Run AVD Manager]. A window similar to the following appears:

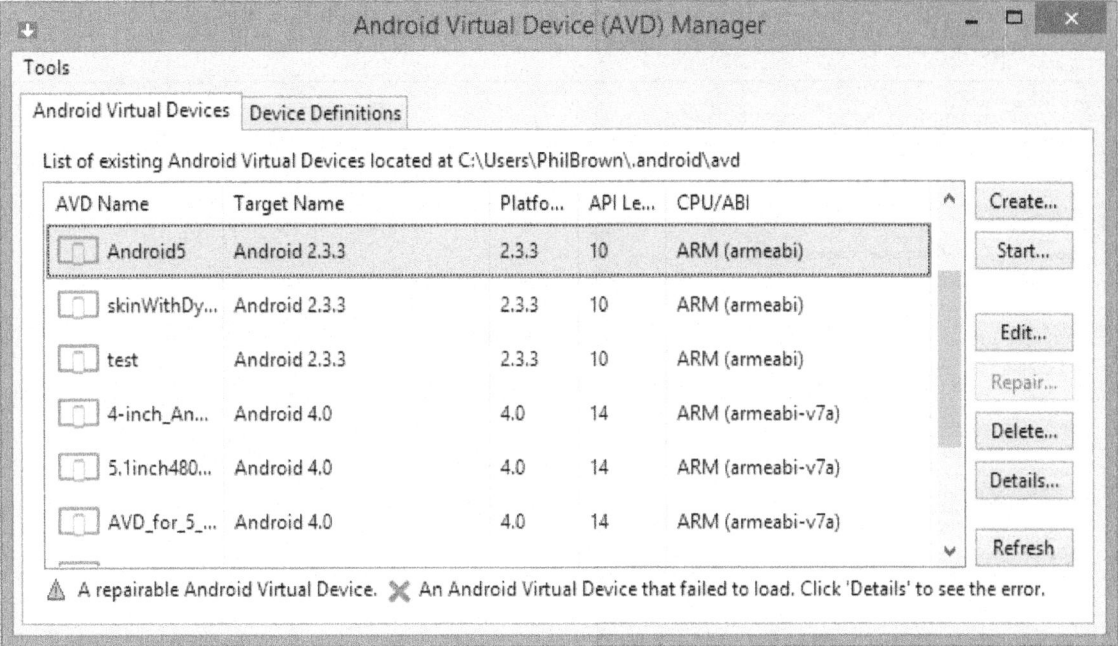

Missing Tabs

Exactly what you see will depend on which Revision of the Android SDK Tools you have installed on your PC. Those with newer versions will see the two tabs, **Android Virtual Devices** and **Device Definitions**, below the menu. Those with older versions will simply see a list of the existing Android Virtual Devices.

How to upgrade

If you need access to the Device Definitions tab, described below, then you should use the [Tools > Manage SDK...] menu and upgrade to a later version of the Android SDK Tools, for example 22.n.n:

Name	API	Rev.	Status
◢ ☐ ▢ Tools			
☐ 🔧 Android SDK Tools		22.0.5	☑ Installed

Android Virtual Devices (AVDs)

The emulators you will run are Android Virtual Devices (AVD). Each one is based upon a Device Definition. Initially, the AVD list will be empty, but there is a pre-populated list of Device Definitions.

Creating an AVD

Every virtual device is based upon a Device Definition. The emulator comes with a list of device definitions pre-defined, and you can create new ones using the Device Definitions tab. Choose "New" or "Create" (depending which version of the AVD manager you have).

A dialog box will open for creating a new emulator similar to the following:

AVD Name (Required)

A name for your Virtual device. Spaces are not allowed in this field. You can give it a name like "HTCDesireHD" or "Xoom10.1", but since you can use a particular size to emulate different devices which have the same specs, you may want to use names like "480x800-API-10".

Device (Required)

Choose the device upon which this AVD will be based. **Note**: you can also create new devices using the Device Definitions tab in the AVD Manager.

Target (Required)

The options available here depend upon which Android APIs you have installed using the Android SDK Manager. B4A supports all versions of the API from 1.6.

CPU / ABI (Required)

The options might include ARM (armeabi) and Intel Atom (x86). The latter requires hardware acceleration, and requires Intel HAXM to be installed on your PC.

Keyboard

This option is intended for devices which have an external hardware keyboard.

It is recommended to leave this option selected. This allows you to use the keyboard on your computer to enter data into fields in the emulator. Otherwise, you have to use the emulator's keyboard.

Skin (Required)

This can include options such as Skin with dynamic hardware controls, No skin, HVGA etc. If you select Skin with dynamic hardware controls, you will see a keyboard to the right of the emulator screen

The **keyboard** option determines whether these keys are active.

If you select No skin, these buttons are not displayed.

Front / Back Camera

This allows you to specify whether a front and/or back camera (if present in this Device Definition) is inactive, emulated or uses a webcam attached to the computer on which the AVD is running. The options usually are: None, Emulated or Webcam0.

Memory Options

These will be set by the Device Definition you have selected but can be over-ridden.

RAM

Set the amount of RAM in Mb. Under Windows, emulating RAM greater than 768 Mb might fail if you do not have enough RAM available on your PC. If the emulator fails to run, reduce the amount of RAM allocated.

VM Heap

The VM Heap specifies the heap size of the virtual machine in MB. You should increase the heap size if you allocate more RAM. The heap is used to store instance variables of instantiated class objects. Garbage collection is used by the VM to free the heap space.

Internal Storage

This assumes a default value of 200 Mb but can be changed. Enter the number and select the units (Kb, Mb or Gb).

SD Card

Size

This allows you to specify the size of the SD card fitted to your device. **Note**: this will consume hard disk space, so don't be tempted to create a 32GB card by entering 32000 or else you will be waiting a long time as the SDK creates the SD card, and consumes 32GB of your drive!

The minimum size is 9Mb, and a useful size is probably 16 or 32 MB. Enter the number and select the units (Kb, Mb or Gb). It might be useful to have an emulator without an SD card so you can check that your app will still work.

File

This allows you to specify a File which represents an SD card. This allows you to share virtual SD cards between emulators.

In order to create a File, you need to use a tool which is provided by the Android SDK, "mksdcard.exe". A reference to this tool can be found in the Android Documentation here (http://bit.ly/1IjNTXm).

For example, if you wanted to create a file with a volume name of "mySDCard", and a size of 128M, you would follow these steps:
– Open a Command Prompt Window (on Windows 7 for example, this is found under "[All Programs > Accessories > Command Prompt]")
– If your computer's Path does not contain the Android SDK (which it probably doesn't), you will need to use the DOS commands to navigate to the folder <android-sdk-windows>\tools where <android-sdk-windows> depends on where you installed the Android SDKs. The commands might be:
- If necessary, move to the C drive with the DOS command `c:`
- Move to the correct directory with `cd android-sdks\tools`
- Create the file with `mksdcard -l mySDCard 128M c:\temp\mySDCardFile.img`
This will create a file called **mySDCardFile.img** in the c:\temp directory.
You can then use this as your SD Card file in the AVD Manager.
For Mac users, If you are running B4A inside a Virtual machine running a Windows O/S, you can go back to the Mac O/S and mount this SD image file. This allows you to copy files onto the SD Card. These files will be available on the SD Card when viewed on a Virtual Device using this SD Card file.

Emulation Options

Snapshot

Taking a snapshot means that the emulator will launch to that saved state, thus launching faster. For example, adding the Snapshot option can change the startup time from 24 seconds to 2 seconds! The first time it runs after you enble this option, the launch dialog box shows options to save snapshop and launch from the snapshop:

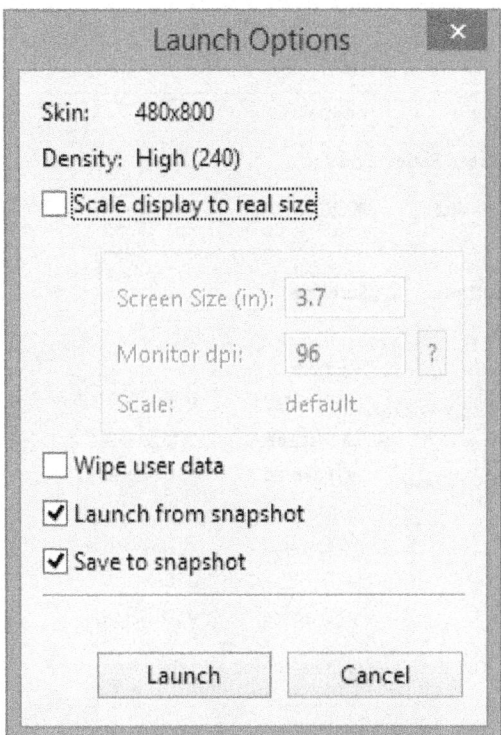

The first time it runs, the emulator starts normally. But when it closes, a snapshot will be saved so the next time it starts, this saved state will be used to launch the emulator much more quickly.

Use Host GPU

This option allows the emulator to use the graphics processing unit (GPU) of the host machine the emulator is running on. This results in a faster emulator. This option is not available in some older version of the SDK.

Creating a Device Definition

As well as using the pre-defined device definitions, you can create your own. Within the AVD Manager, click **Device Definitions** tab and click the **Create Device...** button:

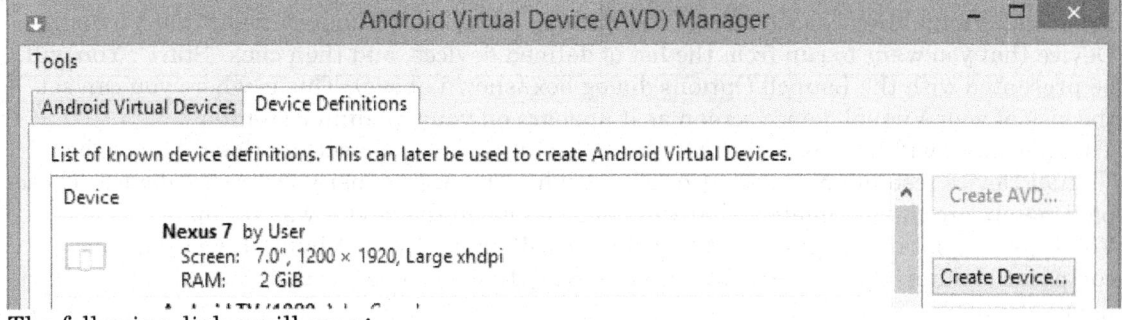

The following dialog will open:

Create New Device

Name:		Size:	normal ⌄
Screen Size (in):		Screen Ratio:	long ⌄
Resolution (px):	□ x □	Density:	400dpi ⌄

Sensors: ☑ Accelerometer ☑ Gyroscope
            ☑ GPS   ☑ Proximity Sensor

Buttons: Software ⌄

Cameras   ☐ Front   ☑ Rear

Portrait:
☑ Enabled   ☑ Navigation
Landscape:
☑ Enabled   ☑ Navigation

Device States:

Input: ☐ Keyboard
            ⦿ No Nav   ○ DPad   ○ Trackball

Portrait with keyboard:
☑ Enabled   ☑ Navigation
Landscape with keyboard:
☑ Enabled   ☑ Navigation

RAM: □   MiB ⌄

☐ Override the existing device with the same name

⚠ Please enter a name for the device.

Create Device   Cancel

All the parameters on the left are required: **Name, Screen Size** (in inches), **Resolution** (width and height in pixels) and **RAM** amount.

The parameters on the right are preset and their default values are often acceptable. More information can be found here (http://bit.ly/1MzwvvE).

Running a Virtual Device and scaling for Real Size Emulation

From the "Virtual Devices" section of the Android SDK AVD Manager, select the Virtual Device that you want to run from the list of defined devices, and then click "Start". You will be presented with the Launch Options dialog box (shown above). This is where you can set the size of your Virtual device screen as it appears on your computer monitor.

The dialog box will tell you what the screen resolution has been set to - this refers to the Virtual Device resolution. It will also tell you what the pixel density is for that device. These parameters are the parameters that were entered when the device was set up.

You have two options as to how AVD Manager will present your Virtual Device on your computer monitor: **No Scaling** and **Scale display to real size**. These are described next.

No Scaling

If you leave the `Scale display to real size` option unchecked, then AVD Manager will directly map the Virtual Device screen's pixels to your monitor's pixels, one for one. A 1280 by 800 screen will therefore take up 1280x800 pixels on your monitor. A 480 by 800 screen will take up 480 by 800 pixels on your monitor. This could create problems for you - for example, if you're running on a 1024 by 768 monitor and you try and run a 1280 by 800 Virtual device, the Virtual Device screen will be bigger than your monitor, so you'll only see part of the Virtual Device screen.

Scale display to real size

If you select the `Scale display to real size` option, then AVD Manager will attempt to scale your device so that it shows with the correct physical dimensions on your computer monitor. To do this, AVD Manager needs some more information about your requirement, so you need to fill in the following fields:

Screen Size (inches)

This is the length of the diagonal measured from top left to bottom right across your desired device screen. (This is the standard used when quoting screen sizes). So if you want to emulate an HTC Desire HD, you would enter 4.3 here as that device has a 4.3in screen. For something like the Xoom, you would enter 10.1, as that device has a 10.1 inch screen. The emulator will try and make your emulated device screen match that size on your computer monitor.

Monitor dpi

Scaling involves interpolating between real pixel sizes (on your computer monitor) and emulated device pixel sizes (on your emulated device), so AVD Manager needs to know about your monitor. Click on the "?" next to this option, and you will see the `Monitor Density` dialog box. These values refer to your computer monitor, not the emulated device. This little dialog will try and work out a monitor density for you.

The resolution shown in the `Resolution` dropdown menu should match your computer monitor's resolution. The one bit that this dialog doesn't know is your computer monitor size - so you need to enter that into the `Screen Size` dropdown box. With that piece of information, AVD Manager can now scale the Virtual Device correctly so that it appears to be the correct size on your computer monitor.

Having set all the required parameters, click on `Launch` to launch the desired Virtual Device. There will be a delay as the Virtual Device is created (if this is the first time it has been used) or launched. Be patient - this can take some time.

Eventually your device will appear in a window of its own. You may have to unlock the device by sliding the green Android button across the screen.

Interacting with your Virtual Device

When the emulator is running, you can interact with the emulated mobile device just as you would an actual mobile device, except that you use your mouse pointer to "touch" the touchscreen and your keyboard keys to "press" the simulated device keys. The table below summarizes the mappings between the emulator keys and and the keys of your keyboard.

One of the most useful functions is CTRL-F11 - this rotates the Virtual Display from landscape to portrait and back.

PC Keyboard Shortcuts

Emulator Function	PC Keyboard Key
Home	Home
(left softkey)	F2 or Page-up button
Star (right softkey)	Shift-F2 or Page Down
Back	ESC
Call/dial button	F3
Hangup/end call button	F4
Search	F5
Power button	F7
Audio volume up button	KEYPAD_PLUS, Ctrl-5
Audio volume down button	KEYPAD_MINUS, Ctrl-F6
Camera button	Ctrl-KEYPAD_5, Ctrl-F3
Switch to previous layout orientation (for example, portrait, landscape)	KEYPAD_7, Ctrl-F11
Switch to next layout orientation (for example, portrait, landscape)	KEYPAD_9, Ctrl-F12
Toggle cell networking on/off	F8
Toggle code profiling	F9 (only with -trace startup option)
Toggle fullscreen mode	Alt-Enter
Toggle trackball mode	F6
Enter trackball mode temporarily (while key is pressed)	Delete
DPad left/up/right/down	KEYPAD_4/8/6/2
DPad center click	KEYPAD_5
Onion alpha increase/decrease	KEYPAD_MULTIPLY(*) / KEYPAD_DIVIDE(/)

Mac Keyboard Shortcuts

The following assumes you are using Parallels (http://bit.ly/1IjNYKJ) to run Windows on a Mac.

Emulator Function	Mac Keyboard Key (in Parallels)
(left softkey)	fn-F2
Back	ESC
Call/dial button	fn-F3
Hangup/end call button	fn-F4
Search	fn-F5
Power button	fn-F7
Toggle cell networking on/off	fn-F8
Toggle code profiling	fn-F9

Exchanging files with the PC

To get access to files in the Emulator, you can use the Android Device Monitor. The replaces the earlier **Dalvik Debug Monitor**.

This can be run by double-clicking the batch file **monitor.bat** which is located in the tools folder where you copied the Android SDK, for example **C:\android-sdks\tools**

You might see a message from Google asking if you are willing to send them certain statistics. You can decide whether you agree or not. Then you should see something like this:

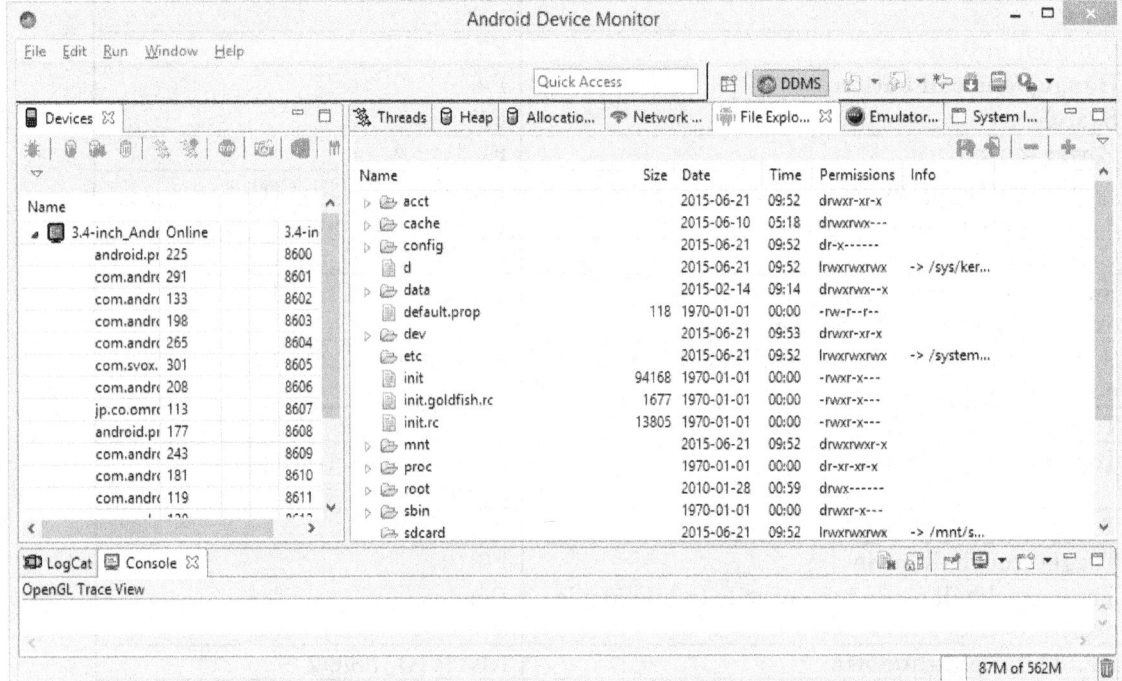

In the Devices panel (upper-left) you should see a reference to the currently running Emulator. Select it. Then select the Files Explorer panel in the right-hand side.

Where to find your files

In **data\data** , you will find files your app has copied to **File.DirAssets**. You need to search for the Package Name you gave your app in the IDE [Project > Build Configurations] menu. In the **mnt\sdcard** folder, you should find files your app has created in **File.DirRootExternal**. If you cannot find them, you could search for the Package Name in **mnt\shell\emulated\0\Android\data**.

How to manage files

When a file has been selected in the File Explorer, you see some icons in the upper right corner:

     Pull file from device, copies the file to the PC

     Push file onto device, copies a file to the device

    Deletes the file

   New folder (only active if another folder is selected in the tree)

Clicking on either ![icon] or ![icon] shows the standard Windows file explorer to select the destination or source folder for the selected file.

Troubleshoot Connection Problems

Sometimes when you run an app or try connect to the Emulator, you will see the following error:

Process is running longer than expected. Do you want to cancel it?

This indicates that Emulator is still running a program or that the Emulator is still connected to another project. In this case try one of the following:

– Use the [Tools > IDE Options > Restart ADB Server (page 72)] menu option

– Go to the Emulator and press the Back button until you reach the Emulator's home screen, then try to connect again.

– Close the Emulator and start another.

– If this problem happens repeatedly, try increasing the Process Timeout in the [Tools > Configure Process Timeout (page 77)] menu.

2.7 Graphics and Drawing

The details of the core B4A drawing types (page 352) are explained in the Core Objects (page 336) chapter. Here we explain how to use them.

Drawing Methods

There are several ways you can draw:
- By setting the background of a View or of the Activity to a Drawable or a Bitmap
- By drawing lines or other shapes, Drawables or Bitmaps onto a Canvas and later copying the Canvas bitmap onto a View or the Activity.

We deal with these separately below.

Setting Backgrounds of Views and the Activity

First we discuss some basic concepts and how to set the backgrounds of Views and the Activity.

View Drawables

Views (page 443) are the objects shown on an Activity (page 337). They each have default backgrounds when they are defined either in the Designer or by code. Their backgrounds can be drawn onto by a Drawable (see below) or set to a Bitmap.

Bitmaps

A bitmap is an object which is typically read from a file and copied into the background of a View or onto a Canvas, as illustrated in this diagram:

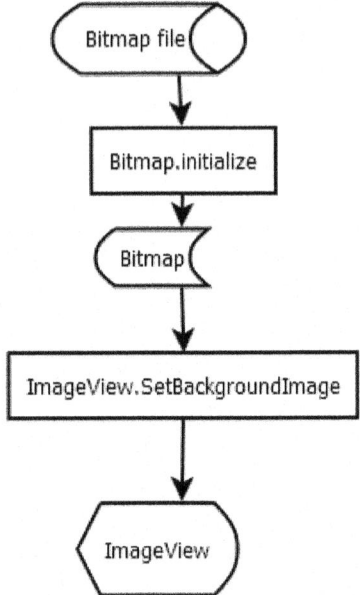

Drawables

Objects such as `BitmapDrawable`, `ColorDrawable`, `GradientDrawable` and `StateListDrawable` are termed "drawables" in Android, which is a concept meaning "capable of being drawn onto the screen". The background of a View or the Activity can be set from a drawable, as shown in this diagram:

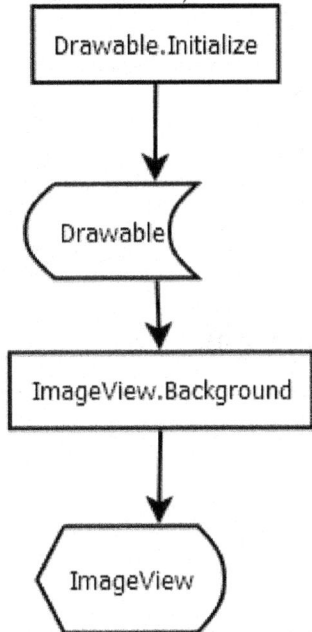

Background Property

There exist three drawables which can be assigned to the `Background` property of various Views and of the `Activity` itself:

ColorDrawable

The `ColorDrawable` object has a solid single color. The corners can be rounded or not.

GradientDrawable

The `GradientDrawable` object has two colors with a gradient change from the first to the second color.

BitmapDrawable

The `BitmapDrawable` object has two properties: `Bitmap` and `Gravity`. The `BitmapDrawable` object has no rounded corner property; if you want rounded corners; they must be part of the bitmap.

You can define all of these properties in the Designer, but in the following example; we define them in code as backgrounds of panels. (If you want to run this you will need to provide your own background.png file, which you would add to the Files folder of your project).

Example Code

```
Sub Globals
 Dim pnlColor As Panel
 Dim pnlGradient As Panel
 Dim pnlBitmap As Panel
End Sub

Sub Activity_Create(FirstTime As Boolean)
 pnlColor.Initialize("")
 Activity.AddView(pnlColor, 10%x, 40dip, 80%x, 80dip)
 Dim cdwColor As ColorDrawable
 cdwColor.Initialize(Colors.Red, 5dip)
 pnlColor.Background = cdwColor

 pnlGradient.Initialize("")
 Activity.AddView(pnlGradient, 10%x, 140dip, 80%x, 80dip)
 Dim gdwGradient As GradientDrawable
 Dim Cols(2) As Int
 Cols(0) = Colors.Blue
 Cols(1) = Colors.White
 gdwGradient.Initialize("TOP_BOTTOM", Cols)
 gdwGradient.CornerRadius = 10dip
 pnlGradient.Background = gdwGradient

 pnlBitmap.Initialize("")
 Activity.AddView(pnlBitmap, 10%x, 250dip, 80%x, 80dip)
 Dim bdwBitmap As BitmapDrawable
 bdwBitmap.Initialize(LoadBitmap(File.DirAssets, "background.png"))
 bdwBitmap.Gravity = Gravity.FILL
 pnlBitmap.Background = bdwBitmap
End Sub
```

The result would be:

StateListDrawable

In addition to the above drawables, a **StateListDrawable** is a drawable object that holds other drawables and chooses the current one based on a button's state. It can be defined either in code:

```
Dim sld As StateListDrawable
```

or in the Designer as the **Background** property of **Buttons**.

There are two options for the **Drawable** property of a button:

- **DefaultDrawable**, which is set by default and uses default colors
- **StatelistDrawable**, which allows you to chose custom colors

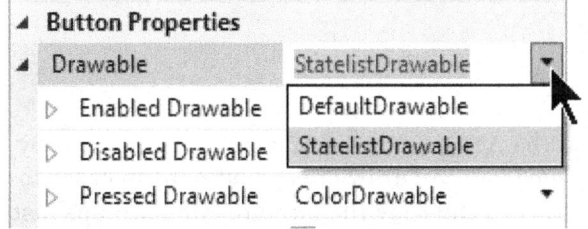

A button with the StatelistDrawable property has three states:

- Enabled Drawable – What you see when the button is enabled
- Disabled Drawable – What you see when it's disabled
- Pressed Drawable – What it looks like when pressed

Each state has its own Drawable, which could be either **ColorDrawable**, **GradientDrawable** or **BitmapDrawable**.

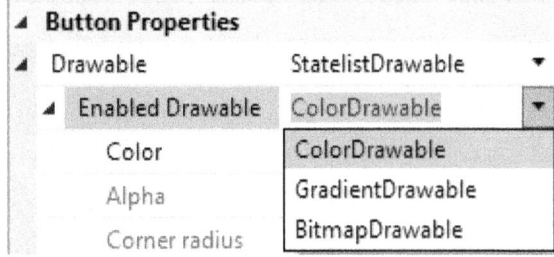

Example Project

For a sample project which uses both code and a Designer-created layout to create buttons with a **StateListDrawable** set to **ColorDrawable, GradientDrawable** and **BitmapDrawable**, download the ButtonStateDrawables project from this book's resources page (http://bit.ly/1IjLiwC).

NinePatchDrawable

Android supports a special format of PNG images that can be resized by replicating specific parts of the image. These images also include padding information. Such images are named "nine-patch images". You can read more about this format here (http://bit.ly/1MzxxYu). The Android SDK includes a tool named **draw9patch.bat** that can help you with building and modifying such images. This tool is available in the Tools folder of your Android SDK. You can read more about it here (http://bit.ly/1MzxETT).

Example Project

NinePatchExample is a simple example of a project which uses SetNinePatchDrawable to demonstrate the power and usage of NinePatchDrawable.

Note: this project requires the use of the Reflection library (page 579), so it cannot be run with the Trial Version of B4A. The project is available from this book's resources page (http://bit.ly/1IjLiwC).

Canvas Object

As well as setting the background of Views and the Activity, the second way of drawing is by using a **Canvas**. A **Canvas** is an object upon which you can draw or copy bitmaps in order to prepare your drawing and then, when it is ready, you can copy the bitmap onto (perhaps just a part of) the background of a View or the Activity.

A **Canvas** can draw onto the following views: Activity (page 337), ImageView (page 416), Panel (page 425) and Bitmap (page 352)

A bitmap must be "mutable" in order for a **Canvas** to draw upon it.

A Canvas is an **Activity** object; it cannot be declared under **Sub Process_Globals**.

Initializing a Canvas

When we initialize the **Canvas**, we must specify which view or bitmap it will eventually draw onto, either a View or the Activity, as shown in this diagram:

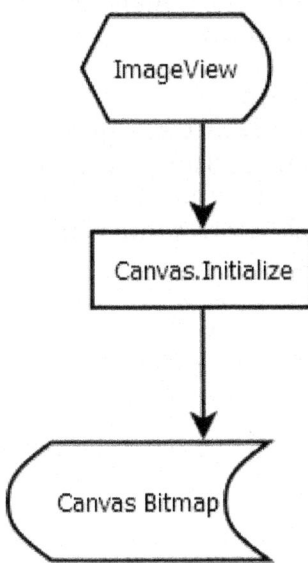

When a **Canvas** is initialized and set to draw on a view (or the Activity), a new mutable bitmap is created for Canvas to draw on and the current view's background is first copied to the new bitmap. In this way, we can prepare our drawing over the top of the old background. You can get the bitmap that the **Canvas** draws on with the **Bitmap** property.

For example you could set a Canvas to draw onto the **Activity** background and at the same time take a copy of the Activity's current background bitmap:

```
Dim Canvas1 As Canvas
Canvas1.Initialize(Activity)
```

Drawing onto a Canvas

You can then draw onto the Canvas's bitmap by calling one of the Canvas's drawing methods. This draws onto the Canvas (still invisible) bitmap.

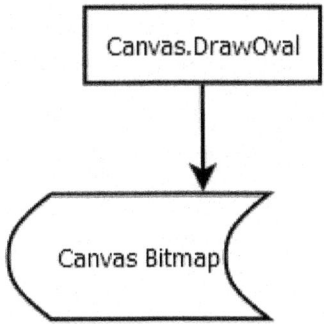

`Canvas` drawings are not immediately updated on the screen. This is useful as it allows you to draw several things and only refresh the display when everything is ready.

For example, you could draw onto `Canvas1`:

```
Canvas1.DrawLine(0, 0, 100dip, 200dip, Colors.Red, 3dip)
```

The `Canvas` object has the following methods which allow you to draw: DrawCircle (page 356), DrawLine (page 357), DrawOval (page 358), DrawOvalRotated (page 358), DrawPath, DrawPoint (page 358), DrawRect (page 359), DrawRectRotated (page 359), DrawText (page 359) and DrawTextRotated (page 359). You can specify their positions, colors, width of the line and (for closed shapes) whether they are filled.

Importing a Bitmap file into Canvas

The following diagram illustrates the required steps:

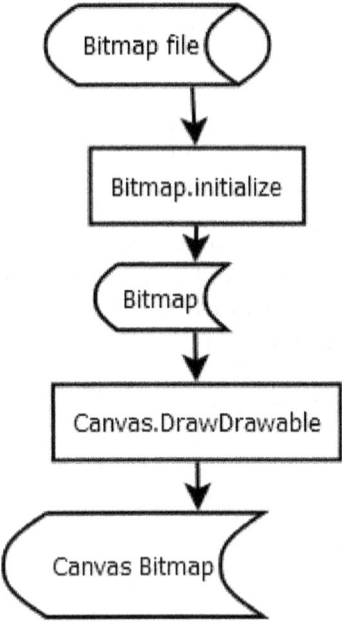

Copying a Drawable onto a Canvas

The following diagram illustrates the steps:

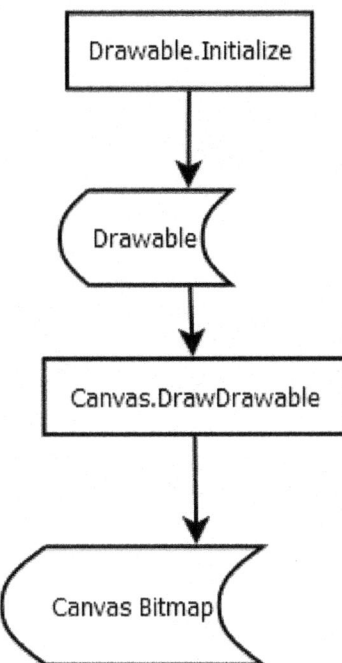

Making the Canvas Draw Itself

When your drawing is complete, you make the **Canvas** draw itself onto its target by making the target invalid by calling the target view **Invalidate** method.:

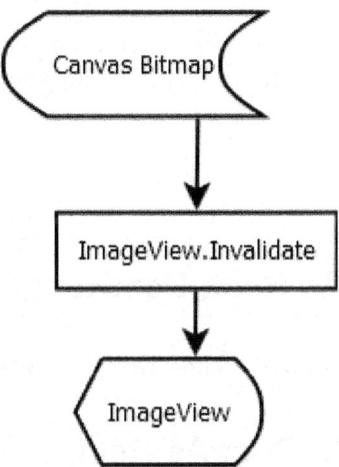

For example, you could make **Canvas1** draw itself using the code:

```
Activity.Invalidate
```

The result would have the following measurements:

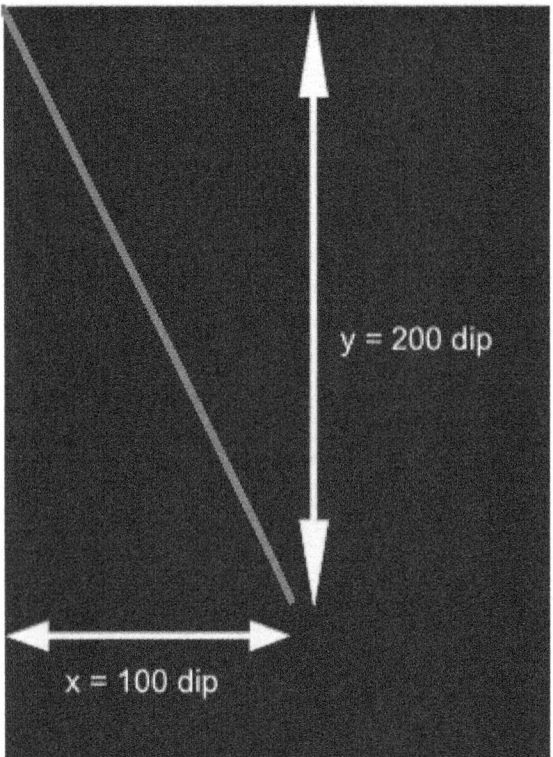

Note the first four parameters of DrawLine are in the order left, top, right, bottom.

Restricting the Drawing Area

The `Canvas` can be limited to a path defining a specific area of the target, and thus only drawing onto that region. This is done by calling `ClipPath`. See Canvas.ClipPath (page 355) for an example.

Most common Canvas functions

See the Canvas (page 354) object for details.

DrawBitmap (Bitmap1 As Bitmap, SrcRect As Rect, DestRect As Rect)

Draws a source bitmap (or part of it) onto a destination. If the source and destination sizes are different, the destination drawing is stretched or shrunk.

DrawBitmapRotated (Bitmap1 As Bitmap, SrcRect As Rect, DestRect As Rect, Degrees As Float)

Same functionality as DrawBitmap, but with a rotation around the centre of the bitmap.

DrawCircle (x As Float, y As Float, Radius As Float, Color As Int, Filled As Boolean, StrokeWidth As Float)

Draws a circle with left edge of x and top of y. It can be filled with a given color (page 345) and, if filled, the perimeter can be outlined with a stroke of a given width.

DrawColor (Color As Int)

Fills the whole view with the given color. The color can be Colors.Transparent making the whole view transparent.

DrawLine (x1 As Float, y1 As Float, x2 As Float, y2 As Float, Color As Int, StrokeWidth As Float)

Draw a straight line from (x1,y1) to (x2,y2) with specified color (page 345) and stroke width (in dips (page 163)).

DrawRect (Rect1 As Rect, Color As Int, Filled As Boolean, StrokeWidth As Float)

Draw a rectangle with given size, color, whether filled, and line width.

DrawRectRotated (Rect1 As Rect, Color As Int, Filled As Boolean, StrokeWidth As Float, Degrees As Float)

Same as `DrawRect`, but rotated by the given angle

DrawText (Text As String, x As Float, y As Float, Typeface1 As Typeface, TextSize As Float, Color As Int, Align1 As Align)

Draws the given text in the given typeface, size and color.

Align1 is the alignment relative to the chosen position, and can have one of the following values: LEFT, CENTER, RIGHT.

DrawTextRotated (Text As String, x As Float, y As Float, Typeface1 As Typeface, TextSize As Float, Color As Int, Align1 As Align, Degree As Float)

Same as `DrawText`, but with the text rotated.

Full details of all `Canvas` methods can be found here (page 354).

Example Program

In this example, we draw some sample shapes on the Main Activity. We put the code in the `Sub Activity_Resume` because this is always run whenever the app starts or restarts. Thus, we do not need to call `Activity.Invalidate`. We also add a button and draw a circle when it is pressed. In this case, we need to call `Activity.Invalidate` so that the `Canvas` will be transferred to the `Activity`'s background.

```
Sub Globals
  Dim cvsActivity As Canvas
  Dim btnTest As Button
End Sub


Sub Activity_Create(FirstTime As Boolean)

End Sub
```

```
Sub Activity_Resume
 ' create a button
 btnTest.Initialize("btnTest")
 Activity.AddView(btnTest,10dip, 240dip, 200dip, 50dip)
 btnTest.Text = "Draw Another Circle"
 ' initialize the canvas
 cvsActivity.Initialize(Activity)
 ' draw a horizontal line
 cvsActivity.DrawLine(20dip, 20dip, 160dip, 20dip, Colors.Red, 3dip)
 ' draw an empty rectangle
 Dim rect1 As Rect
 rect1.Initialize(50dip, 40dip, 150dip, 100dip)
 cvsActivity.DrawRect(rect1, Colors.Blue, False, 3dip)
 ' draw an empty circle
 cvsActivity.DrawCircle(50dip, 200dip, 30dip, Colors.Green, False,
3dip)
 ' draw a text
 cvsActivity.DrawText("Test text", 50dip, 150dip, Typeface.DEFAULT,
20, Colors.Yellow, "LEFT")
 ' draw a filled circle with a boarder
 cvsActivity.DrawCircle(50dip, 340dip, 30dip, Colors.Green, True,
3dip)
 ' the above will always be drawn because
 '  the Activity is automatically redrawn on activity_resume
End Sub

Sub btnTest_Click
 cvsActivity.DrawCircle(100dip, 40dip, 30dip, Colors.Green, False,
3dip)
 ' make the drawing visible
 Activity.Invalidate
End Sub
```

The resulting screen is:

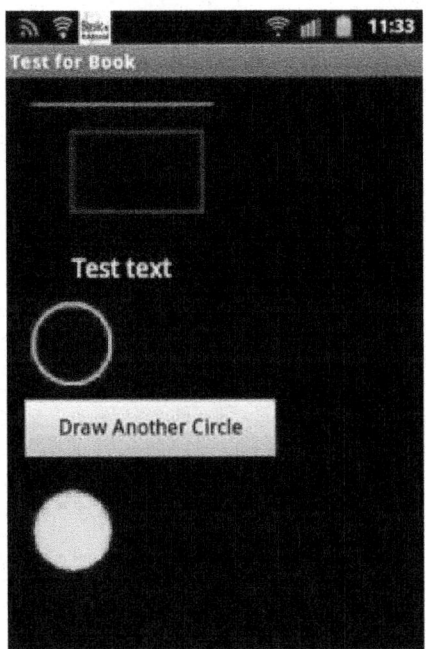

More Complex Examples

A good way to learn is to play with projects and figure out how they work. You can download several graphics example projects from this book's resource page (http://bit.ly/1IjLiwC). The RotatingNeedle project (shown on left below) will draw a compass which will rotate either the compass or the needle. It uses a `Timer` to control the rotation.

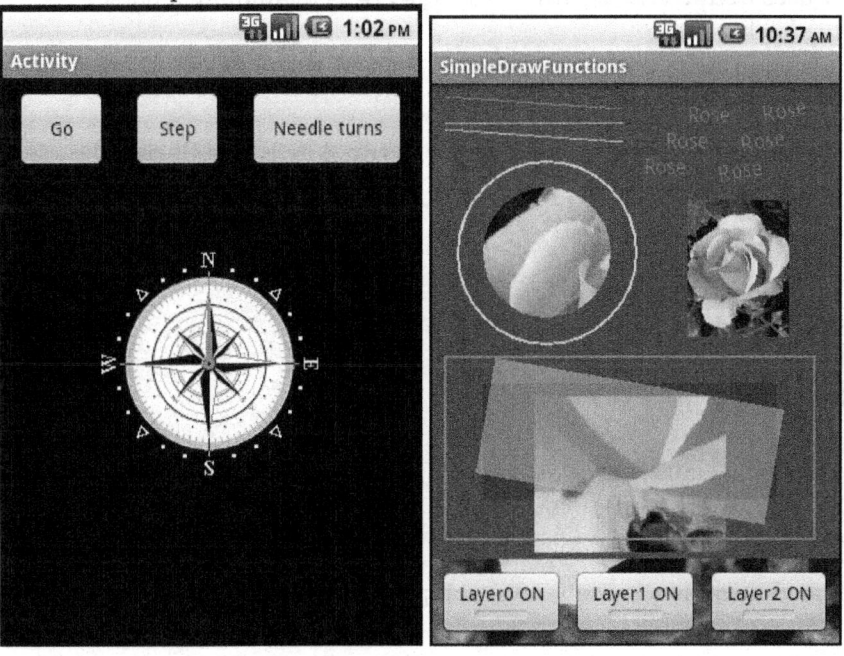

The SimpleDrawFunctions project (on right above) uses more common drawing functions and Panels which can be shown or hidden with buttons.
The blue circle with a transparent center can be dragged around the screen.

Animating Bitmaps

You can animate a bitmap (page 352) by having several **Panels** or **ImageViews** superimposed, and revealing each of them in turn. The illusion of movement can be created by moving a background image across the screen. If the images need to be changed often, then you could draw onto a canvas first. The code to draw is essentially:

```
Dim cvs As Canvas
Dim imv As ImageView
Dim img As Bitmap
Dim Rect1 As Rect

imv.Initialize("")
Activity.AddView(imv, 0, 0, 100%x, 100%y)
cvs.Initialize(imv)
img.Initialize(File.DirAssets, "horse.png")
Rect1.Initialize(0, 45%y, img.Width, 45%y + img.Height)

cvs.DrawBitmap(img, Null, Rect1)
imv.Invalidate2(Rect1)
```

"Layers" is an example project, whose source code is available from this book's resources page (http://bit.ly/1IjLiwC). It uses **DrawBitmap** with two **ImageViews** to animate a horse galloping across a moving background.

Diagrams / Charts

Oscilloscope is a demonstration of drawing onto a Canvas, written by Klaus Christl.

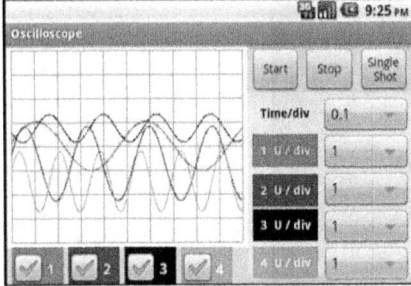

The project can be downloaded from this book's resources page (http://bit.ly/1IjLiwC).

Charts Framework

The Charts Framework module allows to draw several types of diagrams:
- Pie charts
- Bar charts
- Stacked Bar charts

- Curves

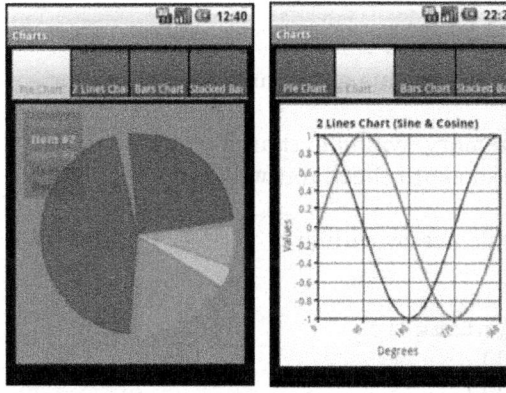

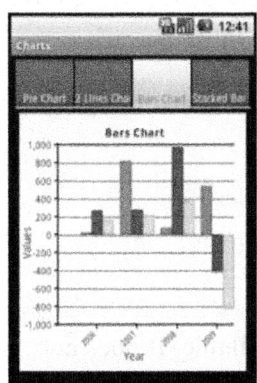
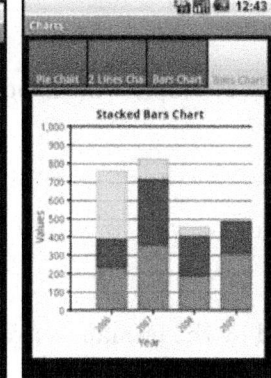

The Charts Framework is a code module (not a library) **charts.bas** which must be included in your project if you wish to use it. It can be downloaded here: Charts Framework (http://bit.ly/10enSTK)

Out of Memory Errors

A device's memory is limited, and it is possible for your app to use up the available memory and eventually run out, leading to an exception:

```
java.lang.RuntimeException: Error loading bitmap (OutOfMemoryError)
```

If you don't try and catch (page 304) this exception then your app will crash.

The most common cause of consuming memory is by loading bitmaps into memory, typically with the **LoadBitmap** command. You can also have a memory leak if the user changes the orientation of the screen and the app has to reload the bitmaps.

You can reduce memory consumption by calling **LoadBitmapSample** instead of **LoadBitmap**, but even then memory consumption is possible if too many bitmaps are loaded. The best way to minimise this problem is to ensure that your sampled bitmaps are stored as Process_Globals, so they only need to be loaded once.

It is also possible to allocate more memory space by using the manifest LargeHeap command using

```
SetApplicationAttribute(android:largeHeap,"true")
```

The heap is one sort of memory used by Android. Note that this only works for SDK 11 or above.

Also note that when you Debug an app it has less memory available than it would do in Release mode, so you could try switching to Release mode to check if it will run.

Your app can see the amount of free memory on the device by calling

```
Sub GetFreeMemory As Long
  Dim jo As JavaObject
  jo = jo.InitializeStatic("java.lang.Runtime")
  jo = jo.RunMethodJO("getRuntime", Null)
  Return jo.RunMethod("totalMemory", Null)
End Sub
```

Note that is requires the JavaObject (page 491) library.

In theory you can free up memory of objects (such as bitmaps) which you no longer need by calling:

```
Sub recycle (bmp As Bitmap)
  Dim Obj1 As Reflector
  Obj1.Target = bmp
  Obj1.RunMethod ("recycle")
  bmp = Null
End Sub
```

But note that this only marks the memory occupied by the bitmap as available. It does not actually free the memory immediately. See here (http://bit.ly/1c4VJVH) for more details.

2.8 Databases

Storing Data

B4A provides the developer with several different ways to store data to persistent storage so it will be available when the user pauses (page 245) or quits your app. You should choose the right method for the type of data you want to store. The following options are available to store data to persistent storage:

- Using the KeyValueStore (page 564) class which uses an SQLite database
- Using the StateManager (page 566) code module which saves the UI state and settings to a file
- Using your own Database, as described below

You could also store data in a random access file (page 531) using your own code, although this is perhaps not normally the preferred method.

Database fundamentals

Android supports the SQLite database engine which your app can use to store data on the device. B4A provides DBUtils which allow you to easily manipulate tables and data without any special knowledge. If you need something more sophisticated, you can write commands in the SQL database manipulation language.

First, let's look at some fundamental facts about databases.

Database

A database is a collection of data organised into tables, fields and records. A database management system (DBMS) such as SQLite allows the creation of these structures and lets you enter and retrieve data.

Table

Data within a database is organised into tables. A table corresponds to an object about which data is to be stored. For example, a table could contain information about cities or countries.

Record

A record is the data about one object in a table. Thus, the city table might contain one record for Toyko and a different one for London.

A table is often pictured as an array, like a spreadsheet in which the rows contain the records.

Field

The fields within a table are the individual pieces of information which need to be stored for the objects in the table. For example, the city table might store City Name, Country and Population fields.

If a table is pictured like a spreadsheet, then the columns would contain the fields and the rows would hold the records:

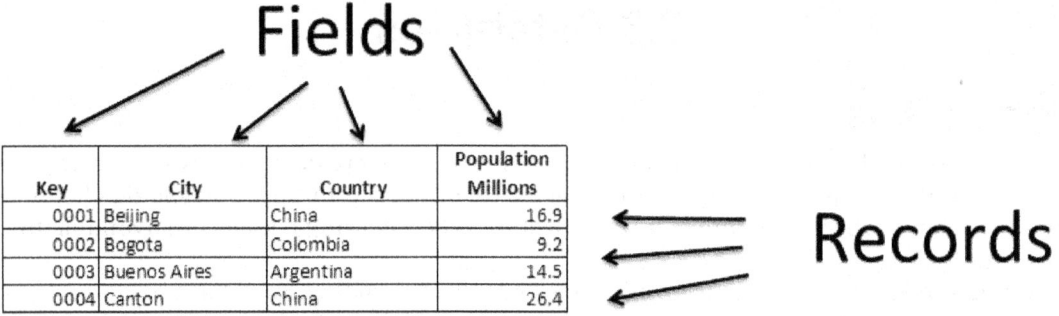

Primary Key

Every table normally contains one special field, called the primary key, which is used to quickly identify and locate a single record. In the country table, we might want to use the city name as the key, but that would cause a problem if two cities in different countries share the same name. So it is safest to create a special key field, using an integer, which is usually incremented automatically when a new record is added.

Field Type

Most DBMS need to know what type of data will be added to each field. Typical types are:

NULL: The value is a `Null` value.

INTEGER: The value is a signed integer, stored in 1, 2, 3, 4, 6, or 8 bytes depending on the magnitude of the value.

REAL: The value is a floating point value, stored as an 8-byte IEEE floating point number.

TEXT: The value is a text string, stored using the database encoding (UTF-8 by default for Android).

BLOB: The value is a blob of data, stored exactly as it was input.

Note that SQLite is Different

However note that SQLite (the Android DBMS) does not comply with this standard for most fields. See Manifest Typing (page 226) for more details.

Relational Data

Let us look again at our Country table.

Key	City	Country	Population Millions
0001	Beijing	China	16.9
0002	Bogota	Colombia	9.2
0003	Buenos Aires	Argentina	14.5
0004	Canton	China	26.4

Because countries contain thousands of cities, the name of each country may occur more than once (China in this small example). So if the name of the country changes, we would need to change many records. Also, it would be very slow to find every city belonging to a particular country. A better way to store this data would be to have two tables, one for cities and one for countries:

City Table

CityID	Name	CountryID	Population Millions
0001	Beijing	0001	16.9
0002	Bogota	0002	9.2
0003	Buenos Aires	0003	14.5
0004	Canton	0001	26.4

Country Table

CountryID	Name
0001	China
0002	Colombia
0003	Argentina

One of the benefits of most DBMS is that you can establish links (or relationships) between tables. Thus, for example, you might have a city table and a country table. Instead of the name of the country, we store only its key in the city table. To find which country a city belongs to, we look up its country key in the country table.

Database Files

In SQLite, a database is contained within a single file. You can create this file before you publish your app, or your app can create the database from scratch. If you want to ship your database file with your app, you should copy the file into the Files folder of your project. You can use any file extension you like, or even no extension, but .db might be a good choice to remind you what sort of data the file contains.

Your app will need to copy the database to a writable location because it is not possible to access a database located in File.DirAssets. You can use CopyDBFromAssets (page 220) **to copy it.**

KeyValueStore Class

Note: the additional KeyValueStore (page 564) class provides a useful way to easily store data to persistent storage using an SQLite database in a transparent fashion. It can be used, for example, to store user preferences before Android calls `Activity_Pause`, then restore them on `Activity_Resume`.

Encrypting Databases

The SQLCipher (http://bit.ly/165Z6Uq) additional library allows you to encrypt the SQLite database file.

Showing Tables to the User

You can show an SQL table in a WebView, and detect which row and column a user clicks in, by using the `ShowTableInWebView` call in the DBUtils code module. For a more flexible and powerful way of showing a table using the ScrollView2D library see the tutorial here (http://bit.ly/1L0R59m).

Database Administration

DBMS Tools
While it is possible to create a database from within your app using SQL, it might be easier to create it during the development process and ship it with your app (see the previous section). The easiest way to create a database is to use one of the following tools.

SQLiteBrowser
SQLite Database Browser is a freeware, public domain, open source visual tool used to create, design and edit database files compatible with SQLite. It is meant to be used for users and developers that want to create databases, and edit and search data using a familiar spreadsheet-like interface, without the need to learn complicated SQL commands. It has an excellent GUI which lets you create and manipulate SQLite databases without SQL, but also lets you run SQL against them.
This tool (http://bit.ly/1IjOpVw) is not currently being maintained, but it is very valuable nevertheless.

SQLiteSpy
For those who know SQL, if you want an SQL-based database management tool to create SQLite databases, try SQLiteSpy, a fast and compact GUI database manager for SQLite. It reads SQLite3 files and executes SQL against them. Its graphical user interface makes it very easy to explore, analyze, and manipulate SQLite3 databases.
It is frequently updated. The problem with it is that it relies entirely upon SQL. Unlike SQLiteBrowser, it has no GUI tools for table manipulation. http://bit.ly/1agKxQx

DBMS Apps
There are several Android apps available to manage databases. The features they offer vary. Some will allow you to create databases, some to browse existing databases, some to add records but if you want to edit databases created by other apps, they all require you to have a rooted device in order to overcome Android's security limitations.

SQL Object

This is the main B4A object which accesses a database. It is defined in the SQL Library (page 544). Before you can use SQL, you need to reference the library and declare the object, as follows.

Reference SQL Library
Your project needs to reference the SQL library, even if you do not want to write SQL yourself, since DBUtils needs it. Use the Libraries Manager (page 87) window within the IDE to create the reference.

Declare SQL Object
For the SQL Library to work, you need to declare an SQL object in **Process_Globals**:

```
Sub Process_Globals
  Dim SQL1 As SQL
End Sub
```

Initialize SQL Object

As well as declaring the SQL Object, you must initialize it. This ties the SQL to the named database file and opens the database file.

Note that a new database will be created if it does not exist and if Initialize's third parameter `CreateIfNecessary` is true.

You can have several database files open by using multiple SQL Objects. See the File Location (page 366) section for information on where to store your files.

Example

```
Sub Activity_Create(FirstTime As Boolean)
  If FirstTime Then
    SQL1.Initialize(File.DirRootExternal, "1.db", True)
  End If
End Sub
```

DBUtils

DBUtils Fundamentals

DBUtils is a code module which lets you manipulate databases without writing much SQL. However, it is probable you will still need a little SQL, which we explain in the SQLite (page 226) Reference section.

Installing DBUtils

DBUtils is a code module and not a library, so you have to include it in your project:
– First, see here (http://bit.ly/1cUgfEi) to find the DBUtils web page, scroll down to the bottom of the tutorial and download the zip file.
– Unzip the file into a folder. You might want to study the project contained in that folder to learn about how to use DBUtils.
– When you want to use it in your own project, add **DBUtils.bas** to your project with the menu [Project > Add Existing Module]. Navigate to the DBUtils project and select DBUtils.bas.
– Click Open. A message will appear telling you the file has been copied to your project, and "DBUtils" will appear in the Modules window (on the right of the IDE) and in the modules tabs (near the top of the IDE).

Preliminary SQL Steps

SQL Object

You need to reference the SQL Library and declare the object, as described above.

Versioning

Your database structure might change over time.
DBUtils introduces the concept of database version, so that your code can set and test the version number of the database and update it if necessary. Use the functions `GetDBVersion` and `SetDBVersion` to control the version of your database.

DBUtils Field Types

DBUtils includes the following which are used as constants for defining field types:
```
DB_BLOB
DB_INTEGER
DB_REAL
DB_TEXT
```
For an example, see CreateTable

DBUtils Functions

CopyDBFromAssets (FileName As String) As String

If you have shipped your database file with your app (by adding it in the Files tab), then the database must be copied to a writable location because it is not possible to access a database located in `File.DirAssets`. You can use `CopyDBFromAssets` to copy it. **Note**: If the database file already exists, then no copying is done. If you want to replace the database, you need to delete the earlier destination file.

Location of Database

If external storage (page 366) is available, this method copies the database to folder `File.DirDefaultExternal`. If the storage card is not available, the file is copied to the internal folder `File.DirInternal`.
The target folder is returned.

CreateTable (SQL As SQL, TableName As String, FieldsAndTypes As Map, PrimaryKey As String)

This function creates a new table with the given name within the file previously opened when the `SQL` object was initialized.
FieldsAndTypes – A map with the field names as keys and the types as values.
You can use the DBUtils Field Types for the types.
PrimaryKey – The column that will be the primary key (page 216). Pass an empty string if not needed.
Example:
```
Dim SQL As SQL
Dim m As Map
m.Initialize
m.Put("Id", DBUtils.DB_INTEGER)
m.Put("First Name", DBUtils.DB_TEXT)
m.Put("Last Name", DBUtils.DB_TEXT)
m.Put("Birthday", DBUtils.DB_INTEGER)
DBUtils.CreateTable(SQL, "Students", m, "Id")
```

DeleteRecord (SQL As SQL, TableName As String, WhereFieldEquals As Map)

Deletes the specified record in **TableName**.
WhereFieldEquals is a map in which the field names are the keys and the values to search for are the map's values.

DropTable (SQL As SQL, TableName As String)

Deletes the given table.

ExecuteHtml(SQL As SQL, Query As String, StringArgs() As String, Limit As Int, Clickable As Boolean) As String

Creates HTML which, when viewed in a `WebView`, displays the data in a table. This method can be used rapidly to visualize data during development, or to show reports to users. You can change the table style by modifying the Cascading Style Sheet (CSS) variable `HtmlCSS` within `Process_Globals` of the DBUtils module.

StringArgs() – Array of values to replace question marks in the query. Pass `Null` if not needed.

Limit – Limits the number of records returned. Pass 0 to get all the records.

Clickable – Defines whether the values will be clickable or not. If the values are clickable, you should catch the WebView_OverrideUrl event to find the clicked cell. Example:

```
Sub WebView1_OverrideUrl (Url As String) As Boolean
  'parse the row and column numbers from the URL
  Dim values() As String
  values = Regex.Split("[.]", Url.SubString(7))
  Dim col, row As Int
  col = values(0)
  row = values(1)
  ToastMessageShow("User pressed on column: " & col & " and row: " &
row, False)
  Return True 'Don't try to navigate to this URL
End Sub
```

Note: By default, hyperlinks are not differentiated from other text within the HTML. You might want to modify the Cascading Style Sheet (CSS) variable `HtmlCSS` within `Process_Globals` of the DBUtils module to change the table style to make it obvious that there is a hyperlink. Thus, you might change the CSS code from the default:

```
a { text-decoration:none; color: #000;}
```

to make hyperlinks underlined and blue using the following:

```
a { text-decoration:underline; color: #0000FF;}
```

ExecuteJSON(SQL As SQL, Query As String, StringArgs() As String, Limit As Int, DBTypes As List) As Map

Executes the given query and creates a Map that you can pass to JSONGenerator and generate JSON (page 492) text.

StringArgs() – Values to replace question marks in the query. Pass `Null` if not needed.

Limit – Limits the number of records returned. Pass 0 to get all the records.

DBTypes – Lists the type of each column in the result set.

Usage example (requires a reference to the JSON library (page 492)):

```
Dim gen As JSONGenerator
gen.Initialize(DBUtils.ExecuteJSON(SQL, "SELECT Id, Birthday FROM
Students", Null, 0, Array As String(DBUtils.DB_TEXT,
DBUtils.DB_INTEGER)))
Dim JSONString As String
JSONString = gen.ToPrettyString(4)
Msgbox(JSONString, "")
```

ExecuteListView(SQL As SQL, Query As String, StringArgs() As String, Limit As Int, ListView1 As ListView, TwoLines As Boolean)

Executes the **Query** and fills the ListView (page 420) with the values, one row for each record.

StringArgs() – Values to replace question marks in the **Query**. Pass `Null` if not needed.

Limit – Limits the number of records returned. Pass `0` to get all the records.

TwoLines – if `True`, then the first column in the ListView is mapped to the first field and the second column is mapped to the second field.

Example:
```
'Find all tests of this student with grade lower than 55.
DBUtils.ExecuteListView(SQL, "SELECT test, grade FROM Grades WHERE id
= ? AND grade <= 55", Array As String(StudentId), 0, lstFailedTest,
True)
```

The result will be as follows, depending on whether TwoLines is **True** or **False**

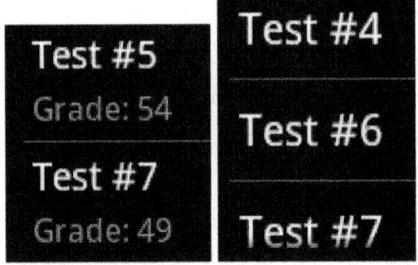

ExecuteMap(SQL As SQL, Query As String, StringArgs() As String) As Map

Executes **Query** and returns a `Map` with the column names as the keys and the first record values as the map's values.

StringArgs() – Values to replace question marks in the **Query**. Pass `Null` if not needed.

The keys are lower-cased. Returns `Null` if no results found.

Example:
```
mFirstRecord = DBUtils.ExecuteMap(SQL, "SELECT Id, [First Name], [Last
Name], Birthday FROM students WHERE id = ?", Array As String(Value))
```

ExecuteMemoryTable(SQL As SQL, Query As String, StringArgs() As String, Limit As Int) As List

Executes the **Query** and returns the result as a `List` of arrays. Each item in the list is an array of strings.

StringArgs() – Values to replace question marks in the **Query**. Pass `Null` if not needed.

Limit – Limits the number of records returned. Pass `0` to get all the records.

Example:

```
Dim lstTable As List
Dim strFields() As String
Dim lstRecords As List
Dim iCountStudents As Int

'lstTable is a list of string arrays. Each array holds a single
record.
lstTable = DBUtils.ExecuteMemoryTable(SQL, "SELECT Id, [First Name]
FROM Students", Null, 0)
lstRecords.Initialize
For iCountStudents = 0 To lstTable.Size - 1
 strFields = lstTable.Get(iCountStudents)
 Log("Id: " & strFields(0))
 Log("Name: " & strFields(1))
Next
```
Example using `StringArgs`:
```
lstTable = DBUtils.ExecuteMemoryTable(SQL, "SELECT Id FROM Students
where Id > ?", Array As String(intMinID), 0)
```

ExecuteSpinner(SQL As SQL, Query As String, StringArgs() As String, Limit As Int, Spinner1 As Spinner)

Executes the **Query** and fills the **Spinner** with the values in the first column.

StringArgs() – Values to replace question marks in the query. Pass Null if not needed.

Limit – Limits the results. Pass 0 for all results.

Examples:
```
'If parameter is known to developer
DBUtils.ExecuteSpinner(SQL, "SELECT * FROM Students WHERE Id < 40000",
Null, 0, spnrStudentId)
'If parameter is a variable Value
DBUtils.ExecuteSpinner(SQL, "SELECT * FROM Students WHERE Id = ?",
Array As String(Value), 0, spnrStudentId)
```

GetDBVersion(SQL As SQL) As Int

Gets the current version (page 219) of the database.

If the DBVersion table does not exist within the initialized database, it is created and the current version is set to version 1.

Example:

```
Dim DBVersion, CurrentDBVersion As Int
DBVersion = DBUtils.GetDBVersion(SQL)
CurrentDBVersion = 2
Do While DBVersion < CurrentDBVersion
 Select DBVersion
 Case 1
 UpdateDB1_2(SQL)
 Case 2
 UpdateDB2_3
 End Select
 DBVersion = DBUtils.GetDBVersion(SQL)
Loop
```

InsertMaps (SQL As SQL, TableName As String, ListOfMaps As List)

This is the way to insert one or more records into a table. The data is passed as a **List** that contains maps as items. Each map holds the fields for one record and their values.

ListOfMaps – A list with maps as items. Each **Map** represents a record, where the map keys are the field names and the map values are the values.

Note: you should create a new map for each record (this can be done by calling **Dim** to redim the map). Example:

```
Dim allRecords As List
allRecords.Initialize
Dim id As Int
For id = 1 To 40
 Dim oneRecord As Map
 oneRecord.Initialize
 oneRecord.Put("Id", id)
 oneRecord.Put("First Name", "John")
 oneRecord.Put("Last Name", "Smith" & id)
 allRecords.Add(oneRecord)
Next
DBUtils.InsertMaps(SQL, "Students", allRecords)
```

SetDBVersion(SQL As SQL, Version As Int)

Sets the database version (page 219) to the given version number.

UpdateRecord(SQL As SQL, TableName As String, Field As String, NewValue As Object, WhereFieldEquals As Map)

Update (that is change) an existing record in the database.

TableName – The table where the record exists.

Field – The name of the field to update.

NewValue – The new value.

WhereFieldEquals – This identifies which record to update. It is a Map, where the keys are the column names and the map values are the values to look for.

Example:

```
Dim WhereFields As Map
WhereFields.Initialize
WhereFields.Put("id", spnrStudentId.SelectedItem)
WhereFields.Put("test", spnrTests.SelectedItem)
DBUtils.UpdateRecord(SQL, "Grades", "Grade", txtGrade.Text,
WhereFields)
```

UpdateRecord2(SQL As SQL, TableName As String, Fields As Map, WhereFieldEquals As Map)

Update (that is change) several fields in an existing record in the database.

TableName – The table where the record exists.

Fields – A map of the fields to update, where the field names to update are the keys and the values are the new values these fields should be given.

WhereFieldEquals – This identifies which record to update. It is a Map where the keys are the column names and the map values are the values to look for.

Example:

```
Dim mapNewFieldsValues As Map
mapNewFieldsValues.Initialize
mapNewFieldsValues.Put("tries", iTries + 1)
Dim mapWhere As Map
mapWhere.Initialize
mapWhere.Put("id", iRandRecord)
mapNewFieldsValues.Put("correct", iCorrect + 1)
DBUtils.UpdateRecord2(SQL1, "aorde", mapNewFieldsValues, mapWhere)
```

Sample DBUtils Program

A sample project using DBUtils is **SQLiteViewer**, an Android-based database browser. It is available from this book's on-line resource page (http://bit.ly/1IjLiwC). Screen shots:

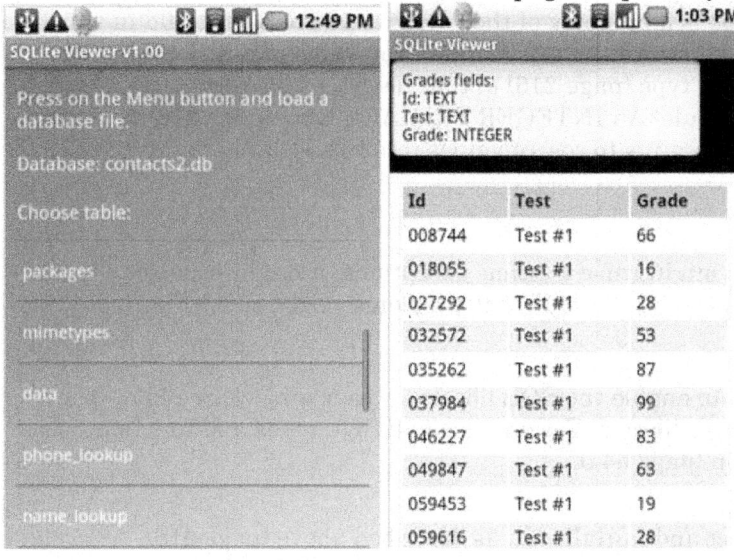

SQLite

SQL

If DBUtils is not adequate for your needs, you are going to have to write code in your app using Structured Query Language (SQL). This allows you to create tables, define their fields and other attributes, and add, retrieve and manipulate records.

There are many websites which help you to learn SQL, for example W3Schools SQL (http://bit.ly/1IjOUyO).

SQLite

SQLite is the database management system (DBMS) built into Android. It is the most widely deployed SQL DBMS in the world. Below, we give an outline of how to write SQLite without using DBUtils (page 219).

More Information on SQLite

You can find more about SQLite here: http://www.sqlite.org/. Here (http://bit.ly/1IjOYyy) you will find the SQLite syntax. See here (http://bit.ly/1IjP9de) for details of keywords and commands.

Sample SQLite Program

SQLExample is a demonstration program, available from this book's Resource page (http://bit.ly/1IjLiwC), which uses SQLite to create and manipulate a database.

Manifest Typing

Most DBMS use "static typing", in which one datatype is associated with each field in a table, and only values of that particular datatype are allowed to be stored in that field. SQLite, on the other hand, uses "manifest typing".

In "manifest typing", the datatype is a property of the value itself, not of the field in which the value is stored. SQLite thus allows you to store almost any value of any datatype into any field regardless of the declared type (page 216) of that field.

There are some exceptions to this rule: An INTEGER PRIMARY KEY (page 216) field may only store integers. And SQLite attempts to coerce values into the declared datatype of the field when it can.

SQLiteExceptions

Because interacting with SQLite might raise runtime exceptions, it might be wise to wrap your code in **TRY-CATCH** blocks so you can handle any problems.

SQL Library

In order to use SQLite, you need to enable the SQL library in your project. See here (page 452) for the method of referencing a library. For details of all SQL types and functions, see the SQL Library reference section (page 544).

SQL Object

You need to declare an SQL object and initialize it, as described above (page 218).

ExecQueries and ExecNonQueries

B4A SQL functions consist largely of queries which return results (`ExecQueries`), or commands which perform actions on the database but do not return results (`ExecNonQueries`). Several flavors are available in each category.

Cursor

A `Cursor` is the object returned from an `ExecQuery`. It consists of a set of records and a pointer to the current record. It is similar to a **recordset** in Visual Basic. More details in the SQL Library section (page 544).

Transactions

A transaction consists of a set of SQL statements. No changes will be made to the database unless all the statements are completed successfully. This ensures the integrity of the database. Statements inside a transaction will be executed significantly faster than separate statements.

It is very important to close transactions in order to commit the changes. This is a situation where the Try-Catch block (page 304) is useful.

Example:

```
SQL.BeginTransaction
Try
 'block of statements
 For i = 1 To 10
 SQL.ExecNonQuery2("INSERT INTO demo VALUES (?,?)", Array As Object(i,
"Tom Brown"))
 Next
 SQL.TransactionSuccessful
Catch
 Log(LastException.Message)  'no changes will be made
End Try
SQL.EndTransaction
```

Note: a transaction is implicitly created for every normal statement and automatically closed.

SQLite Commands

Note that what follows is only an introduction to SQL programming. Consult this page (http://bit.ly/1IjP9de) on the SQLite website for complete details of the language.

Database Creation

You can create a database (that is, a file containing all the tables of the database) using the `SQL.Initialize` statement, for example:

```
SQL.Initialize(File.DirRootExternal, "mydatabase.db", True)
```

Note: if the database file already exists, it will be opened rather than created.

Table creation

Having created your database, you need to add tables using the SQLite command CREATE TABLE. A simple example would be:

```
CREATE TABLE Country (CountryId INTEGER PRIMARY KEY, CountryName TEXT)
```

Note: in this example we are declaring the field types despite the fact that SQLite uses Manifest Typing. We consider this is good practice as it helps to make the code self-documenting.

Execute the above command with the ExecNonQuery (page 547) function, or the ExecNonQuery2 (page 547) function which allows you to easily parameterize this type of command.

The parameters of **CREATE TABLE** are:

TableName: It is usually an error to attempt to create a new table in a database that already contains a table, index or view of the same name.

Field List: TableName is followed by parentheses, containing a list of fields separated by commas. Thus, the example above defines 3 fields.

Field Definition: Each field is defined by its name and, optionally, a type and a contraint.

Field Type: This is the word after the field name. It is optional except in the case of INTEGER PRIMARY KEYS. As mentioned above, SQLite uses Manifest Typing, so the type declaration is not necessary. If you declare it, variables of other types can still be stored here but will be converted to the specified type, if possible.

The declaration merely determines the **Type Affinity** of the field, the preferred type of data. The type affinities available are: TEXT, NUMERIC, INTEGER, REAL and NONE.

A field with TEXT affinity stores all data using storage classes NULL, TEXT or BLOB. If numerical data is inserted into a field with TEXT affinity, it is converted into text form before being stored.

IF NOT EXISTS: It is usually an error to attempt to create a new table in a database that already contains a table, index or view of the same name. However, if the **IF NOT EXISTS** clause is specified as part of the **CREATE TABLE** statement and a table or view of the same name already exists, the **CREATE TABLE** command simply has no effect (and no error message is returned).

```
CREATE TABLE IF NOT EXISTS Country (CountryId INTEGER PRIMARY KEY,
CountryName TEXT)
```

An error is still returned if the table cannot be created because of an existing index, even if the **IF NOT EXISTS** clause is specified.

PRIMARY KEY: A primary key is one or more fields which are indexed to ensure rapid access and are required to contain unique data. Usually it is an integer. Note that a table does not require a primary key, but many do as shown in the previous example.

To specify a composite key, you need to add a primary key clause:

```
CREATE TABLE TableName (ID1 INTEGER, ID2 INTEGER, Col1 TEXT, Col2
REAL, CONSTRAINT PrimaryKeyName PRIMARY KEY (ID1, ID2))
```

Dropping a Table

If you are certain you want to replace the original table with a new one of the same name, and lose all the original data, you can avoid the above error by deleting or "dropping" the table before you re-create it, with SQL statements such as:

```
DROP TABLE IF EXISTS Country
```

Adding records

Use the **INSERT INTO** command to add records to a table. There are two main ways to specify the data to add.

1) Either you specify the names of specific fields and the values to inserted, for example:

```
INSERT INTO Country (CountryName) VALUES ('China')
```
In this case, a new record will be inserted into table called "Country", the "CountryName" field will be set to the value "China" and the primary key will be automatically incremented.
2) Or you specify the values of all fields in the correct sequence, in which case you do not need to include their names:
```
INSERT INTO TableName VALUES (NULL, 'Tom', 26)
```
Note: passing **NULL** will automatically increment the integer primary key for this record. Execute this command with the ExecNonQuery (page 547) function, or the ExecNonQuery2 (page 547) function which allows you to easily parameterize this type of command.

Updating records
Now suppose China changes its name to Chingha. You can change the existing record:
```
UPDATE Country Set CountryName = 'Chingha' WHERE CountryName = 'China'
```
Execute this command with the ExecNonQuery (page 547) function, or the ExecNonQuery2 (page 547) function which allows you to easily parameterize this type of command.

Retrieving data
The SQL command **SELECT** is used to retrieve data from a database. Specify the fields you want and which table to read:
```
SELECT col1, col2 FROM table1
```
To select all fields from a table, use an asterisk (*):
```
SELECT * FROM TableName
```

Processing the SQL
In B4A, execute the **SELECT** command with the ExecQuery (page 547) function, which returns a Cursor (page 544) object:
```
Dim Cursor1 As Cursor
Cursor1 = SQL1.ExecQuery("SELECT col1, col2 FROM table1")
For i = 0 To Cursor1.RowCount - 1
  Cursor1.Position = i
  Log(Cursor1.GetString("col1"))
  Log(Cursor1.GetInt("col2"))
Next
```

Parameterize the Command
Use ExecQuery2 (page 547) to parameterize the **SELECT** command with variables:
```
Dim Cursor1 As Cursor
Cursor1 = SQL.ExecQuery2("SELECT col1 FROM table1 WHERE id = ?", Array
As String(intId))
```

Filtering
Specify which records you want to read using **WHERE**:
```
SELECT id, col1 FROM Tablename WHERE id >= 2
```
The percent character (%) can be used as a wildcard, substituting zero or more characters:
```
SELECT * FROM TableName WHERE  Col1 LIKE  'T%'
SELECT * FROM Customers WHERE City LIKE '%es%'
```

Max and Min Values
Find the maxiumum/minimum value of a field:

```
SELECT MAX(Col1) FROM TableName
SELECT MIN(Col1) FROM TableName
```

Count Records
Find the total number of records in a table:
```
SELECT COUNT() FROM TableName
```

Ordering
Specify how you want the results sorted, either in ascending order:
```
SELECT * FROM TableName ORDER BY Col1
```
or in descending order:
```
SELECT * FROM TableName ORDER BY Col1 DESC
```

ExecQueryAsync
If a query will take a long time to run, you can issue an ExecQueryAsync (page 547) command which will raise an event when it finishes.

Deleting data
Delete selected records from a table:
```
DELETE FROM TableName WHERE ID = idVal
```
Delete ALL records from a table!
```
DELETE FROM TableName
```
Execute this command with the ExecNonQuery (page 547) function.

Rename a table
Rename a given table with:
```
ALTER TABLE TableName RENAME TO NewTableName
```
Execute this command with the ExecNonQuery (page 547) function.

Add a field
Add a new field to a table.
```
ALTER TABLE TableName ADD COLUMN Age REAL
```
Execute this command with the ExecNonQuery (page 547) function.

Using SQLite to Convert Ticks to Strings
Sometimes you store DateTime (page 349) long values (ticks) in a database, but you want to extract the data as a string so you can use it directly, for example to show tables (page 217) to the user. Suppose you have stored the data in a field called **DateTime**, then you can retrieve and convert it using the SQLite function:
```
SELECT
strftime('%H:%M:%S %d-%m-%Y', DateTime / 1000, 'unixepoch', _
  'localtime') as DT2
FROM Test
```
Where **unixepoch** ensures that SQLite will calculate the data using the same basis of B4A, that is, the number of milliseconds since January 1, 1970 00:00:00 UTC (Coordinated Universal Time) and **localtime** tries to convert the time to allow for local daylight saving.

Implementing a Database Relationship
Let us suppose we have created the two tables as shown here:

City Table

CityID	Name	CountryID	Population Millions
0001	Beijing	0001	16.9
0002	Bogota	0002	9.2
0003	Buenos Aires	0003	14.5
0004	Canton	0001	26.4

Country Table

CountryID	Name
0001	China
0002	Colombia
0003	Argentina

We could select the names of all the cities and the names of the countries they belonged to by using SQL code such as:

```
SELECT City.CityName, Country.CountryName
FROM City, Country
WHERE City.CountryID = Country.CountryId
```

The last line establishes the relationship between the two tables. For this reason, databases of this type are often called "Relational Databases".

2.9 Modules

A B4A application is made of one or more **activities** (screens). Android supports several other "main" components. These will be added to B4A in the future.

An app consists of code files called modules. At least one module exists, the main one. Its name is always **Main** and cannot be changed. An app can contain four different types of modules:

- Activity modules (page 239)
- Class modules (page 248)
- Code modules (page 254)
- Service modules (page 254)

All these modules run in a Process, which we discuss next.

Process

Each B4A program runs in its own **process**. Android is based on Linux, in which a process is simply a running program. Each process has one main **thread** (sequence of instructions, also called the "UI thread") which lives as long as the process lives. A process can have more threads, which can be useful for background tasks. You can even run Subs in separate threads (as demonstrated in this threading library (http://bit.ly/1AGl1y9)).

A **process starts** when the user launches your application (assuming it is not running already in the background). The **end** of the process is more variable. It will happen sometime after the user or system has closed all the activities.

If, for example, you have one activity and the user pressed on the back key, the activity is closed. Later, when the device gets low on memory, the process will be ended. If the user launches your app again and the process has not yet been killed, then the same process will be reused.

When Does Android Kill a Process?

When Android is low on memory, it will select a process to kill. If the process is needed later, it will be re-created. It is important to understand how Android chooses which process to kill. A process can be in one of the three following states:

Paused - There are no visible activities and no started services.

Paused processes are the first to be killed when needed.

Background - None of the activities of the process are visible, however there is a started service.

If there is still not enough memory, background processes will be killed.

Foreground - The user currently sees one of the process activities.

Foreground processes will usually not be killed. A service can bring a process to the foreground.

Creating or Adding Modules

You can add either an existing module or a new module.

To create a new module, select the IDE menu [Project > Add New Module]:

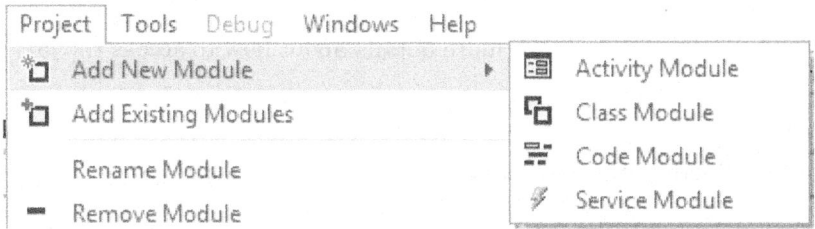

Click on either Activity, Class, Code or Service Module.

Each new module (except **Main**) is saved in a **.bas** file within the project folder. (Main is part of the **.b4a** file.)

To include an existing module (and so reuse the code), click on [Project > Add Existing Modules] in the IDE menu. You have two options:

- If you select to add a module from an existing project, then a copy of the module is placed in the current project. So you have two independent copies of the module

- If you select to add a module from the Shared Module folder (see below), then the module will not be copied to the current project, and you only have one copy of the module.

You can add several existing modules at the same time by checking all those you want to add.

Shared Modules

Sharing modules between projects can make development more efficient. One use would be a module including specialized mathematical calculations. You can share any of the four types of module mentioned above. It is an alternative to creating a shared library.

Modules you wish to use in several projects should be placed in the Shared Modules folder (page 108). This is defined in the [Tools > Configure Paths] dialog.

You add these modules to your project in the normal way using [Project > Add New Module] which is described next.

If you want to convert an existing module into a shared module, simply close the project, move the module into the Shared Modules folder and re-open the project. If B4A does not find the module in the project folder it will automatically look in the Shared Modules folder.

A shared module shows in the Modules Window (page 89) with a shared module icon:

Note: If you have two modules with the same name, one in the project folder and one in the shared modules folder, and if you try to add the one in shared modules folder to your project, B4A will actually add the local one not the shared one. You can tell this because the icon in the Modules window will not show the shared module icon but one of the icons in the diagram below.

Module Attributes

Module Attributes can be used to specify parameters of any type of module.

#AdditionalJar

This allows the code to reference an external jar (a file into which java code has been compressed in "zip" format), typically from another developer. Copy the jar (for example abc.jar) into the Additional Libraries folder, and add a reference to it using code such as:

```
#AdditionalJar: abc
```
Note that the file extension **jar** is not required. For more details about how to access the jar, see this tutorial (http://bit.ly/1zsCIAF).

#ExcludeFromLibrary
Whether to exclude this module during library compilation. Values: **True** or **False**.

In addition there are other attributes specific to specific types of modules, as described below.

Visibility and Lifetime of Variables and Subs

The "visibility" or "scope" of a variable determines from where the variable can be accessed. Their lifetime determines how long they endure.

There are two access modifiers which can change the visibility between modules of certain variables and subroutines: **Public** and **Private**.

Public Variables
Process_Globals variables in a module and **Sub Class_Globals** in a class module are public by default. **Public** means that the variable can be accessed from other modules as well as the one in which it is declared.
You can declare them with either :
```
Sub Process_Globals
  Dim intLocal As Int
  Public intGlobal As Int
End Sub
```
You can make them invisible to other modules by using the Private modifier (see below).
You might want to use **Public** instead of **Dim** if you have a mixture of public and private **Process_Globals** variables and want the difference to be clear to other programmers (or to yourself in later months).
Public variables are declared only once. They retain their value for the lifetime of the Process in which they are running.

Private Variables
Variables declared in **Process_Globals** are always **Private**, which means they are hidden from other modules.
```
Sub Globals
  Dim intThisIsPrivate As Int
End Sub
```

In addition, you can declare **Process_Globals** variables to be hidden from other modules by using the **Private** modifier:

```
Sub Process_Globals
  Private intPrivate As Int
End Sub
```

Variables within Other Subs

Variables declared in any Sub other than `Sub Process_Globals` or `Sub Globals` are visible only within the Sub in which they are declared. Hence they are even more restricted than Private variables.

```
Sub runMe
  Dim iTemporary As Int
End Sub
```

`iTemporary` is created when Sub runMe runs and is deleted when it ends.

Visibility of Subroutines

There are two different cases to consider:
- Subs within a class or a code module
- Subs within an activity or service module

Subs within a Class or Code Module

Subs within a class or code module are public by default. This means they can be called directly by calls such as `CodeModule.mySub` or `myClassInstance.mySub`
These subs can be called by any other type of module.

However, note that subs within a class or code module which are declared with the `Private` modifier, such as `myPrivateSub` below, can only be called from other subs within that module.

Example:

myClass module
```
' The following is public by default
Sub myPublicSub As Int
 Return 21
End Sub


' The following is private so cannot be called by any other module
private Sub myPrivateSub As Int
Return 22
End Sub
```

CodeModule
```
' The following is public by default
Sub myPublicSub
 If IsPaused(Main) = True Then
  Log ("Main is paused")
 Else
  Log ("Main is not paused")
  CallSub(Main, "runMe")
 End If
End Sub


' This cannot be called from outside this code module
private Sub myPrivateSub
 Msgbox("myPrivateSub is running", "Surprise")
End Sub
```

Activity Module
```
'create instance of myClass and call a public sub
Dim test As myClass
test.Initialize
Log(test.myPublicSub)
CodeModule.myPublicSub
```

Subs within Activity and Service Modules

Subs declared in Activity and Service modules are sometimes described as "private" because they **cannot** be called directly with calls such as:
```
Main.mySub ' This does not work!!!
```
Nevertheless subs within activity or service modules can be called by any other module using the CallSub (page 307) or CallSubDelayed (page 308) functions, provided the activity is not paused or the service has started:
```
Sub Activity_Create(FirstTime As Boolean)
 StartService(ServiceModule)
End Sub
'allow the service to start
Sub Button1_Click
 CallSub(ServiceModule, "Test")
End Sub
```
A sub in an activity cannot be called if the activity is paused. Test this as follows:

```
If IsPaused(Main) = False Then
 CallSub(Main, "mainRunMe")
End If
```

Note the CallSub (page 307) or CallSubDelayed (page 308) functions can be used to access both private and public subs in activity and service modules. Hence the **Private** modifier has no effect for these modules.

Activity Global Variables

Variables defined in **Sub Globals** of an activity module are always Private (visible only to subs within this activity).

All object types including views can be declared as Global variables. Example:

```
Sub Globals
 Dim EditText1 As EditText
 Dim strTest As String
 Dim intMaxRuns As Int = 20
End Sub
```

You can initialize primitive type globals here as shown for **intMaxRuns** above.

Global variables are created before **Activity_Resume** is run.

As soon as the activity is paused, Global variables are destroyed.

If the activity is resumed, these variables will be declared again.

See Activity Life Cycle (page 241) for details of when **Sub Globals** is run.

Views Must be Global

Views must be declared inside an activity's **Sub Globals**, not **Sub Process_Globals** nor within any other Sub. The reason is as follows. We do not want to hold a reference to objects that should be destroyed together with the activity. When the activity is paused, all of the views which are contained in the activity are destroyed. If we hold a reference to a view in a **Process_Globals** variable, the garbage collector would not be able to free the resource and we would have a memory leak. Therefore, the B4A compiler enforces this requirement! Likewise, views cannot be local variables (that is, within Subs other than **Sub Globals** or **Sub Process_Globals**) as such variables only endure while the Sub is running, whereas views endure while the activity exists.

Summary: views must be declared inside the **Sub Globals**.

Class_Globals

Variables declared in **Sub Class_Globals** of a class module are public by default, but can be hidden by using the **Private** modifier, as above.

Local variables in Subs

Variables that are declared inside a Sub (other than **Process_Globals** or **Globals**) are local to this subroutine. They are always private and can only be accessed from within the subroutine where they were declared. Once the sub ends, these variables no longer exist. All object types can be declared as local variables. At each call of the subroutine, the local variables are initialized to their default value or to any other value you have defined in the code and are destroyed when the subroutine ends.

Sub Process_Globals

Modules Containing Process_Globals

Activity, Code and Service Modules include `Sub Process_Globals`, all of which are executed once, when the application starts.

`Sub Process_Globals` contains declarations of variables which will be valid during the whole lifetime of the process (normally the same as the app).

```
Sub Process_Globals
  Dim lstHistory As List
End Sub
```

Note: a class module, on the other hand, can only contain global variables, declared in `Sub Class_Globals` (page 250).

Process_Globals Variables

Variables defined in `Sub Process_Globals` are public (page 234) by default, meaning they are accessible from every module in the program. To access them from the current module, you simply use their name:

```
lstHistory.Initialize
```

To access them from a different module, you must prefix the variable name with the name of the module and a period:

```
Main.lstHistory.Get(0)
```

You declare variables in `Process_Globals` and use them inside Subroutines.

You can hide them by using the `Private` (page 234) modifier:

```
Sub Process_Globals
  ' define a variable visible from any module
  Dim strThisIsAPublicVariable As String
  ' define a variable only visible in this module
  Private strThisIsAPrivateVariable As String
End Sub
```

Initialization of Process_Globals

You can also initialize primitive type (page 274) `Process_Globals` (such as integers) when you declare them:

```
Dim bFreeVersion As Boolean = True
```

It is recommended to initialize more complex types within `Sub Activity_Create` when the Activity first runs (check this using the `FirstTime` parameter).

Lifetimes of Process_Globals Variables

`Sub Process_Globals` is declared in all modules once when the process (page 232) starts. Variables declared inside `Sub Process_Globals` live as long as the process lives.

Process_Globals in Starter Service

Note that if you declare Process_Globals within an activity module, but want to access them within a service module, then your app will crash if the activity where they were declared has been closed in the meantime, either by the user or by the system.

To avoid this error, B4A includes a service called Starter (page 110), and it is recommended that you declare all Process_Globals there.

Restriction of Process_Globals Variables

Views (and Class or Type variables which include views) are not allowed within `Process_Globals`. The reason is that under certain circumstances, for example when a device is rotated, all views are destroyed and re-created. This would lead to a memory leak if they were declared within `Process_Globals`. For this reason they must be declared in `Sub Globals`.

If you declare a view in `Process_Globals`, you will see a warning in the Log:

```
Cannot access activity object from sub Process_Globals
```

If you try to run the app, the compiler will report the same error.

Rotating Device

If you need variables to retain their value when the user rotates the device, you should put the variables in `Process_Globals` and not in `Globals`. Because you cannot include views in `Process_Globals`, you would need to copy their data to a `Process_Globals` variable during `Activity_Pause` and then copy it back to the view during `Activity_Resume`. See Activity Life Cycle for details of when these Subs are run.

How to Access Process_Globals Variables

To access `Process_Globals` variables in other modules than the module where they were declared, their names must be prefixed by the name of the module where they were declared followed by a period. Example:

In MyModule
```
'declare the variable
Sub Process_Globals
 Dim MyVar As String
End Sub

...
'use the variable
MyVar = "Text"
```
In OtherModule
```
'use the variable
MyModule.MyVar = "Text"
```

Activity Module

The Activity Concept

A fundamental concept within most apps is the `Activity`. This normally corresponds to a page which is displayed to the user. It might have a Layout (created with the Designer) which determines the views (elements of the page) and their position, or they might be created in code and added to the activity. Your app can have multiple activities (page 127).

Activity Module

An Activity Module is where you write the code for an Activity. Every B4A app must have at least one `Activity` called Main, although it may have more.

If you want to add a new Activity in your app, you would use the menu [Project > Add New Module > Activity Module].

There is one Module for every Activity.

In order to call the second activity from the first, use `StartActivity(Activity2)`.

For details of an **Activity Module**'s events and members, see the Activity (page 337) reference section in the Core Views Chapter.

Activities have Attributes, two types of global variables (Process_Globals and Globals) and three special life-cycle related events: Activity_Create (page 243), Activity_Pause (page 245) and Activity_Resume (page 244).

Activity Attributes

You can set attributes which are valid for the current activity.

Note: Activity Attributes are normally placed within the Activity Attributes Region at the top of an **Activity Module**, as shown in the following example, but that this is purely a convenience. Attributes and can be placed anywhere in the code.

Note also that attributes also exist for the Project (page 111) and for Library compilation (page 454).

Defaults

By default, Attributes are set as follows:

```
#Region  Activity Attributes
  #FullScreen: False
  #IncludeTitle: True
#End Region
```

#FullScreen: Value

Whether to show the Status Bar (page 120) at the top of the screen. Values: `True` or `False`, default `False`. You should not hide the Status Bar unless absolutely necessary.

Note you should set the Visual Designer Activity Property (page 145) **Full Screen** to be the same as this if you want the Visual Designer to accurately show the screen size. But it is this attribute which actually controls whether the Status Bar is shown.

#IncludeTitle: Value

Whether to include a Title Bar (page 121) at the top of your app. Values: `True` or `False`. Default value `True`.

Note you should set the Visual Designer Activity Property (page 145) **Show Title** to be the same as this if you want the Visual Designer to accurately show the screen size. But it is this attribute which actually controls whether the Title is shown.

Other Activity Attributes

The following is also available:

#Extends: ClassOrActivity

Allows you to create activities that extend other classes or activities, usually in an imported SDK jar. Method of use:

```
#Extends: uk.co.mycompany.novelActivities.Activity
```

An example of its use is available here (http://bit.ly/1NbvBat).

Variables within an Activity

Variables can be either local or global. There are two types of globals: Process_Globals and Globals.

Sub Process_Globals

This sub contains variables which are visible from all modules and are valid during the entire lifetime of the app. See above (page 238) for details.

Sub Globals

This sub contains variables which are valid only during the lifetime of this activity and are accessible only to subs belonging to this activity.

We discuss the visibility of Globals variables here (page 237).

Local Variables

Local variables are variables that are declared inside a `Sub` other than `Process_Globals` or `Globals`. Local variables are local to the containing `Sub`. Once the `Sub` ends, these variables no longer exist.

Comparison of Process_Globals and Globals Variables

Process_Globals Variables retain their values when an activity is paused. This differentiates them from Sub Globals, which are destroyed when the activity is paused. Thus if you want to preserve variables, such as data that the user has entered, you might think it would be a good idea to copy the data from a Global to a Process Global when the activity is paused, and restore the data when it resumes. However note that you can never be sure whether the activity will be restored, so this might not be a good solution. A better one might be to store the data to permanent storage, and retrieve it if and when the app resumes. See Saving Data (page 245) below.

You cannot declare activity objects in sub Process_Globals, since activity objects are destroyed when the activity is paused, whereas Process_Globals endure for the lifetime of the app. Thus views and classes which contain views cannot be declared here.

When the device destroys the app, all Process_Global variables are lost.

Activity Life Cycle

Here we discuss which subs are run under various circumstances.

When the user first launches your app or brings it to the front after quitting

(Quitting could be by pressing the Back button or your app calling Activity.Finish.)

- If the user has not previously run your app, or if she has and the Process has been killed:
A new Process is created.

`Process_Globals` is run in all activities.

`Globals` is run.

`Activity_Create` is run with `FirstTime` parameter set to `True`.

`Activity_Resume` is run.

- If the user has previously run your app and the Process has not yet been killed:

`Process_Globals` is run in all activities.

`Globals` is run.

`Activity_Create` is run with `FirstTime` parameter set to `True`.

`Activity_Resume` is run.

When the user runs another app

`Activity_Pause` is run with the `UserClosed` parameter set to `False`.

(Android will determine when the Process ends.)

When the screen is turned off

`Activity_Pause` is run with the `UserClosed` parameter set to `False`.

When the screen is turned back on

`Activity_Resume` is run.

When the user clicks the Back button

`Activity_Pause` is run with the `UserClosed` parameter set to `True`.
(Android will determine when the Process ends.
The next time the app is run, `Process_Globals` will be run.)

When the user brings your app to front after running a different app

- If Android has not killed your app's Process:
`Globals` is run.
`Activity_Resume` is run.
- If Android has killed your app's Process:
`Process_Globals` is run.
`Globals` is run.
`Activity_Create` is run with `FirstTime` parameter set to `True`.
`Activity_Resume` is run.

When the user rotates the device

`Activity_Pause` is run with the `UserClosed` parameter set to `False`.
The screen takes on its new configuration.
`Globals` is run.
`Activity_Create` is run with `FirstTime` parameter set to `False`.
`Activity_Resume` is run.

When your app calls Activity.Finish

(You might have an Exit button which calls this.)
`Activity_Pause` is run with the `UserClosed` parameter set to `True`.
Android will determine when the Process ends.

When one activity opens another using StartActivity

First activity calls StartActivity(SecondActivity)
Sub in first activity finishes running.
First Activity calls `Activity_Pause` with the `UserClosed` parameter set to `False`.
Second activity runs `Process_Globals`.
Second activity runs `Globals`.
Second activity runs `Activity_Create`.
(`FirstTime` parameter is either `True` or `False` depending whether second activity has run before.)
Second activity runs `Activity_Resume`.

When second activity closes and first activity resumes

(For example if second activity calls `Activity.Finish`)
Second activity calls `Pause` with `UserClosed` set to `True`.
First activity runs `Resume`.

Activity Events

The Activity can respond to several user events, for example:

Touch (Action As Int, X As Float, Y As Float) Event

The Touch (page 338) event can be used to handle user touches.

Action: specifies the user's action. Its values can be:

- `Activity.ACTION_DOWN`: The user has touched the screen at **X,Y**.
- `Activity.ACTION_MOVE`: The user's touch has moved to **X,Y**.
- `Activity.ACTION_UP`: The user has stopped touching the screen at **X,Y**.

KeyPress and KeyUp

The KeyPress (page 338) and KeyUp (page 338) events occur when the user presses or releases a key on a physical keyboard attached to the device or on Android's-on-screen keyboard. **Note**: it is possible for a view (such as a `EditText`) to consume this event, in which case the Activity will not see it. When handling the **KeyPress** or **KeyUp** event, you should return a boolean value which tells whether the event has been consumed by your code. For example, if the user pressed on the Back key and you return **True** then Android will not see the back key and so will not close your activity.

```
Sub Activity_KeyPress (KeyCode As Int) As Boolean
  If Keycode = KeyCodes.KEYCODE_BACK Then
      Return True
  Else
      Return False
  End If
End Sub
```

For a complete list of Activity events, see here (page 338).

Sub Activity_Create (FirstTime As Boolean)

Sub Activity_Create is automatically called when the activity is created.
The activity is created when:
- the user first launches the application (in which case **FirstTime = True**).
- the device configuration has changed (user rotated the device) and the activity was destroyed (in which case **FirstTime = False**).
- the user re-launches the application (either through the recents list or clicking on the app launcher icon) after the operating system has destroyed it in order to free memory. In all these cases, **FirstTime = True**.
- one activity calls **StartActivity** and starts another activity.

Note that Activity_Create is **not** called when an activity, which has moved to the background, then returns to the foreground. Under these circumstances, only Activity_Resume is called.

The primary purpose of Activity_Create is to initialize activity variables and load or create the layout:

```
Sub Process_Globals
    Dim strUserData As String
End Sub
Sub Activity_Create(FirstTime As Boolean)
 Activity.LoadLayout("Main") ' Must be loaded every time
 If FirstTime Then
  LoadLstHistory
 End If
End Sub
```

FirstTime parameter

The `FirstTime` parameter tells the app if this is the first time that this activity has been created during the current process. If the user exits the app, or restarts the device, then the next time the app runs, `FirstTime` is reset to `True`. You can use `FirstTime` to initialize those variables or objects which must be initialized only once, such as process variables. For example, suppose you have a file with a list of values that you need to read. You can read the file if `FirstTime` is `True` and store the list as a process variable by declaring the list variable within `Process_Globals` so it will be available as long as the process lives. There will be no need to reload it when the activity is recreated.

Note that if a layout is used by this Activity then `LoadLayout` must be called every time that `Activity_Create` runs, not just when `FirstTime = True`. This regenerates all the views belonging to the layout, which are declared in Sub Globals.

To summarize, you can test whether `FirstTime` is `True` and then initialize the process variables that are declared in `Sub Process_Globals`.

Creating the Page

An Activity can either have a Layout which determines the views (elements of the page) and their position, or the views can be created in the code itself. You load a layout file with `LoadLayout`. You can add views to this activity with AddView (page 340), and remove them with RemoveViewAt (page 342).

Sub Activity_Resume

`Activity_Resume` is automatically called every time an activity is launched or re-activated. Two different circumstances need to be distinguished:

- When an app is started or the orientation of the device changes, `Activity_Resume` is called right after `Activity_Create` finishes.

- It is also called when a paused activity is restarted, typically when an activity which has moved to the background then returns to the foreground or when the screen which has gone into sleep mode is awoken. **Note** that in these circumstances, `Activity_Resume` runs but `Activity_Create` does not.

See Activity Life Cycle (page 241) for details.

Use `Activity_Resume` to restore any activity parameters which you stored when `Activity_Pause` was called.

Note: when you open a different activity (by calling StartActivity (page 324)), the current activity is first paused and then the other activity will be created if needed and (always) resumed.

Note also that `Activity_Resume` is called when the user rotates the device. Thus you might want `Activity_Resume` to check the screen dimensions, or you might have a Designer Script (page 162) to handle this.

Sub Activity_Pause (UserClosed As Boolean)

This Sub is called when the activity is going to be paused. Here you need to save any activity parameters which you want to recover when the activity is resumed.

When is Activity_Pause called?

`Activity_Pause` is called when one of the following happens:

– A different activity was started. Note that when you open a different activity (by calling StartActivity (page 324)), the current activity is first paused and then the other activity will run its own versions of `Activity_Create` and `Activity_Resume`.

– The Home button was pressed

– A configuration changed event was raised (device rotated for example). This is one of the most frequent reasons that `Activity_Pause` is called. In this case, the following subs are called:

```
Sub Activity_Pause (with UserClosed = False)
Sub Globals
Sub Activity_Create (with FirstTime set to False)
Sub Activity_Resume
```

– The Back button was pressed.

– Any time the Activity moves from the foreground to the background.

UserClosed parameter

The parameter `UserClosed` can be used to decide whether the Activity has been paused by the Operating System (for example by an orientation change) or by the user (for example by a back button click). The `UserClosed` parameter will be `True` either when the user clicks the Back button or when the program calls `Activity.Finish`. You can use the `UserClosed` parameter to decide which data to save and whether to reset any related process variables to their initial state, as we discuss next.

Saving Data

`Activity_Pause` is the last place to save important information before your activity is paused. Generally there are two types of mechanisms that allow you to save the activity state.

Saving Temporary Data

Information that is only relevant to the current run (for example the current orientation of the device) can be stored in one or more `Process_Globals` variables. Later, when Android calls your `Sub Activity_Resume`, you can restore this data. For example:

```
Sub Process_Globals
  ' These data are preserved while the app is in the background
  Dim strUserData As String
End Sub

Sub Activity_Pause (UserClosed As Boolean)
  ' save the user data
  strUserData = txtName.Text
End Sub

Sub Activity_Resume
  ' restore the user data
  txtName.Text = strUserData
End Sub
```

Saving Permanent Data

Information which you want to keep between one run of your app and the next, for example the user's settings, should be saved to **persistent storage** (a file or database).

Note that when the app pauses, you have no idea whether it will be restarted or killed, so be sure you keep any data you might want to use in future runs.

One way to store data to persistent storage is provided by the KeyValueStore (page 564) class. But you might prefer to use the StateManager (page 566) code module to save the current state as well as settings. For example, if the user has entered some text in an `EditText` view, then you might want to keep this text and restore it when the activity resumes.

StartActivity (Activity As Object)

`StartActivity` will start an `Activity` or bring it to front if it already exists. The `Activity` can be a string with the target activity name, or it can be the actual activity. An **Activity Module** with this name must exist.

Examples:

```
StartActivity(Activity2)
StartActivity("Activity2")
```

The target activity will be started once the program is free to process its message queue. After this call, the current activity will be paused and the target activity will be resumed. This method can also be used to send Intents (page 378) objects to the system.

Note: contrary to some documentation on the B4A website, it IS possible to call StartActivity from a Service.

Activity.Finish vs ExitApplication

There are two ways to end your app: `Activity.Finish` and `ExitApplication`.

Most applications should **not** use `ExitApplication` but prefer `Activity.Finish`, which lets Android decide when the process is killed. You should only use `ExitApplication` if you really need to fully kill the process. An interesting article about the functioning of Android can be found here: Multitasking the Android Way (http://bit.ly/1Vo0mgC).

Should we use `Activity.Finish` before starting another activity? Consider first the following example, which shows the flow of execution of code which does not use `Activity.Finish`:

Main activity
StartActivity(SecondActivity)
   SecondActivity activity
   StartActivity(ThirdActivity)
      ThirdActivity activity
      Click on Back button
      Android goes back to previous activity, SecondActivity
   SecondActivity activity
   Click on Back button
   Android goes back to previous activity, Main
Main activity
Click on Back button
Android leaves the program

Now consider following example, which calls `Activity.Finish` before each
`StartActivity`:
Main activity
Activity.Finish
StartActivity(SecondActivity)
   SecondActivity activity
   Activity.Finish
   StartActivity(ThirdActivity)
      ThirdActivity activity
      Click on Back button
      Android leaves the program

We should use `Activity.Finish` before starting another activity only if we don't want to go back to this activity with the Back button.

Creating a Menu

You can add menu items to the activity with Activity.AddMenuItem (page 339) method. The menu is shown if the user presses the Menu button (on older devices) or selects the overflow (page 123) symbol (3 vertical dots) on the Action Bar. **Note**: `AddMenuItem` should only be called inside the `Activity_Create` event.

Activities vs Windows Forms

Activities are similar to what are called Forms in Microsoft Visual Basic. One major difference is that, while an activity is not in the foreground, it can be killed in order to preserve memory. Usually, you will want to save the state of the activity before the data is lost. It can be stored either in persistent storage or in memory that is associated with the process. Later, this activity will be recreated when needed.
Another delicate point happens when there is a major configuration change in the device. The most common is an orientation change (the user rotates the device). When such a change occurs, the current activities are destroyed and then recreated by calling

`Activity_Create()`. Then it is possible to create the activity according to the new configuration (for example, the new screen dimensions).

Variables in other Activity Modules

If there are several Activity Modules in an application, they can access the `Process_Globals` variables in other modules using references such as

  `Main.Value2`

where Main is an activity name.

More Information

See Process and Activity (page 241) for more information about Activities and Processes Life Cycle.

Multiple Activity Modules

An app might need several different screens. Each one of these will (normally) require its own activity module. To access any object or variable in a module other than the module where they were declared, you must add the module name as a prefix to the object or variable name separated by a dot. For example, suppose variables Value1 and Value2 are declared in Main module in **Sub Process_Globals**:

```
Sub Process_Globals
  Dim Value1, Value2, Value3 As String
End Sub
```

To access these variables from another module, the variable name is Main.Value1 or Main.Value2.

```
Sub Activity_Pause (UserClosed As Boolean)
  Main.Value2 = edtValue2_P2.Text
End Sub
```

It is not possible to access any view from another activity module, because when a new activity is started, the current activity is paused and it is no longer accessible.

Class module

Note: A class module cannot be given the name "Class" as this causes a compiler error.

What is a Class?

A class represents an object such as a person, place or thing and encapsulates the data and functionality of that object. For example, a "Customer" class would represent your customers. A single, particular customer would be an **instance** of the "Customer" class, an object of the class "Customer".

A class contains **properties**, such as strForeName, which gives the state of a particular instance, and **methods**, such as AddOrder ( ), which allow the properties of an instance to be manipulated or queried.

Benefits of Classes

Writing code which focuses on the objects involved is called object-oriented programming. There are number of benefits to this style of coding:

– It provides a clear, modular structure, which makes it good for defining abstract datatypes where implementation details are hidden and the unit has a clearly defined interface.

– It simplifies code maintenance, as new objects can be created with small differences to existing ones.

– It delivers a framework for code libraries where supplied software components can be easily adapted and modified.

Example

We give here an example of a class module. (You can download the complete Classes example project here (http://bit.ly/1IjLiwC)). Consider a "Person" class. In the Main module we create in object of this class with

```
Dim Fred As Person
```

We want to store Fred's forename, last name and date of birth. We do this by calling Fred.Initialize and passing in the relevant details. A class object must always be initialized before you can use it.

We want to make it easy to change Fred's, so we make these values public. They could be accessed directly using code such as **Fred.LastName**

The date of birth, on the other hand, will be stored as a **Long** so we can do calculations on it, such as working out the current age. Therefore, this value must be private (hidden and accessed only through functions within the class. See Visibility of Variables (page 234) for details.

Here is the code:

```
'Class Person module
Sub Class_Globals
  Public FirstName, LastName As String
  Private BirthDate As Long
End Sub

Sub Initialize (strFirstName As String, strLastName As String,
strBirthDate As String)
  FirstName = strFirstName
  LastName = strLastName
  Try
    BirthDate = DateTime.DateParse(strBirthDate)
  Catch
    Msgbox (strBirthDate, "Invalid Date Format")
  End Try
End Sub

Public Sub GetName As String
  Return FirstName & " " & LastName
End Sub

Public Sub GetCurrentAge As Int
  Return GetAgeAt(DateTime.Now)
End Sub

Public Sub GetAgeAt(Date As Long) As Int
  Dim diff As Long
  diff = Date - BirthDate
  Return Floor(diff / DateTime.TicksPerDay / 365)
End Sub
```

Main module.

```
Sub Activity_Create(FirstTime As Boolean)
  Dim Fred As Person
  Fred.Initialize("Fred", "Smith", "1/2/1950")
  Log (Fred.GetName & " is aged " & Fred.GetCurrentAge)
  Fred.LastName = "Jones"
  Log (Fred.GetName & " is aged " & Fred.GetCurrentAge)
End Sub
```

The log shows
```
  Fred Smith is aged 63
  Fred Jones is aged 63
```

Sub Class_Globals

Public vs Private Variables

Public variables can be read and written to directly:

```
Fred.LastName = "Jones"
```
Private variables are hidden, and we must provide special functions to access them:
```
Fred.GetCurrentAge
```
We might do this because we want to store the data in a special format which the user would never want to access, for example storing the date of birth as a **Long**.

Public vs Private Subs
See Visibility of Subroutines (page 235) for details.

Classes vs Types
B4A allows you to declare simple data structures using the **Type** keyword, for example
```
Type Person( _
  LastName As String, FirstName As String, _
  Address As String, City As String _
  )
```
More details here (page 285).

What are the similaries and differences between a Class module and a Type?

– Both **classes** and **types** are templates. From these templates, you can instantiate any number of objects.

– **Type** fields are similar to the global variables of a **class**. However, unlike types which only define the data structure, classes also define the data's behavior. The behavior is defined in the class's subs.

– The fields of types are always public (page 234), while the fields of a class can be private.

Classes vs Code Modules
How does a class module compare with a code module (page 254)?

– A **code module** is a collection of subs, unlike a **class**, which is a template for an object.

– A **code module** always runs in the context of the calling sub (the activity or service that called the sub) and the code module doesn't hold a reference to any context. For that reason, it is impossible to handle events or use **CallSub** within code modules. A **class**, on the other hand, stores a reference to the context of the activity or service module that called the Initialize sub. This means that class objects share the same life cycle as the service or activity that initialized them.

– A **code module** has a Sub Process_Globals, which contains variables visible from all other modules. A class module, on the other hand, can only contain variables accessible from this module.

Adding a class module
Add a new or existing class module by choosing [Project > Add New Module > Class Module] or [Project > Add Existing Module]. Like other modules, classes are saved as files with a "bas" extension.

Class structures
Classes must have the following two subs:

Sub Class_Globals - This sub is similar to the activity Globals sub. These variables will be the class global variables (sometimes referred to as instance variables or instance members). They can either public or private. They are public by default.

`Sub Initialize` - A class object should be initialized before you can call any other sub. Initializing an object is done by calling the `Initialize` sub. When you call `Initialize`, you set the object's context (the parent activity or service).

Note that you can chose the arguments you need to instantiate an instance of your class. In the above code, we created a class named Person and later instantiated an object of this type:

```
Dim Fred As Person
Fred.Initialize("Fred", "Smith", "1/2/1950")
```

Note that `Initialize` is not required if you make a copy of an object which was already initialized:

```
Dim p2 As Person
p2 = Fred 'both variables now point to the same Person object.
Log(p2.GetCurrentAge)
```

Polymorphism

Polymorphism allows you to treat different classes of objects that adhere to the same interface in the same way. As an example, we will create two classes named: Square and Circle. Each class has a sub named Draw that draws the object on a canvas:

Class Square module

```
Sub Class_Globals
  Private mx, my, mLength As Int
End Sub


'Initializes the object. You can add parameters to this method if
needed.
Sub Initialize (x As Int, y As Int, length As Int)
  mx = x
  my = y
  mLength = length
End Sub


Sub Draw(c As Canvas)
  Dim r As Rect
  r.Initialize(mx, my, mx + mLength, my + mLength)
  c.DrawRect(r, Colors.White, False, 1dip)
End Sub
```

Class Circle module

```
Sub Class_Globals
  Private mx, my, mRadius As Int
End Sub


'Initializes the object. You can add parameters to this method if
needed.
Sub Initialize (x As Int, y As Int, radius As Int)
  mx = x
  my = y
  mRadius = radius
End Sub


Sub Draw(cvs As Canvas)
```

```
    cvs.DrawCircle(mx, my, mRadius, Colors.Yellow, False, 1dip)
  End Sub
```

In the main module

Create a list with Squares and Circles. We then go over the list and draw all the objects:

```
  Sub Process_Globals
  End Sub

  Sub Globals
   Dim shapes As List
   Dim cvs As Canvas
  End Sub

  Sub Activity_Create(FirstTime As Boolean)
   cvs.Initialize(Activity)
   Dim sq1, sq2 As Square
   Dim circle1 As Circle
   sq1.Initialize(100dip, 100dip, 50dip)
   sq2.Initialize(2dip, 2dip, 100dip)
   circle1.Initialize(50%x, 50%y, 100dip)
   ' add the items to the list
   shapes.Initialize
   shapes.Add(sq1)
   shapes.Add(sq2)
   shapes.Add(circle1)
   DrawAllShapes
  End Sub

  Sub DrawAllShapes
   For i = 0 To shapes.Size - 1
     Log(shapes.Get(i))
     CallSub2(shapes.Get(i), "Draw", cvs)
   Next
   Activity.Invalidate
  End Sub
```

We do not need to know the specific class of each object in the list. We know that it has a Draw method that expects a single Canvas argument. Later we can easily add more classes of shapes. You can use the **SubExists** keyword to check whether an object includes a specific sub. You can also use the **Is** keyword to check if an object is of a specific type.

Self reference

The **Me** keyword returns a reference to the current object. **Me** cannot be used inside a code module. Consider the above example. We could have passed the shapes list to the **Initialize** sub and then added each object to the list from the **Initialize** sub:

```
Sub Initialize (Shapes As List, x As Int, y As Int, radius As Int)
  mx = x
  my = y
  mRadius = radius
  Shapes.Add(Me)
End Sub
```

In that case, the calls from Main to Initialize would have been:

```
sql.Initialize(shapes, 100dip, 100dip, 50dip)
```

Classes and Activity Object

Android user interface elements, such as views, hold a reference to the parent activity. But, since Android is allowed to kill background activities in order to free memory, UI elements cannot be declared as `Sub Process_Globals` variables because these variables live as long as the process lives. They should be declared in `Sub Globals` instead. This is discussed further in the Process and Activity (page 241) chapter.

The same is true for instances of a class. If one or more of the class global variables is a view (or any activity object type), then the class will be treated as an "activity object", meaning that instances of this class cannot be declared as `Sub Process_Globals` variables.

Activities that Extend Classes

You can use the #Extends (page 240) attribute to change the parent class of an Activity.

Limitations of Classes

B4A's implementation of classes is only partial. For example, it does not support inheritance, overriding or overloading.

Classes which contain views cannot be declared in sub Process_Globals of an Activity, because Process_Globals endure for the lifetime of the app so you cannot declare activity objects (such as views), here.

Code module

Code modules contain only code. No Activity is allowed in Code modules. The purpose and advantage of code modules is that they allow the same code to be shared in different programs, mainly for calculations or other general management.

Examples of code modules are:

DBUtils (page 219), database management utilities.

StateManager (page 566), helps managing Android application settings and states.

Service Module

Within Android, code written in an activity module is paused once the activity is not visible. So, by only using activities, it is not possible to run any code while your application is not visible. A service, on the other hand, is (almost) unaffected by the currently visible activity. This allows you to run tasks in the background.

Why use a Service

If you want to run code when your app is not visible, you need to use a service. Activity modules are paused when they are not visible, so it is not possible to run any code while your

application is not visible if you only use activities. A service is almost unaffected by the currently visible activity. This allows you to run tasks in the background.
If you want to create a widget (page 130), it must be tied to a service module.

Services usually use status bar notifications (page 389) to interact with the user. They do not have any other visible elements. Services cannot show any dialog (except toast messages (page 326)).
Note: when an error occurs in a service code module, you will not see the "Do you want to continue?" dialog. Android's regular "Process has crashed" message will appear instead.

Alternative to an Activity

Because a service is never paused or resumed, and because services are not re-created when the user rotates the screen, services are often easier to code than activities. There is nothing special about the code written in a service.
Code in a service module runs in the same process and the same thread as all other code.

Android's View of Services

For more about how Android sees services, see here (http://bit.ly/1CMP3sx).

How to Start a Service

Call StartService (page 324) during `Activity_Create`. This will run `Sub Service_Create` followed by `Sub Service_Start` (see below).
You can then use the service's code.

Service Code

Adding a service module is done using the menu [Project > Add New Module > Service Module].
This creates a new service with the skeleton code:

```
#Region  Service Attributes
 #StartAtBoot: False
#End Region

Sub Process_Globals
 'These global variables will be declared once when the application starts.
 'These variables can be accessed from all modules.
End Sub

Sub Service_Create
End Sub

Sub Service_Start (StartingIntent As Intent)
End Sub

Sub Service_Destroy
End Sub
```

You can also schedule a service to run at a specific time by calling StartServiceAt (page 325) or StartServiceAtExact (page 325).

Service Attributes

These are defined in the #Region at the top of the code.

The possible options are:

#StartAtBoot: Whether this service should start automatically after boot. Values: **True** or **False**. Defaults to **False**.

#StartCommandReturnValue: (advanced) Sets the value that will be returned from onStartCommand. The default value is android.app.Service.START_NOT_STICKY. For details, see Android's view of services (http://bit.ly/1CMP3sx).

SubRoutines

Every service module must include at least the following subs:

Sub Process_Globals

The place to declare the service global variables. Unlike an Activity, there is no Globals sub as Services do not support Activity objects. **Sub Process_Globals** should only be used to declare variables. It should not run any other code as it might fail. This is true for other modules as well. **Note**: Process_Globals variables are kept as long as the process runs and are accessible from other modules.

Sub Service_Create

This is called when the service is first started. This is the place to initialize and set the **Sub Process_Globals** variables. Once a service is started, it stays alive until you call **StopService**, or until the whole process is destroyed.

Sub Service_Start (StartingIntent As Intent)

This is called **each time** you call StartService (page 324) (or StartServiceAt (page 325) or StartServiceAtExact (page 325)). It can also be called if this service is a broadcast receiver. For more on this, see here (http://bit.ly/12QWZBw). When this sub runs, the process is moved to the foreground state, which means that Android will not kill your process until this sub finishes running. If you want to run some code periodically, you should schedule the next task with StartServiceAt (page 325) or StartServiceAtExact (page 325) inside this sub.

StartingIntent: The argument will be set by Android if this service is a broadcast receiver. For more information, see this page (http://bit.ly/12QWZBw) on the B4A website. See here (page 378) for more on **Intent**s.

Sub Service_Destroy

This is called when you call StopService. The service will not be running until you call StartService again.

When to Use a Service

There are probably four main use-cases for services:

1) Separating the user interface (UI) code from logical code.

Writing the non-UI code in a service is easier than implementing it inside an Activity module as the service is not paused and resumed and it will usually not be recreated (whereas an Activity can be).

You can call StartService (page 324) during **Activity_Create** and from then-on work with the service module.

A good design is to make the activity fetch the required data from the service in Sub `Activity_Resume`. The activity can fetch data stored in a `Sub Process_Globals` variable or it can call a service Sub with the `CallSub` method.

2) Running a long operation.

For example, downloading a large file from the internet. In this case you can call `Service.StartForeground` (from the service module). This will move your service to the foreground state and will make sure that Android doesn't kill it. Make sure to eventually call `Service.StopForeground`.

3) Scheduling a repeating task.

By calling StartServiceAt (page 325) or StartServiceAtExact (page 325) you can schedule your service to run at a specific time. You can call these methods in `Sub Service_Start` to schedule the next time and create a repeating task (for example, a task that checks for updates every couple of minutes).

4) Run a service after the device boots, that is, when it powers up.

Your service will run after boot is completed if you set:

```
#Region   Service Attributes
  #StartAtBoot: True
#End Region
```

Notifications

Both activities and services can display status bar notifications, but for services it is their main way of interacting with the user.

The notification displays an icon in the status bar.

The user can swipe down the notifications screen and see more details.

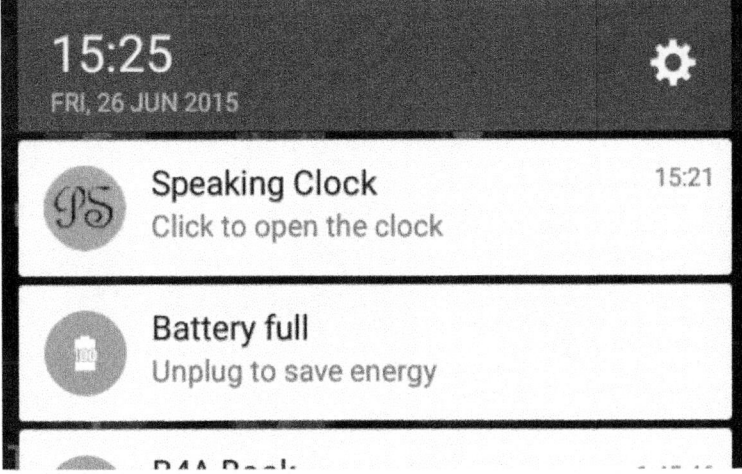

The user can press on the message, which will open an activity as configured by the Notification object (page 389).

Accessing other modules

`Sub Process_Globals` objects are public and can be accessed from other modules. Using the `CallSub` method you can also call a sub in a different module, provided the other module is not paused. You can use `IsPaused` to check if the target module is paused.

This means that one activity can never access a sub of a different activity as there could only be one running activity. However, an activity can access a running service and a service can access a running activity. **Note**: if the target component is paused, then an empty string is returned. No exception is thrown. For example, suppose a service has finished downloading some new information. It can call:

```
CallSub(Main, "RefreshData")
```

If the Main activity is running, it can fetch the data from the service `Process_Globals` variables and update the display. It is also possible to pass the new information to the activity sub, but it is better to keep the information as a `Process_Globals` variable. This allows the activity to call the required sub (in this case RefreshData) whenever it wants and fetch the information (as the activity might be paused when the new information arrived). **Note**: it is NOT possible to use `CallSub` to access subs of a Code module.

Sample Projects Using Services

Examples of projects using services are available from the B4A website:
Downloading a file using a service module (http://bit.ly/17yeXPZ)
Periodically checking Twitter feeds (http://bit.ly/17yfyRP)

2.10 Publishing and Monetizing Your App

Once you have developed your app, you will want to distribute it. This can be done either through the Google Play website or one of the other distribution channels such as Amazon, or by distributing the APK file from a website or via email.

This chapter will take you through the whole process of preparing your app for publication, including ways to make money from it, then sending it out into the world.

User Help

Users will probably need help about how to use your app most effectively. You can provide some information in a splash screen (http://bit.ly/13WB1xW), in an activity or on a web page which you display in a WebView (page 445).

Branding and Marketing

Before you begin to distribute your app, you will need to think about what to call it, whether it needs its own website, and if so, whether the domain name is available, the design of your logo, whether you need to register the trademark, and how you are going to advertise and market the product. To do all these things effectively requires a different set of skills from development, and you might want to find a partner who can spend time on these important aspects of app distribution.

Setting Your Project Parameters

Before generating the APK, you should check that the following parameters are set correctly:

Package Name
This is set in [Project > Build Configurations]. See Package Name (page 114) for what is required.

Project Attributes
A number of attributes should be set in the Project Attributes Region at the top of the Main Activity. See here (page 111) for details.

Setting Icons

Your app will need a number of icons before it can be distributed. There are several sorts of icons you might consider: launcher, menu, action bar, status bar, tab, dialog and list view icons are all possible. Your app may also need to display icons in the Notification Area (page 389). We discuss some of these below. For more details, see here (http://bit.ly/1CMQc3a). See here for Launcher Icon tips (http://bit.ly/1DSoPic) and a wider view of Android Icons.

Google Play Store Icon
For the Google Play Store you will need an icon 512x512 pixels, 32-bit PNG with an alpha channel and maximum size of 1024KB (more details here (http://bit.ly/1GjjK4Q)).

Launcher Icon

Every app needs a Launcher Icon so the user can identify and run it.
This icon will be shown in several places on the user's device:
– on the installation panel
– in the Title Bar (for later versions of Android)
– on the Home page
– in the [Settings > Apps] list
The Launcher Icon should have a distinctive silhouette, should look three-dimensional as if
seen from the front, with a slight perspective as if viewed from above so that users perceive
some depth.

The Launcher icon always shows as 48x48 dip (page 163), but when translated into pixels on
screens with different resolutions, this can become 48, 72, 96, 144 or even 192 pixels square.
You should ideally provide versions of your icon in all these sizes, distributed in folders
whose names include the word **mipmap**. Luckily this is easy to do using the on-line Launcher
Icon Generator (http://bit.ly/1CH1rZM). This not only generates the images but puts them
into the correct folders.
When your app runs, Android can then check the characteristics of the device screen and
load the appropriate density-specific assets for your app.
You might decide that it would be easier to simply create a single icon at a high resolution,
such as 192 pixels, which the device will then scale down. This works for displaying a simple
logo, but there can be circumstances when Android might extract a part of your logo and
display that, creating an unprofessional impression.

Is it worth the effort using mipmap? You can test out the result of using a fixed launcher icon
using 48x48 or 192x192 pixels on various devices and compare that with the result of using
mipmap by using the three sample apps included on this book's resources page
(http://bit.ly/1IjLiwC).
As we describe below, it is very easy to implement mipmap, but in case you decide to just use
a single icon, we will discuss this first, then explain how to implement mipmap later.

[Project > Choose Icon]

If you decide just to use a single logo, you can set the Launcher Icon with the menu [Project >
Choose Icon]. You can navigate to any folder and choose any file with an extension of BMP,
JPG, GIF or PNG. The file will be copied into the project's **Objects\res\drawable** folder and
automatically renamed to icon.xxx, where xxx is the original filename extension. Android
will search for a file with this name to use for the Launcher, therefore you should not rename
it once it has been copied, although you can select a new Launcher Icon at any time.
The location of this file is actually specified in the Manifest:

```
SetApplicationAttribute(android:icon, "@drawable/icon")
```

You will not need to change this if you use the [Project > Choose Icon] option.

Action Bar Icons

You can show icons on the Action Bar (page 121). Each one should be 32 dip. Google provides
a downloadable Action Bar Icon Pack (http://bit.ly/1g0MCZ9).

Creating Icons

An icon is a file in BMP, JPG, GIF or PNG format.

You can create a PNG file using the free Inkscape program (http://inkscape.org/). This allows you to control the opacity (alpha channel) of your image, which is important in achieving a good result, as explained here (http://bit.ly/1DSoPic).

Tip: Use filenames which contain only lower case letters, numbers and underscores so when you export the image to PNG, it's name will be acceptable to B4A.

Because of the various sized icons you will need to generate, it is recommended you start your icon artwork with a resolution of 864x864 pixels, then scale it down to suit the various required sizes.

Sources of Icons

You can find some ready-made icons at iconarchive.com (http://bit.ly/1IjPGMi)

Implementing MipMap

MipMap is very easy to implement. If you decide to implement mipmap, you do not need to use [Project > Choose Icon]. Instead, you need to generate a master image for your icon. Since you will also need an image 512x512 pixels in 32-bit PNG format for Google Play, you might decide to start your artwork in that size and then resize it to produce the smaller format images. But it might be better to start with an image of 864x864 pixels, which can be accurately be downsized to all the sizes needed by mipmap.

You can convert your icon to images with sizes of 48, 72, 96, 144 and 192 pixels square ready for mipmap using the on-line Launcher Icon Generator (http://bit.ly/1CH1rZM). This will also create a folder called \res containing other folders called \mipmap-hdpi, \mipmap-mdpi and so on.

Each of these folders contains an image with the same name but with different sizes. They can have any name, but the commonest name is ic_launcher.png

You need to copy these folders to your project's Objects\res folder, so you have \Objects\res\mipmap-hdpi etc. Once copied, you must set these folders and files to be read only by selecting all the folders, right-clicking and selecting Properties from the pop-up menu, then checking the Read-only option. Or, if you frequently edit your icons, you could use the #CustomBuildAction attribute to mark them all as read-only. To mark all files under the **res** folder as read-only:

```
#CustomBuildAction: 1, c:\windows\system32\attrib.exe, +r res\*.* /s
```

The final step is to let Android know where to look for your icons by editing the Manifest. Edit the line

```
SetApplicationAttribute(android:icon, "@drawable/icon")
```

and change it to

```
SetApplicationAttribute(android:icon, "@mipmap/ic_launcher")
```

Where the word `ic_launcher` matches the names of your icons. You do not need to specify the file extension.

Notification Icon Recommendations

Notification icons are shown in the notification area at the top of the screen. They must be 24x24 dip.

The table below converts this into pixels for various screen resolutions.

You can specify which icon to use using the notification Icon (page 390) property.

Icon Sizes

Provide icons for use within your app in all prescribed sizes to make sure it looks good at all resolutions. Otherwise, Android can downsize large images, but that may result in jagged edges. More information here (http://bit.ly/1MzwvvE). Also, if you use large icons, they might be trimmed instead of resized when shown in the notifications pull-down list, resulting in inappropriate images. However, if for some reason you can only provide a single icon, 48x48 pixels is the best size to use. It looks passable on most devices.

Prescribed Resolutions

There are several prescribed resolutions, and each have their own recommended icon sizes, as shown below. **Note**: "**px**" means pixels. The baseline is MDPI. Icons for devices with lower resolution will be automatically generated from this. The significance of Folder is explained above.

MDPI

dpi.. 160
Scale....................................... 1
Notification Drawable (px)............. 22x22
Notification Icon Size (px)............. 24x24
Launcher Icon Size (px)..................48x48
Folder... drawable-mdpi

HDPI

dpi.. 240
Scale....................................... 1.5
Notification Drawable (px)............. 33x33
Notification Icon Size (px)............. 36x36
Launcher Icon Size (px)................. 72x72
Folder... drawable-hdpi

XHDPI

dpi.. 320
Scale....................................... 2
Notification Drawable (px)............. 44x44
Notification Icon Size (px)............. 48x48
Launcher Icon Size (px)................. 96x96
Folder... drawable-xhdpi

XXHDPI

dpi.. 480
Scale....................................... 3
Notification Drawable (px)............. 66x66
Notification Icon Size (px)............. 72x72
Launcher Icon Size (px)................. 144x144
Folder... drawable-xxhdpi

XXXHDPI

dpi.. 640
Scale....................................... 4
Notification Drawable (px)............. 88x88
Notification Icon Size (px)............. 96x96

Launcher Icon Size (px)................. 192x192
Folder.. drawable-xxxhdpi

Installing Icons

See the section Implementing MipMap above for details on how to install your icons.

Generating Your APK

Now you are ready to create your APK.

APK File

The APK is a package which contains the compiled source code and the assets files. The apk is placed in the Objects folder.

Note that the name of the apk will be the same as the name of the b4a file unless the b4a file name contains spaces, in which case the apk will be called **result.apk**

Keys and Certificates

Electronic documents (such as APKs) can be "signed" using other electronic documents called Certificates. Certificates contain the identity of the owner and a key. Certificates occur in pairs, one containing a private key, the other a public key. Some certificates are issued by certificate authorities, who authenticate the owner's identity. Other certificates are simply generated by the owner, without any authentication.

Signing

Android requires that all installed apps **must be signed** before they can be installed. Details from the Android Developer website (http://bit.ly/1CMQUNW). Android devices will not install an unsigned APK. The Android system uses certificates as a means of identifying the author of an application and establishing trust relationships between applications. The certificate is not used to control which applications the user can install.

The developer signs his app using the private key and then distributes it along with the certificate containing the public key. After an app is signed, it is not possible to modify it without the private key that was used to sign it.

Important note: Do not use the B4A key to sign your app. Google Play will not accept it. Instead, follow the instructions below for creating and using your own key.

Debugging Certificates

To test and debug your app, B4A signs it with a special debug key that is created by the Android SDK build tools. B4A uses a default "debug key" to sign apps. This key is fine during debugging. However, Google Play doesn't accept APK files signed with this key.

For an app called "abc", the debug key would be stored in a file called **abc_DEBUG.apk** in the **Objects** folder of the **abc** project.

During testing, installation will fail if you try to install the release version of your app on a device where you previously installed a debug version using B4A's own key. In that case you will need to manually uninstall the existing application from the device before you can install with your own key.

Signing for Distribution

An Android certificate does not need to be signed by a certificate authority; it is perfectly allowable, and typical, for Android applications to use self-signed certificates, but before you can distribute your app, you must sign it with a certificate whose private key you hold. Also, it is very important that you keep this certificate safe. See below.

Creating or Loading a Private Key

You therefore need to create your own private key. B4A makes it easy to create such a key. Select [Tools > Private Sign Key] to see the following dialog:

A Private Sign Key		✕
First and last name:	Unknown	⦿ Create new key
Organization:	Unknown	◯ Load existing key
Country (two letters):	Unknown	
Password (at least 6 characters):		
File:		Save As
Signature (read-only):	Create or load a key and reopen this dialog to see the signatures.	
	Use debug key Cancel Ok	

You can create a new key, load an existing one or use the debug key.

Creating a New Key

If you create a new key, you need to include your two-letter Country Code. There is a list of codes here (http://bit.ly/1CMQYgH). See below for more about keystores.

The private key which B4A generates will have an expiry date set to the maximum allowed by the certificate system, a date about 38 years in the future. B4A uses the DSA 1024 algorithm to generate keys.

The KeyStore

Keys are stored in a "keystore" file. You can store the key in any file with any name you wish. It might be a good idea to give it the extension "keystore" so you will know what it is. It is not possible to read such a file without its password, so **make sure you can remember the password**.

Once you have created a new keystore file, B4A will use this key for all your projects. **You should be very careful with this file. If you lose this file, you will not be able to update your applications in the market. You will need to publish updates as new applications.** Therefore, it is recommended to backup this file.

Note: while it is possible to have several keystores, it then becomes difficult to keep track of which key is in which keystore. It is probably best to use a single key in a single keystore to sign all your apps. However, problems might arise if you wish to sell your app to another developer in the future, as you would then need to give them a copy of your keystore and its password.

After signing, you can continue to debug. Your private key will then be used to sign the APK. If you wish, you can revert to using a debug key, but there is no need.

Keystore Explorer

If you need to, Keystore Explorer allows you to explore your keystore. Download it free here (http://bit.ly/1IjPP2m). Note the first time you run it you will probably need to upgrade your Java SE with the Java Cryptography Extension (JCE) Unlimited Strength Jurisdiction Policy Files 8 Download. In order to do this, we advise that you run Keystore Explorer the first time as an Administrator, to give you the required permissions.

Compiling the APK

Compile your app, either in Release Mode or Release Obfuscated Mode. See the Compilation Modes (page 172) section for details.

This will create an APK file in the Objects folder of your project.

SHA1 Certificate Fingerprint

Sometimes you need to know the SHA1 fingerprint of your certificate. For example, if you wish to use one of the Google APIs within your app. For details see here (http://bit.ly/1CMRdZa).

In order to find the SHA1 fingerprint, you should open your keystore file with Keystore Explorer (see above), double click on the certificate or right-click the certificate and select [View Details > Certificate Chain Details]. The certificate chain details include the fingerprint, which can be viewed in various formats including SHA-1. Copy the string, which looks like:

45:B5:E4:6F:36:AD:0A:98:94:B4:02:66:2B:12:17:F2:56:26:A0:E0

In order to create the Google API key you need to also state the package name of your app, which comes from the [Project > Build Configurations]. You should add this to the fingerprint, separated by a semi-colon.

Monetising Your App

Before you publish your app, you need to consider whether you are going to try to make money from it. If not then you can skip this section.

Ways of Monetizing Your App

There are a number of ways you can earn money from your app:
- Give your app away but include advertisements
- Sell it, perhaps as an add-free alternative
- Ask for donations if people find your app useful
- Use in-app billing
- Verify the user is licensed to use the app
- Find a sponsor and link your app to their site
- Write an app for a client and sell your time
- Use the PayPal library (page 565)

Libraries Supporting Advertising

There are several B4A libraries which allow you to easily include advertisements in your app. Some are official libraries (that is, produced by Anywhere Software) but are not included in the core distribution, so they require the library (or wrapper) to be downloaded. Others are developed by users. Mobile advertising is a fast-developing and profitable field, so the following may not include the latest developments or opportunities.

Note that advertisements take up space on the device's display, so you need to consider the implications when designing the user interface.

AdMob

Google is perhaps the best-known source of advertising. Use the AdMob library to display Google ads in your applications. This has the benefit that you can also use Google Analytics to analyse your results. Note this library requires resources which are part of Google Play services.

Library and Tutorial

Download the AdMob library here (http://bit.ly/19UeAy4). This library also requires configuration. Of course, in order to get your ads and get paid, you will need to register with Google's Admob site. See here (http://bit.ly/19UeDcY) for a tutorial with all the details.

AdBuddiz

This site (http://bit.ly/1CMTrHR) provides a B4A library which delivers full-page interstitial ads. See here (http://bit.ly/1CMTmDW) for a discussion of using it in a B4A app.

AdiQuity

AdiQuity is another advertisement solution. See here (http://bit.ly/1CMRXgN) for details of Adiquity and see here (http://bit.ly/19UgZbZ) for the library and a tutorial.

TapForTap

Tap for Tap offers a way to promote your app and a way of generating ad revenue, or perhaps to do both. When users "tap" on a link in your app and install an app advertised on the tap exchange, you can either earn credits (and hence have your app advertised) or you can make money; or you can choose a mix of these options.

For more information about the service, see here (https://tapfortap.com/). See here (http://bit.ly/14Lhsrc) for the B4A wrapper around the SDK.

AppLovin

This site (http://bit.ly/1OwfbJh) provides ads which take advertisers' existing customer data and uses targeted mobile ads to find similar consumers. Also, a customer who bought a dress in your app might then see ads promoting a deal on matching shoes.

See here (http://bit.ly/1CMSyPG) for an B4A library which supports this service.

Selling Your App

Google Play (http://bit.ly/1OwfeVp) is the main place users go to find new apps, although you can distribute your app through other channels. If you charge for your app, then the distributor will charge you a transaction fee.

Note: once you publish an app as free on Google Play, you can't change it to a paid app later. However you can sell a license within your app via in-app billing.

In-App Billing

Google Play provides an in-app billing service which you can use to accept payments from within your app. You define your products (using Google Play Developer Console) including product type, SKU, price, description, and so on. This could include a key which removes advertisements.

In-app products, which are declared in the Google Play Developer Console, can include licenses, subscriptions and managed items which your app can consume. You would typically implement consumption for items that can be purchased multiple times (such as in-game currency, fuel, or magic spells). Once purchased, a managed item cannot be purchased again until you consume the item, by sending a consumption request to Google Play. Read the official documentation here (http://bit.ly/1GyiGIy). Get the library here (http://bit.ly/19UimHB) and read the tutorial here (http://bit.ly/19UidUJ).

Licensing

A good way to protect your app is to use Google Play App Licensing, a service that lets you enforce licensing policies for applications that you publish on Google Play. Your app can query Google Play at run time to obtain the licensing status for the current user, then allow or disallow further use as appropriate. This way you can be sure that the user has the right to use your app. For more information about licensing, see here (http://bit.ly/14Li2VV). To download the library see here (http://bit.ly/14LiaF2). For a tutorial on how to use it, follow this link (http://bit.ly/14LikMx).

Registering as a Google Play Developer

Whether you want to sell your app or give it away, the best outlet for Android Apps is the Google Play store, and before you can publish there, you must register as a Developer. This has a one-time registration fee of $25. Any number of apps can be distributed once you have registered.

Register as a Google Play Developer

You will need a Google account. Log in and go to the Google Play Developer sign-up page (http://bit.ly/1Iheh4n).

Review and agree to the Google Play Developer distribution agreement (http://bit.ly/1VorOe9). This includes important information about user privacy and legal rights.

Review the distribution countries where you can distribute and sell applications to ensure you can sell into your target markets.

Check if you can have a merchant account in your country.

Pay your one-time registration fee of $25. You will need a credit card if you have not already registered one with Google Wallet (http://bit.ly/1Owfofy).

Merchant Account

If you are planning to sell apps or in-app products, you will need a Merchant Account. Before you register as a developer, you need to check if you can have a merchant account in your country. If you have a Google Wallet (http://bit.ly/1Owfofy), this will automatically be used as your merchant account.

Prepare Your App's Google Play Page

You must upload at least two screenshots of your app in approved formats, and a large 512 x 512-pixel icon for your app, as well as listing details.

It's worth spending some time on these details, since they'll represent the entirety of your "shopfront" in Google Play.

User Support

Before you begin selling your app (or even distributing it free), consider how you are going to support your users. On Google Play for example, you will be solely responsible for support and maintenance of your products and any complaints about them. Your contact information will be displayed in each application detail page and made available to users for customer support purposes. You need to respond to these complaints quickly, otherwise your ratings will go down.

Google Play Developer Console

For information on how to use the Google Play Developer Console to upload and manage your app, see this page (http://bit.ly/1OjzGYO).

Upload your App to Google Play

You will need to choose a title and decide whether to just upload the APK or prepare a store listing. An app you upload is a draft until you publish it, at which time Google Play makes your store listing page and app available to users. You can unpublish the app at any time.

Distributing Apps elsewhere

There are several other ways to distribute your app in addition to Google Play.

Preparing the User's Device

If they obtain the app from anywhere other than Google Play, users will need to allow their device to run it by selecting

either: [Settings > Applications > Unknown sources]

or: [Settings > Security > Unknown sources]

(This might frighten some users!)

Amazon Appstore

The Amazon Mobile App Distribution Program enables developers to make their apps available for sale on any Android device running Android 2.2 and higher. This costs $99 per year, although the first year may be free. Details here (http://amzn.to/1RM6UWW). Full terms and conditions here (http://amzn.to/1MEYUAw).

To install your app, users need to install an app called "Appstore for Android". It is pre-installed on Kindle Fire devices or can be downloaded from the Amazon website to other Android devices. The sites are here (http://amzn.to/1Sz3SQT) or here (http://amzn.to/1CMXbsO).

By Email

If you attach your app to an email, when a user running Gmail on Android 4 tries to download the attachment, they will be asked whether they want to install it.

Downloading from a website

If you upload your app to a web-server, then you can publish a link to your app on any web page. If a user clicks the link, it will be saved by their browser, then their device will show a notification (in the status bar at the top of the screen) which they can tap to install the app.

Other App Publishers

Other places you might want to consider publishing your app include the following. You will have to pay to advertise on some of these. In addition users might be wary of downloading APKs because of security worries.

The appearance of sites in this list is NOT meant as an endorsement of these sites:

android.brothersoft.com (http://bit.ly/1Owftjc)

appszoom.com/android (http://bit.ly/1OwfzaJ)

androidfreedownload.net (http://bit.ly/1OwfAvb)

androidfreeware.net (http://bit.ly/1OwfDr2)

appsapk.com (http://bit.ly/1OwfKD0)

freewarelovers.com (http://bit.ly/1OwfMdO)

mobogenie.com (http://bit.ly/1OwgrMA)

softonic.com (http://bit.ly/1OwgwQb)

2.11 Getting More Help

Anywhere Software

The producers of B4A provide an excellent level of service, usually answering queries very rapidly via the Forum (see below).

The on-line documentation for B4A is available here (http://bit.ly/1CMZ6xz).

Forum

The main place to find help and support is here (http://bit.ly/1CMZ9JU).

There is a lively on-line community of enthusiastic B4A developers who not only contribute their own Additional Libraries (page 562), but also support other users by answering questions. This is one of the reasons that B4A is such a valuable development tool.

Here you can find information on updates, get answers to questions and, if you have bought a copy of B4A, download the Additional Libraries.

Chat Room

You can chat live with other B4A enthusiasts and get help and support. Follow this link (http://bit.ly/1JQSFMC) to find it.

When you see the sign-on screen...

B4A Chat

Username:

Password*:

Channel:
B4Achat ▾

Language:
English ▾

Login

* Registered Users

AJAX Chat © blueimp.net

...simply enter a Username. You can enter without a password.

The busiest times are between 17:00 and 00:00 GMT. To convert 17:00 GMT to your local time, you could use this website (http://bit.ly/1edIaoa).

Video Tutorials

Andy McAdam has published several tutorials on YouTube (http://bit.ly/1edIeUG). Erel Uziel has also put some videos on YouTube (http://bit.ly/15IGy13).

On-Line Tutorials

The B4A website includes many tutorials covering many aspects of developing apps and using the IDE. See here (http://bit.ly/1edIkfd) for a list. Andy McAdam is a developer who is so keen to help others to use B4A that he has created a website (http://bit.ly/1edIoLQ) containing tutorials.

Twitter

B4A has a Twitter (http://bit.ly/1edIwuJ) account @Basic4Android.

Linked In

There is a small LinkedIn group called Basic4Android Developers.

On-line Documentation

The main on-line source for documentation is here (http://bit.ly/1CMZ6xz).

PDF Guides

Although most of the material is covered in this book, you might want to refer to the valuable assistance with using B4A which can be found in the following two guides, written by Klaus Christl: his Beginner's Guide, whose zip file (http://bit.ly/1RMaYXn) includes many example programs and a pdf with tutorials; and the User's Guide (http://bit.ly/1GynRZ3), which explains advanced features and also includes example programs and accompanying files.

Library Browsers

The XML files that describe a library to B4A contain descriptions of object members and sometimes an overall description of the library itself and of each object within the library. This information is shown in the on-line help but is not accessible in the IDE. There are two programs you can download to your PC which will browse through the library XML files:

B4a Object Browser

Vader has produced the B4A Object Browser (http://bit.ly/12RRrcI) (also called the DocLoader Help Documentation) which allows you to browse the help information contained in the XML files in your B4A installation library, similar to the Visual Studio Object Browser. It requires .NET Framework 3.5 and B4A to be installed on your PC.

B4AHelp

B4AHelp is another XML browser program written by Andrew Graham (agraham) which shows this help information. It can be downloaded here (http://bit.ly/13uEAxN).

Part 3: Language and Core Objects

Part 3 includes reference material which cover every part of B4A's language and core objects (that is, objects accessible from every app).

We also compare B4A's language with Microsoft's Visual Basic, and discuss the way to embed Java directly within your BASIC code.

3.1 B4A's Language

BASIC

B4A is a dialect of BASIC (Beginner's All-purpose Symbolic Instruction Code), a family of high-level programming languages designed to be easy to use. Created in 1964 at a time when writing programs was still technically difficult, BASIC was designed to be easy to use and became widespread as microcomputers were introduced.

Many dialects appeared and the ones written by the young Microsoft were especially popular. The company's Visual Basic is widely used to develop programs for Windows.

B4A

In 2005, Israeli company Anywhere Software created "Basic for PPC", a system for developing apps for Pocket PC computers. In 2010, a version appeared which could create apps for Android devices and this evolved into Basic4Android in 2011, renamed B4A in 2014.

Lexical Rules

Lexical rules determine how code should be written. Ground rules are:
– B4A is not case sensitive. The editor will automatically change the case of keywords.
– Unlike some languages, a semi-colon(;) is not required at the end of each line. They are simply terminated by a carriage return.

Statement Separator

Two statements can be written on one line by separating them with a colon:
```
Dim intX As Int: If intY > 3 Then intX = 2 Else intX = 9
```
(You might consider your code would be easier to read if such code were placed on separate lines.)

Comments

For many apps, more time is spent maintaining and enhancing the code than was originally spent writing them, so it is essential that they are easy to read and understand. For this purpose, comments are important. They explain the purpose of variables and subs. The single quote is used to add a comment on a line. For example:
```
'Send a POST request with the given file as the post data.
'This method doesn't work with assets files.
Public Sub PostFile(Link As String, Dir As String, FileName As String)
  If Dir = File.DirAssets Then ' Dir is not valid
   Msgbox("Cannot send files from the assets folder.", "Error")
     Return
  Else
   '...
  End If
End Sub
```
This illustrates some important principles which will help improve the ease of maintenance of your code:

Meaningful names

Choose meaningful names for variables and subs, so their function is clear.

Comments as Documentation
Document your subs by adding comments before them. See here for more information (page 85).

Splitting Long Lines
Long lines of code are difficult to read:
```
Sub dblSecsToJ2000 (intYear As Int, intMonth As Int, intDay As Int,
intHour As Int, intMin As Int, intSec As Int, floLat As Float, floLong
As Float, bRound As Boolean) As Double
```
The underscore character can be used to split long lines. For example:
```
Sub dblSecsToJ2000 ( _
  intYear As Int, intMonth As Int, intDay As Int, _
  intHour As Int, intMin As Int, intSec As Int, _
  floLat As Float, floLong As Float, bRound As Boolean _
  ) As Double
```
Note that Smart Strings (page 395) can define multi-line strings without needing the underscore.

Variables

A **variable** is a symbolic name given to some quantity or information to allow the data to be easily manipulated and changed.

Constants

To define a constant, use the `Const` keyword:
```
Dim Const dblDiameterEarth As Double = 12756.2
```
Once declared, the value of a constant cannot be changed

Types

The **type** of a variable is the sort of data which it can contain. The B4A type system is derived directly from the Java type system. There are two types of variables: primitive and non-primitive types.

Primitive Types
These are the fundamental types in B4A.
In the following list of primitive types with their ranges, "~" means "approximately equal to"

Boolean
Type....................................... boolean
min value.............................. FALSE
max value.............................. TRUE
Note that FALSE is stored as 0.

Byte
Type....................................... 8 bits (1 byte signed)
min value.............................. $-2^7 = -128$
max value.............................. $2^7 - 1 = 127$

Short

Type............................... integer 16 bits (2 bytes signed)
min value............................... - 2^{15} = -32768
max value............................... 2^{15} -1 = 32767

Int

Type............................... integer 32 bits (4 bytes signed)
min value............................... - 2^{31} = -2147483648
max value............................... 2^{31} -1 = 2147483647

Long

Type............................... long integer 64 bits (8 bytes signed)
min value............................... - 2^{63} = -9,223,372,036,854,775,808
max value............................... 2^{63} -1 = 9,223,372,036,854,775,807

Float

Type............................... floating point number 32 bits (4 bytes, ~7 digits)
max negative value................. - $(2 - 2^{-23}) * 2^{127} \sim$ - $3.4028235*10^{38}$
min negative value................. - $2^{-149} \sim$ - $1.4*10^{-45}$
min positive value................. $2^{-149} \sim 1.4*10^{-45}$
max positive value................. $(2 - 2^{-23}) * 2^{127} \sim 3.4028235*10^{38}$

Double

Type............................... double precision number 64 bits (8 bytes, ~15 digits)
max negative value................. - $(2 - 2^{-52}) * 2^{1023} \sim$ - $1.7976931348623157*10^{308}$
min negative value................. - $2^{-1074} \sim$ - $2.2250738585072014*10^{-308}$
min positive value................. $2^{-1074} \sim 2.2250738585072014*10^{-308}$
max positive value................. $(2 - 2^{-52}) * 2^{1023} \sim 1.7976931348623157*10^{308}$

Char

Type............................... character, 2 bytes unsigned

String

Type............................... array of characters

Hex Literals

B4A supports the writing of integers in hexadecimal notation, (often shortened to "hex"). For more details about hex, see here (http://bit.ly/1OwgyYr).
You must prefix the number with 0x (the 0 is the number zero). Thus you can write

```
Dim iSize As Int
iSize = 0x2C
Log (iSize) ' produces 44
```

Non-Primitive Types

All other types, including arrays (page 282) of primitive types, are categorized as non-primitive types.

Core Types

In the following sections, we give details of the non-primitive types built into B4A; the so-called Core Types.

Reference to Non-Primitives

When you pass a non-primitive to a Sub, or when you assign a non-primitive to a different variable, a copy of the reference is passed. This means that the data itself isn't duplicated. For examples, see below Pass by Reference (page 280).

Type Conversion

In B4A, variable types are automatically converted as needed. For example:

```
Dim str As String
Dim i As Int
i = 3
str = i ' automatic type conversion
Log (str) ' produces 3

' conversion string to int
str = "4"
i = str ' automatic type conversion
Log (i) ' produces 4
```

Error converting String to Int

```
str = "hello"
i = str
```

The last line cannot be executed and produces a runtime error (page 302):
NumberFormatException
This problem can be solved by using code like:

```
If IsNumber(str) Then
  i = str
End If
```

Error converting Floating Point numbers to Strings

Floating point numbers (Floats and Doubles) are only held as approximate values in B4A, and hence converting them to strings can lead to errors:

```
Dim flt As Float = 1.23
Dim str As String = flt
Log ("str from flt gives " & str)
```

The log contains

```
str from flt gives 1.2300000190734863
```

Similar errors can arise when converting Double to String.
The solution is to use Round2 (page 323) or NumberFormat (page 321) or NumberFormat2 (page 321), for example:

```
Dim flt As Float = 1.23
str = Round2(flt, 4)
Log ("Round2 flt gives " & str)
```

The log contains

```
Round2 flt gives 1.23
```

Rank

You might sometimes see a compile-time error such as:

```
Cannot cast type: {Type=Int,Rank=0} to: {Type=Int,Rank=1}
```

Rank=0 is a simple variable, Rank=1 means an array (page 282).

Creating Your Own Types

You can create a new type using the Type keyword. See here for details (page 285).

Objects

An Object is a useful concept in computer programming which allows us to represent real-world objects in our code. This helps us to design better and more robust apps. Objects can have attributes (also called properties) and behaviours (also called functions or methods). In B4A, these are collectively called Members.

In addition, an object can respond to user actions by raising Events, which we describe elsewhere (page 297).

For example, a Button has attributes of **Left** and **Top** (which determine its position on the screen), and it has behaviours which determine how it responds to commands.

```
Dim btn As Button
btn.Initialize("Menu")
btn.Left = 20dip
btn.BringToFront
```

If we are not sure what type of variable we will be dealing with, we can declare a variable to be an Object. An Object can contain any type of variable.

```
Dim objThing As Object
```

Later we can test its type:

```
If objThing Is Bitmap Then
```

If one variable containing an Object is assigned to a second variable, they both refer to the same Object:

```
Dim btnTest As Button
Dim btnSameAsTest As Button
btnSameAsTest = btnTest
```

Now anything you do to **btnSameAsTest** also affects **btnTest**. This is an example of passing by reference (page 280).

A collection, such as a **List** or a **Map**, works with objects and therefore can store any type of data. It is not necessary that all its elements contain the same type. On the other hand, an array (page 282) can store only a single type in all of its elements.

Initialization of Objects

Objects must be initialized (i.e. assigned a value) before use. Otherwise they cannot be used. Consider a button, for example. First we declare it:

```
Sub Globals
  Dim btnAddRoute As Button
End Sub
```

Then we initialize it and declare the event name which will be used to handle its events:

```
Sub Activity_Create(FirstTime As Boolean)
  btnAddRoute.Initialize("GetPath")
End Sub
```

Then we create subs to handle each required event:

```
Sub GetPath_click
  ' do something
End Sub
Sub GetPath_LongClick
  ' do something
End Sub
```

The IDE provides the AutoComplete (page 84) system, which is an easy way to create these subs and ensure they have the correct arguments.

Declaring Variables

The "declare a variable" means "to tell B4A the name, type and (perhaps) number of dimensions of a variable".

Dim Statement

The way you declare a variable is to use the **Dim** statement. The word "Dim" comes from "dimension" because, if you wish to use an array (page 282), it has to be declared and the number of dimensions specified.

In B4A, it is not essential to declare a variable before you use it, but it is good practice to do so. This is a good way to reduce logical errors within your code, because it tells the compiler to only allow values of a specific type to be assigned to that variable. If you do not declare a variable before you use it, B4A assumes it is a **String** type.

Variables are declared with the **Dim** keyword followed by the variable name, the **As** keyword and the variable's **type (page 274)**. If it is an array, the variable name is followed by parentheses enclosing the number of dimensions. Variables can also be initialized when they are declared. Examples:

```
Dim dblCapital As Double
Dim dblExpenses(10) As Double
Dim i = 0 As Int
Dim intData(3, 5, 10) As Int
```

Variables of the same type can be declared together with their names separated by commas and followed by the type declaration. They can be initialized at the same time:

```
Dim dblCapital, dblInterest, dblRate As Double
Dim i = 0, j = 2, k = 5 As Int
```

Variables of different types can be declared on the same line:

```
Dim txt As String, value As Double, flag As Boolean
```

However, this can be difficult to read:

```
Dim txt = "test" As String, value = 1.05 As Double, flag = False As
Boolean
```

These might be better spread over several Dim statements. It is usually best to make your code as easy as possible for humans to read and understand, in particular yourself, when you have to maintain your own app!

No Option Explicit

Programmers can sometimes waste time searching for errors caused by mis-spelt variable names. Unlike Microsoft Visual Basic, there is no Option Explicit in B4A. Option Explicit required that all variables were declared using the Dim statement before they were used, but you do not have to declare variables in B4A. Thus the following lines will compile without problem with B4A:

```
Sub Activity_Create(bFirstTime As Boolean)
  intX = 16
  Log (intX)
End Sub
```

Editor Warnings of Undeclared Variables

The IDE editor highlights an undeclared variable in red (such as `intX` shown above) as a warning that it is being used before it has been declared, and also puts that message in the warning area at the top of the Logs (page 90) window, but the code will nevertheless compile. **Note**: `intX` will be automatically declared as a **String**, which is clearly not the programmer's intention!

Allocating Values

To allocate a value to a variable, write its name followed by the equal sign, followed by the value, for example:

```
Capital = 1200
LastName = "SMITH"
```

Note: the values of strings (page 394), such as `LastName`, must be written between double quotes.

Type Checking

The main benefit of declaring a variable is that, if you try to assign the wrong type (page 274) of data to a variable (which indicates a logical error on your part):

```
Dim yourAge As Int
yourAge = "Seventeen"
```

there will be a run-time error and the program will stop, showing the error in the Log window:

```
Error occurred on line: 35 (Main)
java.lang.NumberFormatException: Invalid double: "Seventeen"
```

Such errors should be caught during testing, if your testing is effective!

Use of Unassigned Variables

Variables, whether declared or not, cannot be used before they are assigned a value. The following (which mis-types the variable name) will produce an error when you try to compile the code:

```
myAge = 16
yourAge = myAg * 2
```

The error produced will be:

```
Parsing code.      Error
Error parsing program.
Error description: Undeclared variable 'myag' is used before it was
assigned any value.
Occurred on line: 37
yourAge = myag * 2
```

Pass by Value

Primitive types are always passed by value to other subs or when assigned to other variables. The alternative, passing a reference to a primitive variable, is not implemented. This means you cannot alter the original value from within a subroutine.
Example:

```
Sub S1
  Dim A As Int
  A = 12
  ' pass a copy of A's value to routine S2
  S2(A)
  Log(A)
  ' Prints 12. This value of A is unchanged
End Sub

Sub S2(A As Int)
  ' This A Is a local copy
  A = 45
  ' Only the value of the local copy is changed
End Sub
```

Pass by Reference

Non-primitive types, such as arrays, objects and types are always passed to other subs by reference. If you change the reference, you actually change the original object. For example:

```
Sub S1
  Dim A(3) As Int
  A(0) = 12
  ' pass a reference to A to routine S2
  S2(A)
  Log(A(0))
  ' Prints 45
End Sub

Sub S2(B() As Int)
  ' This B Is a reference to the original
  B(0) = 45
  ' The original value A(0) is changed
End Sub
```

The same is true when a non-primitive such as an array is assigned to another variable. The second variable is a reference to the first. Example:

```
Dim A(3), B(3) As Int
A(0) = 12
B = A
' B is a reference to A
Log(B(0)) ' prints 12
' Change both A and B
A(0) = 45
Log(B(0)) ' prints 45
```

The same is true for any non-primitive, such as an object:

```
Dim lbl1, lbl2 As Label
lbl1.Initialize("")
lbl2.Initialize("")
lbl1.TextSize = 20
Log (lbl1.TextSize) ' prints 20
lbl2 = lbl1
' lbl2 is a reference to lbl1
' if change lbl2 we also change lbl1
lbl2.TextSize = 40
Log (lbl1.TextSize) ' prints 40
```

Naming of Variables

You must identify your variables by giving them names. A variable name must begin with a letter and must be composed of the following characters: A-Z, a-z, 0-9, and underscore "_". You cannot use spaces, brackets, etc.

Variable names are not case-sensitive. This means that "Index" and "index" refer to the same variable. The editor automatically changes the case of a variable name to match the case you used when you declare it.

You cannot use reserved words (keywords listed in this chapter) as variable names. However, you can use Object types such as Bitmap. Thus:

```
Dim Int As Int        ' this is an error
Dim Bitmap As Bitmap    ' this is OK, although not good practice
Dim Bitmap1 As Bitmap   ' this is good
Dim bmpMyPhoto As Bitmap ' this is perfect
```

Note: using Object types as variable names (**Bitmap**, for example) is widely regarded as bad practice, since it can cause confusion; for example, the IDE will color-code the variable wrongly. The best practice is to use Hungarian notation (see below).

Hungarian Notation

It can help to remember which type of data a variable needs by using the so-called Hungarian notation. In Hungary (and other cultures), the family name is cited before the given name. So, in variables which use this convention, the first part of the variable's name tells you what type of object you are handling. For example, an integer could be named intMyAge, a string could be called strMyName and so on. Some suggested prefixes:

```
Dim bMale As Boolean
Dim btnNext As Button
Dim byteMyData As Byte
Dim chkFavorite As CheckBox
Dim chrInitial As Char
Dim dblSunDistance As Double
Dim edtInterest As EditText
Dim fltWeight As Float
Dim intAge As Int
Dim lblCapital As Label
Dim lngDate As Long
Dim lstNames As List
Dim mapPeople As Map
Dim pnlBackground As Panel
Dim shrtAge As Short
Dim strName As String
Dim spnChoice As Spinner
Dim wbvMyPage As WebView
```

Arrays

An array is a collection of values or objects of the same type. These elements are held within the array in a fixed order and individual elements can be selected by specifying their position using an index number.

Dimensions

Arrays can have multiple dimensions. Think of a one-dimensional array as a row of objects. You pick one of them by counting along the row until you find the one you want. A two-dimensional array is like a chequer-board with each square containing an object. To pick one of them, you must specify two numbers, one for the horizontal position and one for the vertical. This plan can be extended to any number of dimensions, although they get increasing difficult to imagine!

Declaring an Array

A one-dimensional array is declared as follows:

```
Dim strLastName(50) As String
```

The declaration contains the `Dim` keyword followed by the variable name `strLastName`, the dimensions between brackets `(50)`, the keyword `As` and, optionally, the variable type for example `String`. This array can hold a total of 50 Strings, from **strLastName(0)** to **strLastName(49)**.

Default Type

If the type is omitted, it defaults to String.

```
Dim arr(3) ' this array can hold 3 Strings
```

Other Examples

Two dimensional array of Doubles, total number of items 9:

```
Dim dblMatrix(3, 3) As Double
```

Three dimensional array of integers, total number of items 150:

```
Dim intData(3, 5, 10) As Int
```

Cannot Change Dimensions

Unlike in Visual Basic, it is not possible to change the number of dimensions of an array. If you need this, you would be better to use a list or map.

Saving and Retrieving Data

To store data in an array, you have to specify at which position you want to store it. You do this by giving an index-number, starting with 0 as the first position.

```
Dim strLastName(2) As String
strLastName(0) = "Jones"
strLastName(1) = "Smith"
```

You can read data from an array if you know its position within the structure. For example, to pick the first item, you would say:

```
Dim strPatient As String
strPatient = strLastName(0)
```

Now strPatient will be "Jones"

The first index of each dimension in an array is 0:

```
strLastName(0), dblMatrix(0,0), intData(0,0,0)
```

The last index is equal to the number of items in each dimension minus 1.

```
Dim dblMatrix(3,3) As Double
dblMatrix(2,2) = 1.233
Dim intData(3,5,10) As Int
intData(2,4,9) = 36676
```

The following example shows how to access all items in a three dimensional array:

```
Dim intData(3,5,10) As Int
For i = 0 To 2
  For j = 0 To 4
    For k = 0 To 9
      intData(i,j,k) = i + j + k
    Next
  Next
Next
```

Variable Can Specify Dimensions

The above example demonstrates that you can use variables (i, j and k) to specify the index when you store or retrieve data. You can also use variables to specify the number of elements when you declare an array, as shown in the last line of this code:

```
Dim intFriends As Int
' read number of friends from user input
intFriends = txtNumFriends.Text
' declare array to hold friends names
Dim strLastName(intFriends) As String
```

Filling an array using the Array keyword

An array can be declared without specifying its length:

```
Dim strNames() As String
```
The array can then be filled using the **Array** keyword:
```
strNames = Array As String("Miller", "Smith", "Johnson", "Jordan")
```
In fact this creates a new array and then sets **strNames** as a reference to it.

Length of an Array
You can find how many objects there are in an array by using the Length method:
```
Dim strNames() As String = Array As String( _
  "Miller", "Smith", "Johnson", "Jordan")
Log(strNames.Length) ' produces 4
```
Note that Length only tells you how many elements are in the first dimension, so
```
Dim x(3,4) As Int
Log(x.Length) ' produces 3
```

Arrays of Objects
Views or other objects can be stored in an Array. An example is given in the Shared Event Handler (page 298) section. If the Array keyword is used without a type then Object is assumed:
```
Dim person() As Object = Array ("Tom", 37, tomsPhoto)
```

Array Dimensions are Fixed
One of the limitations of arrays is that their dimensions are fixed. Once you have created an array, the number of elements it can hold is fixed. You cannot later decide to make it bigger unless you replace it with a new array:
```
strNames = Array As String("Jones", "Windor")
 ' replace the original data with some new strings
strNames = Array As String("Miller", "Smith", "Johnson", "Jordan")
```
The array has changed its dimensions but the original data is lost.

This limitation can be overcome by using **Lists** or **Maps**, which allow you to add data to existing structures:

Lists

Lists are similar to arrays but they are dynamic: you can add and remove items from a list and it will change its size accordingly:
```
Dim lstNames As List
lstNames.Initialize
lstNames.Add("David")
lstNames.Add("Goliath")
```
Lists resemble arrays in that you access their elements by using an index number:
```
Dim strName As String
strName = lstNames.Get(1)
Log(strName) ' logs Goliath
lstNames.RemoveAt(1)
```
There are other benefits of using lists. For example, lists can hold any type of object. A detailed description of all functions is in the List section (page 380).

Maps

A `Map` resembles a `List`, but you access its members not only with an index number but also with a key. A key can be a string or a number. Like a `List`, a `Map` can store any type of object.

```
Dim mapPerson As Map
mapPerson.Initialize
Dim photo As Bitmap
...
mapPerson.Put("name", "smith")
mapPerson.Put("age", 23)
mapPerson.Put("photo", photo)
```

More details in the Map section (page 384).

Type variables

The `Type` keyword is used to create your own types or structures. You can use such types to create simple structures that group some values. However, you can also use it to create more complex collections. Define a type with the Type keyword:

```
Sub Process_Globals
  Type Person( _
  LastName As String, FirstName As String, Age As Int, _
  Address As String, City As String _
  )
End Sub
```

We can declare either single variables or arrays of this type:

```
Dim CurrentUser As Person
Dim User(10) As Person
```

To access a particular item, we use the variable name and its data item, separated by a period:

```
CurrentUser.FirstName = "Wyken"
CurrentUser.LastName = "Seagrave"
```

If the variable is an array, then the name is followed by the desired index between parentheses:

```
User(1).LastName = "Seagrave"
```

It is possible to assign a typed variable to another variable of the same type:

```
CurrentUser = User(1)
```

Declaring Types

A Type cannot be private. Types must be declared in Process_Globals.
Once declared, it is available everywhere (similar to Class modules).

Recursive Types

It is possible to use the current type as a type for one of the variable's fields.

```
Sub Process_Globals
  Type Element (NextElement As Element, Val As Int)
  Dim Head As Element 'declare a variable of that type
  Dim Last As Element
End Sub
```

The ability to declare such recursive types is very powerful. The above example could be used for a linked list, as explained in this on-line tutorial (http://bit.ly/13uxb1r)

Initializing a Recursive Type

Before we can access any of the type fields in a recursive type, it should be initialized by calling its Initialize method:

```
Head.Initialize
```

Note: if your type only includes numeric fields and strings, then there is no need to call Initialize (although there is no harm in calling it).

Casting

Casting means changing an object's type (page 274). B4A casts types automatically as needed. It also converts numbers to strings and vice versa automatically. Sometimes you need to explicitly cast an Object to a specific type.

For example, you might have an event handler which needs to read data from the object which raised the event. You can get a reference to that object by using the **Sender** keyword, but to use the properties of that object, you must cast it to the correct type. This can be done by assigning the Object to a variable of the required type.

```
Sub Btn_Click
  ' Create an object of the correct type so we can access its
  properties
  Dim btn As Button
  ' Copy the Object which raised this event.
  '  This will cast its type to Button
  btn = Sender
  ' Now we can access its properties
  btn.Color = Colors.RGB(Rnd(0, 255), Rnd(0, 255), Rnd(0, 255))
End Sub
```

Visibility of Variables

We discuss this issue here (page 234).

Expressions and Operators

An expression is a combination of values, constants, variables, operators, and functions which are combined using operators to produce a value, for example:

```
2 + intAge
strName.Length - 1
```

Mathematical expressions

The mathematical operators ("+", "-" etc) have to be executed in a particular order. This is called their precedence. **Precedence 1 is highest.** Precedence Level is abbreviated PL in the following table:

Operator	Example	PL	Operation
Power	Power(x,y)	1	Power of, x^y
Mod	x Mod y	2	Modulo
*	x * y	2	Multiplication
/	x / y	2	Division
+	x + y	3	Addition
-	x - y	3	Subtraction

Thus, for example, in the expression 4 + 5 * 3 + 2, the multiplication is evaluated first, to produce 4 + 15 + 2, so the returned value is 21.

Power means multiplying a number by itself several times, so Power(2,3) means 2 * 2 * 2. **Mod** (short for modulo or modulus) returns the remainder after a division. Thus, 11 Mod 4 is the remainder of 11 / 4, so it returns 3.

Relational Operators

Relational operators compare two values and decide if they are equal, if one is larger than the other, etc. These operators return **True** or **False**.

Operator	Example	Returns **True** if
=	x = y	the two values are equal
<>	x <> y	the two values are not equal
>	x > y	the value of the left expression is greater than that of the right
<	x < y	the value of the left expression is less than that of the right
>=	x >= y	the value of the left expression is greater than or equal to that of the right
<=	x <= y	the value of the left expression is less than or equal to that of the right

Logical Operators

Logical or "Boolean" operators are used to determine whether an expression is **True** or **False**. They are typically used in conditional statements such as **If-Then**. They return values of **True** or **False**

Operator	Example	Returns **True** if
Or	X Or Y	if either X or Y is **True**, or if both are **True**
And	X And Y	**True** only if both X and Y are **True**
Not ( )	Not(X)	**True** only if X is **False**

Regular Expressions

Regular Expressions occur several times in B4A, and provide a very powerful (although not very programmer-friendly) method of specifying a pattern (sometimes very complex) to search for within a string. For example:

– to search for a tab character you would use the expression "\t"

– to match any single character you use a dot "."

– to match one or more characters you would use ".*"

Thus, for example:

"c.t" would match "cat" and "cot" but not "cart"

"c.*t" would match "cat", "cot" and "cart" but not "ct"

There are many of these rules.

There are also various flavors of regular expressions. B4A uses the Java flavor.

In B4A, regular expressions can be processed using the Regex object (page 391) and its associated Matcher Object (page 318).

Regular expressions are used in the delimiters of the String Functions Library (http://bit.ly/15HuBDW).

There is a B4A tutorial on regular expressions here (http://bit.ly/1BSPux0).

Examples of Java Regex Constructs

The following is a partial list:

x	The character x
\\	The backslash character
.	Any character (may or may not match line terminators)
X*	X, zero or more times
X?	X, once or not at all
X+	X, one or more times
[abc]	a, b, or c (simple class)
[^abc]	Any character except a, b, or c (negation)
[a-z]	a to z inclusive (range)
\d	A digit: [0-9]
\D	A non-digit: [^0-9]
\s	A whitespace character: [\t\n\x0B\f\r]
\S	A non-whitespace character: [^\s]
\w	A word character: [a-zA-Z_0-9]
\W	A non-word character: [^\w]
^	The beginning of a string
$	The end of a string
\b	A word boundary
\B	A non-word boundary

Simple Example of Usage

```
' check that date is of format nn-nn-nnnn
If Regex.IsMatch("\d\d-\d\d-\d\d\d\d", "26-12-16") Then
 Log ("Valid")
Else
 Log ("Invalid")
End If
' log says Invalid
```

Getting More Help with Regular Expressions

For an on-line primer see here (http://bit.ly/1TO2bSb). For a complete list of Java regex constructs see here (http://bit.ly/1KfNbtY).

You can test your B4A regular expressions on-line here (http://bit.ly/1TO2ah0) .

If you need to use regular expressions regularly, I recommend you invest in RegexBuddy (http://bit.ly/1OwgCr1). It not only provides a tool for creating and testing regular expressions, but it has useful (although not easily digested) tutorials to explain the more abstruse parts of the arcane syntax.

Conditional statements

Various conditional statements are available in B4A.

If – Then

A simple test which executes a single statement when the condition is **True**,

```
If intA = 20 Then intA = intA - 3
```

If-Then-End If

If several statements need to be executed when the test is true, it is common to list them on separate lines and terminate them with an **End If** statement:

```
If intA = 20 Then
 intA = intA - 3
 intB = intB + 3
End If
```

If-Then-Else-End If

If some statements need to be executed when the test is fails, an **Else** statement is used:

```
If intA = 20 Then
 intA = intA - 3
Else
 intA = intA + 1
End If
```

Note that this could be written as:

```
If intA = 20 Then intA = intA - 3 Else intA = intA + 1
```

But you might decide that having the structure spread over several lines makes the code more readable.

Detailed explanation of how If-Then-Else-End If works

Consider this general case:

```
If test1 Then
  ' code1
Else If test2 Then
  ' code2
' more tests are possible
Else
  ' codeN
End If
```

– When reaching the line with the **If** keyword, "test1" is evaluated. The test can be any kind of conditional test with two possibilities: **True** or **False**.

– If the test result is **True**, then "code1" is executed until the line with the **Else If** keyword, then execution jumps to the line following the **End If** keyword and continues.

– If the result of test1 is **False**, then "test2" is evaluated.

– The same thing is repeated.

– If all tests fail, then the code after the **Else** keyword is executed.

Differences between B4A and Visual Basic

1. B4A uses **Else If** whereas VB uses: **ElseIf**

2. The following line is interpreted differently in B4A and VB:
```
If b = 0 Then a = 0: c = 1
```
In B4A this is equivalent to:
```
If b = 0 Then
  a = 0
End If
c = 1
```
But in VB it is:
```
If b = 0 Then
  a = 0
  c = 1
End If
```

Select – Case

The **Select - Case** structure allows you to compare a test expression with other expressions and to execute different code sections according to the matches with the test expression. This is similar to the **switch** command in C, PHP and other languages.
```
Select TestExpression
  Case ExpressionList1
    ' code1
  Case ExpressionList2
    ' code2
  Case Else
    ' code3
End Select
```
"TestExpression" is any expression or value.

"ExpressionList1" is a list of any expressions or values, separated by commas.

The **Select - Case** structure works as follows:

– "TestExpression" is evaluated.

– If one element in the "ExpressionList1" matches "TestExpression", then "code1" is executed and control passes to the line following the **End Select** keyword.

– Otherwise, if one element in the "ExpressionList2" matches "TestExpression", then "code2" is executed and control passes to the line following the **End Select** keyword.

– Otherwise, if no expression matches "TestExpression", then "code3" is executed and control continues at the line following the **End Select** keyword.

Note: the type of each value in each ExpressionList has to be the same as the type of the TestExpression. If not, either a compiletime error or a runtime error will result.

Some examples:

```
Dim intA As Int
intA  = Rnd(1,100)
Select intA
 Case 1, 2, 99
 ' code
 Case 5
 ' code
 Case Else
 ' code
End Select
```

Note: if you accidentally use the same expression in two Case statments, a compile error is reported. Some more examples:

```
Dim intA, intB  As Int
intA = Rnd(1,100)
intB = Rnd(1,100)
Select intA + intB
Case 2,3,4,5
 Log("small")
Case Else
 Log("big")
End Select
'----------
Dim strCode As String
Select strCode
 Case "walk"
 ' code
 Case "run"
 ' code
 Case Else
 ' code
End Select
'----------
Sub Activity_Touch (Action As Int, X As Float, Y As Float)
 Select Action
  Case Activity.ACTION_DOWN
   ' code
  Case Activity.ACTION_MOVE
   ' code
  Case Activity.ACTION_UP
```

```
' code
  End Select
End Sub
```

Differences between B4A and Visual Basic:

– B4A uses `Select`, where VB uses `Select Case`.

– B4A allows only a list for example: `Case 1,2,3`, where VB also allows a range for example: `Case 1 To 3`

Loop structures

Various loop structures are available in Basic:

For – Next

In a `For-Next` loop, the same code will be executed a number of times controlled by a variable called an "iterator". For example:

```
For i = 1 To 9 Step 2
  ' your code
Next
```

In this case `i` is the iterator. This is how the code is executed:

– Iterator `i` set to the first value `1` and `your code` will be executed.

– When execution reaches `Next`, execution will return to the `For` statement and `i` will be incremented by the `Step` value `2` to 1+2 or 3.

– If `i` is less than or equal to the upper value `9`, then your code will be executed again.

– This will be repeated until `i` is greater than the upper value

– Control then passes the line after `Next`.

So `your code` in the above example will execute exactly five times, when `i` = 1,3,5,7 and 9. If the iterator variable `i` was not previously declared, it will be of type `Int`.

Note: the loop limits (in the above case, 1 and 9) might be expressions which depend on variables. In that case, they will only be calculated once, before the first iteration.

Step Value

Note: if the `Step` value is omitted, then it is assumed to be 1, no matter what the starting value of the iterator. So:

```
For i = 1 To 10
```

is the same as

```
For i = 1 To 10 Step 1
```

`Step` variable can be negative:

```
For i = 10 To 6 Step -1
```

Non-integer Iterators

Note that the iterator (`i` in the above examples) is assumed to be in integer, unless it is declared beforehand. But if declared correctly, then any numeric value can be used as the iterator:

```
Dim i As Float
For i = 1.1 To 1.4 Step 0.1
 ' your code
Next
```

Exit

It is possible to exit a **For-Next** loop with the **Exit** keyword. When code execution meets the **Exit** keyword, it continues on the line after **Next**. The following will log 1-4:

```
For i = 1 To 10
 If i = 5 Then Exit
 Log (i)
Next
```

Continue

If you want to stop executing the current iteration but continue with the next one, use **Continue**:

```
For i = 1 To 10
 If i = 5 Then Continue
 Log (i)
Next
```

This will log 1-4 and 6-10, but not 5.

Differences between B4A and Visual Basic

– B4A uses **Next**, whereas VB uses **Next i**
– B4A uses **Exit**, VB uses **Exit For**

For-Each

For-Each is a variant of the **For-Next** loop, but while **For-Next** is limited to using an integer to control the loop, **For-Each** can use arrays, lists, maps or any other "IterableList" you may create. Example:

```
Dim strName() As String = Array As String("a", "b", "c")
For Each name As String In strName
 Log (name)
Next
```

Each value of strName is assigned, in turn, to the variable name, so the result is:

```
a
b
c
```

An example iterating over a **Map**:

```
Dim balances As Map
balances.Initialize
balances.Put("Fred", 123.45)
balances.Put("Tom", 543.21)
Dim value As Float
For Each Person As String In balances.Keys
 value = balances.Get(Person)
 Log (Person & " has balance " & value)
Next
```

You can also get the values in a map as an iterable list:

```
For Each v As Int In map1.Values
  Log(v)
Next
```

The views in an activity are an IterableList:

```
For Each vw As View In Activity
  ' check its type
  If vw Is Button Then
  ' need object with correct type so
  '  can gain access to properties
  Dim btn As Button
  ' make copy of original view
  btn = vw
  Log (btn.Text)
  End If
Next
```

You can also iterate over all the views belonging to a panel:

```
For Each vw As View In pnlMain.GetAllViewsRecursive
  vw.Color = Colors.RGB(Rnd(0,255), Rnd(0,255), Rnd(0,255))
Next
```

Do-While

You can loop while a certain condition is **True**. For example, this will randomly decrease a number starting with 10000 and log the result while it is greater than 0:

```
Dim i As Int = 10000
Do While i > 0
  ' randomly decrease i
  i = i - Rnd(20, 200)
  Log (i)
Loop
```

Do-While is useful if you know the starting condition when the loop starts. For example, when you read a text file. The following reads a text file and uses it as the text for a **Label**:

```
Dim lbl As Label
Dim strLines As String
Dim tr As TextReader
tr.Initialize(File.OpenInput(File.DirAssets, "test.txt"))
lbl.Initialize("")

strLines = tr.ReadLine
Do While strLines <> Null
  lbl.Text = lbl.Text & CRLF & strLines
  strLines = tr.ReadLine
Loop
tr.Close
Activity.AddView(lbl, 10dip, 10dip, 100dip, 100dip)
```

Do-While may not be executed

Note: in some languages, such as C, the syntax causes a do-while loop to always be executed at least once, because the condition which controls the loop is not tested until **after** the code is run. For example:

```
// Example of C code
do {
 /* "Hello, world!" is printed at least one time
 even though the condition is false */
 printf( "Hello, world!\n" );
} while ( x != 0 );
```

In B4A, on the other hand, the condition is tested **before** the loop is executed. For example, the following B4A code will produce NO log entries:

```
Dim i As Int = 0
Do While i > 3
 Log (i)
 i = i - 1
Loop
```

Do-Until

Sometimes, we do not know the initial value which we want to use. We only know when we want to stop the loop. In this case, we use the `Do Until` loop:

```
i = Rnd(20, 200)
Do Until i <= 0
 ' randomly decrease i
 i = i - Rnd(20, 200)
 Log (i)
Loop
```

Exit a Loop

It is possible to exit either of these Do-Loop structures by using the `Exit` keyword.

```
Dim i As Int = 10000
Dim magicNumber As Int = 1234
Do While i > 0
 ' randomly decrease i
 i = i - Rnd(20, 200)
 Log (i)
 If i = magicNumber Then
  Log ("Hit magic number so ending loop")
  Exit
 Else
  Log (i)
 End If
Loop
```

Differences between B4A and Visual Basic

In Visual Basic, the loop type is specified after `Exit`, for example, `Exit Loop`

In B4A, only `Exit` is used.

Visual Basic also accepts the following loops:

```
Do ... Loop While test
Do ... Loop Until test
```

These are NOT supported in B4A.

Subs

A Subroutine ("**Sub**") is a piece of code. It has a distinctive name and a defined visibility (as discussed earlier (page 235)). In B4A, a subroutine is called **Sub**, and is equivalent to procedures, functions, methods and subs in other programming languages.

Using Subs to encapsulate logical units of your code can help it to be more readable and more robust, since you can test each **Sub** separately from all the other code. It is not recommended to have Subs that are too long; they tend to be less readable.

Declaring a Sub

A Sub is declared in the following way:

```
Sub CalcInterest(Capital As Double, Rate As Double) As Double
  Return Capital * Rate / 100
End Sub
```

It starts with the keyword **Sub**, followed by the Sub's name **CalcInterest**, followed by a parameter list enclosed in parentheses **(Capital As Double, Rate As Double)**, followed by the return type **Double**. This is followed by the code which the sub executes. The sub ends with the keywords **End Sub**.

There is no limit on the number of subs you can add to your program, but you are not allowed to have two subs with the same name in the same module.

Subs are always declared at the top level of the module. That is so say, you CANNOT nest two Subs one inside the other.

Naming

For a **Sub**, you can use any name that's legal for a variable (page 281). It is highly recommended to name the **Sub** with a meaningful name so that your code is self-documenting.

Calling a Sub

When you want to execute a Sub in the same module, you simply use the Sub's name.

```
Sub Activity_Resume
  doSomething
End Sub

Sub doSomething
  ' code goes here
End Sub
```

Calling a Sub from another module

As we discuss at greater length in the Visibility of Subroutines (page 235) section, public Subs within a class or code module can be called directly by calls in any other type of module such as **CodeModule.mySub** or **myClassInstance.mySub**

Subs declared in Activity and Service modules, on the other hand, **cannot** be called directly with such calls as shown above, but can be called by any other module using the CallSub (page 307) or CallSubDelayed (page 308) functions, provided the activity is not paused or the service has started.

Parameters

Input parameters can be transmitted to the Sub. This allows you to make the sub do different things depending on its inputs. The parameter list is enclosed in parentheses, and their types are required:

```
Sub CalcInterest(Capital As Double, Rate As Double) As Double
  Return Capital * Rate / 100
End Sub
```

To invoke a sub which needs parameters, add the parameters to the call:

```
Interest = CalcInterest(1234.56, 3.2)
```

If a sub needs no parameters, then the parentheses are not required when the sub is defined or called:

```
i = getRate
...
Sub getRate
  Return 3
End Sub
```

Returned value

A sub can return a value. This can be any object. Returning a value is done with the **Return** keyword. The type of the return value is defined after the parameter list. So the following will return a **Double**

```
Sub CalcInterest(Capital As Int, Rate As Int) As Double
```

Creating Tooltips for Subs

You can create a tooltip to remind yourself what a Sub does. See Comments As Documentation (page 85) for more information.

Events

In Object-oriented programming, objects can react to Events. These could be actions by the user or system-generated events. The number and the type of events an object can raise depends on the type of the object.

Core Object Events

Many Core Objects generate events. Examples are **Animation**, **AudioRecordApp**, **Camera**, **DayDream**, **GameView**, **GPS**, **HTTPClient**, **IME**, **MediaPlayerStream**, **Timer**, etc. Consult the documentation for each of these objects to discover what events they can raise.

Reacting to an Event

To react to an event, you must write a subroutine with the correct name. You must write a **Sub** with the name of the object which is raising the event, followed by an underscore followed by the event name. For example:

```
Sub Timer1_Tick
```

Timer1 is the name of the object which is raising the event. You decide this name when you initialize the object, for example

```
Timer1.Initialize("Timer1", 1000)
```

The `Tick` part of the subroutine name is the name of the event. This is determined by the object itself. You need to consult the object's documentation to discover what events it can raise. Some objects can raise several events.

You must join these two parts of the name together with an underscore _, for example `Timer1_Tick`.

Note: the IDE provides a way of easily autocompleting Event Subroutines (page 84).

Example

To give a concrete example, a `Timer` will run in the background until it has finished its task, then it will raise an event (in this case `Tick`) which your code needs to respond to. For example, `Timer1_Tick` as in the following sample:

```
Sub Process_Globals
  ' declare here so dont get multiple timers when activity recreated
  Dim Timer1 As Timer
End Sub

Sub Globals
End Sub

Sub Activity_Create(FirstTime As Boolean)
  ' make the timer last 1000 milliseconds
  Timer1.Initialize("Timer1", 1000)
  ' start the timer
  Timer1.Enabled = True
End Sub

Sub Timer1_Tick
  ' timer has ended
  Log ("Timer finished")
End Sub
```

Shared Event Handler

You can use a single Sub to handle the events of many objects. For example, you might have several buttons, all of which perform a similar function, so you only need a single event handler. You can determine which object raised the event by using the **Sender** keyword. The following produces a column of buttons labeled Test 1 to Test 7, all of which share the same handler `Buttons_Click`:

```
Sub Globals
 Dim b1, b2, b3, b4, b5, b6, b7 As Button
 Dim Buttons() As Button
End Sub

Sub Activity_Create(FirstTime As Boolean)
 ' index to handle buttons
 Dim i As Int
 Buttons = Array As Button(b1, b2, b3, b4, b5, b6, b7)

 For i = 0 To 6
   ' all buttons share same event handler
   Buttons(i).Initialize("Buttons")
   ' use index to position buttons correctly
   Activity.AddView(Buttons(i), 10dip, 10dip + i * 60dip, _
     150dip, 50dip)
   ' add tag so can identify which button this is
   Buttons(i).Tag = i + 1
   Buttons(i).Text = "Test " & (i + 1)
 Next
End Sub

Sub Buttons_Click
 ' event handler for all buttons
 Dim btn As Button
 btn = Sender
 Activity.Title = "Button " & btn.Tag & " clicked"
End Sub
```

View Events

Many events are raised by Views (page 443) which are handled by your code in the same way as Core Object Events. The Designer is able to generate the skeleton subs (page 141) for you, such as:

```
Sub btnTest_Click
 ' add your code here
End Sub
```

Here is a summary of the events for different views:

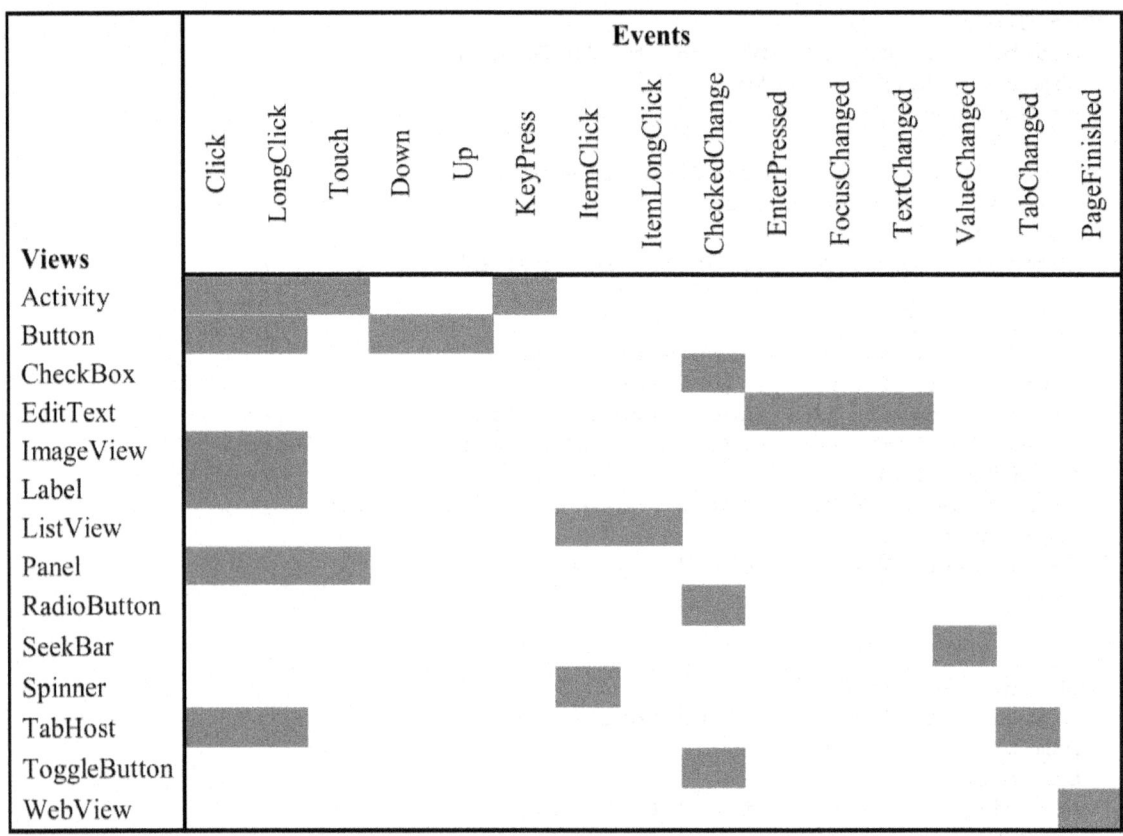

Views	Events Click	LongClick	Touch	Down	Up	KeyPress	ItemClick	ItemLongClick	CheckedChange	EnterPressed	FocusChanged	TextChanged	ValueChanged	TabChanged	PageFinished
Activity	■	■				■									
Button	■	■	■	■											
CheckBox									■						
EditText										■	■	■			
ImageView	■	■													
Label															
ListView							■	■							
Panel	■	■	■												
RadioButton									■						
SeekBar													■		
Spinner							■								
TabHost	■	■												■	
ToggleButton									■						
WebView															■

Commonest View Events

The most common events are as follows. Note that the events supported vary with the type of view:

Click

Event raised when the user clicks on the view. Example:

```
Sub Button1_Click
  ' Your code
End Sub
```

LongClick

Event raised when the user clicks on the view and holds it pressed for about one second. Example:

```
Sub Button1_LongClick
  ' Your code
End Sub
```

Touch(Action As Int, X As Float, Y As Float)

Event raised when the user touches the screen.

Three different actions are handled:

– Activity.Action_DOWN: the user makes contact with the screen.
– Activity.Action_MOVE: the user moves the finger without leaving the screen.
– Activity.Action_UP: the user stops touching the screen.

The X and Y coordinates of the finger position are given. Example:

```
Sub Activity_Touch (Action As Int, X As Float, Y As Float)
  Select Action
  Case Activity.ACTION_DOWN
    ' Your code for DOWN action
  Case Activity.ACTION_MOVE
    ' Your code for MOVE action
  Case Activity.ACTION_UP
    ' Your code for UP action
  End Select
End Sub
```

CheckChanged (Checked As Boolean)

Event raised when the user clicks on a **CheckBox** or a **RadioButton**.

Checked is equal to **True** if the view is checked or **False** if not checked.

Example:

```
Sub CheckBox1_CheckedChange(Checked As Boolean)
  If Checked = True Then
    ' Your code if CheckBox1 is checked
  Else
    ' Your code if CheckBox1 is not checked
  End If
End Sub
```

KeyPress (KeyCode As Int) As Boolean

This event (which only belongs to the **Activity** object) is raised when the user presses a physical or virtual key (except the Home key, which calls **Activity_Pause**).

KeyCode is the code of the pressed key. You can get a list of them in the IDE by typing **KeyCodes** and a dot, or in this book here (page 347).

Your **KeyPress** event should return either **True**, in which case the event is consumed and never seen by the operating system, or **False**, in which case the event is transmitted to the system for further action.

Example:

```
Sub Activity_KeyPress(KeyCode As Int) As Boolean
 ' Confirm user wants to quit if press back key
 Dim Answ As Int
 Dim Txt As String

 ' Check if KeyCode is BackKey
 If KeyCode = KeyCodes.KEYCODE_BACK Then
  ' Confirm user wants to quit
  Txt = "Do you really want to quit the program ?"
  Answ = Msgbox2(Txt, "A T T E N T I O N", "Yes", "", "No", Null)
  If Answ = DialogResponse.POSITIVE Then
   ' User wants to quit
   Return False
  Else
   ' Do not quit
   Return True
  End If
 End If
End Sub
```

Error Handling

Runtime Errors

Some errors are caught by the compiler, but some more subtle errors are only revealed when the code runs. Such a "runtime error" is produced by the following example:

```
Dim str As String
Dim i As Int
str = "hello"
i = str
```

The last line produces a runtime error because Java (which is what Android uses) cannot convert a non-numeric string to a number.

Exceptions

When a runtime error occurs, a Java language Exception (page 365) is raised. You can add Try-Catch code to your app to handle Exceptions. If you have not added this code, when an Exception occurs the program stops and an error is shown on the device or emulator, as described next.

Uncaught Runtime Exceptions

If a runtime error occurs outside a Try-Catch block, what the user sees will depend on how you have distributed the app.

Default Uncaught Runtime Exception Handling

If you distribute via Google Play and your application raises an error which is not caught internally, the user will be asked to send a crash report. This happens automatically. If the user agrees to send the report, you can see the result in Google Play Developer Console (page 268).

If you distribute your application directly with an apk file and your application raises an error which is not caught internally, and the error happens within an activity, by default the user will see an error crash report which asks if they wish to continue, as shown below.

But the user does not know whether the app can continue correctly after the uncaught exception. The dialog is also inconsistent, since it only appears when the error happens within an Activity, but not within any other sort of module.

Better Uncaught Runtime Exception Handling

So it is preferable to override this behavior and handle the error yourself, for example by sending the error in an email.

This requires that your app contains a Starter Service (page 110). By default, the Starter Service contains a Sub called `Application_Error`:

```
'Return true to allow the OS default exceptions handler to handle the
uncaught exception.
Sub Application_Error (Error As Exception, StackTrace As String) As
Boolean
    Return True
End Sub
```

You could use this Sub to, for example, catch the log and send it via email or use HttpUtils2 to send the StackTrace to your server and then kill the process in the JobDone event.

An example of sending the logs via email is shown here (http://bit.ly/20GnuJZ).

Note the following

If you return True from `Sub Application_Error` then the OS default exceptions handler is called. The result is that the app will crash and the crash report will be sent to Google Play (if the user allows it). This is probably the best way to handle most errors.

If you return False, the default exceptions handler will not be called and the app will continue to run.

Sub Application_Error will only be called in Release mode. In Debug mode the program will print the error message in the logs and will end.

Errors that happen when the app is started, before the Starter service is ready will not be trapped. The OS default exceptions handler will handle those errors.

The starter service must be running for this sub to be raised. It will be running unless you explicitly stop it.

Try-Catch

B4A provides a mechanism to handle runtime errors, called a **Try-Catch** block. Example:

```
Try
  'block of statements
Catch
  Log(LastException.Message)
  'handle the problem if necessary
End Try
```

Now when the Exception occurs in the **Try** block, control moves to the **Catch** block. Your program can take steps to handle the problem.

When to use a Try-Catch

Try-Catch should not be used to protect from programming mistakes. You should make sure your code is logically and syntactically correct by testing before distribution.

Try-Catch should only be used when there might be a problem which you cannot control. For example, when you parse a downloaded feed, the feed itself might have problems. Or when you try to update a database using a Transaction (page 227) and there is a problem. For example:

```
SQL.BeginTransaction
Try
  'block of statements
  For i = 1 To 10
  SQL.ExecNonQuery2("INSERT INTO demo VALUES (?,?)", Array As Object(i,
"Tom Brown"))
  Next
  SQL.TransactionSuccessful
Catch
  Log(LastException.Message)  'no changes will be made
End Try
SQL.EndTransaction
```

Try-Catch is of use mainly during development.

Note: if an error is caught in the middle of a large subroutine, you cannot make a correction and then go back and resume execution where the error occurred. Only the code in the **Catch** block gets executed.

String manipulation

B4A allows string manipulations like other Basic languages, but with some differences. These manipulations can be done directly on a string.
Example:

```
strTxt = "123,234,45,23"
strTxt = strTxt.Replace(",", ";")
```

Result: 123;234;45;23

Mutable Strings

Repetitive manipulation of strings can be very slow. Since they are immutable (page 394), a new string has to be created every time you want to change a string. If you are doing extensive string manipulation, you should consider using StringBuilder (page 399).

The String functions

Here we list the string functions. For more details, see below (page 394).

CharAt(Index)
.... Returns the character at the position given by `Index`, where the first character is at 0.

CompareTo(Other)
.... Lexicographically compares the string with the `Other` string.

Contains(SearchFor)
.... Returns `True` if the string contains the given `SearchFor` string.

EndsWith(Suffix)
.... Returns `True` if the string ends with the given `Suffix` substring.

EqualsIgnoreCase(Other)
.... Returns `True` if both strings are equal ignoring their case. Example:
```
If firstString.EqualsIgnoreCase("Abc") Then
```

GetBytes(Charset)
... Encodes the `Charset` string into a new array of bytes.

IndexOf(SearchFor)
... Returns the index of the first occurrence of `SearchFor` in the string, or `-1` if not found.

IndexOf2(SearchFor, Index)
.... Returns the index of the first occurrence of `SearchFor` in the string, or `-1` if not found. Starts searching from the given `Index`.

LastIndexOf(SearchFor)
.... Returns the index of the first occurrence of SearchFor in the string, or `-1` if not found. Starts searching from the end of the string.

Length
.... Returns the number of characters in the string.

Replace(Target, Replacement)
.... Returns a new string resulting from the replacement of all the occurrences of Target with Replacement.

StartsWith(Prefix)
.... Returns `True` if this string starts with the given `Prefix`.

Substring(BeginIndex)
.... Returns a new string which is a substring of the original string. The new string will include the character at `BeginIndex` and will extend to the end of the string.

Substring2(BeginIndex,EndIndex)
... Returns a new string which is a substring of the original string. The new string will include the character at `BeginIndex` and will extend to the character before `EndIndex`.

ToLowerCase
.... Returns a new string which is the result of lower casing this string.

ToUpperCase
.... Returns a new string which is the result of upper casing this string.

Trim

.... Returns a copy of the original string without any leading or trailing white spaces.

Number formatting

Numbers can be displayed as strings with different formats. There are two keywords:
`NumberFormat` and `NumberFormat2`.

NumberFormat (page 321) (Number As Double, MinimumIntegers As Int, MaximumFractions As Int)

Follow the link for the meaning of the arguments. Examples:

```
NumberFormat(12345.6789, 0, 2)
' produces 12,345.68
NumberFormat(1, 3 ,0)
' produces 001
NumberFormat(Value, 3 ,0)
' variables can be used.
NumberFormat(Value + 10, 3 ,0)
' arithmetic operations can be used.
NumberFormat((lblscore.Text + 10), 0, 0)
' parentheses needed If one variable Is a String.
```

NumberFormat2 (page 321)(Number As Double, MinimumIntegers As Int, MaximumFractions As Int, MinimumFractions As Int, GroupingUsed As Boolean)

Follow the link for the meaning of the arguments. Example:

```
NumberFormat2(12345.67, 0, 3, 3, True)
' This will produce "12,345.670".
```

Keywords

In this section we list alphabetically the keywords used by B4A and define their functions.
We list separately the objects (page 336) which are included in the core of the language.

♔Abs (Number As Double) As Double

Returns the absolute value of a number, that is, the value of the number but with negative numbers changed to positive. Thus both of the following produce 123.45:

```
Log (Abs(123.45))
Log (Abs(-123.45))
```

♔ACos (Value As Double) As Double

Given a cosine, this function returns the angle, measured as radians. Thus

```
Log (ACos(0.5))
```

will produce 1.04719755119659799 since 60° is just over 1 radian.

♔ACosD (Value As Double) As Double

Given a cosine, this returns the angle measured in degrees. Thus

```
Log (ACosD(0.5))
```

will produce 60 (or something very close).

♔Array

Creates a one-dimensional array of the specified type.
The syntax is: Array As type (list of values).

Example
```
Dim Days() As String
Days = Array As String("Sunday", "Monday", ...)
```
See Arrays (page 282) for more details.

⬡Asc (Char As Char) As Int

Returns the unicode code point (http://bit.ly/10alZFl) of the given character or first character in the given string. Thus, `Log (Asc("A"))` and `Log (Asc("ABC"))` will both produce 65. See here (http://bit.ly/1OwgFDm) for a list of characters and their codes.

⬡ASin (Value As Double) As Double

Given the sine of an angle, this function returns the angle measured in radians.

⬡ASinD (Value As Double) As Double

Given the sine of an angle, this function returns the angle measured in degrees.

⬡ATan (Value As Double) As Double

Given the tangent of an angle, this function returns the angle measured in radians. Thus, the following returns 0.7853981633974483
```
Log (ATan(1))
```

⬡ATan2 (Y As Double, X As Double) As Double

Given the opposite Y and adjacent X sides of a right-triangle, this function returns the tangent of the angle measured in radians. Thus, `Log (ATan2(1,1))` returns 0.7853981633974483

⬡ATan2D (Y As Double, X As Double) As Double

Given the opposite Y and adjacent X sides of a right-triangle, this function returns the angle measured in degrees. Thus, `Log (ATan2D(1,1))` returns 45

⬡ATanD (Value As Double) As Double

Given the tangent of an angle, this function returns the angle measured in degrees. Thus, `Log (ATanD(1))` returns 45

⬡BytesToString (Data() As Byte, StartOffset As Int, Length As Int, CharSet As String) As String

Decodes the given byte array as a string.
Data - The byte array.
StartOffset - The first byte to read.
Length - Number of bytes to read.
CharSet - The name of the character set. See Text Encoding (page 368) for details.
The following example will produce ABCDE:

```
Dim Buffer() As Byte = Array As Byte(65,66,67,68,69)
Dim str As String
str = BytesToString(Buffer, 0, Buffer.Length, "UTF-8")
Log (str)
```

CallSub (Component As Object, Sub As String) As String

CallSub allows an activity to call a Sub in a service module or a service to call a Sub in an activity. CallSub can also be used to call subs in the current module. Pass an empty string as the component in that case.

Component - name of a module. Should not be a string.

Sub – name of Sub to call. Must be a string.

Example

```
CallSub(Main, "RefreshData")
```

Restrictions

A sub will only be called if the called module is not paused. But if it is paused, an empty string will be returned. This is why one activity cannot call a sub of a different activity since the other activity will certainly be paused. You can use **IsPaused** to test whether a module is paused.

Nor is it possible to use this function to call Subs of code modules. To call a Sub in a code module, use a call like **moduleName.subName**.

CallSub2 (Component As Object, Sub As String, Argument As Object) As String

Similar to **CallSub**. Calls a sub with a single argument.

CallSub3 (Component As Object, Sub As String, Argument1 As Object, Argument2 As Object) As String

Similar to **CallSub**. Calls a sub with two arguments.

CallSubDelayed (Component As Object, Sub As String)

CallSubDelayed is a combination of **StartActivity**, **StartService** and **CallSub**. Unlike CallSub (which only works with currently running components), CallSubDelayed will first start the target component if needed.

CallSubDelayed can also be used to call subs in the current module. Instead of calling these subs directly, a message will be sent to the message queue.

The sub will be called when the message is processed. This is useful in cases where you want to do something "right after" the current sub (usually related to user interface events).

Note: if you call an Activity while the whole application is in the background (no visible activities), the sub will be executed once the target activity is resumed. The sub will be called before Activity_Resume.

CallSubDelayed2 (Component As Object, Sub As String, Argument As Object)

Similar to CallSubDelayed. Calls a sub with a single argument.

⊕CallSubDelayed3 (Component As Object, Sub As String, Argument1 As Object, Argument2 As Object)

Similar to `CallSubDelayed`. Calls a sub with two arguments.

⊕CancelScheduledService (Service As Object)

Cancels previously scheduled tasks for this service.

⊕Catch

Any exception thrown inside a `Try` block will be caught in the `Catch` block.
Call LastException to get the caught exception. See Try-Catch (page 304) for details.
Syntax
```
Try
...
Catch
...
End Try
```

⊕cE As Double

e (natural logarithm base) constant, approximately 2.718281828459045

⊕Ceil (Number As Double) As Double

Returns the smallest whole number that is greater than or equal to the specified number.
Thus, `Ceil(4.321)` will return 5. The word is an abbreviation of "ceiling". For the opposite function, see Floor (page 312).

⊕CharsToString (Chars() As Char, StartOffset As Int, Length As Int) As String

Creates a new String by copying the characters from the array `Chars()`.
Copying starts from `StartOffset` and the number of characters copied is specified by `Length`. The following will produce "cd":
```
Dim chars() As Char
chars = Array As Char("a", "b", "c", "d", "e")
Log (CharsToString(chars, 2,2))
```

⊕Chr (UnicodeValue As Int) As Char

Returns the character that is represented by the given unicode value. Thus, `Log (Chr(65))` will produce "A". See here (http://bit.ly/1OwgFDm) for a list of characters and their codes.

⊕ConfigureHomeWidget (LayoutFile As String, EventName As String, UpdateIntervalMinutes As Int, WidgetName As String) As RemoteViews

At compile time, the compiler generates the required XML files based on the arguments of this keyword. At runtime, this command creates a `RemoteViews` object based on the `LayoutFile`. Note that all parameters must be strings or numbers (not variables) so they can be read by the compiler.
LayoutFile - The widget layout file.

EventName - Sets the `Sub` that will handle events from `RemoteViews`, such as `RequestUpdate` event in the example below.

UpdateIntervalMinutes - Sets the update interval in minutes. Pass 0 to disable automatic updates. Otherwise, the minimum value is 30.

WidgetName - The name of the widget as it appears in the widgets list.

Example
```
Sub Process_Globals
  Dim rv As RemoteViews
End Sub

Sub Service_Create
  rv = ConfigureHomeWidget("LayoutFile", "rv", 0, "Widget Name")
End Sub

Sub rv_RequestUpdate
  rv.UpdateWidget
End Sub
```

Reference
See here for more information (page 130) about Widgets.

Continue
Stops executing the current iteration and continues with the next one. The following will log 1-4 and 6-10 but not 5:
```
For i = 1 To 10
  If i = 5 Then Continue
  Log (i)
Next
```
Compare to Exit.

Cos (Radians As Double) As Double
Calculate the cosine of the angle given in radians.

CosD (Degrees As Double) As Double
Calculate the cosine of the angle given in degrees.

cPI As Double
The constant PI, approximately 3.141592653589793

CreateMap() As Map
Create and fill a map. For example:
```
Dim mapPerson As Map = CreateMap("name": "smith", "age": 23, "photo": photo)
```

CRLF As String
The line feed character whose value is Chr(10).

Note: The name CRLF sometimes causes confusion. Despite its name, this is NOT the combination of

CR = Carriage Return = Chr(13) and LF = Line Feed =Chr(10)

which Windows uses in its documents! Android is a Linux-based system in which lines are terminated just by a LF.

⬡Density As Float

Returns the screen's density, which is number of dots per inch / 160.
More information about the screen can be found using GetDeviceLayoutValues

⬡Dim

Declares a variable.
To declare a single variable:
Dim variable name [As type]

```
Dim intSize As Int
```

The default type is String.

To declare and initialize a single variable, two alternatives are possible:
Dim variable name [As type] [= expression]
Dim variable name [= expression] [As type]

```
Dim intA As Int = 1
Dim intB = 2 As Int
```

To declare multiple variables, all of the same type:
Dim variable1 [= expression], variable2 [= expression], ..., [As type]

```
Dim intA, intB, intC As Int
Dim intA = 1, intB = 2, intC = 3 As Int
```

Declare an array and specify the size of each dimension:
Dim variable(size1, size2, ...) [As type]

```
Dim strDayNames(7) As String
```

The size can be omitted for zero length arrays:

```
Dim payments() As Long
Log(payments.Length) ' this will produce 0
```

⬡DipToCurrent (Length As Int) As Int

DipToCurrent(Length as Int) scales Length given in dips (page 163). For example, the following code will set the width value of an EditText to be 1 inch wide on all devices.

```
EditText1.Width = DipToCurrent(160)
```

Note: a shorthand syntax for this method is available. Any number followed by the string dip (page 163) will be converted in the same manner (no spaces are allowed between the number and "dip").
So the previous code is equivalent to

```
EditText1.Width = 160dip
```

⬡DoEvents

Processes waiting messages in the message queue. DoEvents can be called inside lengthy loops to allow your app to update the screen. Other waiting events will not be handled by DoEvents.

⬡Exit

Exits the inner ‑most loop. The following will log 1‑4:
```
For i = 1 To 10
 If i = 5 Then Exit
 Log (i)
Next
```
Compare to Continue.

⬡ExitApplication

Immediately ends the application and stops the process. Most applications should not use this method, with the use of `Activity.Finish` being the preferred method to allow Android to decide when the process will be killed. See Activity.Finish vs ExitApplication (page 246) for a discussion.

⬡False As Boolean

A constant which can be used to compare or set logical values, for example:
```
#Region  Activity Attributes
 #FullScreen: False
 #IncludeTitle: True
#End Region
```

⬡File As File

File‑related methods. See the File Object (page 370) for details of its members and here (page 365) for a discussion of its usage.

⬡Floor (Number As Double) As Double

Returns the largest whole number that is smaller than or equal to the specified number. Thus, `Floor(123.456)` is 123.

For the opposite function, see Ceil (page 309).

⬡For

Begins a loop controlled by a variable called an "iterator". Syntax:
```
For variable = value1 To value2 [Step interval]
  . . .
Next
```
`Step` is optional. If not specified it defaults to 1. Example:
```
For i = 1 To 10
  Log(i) 'Will print 1 to 10 (inclusive).
Next
```
If the iterator variable i was not previously declared, it will be of type `Int`.

Note: the loop limits will only be calculated once, before the first iteration.

⬡For Each

Iterates a loop over an IterableList. Syntax:

```
For Each variable As Type In collection
 ...
Next
```

Examples

```
Dim strName() As String = Array As String("a", "b", "c")
For Each name As String In strName
 Log (name)
Next


For Each vw As View In Activity
 If vw Is Button Then
 ...
 End If
Next
```

✿GetDeviceLayoutValues As LayoutValues

Returns the device LayoutValues (page 379). For example:

```
Dim lv As LayoutValues
lv = GetDeviceLayoutValues
Log(lv)
Dim scale As Float
scale = lv.Scale
```

This will print the following line to the log:

320 x 480, scale = 1.0 (160 dpi)

✿GetType (object As Object) As String

Returns a string representing the object's java type.

✪If

Single line

```
If condition Then true-statement [Else false-statement]
```

Multiline

```
If condition Then
  statements
  . . .
Else If condition Then
  statements
  . . .
Else
  statements
  . . .
End If
```

✪InputList (Items As List, Title As String, CheckedItem As Int) As Int

Shows a modal dialog with a list of items and radio buttons. Pressing on an item will close the dialog and return the index of the selected item or `DialogResponse.Cancel` if the user pressed on the **Back** key.

List - Items to display.

Title - Dialog title.

CheckedItem - The index of the item that will be preselected. If you want the top item to be selected, set this to 0. Pass **-1** if no item should be preselected.

Example which makes a label act like a spinner (page 435):

```
Sub tgtLabel_Click
  Dim myarray(4) As String
  myarray(0)="January"
  myarray(1)="February"
  myarray(2)="March"
  myarray(3)="May"
  choice = InputList(myarray, "Select Month", 1)
  tgtlabel.Text = myarray(choice)
End Sub
```

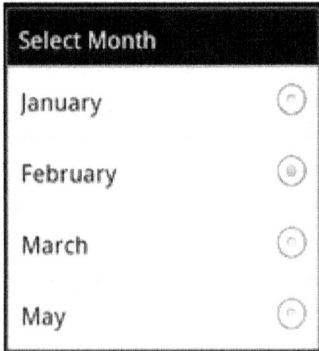

☺InputMap (Items As Map, Title As String)

Shows a modal dialog with a title, a list of items and checkboxes, and an **Ok** button . The user can select multiple items. The dialog closes when the user presses **Ok** or the **Back** button.

The text displayed are the keys of the **Items** map. The values of this map determine whether they are checked. Items with a value of `True` will be checked.

When the user checks or unchecks an item, the related item value gets updated.

The updated values are returned whether the user presses **Ok** or **Back**.

Items - A map object with the items as keys and their checked state as values.

Example:

```
Dim m As Map
m.Initialize
m.Put("Apples", True)
m.Put("Bananas", False)
m.Put("Mangos", False)
m.Put("Oranges", True)
InputMap(m, "Select all the fruits you want")
```

The InputMap looks something like this:

Its exact appearance will vary, depending on the device and the version of Android running.

☺InputMultiList (Items As List, Title As String) As List

Shows a modal dialog with a title, a list of items and checkboxes, and an **Ok** button. The user can select multiple items. The dialog is closed when the user presses **Ok** or **Back**.

If the user presses **Ok**, it returns a list with the indices of the selected items, sorted in ascending order.

It returns an empty list if the user has pressed on the **Back** key.

```
Dim choice As Int
Dim lstInput, lstOutput As List
lstInput.Initialize2(Array As String("Apples", "Bananas", "Mangos",
"Oranges"))
lstOutput = InputMultiList (lstInput, "Select all the fruits you
want")
For Each index As Int In lstOutput
  Log (index)
Next
```

The InputMultiList will appear to the user as:

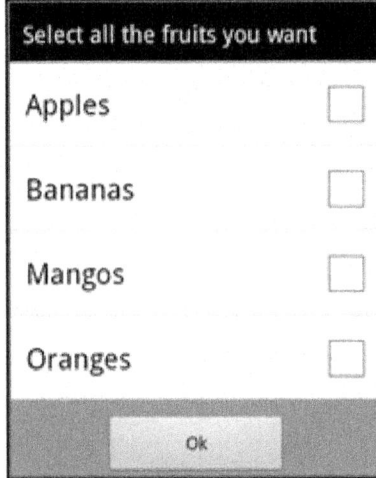

If Bananas and Oranges are selected, the numbers 1 and 3 will be logged.

Is

Returns TRUE if the object is of the given type. Example:

```
For i = 0 To Activity.NumberOfViews - 1
If Activity.GetView(i) Is Button Then
  Dim b As Button
  b = Activity.GetView(i)
  b.Color = Colors.Blue
End If
Next
```

IsBackgroundTaskRunning (ContainerObject As Object, TaskId As Int) As Boolean

Returns TRUE if a background task is running which was submitted by the container object and with the specified id. Example:

```
Dim hc As HttpClient
Dim req As HttpRequest
Dim TaskID As Int = 1

req.InitializePost2("http://abc.com/query.php",
Query.GetBytes("UTF8"))
hc.Execute(req, TaskId)

If IsBackgroundTaskRunning(hc, TaskId) Then
  ToastMessageShow("Wait for previous call to finish.", False)
End If
```

⬡IsDevTool (ToolName As String) As Boolean

Returns TRUE if ToolName = "b4a" (case is ignored). It allows the developer who is re-using the same code across Anywhere Software's (http://www.b4x.com/) development tools (B4A, B4J or B4I) to check which of these tools is currently running, and make appropriate adjustments.

```
If IsDevTool("B4A") Then ' returns TRUE
If IsDevTool("B4J") Then ' returns FALSE
```

⬡IsNumber (Text As String) As Boolean

Returns TRUE if the specified string can be converted to a number.

⬡IsPaused (Component As Object) As Boolean

Returns TRUE if the given component is paused. Will also return True for components that were not started yet. Example:

```
If IsPaused(Main) = False Then CallSub(Main, "RefreshData")
```

⬡LastException As Exception

Returns the last exception (page 365) that was caught (if such exists). If there has not been an exception, LastException will be uninitialized. Thus you should only check for LastException inside the Catch block of a Try-Catch (page 304). Example:

```
Try
  'block of statements
Catch
  Log(LastException.Message)
  'handle the problem if necessary
End Try
```

⬡LoadBitmap (Dir As String, FileName As String) As Bitmap

Loads the bitmap (page 352). Note: the Android file system is case sensitive.
You should consider using LoadBitmapSample if the image size is large.
The actual file size is not relevant as images are usually stored compressed.
Example:

```
Activity.SetBackgroundImage(LoadBitmap(File.DirAssets,
"SomeFile.jpg"))
```

⬡LoadBitmapSample (Dir As String, FileName As String, MaxWidth As Int, MaxHeight As Int) As Bitmap

Loads the bitmap (page 352). The decoder will sub-sample the bitmap if either MaxWidth or MaxHeight is smaller than the bitmap dimensions. This can save a lot of memory when loading large images. The width / height ratio is preserved. Example:

```
Activity.SetBackgroundImage(LoadBitmapSample(File.DirAssets,
"SomeFile.jpg", Activity.Width, Activity.Height))
```

⬡Log (Message As String)

Logs a message. When debugging, the log can be viewed in the Logs tab. When the app is released, this command has no effect.

⬡Logarithm (Number As Double, Base As Double) As Double

The power you need to raise Base to in order to create Number. Examples:

```
Logarithm(10,10) is 1, Logarithm(8,2) is 3 and Logarithm(100,10) is 2.
```

⬤Matcher

A Matcher object can be used to find matches of the given pattern in the text. It is created by the Regex object (page 322).

Matcher Groups

It can search for groups of characters, which are enclosed in parentheses ( ).
Example:

```
'Check two numbers and swap if first > second
strPattern = "(\d+)-(\d+)"
strText = "456-123"
matcher1 = Regex.Matcher(strPattern, strText)
matcher1.Find
Log("GroupCount: " & matcher1.GroupCount)
If matcher1.Group(1) <= matcher1.Group(2) Then
 strOutput = strText
Else
 ' swap numbers
 strOutput = matcher1.Group(2) & "-" & matcher1.Group(1)
End If
Log ("Result: " & strOutput)
```

The result is:

```
GroupCount: 2
Result: 123-456
```

Matcher Methods

⬡*Find as Boolean*

Searches for the next substring that matches the pattern.
Returns True if such a match was found.

⬡*GetEnd (Index as Int) as Int*

Returns the end offset of the specified captured group. Example:

```
strPattern = "(\d+-\d+)"
strText = "123:456-789:000"
matcher1 = Regex.Matcher(strPattern, strText)
If matcher1.Find Then
 Log("Group(1): " & matcher1.Group(1))
 Log("GetStart of Group(1): " & matcher1.GetStart(1))
 Log("GetEnd of Group(1): " & matcher1.GetEnd(1))
Else
 Log("No match found")
End If
```
Result:
```
Group(1): 456-789
GetStart of Group(1): 4
GetEnd of Group(1): 11
```
Use GetEnd(0) to get the end offset of the whole match.

❦ GetStart (Index as Int) as Int
Returns the start offset of the specified captured group. See GetEnd example.
Use GetStart(0) to get the start offset of the whole match.

❦ Group (Index as Int) as Int
Returns the value of the specified captured group. See Matcher Groups above for example.
Group(0) returns the whole match. Example:
```
strPattern = "(\d+)-(\d+)"
strText = "123-456-789-000"
matcher1 = Regex.Matcher(strPattern, strText)
matcher1.Find
Log("group(0): " & matcher1.Group(0))
```
Result
group(0): 123-456

⚡ GroupCount as Int
Returns the number of capturing groups in the pattern. See Matcher Groups above for example.
Note that the number returned does not include group(0) which is the whole match.

❦ IsInitialized as Boolean
Whether the Match object has been initialized.

⚡ Match
Returns the matched value. This is the same as calling Group(0).

❦ Max (Number1 As Double, Number2 As Double) As Double
Returns the larger number of two numbers.

❦ Me As Object
For classes: returns a reference to the current instance.
For activities and services: returns a reference to an object that can be used with CallSub, CallSubDelayed and SubExists keywords. Example:
```
CallSub(Me, "test")
```
Cannot be used in code modules.

🔷Min (Number1 As Double, Number2 As Double) As Double

Returns the smaller of two numbers.

🔷Msgbox (Message As String, Title As String)

Shows a modal message box with the specified message and title.
The dialog will show one OK button.
Example:

```
Msgbox("Hello world", "This is the title")
```

See Modal Dialogs (page 132) for more.

🔷Msgbox2 (Message As String, Title As String, Positive As String, Cancel As String, Negative As String, Icon As Bitmap) As Int

Shows a modal message box with the specified message and title.
Message - The dialog message.
Title - The dialog title.
Positive - The text to show for the "positive" button. Pass "" if you don't want to show the button.
Cancel - The text to show for the "cancel" button. Pass "" if you don't want to show the button.
Negative - The text to show for the "negative" button. Pass "" if you don't want to show the button.
Icon - A bitmap that will be drawn near the title. Pass Null if you don't want to show an icon.
Returns one of the DialogResponse values. Example:

```
Dim bmp As Bitmap
Dim choice As Int
bmp.Initialize(File.DirAssets, "question.png")
choice = Msgbox2("Would you like to select a route?", "Please specify
your choice", "Yes please", "", "No thank you", bmp)
If choice = DialogResponse.POSITIVE Then ...
```

See Modal Dialogs (page 132) for more.

🔷Not (Value As Boolean) As Boolean

Inverts the value of the given boolean. Example:

```
If Not (startMarker.IsInitialized) Then
```

🔷Null As Object

The value of an object which does not exist. It will be returned, for example, if you try to access a non-existent key in a map. In the following, **obj** has the value null:

```
Dim m As Map
m.Initialize
Dim obj As Object
obj = m.Get("test")
If obj = Null Then …
```

⬡NumberFormat (Number As Double, MinimumIntegers As Int, MaximumFractions As Int) As String

Converts **Number** to a string with at least **MinimumIntegers** integer digits and at most **MaximumFractions** decimal digits. Examples:

```
NumberFormat(12345.6789, 0, 2) '12,345.68
NumberFormat(1, 3 ,0)           '001
```

⬡NumberFormat2 (Number As Double, MinimumIntegers As Int, MaximumFractions As Int, MinimumFractions As Int, GroupingUsed As Boolean) As String

Converts **Number** to a string with at least **MinimumIntegers**, at most **MaximumFractions** decimal digits and at least **MinimumFractions** decimal digits.

GroupingUsed - Determines whether to group every three integers. Example:

```
NumberFormat2(12345.67, 0, 3, 3, false) ' 12345.670
NumberFormat2(12345, 0, 2, 2, True)      ' 12,345.00
```

⬡PerXToCurrent (Percentage As Float) As Int

Returns the actual size of the given percentage of the activity width.
Example: set the width of Button1 to 50% of the width of the current activity:

```
EditText1.Width = PerXToCurrent(50)
```

A shorthand syntax for this method is available. Any number followed by %x will be converted in the same manner.
So the previous code is equivalent to

```
EditText1.Width = 50%x
```

Note: there is no space between the 0 and the %.

⬡PerYToCurrent (Percentage As Float) As Int

Returns the actual size of the given percentage of the activity height.
Example: set the height of Button1 to 50% of the current activity:

```
EditText1.Height = PerYToCurrent(50)
```

A shorthand syntax for this method is available. Any number followed by %y will be converted in the same manner.
So the previous code is equivalent to

```
EditText1.Height = 50%y
```

Note: there is no space between the 0 and the %.

⬡Power (Base As Double, Exponent As Double) As Double

Returns the Base value raised to the Exponent power.

⬡ProgressDialogHide

Hides a visible progress dialog. Does not do anything if no progress dialog is visible.

⬡ProgressDialogShow (Text As String)

Shows a dialog with a circular spinning bar and the specified **Text**.
Unlike **Msgbox** and **InputList** methods, the code will not block, or in other words, the program will continue to run and not wait for the user to take some action.

You should call ProgressDialogHide to remove the dialog.
The dialog will also be removed if the user presses on the **Back** key.

⬡ProgressDialogShow2 (Text As String, Cancelable As Boolean)

Shows a dialog with a circular spinning bar and the specified **Text**.

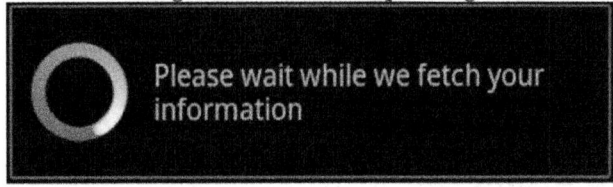

Unlike `Msgbox` and `InputList` methods, the code will not block, or in other words, the
program will continue to run and not wait for the user to take some action.
You should call `ProgressDialogHide` to remove the dialog.
Cancelable - Whether the user can dismiss the dialog by pressing on the **Back** key.

⬡QUOTE As String

Quote character. The value of Chr(34).

⬡Regex As Regex

Regex is a predefined object which contains regular expression (page 288) related methods.
Follow the link for more on this subject. All methods receive a pattern string.
Suppose we want to check that the user has entered a date in the format 99-99-9999. We
could use the expression:

```
If Not(Regex.IsMatch("\d\d-\d\d-\d\d\d\d", strText)) Then
```

For more information about the constructs used in regular expressions, see here (page 288).

Regex Options

CASE_INSENSITIVE

This option enables matching to be case insensitive when used in `IsMatch2` and `Split2`.

MULTILINE

Normally the regex character ^ matches the start of a string and $ matches the end, but the
MULTILINE option changes them to match the start and end of each line instead of the
whole string when used in `IsMatch2` and `Split2`.
These two options can both be applied by using

```
Bit.Or(Regex.MULTILINE, Regex.CASE_INSENSITIVE)
```

Regex Methods

IsMatch (Pattern as String, Text as String) as Boolean

Tests whether the whole of **Text** is the same as **Pattern**. See the example above.
Use a `Matcher` (page 318) if you need to find a substring that matches the pattern.

IsMatch2 (Pattern as String, Options as String, Text as String)

Tests whether Text is a match for Pattern.
Options - One or more pattern options. These options can be combined with Bit.Or.

Matcher (Pattern as String, Text as String) as Matcher

This creates a Matcher (page 318) object which can be used to find matches Pattern in Text.

Matcher2 (Pattern as String, Options as String, Text as String)

Same as Matcher with the additional pattern options.

Split (Pattern as String, Text as String)

Splits the given text around matches of the pattern. Example:

```
Dim components() As String
components = Regex.Split(",", "abc,def,,ghi")
```

The result is "abc", "def", "", "ghi"

Split2 (Pattern as String, Options as String, Text as String)

Same as Split with the additional pattern Options.

⬡Return

Returns from the current sub and optionally returns the given value.
Syntax: Return [value]

⬡Rnd (Min As Int, Max As Int) As Int

Returns a random integer between Min (inclusive) and Max (exclusive).

⬡RndSeed (Seed As Long)

Sets the random seed value.
This method can be used for debugging as it allows you to get the same results each time.

⬡Round (Number As Double) As Long

Returns the closest long number to the given number.

⬡Round2 (Number As Double, DecimalPlaces As Int) As Double

Rounds **Number**, retaining **at most** the specified number of decimal digits.

```
Log(Round2(1234.5678, 2)) ' result is 1234.57
Log(Round2(1234, 2)) ' result is 1234
```

⬡Select

Compares a single value to multiple values.
Example

```
Dim value As Int
value = Rnd(-10, 10)
Log("Value = " & value)
Select value
 Case 1
   Log("One")
 Case 2, 4, 6, 8
   Log("Positive even")
 Case 3, 5, 7, 9
   Log("Positive odd")
 Case Else
  If value < 1 Then
   Log("Less than 1")
  Else
   Log("Larger than 9")
  End If
End Select
```

❤Sender As Object

Returns the object that raised the event. Only valid while inside the event sub. Example:

```
Sub Button_Click
  Dim b As Button
  b = Sender
  b.Text = "I've been clicked"
End Sub
```

Note that **Sender** correctly manages events from multiple threads.

❤Sin (Radians As Double) As Double

Calculates the trigonometric sine function. Angle measured in radians.

❤SinD (Degrees As Double) As Double

Calculates the trigonometric sine function. Angle measured in degrees.

❤Sqrt (Value As Double) As Double

Returns the positive square root.

❤StartActivity (Activity As Object)

Starts an activity or brings it to the front if it already exists.

The target activity will be started once the program is free to process its message queue.

Activity can be a string with the target activity name or it can be the actual activity.

After this call, the current activity will be paused and the target activity will be resumed.

This method can also be used to send Intents (page 378) objects to the system.

Note: you should usually **not** call **StartActivity** from a Service.

Example: StartActivity (Activity2)

❤StartService (Service As Object)

Starts the given **Service**. The **Service** will be first created if it was not previously started.

The target **Service** will be started once the program is free to process its message queue.

Service - The service module or the service name.

Note: you cannot show a Msgbox after this call and before the service starts.
Example: `StartService(SQLService)`

⚙ StartServiceAt (Service As Object, Time As Long, DuringSleep As Boolean)

Schedules the given **Service** to start at the given **Time**. This is an alternative to using a timer (page 401). A service has the benefit that it continues to run when your app is not running and can even run when the device is sleeping.

Starting from Android 4.4, the operating system may group scheduled tasks to save battery and hence not use the exact time. If you need to use the exact time you should use `StartServiceAtExact`.

Service - The service module or service name. Pass an empty string when calling from a service module that schedules itself.

Time - The time to start the service, specified as a **Long**. You can use the DateTime (page 349) object to calculate this, for example, to specify 1 hour from now:
```
DateTime.Now + 3600 * 1000
```
.... If the selected time has already passed, the **Service** will be started immediately.

DuringSleep - Whether to start the **Service** when the device is sleeping. If set to **False** and the device is sleeping at the specified time, the **Service** will be started when the device wakes up.

`StartServiceAt` can be used to schedule a repeating task. You should call it under **Sub Service_Start** to schedule the next task. This call cancels previous scheduled tasks (for the same service).

Example:
```
StartServiceAt(SQLService, DateTime.Now + 30 * 1000, false) 'will
start after 30 seconds.
```

⚙ StartServiceAtExact (Service As Object, Time As Long, DuringSleep As Boolean)

For Android up to and including 4.3 (API 18) this is the same as `StartServiceAt`. On Android 4.4 and later, when `StartServiceAt` may not give the exact time, `StartServiceAtExact` forces the operating system to start the service at the exact **Time**. This method will have a larger impact on the battery compared to StartServiceAt. The parameters are the same as `StartServiceAt`.

⚙ StopService (Service As Object)

Stops the given service. **Sub Service_Destroy** will be called. Calling `StartService` afterwards will first create the **Service**.

Service - The service module or service name. Pass an empty string to stop the current service (from the service module).

Example:
```
StopService(SQLService)
```

⚙ Sub

Declares a sub with the parameters and return type. Syntax:

```
Sub name [(list of parameters)] [As return-type]
```

Any parameters which are given must include a name and type. You can pass an array as a parameter but it must be one-dimensional. The size of the dimension should not be included. Multi-dimensional arrays are not allowed. For example, a sub which requires a parameter iScores which is a one-dimensional array would be declared as:

```
Sub dWeightedMean (strName As String, iScores() As Int) As Double
```

A sub can return an object of any type. It can also return a one-dimensional array. For example, a sub which returns an array of Double would be declared as:

```
Sub getArray (iCount As Int) As Double()
```

SubExists (Object As Object, Sub As String) As Boolean

Returns TRUE if the **Object** includes the specified method.

Returns False if the **Object** was not initialized, or is not an instance of a user class.

TAB As String

Tab character equivalent to Chr(9).

Tan (Radians As Double) As Double

Calculates the trigonometric tangent function. Angle measured in radians.

TanD (Degrees As Double) As Double

Calculates the trigonometric tangent function. Angle measured in degrees.

ToastMessageShow (Message As String, LongDuration As Boolean)

Shows a small message that fades automatically.

Message - The text message to show.

LongDuration - If True, shows the message for a long period. If False, shows the message for a short period.

True As Boolean

A constant which can be used to compare or set logical values, for example:

```
ToastMessageShow("Email sent", True)
```

Try

Any exception thrown inside a **Try** block will be caught in the **Catch** block.

Call **LastException** to get the caught exception. Syntax:

```
Try
. . .
Catch
. . .
End Try
```

See Try-Catch (page 304) for more details.

Type

Declares a structure. Can only be used inside sub Globals or **Sub Process_Globals**. Syntax:

```
Type type-name (field1, field2, ...)
```
Fields must include their name and type. Example:
```
Type MyType (Name As String, Items(10) As Int)
Dim a, b As MyType
a.Initialize
a.Items(2) = 123
```
See here for details (page 285).

Until

Loops until the condition is **True**. Syntax:
```
Do Until condition
...
Loop
```
See Do-Until (page 295) for more details.

While

Loops while the condition is **True**. Syntax:
```
Do While condition
...
Loop
```
See Do-While (page 294) for more details.

3.2 VB6 versus B4A

There are some differences between B4A and Visual Basic from Microsoft. The following analysis of the differences between B4A and Visual Basic 6 is extracted from work by nfordbscndrd, a member of the B4A forum. It highlights some of the differences between the two IDEs and their languages. It might be useful for experienced VB6 programmers.

Controls vs. Views

The objects which B4A calls Views (page 443) (buttons, edittext, labels, etc.) are called Controls in Visual Basic.

In the VB6 code window, the top left drop-down list contains all the controls you have placed in the current form and the right list contains all the events for each control. The equivalent in B4A can be found by clicking on the Designer menu [Tools > Generate Members]. Once you have created Subs in the program coding window, the Modules window will list each of the Subs in the current module, below a list of all the modules.

In B4A, you start by typing "Sub" followed by a space. The IDE will then prompt you for details. We describe this in the Autocomplete Event Subroutines (page 84) section.

In VB6, you can leave ".Text" off the names of controls when assigning text to them, but this is not allowed in B4A.

Dim

VB6: Dim name(n) will give you n+1 elements with index 0 to n. For example, `Dim strName(12)` will give you 13 strings.

B4A: Dim name(n) will give you n elements with index 0 to n-1. This can be confusing since, for `Dim strName(12)`, the last element is actually `strName(11)`.

ReDim

VB6: ReDim name(n) does not exist in B4A, where you would simply use another `Dim name(n)`. Likewise, VB6 "ReDim Preserve" does not exist. If you need this, you would be better to use a list or map.

Boolean Operations

Suppose the following have been declared in either language:
```
Dim i Int
Dim b as Boolean
```

Not
VB6 does not require parentheses: "If Not b Then"
In B4A, parentheses are reqired: `If Not(b) Then`

Using Integers as Boolean
In VB6, an integer that equals zero is considered as the same as a Boolean FALSE; anything non-zero is TRUE. For example: "If i Then"

In B4A, a Boolean value CANNOT be used in a math function. Instead, you must test the value of a variable, for example:

```
If i > 0 Then
```

Global Const

B4A does not have a Global Const function.
In VB6 you can say

```
Global Const x=1
```

In B4A you say
Sub Globals

```
Dim x as Int = 1
```

However, x is not a constant. Its value can be changed.

Repeating Structures

For...Next
VB6: For i...Next i
B4A: For i...Next

Loops, If-Then, Select Case
VB6: Loop...Until, Loop...While
This structure is not allowed in B4A. You can, however, use the alternative form:
B4A: Do While...Loop, Do Until... Loop
See Do-While (page 294) and Do-Until (page 295) for more details.

Exit
VB6: Exit Do/For
B4A: Exit

ElseIf/EndIf
VB6: ElseIf/EndIf
B4A: Else If/End If

Colors

In VB6, colors have names such as "vbRed". In B4A, you use the Colors object, for example:
```
Colors.Red
```

Subroutines

Declaring a Sub
VB6: Sub SubName()
B4A: Sub SubName() As Int/String/etc.

Calling a sub
VB6: SubName x, y

B4A: SubName(x, y)

Functions

Functions do not exist in B4A. Instead, any **Sub** can be used as a Function by adding a variable type.
VB6: Function FName() As Int
B4A: **Sub FName() As Int**
If no **Return** is given, then zero or **False** or "" is returned.

Exit Sub

Exit Sub does not exist in B4A. Use Return instead.
VB6: Exit Sub / Exit Function
B4A: Return / Return [value]

DoEvents

While **DoEvents** exists in B4A, calling DoEvents in a loop consumes a lot of resources and uses excessive battery power because Android will never get back to the main "idle loop" where the hardware power saving measures are invoked. Also, **DoEvents** doesn't allow the system to process all waiting messages properly. In short, **looping for long periods should be avoided where possible on mobile devices**.

Format

VB6: Format()
B4A: NumberFormat (page 321) & NumberFormat2 (page 321)

InputBox

In VB6, InputBox() shows a dialog box and waits for the user to input text or click a button, and then returns a string containing the contents of the text box.
B4A has no dialog box which allows the user to enter text. Instead, you create something similar using an EditText on a layout. Alternatively, you could use one of the following:
– The user-created Dialogs Library (page 568), which offers InputDialog for text, a TimeDialog for times, a DateDialog for dates, both a ColorDialog and a ColorPickerDialog for colors, a NumberDialog for numbers, a FileDialog for folders and file names, and a CustomDialog.
– InputList (page 314) to show a modal dialog with a list of choices and radio buttons and return an index indicating which one the user has selected.
– InputMultiList (page 315) to show a list from which the user can select multiple items before returning.
– InputMap (page 315) to show a modal dialog with a list of items and checkboxes. The user can select multiple items.

Loop

VB6: Loop ... Until / While
B4A: Do While / Do Until ... Loop

MsgBox

VB6: MsgBox "text" / i=MsgBox()
B4A: has several alternatives:
MsgBox (page 320)("text", "title")
MsgBox2 (page 320)(Message, Title, Positive, Cancel, Negative, Icon) as Int
ToastMessageShow (page 326)(text, b)

Random Numbers

Random numbers generated by computers are not really random. They are "pseudo-random" and are created using an algorithm which starts from one number, the "seed", to generate the next.

Rnd

In VB6, `Rnd()` returns a float < 1.
In B4A, `Rnd(min, max)` returns an integer >= min and < max.

RndSeed

If # is a number, then in VB6, Rnd(-#) sets the "seed" of the random number generator to #. After this call, Rnd will return the same series of numbers every time.
In B4A, `RndSeed(#)` sets the random number generator seed in the same way. # must be a `Long` type number.

Randomize

If # is a number, then in VB6, Randomize(#) uses # to initialize the Rnd function's random number generator, using # as the new seed value. Randomize() without the number uses the value returned by the system timer as the new seed value. If Randomize is not used, the Rnd function (with no arguments) always uses the same number as a seed the first time it is called, and thereafter uses the last-generated number as a seed value.
In B4A, there is no equivalent of Randomize, because the seed of Rnd is always randomized automatically.

Round

VB6: Round(n) where n is a floating point number.
B4A: `Round(n)` or `Round2(n, x)` where n is a `Double` and x=number of decimal places

Val()

VB6: i = Val(string)
B4A: If IsNumber(string) Then i = string Else i = 0

An attempt to use i=string throws a NumberFormatException if the string is not a valid number.

SetFocus

VB6: control.SetFocus
B4A: `view.RequestFocus`

Divide by Zero

VB6 throws an exception for division by 0. B4A returns either 2147483647 or Infinity, depending whether the result is set to an integer or a string:

```
Dim i As Int
i = 12/0
Log (i) ' 2147483647

Dim str As String
str = 12/0
Log (str) ' Infinity
```

Shell

VB6: x = Shell("...")
B4A: See "Intent (page 378)".
This is not a complete replacement, but allows code such as the following:

```
Dim Intent1 As Intent
Intent1.Initialize(Intent1.ACTION_MAIN, "")
Intent1.SetComponent("com.google.android.youtube/.HomeActivity")
StartActivity(Intent1)
```

Timer

VB6: t = Timer
B4A: `t = DateTime.Now`, which returns the number of milliseconds since 1-1-70

TabIndex

In VB6, TabIndex can be set to control the order in which controls get focus in a form when Tab is pressed.
On an Android device, Android handles the sequence according to their position. However, in the Designer or in code, you can set `EditText.ForceDone` to `True` in all your EditTexts: `EditText1.ForceDoneButton = True`. This forces the virtual keyboard to show the Done button. You can then catch the `EditText_EnterPressed` event and explicitly set the focus to the next view (with `EditText.RequestFocus`).

Setting Label Transparency

You can control the transparency of a label as follows:
VB6: [Properties > Back Style]

B4A Designer: [Drawable > Alpha]

Constants

There are a number of useful predefined constants in VB6, for example,
VB6: vbCr, vbCrLf
B4A: CRLF (page 310) (Android's equivalent of Windows CRLF, although in fact it is the Line Feed character Chr(10)).

String "Members"

VB6 uses a character position pointer starting with 1.
B4A function CharAt() uses a character Index pointer starting with 0.
All the following produce "a":
VB6: Mid$("abcde", 1)
VB6: Mid$("abcde", 1, 1)
B4A: "abcde".CharAt(0)
B4A: "abcde".SubString2(0,1)
The following produce "abc":
VB6: Mid$("abcde", 1, 3)
B4A: "abcde". SubString2(0, 3)

Left$ and Right$

These do not exist in B4A. You can recreate them as follows:

VB6: Left$("abcde", 3)
B4A: "abcde".SubString2(0, 3)

VB6: Right$("abcde", 2)
B4A: "abcde".SubString("abcde".Length - 2)

VB6: If Right$(text, n) = text2
B4A: If text.EndsWith(text2)...

VB6: If Left$(text, n) = text2
B4A: If text.StartsWith(text2)...

VB6: If Lcase$(text) = Lcase$(text2)
B4A: If text.EqualsIgnoreCase(text2)

Len

VB6: x = Len(text)
B4A: x = text.Length

Replace

VB6: text = Replace(text, str, str2)
B4A: text.Replace(str, str2)

Case

VB6: Lcase(text)
B4A: text.ToLowerCase
VB6: Ucase(text)
B4A: text.ToUpperCase

Trim

VB6: Trim(text)
B4A: text.Trim
There is no LTrim or RTrim in B4A

Instr

VB6: Instr(text, string)
B4A: text.IndexOf (page 398)(string)

VB6: Instr(int, text, string)
B4A: text.IndexOf2 (page 399)(string, int)

VB6: If Lcase$(x) = Lcase$(y)
B4A: If x.EqualsIgnoreCase(y)

VB6: text = Left$(text, n) & s & Right$(Text, y)
B4A: text.Insert(n, s)

Error Trapping

VB6

```
Sub SomeSub
  On [Local] Error GoTo ErrorTrap
  ...some code...
  On Error GoTo 0 [optional end to error trapping]
  ...optional additional code...
  Exit Sub [to avoid executing ErrorTrap code]
ErrorTrap:
  ...optional code for error correction...
  Resume [optional: "Resume Next" or "Resume [line label]".
End Sub
```

B4A

```
Sub SomeSub
  Try
    ...some code...
  Catch [only executes if error above]
   Log(LastException) [optional]
    ...optional code for error correction...
  End Try
  ...optional additional code...
End Sub
```

With B4A, if you get an error caught in the middle of a large subroutine, you CANNOT make a correction and resume within the code you were executing. Only the code in "Catch" gets executed. That would seem to make **Try-Catch-End Try** of use mainly during development.

"Immediate Window" vs. "Logs" Tab

Comments, variable values, etc., can be displayed in VB6's Immediate Window by entering into the code "Debug.Print ...".
In B4A, show values of variables, etc. in the Logs tab (page 56).
Both VB6 and B4A allow single-stepping through the code while it is running and viewing the values of variables. VB6 also allows changing the value of variables, changing the code, jumping to other lines from the current line, etc. Because B4A runs on a PC while the app runs on a separate device, B4A is currently unable to duplicate all of these VB6 debug features.

3.3 Core Objects

These objects are in the core library of the IDE and can be used without referring to any other libraries. These are included in both the Trial and the Full versions of B4A.
For example your code can simply say:

```
Sub Globals
  Dim map1 As Map
  Dim match1 As Matcher
  Dim mediaPlayer1 As MediaPlayer
End Sub
```

List of Core Objects

In the following lists, we group the core objects (and constants) according to their function where possible. The remainder we group under "General".

General

Activity
Application (page 343)
Bit (page 343)
DateTime (page 349)
Exception (page 365)
Intent (page 378)
LayoutValues (page 379)
List (page 380)
Map (page 384)
MediaPlayer (page 388)
Notification (page 389)
RemoteViews (page 393)
Service (page 394)
String (page 394)
StringBuilder (page 399)
Timer (page 401)

Constants

Colors (page 345)
DialogResponse (page 346)
Gravity (page 346)
KeyCodes (page 347)
Typeface (page 349)

Drawing Objects

Bitmap (page 352)
BitmapDrawable (page 354)
Canvas (page 354)
ColorDrawable (page 361)
GradientDrawable (page 361)

File Objects

Views

Activity

Activities are the main components of your application. We describe its usage in the Activity Concept (page 239) Chapter. In the following section, we detail its events and members. Note your app can have multiple activities (page 127).

Views within an Activity

If you iterate over an Activity, you will find each of the views it consists of:

```
For Each vw As View In Activity
  ' check its type
  If vw Is Button Then
    ' need object with correct type so
    '  can gain access to properties
    Dim btn As Button
    ' make copy of original view
    btn = vw
    Log (btn.Text)
  End If
Next
```

Activity Events

ActionBarHomeClick

This event is generated when the user touches the Up Button (page 122), the Action Bar icon (page 123) or the Action Bar Title (page 123). It replaces the **ButtonClicked** event from the StdActionBar library (page 566), which no longer fires in Android 5 (API 21).

Click

This event is generated when the user touches the screen, provided that no other view has consumed the event (such as an **EditText**), and provided that no handler exists for the **Touch** event. **Touch** takes priority over **Click**.

KeyPress and KeyUp Events

The **KeyPress** and **KeyUp** events occur when the user presses or releases a key on the Android keyboard, assuming that no other view has consumed this event (like EditText). When handling the KeyPress or KeyUp event, you should return a boolean value which tells whether the event was consumed. Return **True** to consume the event. For example, if the user pressed on the Back key and you return **True**, then Android will not close your activity.

```
Sub Activity_KeyPress (KeyCode As Int) As Boolean
  If Keycode = KeyCodes.KEYCODE_BACK Then
    Return True
  Else
    Return False
  End If
End Sub
```

LongClick

This event is generated when the user touches the screen for a long time (about one second) provided that no other view has consumed the event (such as an **EditText**), and provided that no handler exists for the **Touch** event. **Touch** takes priority over **LongClick**.

Touch (Action As Int, X As Float, Y As Float)

The Touch event can be used to handle user touches. If a handler exists for the Touch event, then handlers for the **Click** and **LongClick** events will not work.

The **Action** parameter values can be:

– Activity.ACTION_DOWN: The user has touched the screen at X,Y.

– Activity.ACTION_MOVE: The user's touch has moved to X,Y.

– Activity.ACTION_UP: The user has stopped touching the screen at X,Y.
Use this value to find the user current action.

Activity Members

●ACTION_DOWN As Int

●ACTION_MOVE As Int

●ACTION_UP As Int

♥AddMenuItem (Title As String, EventName As String)

Adds a menu item to the activity. On devices running Android less than 3.0, the menu is
evoked by pressing the menu key. On 3.0 and above it is shown as an overflow (page 123)
symbol (3 vertical dots) on the Action Bar (page 121).

Title – Text shown in menu.
EventName - The prefix name of the sub that will handle the click event.
This method should only be called inside `Sub Activity_Create`.
Note: the `Sender` (page 324) keyword inside the click event equals the clicked menu item
text.
Example:

```
Activity.AddMenuItem("Test Menu", "TestMenu")
' ...
Sub TestMenu_Click
  Log (Sender) ' will log "Test Menu"
End Sub
```

♥AddMenuItem2 (Title As String, EventName As String, Bitmap1 As Bitmap)

Adds a menu item with a `Bitmap` to the activity. See previous topic for more details.
Title – Text shown in menu. If blank then only `Bitmap1` will be shown.
EventName – The prefix name of the sub that will handle the click event.
Bitmap – Bitmap to draw as the item background.
Only the first five (or six if there are six total) menu items display icons.
This method should only be called inside `Sub Activity_Create`.
Note: the `Sender` keyword inside the click event equals the clicked menu item text.
Example:

```
Activity.AddMenuItem2("Open File", "OpenFile",
LoadBitmap(File.DirAssets, "SomeImage.png"))
...
Sub OpenFile_Click
...
End Sub
```

❦AddMenuItem3 (Title As String, EventName As String, Bitmap1 As Bitmap, AddToActionBar As Boolean)

Adds a menu item with a `Bitmap` to the activity, with the option to add the action bar (page 121) on Android 3.00+ devices. See below for more details.

Title – Text shown in menu. If blank then only `Bitmap1` will be shown.

EventName – The prefix name of the sub that will handle the click event.

Bitmap – Bitmap to draw as the item background.

AddToActionBar – if `True`, then the item will be displayed in the action bar (page 121) (on Android 3.0+ devices) if there is enough room. If there is not enough room, then the item will be displayed together with the other menu items in the overflow (page 123) options. See here (http://bit.ly/19E7ppF) for more about the options menu in Android 3.0+

Note: the `Sender` keyword inside the click event equals the clicked menu item text.

Example
```
Dim bm As Bitmap
bm.Initialize (File.DirAssets, "menuIcon.png")
Activity.AddMenuItem3 ( "Open File", "OpenFile", bm, True)
...
Sub OpenFile_click()
...
End Sub
```

❦AddView (View1 As View, Left As Int, Top As Int, Width As Int, Height As Int)

Adds a view to this activity.

⚒Background As Drawable

Gets or sets the background drawable.

❦CloseMenu

Programmatically closes the menu.

⚒Color As Int [write only]

Sets the background of the view to be a `ColorDrawable` with the given color. If the current background is of type `GradientDrawable` or `ColorDrawable`, the round corners will be kept.

❦DisableAccessibility (Disable As Boolean)

This method was added as a workaround for a bug (http://bit.ly/1za8Klh) which mades Android crash when sorting view children if accessibility is enabled. By setting Disable to True, the child views of all Activities will not be added to the accessibility enabled list.

✤Finish

Closes this activity. See Activity.Finish vs ExitApplication (page 246) for details of when you should use Finish.

✤GetAllViewsRecursive As IterableList

Returns an iterator that iterates over all the views belonging to the Activity, including views which are children of other views. Example:

```
For Each vw As View In Activity.GetAllViewsRecursive
  vw.Color = Colors.RGB(Rnd(0,255), Rnd(0,255), Rnd(0,255))
Next
```

✤GetStartingIntent As Intent

(Advanced) Gets the intent object that started this Activity.

This can be used together with **SetActivityResult** to return results to 3rd party applications.

✤GetView (Index As Int) As View

Gets the view that is stored at the specified index.

✦Height As Int

Gets or sets the Activity's height.

✤Initialize (EventName As String)

Initializes the Activity and sets the subs that will handle the events.

Note: this function is never needed since the Activity will be automatically initialized. It only exists because, technically, Activity is a sub-type of View.

✤Invalidate

Invalidates the whole Activity, forcing the view to redraw itself. Redrawing will only happen when the program can process messages, usually when it finishes running the current code. If you only need to redraw part of the view, it is usually quicker to use **Invalidate2** or **Invalidate3**.

✤Invalidate2 (Rect1 As Rect)

Invalidates anything inside the given rectangle that is part of this Activity. Redrawing will only happen when the program can process messages, usually when it finishes running the current code.

✤Invalidate3 (Left As Int, Top As Int, Right As Int, Bottom As Int)

Invalidates anything inside the given rectangle that is part of this Activity. Redrawing will only happen when the program can process messages, usually when it finishes running the current code.

✤IsInitialized As Boolean

This always returns **True**. It only exists because, technically, Activity is a sub-type of View.

✦Left As Int

This is always 0 for an Activity.

⬡LoadLayout (Layout As String) As LayoutValues

Loads a layout file (.bal). Returns the LayoutValues of the actual layout variant that was loaded.

⚲NumberOfViews As Int [read only]

Returns the number of child views.

⬡OpenMenu

Programmatically opens the menu.

⬡RemoveAllViews

Removes all child views.

⬡RemoveViewAt (Index As Int)

Removes the view that is stored at the specified index. Example:

```
Dim vw As View
For i = 0 To Activity.NumberOfViews - 1
 vw = Activity.GetView(i)
 If vw.Tag = "btnNew" Then
  Activity.RemoveViewAt(i)
 End If
Next
```

⬡RequestFocus As Boolean

This function is never needed. It will always return **False**. It only exists because, technically, Activity is a sub-type of View.

⬡RerunDesignerScript (Layout As String, Width As Int, Height As Int)

Runs the designer script again with the specified width and height. See the designer scripts (page 162) chapter for more information.

⬡SendToBack

This function is never needed. It only exists because, technically, Activity is a sub-type of View.

⬡SetActivityResult (Result As Int, Data As Intent)

This advanced feature allows an Activity to return a result to an external app that calls **startActivityForResult** to start the app and get a result. For example, you can use it to build a file chooser app with a defined external API. **SetActivityResult** sets the result that the calling Activity will get after calling **StartActivityForResult**.

Note: **IOnActivityResult**, **OnActivityResult**, **SetActivityResult** and **StartActivityForResult** are all advanced features which are beyond the scope of this book. For more information, see here (http://bit.ly/1gvOvso).

⬡SetBackgroundImage (Bitmap1 As Bitmap)

⬡SetLayout (Left As Int, Top As Int, Width As Int, Height As Int)

Changes the view position and size.

⚹Tag As Object

Gets or sets the Activity's Tag value. This can be used to store additional data.

⚹Title As CharSequence

Gets or sets the Activity's title.

⚹TitleColor As Int

Gets or sets the title color.

Note: the title color doesn't have any effect on devices using the holo style, which was introduced in Android 4. For more about Themes, see here (page 125).

⚹Top As Int

This is always 0 for an Activity.

⚹Width As Int

Gets or sets the view's width.

Application

Your program can read various parameters about your app using this object.

Application Members

⚹ LabelName As String

Returns the application name, specified in your #ApplicationLabel (page 111) attribute.

⚹ PackageName As String

Returns the application package name, specified in [Project > Build Configurations (page 171)].

⚹ VersionCode As Int

Returns the application version code, specified in your #VersionCode (page 113) attribute.

⚹ VersionName As String

Returns the application version name, specified in your #VersionName (page 113) attribute.

Bit

`Bit` is a predefined object containing bitwise related methods.
Example:

```
Dim flags As Int
flags = Bit.Or(100, 200)
```

Bitwise Operations

In bitwise operations, the numbers are first converted to their binary form (which consists of 1 and 0 digits). Then the operation is performed on each pair of binary digits, and the result assembled into a new binary number which is then converted back into a decimal form. For example, `Bit.AND(3,6)` would be processed as follows to produce the decimal number 2:

– 3 is converted to binary 011
– 2 is converted to binary 110
– The left-hand digits are ANDED together: 0 AND 1 evaluate to 0
– The middle two digits are ANDED; 1 AND 1 = 1
– The right-hand digits are ANDED; 1 AND 0 evaluate to 0
– The three results are assembled to make the binary number 010
– The binary number 010 is converted to decimal 2

Members:

And (N1 As Int, N2 As Int) As Int

Returns the bitwise AND of the two values. For each pair of corresponding bits in N1 and N2, the result is 1 if both both bits are 1, otherwise it is 0.

InputStreamToBytes (In As Inputstream) As Byte()

Reads data from an input stream, writes it into an array of bytes, closes the stream and returns the array.

```
Dim input As InputStream
input = File.OpenInput (File.DirRootExternal, "source.xxx")
Dim bytes() As Byte
bytes = Bit.InputStreamToBytes(input)
```

Not (N As Int) As Int

Returns the bitwise complement of the given value. For each bit in N, the corresponding bit in the result has the opposite value (1s are replace by 0s and 0s by 1s).

Or (N1 As Int, N2 As Int) As Int

Returns the bitwise OR of the two values. For each pair of corresponding bits in N1 and N2, the result is 0 if both both bits are 0, otherwise it is 1.

ParseInt (Value As String, Radix As Int) As Int

Converts **Value** from base **Radix** to base 10. So the following example will convert 100 in base 2 to base 10, and produce the result 4:

```
Log ( Bit.ParseInt("100",2))
```

Radix should be from 2 to 36. Other examples:

```
Log ( Bit.ParseInt("100",8))  ' 64
Log ( Bit.ParseInt("100",10))  ' 100
Log ( Bit.ParseInt("100",13))  ' 169
```

ShiftLeft (N As Int, Shift As Int) As Int

Shifts the bits in N to the left. The new right-most bits are set to 0.

Shift - Number of positions to shift.

⬡ShiftRight (N As Int, Shift As Int) As Int

Shifts the bits in N to the right. Keeps the original value sign, meaning that the new left-most bits have the same value as the original left-most bit.
Shift - Number of positions to shift.

⬡ToBinaryString (N As Int) As String

Returns a string representation of N in base 2.

⬡ToHexString (N As Int) As String

Returns a string representation of N in base 16.

⬡ToOctalString (N As Int) As String

Returns a string representation of N in base 8.

⬡UnsignedShiftRight (N As Int, Shift As Int) As Int

Shifts **N** right and inserts a zero in the left-most position for each shift performed.
Shift - Number of positions to shift.

⬡Xor (N1 As Int, N2 As Int) As Int

Returns the bitwise "exclusive or" of the two values. For each pair of bits, the result is 1 if only one of the two is 1, otherwise the result is 0.

Constants

Colors

A predefined object containing color constants.
For example: `Activity.Color = Colors.Green`

Members:

⬡ *ARGB (Alpha As Int, Red As Int, Green As Int, Blue As Int) As Int*

Returns an integer value representing the color built from the three components **Red**, **Green** and **Blue**, and with the specified **Alpha** value, which determines the transparency of the color. Each component should be a value from 0 to 255 (inclusive).
Alpha - A value from 0 to 255, where 0 is fully transparent and 255 is fully opaque.
Note: you can get the same result by using a hex literal (page 275). Thus Colors.ARGB(255,0,0,0) is the same as 0xFF000000.

⬢ *Black As Int*

⬢ *Blue As Int*

⬢ *Cyan As Int*

⬢ *DarkGray As Int*

⬢ *Gray As Int*

⬢ *Green As Int*

⬢ *LightGray As Int*

⬢ *Magenta As Int*

⬢ *Red As Int*

⬢ *RGB (Red As Int, Green As Int, Blue As Int) As Int*

Returns an integer value representing the color built from the three components **Red**, **Green** and **Blue**. Each component should be a value from 0 to 255 (inclusive). This is the same as ARGB with Alpha set to 255 (opaque).

Note: you can get the same result by using a hex literal (page 275). Thus Colors.RGB(255,0,0) is the same as 0xFF0000.

⬢ *Transparent As Int*

⬢ *White As Int*

⬢ *Yellow As Int*

DialogResponse

A predefined object containing the possible values that dialogs return. For example:

```
Dim result As Int
result = Msgbox2("Save changes?", "", "Yes", "", "No", Null)
If result = DialogResponse.POSITIVE Then
   'save changes
End If
```

⬢ *CANCEL As Int*

⬢ *NEGATIVE As Int*

⬢ *POSITIVE As Int*

Gravity

Predefined object containing "gravity" values. These values affect the alignment of text or images. Example:

```
Dim EditText1 As EditText
EditText1.Initialize("")
EditText1.Gravity = Gravity.CENTER
```

🔹 **BOTTOM As Int**

🔹 **CENTER As Int**

🔹 **CENTER_HORIZONTAL As Int**

🔹 **CENTER_VERTICAL As Int**

🔹 **FILL As Int**

🔹 **LEFT As Int**

🔹 **NO_GRAVITY As Int**

🔹 **RIGHT As Int**

🔹 **TOP As Int**

KeyCodes

A predefined object with the **KeyCode** constants. These constants are passed to the **Activity KeyPressed** event, for example:

```
Sub Activity_KeyPress(KeyCode As Int) As Boolean
 If KeyCode = KeyCodes.KEYCODE_BACK Then
  Log ("KEYCODE_BACK")
  Return False
 End If
End Sub
```

Events

None

Members

All the following are integer constants:

KEYCODE_0	KEYCODE_ALT_LEFT
KEYCODE_1	KEYCODE_ALT_RIGHT
KEYCODE_2	KEYCODE_APOSTROPHE
KEYCODE_3	KEYCODE_AT
KEYCODE_4	KEYCODE_B
KEYCODE_5	KEYCODE_BACK
KEYCODE_6	KEYCODE_BACKSLASH
KEYCODE_7	KEYCODE_C
KEYCODE_8	KEYCODE_CALL
KEYCODE_9	KEYCODE_CAMERA
KEYCODE_A	KEYCODE_CLEAR

KEYCODE_COMMA

KEYCODE_D

KEYCODE_DEL

KEYCODE_DPAD_CENTER

KEYCODE_DPAD_DOWN

KEYCODE_DPAD_LEFT

KEYCODE_DPAD_RIGHT

KEYCODE_DPAD_UP

KEYCODE_E

KEYCODE_ENDCALL

KEYCODE_ENTER

KEYCODE_ENVELOPE

KEYCODE_EQUALS

KEYCODE_EXPLORER

KEYCODE_F

KEYCODE_FOCUS

KEYCODE_G

KEYCODE_GRAVE

KEYCODE_H

KEYCODE_HEADSETHOOK

KEYCODE_HOME

KEYCODE_I

KEYCODE_J

KEYCODE_K

KEYCODE_L

KEYCODE_LEFT_BRACKET

KEYCODE_M

KEYCODE_MEDIA_FAST_FORWARD

KEYCODE_MEDIA_NEXT

KEYCODE_MEDIA_PLAY_PAUSE

KEYCODE_MEDIA_PREVIOUS

KEYCODE_MEDIA_REWIND

KEYCODE_MEDIA_STOP

KEYCODE_MENU

KEYCODE_MINUS

KEYCODE_MUTE

KEYCODE_N

KEYCODE_NOTIFICATION

KEYCODE_NUM

KEYCODE_O

KEYCODE_P

KEYCODE_PERIOD

KEYCODE_PLUS

KEYCODE_POUND

KEYCODE_POWER

KEYCODE_Q

KEYCODE_R

KEYCODE_RIGHT_BRACKET

KEYCODE_S

KEYCODE_SEARCH

KEYCODE_SEMICOLON

KEYCODE_SHIFT_LEFT

KEYCODE_SHIFT_RIGHT

KEYCODE_SLASH

KEYCODE_SOFT_LEFT

KEYCODE_SOFT_RIGHT

KEYCODE_SPACE

KEYCODE_STAR

KEYCODE_SYM

KEYCODE_T

KEYCODE_TAB

KEYCODE_U

KEYCODE_UNKNOWN

KEYCODE_V

KEYCODE_VOLUME_DOWN	KEYCODE_X
KEYCODE_VOLUME_UP	KEYCODE_Y
KEYCODE_W	KEYCODE_Z

Typeface

`Typeface` is a predefined object that holds the typeface styles and the default installed fonts. **Note**: unlike most other predefined objects, you can declare new objects of this type. Example:

```
EditText1.Typeface = Typeface.DEFAULT_BOLD
```

Events

None

Members

CreateNew (Typeface1 As Typeface, Style As Int) As Typeface

Returns a typeface with the specified **Style**. Example:

```
Typeface.CreateNew(Typeface.MONOSPACE, Typeface.STYLE_ITALIC)
```

DEFAULT As Typeface

DEFAULT_BOLD As Typeface

IsInitialized As Boolean

Whether this object has been initialized by calling `LoadFromAssets`.

LoadFromAssets (FileName As String) As Typeface

Loads a font file that was added with the file manager. Example:

```
Dim MyFont As Typeface
MyFont = Typeface.LoadFromAssets("MyFont.ttf")
EditText1.Typeface = MyFont
```

ttf files define TrueType (http://bit.ly/1OwgLef) format fonts. Free fonts are available from many sources, for example dafont.com (http://www.dafont.com/).

MONOSPACE As Typeface

SANS_SERIF As Typeface

SERIF As Typeface

STYLE_BOLD As Int

STYLE_BOLD_ITALIC As Int

STYLE_ITALIC As Int

STYLE_NORMAL As Int

DateTime

Date and time related methods. DateTime is a predefined object. You should not declare it yourself. Date and time values are stored as ticks.

Ticks

`Ticks` are the number of milliseconds since January 1, 1970 00:00:00 UTC (Coordinated Universal Time). **This value is too large to be stored in an Int variable. It should only be stored in a Long variable.** The methods `DateTime.Date` and `DateTime.Time` convert the ticks value to a string. You can get the current time with `DateTime.Now`.
Example:

```
Dim now As Long
now = DateTime.Now
Msgbox("The date is: " & DateTime.Date(now) & CRLF & _
    "The time is: " & DateTime.Time(now), "")
```

Members:

Add (Ticks As Long, Years As Int, Months As Int, Days As Int) As Long

Returns a ticks value which is the result of adding the specified time spans to the given **Ticks** value. Pass negative values if you want to subtract the values. Example:

```
Dim Tomorrow As Long
Tomorrow = DateTime.Add(DateTime.Now, 0, 0, 1)
Log("Tomorrow's date is: " & DateTime.Date(Tomorrow))
```

Date (Ticks As Long) As String

Returns a string representation of the date of the `Ticks` value. The date format can be set with the DateFormat keyword. Example:

```
Log("Today is: " & DateTime.Date(DateTime.Now))
```

DateFormat As String

Gets or sets the format used to parse date strings. See this page for the supported patterns: formats (http://bit.ly/1VEl1gr). The default pattern is MM/dd/yyyy (04/23/2002 for example).

DateParse (Date As String) As Long

Parses the given **Date** string and returns its ticks representation. An exception will be thrown if parsing fails. Example:

```
Dim SomeTime As Long
SomeTime = DateTime.DateParse("02/23/2007")
```

DateTimeParse (Date As String, Time As String) As Long

Parses the given date and time strings and returns the ticks representation.

DeviceDefaultDateFormat As String [read only]

Returns the default date format based on the language used by the Android device.

DeviceDefaultTimeFormat As String [read only]

Returns the default time format based on the language used by the Android device.

GetDayOfMonth (Ticks As Long) As Int

Returns the day of month component from the ticks value.
Values are from 1 to 31.

GetDayOfWeek (Ticks As Long) As Int

Returns the day of week component from the ticks value.
Values are from 1 to 7, where 1 means Sunday.
You can use the AHLocale library if you need to change the first day.

GetDayOfYear (Ticks As Long) As Int

Returns the day of year component from the ticks value.
Values are from 1 to 366.

GetHour (Ticks As Long) As Int

Returns the hour of day component from the ticks value.
Values are from 0 to 23.

GetMinute (Ticks As Long) As Int

Returns the minutes within an hour component from the ticks value.
Values are from 0 to 59.

GetMonth (Ticks As Long) As Int

Returns the month of year component from the ticks value.
Values are from 1 to 12.

GetSecond (Ticks As Long) As Int

Returns the seconds within a minute component from the ticks value.
Values are from 0 to 59.

GetTimeZoneOffsetAt (Date As Long) As Double

Returns the difference, measured in hours, between the time used by the Android device and
UTC (Coordinated Universal Time, equivalent to Greenwich Mean Time). You can specify
which **Date** you want to use for the calculation. The offset can change due to daylight-saving
settings. For example, if you were in Paris in the summer, then the following would give the
result of 2, because France is 1 hour ahead of UTC in winter and another hour ahead in the
summer:

```
Log(DateTime.GetTimeZoneOffsetAt(DateTime.Now))
```

GetYear (Ticks As Long) As Int

Returns the year component from the ticks value.

ListenToExternalTimeChanges

Creates a dynamic broadcast receiver that listens to the "time-zone changed" event and "time
set" event. By calling this method, the time-zone will update automatically when the device
time-zone changes. The **DateTime_TimeChanged** event will be raised when the time-zone
changes or when the time is set.

Now As Long [read only]

Gets the current time as ticks (number of milliseconds since January 1, 1970).

♥SetTimeZone (OffsetHours As Double)

Sets the time zone which your application uses to convert dates to ticks and vice versa. **Note**: the time zone used by the Android device is not changed.

♠TicksPerDay As Long

Contains the number of milliseconds in a day: 86400000

♠TicksPerHour As Long

Contains the number of milliseconds in an hour: 3600000

♠TicksPerMinute As Long

Contains the number of milliseconds in a minute: 60000

♠TicksPerSecond As Long

Contains the number of milliseconds in a second: 1000

♥Time (Ticks As Long) As String

Returns a string representation of the time (which is stored as ticks).
The time format can be set with the TimeFormat keyword.
Example:

```
Log("The time now is: " & DateTime.Time(DateTime.Now))
```

✒TimeFormat As String

Gets or sets the format used to parse time strings. The default pattern is HH:mm:ss (23:45:12 for example). See this page for the supported patterns: formats (http://bit.ly/1ErmQmQ).

♥TimeParse (Time As String) As Long

Parses the given **Time** string and returns its ticks representation, based on today's date.
Example:

```
Log(DateTime.TimeParse("13:45:57"))
```

Note: if the format of Time does not match the format specified by `DateTime.TimeFormat`, then a ParseException will be raised and the app will crash.

✒TimeZoneOffset As Double [read only]

Returns the current offset measured in hours from UTC (Coordinated Universal Time).

Drawing Objects

Bitmap

An object that holds a bitmap image. The bitmap can be loaded from a file or other input stream, or can be set from a different bitmap. You can show the Bitmap to the user by assigning it to an ImageView (page 416).
Loading large bitmaps can easily lead to out-of-memory exceptions. This is true even if the file is compressed and not large, as the bitmap is stored uncompressed in memory. For large images, you can call `InitializeSample` and load a subsample of the image. The whole image will be loaded with a lower resolution.

Members:

🔹 GetPixel (x As Int, y As Int) As Int
Returns the color of the pixel at the specified position.

🔸 Height As Int [read only]
Returns the bitmap height.

🔹 Initialize (Dir As String, FileName As String)
Reads the image from the given file and uses it to create the `Bitmap`. Note that the image will be downsampled if there is not enough memory available. Example:
```
Dim Bitmap1 As Bitmap
Bitmap1.Initialize(File.DirAssets, "X.jpg")
```

🔹 Initialize2 (InputStream As java.io.InputStream)
Initializes the bitmap from the given stream.

🔹 Initialize3 (Bitmap1 As Bitmap)
Initializes the bitmap with a copy of the original image (copying is done if necessary).

🔹 InitializeMutable (Width As Int, Height As Int)
Creates a new mutable bitmap with the specified dimensions. You can use a Canvas object to draw on this bitmap.

🔹 InitializeSample (Dir As String, FileName As String, MaxWidth As Int, MaxHeight As Int)
Initializes the bitmap from the given file. The decoder will subsample the bitmap if `MaxWidth` or `MaxHeight` are smaller than the bitmap dimensions. This can save a lot of memory when loading large images. Note that the actual dimensions may be larger than the specified values.

🔹 IsInitialized As Boolean
Whether the `Bitmap` has been initialized using one of the `Initialize` methods.

🔸 Width As Int [read only]
Returns the bitmap width.

🔹 WriteToStream (OutputStream As java.io.OutputStream, Quality As Int, Format As CompressFormat)
Writes the bitmap to the output stream.
Quality - Value from 0 (smaller size, lower quality) to 100 (larger size, higher quality), which is a hint for the compressor for the required quality.
Format – can be "JPEG" or "PNG". Any other format will produce a runtime exception.
Notes: "JPG" is not an allowed format, but you can use ".jpg" as the filename extension if you wish. Also you can read an image in format and write it in the other. Example:

```
Dim bm As Bitmap
bm.Initialize(File.DirAssets, "horse.png")
Dim Out As OutputStream
Out = File.OpenOutput(File.DirRootExternal, "horse.jpg", False)
bm.WriteToStream(Out, 100, "JPEG")
Out.Close
```

BitmapDrawable

A drawable that draws a bitmap. The bitmap is set during initialization. You can change the way the bitmap appears by changing the Gravity (page 346) property. Example:

```
Dim bd As BitmapDrawable
bd.Initialize(LoadBitmap(File.DirAssets, "SomeImage.png"))
bd.Gravity = Gravity.FILL
Activity.Background = bd
```

This is an **Activity** object; it cannot be declared under **Sub Process_Globals**.

Members:

⚑ Bitmap As Bitmap [read only]

Returns the internal Bitmap.

⚑ Gravity As Int

Gets or sets the gravity value. This value affects the way the image will be drawn. Example:

```
BitmapDrawable1.Gravity = Gravity.FILL
```

⚙ Initialize (Bitmap1 As Bitmap)

⚙ IsInitialized As Boolean

Whether the **BitmapDrawable** has been initialized using one of the **Initialize** methods.

Canvas

A **Canvas** is an object that draws on other views or bitmaps which are editable (also called "mutable"). When the canvas is initialized and set to draw on a view, a new mutable bitmap is created for that view's background, the current view's background is copied to the new bitmap and the canvas is set to draw on the new bitmap.

The canvas drawings are not immediately updated on the screen. You should call the target view's **Invalidate** method to make it refresh the view. This is useful as it allows you to make several drawings and only then refresh the display.

The canvas can be temporarily limited to a specific region (and thus only affect this region). This is done by calling **ClipPath**. Removing the clipping is done by calling **RemoveClip**.

You can get the bitmap that the canvas draws on with the **Bitmap** property.

This is an **Activity** object; it cannot be declared under **Sub Process_Globals**.

Members:

⚑ Bitmap As Bitmap [read only]

Returns the bitmap that the canvas draws to. The following example saves the drawing to a file:

```
Dim Out As OutputStream
Out = File.OpenOutput(File.DirRootExternal, "Test.png", False)
Canvas1.Bitmap.WriteToStream(out, 100, "PNG")
Out.Close
```

☢ ClipPath (Path1 As Path)

Clips the drawing area to the given path.

Example: Fills a diamond shape with gradient color.
```
Dim Canvas1 As Canvas
Dim DestRect As Rect
Dim Gradient1 As GradientDrawable
Dim Clrs(2) As Int
Clrs(0) = Colors.Black
Clrs(1) = Colors.White
Gradient1.Initialize("TOP_BOTTOM", Clrs)
Dim Path1 As Path
Path1.Initialize(50%x, 100%y)
Path1.LineTo(100%x, 50%y)
Path1.LineTo(50%x, 0%y)
Path1.LineTo(0%x, 50%y)
Path1.LineTo(50%x, 100%y)
Canvas1.Initialize(Activity)
Canvas1.ClipPath(Path1) 'clip the drawing area to the path
DestRect.Initialize(0%y,0%y,100%x,100%y)
Canvas1.DrawDrawable(Gradient1, DestRect) 'fill the drawing area with
the gradient.
Activity.Invalidate
```

☢ DrawBitmap (Bitmap1 As Bitmap, SrcRect As Rect, DestRect As Rect)

Draws a bitmap.

SrcRect - The subset of the bitmap that will be drawn. If **Null**, then the complete bitmap will be drawn.

DestRect - The rectangle that the bitmap will be drawn to.

The following example first draws the whole bitmap, then draws just the left half . The image must be included in the Files folder of the project:

```
Dim Canvas1 As Canvas
Canvas1.Initialize(Activity)

'draw the whole bitmap to the top half of the Activity
Dim Bitmap1 As Bitmap
Bitmap1.Initialize(File.DirAssets, "horse.png")
Dim DestRect As Rect
DestRect.Initialize(0, 0, 100%x, 50%y)
Canvas1.DrawBitmap(Bitmap1, Null, DestRect)

' draw the left half of the bitmap to bottom half of Activity
Dim SrcRect As Rect
SrcRect.Initialize(0, 0, Bitmap1.Width / 2, Bitmap1.Height)
DestRect.Top = 50%y
DestRect.Bottom = 100%y
Canvas1.DrawBitmap(Bitmap1, SrcRect, DestRect)
Activity.Invalidate
```

DrawBitmapFlipped (Bitmap1 As Bitmap, SrcRect As Rect, DestRect As Rect, Vertically As Boolean, Horizontally As Boolean)

Flips the bitmap and draws it.

SrcRect - The subset of the bitmap that will be drawn. If **Null**, then the complete bitmap will be drawn.

DestRect - The rectangle that the bitmap will be drawn to.

Vertically - Whether to flip the bitmap vertically.

Horizontally - Whether to flip the bitmap horizontally.

Example:
```
Canvas1.DrawBitmapFlipped(Bitmap1, Null, DestRect, False, True)
```

DrawBitmapRotated (Bitmap1 As Bitmap, SrcRect As Rect, DestRect As Rect, Degrees As Float)

Rotates the bitmap and draws it.

SrcRect - The subset of the bitmap that will be drawn. If **Null**, then the complete bitmap will be drawn.

DestRect - The rectangle that the bitmap will be drawn to.

Degrees - Number of degrees to rotate the bitmap clockwise. Negative numbers will rotate anti-clockwise.

Example:
```
Dim Canvas1 As Canvas
Canvas1.Initialize(Activity)
Dim Bitmap1 As Bitmap
Bitmap1.Initialize(File.DirAssets, "horse.png")
Dim DestRect As Rect
DestRect.Initialize(0, 0, 100%x, 50%y)
' draw the bitmap rotated by 70 degrees
Canvas1.DrawBitmapRotated(Bitmap1, Null, DestRect, 70)
```

DrawCircle (x As Float, y As Float, Radius As Float, Color As Int, Filled As Boolean, StrokeWidth As Float)

Draws a circle.

x - the left edge of the circle
y - the top of the circle
Filled - Whether the circle will be filled.
StrokeWidth - The stroke width (only relevant when Filled = `False`)
Example:
```
Dim Canvas1 As Canvas
Canvas1.Initialize(Activity)
Canvas1.DrawCircle(150dip, 150dip, 20dip, Colors.Red, False, 10dip)
```

DrawColor (Color As Int)

Fills the entire canvas with the given color.
Example:
```
'fill with semi-transparent red color
Canvas1.DrawColor(Colors.ARGB(100, 255, 0, 0))
Activity.Invalidate
```

DrawDrawable (Drawable1 As Drawable, DestRect As Rect)

Draws a Drawable into the specified rectangle.
Example:
```
' Fill a rectangle with a Gradient
Dim Canvas1 As Canvas
Dim DestRect As Rect
Dim Gradient1 As GradientDrawable
Dim Clrs(2) As Int

Canvas1.Initialize(Activity)
DestRect.Initialize(0, 0, 100%x, 100%y)
Clrs(0) = Colors.Green
Clrs(1) = Colors.Blue
Gradient1.Initialize("TOP_BOTTOM", Clrs)
Canvas1.DrawDrawable(Gradient1, DestRect)
Activity.Invalidate
```

DrawDrawableRotate (Drawable1 As Drawable, DestRect As Rect, Degrees As Float)

Rotates and draws a Drawable into the specified rectangle.
Degrees - Number of degrees to rotate clockwise. Negative numbers will rotate anti-clockwise.

DrawLine (x1 As Float, y1 As Float, x2 As Float, y2 As Float, Color As Int, StrokeWidth As Float)

Draws a line from (x1, y1) to (x2, y2). StrokeWidth determines the width of the line.
x1 - the left of the starting point
y1 - the top of the starting point
x2 - the left of the end point
y2 - the top of the end point
Example:

```
Canvas1.DrawLine(100dip, 100dip, 200dip, 200dip, Colors.Red, 10dip)
Activity.Invalidate
```

🛡️DrawOval (Rect1 As Rect, Color As Int, Filled As Boolean, StrokeWidth As Float)

Draws an oval shape.

Filled - Whether the rectangle will be filled.

StrokeWidth - The stroke width. Relevant only when Filled = `False`.

Example:
```
Dim Rect1 As Rect
Rect1.Initialize(100dip, 100dip, 200dip, 150dip)
Canvas1.DrawOval(Rect1, Colors.Gray, False, 5dip)
Activity.Invalidate
```

🛡️DrawOvalRotated (Rect1 As Rect, Color As Int, Filled As Boolean, StrokeWidth As Float, Degrees As Float)

Rotates the oval and draws it.

Filled - Whether the rectangle will be filled.

StrokeWidth - The stroke width. Relevant when Filled = `False`.

Degrees - Number of degrees to rotate the oval clockwise. Negative numbers will rotate anti-clockwise.

🛡️DrawPath (Path1 As Path, Color As Int, Filled As Boolean, StrokeWidth As Float)

Draws the path.

Filled - Whether the path will be filled.

StrokeWidth - The stroke width. Relevant when Filled = `False`.

Example:
```
' Draw a magenta diamond
Dim Canvas1 As Canvas
Dim DestRect As Rect
Dim Path1 As Path

Canvas1.Initialize(Activity)
DestRect.Initialize(0, 0, 100%x, 50%y)
Path1.Initialize(50%x, 100%y)
Path1.LineTo(100%x, 50%y)
Path1.LineTo(50%x, 0%y)
Path1.LineTo(0%x, 50%y)
Path1.LineTo(50%x, 100%y)
Canvas1.DrawPath(Path1, Colors.Magenta, False, 10dip)
```

🛡️DrawPoint (x As Float, y As Float, Color As Int)

Draws a point at the specified position and color. Example to draw a point in the middle of the screen.

x - the left of the point

y - the top of the point

Example:

```
Dim Canvas1 As Canvas
Canvas1.Initialize(Activity)
Canvas1.DrawPoint(50%x, 50%y, Colors.Yellow)
```

✪ DrawRect (Rect1 As Rect, Color As Int, Filled As Boolean, StrokeWidth As Float)

Draws a rectangle.

Filled - Whether the rectangle will be filled.

StrokeWidth - The stroke width. Relevant when Filled = `False`

Example to draw an outlined rectangle:

```
Dim Canvas1 As Canvas
Dim Rect1 As Rect
Canvas1.Initialize(Activity)
Rect1.Initialize(100dip, 100dip, 200dip, 150dip)
Canvas1.DrawRect(Rect1, Colors.Gray, False, 5dip)
Activity.Invalidate
```

✪ DrawRectRotated (Rect1 As Rect, Color As Int, Filled As Boolean, StrokeWidth As Float, Degrees As Float)

Rotates the rectangle and draws it.

Filled - Whether the rectangle will be filled.

StrokeWidth - The stroke width. Relevant when Filled = `False`.

Degrees - Number of degrees to rotate the rectangle clockwise. Negative numbers will rotate anti-clockwise.

✪ DrawText (Text As String, x As Float, y As Float, Typeface1 As Typeface, TextSize As Float, Color As Int, Align1 As Align)

Draws the text.

Text - The text to be drawn.

x - the left of the starting point

y - the top of the starting point

Typeface1 - Typeface (font) to use.

TextSize - This value will be automatically scaled, so do not scale it yourself.

Color - Text color.

Align - The alignment related to the origin. One of the following values: "LEFT", "CENTER", "RIGHT". Example to draw text in middle of screen:

```
Dim Canvas1 As Canvas
Canvas1.Initialize(Activity)
Canvas1.DrawText("B4A is fantastic!", _
  50%x, 50%y, Typeface.DEFAULT_BOLD, 20, Colors.Blue, "CENTER")
Activity.Invalidate
```

✪ DrawTextRotated (Text As String, x As Float, y As Float, Typeface1 As Typeface, TextSize As Float, Color As Int, Align1 As Align, Degree As Float)

Rotates the text and draws it.

Text - The text to be drawn.

x - the left of the starting point

y - the top of the starting point

Typeface1 - Typeface (font) to use.

TextSize - This value will be automatically scaled, so do not scale it yourself.
Color - Text color.
Align - The alignment related to the origin. One of the following values: "LEFT", "CENTER", "RIGHT".
Degrees - Number of degrees to rotate clockwise. Negative numbers will rotate anti-clockwise.
Example to draw rotated text in middle of screen:

```
Dim Canvas1 As Canvas
Canvas1.Initialize(Activity)
Canvas1.DrawTextRotated("B4A is fantastic!", _
 50%x, 50%y, Typeface.DEFAULT_BOLD, 20, Colors.Blue, "CENTER", 90)
Activity.Invalidate
```

Initialize (Target As View)

Initializes the canvas for drawing on a view.
The view background will be drawn on the canvas during initialization.
Note that you should not change the view's background after calling this method. Example:

```
Dim Canvas1 As Canvas
Canvas1.Initialize(Activity) 'this canvas will draw on the activity
background
```

Initialize2 (Bitmap1 As Bitmap)

Initializes the canvas for drawing on this bitmap. The bitmap must be mutable. Bitmaps created from files or input streams are NOT mutable.

MeasureStringHeight (Text As String, Typeface As Typeface, TextSize As Float) As Float

Returns the height of the given text. Example of drawing a blue text with white rectangle as the background:

```
Dim Canvas1 As Canvas
Dim Rect1 As Rect
Dim width, height As Float
Dim t As String
Canvas1.Initialize(Activity)
t = "Text to write"
width = Canvas1.MeasureStringWidth(t, Typeface.DEFAULT, 14)
height = Canvas1.MeasureStringHeight(t, Typeface.DEFAULT, 14)
Rect1.Initialize(100dip, 100dip, 100dip + width, 100dip + height)
Canvas1.DrawRect(Rect1, Colors.White, True, 0)
Canvas1.DrawText(t, Rect1.Left, Rect1.Bottom, Typeface.DEFAULT, 14,
Colors.Blue, "LEFT")
Activity.Invalidate
```

MeasureStringWidth (Text As String, Typeface1 As Typeface, TextSize As Float) As Float

Returns the width of the given text. See MeasureStringHeight above for an example.

RemoveClip

Removes previous clipped region.

ColorDrawable

A drawable that has a solid color and can have round corners. Example to color a button green:

```
Dim Button1 As Button
Dim cd As ColorDrawable
Button1.Initialize("test")
Activity.AddView(Button1, 10dip, 10dip, 80dip, 50dip)
cd.Initialize(Colors.Green, 5dip)
Button1.Background = cd
Button1.Text = "Test"
Activity.Invalidate
```

This is an `Activity` object; it cannot be declared under `Sub Process_Globals`.

Initialize (Color As Int, CornerRadius As Int)

Initializes the drawable with the given color and corner radius.

Initialize2 (Color As Int, CornerRadius As Int, BorderWidth As Int, BorderColor As Int)

Initializes the drawable with the given color and corner radius, and with a border of the specified width and color. Changing `cd.Initialize` in the above example; to

```
cd.Initialize2(Colors.Green, 5dip, 5dip, Colors.Red)
```

produces the following:

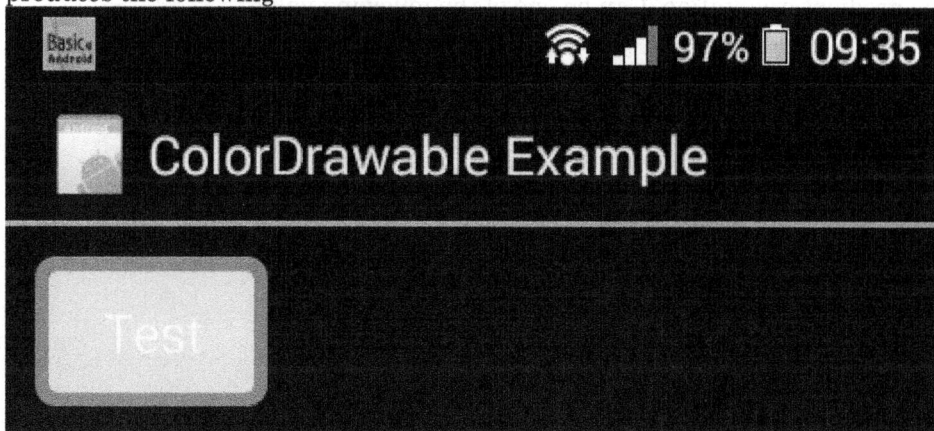

IsInitialized As Boolean

Whether the `ColorDrawable` has been initialized using the `Initialize` method.

GradientDrawable

A drawable that has a gradient color and can have round corners.

This is an `Activity` object; it cannot be declared under `Sub Process_Globals`.

Example to draw a gradient, with rounded corners, within a panel:

```
' create the panel to receive the gradient
Dim pnlTest As Panel
pnlTest.Initialize("")
Activity.AddView(pnlTest,20dip,20dip,100dip,100dip)
' create gradient colors
Dim cols(2) As Int
cols(0) = Colors.Red
cols(1) = Colors.Blue
' create the gradient
Dim gd1 As GradientDrawable
gd1.Initialize("TL_BR",cols)
gd1.CornerRadius = 20dip
' add gradient to panel
pnlTest.Background=gd1
```

Members:

⚡ CornerRadius As Float [write only]

Sets the radius of the "rectangle" corners. Set to 0 for square corners. Example:
```
Gradient1.CornerRadius = 20dip
```

✪ Initialize (Orientation1 As Orientation, Colors() As Int)

Initializes this object.

Orientation - The gradient orientation. Can be one of the following value:
"TOP_BOTTOM"
"TR_BL" (Top-Right to Bottom-Left)
"RIGHT_LEFT"
"BR_TL" (Bottom-Right to Top-Left)
"BOTTOM_TOP"
"BL_TR" (Bottom-Left to Top-Right)
"LEFT_RIGHT"
"TL_BR" (Top-Left to Bottom-Right)

Colors - An array with the gradient colors.
Example:
```
Dim Gradient1 As GradientDrawable
Dim Clrs(2) As Int
Clrs(0) = Colors.Black
Clrs(1) = Colors.White
Gradient1.Initialize("TOP_BOTTOM", Clrs)
```

✪ IsInitialized As Boolean

Whether the `GradientDrawable` has been initialized using the `Initialize` method.

Path

A `Path` is a collection of points that represent a connected path. The first point is set when the path is initialized, and then other points are added with `LineTo`.

Members:

✪ Initialize (x As Float, y As Float)

Initializes the path and sets the value of the first point.
x - the left of the starting point

y - the top of the starting point

🔷 *IsInitialized As Boolean*

Whether the `Path` has been initialized using the `Initialize` method.

🔷 *LineTo (x As Float, y As Float)*

Adds a line from the last point to the specified point.
x - the left of the end point
y - the top of the end point

Rect

Holds four coordinates which represent a rectangle.

Members:

🔧 *Bottom As Int*

🔧 *CenterX As Int [read only]*

Returns the horizontal center measured from the left.

🔧 *CenterY As Int [read only]*

Returns the vertical center measured from the top.

🔷 *Initialize (Left As Int, Top As Int, Right As Int, Bottom As Int)*

🔷 *IsInitialized As Boolean*

Whether the `Rect` has been initialized using the `Initialize` method.

🔧 *Left As Int*

🔧 *Right As Int*

🔧 *Top As Int*

StateListDrawable

A drawable that holds other drawables and chooses the current one based on the view's state, such as `State_Checked`. This is an `Activity` object; it cannot be declared under `Sub Process_Globals`. Example:

```
' create button to use StateListDrawable as background
Dim tb As ToggleButton
tb.Initialize("")
tb.Checked = False
tb.TextColor = Colors.Blue
tb.TextSize = 20
tb.Typeface = Typeface.DEFAULT_BOLD
' create colorDrawables
Dim checked, unchecked As ColorDrawable
checked.Initialize(Colors.Green, 10dip)
unchecked.Initialize(Colors.Red, 10dip)
' create StateListDrawable
Dim sld As StateListDrawable
sld.Initialize
' add colorDrawables to StateListDrawable
sld.AddState(sld.State_Checked, checked)
sld.AddState(sld.State_Unchecked, unchecked)
' add StateListDrawable to button
tb.Background = sld
' show button
Activity.AddView(tb, 100dip, 100dip, 100dip, 100dip)
```

Members:

⬡ *AddCatchAllState (Drawable1 As Drawable)*

Adds the **Drawable** that will be used if no other state matched the current state.
Note: this should always be the last state. States added after this one will never be used.

⬡ *AddState (State As Int, Drawable1 As Drawable)*

Adds a **State** and **Drawable** pair. Example (see above for complete code):
```
sld.AddState(sld.State_Checked, checked)
```
Note: if you add the same state twice, the first one added will be used.

⬡ *AddState2 (State() As Int, Drawable1 As Drawable)*

Adds a **State** and **Drawable** pair. The state is made from a combination of states.
Note: You should not reuse the array specified as it is used internally by
`StateListDrawable`.
Note also: the order of states is very important. The first state that matches will be used.

⬡ *Initialize*

Initializes the object.

⬡ *IsInitialized As Boolean*

Whether the `StateListDrawable` has been initialized using the `Initialize` method.

- **State_Checked As Int**
- **State_Disabled As Int**
- **State_Enabled As Int**
- **State_Focused As Int**
- **State_Pressed As Int**
- **State_Selected As Int**
- **State_Unchecked As Int**

Exception

Holds a thrown exception. You can access the last thrown exception by calling
`LastException`.
Example:
```
Try
   Dim in As InputStream
   in = File.OpenInput(File.DirInternal, "SomeMissingFile.txt")
   ' etc
Catch
   ' come here if there is an exception
   Log(LastException.Message)
End Try
If in.IsInitialized Then in.Close
```

Members:

IsInitialized As Boolean

Whether the `Exception` has been initialized. Example:
```
If LastException.IsInitialized Then
```

Message As String [read only]

File Object

Many applications require access to persistent storage. The two most common storage types
are files and databases. We deal with files here. Databases have a chapter of their own (page
215).

Filenames

Android file names allow the following characters:
a to z, A to Z, 0 to 9 . _ + - % &
Spaces, "*" and "?" are not allowed.
Note that Android file names are case sensitive , so "MyFile.txt" is different from
"myfile.txt".

Adding Files to your Project

If you want to include files with your app, you must add them to the Files folder of your project. One way to do this is by using the Files Manager (page 88) window in the IDE and clicking "Add Files".

Folder locations on Device

Your app can access the following folders in your device:

File.DirAssets

The folder which includes the files that were added to the Files folder in your project. **These files are read-only**. These files are stored within the APK on the device's main memory. **Note:** copies of these files might also be found within a virtual_assets folder of `File.DirDefaultExternal`.

If you have a database file in the DirAssets folder, you need to copy it to another folder before you can use it. You can use the DBUtils.CopyDBFromAssets (page 220) function to achieve this.

"Internal" Storage

There are two locations which use "Internal" or private storage. It is "private" because other apps and the user cannot normally see it. **However note** that if the user has "rooted" the device then they will be able to see it.

Note: since internal storage offers the maximum protection for stored data, you should store sensitive data on internal storage. Specifically, configuration and log files should only be stored on `File.DirInternal` where they can be more effectively protected.

Internal storage is located on the device's main memory.

File.DirInternalCache

File.DirInternalCache is an "internal" directory (see above) where your application should save temporary cache files rather than store it persistently.

When the device is low on internal storage space, Android may delete these cache files to recover space. **But note:** you should not rely on the system to clean up these files for you. You should always maintain the cache files yourself and stay within a reasonable limit of space consumed, such as 1MB.

When the user uninstalls your application, these files are removed.

A typical location is
/data/data/<Build Configuration Package Name>/cache

File.DirInternal

See the note above regarding "Internal" storage.

This is where you store your app's private data such as configuration and log files.

A typical location is:
/data/data/<Build Configuration Package Name>/files

"External" Storage

The next two locations are public storage on the device's main memory. The user and other apps can see and modify this data.

Note: Use of the word "External" can be confusing, since this directory is located on the device's internal storage, not the external SD card!

Access to the external storage card has changed as Android has developed.

Starting from Android 1.0, write access is protected with the WRITE_EXTERNAL_STORAGE permission.

Starting from Android 4.1, read access is protected with the READ_EXTERNAL_STORAGE permission.

Starting from Android 4.4, apps can manage their package-specific directories on external storage without requiring WRITE_EXTERNAL_STORAGE permission. More details here (http://bit.ly/1HjxTxQ).

With B4A, you can check these permissions with **File.ExternalReadable** and **File.ExternalWritable**.

Note: since external storage offers minimal protection for stored data, you should not store sensitive data on external storage. Specifically, configuration and log files should only be stored on **File.DirInternal** where they can be more effectively protected.

File.DirRootExternal

See the note above on "External" storage.

This is the folder used by many applications since it is easy for the user to find and recognize its source.

Note: If you are going to use this location, you will probably want to create a folder here since otherwise your files will tend to clutter up the root of this folder along with other files.

A typical location is: /storage/emulated/0

File.DirDefaultExternal

See the note above on "External" storage.

This is a sub-folder within **File.DirRootExternal** (see above) which Android creates for your app. Like **File.DirRootExternal**, it is publicly readable, but is harder for the user to find than a folder stored there.

You can check whether it is readable and writable with **File.ExternalReadable** and **File.ExternalWritable**.

As noted above, copies of **File.DirAssets** can be stored here, within a virtual_assets folder.

A typical location of **File.DirDefaultExternal** is:
/storage/emulated/0/Android/data/<Build Configuration Package Name >/files

SD Card

Storage specific to your app on the SD card, if one exists. You can find this by using **getExternalFilesDirs**, as shown in the following code.

A typical location is:
/storage/external_SD/Android/data/<Build Configuration Package Name >/files

Finding Your Folder Locations

You can find the location of all of the above folder locations with the following code. Note that **getExternalFilesDirs** will return the same location as **file.DirDefaultExternal** and then the location of your app's storage on the SD card, if there is one:

```
Sub Activity_Create(FirstTime As Boolean)

 Log("File.DirInternal=" & File.DirInternal)
 Log("file.DirDefaultExternal=" & File.DirDefaultExternal)
 Log("File.DirRootExternal=" & File.DirRootExternal)
 Log("File.DirInternalCache=" & File.DirInternalCache)

 Log("Using getExternalFilesDirs")
 Dim paths() As Object = GetContext.RunMethod( _
  "getExternalFilesDirs", Array(Null))
 For Each p As Object In paths
  Log(p)
 Next

End Sub


Sub GetContext As JavaObject
 Return GetBA.GetField("context")
End Sub

Sub GetBA As JavaObject
 Dim jo As JavaObject
 Dim cls As String = Me
 cls = cls.SubString("class ".Length)
 jo.InitializeStatic(cls)
 Return jo.GetFieldJO("processBA")
End Sub
```

Text encoding

Sometimes it is useful to read or write text files using B4A. There are two objects to help you to do this: TextReader (page 375) and TextWriter (page 376). Here we describe how text is encoded and stored within a file. Since your app might deal with different languages and might import files with various formats, basic understanding can help overcome some possible problems.

Encoding is a way of converting a set of characters into binary data in a standard format so the data can be exchanged between systems.

Unicode

Originally, (back in 1963), English characters were encoded in ASCII. As computing spread to other languages, the Unicode system was invented (in 1988), allowing all the world's languages to be encoded. See here (http://bit.ly/1OwgFDm) for a list of characters and their Unicode codes.

Unicode can be implemented by different encoding systems (also called Code Pages or Character Sets). The most commonly used encodings are UTF-8 and UTF-16.

Android Character Sets

Android can use following character sets:

* UTF-8 - default character-set on Android
* UTF-16
* UTF-16 BE

- UTF-LE
- US-ASCII - ASCII character set
- ISO-8859-1 - almost equivalent to the ANSI character-set
- Windows-1252

The default character set in Android is Unicode UTF-8.

Windows Character Sets
In Windows, the most common character sets are ASCII and Windows-1252 .

ASCII
ASCII is a 7 bit encoding, allowing definitions for 128 characters. 33 are non-printing control characters (now mostly obsolete) that affect how text and space is processed.

Windows-1252
Windows-1252 or CP-1252, (often wrongly called ANSI), is a character encoding of the Latin alphabet, used by default in the legacy components of Microsoft Windows in English and some other Western languages with 256 definitions (one byte). The first 128 characters are the same as in the ASCII encoding. See here (http://bit.ly/1JgIvmS) or here (http://bit.ly/1JgIxv5) for details.

Many files generated by Windows programs are encoded with the Windows-1252 character-set in western countries, for example, Excel CSV files and Notepad files by default. (Note that Notepad can also save files with UTF-8 encoding.)

To read Windows files encoded with Windows-1252, you should use the Windows-1252 character-set. If you need to write files for use with Windows, you should also use the Windows-1252 character-set.

To read or write files with a different encoding, you must use the TextReader (page 375) or TextWriter (page 376) objects with the `Initialize2` methods.

End-of-Line Character(s)
Another difference between Windows and Android is the end-of-line character. In Android (following the Linux model), only the Line Feed LF character, Chr(10), is added at the end of a line.

The B4A symbol for the end-of-line is `CRLF`.:

```
lblComments.Text = "Enter the result" & CRLF & "and click on OK"
```

Its name can be slightly confusing, since it is actually only the LF character Chr(10). The name was chosen because it has the same effect as CR+LF in Windows.

In Windows, two characters, Carriage Return CR, Chr(13), and LF, are both added at the end of every line. So, if you need to write files for Windows, you must add CR yourself:

```
str = str.Replace(CRLF, Chr(13) & Chr(10))
```

Reading and Writing Excel Files
Excel can save spreadsheets in CSV ("Comma Separated Values") format. There are two functions, `LoadCSV` and `LoadCSV2` in the StringUtils library, which can read CSV files and one which can save a CSV file. See the StringUtils (page 549) library documentation for examples. You do NOT need to change the format of the files when you move these CSV files between a Windows PC and an Android device.

Byte Order Marks

Windows programs such as NotePad or NotePad++ (http://bit.ly/1OwgPuy) can save files with various encodings such as ANSI (more correctly called Windows-1252), Unicode, Unicode big endian and UTF-8.

- If you save a file encoded as Windows-1252, the text alone is saved.
- If you encode with Unicode, 0xFF 0xFE are added at the beginning and 0x00 bytes are added between each of the Windows-1252 characters.
- If you encode with Unicode big endian, 0xFE 0xFF are added at the beginning and 0x00 bytes are added between each of the Windows-1252 characters.
- If you encode with UTF-8 (the Android standard), `0xEF`, `0xBB`, `0xBF` are added at the beginning but no extra interstitial bytes are added.

You can examine the hex contents of a file using an editor such as HexEdit4 (http://bit.ly/1CWG73p).

The extra bytes added at the beginning of the file are called BOM characters (Byte Order Mark (http://bit.ly/1TTblNc)). If you save a file with UTF-8 encoding and open in a text editor or web browser which interprets the text as Windows-1252, the characters `ï»¿` will be displayed at the beginning.

To avoid this, encode in Windows-1252.

To change text from Windows-1252 to UTF-8, use B4A code such as:

```
Dim var, result As String
var = "Gestió"
Dim arrByte() As Byte
arrByte = var.GetBytes("Windows-1252")
result = BytesToString(arrByte, 0, arrByte.Length, "UTF8")
```

File

File is a predefined object that holds methods for working with files. The File object includes several methods for writing to files and reading from files. To be able to write to a file or to read from a file, it must be opened.

"Predefined" means that you do not need to declare it yourself. Thus, for each of the following, you would prefix the method with File. For example, **File.Exists**.

Note: the Android file system is case sensitive.

Members:

⬙ Combine (Dir As String, FileName As String) As String

Returns the full path to the given file.

This method does not support files in the assets folder.

⬙ Copy (DirSource As String, FileSource As String, DirTarget As String, FileTarget As String)

Copies the specified source file to the target file name.

Note: it is not possible to copy files to the Assets folder.

⬙ Copy2 (In As java.io.InputStream, Out As java.io.OutputStream)

Copies all the available data from the input stream into the output stream.

Input Stream is automatically closed at the end. You need to close OutputStream yourself.

❖*Delete (Dir As String, FileName As String) As Boolean*

Deletes the specified file **FileName** in the specified directory **Dir**. If FileName is the name of a directory, then it must be empty in order to be deleted. Returns **True** if the file was successfully deleted. Example:

```
File.MakeDir(File.DirRootExternal, "A123Test")
If File.Delete(File.DirRootExternal, "A123Test") Then
 ToastMessageShow("Success", False)
Else
 ToastMessageShow("Success", False)
End If
```

Note: files in the assets folder cannot be deleted.

⚙*DirAssets As String [read only]*

Returns a reference to the files added to the Files tab. These files are read-only. See Folder Locations (page 366) for more details.

⚙*DirDefaultExternal As String [read only]*

Returns the application default "external" folder which is based on the package name. The folder is created if needed. See Folder Locations (page 366) for more details.

⚙*DirInternal As String [read only]*

Returns the folder in the device "internal" storage that is used to save application private data. See Folder Locations (page 366) for more details.

⚙*DirInternalCache As String [read only]*

Returns the folder in the device "internal" storage that is used to save application cache data. This data will be deleted automatically when the device runs low on storage. See Folder Locations (page 366) for more details.

⚙*DirRootExternal As String [read only]*

Returns the root folder of the external storage media. See Folder Locations (page 366) for more details.

❖*Exists (Dir As String, FileName As String) As Boolean*

Returns **True** if the specified FileName exists in the specified Dir.
Note that the Android file system is case sensitive.
Example:

```
If File.Exists(File.DirDefaultExternal, "MyFile.txt") Then ...
```

⚙*ExternalReadable As Boolean [read only]*

Returns TRUE if the "external" storage media can be read from. See Folder Locations (page 366) for more details.

⚙*ExternalWritable As Boolean [read only]*

Returns TRUE if the "external" storage media can be written to. See Folder Locations (page 366) for more details.

```
Dim directory As String
If File.ExternalWritable Then
  directory = File.DirDefaultExternal
Else
  directory = File.DirInternal
End If
```

GetText (Dir As String, FileName As String) As String
Reads the entire file and returns its text. The file is assumed to be encoded with UTF8.

IsDirectory (Dir As String, FileName As String) As Boolean
Returns TRUE if the specified file is a directory.

LastModified (Dir As String, FileName As String) As Long
Returns the last modified date of the specified file. This method does not support files in the assets folder. Example:
```
Dim d As Long
d = File.LastModified(File.DirRootExternal, "1.txt")
Msgbox(DateTime.Date(d), "Last modified")
```

ListFiles (Dir As String) As List
Returns a read only list with all the files and directories which are stored in the specified path. Example:
```
Dim List1 As List
List1 = File.ListFiles(File.DirRootExternal)
```
List1 can be declared in Sub Globals.
An uninitialized list will be returned if the folder is not accessible.

MakeDir (Parent As String, Dir As String)
Creates the given folder. Example:
```
File.MakeDir(File.DirInternal, "Pictures")
```
Can also create a subfolder. All folders will be created as needed. Example:
```
File.MakeDir(File.DirInternal, "music/90/pop/favorites")
```
To access a file in the folder use either
```
ImageView1.Bitmap = LoadBitmap(File.DirInternal &
"/music/90/pop/favorites", "test1.png")
```
Or
```
ImageView1.Bitmap = LoadBitmap(File.DirInternal, "
music/90/pop/favorites/test1.png")
```

OpenInput (Dir As String, FileName As String) As InputStream
Opens the file for reading. The file, specified by **FileName, is** located in the folder specified by **Dir**.
Note: the Android file system is case sensitive.

OpenOutput (Dir As String, FileName As String, Append As Boolean) As OutputStream
Opens (or creates) the file specified by **FileName** which is located in the **Dir** folder for writing. If **Append** is True, then the new data will be written at the end of the existing file. If the file doesn't exist, it will be created.
Example:

```
Dim outFile As TextWriter
outFile.Initialize(File.OpenOutput(strMyFolder,"temp.txt",False))
outFile.Write("hello")
outFile.Close
```

ReadList (Dir As String, FileName As String) As List

Reads the entire file and returns all lines as a List of strings.
Example:

```
Dim List1 As List
List1 = File.ReadList(File.DirDefaultExternal, "1.txt")
For i = 0 to List1.Size - 1
  Log(List1.Get(i))
Next
```

ReadMap (Dir As String, FileName As String) As Map

Reads a file which has been previously written by **File.WriteMap**. ReadMap parses each
line as a key-value pair (of strings) and adds them to a Map object, which it then returns.

```
mapCopy = File.ReadMap(File.DirDefaultExternal, "savedMap")
```

The original mapCopy is over-written by the saved data. Note that the order of entries
returned might be different than the original order.

ReadMap2 (Dir As String, FileName As String, Map As Map) As Map

Same as **ReadMap** except the items retrieved from the file are appended to the existing Map.

ReadString (Dir As String, FileName As String) As String

Reads the file and returns its content as a string. Example:

```
Dim text As String
text = File.ReadString(File.DirRootExternal, "1.txt")
```

Size (Dir As String, FileName As String) As Long

Returns the size in bytes of the specified file. This method does not support files in the assets
folder.

WriteList (Dir As String, FileName As String, List As List)

Writes each item in the **List** as a single line in the output file. All values are converted to
string type if required. Each value will be stored in a separate line. If the file already exists it
will be over-written.
Note: a value in **List** containing CRLF, or a new-line character, will be saved as two lines.
When subsequently reading the file with **ReadList**, they will be read as two items.
Example:

```
File.WriteList (File.DirInternal, "mylist.txt", List1)
```

WriteMap (Dir As String, FileName As String, Map1 As Map)

Takes a **Map** object (holding pairs of key and value elements), converts all values to strings,
creates a new text file and stores the key-value pairs, each pair as a single line. This file
format makes it easy to edit the file manually. If the file already exists it will be over-
written.

One common usage of **File.WriteMap** is to save a map of "settings" to a file.
You can use **File.ReadMap** to read this file.

🔷 *WriteString (Dir As String, FileName As String, Text As String)*

Writes the given text to a file. If the file already exists it will be over-written.
Example:

```
File.WriteString(File.DirRootExternal, "1.txt", "Some text")
```

InputStream

A stream that you can read from. Usually you will pass the stream to a "higher level" object like **TextReader** that will handle the reading. You can use **File.OpenInput** to get a file input stream. Example:

```
Dim streamInput As InputStream
streamInput = File.OpenInput(File.DirAssets, "test.txt")
Dim tr As TextReader
tr.Initialize(streamInput)
```

Members:

🔷 *BytesAvailable As Int*

Returns an estimation of the number of bytes available.
Note: if you call **InputStream.ReadBytes** on a network stream, then the thread will wait for at least a single byte to be available. In most cases this will cause your app to crash! So you should always use **InputStream.BytesAvailable** before calling **ReadBytes**, to avoid blocking the main thread.

🔷 *Close*

Closes the stream.

🔷 *InitializeFromBytesArray (Buffer() As Byte, StartOffset As Int, MaxCount As Int)*

Use **File.OpenInput** to get a file input stream. This method should be used to initialize the input stream and set it to read from the the **Buffer()** byte-array.
StartOffset - The first byte that will be read.
MaxCount - Maximum number of bytes to read.

🔷 *IsInitialized As Boolean*

Whether the InpuStream has been initialized using **InitializeFromBytesArray**.

🔷 *ReadBytes (Buffer() As Byte, StartOffset As Int, MaxCount As Int) As Int*

Reads up to **MaxCount** bytes from the stream and writes it to the given **Buffer**. The first byte will be written at **StartOffset**. Returns the number of bytes actually read. Returns **-1** if there are no more bytes to read. Otherwise, returns at least one byte.
Note: if you call **InputStream.ReadBytes** on a network stream, then the thread will wait for at least a single byte to be available. In most cases this will cause your app to crash! So you should always use **InputStream.BytesAvailable** before calling **ReadBytes**, to avoid blocking the main thread. Example:

```
Dim buffer(1024) As byte
count = InputStream1.ReadBytes(buffer, 0, buffer.length)
```

OutputStream

A stream that you can write to. Usually, you will pass the stream to a "higher level" object like **TextWriter** which will handle the writing.

Use `File.OpenOutput` to get a file output stream.

Members:

🦋 *Close*
Closes the stream.

🦋 *Flush*
Flushes any buffered data.

🦋 *InitializeToBytesArray (StartSize As Int)*
Use `File.OpenOutput` to get a file output stream. This method should be used to write data to a byte-array.

StartSize - The starting size of the internal byte-array. The size will increase if needed.

🦋 *IsInitialized As Boolean*
Whether the `OutputStream` has been initialized using `InitializeFromBytesArray`.

🦋 *ToBytesArray As Byte()*
Returns a copy of the internal byte-array. Can only be used when the output stream was initialized with `InitializeToBytesArray`.

🦋 *WriteBytes (Buffer() As Byte, StartOffset As Int, Length As Int)*
Writes the buffer to the stream. The first byte to be written is Buffer(StartOffset), and the last is Buffer(StartOffset + Length - 1).

TextReader
Reads text from the underlying stream. Example:

```
Dim streamInput As InputStream
streamInput = File.OpenInput(File.DirAssets, "test.txt")
Dim tr As TextReader
tr.Initialize(streamInput)
Dim strLine As String
strLine = tr.ReadLine
Do While strLine <> Null
  Log (strLine)
  strLine = tr.ReadLine
Loop
streamInput.Close
```

Members:

🦋 *Close*
Closes the stream.

🦋 *Initialize (InputStream As java.io.InputStream)*
Initializes a TextReader by wrapping the given InputStream using the UTF8 encoding (page 368).
Example:

```
In = File.OpenInput(File.DirAssets, "myFile.txt")
txtReader.Initialize(In)
strRead = txtReader.ReadAll
```

❖ *Initialize2 (InputStream As java.io.InputStream, Encoding As String)*

Initializes this object by wrapping the given InputStream using the specified encoding (page 368). Example:

```
Dim txt As String
Dim tr As TextReader
tr.Initialize2(File.OpenInput(File.DirAssets, "TestCSV1_W.csv"),
"Windows-1252")
txt = tr.ReadAll
tr.Close
```

❖ *IsInitialized As Boolean*

Whether the **TextReader** has been initialized using one of the Initialize methods.

❖ *Read (Buffer() As Char, StartOffset As Int, Length As Int) As Int*

Reads characters from the stream and into the **Buffer**. Reads up to **Length** characters and puts them in the Buffer starting at **StartOffset**. Returns the actual number of characters read from the stream. Returns **-1** if there are no more characters available.

❖ *ReadAll As String*

Reads all of the remaining text and closes the stream.

❖ *ReadLine As String*

Reads the next line from the stream. Any new-line characters at the end of the line are not returned. Returns Null if there are no more characters to read. Example:

```
Dim Reader As TextReader
Reader.Initialize(File.OpenInput(File.InternalDir, "1.txt"))
Dim line As String
line = Reader.ReadLine
Do While line <> Null
  Log(line)
  line = Reader.ReadLine
Loop
Reader.Close
```

❖ *ReadList As List*

Reads the remaining text and returns a List object filled with the lines. Closes the stream when done.

❖ *Ready As Boolean*

Returns **TRUE** if there is at least one character ready for reading without stopping execution of the program (sometimes called blocking).

❖ *Skip (NumberOfCharacters As Int) As Int*

Skips the specified number of characters. Returns the actual number of characters that were skipped (which may be less than the specified value).

TextWriter

Writes text to the underlying stream.
Example:

```
Dim Writer As TextWriter
Writer.Initialize(File.OpenOutput(File.DirDefaultExternal, "1.txt",
False))
Writer.WriteLine("This is the first line.")
Writer.WriteLine("This is the second line.")
Writer.Close
```

Members:

🔩 *Close*

Closes the stream.

🔩 *Flush*

Flushes any buffered data.

🔩 *Initialize (OutputStream As java.io.OutputStream)*

Initializes this object by wrapping the given **OutputStream** using the UTF8 encoding (page 368). Example:

```
Writer.Initialize(File.OpenOutput(File.DirRootExternal, "Test.txt" ,
False))
```

🔩 *Initialize2 (OutputStream As java.io.OutputStream, Encoding As String)*

Initializes this object by wrapping the given **OutputStream** using the specified encoding (page 368).

```
Dim strText As String
strText = "Hello World"
Dim tw As TextWriter
tw.Initialize2(File.OpenOutput(File.DirInternal, "Test.txt", False),
"ISO-8859-1")
tw.Write(strText)
tw.Close
```

🔩 *IsInitialized As Boolean*

Whether the `TextWriter` has been initialized using one of the Initialize methods.

🔩 *Write (Text As String)*

Writes the given Text to the stream.

🔩 *WriteLine (Text As String)*

Writes the given Text to the stream followed by a new-line character Chr(10).
Example:

```
Dim Writer As TextWriter
Writer.Initialize(File.OpenOutput(File.DirDefaultExternal, "1.txt",
False))
Writer.WriteLine("This is the first line.")
Writer.WriteLine("This is the second line.")
Writer.Close
```

🔩 *WriteList (List As List)*

Writes each item in the **List** as a single line. All values will be converted to strings.
Note: a value containing CRLF will be saved as two lines (which will return two items when read with `ReadList`).

Intent

Intent objects are messages which you can send to Android in order to do some external action. A service can also receive an Intent from Android if it is a Broadcast Receiver. For more about this, see this page (http://bit.ly/12QWZBw) on the B4A website. The Intent object should be sent with the **StartActivity** keyword. See this page (http://bit.ly/1Owh0Ge) for a list of Android's standard constants. Example to launch a YouTube application:

```
Dim Intent1 As Intent
Intent1.Initialize(Intent1.ACTION_MAIN, "")
Intent1.SetComponent("com.google.android.youtube/.HomeActivity")
StartActivity(Intent1)
```

Members:

⚡Action As String
Gets or sets the Intent action.

●ACTION_APPWIDGET_UPDATE As String
See here (page 130) for more information about Widgets and here (http://bit.ly/1Owh5tj) for more about the Android AppWidgetmanager.

●ACTION_CALL As String

●ACTION_EDIT As String

●ACTION_MAIN As String

●ACTION_PICK As String

●ACTION_SEND As String

●ACTION_VIEW As String

⬡AddCategory (Category As String)
Adds a category describing the intent required operation.

⬡ExtrasToString As String
Returns a string containing the extra items. This is useful for debugging.

⚡Flags As Int
Gets or sets the **Flags** component.

⬡GetData As String
Retrieves the data component as a string.

⬡GetExtra (Key As String) As Object
Returns the item value with the given **Key**.

⬡HasExtra (Key As String) As Boolean
Returns **TRUE** if an item with the given **Key** exists.

❖Initialize (Action As String, URI As String)

Initializes the object using the given **Action** and data **URI**.
Action - can be one of the action constants or any other string.
URI – a "Uniform Resource Identifier" identifying the resource to initialize. Pass an empty string if a URI is not required.

❖Initialize2 (URI As String, Flags As Int)

Initializes the object by parsing the URI.
URI – the "Uniform Resource Identifier" identifying the resource to initialize.
Flags - Additional integer value. Pass 0 if it is not required.
Example:

```
Dim Intent1 As Intent
Intent1.Initialize2("http://www.basic4ppc.com", 0)
StartActivity(Intent1)
```

❖IsInitialized As Boolean

Whether the `Intent` has been initialized using one of the Initialize methods.

❖PutExtra (Name As String, Value As Object)

Adds extra data to the intent.

❖SetComponent (Component As String)

Explicitly sets the component that will handle this intent.

❖SetType (Type As String)

Sets the MIME type (the Internet media type). See here (http://bit.ly/1f1wI8U) for details of MIME types.
Example:

```
Intent1.SetType("text/plain")
```

❖WrapAsIntentChooser (Title As String)

Wraps the intent in another "chooser" intent. A dialog will be displayed to the user with the available services that can act on the intent.
`WrapAsIntentChooser` should be the last method called before sending the intent.

LayoutValues

This object holds values related to the display. You can get the values of the current display by calling `GetDeviceLayoutValues`. For example:

```
Dim lv As LayoutValues
lv = GetDeviceLayoutValues
Log(lv) 'will print the values to the log
Dim scale As Float
scale = lv.Scale
```

This will print the following line to the log:

```
320 x 480, scale = 1.0 (160 dpi)
```

`Activity.LoadLayout` and `Panel.LoadLayout` return a `LayoutValues` object with the values of the chosen layout variant.

Members:

⚡ApproximateScreenSize As Double [read only]

Returns the approximate diagonal screen size in inches.

⬣Height As Int

The display height (in pixels).

⬣Scale As Float

The device scale value which is equal to 'dots per inch' / 160.

⬣toString As String

⬣Width As Int

The display width (in pixels).

List

Lists are similar to dynamic arrays. You can add and remove items from a list and it will change its size accordingly. A list can hold any type of object. However, if a list is declared as a `Process_Globals` object, it cannot hold activity objects (such as views). B4A automatically converts regular arrays to lists. So, when a List parameter is expected, you can pass an array instead. For example:

```
Dim lstNumbers As List
lstNumbers.Initialize
lstNumbers.AddAll(Array As Int(1, 2, 3, 4, 5))
```

Use the `Get` method to get an item from the list.

```
number = lstNumbers.Get(i)
```

Lists can be saved and loaded from files using `File.WriteList` and `File.ReadList`. You can use a `For` loop to iterate over all the values:

```
For i = 0 To lstNumbers.Size - 1
  Dim number As Int
  number = lstNumbers.Get(i)
  ...
Next
```

How to use a List

We summarise the main points here. Details are given in the reference section below.

Initialize

Before it can be used, a list must be initialized with the `Initialize` method, as shown above. This initializes an empty list.

Add Elements

You can add and remove items from a list and it will change its size accordingly.
To add a value at the end of the list:

```
lstNumbers.Add(Value)
```

To add all elements of an array at the end of the list:

```
lstNumbers.AddAll(Array As Int(1, 2, 3, 4, 5))
```
To insert the specified element at the specified index, and shift down all items with larger index to make room:
```
lstNumbers.InsertAt(5, Value)
```
To insert all elements of an array in the list starting at the given position:
```
lstNumbers.AddAllAt(3, Array As Int(1, 2, 3, 4, 5))
```

Remove Elements
Remove a specified element at the given position from the list.
```
lstNumbers.RemoveAt(12)
```

Retrieve Elements
Use the `Get` method to get an item from the list with:
```
number = lstNumbers.Get(i)
```

Change an Element
A single item can be changed with:
```
lstNumbers.Set(12, Value)
```

Get the size of a List
```
lstNumbers.Size
```

Iterate a List
Either you can use a `For` loop to iterate over all the values:
```
Dim lstNumbers As List
lstNumbers.Initialize2(Array As Int(1, 2, 3, 4, 5))
For i = 0 To lstNumbers.Size - 1
 Log(lstNumbers.Get(i) )
Next
```
Or you can use a `For Each` loop:
```
Dim lstNumbers As List
lstNumbers.Initialize2(Array As Int(1, 2, 3, 4, 5))
For Each i As Int In lstNumbers
 Log (i)
Next
```

Save to and Load from Files
Lists can be saved to and loaded from files:
```
File.WriteList(File.DirRootExternal, "Test.txt", lstNumbers)
lstNumbers = File.ReadList(File.DirRootExternal, "Test.txt")
```

Sort a List
A List whose items are numbers or strings can be sorted with:
```
lstNumbers.Sort(True)            'sort ascending
lstNumbers.Sort(False)           'sort descending
lstNumbers.SortCaseInsensitive(True)
```

Clear a List
```
lstNumbers.Clear
```

Convert Array to List
You can convert an array to a list using **lstNumbers.Initialize2 (SomeArray)**

Notes: If you pass a list to this method, then both objects will share the same list. If you pass an array, the list will be of a fixed size, meaning you cannot later add or remove items.

Members:

⬢ *Add (Item As Object)*
Adds an **Item** at the end of the list.

⬢ *AddAll (List As List)*
Adds all elements in the specified **List** to the end of the list.
Note that you can add an array directly.
Example:
```
List.AddAll(Array As String("value1", "value2"))
```

⬢ *AddAllAt (Index As Int, List As List)*
Adds all elements in the specified collection starting at the specified index.

⬢ *Clear*
Removes all the items from the list.

⬢ *Get (Index As Int) As Object*
Gets the item at the specified index. The item is not removed from the list.

⬢ *IndexOf (Item As Object) As Int*
Returns the index of the specified item, or **-1** if it was not found.

⬢ *Initialize*
Initializes an empty list.

⬢ *Initialize2 (Array As List)*
Initializes a list with the given values. Note that if you pass a list to this method, then both objects will share the same list. Note also that, although this method can be used to convert arrays to lists, the list will be of a fixed size, meaning that you cannot later add or remove items. Example:
```
Dim lstFruit As List
lstFruit.Initialize2(Array As String("apple", "orange", "grape"))
'lstFruit is fixed in size, so the following will produce an error
lstFruit.Add("pear") ' this creates a compiler error
```

⬢ *InsertAt (Index As Int, Item As Object)*
Inserts the specified **Item** at the specified index. As a result, all items with an index larger than the specified **Index** are shifted down to make room.

⬢ *IsInitialized As Boolean*
Whether the **List** has been initialized using one of the Initialize methods.

⬢ *RemoveAt (Index As Int)*
Removes the item at the specified index.

⬢ *Set (Index As Int, Item As Object)*
Replaces the current item at the specified index with the new item.

⚡ *Size As Int [read only]*
Returns the number of items in the list.

🗘 *Sort (Ascending As Boolean)*

Sorts the list. The items must all be numbers or strings.

Ascending - `True` to sort ascending, `False` to sort descending.

🗘 *SortCaseInsensitive (Ascending As Boolean)*

Lexicographically sorts the list, ignoring the characters' case. The items must all be numbers or strings.

Ascending - `True` to sort ascending, `False` to sort descending.

🗘 *SortType (FieldName As String, Ascending As Boolean)*

Sorts a list with items of user defined type. The list is sorted based on the specified field.

FieldName - The case-sensitive field name that will be used for sorting. Field must contain numbers or strings.

Ascending - `True` to sort ascending, `False` to sort descending.

Example:

```
Sub Process_Globals
  Type Person(Name As String, Age As Int)
End Sub

Sub Activity_Create(FirstTime As Boolean)
 Dim Persons As List
 Persons.Initialize
 For i = 1 To 50
  Dim p As Person
  p.Name = "Person" & i
  p.Age = Rnd(0, 121)
  Persons.Add(p)
 Next

Persons.SortType("Age", True) 'Sort the list based on the Age field
 For i = 0 To Persons.Size - 1
  Dim p As Person
  p = Persons.Get(i)
  Log(p)
 Next
End Sub
```

🗘 *SortTypeCaseInsensitive (FieldName As String, Ascending As Boolean)*

Sorts a list with items of user defined type. The list is sorted based on the specified field.

FieldName - The field name that will be used for sorting. The case of strings in this field will be ignored. Field must contain numbers or strings.

Ascending - Whether to sort ascending or descending.

Example:

```
Sub Process_Globals
  Type Person(Name As String, Age As Int)
End Sub

Sub Activity_Create(FirstTime As Boolean)
 Dim Persons As List
 Persons.Initialize
 Persons.Add(makePerson("dick"))
 Persons.Add(makePerson("Harry"))
 Persons.Add(makePerson("alex"))
 Persons.Add(makePerson("Brigit"))
 Persons.Add(makePerson("tom"))
 ' sort the people by name case insensitive
 Persons.SortTypeCaseInsensitive("Name", True)
 For i = 0 To Persons.Size - 1
  Dim p As Person
  p = Persons.Get(i)
  Log(p.Name & "," & p.age)
 Next
End Sub

Sub makePerson(strName As String) As Person
 ' create person with given name and random age
 Dim p As Person
 p.Initialize
 p.Name = strName
 p.Age = Rnd(0, 121)
 Return p
End Sub
```

Map

A collection that holds pairs of keys and values. Keys can be strings or numbers. The strings are case-sensitive. Keys are unique, which means that if you add a key/value pair and the collection already holds an entry with the same key, the previous entry will be removed from the map. Similar to a list, the values of a map can be any type of object.

```
Dim mapPerson As Map
mapPerson.Initialize
Dim photo As Bitmap
photo.Initialize(File.DirAssets, "smith.bmp")
mapPerson.Put("name", "smith")
mapPerson.Put("age", 23)
mapPerson.Put("photo", photo)
```

You can also create and fill a Map at the same time by using the `CreateMap` keyword. Hence the following code is equivalent to the above:

```
Dim mapPerson As Map = CreateMap("name": "smith", "age": 23, "photo":
photo)
```

Fetching an item is done by looking for its key.

```
photo = mapPerson.Get("photo")
```

Accessing data in a map is usually a very fast operation compared to using an array because a Map uses a system called "hashing". A Map is sometimes referred to as a Dictionary, Hashtable or HashMap. Usually you will use **Put** to add items and **Get** or **GetDefault** to get the values based on the key.

If you need to iterate over all the items, you can use a **For Each** loop:
```
For Each key As String In mapPerson.Keys
  Log (key & "=" & mapPerson.Get(key))
Next
```
Note that this iteration does not necessarily return items in the same order as they were added.

Similar to a list, a map that is a **Process_Globals** variable cannot hold activity objects (such as views). Maps are very useful for storing applications settings.
You can save and load maps with **File.WriteMap** and **File.ReadMap**.

How to use a Map
We summarise the main points here. Details are given in the reference section below.

Initialize
A map must be initialized before it can be used.
```
Dim Map1 As Map
Map1.Initialize
```
Note that if the CreateMap keyword is used, the Map is automatically initialized. See above.

Adding Entry
Add a new entry with Put(Key As Object, Value As Object)
```
Map1.Put("Language", "English")
```

Retrieve Entry
Get(Key As Object)
```
Language = Map1.Get("Language")
```

Iteration
You can retrieve each of the items in a map in two different ways:
Method 1
GetKeyAt and **GetValueAt** retrieve items with a given index and can be used to iterate over all the items:
```
For i = 0 To mapPerson.Size - 1
  Log("Key: " & mapPerson.GetKeyAt(i))
  Log("Value: " & mapPerson.GetValueAt(i))
Next
```
Method 2
```
For Each key As String In mapPerson.Keys
  Log ("Key: " & key)
  Log ("Value: " & mapPerson.Get(key))
Next
```
The order in which the items are retrieved may be different for these two methods.

Check if a Map contains an entry
```
If Map1.ContainsKey("Language") Then ...
```

Remove an entry
```
Map1.Remove("Language")
```

Clear all items from the map
```
Map1.Clear
```

Save to and Load from a File
The File (page 370) object contains some useful functions for reading and writing maps.
Save a map to a file:
```
File.WriteMap(File.DirInternal, "settings.txt", mapSettings)
```
Read it back from the file:
```
mapSettings = File.ReadMap(File.DirInternal, "settings.txt")
```
The order in which the elements in a map read from the file will not necessarily be the same as the order in the original map. Normally this is not a problem. If you want to fix the order, see below.

Appending to a Map
You can use `File.ReadMap2` to add items to a Map.
```
mapCopy.Put("newItem", "someValue")
mapCopy = File.ReadMap2(File.DirDefaultExternal, "savedMap", mapCopy)
```
The elements read from the file are appended to the existing elements. If an existing element has the same name as an element in the file, its value is overwritten.

Fixing Order in a Map
Normally we do not care about the order in which elements are stored in a Map. However, if this is important to you, you can use `File.ReadMap2` to force the elements to be added in a particular order. The trick is to first create a Map with the keys in the order you want but with no values. Then read the data from a file. The values from the file will be added to the keys you have specified, (assuming the keys are the same).
```
Dim mapCopy As Map
mapCopy.Initialize
' add empty elements to fix their order in the map
mapCopy.Put("Item #1", "")
mapCopy.Put("Item #2", "")
' now read elements from file
mapCopy = File.ReadMap2(File.DirInternal, "settings.txt", mapCopy)
```

Members:

❖ Clear
Clears all items from the map.

❖ ContainsKey (Key As Object) As Boolean
Returns TRUE if there is an item with the given key.
Example:
```
If Map.ContainsKey("some key") Then ...
```

❖ Get (Key As Object) As Object
Returns the value of the item with the given key. If the key does not exist, it returns Null.

✪*GetDefault (Key As Object, Default As Object) As Object*

Returns the value of the item with the given key. If no such item exists, the specified default value is returned.

✪*GetKeyAt (Index As Int) As Object*

Returns the key of the item at the given index. `GetKeyAt` and `GetValueAt` should be used to iterate over all the items. These methods are optimized for iterating over the items in ascending order. Example:

```
For i = 0 to Map.Size - 1
   Log("Key: " & Map.GetKeyAt(i))
   Log("Value: " & Map.GetValueAt(i))
Next
```

✪*GetValueAt (Index As Int) As Object*

Returns the value of the item at the given index. `GetKeyAt` and `GetValueAt` should be used to iterate over all the items. These methods are optimized for iterating over the items in ascending order. Example:

```
For i = 0 to Map.Size - 1
   Log("Key: " & Map.GetKeyAt(i))
   Log("Value: " & Map.GetValueAt(i))
Next
```

✪*Initialize*

Initializes the object.
Example:

```
Dim Map1 As Map
Map1.Initialize
```

✪*IsInitialized As Boolean*

Whether the `Map` has been initialized using the `Initialize` method.

✪*Keys As IterableList*

Returns an object which can be used to iterate over all the keys with a `For Each` loop.
Example:

```
For Each k As String In map1.Keys
   Log(k)
Next
```

✪*Put (Key As Object, Value As Object) As Object*

Puts a key/value pair in the map, overwriting the previous item with this key (if such exists). Returns the previous item with this key or null if there was no such item. Note that if you are using strings as the keys, then the keys are case sensitive. Example:

```
Map1.Put("Key", "Value")
```

✪*Remove (Key As Object) As Object*

Removes the item with the given key, if such exists. Returns the item removed or null if no matching item was found.

✪*Size As Int [read only]*

Returns the number of items stored in the map.

✿*Values As IterableList*

Returns an object which can be used to iterate over all the values with a **For Each** loop.
Example:

```
For Each v As Int In map1.Values
  Log(v)
Next
```

MediaPlayer

The MediaPlayer can be used to play audio files. See the media player tutorial (http://bit.ly/1Owhhc1) for more information.
Note: The media player should be declared as a **Process_Globals** object.

Event: Complete

The **Complete** event is raised when playback completes. It will only be raised if you initialize the object with **Initialize2**.

Members:

✐Duration As Int [read only]

Returns the total duration of the loaded file (in milliseconds).

✿Initialize

Initializes the object. You should use **Initialize2** if you want to handle the Complete event. Example:

```
Dim MP As MediaPlayer 'should be done in Sub Process_Globals
MP.Initialize2("MP")
MP.Load(File.DirAssets, "SomeFile.mp3")
MP.Play
```

✿Initialize2 (EventName As String)

Similar to Initialize, but raises the **Complete** event when play-back completes.
EventName - The Sub that will handle the **Complete** event.

✿IsPlaying As Boolean

Returns **True** if the media player is currently playing.

✿Load (Dir As String, FileName As String)

Loads an audio file and prepares it for playing.

✐Looping As Boolean

Gets or sets whether the media player will restart playing automatically.

✿Pause

Pauses playback. You can resume playback from the current position by calling **Play**.

✿Play

Starts (or resumes) playing the loaded audio file.

Position As Int

Gets or sets the current position (in milliseconds).

Release

Releases all resources allocated by the media player.

SetVolume (Right As Float, Left As Float)

Sets the playing volume for each channel. The values should be from 0 to 1.

Stop

Stops playing. You must call Load before trying to play again.

Notification

A notification object allows an activity or a service to display an icon on the left of the Status Bar (page 120) at the top of the device's screen:

The user can swipe down the notifications screen and press on the notification.

Ongoing notifications are not removed if the user presses "Clear", whereas normal notifications are. Pressing the notification will start an activity as set by the notification object SetInfo command. Notifications are usually used by services because services are not expected to directly start activities. The notification **must** have an icon and its "info" **must** be set.

Example:

```
Dim n As Notification
n.Initialize
n.Icon = "icon"
n.SetInfo("This is the title", "and this is the body.", Main)
'Change Main to "" if this code is in the main module.
n.Notify(1)
```

Permissions:
android.permission.VIBRATE

Members:

*AutoCancel As Boolean [write only]
Sets whether the notification will be canceled automatically when the user clicks on it.

Cancel (Id As Int)
Cancels the notification with the given Id.

*Icon As String [write only]
Sets the icon displayed. The icon value is the name of the image file without the extension.
The name is case sensitive.
Note: the image file must be manually copied to the following folder within your project:
  `\Objects\res\drawable`
You can use "icon" to specify the application icon (which is also located in this folder):
  `n.Icon = "icon"`

Initialize
Initializes the notification. By default, the notification plays a sound, shows a light and vibrates the phone.

*Insistent As Boolean [write only]
Sets whether the sound will play repeatedly until the user opens the notifications screen.

IsInitialized As Boolean
Whether the `Notification` has been initialized using the `Initialize` method.

*Light As Boolean [write only]
Sets whether the notification will show a light. Example:
  `n.Light = False`

Notify (Id As Int)
Displays the notification.
Id - The notification id. You need to generate and store this number. It can be used to later update this `Notification` (by calling Notify again with the same Id), or to cancel the `Notification`.

*Number As Int
Gets or sets a number that will be displayed on the icon. This is useful to represent multiple events in a single notification.

⚜OnGoingEvent As Boolean [write only]

Sets whether this notification is an "ongoing event". The notification will be displayed in the ongoing section and it will not be cleared.

◈SetInfo (Title As String, Body As String, Activity As Object)

Sets the message text and action.
Title - The message title.
Body - The message body.
Activity - The activity to start when the user presses on the notification.
Pass an empty string to start the current activity (when calling from an activity module).
Example:

```
n.SetInfo("Some title", "Some text", Main)
```

◈SetInfo2 (Title As String, Body As String, Tag As String, Activity As Object)

Similar to SetInfo. Also sets a string that can be later extracted in `Activity_Resume`.
Title - The message title.
Body - The message body.
Tag - An arbitrary string that can be later extracted when the user clicks on the notification.
Activity - The activity to start when the user presses on the notification.
Pass an empty string to start the current activity (when calling from an activity module).
Example of extracting the tag:

```
Sub Activity_Resume
  Dim in As Intent
  in = Activity.GetStartingIntent
  If in.HasExtra("Notification_Tag") Then
    Log(in.GetExtra("Notification_Tag")) 'Will log the tag
  End If
End Sub
```

⚜Sound As Boolean [write only]

Sets whether the notification will play a sound.
Example:

```
n.Sound = False
```

⚜Vibrate As Boolean [write only]

Sets whether the notification will vibrate.
Example:

```
n.Vibrate = False
```

◈Regex As Regex

The Regex object allows you to access regular expression (page 288) related methods. This allows you to search within a string to find substrings which match complicated expressions. Simple example:

```
' check that date is of format nn-nn-nnnn
strPattern = "\d\d-\d\d-\d\d\d\d"
strText = "26-12-16"
If Regex.IsMatch(strPattern, strText) Then
 Log ("Valid")
Else
 Log ("Invalid")
End If
```
Result: `Invalid`

Matcher Object

If you need to run regex several times against some text then you need to create a Matcher object (page 318). For example:

```
strPattern = "\d"
strText = "the date is 26-12-16"
matcher1 = Regex.Matcher(strPattern, strText)
Do While matcher1.Find
 Log("Found: " & matcher1.Match)
Loop
```
Result:
```
Found: 2
Found: 6
Found: 1
Found: 2
Found: 1
Found: 6
```
See the Matcher object (page 318) for more details

More about Regex

There are various different flavours of regular expressions. B4A uses the Java regular expression engine. We show some of the more important constructs here (page 288). More information about the Java regex engine can be found here (http://bit.ly/1BSPhtW). For a tutorial on the use of Regex in B4A see here (http://bit.ly/1BSPux0). You can test B4A regular expressions here (http://bit.ly/1TO2ah0).

Options

Some of the Members can have Options. There are two pre-defined options: CASE_INSENSITIVE and MULTILINE. These can be combined with
```
Bit.Or(Regex.MULTILINE, Regex.CASE_INSENSITIVE)
```

Members:

⬤ CASE_INSENSITIVE

This constant is used as an option to make the pattern matching case insensitive.

⬤ IsMatch (Pattern As String, Text As String) As Boolean

Tests whether the whole of **Text** matches **Pattern**. If you want to search for a substring of Text that matches Pattern, use Matcher. Example:

```
If Regex.IsMatch("\d\d\d", EditText1.Text) = False Then ...
```

🔹 IsMatch2 (Pattern As String, Options As Int, Text As String) As Boolean

Tests whether `Text` is a match for `Pattern`.
`Options` - One or more pattern options.

🔹 Matcher (Pattern As String, Text As String) As Matcher

Returns a Matcher object (page 318) which can be used to find matches of `Pattern` in `Text`.
See the Matcher Object section above for a simple example.

🔹 Matcher2 (Pattern As String, Options As Int, Text As String) As Matcher

Same as Matcher with the additional pattern `Options` (see options).

🔹 MULTILINE

Normally the pattern ^ will match the beginning of the text string and & will match the end.
By using the option MULTILINE, these anchors match the beginning and end of each line instead of the whole string.

🔹 Split (Pattern As String, Text As String) As String()

Splits `Text` around matches of `Pattern`. Example:
```
components = Regex.Split(",", "abc,def,,ghi")
'returns: "abc", "def", "", "ghi"
```

🔹 Split2

Same as Split with the additional pattern `Options` (see options).

RemoteViews

RemoteViews allows indirect access to a home screen widget.
See here for more information (page 130) about Widgets.

Events:
RequestUpdate
Disabled

Members:

🔹HandleWidgetEvents (StartingIntent As Intent) As Boolean

Checks if the intent starting this service was sent from the widget and raises events based on the intent. Returns `True` if an event was raised.
See here for more information (page 130) about Widgets.

🔹SetImage (ImageViewName As String, Image As Bitmap)

Sets the image of the given ImageView. Example:

```
rv.SetImage("ImageView1", LoadBitmap(File.DirAssets, "1.jpg"))
```

❧SetProgress (ProgressBarName As String, Progress As Int)

Sets the progress value of the given ProgressBar. Value should be from 0 to 100.
Example:
```
rv.SetProgress("ProgressBar1", 50)
```

❧SetText (ViewName As String, Text As String)

Sets the text of the given view. Example:
```
rv.SetText("Label1", "New text")
```

❧SetTextColor (ViewName As String, Color As Int)

Sets the text color of the given button or label. Example:
```
rv.SetTextColor("Label1", Colors.Red)
```

❧SetTextSize (ViewName As String, Size As Float)

Sets the text size (page 163) of the given button or label. Example:
```
rv.SetTextSize("Label1", 20)
```

❧SetVisible (ViewName As String, Visible As Boolean)

Sets the visibility of the given view. Example:
```
rv.SetVisibile("Button1", False)
```

❧UpdateWidget

Updates the widget with the changes done. This method is also responsible for configuring the events.
See here for more information (page 130) about Widgets.

Service

Each Service module (page 254) includes a Service object which is used to bring the service in and out of the foreground state. See the Services module section for more information.

Members:

❧StartForeground (Id As Int, Notification1 As Notification)

Brings the current service to the foreground state and displays the given notification.
Id - The notification Id (page 390).
Notification - The notification (page 389) that will be displayed.

❧StopForeground (Id As Int)

Takes the current service out of the foreground state and cancels the notification with the given **Id**.

String

Immutable Strings

Strings are immutable in B4A, which means that you can change the value of a string variable, but you cannot change the text stored in a string object. So methods like

`SubString`, `Trim` and `ToLowerCase` return a new string; **they do not change the value of the current string**. Typical usage:

```
Dim s As String
s = "some text"
s = s.Replace("a", "b")
```

You can use **StringBuilder** if you need a mutable string. **Note** that string literals are also string objects:

```
Log(" some text ".Trim)
```

Mutable Strings

Repetitive manipulation of strings can be very slow. Since they are immutable, a new string has to be created every time you want to change a string. If you are doing extensive string manipulation, you should consider using StringBuilder (page 399).

Number formatting

Numbers can be displayed as strings with different formats. There are two keywords:
– NumberFormat (page 321) (Number As Double, MinimumIntegers As Int, MaximumFractions As Int) As String
– NumberFormat2 (page 321) (Number As Double, MinimumIntegers As Int, MaximumFractions As Int, MinimumFractions As Int, GroupingUsed As Boolean) As String

Smart Strings

Smart strings are useful feature of B4A not found in most other implementations of BASIC. A smart string allows you to:
- Create multi-line strings.
- Include quotation marks inside strings.
- Include variable placeholders (technically called "string interpolation").
- Specify format of numeric placeholders

Note that this is a compile time feature. For example, you cannot load smart strings from a file.

A smart string literal starts with $" and ends with "$.

```
Dim strExample As String = $"This is a smart string"$
```

Multi-line String

Smart strings can extend over several lines without requiring an _ to extend the line:

```
Dim strQuery As String = $"
    SELECT name FROM user
    WHERE usernumber >= 3456
    AND address ISNOTNULL
"$
```

Include Quotation Marks

Smart stings can include either or both single and double quotations marks.

```
Dim strQuotes As String = $"A smart string can include 'single' or
"double" quotation marks."$
Log ("strQuotes=" & strQuotes)
' strQuotes=A smart string can include 'single' or "double" quotation
marks.
```

Variable Placeholders

Smart strings can include placeholders for variables. Simple placeholders are formatted as
```
${variable}
```
For example:
```
Dim strInput As String = "world"
Dim strOutput As String = $"Hello ${strInput}"$
Log (strOutput)
```
The output will be **Hello world**.

Placeholder Calculations

Placeholders can also include calculations. For example:
```
Dim iValue = 3 As Int
Dim strCalc As String = $"5 * ${iValue} = ${5 * iValue}"$
Log ("strCalc=" & strCalc)
```
The output will be **strCalc=5 * 3 = 15**
Another example:
```
Dim iAngle = 5 As Int
strCalc = $"Sin of ${iAngle} = ${Sin(iAngle)}"$
Log ("strCalc=" & strCalc)
' strCalc=Sin of 5 = -0.9589242746631385
```

Formatting Numbers

Smart strings can include an optional number format which allows you to set the minimum number of integers and the maximum number of decimal digits to be output by the smart string. It is similar to the NumberFormat (page 321) keyword. The number formatter has the structure:
```
$MinIntegers.MaxIntegers MaxFractions{number}
```
MinIntegers specifies the minimum number of integers to be output. If greater than the number of digits available, they are padded with zeros and separated by commas.
MaxFractions specifies the maximum number of decimal digits to be output. Note this component is optional. If omitted, all decimal values are included.
Examples:
```
Dim dExample = 123.45678 As Double
Log ($"dExample= $5{dExample}"$)
' dExample= 00,123.45678
Log ($"dExample= $0.2{dExample}"$)
' dExample= 123.46
```

Automatic Conversion of String to Number

If a string contains a numeric value then it is automatically converted to a number by the smart string:

```
Dim iNum As Int = 12
Dim strNum As String = "3"
Log($"$1.2{iNum*strNum}"$)
' result: 36
```

Generating Exceptions

If a calculation does not return a number, the device returns an error and the program crashes with a NumberFormatException:

```
Dim iNum As Int = 12
Dim strNum As String = "Something which is not a number"
Log($"$1.2{iNum*strNum}"$)
```

Formatting Date and Time

There are three formatters which allow a smart string to easily extract the date, the time or both date and time from a long. **Note** that the formatters are case insensitive.

$Date - Equivalent to DateTime.Date (page 206):

```
Log($"Current date is $date{DateTime.Now}"$)
'Exactly the same as
Dim strDate As String = DateTime.Date(DateTime.Now)
Log("Current date is " & strDate)
```

$Time - Equivalent to DateTime.Time (page 352):

```
Log($"Current time is $time{DateTime.Now}"$)
'Exactly the same as
Dim strDate As String = DateTime.time(DateTime.Now)
Log("Current time is " & strDate)
```

$DateTime - Equivalent to DateTime.Date & " " & DateTime.Time:

```
Log($"Current date and time is $datetime{DateTime.Now}"$)
'Exactly the same as
Dim strDate As String = DateTime.Date(DateTime.Now) & " " & _
DateTime.time(DateTime.Now)
Log("Current date and time is " & strDate)
```

Escaping XLM / HTML

Smart strings can also "escape" XML code. To "escape" a string is to reduce ambiguity and so render the string safe for use by parsers. It does this by converting certain characters within the string into other characters.

Smart strings can escape five characters used by XML:

" double quote, which is converted to "
' single quote, which is converted to '
< less than sign, which is converted to <
> greater than sign, which is converted to >
& ampersand, which is converted to &

Note that if you are using the XMLBuilder (http://bit.ly/1663zXh) library then you do not need to escape the XML, but if you are creating your own XML, then this can be useful. Consider this example, in which you ask for user input to create your XML file:

```
Dim dlg As InputDialog
Dim strInputName As String
dlg.Show("What is your name?", "Please enter", "Enter", "", "", Null)
strInputName = dlg.Input
Dim strXML As String = "<name>" & strInputName & "</name>"
File.WriteString(File.DirRootExternal, "user.xml", strXML)
```

If the user enters a string containing < or > or any of the other XML characters listed above, your XML will not be valid. You can prevent this by escaping the user input before saving it, by changing the penultimate line to:

```
Dim strXML As String = $"<name>$xml{strInputName}</name>"$
```

Smart string $xml is identical to the PHP htmlspecialchars function with ENT_QUOTES set, and to the org.apache.commons.lang Java function escapeXml.

Members:

String Functions Library
As well as the following built-in members, the user-generated String Functions Library (http://bit.ly/15HuBDW) is useful.

⬡CharAt (Index As Int) As Char
Returns the character at the given index.

⬡CompareTo (Other As String) As Int
Lexicographically compares the two strings, that is, as they would appear in a dictionary. Returns a value less than 0 if the current string comes before **Other**. Returns 0 if both strings are equal. Returns a value larger than 0 if the current string comes after **Other**. **Note:** upper case characters precede lower case characters. The exact value returned depends in part upon the unicode values of the strings involved. Examples:

```
"abc".CompareTo("da")   ' < 0
"abc".CompareTo("Abc")  ' > 0
"abc".CompareTo("abca") ' < 0
```

⬡Contains (SearchFor As String) As Boolean
Returns TRUE if the string contains the given string parameter.

⬡EndsWith (Suffix As String) As Boolean
Returns True if this string ends with the given Suffix.

⬡EqualsIgnoreCase (other As String) As Boolean
Returns True if both strings are equal (ignoring their case).

⬡GetBytes (Charset As String) As Byte()
Encodes the string into a new array of bytes. Example:

```
Dim Data() As Byte
Data = "Some string".GetBytes("UTF8")
```

⬡IndexOf (SearchFor As String) As Int
Returns the index of the first occurrence of **SearchFor** in the string. Returns −1 if **SearchFor** was not found.

❖IndexOf2 (SearchFor As String, Index As Int) As Int

Returns the index of the first occurrence of **SearchFor** in the string. Starts searching from **Index**. Returns -1 if **SearchFor** was not found.

❖LastIndexOf (SearchFor As String) As Int

Returns the index of the first occurrence of **SearchFor** in the string. The search starts at the end of the string and advances to the beginning.

❖LastIndexOf2 (SearchFor As String, Index As Int) As Int

Returns the index of the first occurrence of **SearchFor** in the string. The search starts at **Index** and advances to the beginning.

❖Length As Int

Returns the length of this string.

❖Replace (Target As String, Replacement As String) As String

Returns a new string resulting from the replacement of all the occurrences of **Target** with **Replacement**.

❖StartsWith (Prefix As String) As Boolean

Returns **True** if this string starts with the given Prefix.

❖SubString (BeginIndex As Int) As String

Returns a new string which is a substring of the original string. The new string will include the character at **BeginIndex** and will extend to the end of the string. Example:
```
"012345".SubString(2) 'returns "2345"
```

❖SubString2 (BeginIndex As Int, EndIndex As Int) As String

Returns a new string which is a substring of the original. The new string will include the character at **BeginIndex**, where first character counts as index 0. The last character returned will be the one before **EndIndex**. Examples:
```
Log("ABCDEF".SubString2(0, 3)) 'result is "ABC"
Log("ABCDEF".SubString2(2, 4)) 'result is "CD"
```

❖ToLowerCase As String

Returns a new string which is the result of lower casing this string.

❖ToUpperCase As String

Returns a new string which is the result of upper casing this string.

❖Trim As String

Returns a copy of the original string without any leading or trailing white spaces.

StringBuilder

StringBuilder is a mutable string, unlike regular strings which are immutable. StringBuilder is especially useful when you need to concatenate many strings. The following code demonstrates the performance boosting of StringBuilder:

```
Dim start As Long
start = DateTime.Now
'Regular string
Dim s As String
For i = 1 To 5000
  s = s & i
Next
Log(DateTime.Now - start)
'StringBuilder
start = DateTime.Now
Dim sb As StringBuilder
sb.Initialize
For i = 1 To 5000
  sb.Append(i)
Next
Log(DateTime.Now - start)
```

Tested on a real device, the first 'for loop' took about 20 seconds and the second took less than one tenth of a second. The reason is that the code: **s = s & i** creates a new string each iteration because strings are immutable.

The method **StringBuilder.ToString** converts the object to a string.

Members:

Append (Text As String) As StringBuilder

Appends the specified text at the end. Returns the same object, so you can chain methods. Example:

```
sb.Append("First line").Append(CRLF).Append("Second line")
```

Initialize

Initializes the object. Example:

```
Dim sb As StringBuilder
sb.Initialize
sb.Append("The value is: ").Append(SomeOtherVariable).Append(CRLF)
```

Insert (Offset As Int, Text As String) As StringBuilder

Inserts the specified text at the specified offset.

IsInitialized As Boolean

Whether the **StringBuilder** has been initialized using the Initialize method.

Length As Int [read only]

Returns the number of characters.

Remove (StartOffset As Int, EndOffset As Int) As StringBuilder

Removes the specified characters.
StartOffset - The first character to remove.
EndOffset - The ending index. This character will not be removed. Examples:

```
Dim sb As StringBuilder
sb.Initialize
sb.Append("ABCDEF")
Log(sb.Remove(0, 3)) 'result is "DEF"
sb.Initialize
sb.Append("ABCDEF")
Log(sb.Remove(2, 4)) 'result is "ABEF"
```

ToString As String
Converts the object to a string.

Timer

A **Timer** object generates **Tick** events at specified intervals. Using a timer is a good alternative to a long loop, as it allows the UI (page 40) thread to handle other events and messages. The timer **Enabled** property is set to **False** by default. To start the timer, you should change **Enabled** to **True**.

Note: timer events will not fire while the UI thread is busy running other code unless you call the **DoEvents** keyword within a loop. In addition, Timer events will not fire when the activity is paused, or if a blocking dialog (like Msgbox) is visible. An alternative approach, which overcomes this limitation, is to start a service (page 394) at a given time using StartServiceAt (page 325).

Timers should be declared in Sub Process_Globals. Otherwise you may get multiple timers running when the activity is recreated. It is **also important** to disable the timer when the activity is pausing and then enable it when it resumes. This will save CPU and battery.

The Timer must be declared in a Sub Process_Globals routine.
```
Sub Process_Globals
' declare here so do not get multiple timers when activity is
recreated
 Dim Timer1 As Timer
End Sub
```
A Timer must be initialized in the Activity_Create routine in the module where the timer tick event routine is used.
```
Sub Activity_Create(FirstTime As Boolean)
  If FirstTime = True Then
    ' Call every 1000 milliseconds
    Timer1.Initialize("Timer1", 1000)
    Timer1.Enabled = True
  End If
End Sub
```

Event: Tick
When a timer is **Enabled**, the **Tick** event is called after the time interval set by the **Initialize** method. **Tick** will continue to be called until **Enabled** is set to **False**. Example:

```
Timer1.Initialize("Timer1", 1000)
Timer1.Enabled = True
' ...
Sub Timer1_Tick
 'Handle tick events
 ProgressBar1.Progress = ProgressBar1.Progress + 10
 If ProgressBar1.Progress = 100 Then
  Timer1.Enabled = False
 End If
End Sub
```

Example:
You find an example of using a Timer in the RotatingNeedle example program available from this book's resources website (http://bit.ly/1IjLiwC).

Members:

⚡Enabled As Boolean
Gets or sets whether the timer is enabled (ticking). **It is False by default**, which means to start a timer you must call:
```
Timer1.Enabled = True
```

⚙Initialize (EventName As String, Interval As Long)
Initializes the timer with the event sub prefix and the specified interval (measured in milliseconds). **Important**: this object should be declared in Sub Process_Globals.
EventName - The name used for the Tick event, for example, Sub Timer1_Tick.
Interval - Sets the timer interval in milliseconds. Interval can be changed by calling TimerName.Interval = Interval, for example:
```
Sub Process_Globals
Dim timer1 As Timer
End Sub

Sub Activity_Create(FirstTime As Boolean)
 timer1.Initialize("Timer1", 1000)
 timer1.Enabled = True
End Sub

Sub Timer1_Tick
 'Handle tick events
 'Shorten the timer interval
 timer1.Interval = timer1.Interval - 10
 If Timer1.Interval <= 0 Then
  Timer1.Enabled = False
 End If
End Sub
```

⚡Interval As Long
Gets or sets the interval between tick events, measured in milliseconds.

⚙️IsInitialized As Boolean

Whether the timer has been initialized.

Views

Most views are objects which can be added to a layout either using the Designer (page 139) or in code. Here we list all views and give their methods. The view types are: AutoCompleteEditText, Button (page 407), CheckBox (page 409), CustomView (page 410), EditText (page 411), ImageView (page 416), HorizontalScrollView (page 414), Label (page 418), ListView (page 420), Panel (page 425) , ProgressBar (page 427), RadioButton (page 429), ScrollView (page 431), SeekBar (page 433), Spinner (page 435), TabHost (page 439), ToggleButton (page 442), WebView (page 446)

Note that Views hold a reference to the parent Activity, and therefore cannot be declared in **Process_Globals**. This is discussed further in the Process and Activity (page 241) chapter.

AutoCompleteEditText

An enhanced version of EditText which shows the user a drop down list with all items matching the currently entered characters. Items matching are items starting with the current input or items that include a word that starts with the current input (words must be separated by spaces).

Call **SetItems** with the list of possible items.

Note: the SearchView (page 567) class offers similar functionality but with faster search and other benefits.

Example:

```
Sub Process_Globals
End Sub
Sub Globals
  Dim ACT As AutoCompleteEditText
End Sub
Sub Activity_Create(FirstTime As Boolean)
  ACT.Initialize("ACT")
  Activity.AddView(ACT, 10dip, 10dip, 500dip, 80dip)
  Dim people() As String
  people = Array As String( _
      "Alan", "Albert", "Algernon", "Alice", "Andorra")
  ACT.SetItems(people)
End Sub
Sub Activity_Pause (UserClosed As Boolean)
End Sub
```

Events:

ItemClick (Value As String)

The ItemClick event is raised when the user clicks on an item from the list.

TextChanged (Old As String, New As String)

This is raised every time the user edits the text in the AutoCompleteEditText. **Old** and **New** contain the text before and after the edit.

EnterPressed

This event is raised when the user presses the "Done" or "Enter" keys on the keyboard.

FocusChanged (HasFocus As Boolean)

This event is raised when the user touches the AutoCompleteEditText, in which case **HasFocus** will be True, or when the user moves from here to another view (when **HasFocus** will be False).

Members:

Background As Drawable

Gets or sets the background drawable.

BringToFront

Changes the Z order of this view and brings it to the front.

Color As Int [write only]

Sets the background of the view to be a ColorDrawable with the given color. If the current background is of type GradientDrawable or ColorDrawable, the round corners will be kept.

DismissDropDown

Forces the drop down list to disappear.

Enabled As Boolean

If set to True then the AutoCompleteEditText will respond to events. If set to False, events are ignored.

ForceDoneButton As Boolean [write only]

By default, Android sets the virtual keyboard action key to display **Done** or **Next** according to the specific layout. You can force it to display **Done** by setting this value to **True**. Example:
```
EditText1.ForceDoneButton = True
```

Gravity As Int

Gets or sets the gravity (page 346) value. This value affects the way the text will be drawn.

Height As Int

Gets or sets the view's height.

Hint As String

Gets or sets the text that will appear when the EditText is empty. Example:
```
EditText1.Hint = "Enter username"
```

HintColor As Int

Gets or sets the hint text color.
Example:
```
EditText1.HintColor = Colors.Gray
```

Initialize (EventName As String)

Initializes the view and sets the subs that will handle the events.
Views added with the designer should NOT be initialized. These views are initialized when the layout is loaded.

INPUT_TYPE_DECIMAL_NUMBERS As Int

Numeric keyboard will be displayed. Numbers, decimal point and minus sign are accepted.

INPUT_TYPE_NONE As Int

No keyboard will be displayed. This could be useful, for example, if you use a read-only `AutoCompleteEditText` for which you do not want a keyboard to be displayed.

INPUT_TYPE_NUMBERS As Int

Numeric keyboard will be displayed. Only numbers are accepted.

INPUT_TYPE_PHONE As Int

Keyboard will be displayed in phone mode.

INPUT_TYPE_TEXT As Int

Default text mode.

InputType As Int

Gets or sets the input type flag. This flag is used to determine the settings of the virtual keyboard. **Note** that changing the input type will set the EditText to be in single line mode. Example:
```
EditText1.InputType = EditText1.INPUT_TYPE_NUMBERS
```

Invalidate

Invalidates the whole view forcing the view to redraw itself. Redrawing will only happen when the program can process messages, usually when it finishes running the current code. If you only need to redraw part of the view, it is usually quicker to use **Invalidate2** or **Invalidate3**.

⟡ *Invalidate2 (Rect1 As Rect)*

Invalidates anything inside the given rectangle that is part of this view. Redrawing will only happen when the program can process messages, usually when it finishes running the current code.

⟡ *Invalidate3 (Left As Int, Top As Int, Right As Int, Bottom As Int)*

Invalidates anything inside the given rectangle that is part of this view. Redrawing will only happen when the program can process messages, usually when it finishes running the current code.

⟡ *IsInitialized As Boolean*

Whether this object has been initialized by calling `Initialize`.

⚒ *Left As Int*

Gets or sets the view's left position.

⚒ *PasswordMode As Boolean [write only]*

Sets whether the EditText should be in password mode and hide the actual characters.

⟡ *RemoveView*

Removes this view from its parent.

⟡ *RequestFocus As Boolean*

Tries to set the focus to this view.
Returns `True` if the focus was set.

⟡ *SelectAll*

Selects the entire text.

⚒ *SelectionStart As Int*

Gets or sets the selection start position (or the cursor position). Returns `-1` if there is no selection or cursor.

⟡ *SendToBack*

Changes the Z order of this view and sends it to the back.

⟡ *SetBackgroundImage (Bitmap1 As Bitmap)*

⟡ *SetItems (Items As List)*

Sets the list of possible items. The items' visual style will be the same as the style of the main text.

⟡ *SetItems2 (Items As List, Typeface1 As Typeface, Gravity As Int, TextSize As Float, TextColor As Int)*

Sets the list of possible items and specifies their style.
Gravity: sets the gravity (page 346) value. This value affects the way the text will be drawn.
Example:

```
Dim act As AutoCompleteEditText
act.Initialize("act")
Activity.AddView(act, 10dip, 10dip, 200dip, 80dip)
act.SetItems2(Array As String("aab", "abc"), act.Typeface,
Gravity.LEFT, 12, Colors.Green)
```

SetLayout (Left As Int, Top As Int, Width As Int, Height As Int)
Changes the view position and size.

ShowDropDown
Forces the drop down list to appear.

SingleLine As Boolean [write only]
Sets whether the EditText should be in single-line mode or multiline mode.

Tag As Object
Gets or sets the Tag value. This is a place holder which can be used to store additional data.

Text As String

TextColor As Int

TextSize As Float

Top As Int
Gets or sets the view's top position.

Typeface As Typeface

Visible As Boolean
Whether the user can see the object.

Width As Int
Gets or sets the view's width.

Wrap As Boolean [write only]
Sets whether the text content will wrap within the EditText bounds. Relevant when the EditText is in multiline mode. Example:
```
EditText1.Wrap = False
```

Button
A Button view. If you change the button's background, you will usually want to use **StateListDrawable** which allows you to set the "default" Drawable and the "pressed" drawable.
This is an **Activity** object; it cannot be declared under **Sub Process_Globals**.

Events:

Down
Occurs when the user first presses on the button.

Up
Occurs when the user releases the button.

Click

Occurs when the user presses and releases the button. The Down and Up events also fire. They are called in this sequence: Down, Up, Click.

LongClick

Occurs when the user presses on the button for roughly one second. The Down and Up events also fire. They are called in this sequence: Down, LongClick, Up.

Members:

Background As Drawable

Gets or sets the background drawable.

BringToFront

Changes the Z order of this view and brings it to the front.

Color As Int [write only]

Sets the background of the view to be a `ColorDrawable` with the given color. If the current background is of type `GradientDrawable` or `ColorDrawable`, the round corners will be kept.

Enabled As Boolean

If set to `True` then the `Button` will respond to events. If set to `False`, events are ignored.

Gravity As Int

Gets or sets the gravity (page 346) value. This value affects the way the text will be drawn.

Height As Int

Gets or sets the view's height.

Initialize (EventName As String)

Initializes the view and sets the subs that will handle the events.
Views added with the designer should NOT be initialized. These views are initialized when the layout is loaded.

Invalidate

Invalidates the whole view forcing the view to redraw itself. Redrawing will only happen when the program can process messages, usually when it finishes running the current code. If you only need to redraw part of the view, it is usually quicker to use `Invalidate2` or `Invalidate3`.

Invalidate2 (Rect1 As Rect)

Invalidates anything inside the given rectangle that is part of this view. Redrawing will only happen when the program can process messages, usually when it finishes running the current code.

Invalidate3 (Left As Int, Top As Int, Right As Int, Bottom As Int)

Invalidates anything inside the given rectangle that is part of this view. Redrawing will only happen when the program can process messages, usually when it finishes running the current code.

IsInitialized As Boolean

Whether this object has been initialized by calling `Initialize`.

Left As Int
Gets or sets the view's left position.

RemoveView
Removes this view from its parent.

RequestFocus As Boolean
Tries to set the focus to this view. Returns **True** if the focus was set.

SendToBack
Changes the Z order of this view and sends it to the back.

SetBackgroundImage (Bitmap1 As Bitmap)

SetLayout (Left As Int, Top As Int, Width As Int, Height As Int)
Changes the view position and size.

Tag As Object
Gets or sets the Tag value. This is a place holder which can be used to store additional data.

Text As String

TextColor As Int

TextSize As Float

Top As Int
Gets or sets the view's top position.

Typeface As Typeface

Visible As Boolean
Whether the user can see the object.

Width As Int
Gets or sets the view's width.

CheckBox

A **CheckBox** view. Unlike **RadioButtons**, each CheckBox can be checked independently. This is an **Activity** object; it cannot be declared under **Sub Process_Globals**.

Events:
CheckedChange(Checked As Boolean)

Members:

Background As Drawable
Gets or sets the background drawable.

BringToFront
Changes the Z order of this view and brings it to the front.

🪶 *Checked As Boolean*

🪶 *Color As Int [write only]*

Sets the background of the view to be a `ColorDrawable` with the given color. If the current background is of type `GradientDrawable` or `ColorDrawable`, the round corners will be kept.

🪶 *Enabled As Boolean*

If set to `True` then the `CheckBox` will respond to events. If set to `False`, events are ignored.

🪶 *Gravity As Int*

Gets or sets the gravity (page 346) value. This value affects the way the text will be drawn.

🪶 *Height As Int*

Gets or sets the view's height.

🎛 *Initialize (EventName As String)*

Initializes the view and sets the subs that will handle the events.
Views added with the designer should NOT be initialized. These views are initialized when the layout is loaded.

🎛 *Invalidate*

Invalidates the whole view forcing the view to redraw itself. Redrawing will only happen when the program can process messages, usually when it finishes running the current code. If you only need to redraw part of the view, it is usually quicker to use `Invalidate2` or `Invalidate3`.

🎛 *Invalidate2 (Rect1 As Rect)*

Invalidates anything inside the given rectangle that is part of this view. Redrawing will only happen when the program can process messages, usually when it finishes running the current code.

🎛 *Invalidate3 (Left As Int, Top As Int, Right As Int, Bottom As Int)*

Invalidates anything inside the given rectangle that is part of this view. Redrawing will only happen when the program can process messages, usually when it finishes running the current code.

🎛 *IsInitialized As Boolean*

Whether this object has been initialized by calling `Initialize`.

🪶 *Left As Int*

Gets or sets the view's left position.

🎛 *RemoveView*

Removes this view from its parent.

🎛 *RequestFocus As Boolean*

Tries to set the focus to this view. Returns `True` if the focus was set.

🎛 *SendToBack*

Changes the Z order of this view and sends it to the back.

⬙ **SetBackgroundImage (Bitmap1 As Bitmap)**

⬙ **SetLayout (Left As Int, Top As Int, Width As Int, Height As Int)**

Changes the view position and size.

🔑 **Tag As Object**

Gets or sets the Tag value. This is a place holder which can be used to store additional data.

🔑 **Text As String**

🔑 **TextColor As Int**

🔑 **TextSize As Float**

🔑 **Top As Int**

Gets or sets the view's top position.

🔑 **Typeface As Typeface**

🔑 **Visible As Boolean**

Whether the user can see the object.

🔑 **Width As Int**

Gets or sets the view's width.

CustomView

A Custom View allows you to create your own types of views which you implement either as a class or in Java. Your class could also be compiled into a library.

DoubleClickButton is a working example using a class, available for download from this book's resources page (http://bit.ly/1IjLiwC).

Steps for Creating a Custom View Class

1) Add a class to your project.
2) Declare the events which your view will support, for example:

```
#Event: DoubleClick
#Event: SingleClick
```

3) Modify the `Initialize` sub so it has two arguments:

```
Public Sub Initialize (TargetModule As Object, EventName As String)
```

TargetModule - references the module that loads the layout file.

EventName - the event's name property.

These two parameters allow you to later raise events like all standard views.

4) Add a sub

```
Public Sub DesignerCreateView(Base As Panel, Lbl As Label, Props As
Map)
```

Base - a panel that will be the parent for your custom view. The panel background and layout will be based on the values from the designer. Note that you are free to do whatever you need with this panel.

Lbl - the purpose of the label is to hold all the text related properties. The label will not appear (unless you explicitly add it).

Props - a Map with additional entries. Currently the only entry is an "activity" key that holds a reference to the parent Activity object.

5) Add any other subs and variables you need to make your CustomView work.

6) Open the Visual Designer

7) Use the menu [Add View > CustomView] to add a custom view to a layout

8) Select the custom type from to the Custom Type list. The name will be the same as the name of the class you created.

9) Set the view properties and if required use it in the designer script.

10) Use the Designer menu [Tools > Generate Members] or the context menu in the Abstract Designer (page 160) to generate `Dim` statements in your **Activity Module** for the Custom View.

EditText

EditText is a view that allows the user to write free text (similar to TextBox in VB forms). The EditText has two modes; `SingleLine` and `MultiLine`. You can set it to be multiline by calling `EditText1.SingleLine = False`

On most devices, the soft keyboard will show automatically when the user presses on the EditText. You can change the InputType property and change the type of keyboard that appears. For example:

```
EditText1.InputType = EditText1.INPUT_TYPE_NUMBERS
```

will cause the numeric keyboard to appear when the user presses on the EditText. **Note** that it will also cause the EditText to only accept numbers. Note also that most views are not focusable. For example, pressing on a Button will not change the focus state of an EditText. This is an `Activity` object; it cannot be declared under `Sub Process_Globals`.

TextChanged (Old As String, New As String)

The **TextChanged** event fires whenever the text changes and it includes the old and new strings.

EnterPressed

The **EnterPressed** event fires when the user presses on the enter key or action key (Done or Next).

FocusChanged (HasFocus As Boolean)

The FocusChanged event fires when the view is focused or loses focus. The **HasFocus** parameter value will be set accordingly.

Members:

Background As Drawable

Gets or sets the background drawable.

BringToFront

Changes the Z order of this view and brings it to the front.

Color As Int [write only]

Sets the background of the view to be a `ColorDrawable` with the given color. If the current background is of type `GradientDrawable` or `ColorDrawable`, the round corners will be kept.

Enabled As Boolean

If set to `True` then the `EditText` will respond to events. If set to `False`, events are ignored.

🔧 ForceDoneButton As Boolean [write only]

By default, Android sets the virtual keyboard action key to display Done or Next according to the specific layout. You can force it to display Done by setting this value to **True**.
Example:
```
EditText1.ForceDoneButton = True
```

🔧 Gravity As Int

Gets or sets the gravity (page 346) value. This value affects the way the text will be drawn.

🔧 Height As Int

Gets or sets the view's height.

🔧 Hint As String

Gets or sets the text that will appear when the EditText is empty.
Example:
```
EditText1.Hint = "Enter username"
```

🔧 HintColor As Int

Gets or sets the hint text color.
Example:
```
EditText1.HintColor = Colors.Gray
```

🔷 Initialize (EventName As String)

Initializes the view and sets the subs that will handle the events.
Views added with the designer should NOT be initialized. These views are initialized when the layout is loaded.

🔶 INPUT_TYPE_DECIMAL_NUMBERS As Int

Numeric keyboard will be displayed. Numbers, decimal point and minus sign are accepted.

🔶 INPUT_TYPE_NONE As Int

No keyboard will be displayed and clicking on the EditText will do nothing.

🔶 INPUT_TYPE_NUMBERS As Int

Numeric keyboard will be displayed. Only numbers are accepted.

🔶 INPUT_TYPE_PHONE As Int

Keyboard will be displayed in phone mode.

🔶 INPUT_TYPE_TEXT As Int

Default text mode.

🔧 InputType As Int

Gets or sets the input type flag. This flag is used to determine the settings of the virtual keyboard. **Note** that changing the input type will set the EditText to be in single line mode.
Example:
```
EditText1.InputType = EditText1.INPUT_TYPE_NUMBERS
```

🔷 Invalidate

Invalidates the whole view forcing the view to redraw itself. Redrawing will only happen when the program can process messages, usually when it finishes running the current code.

If you only need to redraw part of the view, it is usually quicker to use `Invalidate2` or `Invalidate3`.

⬡ *Invalidate2 (Rect1 As Rect)*

Invalidates anything inside the given rectangle that is part of this view. Redrawing will only happen when the program can process messages, usually when it finishes running the current code.

⬡ *Invalidate3 (Left As Int, Top As Int, Right As Int, Bottom As Int)*

Invalidates anything inside the given rectangle that is part of this view. Redrawing will only happen when the program can process messages, usually when it finishes running the current code.

⬡ *IsInitialized As Boolean*

Whether this object has been initialized by calling `Initialize`.

⚒ *Left As Int*

Gets or sets the view's left position.

⚒ *PasswordMode As Boolean [write only]*

Sets whether the EditText should be in password mode and hide the actual characters.

⬡ *RemoveView*

Removes this view from its parent.

⬡ *RequestFocus As Boolean*

Tries to set the focus to this view. Returns `True` if the focus was set.

⬡ *SelectAll*

Selects the entire text.

⚒ *SelectionStart As Int*

Gets or sets the selection start position (or the cursor position). Returns `-1` if there is no selection or cursor.

⬡ *SendToBack*

Changes the Z order of this view and sends it to the back.

⬡ *SetBackgroundImage (Bitmap1 As Bitmap)*

⬡ *SetLayout (Left As Int, Top As Int, Width As Int, Height As Int)*

Changes the view position and size.

⚒ *SingleLine As Boolean [write only]*

Sets whether the EditText should be in single-line mode or multiline mode.

⚒ *Tag As Object*

Gets or sets the Tag value. This is a place holder which can be used to store additional data.

🔥 *Text As String*

🔥 *TextColor As Int*

🔥 *TextSize As Float*

🔥 *Top As Int*

Gets or sets the view's top position.

🔥 *Typeface As Typeface*

🔥 *Visible As Boolean*

Whether the user can see the object.

🔥 *Width As Int*

Gets or sets the view's width.

🔥 *Wrap As Boolean [write only]*

Sets whether the text content will wrap within the EditText bounds. Relevant when the EditText is in multiline mode. Example:

```
EditText1.Wrap = False
```

HorizontalScrollView

HorizontalScrollView is a view that contains other views and allows the user to horizontally scroll those views. The HorizontalScrollView is similar to ScrollView which scrolls vertically. See the ScrollView tutorial (http://bit.ly/1Owhtbg) for more information.

The HorizontalScrollView has an inner panel which actually contains the child views. You can add views by calling: `HorizontalScrollView1.Panel.AddView(...)`

Note that it is not possible to nest scrolling views.

This is an `Activity` object; it cannot be declared under `Sub Process_Globals`.

Events:

ScrollChanged(Position As Int)

Members:

🔥 *Background As Drawable*

Gets or sets the background drawable.

♻ *BringToFront*

Changes the Z order of this view and brings it to the front.

🔥 *Color As Int [write only]*

Sets the background of the view to be a `ColorDrawable` with the given color. If the current background is of type `GradientDrawable` or `ColorDrawable`, the round corners will be kept.

🔥 *Enabled As Boolean*

If set to `True` then the `HorizontalScrollView` will respond to events. If set to `False`, events are ignored.

♻ *FullScroll (Right As Boolean)*

Set to `True` to scroll the view to the right. Set to `False` to scroll to the left.

✦ Height As Int

Gets or sets the view's height.

✿ Initialize (Width As Int, EventName As String)

Initializes the object.

Width - The width of the inner panel.

EventName - Sets the sub that will handle the event.

✿ Invalidate

Invalidates the whole view forcing the view to redraw itself. Redrawing will only happen when the program can process messages, usually when it finishes running the current code. If you only need to redraw part of the view, it is usually quicker to use `Invalidate2` or `Invalidate3`.

✿ Invalidate2 (Rect1 As Rect)

Invalidates anything inside the given rectangle that is part of this view. Redrawing will only happen when the program can process messages, usually when it finishes running the current code.

✿ Invalidate3 (Left As Int, Top As Int, Right As Int, Bottom As Int)

Invalidates anything inside the given rectangle that is part of this view. Redrawing will only happen when the program can process messages, usually when it finishes running the current code.

✿ IsInitialized As Boolean

Whether this object has been initialized by calling `Initialize`.

✦ Left As Int

Gets or sets the view's left position.

✦ Panel As Panel [read only]

Returns the panel which you can use to add views to. Example:
```
HorizontalScrollView1.Panel.AddView(...)
```

✿ RemoveView

Removes this view from its parent.

✿ RequestFocus As Boolean

Tries to set the focus to this view. Returns `True` if the focus was set.

✦ ScrollPosition As Int

Gets or sets the scroll position. If setting, scrolls the View with animation.

✿ ScrollToNow (Scroll As Int)

Immediately scrolls the HorizontalScrollView without animation.

✿ SendToBack

Changes the Z order of this view and sends it to the back.

✿ SetBackgroundImage (Bitmap1 As Bitmap)

✿ SetLayout (Left As Int, Top As Int, Width As Int, Height As Int)

Changes the view position and size.

🪶 *Tag As Object*

Gets or sets the Tag value. This is a place holder which can be used to store additional data.

🪶 *Top As Int*

Gets or sets the view's top position.

🪶 *Visible As Boolean*

Whether the user can see the object.

🪶 *Width As Int*

Gets or sets the view's width.

ImageView

A view that shows an image. You can assign a bitmap (page 352) using the `Bitmap` property. The `Gravity` property changes the way the image appears. The two most relevant values are:

`Gravity.FILL` (which will cause the image to fill the entire view)

and `Gravity.CENTER` (which will draw the image in the view's center).

This is an `Activity` object; it cannot be declared under `Sub Process_Globals`.

Events:

Click

Occurs when the user presses and releases the ImageView.

LongClick

Occurs when the user presses on the ImageView for roughly one second.

Members:

🪶 *Background As Drawable*

Gets or sets the background drawable.

🪶 *Bitmap As Bitmap*

Gets or sets the bitmap assigned to the ImageView.
Example:

```
ImageView1.Bitmap = LoadBitmap(File.DirAssets, "someimage.jpg")
```

🔩 *BringToFront*

Changes the Z order of this view and brings it to the front.

🪶 *Color As Int [write only]*

Sets the background of the view to be a `ColorDrawable` with the given color. If the current background is of type `GradientDrawable` or `ColorDrawable`, the round corners will be kept.

🪶 *Enabled As Boolean*

If set to `True` then the `ImageView` will respond to events. If set to `False`, events are ignored.

🪶 *Gravity As Int*

Gets or sets the gravity (page 346) assigned to the bitmap.
Example:

```
ImageView1.Gravity = Gravity.Fill
```

🔧 *Height As Int*
Gets or sets the view's height.

🔷 *Initialize (EventName As String)*
Initializes the view and sets the subs that will handle the events.
Views added with the designer should NOT be initialized. These views are initialized when the layout is loaded.

🔷 *Invalidate*
Invalidates the whole view forcing the view to redraw itself. Redrawing will only happen when the program can process messages, usually when it finishes running the current code. If you only need to redraw part of the view, it is usually quicker to use `Invalidate2` or `Invalidate3`.

🔷 *Invalidate2 (Rect1 As Rect)*
Invalidates anything inside the given rectangle that is part of this view. Redrawing will only happen when the program can process messages, usually when it finishes running the current code.

🔷 *Invalidate3 (Left As Int, Top As Int, Right As Int, Bottom As Int)*
Invalidates anything inside the given rectangle that is part of this view. Redrawing will only happen when the program can process messages, usually when it finishes running the current code.

🔷 *IsInitialized As Boolean*
Whether this object has been initialized by calling `Initialize`.

🔧 *Left As Int*
Gets or sets the view's left position.

🔷 *RemoveView*
Removes this view from its parent.

🔷 *RequestFocus As Boolean*
Tries to set the focus to this view. Returns `True` if the focus was set.

🔷 *SendToBack*
Changes the Z order of this view and sends it to the back.

🔷 *SetBackgroundImage (Bitmap1 As Bitmap)*

🔷 *SetLayout (Left As Int, Top As Int, Width As Int, Height As Int)*
Changes the view position and size.

🔧 *Tag As Object*
Gets or sets the Tag value. This is a place holder which can be used to store additional data.

🔧 *Top As Int*
Gets or sets the view's top position.

🔧 *Visible As Boolean*
Whether the user can see the object.

⚜ *Width As Int*
Gets or sets the view's width.

Label
A Label view that shows read-only text.
This is an `Activity` object; it cannot be declared under `Sub Process_Globals`.

Events:

Click
Occurs when the user presses and releases the label.

LongClick
Occurs when the user presses on the label for roughly one second.

Members:

⚜ *Background As Drawable*
Gets or sets the background drawable.

⚙ *BringToFront*
Changes the Z order of this view and brings it to the front.

⚜ *Color As Int [write only]*
Sets the background of the view to be a `ColorDrawable` with the given color.
If the current background is of type `GradientDrawable` or `ColorDrawable`, the round corners will be kept.

⚜ *Enabled As Boolean*
If set to `True` then the label will respond to the `Click` and `LongClick` events. If set to `False`, these events are ignored.

⚜ *Gravity As Int*
Gets or sets the gravity (page 346) value. This value affects the way the text will be drawn.

⚜ *Height As Int*
Gets or sets the view's height.

⚙ *Initialize (EventName As String)*
Initializes the view and sets the subs that will handle the events.
Views added with the designer should NOT be initialized. These views are initialized when the layout is loaded.

⚙ *Invalidate*
Invalidates the whole view forcing the view to redraw itself. Redrawing will only happen when the program can process messages, usually when it finishes running the current code. If you only need to redraw part of the view, it is usually quicker to use `Invalidate2` or `Invalidate3`.

⚙ *Invalidate2 (Rect1 As Rect)*
Invalidates anything inside the given rectangle that is part of this view. Redrawing will only happen when the program can process messages, usually when it finishes running the current code.

⬡ *Invalidate3 (Left As Int, Top As Int, Right As Int, Bottom As Int)*

Invalidates anything inside the given rectangle that is part of this view. Redrawing will only happen when the program can process messages, usually when it finishes running the current code.

⬡ *IsInitialized As Boolean*

Whether this object has been initialized by calling `Initialize`.

⚡ *Left As Int*

Gets or sets the view's left position.

⬡ *RemoveView*

Removes this view from its parent.

⬡ *RequestFocus As Boolean*

Tries to set the focus to this view.
Returns `True` if the focus was set.

⬡ *SendToBack*

Changes the Z order of this view and sends it to the back.

⬡ *SetBackgroundImage (Bitmap1 As Bitmap)*

⬡ *SetLayout (Left As Int, Top As Int, Width As Int, Height As Int)*

Changes the view position and size.

⚡ *Tag As Object*

Gets or sets the Tag value. This is a place holder which can be used to store additional data.

⚡ *Text As String*

Get or set the text which this label shows.

⚡ *TextColor As Int*

The color (page 345) of the text used by this label.

⚡ *TextSize As Float*

The size of the text this label uses.

⚡ *Top As Int*

Gets or sets the view's top position.

⚡ *Typeface As Typeface*

The typeface (page 349) this label uses.

⚡ *Visible As Boolean*

Whether the user can see this label.

⚡ *Width As Int*

Gets or sets the label's width.

ListView

ListView is a view that displays lists. The ListView can have one or two lines. A two-line item can also have an icon. You can mix all three types of lines in a single ListView:

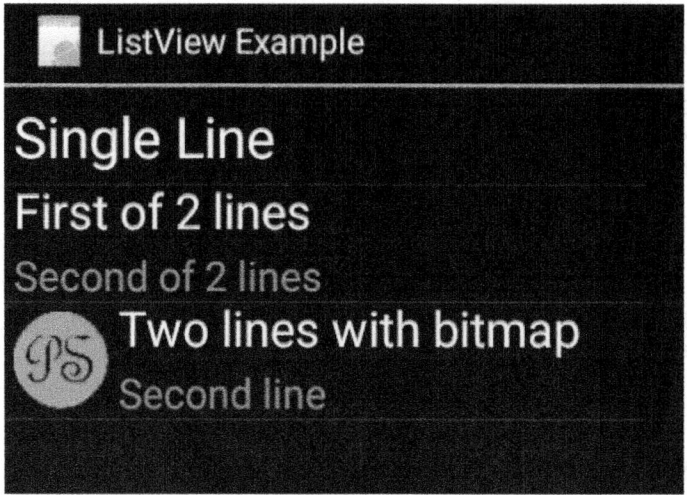

ListView has two events which allow you to determine which item the user clicked. Unfortunately, you cannot respond by changing the appearance of the selected item, so you might want to consider using a Custom List View (page 565) instead.

This is an `Activity` object; it cannot be declared under `Sub Process_Globals`.

Changing Text Appearance

You can change the appearance of each of these three types of line by editing the layout, for example:

```
Dim label1 As Label
label1 = ListView1.SingleLineLayout.Label
label1.TextSize = 20
label1.TextColor = Colors.Blue
```

This will change the appearance of all items in the list with SingleLineLayout.

Note that a TwoLine item has two labels, one for each line:

```
Dim Label1 As Label
Label1 = ListView1.TwoLinesLayout.SecondLabel
Label1.TextSize = 20
Label1.TextColor = Colors.Green
```

ListView as a Menu

You can use a ListView as a popup menu on any Activity. For example:

```
Sub Globals
  ' Could create either in Layout or here
  Dim lstMenu As ListView
End Sub

Sub Activity_Create(FirstTime As Boolean)
  Activity.LoadLayout("main")

  lstMenu.Initialize("lstMenu")
  Activity.AddView(lstMenu, 10%x, 10%y, 80%x, 80%y)
  lstMenu.AddSingleLine2("Help", "help")
  lstMenu.AddSingleLine2("Settings", "settings")
```

```
    ' Set colors since default background is transparent
    lstMenu.Color = Colors.White
    Dim lstLabel As Label
    lstLabel = lstMenu.SingleLineLayout.Label
    ' default text color is white
    lstLabel.TextColor = Colors.Black
    lstMenu.Visible = False
End Sub


Sub btnTest_Click
    ' StartActivity(test) will hide this activity
    ' Activity.LoadLayout("testActivity")
    lstMenu.Visible = True
End Sub

Sub lstMenu_ItemClick (Position As Int, Value As Object)
    Select Value
    Case "help"
      lstMenu.Visible = False
      StartActivity("help")
    Case "settings"
      lstMenu.Visible = False
      StartActivity("settings")
    End Select
End Sub
```

Tutorial

See the ListView tutorial (http://bit.ly/181bNV6) for more information.

Events:

ItemClick (Position As Int, Value As Object)

ItemClick is raised when an item is touched and released.

ItemLongClick (Position As Int, Value As Object)

ItemLongClick is raised when an item is touched and held.

Members:

⬡ AddSingleLine (Text As String)

Adds a single line item.
Example:
```
  ListView1.AddSingleLine("Sunday")
```

⬡ AddSingleLine2 (Text As String, ReturnValue As Object)

Adds a single line item.
The specified return value will be returned when calling GetItem or in the ItemClick event.
Example:
```
  ListView1.AddSingleLine2("Sunday", 1)
```

⬡ AddTwoLines (Text1 As String, Text2 As String)

Adds a two-lines item.

Example:
```
ListView1.AddTwoLines("This is the first line.", "And this is the
second")
```

🔷 AddTwoLines2 (Text1 As String, Text2 As String, ReturnValue As Object)

Adds a two-lines item. **ReturnValue** will be returned when calling `GetItem` or in the
`ItemClick` event.

🔷 AddTwoLinesAndBitmap (Text1 As String, Text2 As String, Bitmap1 As Bitmap)

Adds two lines and a bitmap item.
Example:
```
ListView1.AddTwoLinesAndBitmap("First line", "Second line",
LoadBitmap( File.DirAssets, "SomeImage.png"))
```

🔷 AddTwoLinesAndBitmap2 (Text1 As String, Text2 As String, Bitmap1 As Bitmap, ReturnValue As Object)

Adds two lines and a bitmap item. **ReturnValue** will be returned when calling `GetItem` or in
the `ItemClick` event.

🔥 Background As Drawable

Gets or sets the background drawable.

🔷 BringToFront

Changes the Z order of this view and brings it to the front.

🔷 Clear

Clears all items from the list.

🔥 Color As Int [write only]

Sets the background of the view to be a `ColorDrawable` with the given color.
If the current background is of type `GradientDrawable` or `ColorDrawable`, the round
corners will be kept.

🔥 Enabled As Boolean

If set to `True` then the `ListView` will respond to the `ItemClick` and `ItemLongClick`
events. If set to `False`, these events are ignored.

🔥 FastScrollEnabled As Boolean

Gets or sets whether the fast scroll icon will appear when the user scrolls the list.
The default is `False`.

🔷 GetItem (Index As Int) As Object

Returns the value of the item at the specified position. Returns the "return value" if it was
set, and if not, returns the text of the first line.

🔥 Height As Int

Gets or sets the view's height.

🔷 Initialize (EventName As String)

Initializes the view and sets the subs that will handle the events.

Views added with the designer should NOT be initialized. These views are initialized when the layout is loaded.

Invalidate

Invalidates the whole view forcing the view to redraw itself. Redrawing will only happen when the program can process messages, usually when it finishes running the current code. If you only need to redraw part of the view, it is usually quicker to use `Invalidate2` or `Invalidate3`.

Invalidate2 (Rect1 As Rect)

Invalidates anything inside the given rectangle that is part of this view. Redrawing will only happen when the program can process messages, usually when it finishes running the current code.

Invalidate3 (Left As Int, Top As Int, Right As Int, Bottom As Int)

Invalidates anything inside the given rectangle that is part of this view. Redrawing will only happen when the program can process messages, usually when it finishes running the current code.

IsInitialized As Boolean

Whether this object has been initialized by calling `Initialize`.

Left As Int

Gets or sets the view's left position.

RemoveAt (Index As Int)

Removes the item at the specified position.

RemoveView

Removes this view from its parent.

RequestFocus As Boolean

Tries to set the focus to this view. Returns `True` if the focus was set.

ScrollingBackgroundColor As Int [write only]

Sets the background color that will be used while scrolling the list. This is an optimization done to make the scrolling smoother. Set to `Colors.Transparent` if the background behind the list is not a solid color. The default is black.

SendToBack

Changes the Z order of this view and sends it to the back.

SetBackgroundImage (Bitmap1 As Bitmap)

SetLayout (Left As Int, Top As Int, Width As Int, Height As Int)

Changes the view position and size.

SetSelection (Position As Int)

Sets the currently selected item. Calling this method will make this item visible. If the user is interacting with the list with the keyboard or the wheel button, the item will also be visibly selected. Example:

```
ListView1.SetSelection(10)
```

SingleLineLayout As SingleLineLayout [read only]

Returns the layout that is used to show single line items. You can change the layout values to change the appearance of such items. Example:

```
Dim Label1 As Label
Label1 = ListView1.SingleLineLayout.Label
Label1.TextSize = 20
Label1.TextColor = Colors.Green
```

Size As Int [read only]

Returns the number of items stored in the list.

Tag As Object

Gets or sets the Tag value. This is a place holder which can be used to store additional data.

Top As Int

Gets or sets the view's top position.

TwoLinesAndBitmap As TwoLinesAndBitmapLayout [read only]

Returns the layout that is used to show items containing two lines and bitmap. You can change the layout values to change the appearance of such items. For example, if you want to remove the second label (in all items with this layout):

```
ListView1.TwoLinesAndBitmap.SecondLabel.Visible = False
```

TwoLinesLayout As TwoLinesLayout [read only]

Returns the layout that is used to show two-lines items.

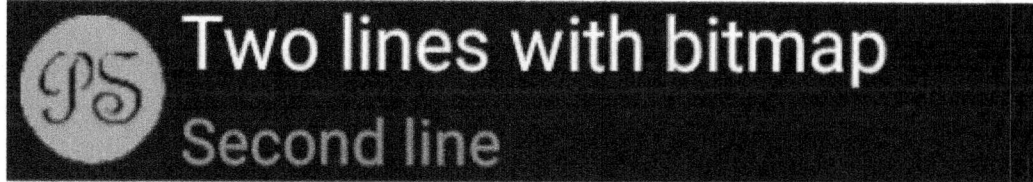

You can change the layout values to change the appearance of such items.
Example:

```
Dim Label1 As Label
Label1 = ListView1.TwoLinesLayout.SecondLabel
Label1.TextSize = 20
Label1.TextColor = Colors.Green
```

Visible As Boolean

Whether the user can see the object.

Width As Int

Gets or sets the view's width.

Panel

A Panel is a view that holds other child views. You can add child views programmatically or by loading a layout file. This is an `Activity` object; it cannot be declared under `Sub Process_Globals`.

Events:

Touch (Action As Int, X As Float, Y As Float)

When the user touches a Panel, it raises the Touch event. The first parameter of this event is the Action which is one of the Activity action constants. X and Y indicate where the panel was touched.

If the user keeps touching the panel, it will continue to raise the Touch event.

Return **True** from the Touch event sub to consume the event (otherwise other views behind the Panel will receive the event).

Click

If there is no Touch event handler in your app, then Android will raise the Click event if the user touches the panel briefly.

LongClick

If there is no Touch event handler in your app, then Android will raise the LongClick event if the user touches the panel for an extended period.

Members:

AddView (View1 As View, Left As Int, Top As Int, Width As Int, Height As Int)

Adds a view to this panel.

Background As Drawable

Gets or sets the background drawable.

BringToFront

Changes the Z order of this view and brings it to the front.

Color As Int [write only]

Sets the background of the view to be a **ColorDrawable** with the given color. If the current background is of type **GradientDrawable** or **ColorDrawable**, the round corners will be kept.

Elevation As Float

Gets or sets the panel's elevation in dip. Only effective on Android 5 or later.

Enabled As Boolean

If set to **True** then the Panel will respond to events. If set to **False**, events are ignored.

GetAllViewsRecursive As IterableList

Returns an iterator that iterates over all the views belonging to the panel, including views which are children of other views. Example:

```
For Each vw As View In pnlMain.GetAllViewsRecursive
  vw.Color = Colors.RGB(Rnd(0,255), Rnd(0,255), Rnd(0,255))
Next
```

GetView (Index As Int) As View

Gets the view that is stored at the specified index.

Height As Int

Gets or sets the view's height.

Initialize (EventName As String)

Initializes the view and sets the subs that will handle the events.
Views added with the designer should NOT be initialized. These views are initialized when the layout is loaded.

Invalidate

Invalidates the whole view forcing the view to redraw itself. Redrawing will only happen when the program can process messages, usually when it finishes running the current code. If you only need to redraw part of the view, it is usually quicker to use `Invalidate2` or `Invalidate3`.

Invalidate2 (Rect1 As Rect)

Invalidates anything inside the given rectangle that is part of this view. Redrawing will only happen when the program can process messages, usually when it finishes running the current code.

Invalidate3 (Left As Int, Top As Int, Right As Int, Bottom As Int)

Invalidates anything inside the given rectangle that is part of this view. Redrawing will only happen when the program can process messages, usually when it finishes running the current code.

IsInitialized As Boolean

Whether this object has been initialized by calling `Initialize`.

Left As Int

Gets or sets the view's left position.

LoadLayout (Layout As String) As LayoutValues

Loads a layout file to this panel. Returns the value of the chosen layout variant.

NumberOfViews As Int [read only]

Returns the number of child views.

RemoveAllViews

Removes all child views.

RemoveView

Removes this view from its parent.

RemoveViewAt (Index As Int)

Removes the view that is stored at the specified index.

RequestFocus As Boolean

Tries to set the focus to this view. Returns `True` if the focus was set.

SendToBack

Changes the Z order of this view and sends it to the back.

SetBackgroundImage (Bitmap1 As Bitmap)

SetElevationAnimated (Duration As Int, Elevation As Int)

Sets the duration in seconds and height in dip for the animated elevation of the panel. Only effective on Android 5 or later. Note: this may not have any effect in an emulator, so you may require a connected real device to test this. Note that you can set a panel's initial elevation property in the Visual Designer.

⬡ SetLayout (Left As Int, Top As Int, Width As Int, Height As Int)
Changes the view position and size.

⚒ Tag As Object
Gets or sets the Tag value. This is a place holder which can be used to store additional data.

⚒ Top As Int
Gets or sets the view's top position.

⚒ Visible As Boolean
Whether the user can see the object.

⚒ Width As Int
Gets or sets the view's width.

ProgressBar
A progress bar view which lets you show the progress of a long-running process.
Example:

```
Sub Activity_Create(FirstTime As Boolean)
  Activity.LoadLayout("Main")
  ProgressBar1.Progress = 0
  Timer1.Initialize("Timer1", 1000)
  Timer1.Enabled = True
End Sub


Sub timer1_Tick
  'Handle tick events
  ProgressBar1.Progress = ProgressBar1.Progress + 10
  If ProgressBar1.Progress = 100 Then
  Timer1.Enabled = False
  End If
End Sub
```

The exact nature of the visible bar depends upon the device and the size you have chosen. Here is one example:

The Progress property sets the progress value which is from 0 to 100.
This is an **Activity** object; it cannot be declared under **Sub Process_Globals**.

Members:

⚒ Background As Drawable
Gets or sets the background drawable.

⬡ BringToFront
Changes the Z order of this view and brings it to the front.

♪ Color As Int [write only]

Sets the background of the view to be a `ColorDrawable` with the given color. If the current background is of type `GradientDrawable` or `ColorDrawable`, the round corners will be kept.

♪ Enabled As Boolean

This property has no effect since a `ProgressBar` has no events.

♪ Height As Int

Gets or sets the view's height.

♪ Indeterminate As Boolean

Gets or sets whether the progress bar is in indeterminate mode (cyclic animation).

♲ Initialize (EventName As String)

Initializes the view and sets the subs that will handle the events.
Views added with the designer should NOT be initialized. These views are initialized when the layout is loaded.

♲ Invalidate

Invalidates the whole view forcing the view to redraw itself. Redrawing will only happen when the program can process messages, usually when it finishes running the current code. If you only need to redraw part of the view, it is usually quicker to use `Invalidate2` or `Invalidate3`.

♲ Invalidate2 (Rect1 As Rect)

Invalidates anything inside the given rectangle that is part of this view. Redrawing will only happen when the program can process messages, usually when it finishes running the current code.

♲ Invalidate3 (Left As Int, Top As Int, Right As Int, Bottom As Int)

Invalidates anything inside the given rectangle that is part of this view. Redrawing will only happen when the program can process messages, usually when it finishes running the current code.

♲ IsInitialized As Boolean

Whether this object has been initialized by calling `Initialize`.

♪ Left As Int

Gets or sets the view's left position.

♪ Progress As Int

Gets or sets the progress value.

♲ RemoveView

Removes this view from its parent.

♲ RequestFocus As Boolean

Tries to set the focus to this view.
Returns `True` if the focus was set.

☙ SendToBack
Changes the Z order of this view and sends it to the back.

☙ SetBackgroundImage (Bitmap1 As Bitmap)

☙ SetLayout (Left As Int, Top As Int, Width As Int, Height As Int)
Changes the view position and size.

☙ Tag As Object
Gets or sets the Tag value. This is a place holder which can be used to store additional data.

☙ Top As Int
Gets or sets the view's top position.

☙ Visible As Boolean
Whether the user can see the object.

☙ Width As Int
Gets or sets the view's width.

RadioButton
A RadioButton view. Only one RadioButton in a group can be checked. When a different RadioButton is checked, all others will automatically be unchecked.
Note that the `CheckedChange` event only runs for the button which has been checked. Grouping is done by adding RadioButtons to the same activity or panel.
This is an `Activity` object; it cannot be declared under `Sub Process_Globals`.

Event:

CheckedChange(Checked As Boolean)
Note that the `CheckedChange` event only runs for the button which has been checked. Thus, **Checked** is never `False`, and your code should test whether each RadioButton has been checked.

Members:

☙ Background As Drawable
Gets or sets the background drawable.

☙ BringToFront
Changes the Z order of this view and brings it to the front.

☙ Checked As Boolean

☙ Color As Int [write only]
Sets the background of the view to be a `ColorDrawable` with the given color. If the current background is of type `GradientDrawable` or `ColorDrawable`, the round corners will be kept.

☙ Enabled As Boolean
If set to `True` then the `RadioButton` will respond to events. If set to `False`, events are ignored.

☙ Gravity As Int
Gets or sets the gravity (page 346) value. This value affects the way the text will be drawn.

🪶 *Height As Int*

Gets or sets the view's height.

🎲 *Initialize (EventName As String)*

Initializes the view and sets the subs that will handle the events.

Views added with the designer should NOT be initialized. These views are initialized when the layout is loaded.

🎲 *Invalidate*

Invalidates the whole view forcing the view to redraw itself. Redrawing will only happen when the program can process messages, usually when it finishes running the current code. If you only need to redraw part of the view, it is usually quicker to use `Invalidate2` or `Invalidate3`.

🎲 *Invalidate2 (Rect1 As Rect)*

Invalidates anything inside the given rectangle that is part of this view. Redrawing will only happen when the program can process messages, usually when it finishes running the current code.

🎲 *Invalidate3 (Left As Int, Top As Int, Right As Int, Bottom As Int)*

Invalidates anything inside the given rectangle that is part of this view. Redrawing will only happen when the program can process messages, usually when it finishes running the current code.

🎲 *IsInitialized As Boolean*

Whether this object has been initialized by calling `Initialize`.

🪶 *Left As Int*

Gets or sets the view's left position.

🎲 *RemoveView*

Removes this view from its parent.

🎲 *RequestFocus As Boolean*

Tries to set the focus to this view. Returns `True` if the focus was set.

🎲 *SendToBack*

Changes the Z order of this view and sends it to the back.

🎲 *SetBackgroundImage (Bitmap1 As Bitmap)*

🎲 *SetLayout (Left As Int, Top As Int, Width As Int, Height As Int)*

Changes the view position and size.

🪶 *Tag As Object*

Gets or sets the Tag value. This is a place holder which can be used to store additional data.

Text As String

TextColor As Int

TextSize As Float

Top As Int

Gets or sets the view's top position.

Typeface As Typeface

Visible As Boolean

Whether the user can see the object.

Width As Int

Gets or sets the view's width.

ScrollView

ScrollView is a view that contains other views and allows the user to vertically scroll those views. See the ScrollView example (http://bit.ly/ZQMe5Q) for more information.

The ScrollView has an inner panel which actually contains the child views. You can add views by calling: `ScrollView1.Panel.AddView(...)`

Note that you cannot use the Designer to add views to a ScrollView, since the panel which actually holds sub-views is not available at the design stage. You must add views to the ScrollView's panel using code such as

```
scrollViewMenu.Panel.AddView (…)
```

Note also that it is not possible to nest scrolling views. For example, a multiline EditText cannot be located inside a ScrollView.

This is an `Activity` object; it cannot be declared under `Sub Process_Globals`.

Events:

ScrollChanged(Position As Int)

Members:

Background As Drawable

Gets or sets the background drawable.

BringToFront

Changes the Z order of this view and brings it to the front.

Color As Int [write only]

Sets the background of the view to be a `ColorDrawable` with the given color. If the current background is of type `GradientDrawable` or `ColorDrawable`, the round corners will be kept.

Enabled As Boolean

If set to `True` then the `ScrollView` will respond to events. If set to `False`, events are ignored.

FullScroll (Bottom As Boolean)

Scrolls the scroll view to the top or bottom.

Height As Int
Gets or sets the view's height.

Initialize (Height As Int)
Initializes the ScrollView and sets its inner panel height to the given height. You can later change this height by calling ScrollView.Panel.Height.
```
Dim ScrollView1 As ScrollView
ScrollView1.Initialize(1000dip)
```

Initialize2 (Height As Int, EventName As String)
Similar to Initialize. Sets the Sub that will handle the ScrollChanged event.

Invalidate
Invalidates the whole view forcing the view to redraw itself. Redrawing will only happen when the program can process messages, usually when it finishes running the current code. If you only need to redraw part of the view, it is usually quicker to use **Invalidate2** or **Invalidate3**.

Invalidate2 (Rect1 As Rect)
Invalidates anything inside the given rectangle that is part of this view. Redrawing will only happen when the program can process messages, usually when it finishes running the current code.

Invalidate3 (Left As Int, Top As Int, Right As Int, Bottom As Int)
Invalidates anything inside the given rectangle that is part of this view. Redrawing will only happen when the program can process messages, usually when it finishes running the current code.

IsInitialized As Boolean
Whether this object has been initialized by calling **Initialize**.

Left As Int
Gets or sets the view's left position.

Panel As Panel [read only]
Returns the panel (page 425) which you can use to add views to. Example:
```
ScrollView1.Panel.AddView(...)
```

RemoveView
Removes this view from its parent.

RequestFocus As Boolean
Tries to set the focus to this view.
Returns **True** if the focus was set.

ScrollPosition As Int
Gets or sets the scroll position. If setting, scrolls the View with animation.

ScrollToNow (Scroll As Int)
Immediately scrolls the ScrollView without animation.

SendToBack
Changes the Z order of this view and sends it to the back.

⬢ *SetBackgroundImage (Bitmap1 As Bitmap)*
⬢ *SetLayout (Left As Int, Top As Int, Width As Int, Height As Int)*
Changes the view position and size.

⬥ *Tag As Object*
Gets or sets the Tag value. This is a place holder which can be used to store additional data.

⬥ *Top As Int*
Gets or sets the view's top position.

⬥ *Visible As Boolean*
Whether the user can see the object.

⬥ *Width As Int*
Gets or sets the view's width.

SeekBar
A view that allows the user to set a value by dragging a slider. Similar to WinForms TrackBar. The ValueChanged event is raised whenever the value is changed. The UserChanged parameter can be used to distinguish between changes done by the user and changes done programmatically.
This is an `Activity` object; it cannot be declared under `Sub Process_Globals`.

Events:
ValueChanged (Value As Int, UserChanged As Boolean)

Members:
⬥ *Background As Drawable*
Gets or sets the background drawable.

⬢ *BringToFront*
Changes the Z order of this view and brings it to the front.

⬥ *Color As Int [write only]*
Sets the background of the view to be a `ColorDrawable` with the given color. If the current background is of type `GradientDrawable` or `ColorDrawable`, the round corners will be kept.

⬥ *Enabled As Boolean*
If set to `True` then the `SeekBar` will respond to events. If set to `False`, events are ignored.

⬥ *Height As Int*
Gets or sets the view's height.

⬢ *Initialize (EventName As String)*
Initializes the view and sets the subs that will handle the events.
Views added with the designer should NOT be initialized. These views are initialized when the layout is loaded.

⬢ *Invalidate*
Invalidates the whole view forcing the view to redraw itself. Redrawing will only happen when the program can process messages, usually when it finishes running the current code.

If you only need to redraw part of the view, it is usually quicker to use `Invalidate2` or `Invalidate3`.

Invalidate2 (Rect1 As Rect)

Invalidates anything inside the given rectangle that is part of this view. Redrawing will only happen when the program can process messages, usually when it finishes running the current code.

Invalidate3 (Left As Int, Top As Int, Right As Int, Bottom As Int)

Invalidates anything inside the given rectangle that is part of this view. Redrawing will only happen when the program can process messages, usually when it finishes running the current code.

IsInitialized As Boolean

Whether this object has been initialized by calling `Initialize`.

Left As Int

Gets or sets the view's left position.

Max As Int

Gets or sets the maximum allowed value.

RemoveView

Removes this view from its parent.

RequestFocus As Boolean

Tries to set the focus to this view. Returns `True` if the focus was set.

SendToBack

Changes the Z order of this view and sends it to the back.

SetBackgroundImage (Bitmap1 As Bitmap)

SetLayout (Left As Int, Top As Int, Width As Int, Height As Int)

Changes the view position and size.

Tag As Object

Gets or sets the Tag value. This is a place holder which can be used to store additional data.

Top As Int

Gets or sets the view's top position.

Value As Int

Gets or sets the current value.

Visible As Boolean

Whether the user can see the object.

Width As Int

Gets or sets the view's width.

Spinner

A folded list that opens when the user clicks on it and allows the user to choose an item. Similar to WinForms ComboBox.

This is an **Activity** object; it cannot be declared under **Sub Process_Globals**.
A spinner behaves and looks like an InputList (page 314).

Example

```
Sub Globals
  Dim i As Int
  Dim tgtlabel As Label
  Dim tgtspin As Spinner
  Dim myarray(4) As String
End Sub

Sub Activity_Create(FirstTime As Boolean)
  Activity.LoadLayout("main")
  myarray(0)="January"
  myarray(1)="February"
  myarray(2)="March"
  myarray(3)="May"
  tgtspin.Initialize("spin")
  tgtspin.Prompt="Select Month"
  tgtspin.AddAll(myarray)
  Activity.AddView(tgtspin,10dip,10dip,200dip,40dip)
End Sub

Sub spin_ItemClick (Position As Int, Value As Object)
  ' what to do when the user selects an option
End Sub
```

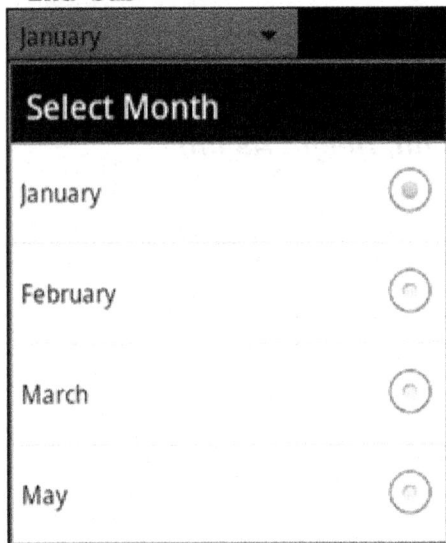

Event:

ItemClick (Position As Int, Value As Object)

The **ItemClick** event is raised each time a user presses on an item (even if the item is already selected). The arguments indicate which item has been clicked, both its position within the list of items and its value.

Members:

Add (Item As String)

Adds an item.
Example:
```
Spinner1.Add("Sunday")
```

AddAll (List As List)

Adds multiple items.
Example:
```
Spinner1.AddAll(Array As String("Sunday", "Monday", ...))
```

Background As Drawable

Gets or sets the background drawable.

BringToFront

Changes the Z order of this view and brings it to the front.

Clear

Clears all items.

Color As Int [write only]

Sets the background of the view to be a `ColorDrawable` with the given color. If the current background is of type `GradientDrawable` or `ColorDrawable`, the round corners will be kept.

DropdownBackgroundColor As Int

Gets or sets the color of the background behind the spinner's dropdown items.

DropdownTextColor As Int

Gets or sets the color of the text of the spinner's dropdown items.

Enabled As Boolean

If set to `True` then the `Spinner` will respond to events. If set to `False`, events are ignored.

GetItem (Index As Int) As String

Returns the item at the specified index.

Height As Int

Gets or sets the view's height.

IndexOf (value As String) As Int

Returns the index of the given item.

Initialize (EventName As String)

Initializes the view and sets the subs that will handle the events.
Views added with the designer should NOT be initialized. These views are initialized when the layout is loaded.

Invalidate

Invalidates the whole view forcing the view to redraw itself. Redrawing will only happen when the program can process messages, usually when it finishes running the current code.

If you only need to redraw part of the view, it is usually quicker to use `Invalidate2` or `Invalidate3`.

Invalidate2 (Rect1 As Rect)

Invalidates anything inside the given rectangle that is part of this view. Redrawing will only happen when the program can process messages, usually when it finishes running the current code.

Invalidate3 (Left As Int, Top As Int, Right As Int, Bottom As Int)

Invalidates anything inside the given rectangle that is part of this view. Redrawing will only happen when the program can process messages, usually when it finishes running the current code.

IsInitialized As Boolean

Whether this object has been initialized by calling `Initialize`.

Left As Int

Gets or sets the view's left position.

Prompt As String

Gets or sets the title that will be displayed when the spinner is opened.
Not visible for SDK 14 or later. You need to add the prompt as the first item, and ensure the user does not select it.

RemoveAt (Index As Int)

Removes the item at the specified index.

RemoveView

Removes this view from its parent.

RequestFocus As Boolean

Tries to set the focus to this view. Returns `True` if the focus was set.

SelectedIndex As Int

Gets or sets the index of the selected item. Returns `-1` if no item is selected.

SelectedItem As String [read only]

Returns the value of the selected item.

SendToBack

Changes the Z order of this view and sends it to the back.

SetBackgroundImage (Bitmap1 As Bitmap)

SetLayout (Left As Int, Top As Int, Width As Int, Height As Int)

Changes the view position and size.

Size As Int [read only]

Returns the number of items.

Tag As Object

Gets or sets the Tag value. This is a place holder which can be used to store additional data.

✔ *TextColor As Int*

Gets or sets the text color. The color should be set before adding items. Setting the color to transparent will make the spinner use the default text color.

✔ *TextSize As Float*

Gets or sets the text size (page 163). The size should be set before adding items.

✔ *Top As Int*

Gets or sets the view's top position.

✔ *Visible As Boolean*

Whether the user can see the object.

✔ *Width As Int*

Gets or sets the view's width.

TabHost

TabHost is a view that contains multiple tab pages. Each tab page contains other child views.

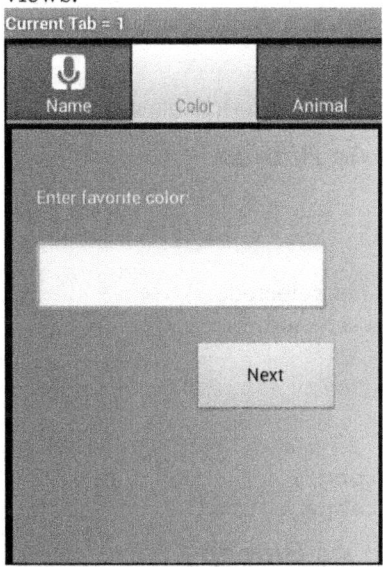

At present you can use the Designer to add a TabHost to a Layout, but you must use code to add pages to it. The simplest way to do this is to create separate layouts for each page. For example, if layout "main" contains TabHost1 and "page1", "page2" and "page3" contain the pages to be added to it, then your code might say:

```
Activity.LoadLayout("main")
TabHost1.AddTab("Name", "page1")
TabHost1.AddTab("Color", "page2")
TabHost1.AddTab("Animal", "page3")
```

A TabHost is an `Activity` object; it cannot be declared under `Sub Process_Globals`. See the TabHost tutorial (http://bit.ly/1OwhtYZ) for more information. **Note** that TabHostExtras Library (page 587) is a user-generated extension of this view which gives you more power over its appearance.

Events:

TabChanged
This event is raised when the user presses on the TabHost menu to select a different page.

Click
This event is never actually fired. It exists because it is inherited from the view object.

LongClick
This event is raised when the user presses and holds one of the pages of the TabHost.

Members:

⬡ AddTab (Title As String, LayoutFile As String)
Adds a tab page.
Title - The page title.
LayoutFile - A layout file describing the page layout.
Example:
```
TabHost1.AddTab("Page 1", "page1.bal")
```

⬡ AddTab2 (Title As String, View1 As View)
Adds a tab page.
Title - The page title.
View - The page content. Usually the view should be a panel containing other views.

⬡ AddTabWithIcon (Title As String, DefaultBitmap As Bitmap, SelectedBitmap As Bitmap, LayoutFile As String)
Adds a tab page. The tab title includes an icon.
Title - The page title.
DefaultBitmap - The icon that will be drawn when the page is not selected.
SelectedBitmap - The icon that will be drawn when the page is selected.
LayoutFile - A layout file describing the page layout.
Example:
```
Dim bmp1, bmp2 As Bitmap
bmp1 = LoadBitmap(File.DirAssets, "ic.png")
bmp2 = LoadBitmap(File.DirAssets, "ic_selected.png")
TabHost1.AddTabWithIcon("Page 1", bmp1, bmp2,"tabpage1.bal")
```

⬡ AddTabWithIcon2 (Title As String, DefaultBitmap As Bitmap, SelectedBitmap As Bitmap, View1 As View)
Adds a tab page. The tab title includes an icon.
Title - The page title.
DefaultBitmap - The icon that will be drawn when the page is not selected.
SelectedBitmap - The icon that will be drawn when the page is selected.
View - The page content. Usually the view should be a panel containing other views.

⌁ Background As Drawable
Gets or sets the background drawable.

⬡ BringToFront
Changes the Z order of this view and brings it to the front.

🔧 Color As Int [write only]

Sets the background of the view to be a `ColorDrawable` with the given color. If the current background is of type `GradientDrawable` or `ColorDrawable`, the round corners will be kept.

🔧 CurrentTab As Int

Gets or sets the current tab.
Example:
```
TabHost1.CurrentTab = (TabHost1.CurrentTab + 1) Mod TabHost1.TabCount
'switch to the next tab.
```

🔧 Enabled As Boolean

If set to `True` then the `TabHost` will respond to events. If set to `False`, events are ignored.

🔧 Height As Int

Gets or sets the view's height.

⚙ Initialize (EventName As String)

Initializes the view and sets the subs that will handle the events.
Views added with the designer should NOT be initialized. These views are initialized when the layout is loaded.

⚙ Invalidate

Invalidates the whole view forcing the view to redraw itself. Redrawing will only happen when the program can process messages, usually when it finishes running the current code. If you only need to redraw part of the view, it is usually quicker to use `Invalidate2` or `Invalidate3`.

⚙ Invalidate2 (Rect1 As Rect)

Invalidates anything inside the given rectangle that is part of this view. Redrawing will only happen when the program can process messages, usually when it finishes running the current code.

⚙ Invalidate3 (Left As Int, Top As Int, Right As Int, Bottom As Int)

Invalidates anything inside the given rectangle that is part of this view. Redrawing will only happen when the program can process messages, usually when it finishes running the current code.

⚙ IsInitialized As Boolean

Whether this object has been initialized by calling `Initialize`.

🔧 Left As Int

Gets or sets the view's left position.

⚙ RemoveView

Removes this view from its parent.

⚙ RequestFocus As Boolean

Tries to set the focus to this view. Returns `True` if the focus was set.

⚙ SendToBack

Changes the Z order of this view and sends it to the back.

🕸️ **SetBackgroundImage (Bitmap1 As Bitmap)**

🕸️ **SetLayout (Left As Int, Top As Int, Width As Int, Height As Int)**

Changes the view position and size.

⚡ **TabCount As Int [read only]**

Returns the number of tab pages.

⚡ **Tag As Object**

Gets or sets the Tag value. This is a place holder which can be used to store additional data.

⚡ **Top As Int**

Gets or sets the view's top position.

⚡ **Visible As Boolean**

Whether the user can see the object.

⚡ **Width As Int**

Gets or sets the view's width.

ToggleButton

A ToggleButton view. This view, which is similar to a button, has two modes: ON and OFF. When the user presses on it, it will change its mode. You can set the text with the **TextOn** and **TextOff** properties.

This is an **Activity** object; it cannot be declared under **Sub Process_Globals**.

Event:

CheckedChange(Checked As Boolean)

Members:

⚡ **Background As Drawable**

Gets or sets the background drawable.

🕸️ **BringToFront**

Changes the Z order of this view and brings it to the front.

⚡ **Checked As Boolean**

⚡ **Color As Int [write only]**

Sets the background of the view to be a **ColorDrawable** with the given color. If the current background is of type **GradientDrawable** or **ColorDrawable**, the round corners will be kept.

⚡ **Enabled As Boolean**

If set to **True** then the **ToggleButton** will respond to events. If set to **False**, events are ignored.

⚡ **Gravity As Int**

Gets or sets the gravity (page 346) value. This value affects the way the text will be drawn.

⚡ **Height As Int**

Gets or sets the view's height.

❂ *Initialize (EventName As String)*

Initializes the view and sets the subs that will handle the events.
Views added with the designer should NOT be initialized. These views are initialized when the layout is loaded.

❂ *Invalidate*

Invalidates the whole view forcing the view to redraw itself. Redrawing will only happen when the program can process messages, usually when it finishes running the current code. If you only need to redraw part of the view, it is usually quicker to use `Invalidate2` or `Invalidate3`.

❂ *Invalidate2 (Rect1 As Rect)*

Invalidates anything inside the given rectangle that is part of this view. Redrawing will only happen when the program can process messages, usually when it finishes running the current code.

❂ *Invalidate3 (Left As Int, Top As Int, Right As Int, Bottom As Int)*

Invalidates anything inside the given rectangle that is part of this view. Redrawing will only happen when the program can process messages, usually when it finishes running the current code.

❂ *IsInitialized As Boolean*

Whether this object has been initialized by calling `Initialize`.

⚑ *Left As Int*

Gets or sets the view's left position.

❂ *RemoveView*

Removes this view from its parent.

❂ *RequestFocus As Boolean*

Tries to set the focus to this view. Returns `True` if the focus was set.

❂ *SendToBack*

Changes the Z order of this view and sends it to the back.

❂ *SetBackgroundImage (Bitmap1 As Bitmap)*

❂ *SetLayout (Left As Int, Top As Int, Width As Int, Height As Int)*

Changes the view position and size.

⚑ *Tag As Object*

Gets or sets the Tag value. This is a place holder which can be used to store additional data.

⚑ *TextColor As Int*

⚑ *TextOff As String*

Gets or sets the text that will appear in the OFF mode.

⚑ *TextOn As String*

Gets or sets the text that will appear in the ON mode.

✒ TextSize As Float

✒ Top As Int
Gets or sets the view's top position.

✒ Typeface As Typeface

✒ Visible As Boolean
Whether the user can see the object.

✒ Width As Int
Gets or sets the view's width.

View

View is a special type of object. You cannot create new View objects. However, all view types can be assigned to a view variable. This allows you to access the shared properties of all views. For example, this code hides all views of an activity:

```
For Each vw As View In Activity.GetAllViewsRecursive
  vw.Visible = False
Next
```

This is an `Activity` object; it cannot be declared under `Sub Process_Globals`.

Note there are five ways in which you can animate (page 125) views on devices with Android 3 or later.

Events:

Click
This event is raised when the user presses on the View.

LongClick
This event is raised when the user presses on the View and holds for about one second.

Members:

✒ Background As Drawable
Gets or sets the background drawable.

🔧 BringToFront
Changes the Z order of this view and brings it to the front.

✒ Color As Int [write only]
Sets the background of the view to be a `ColorDrawable` with the given color. If the current background is of type `GradientDrawable` or `ColorDrawable`, the round corners will be kept.

✒ Enabled As Boolean
If set to `True` then the `View` will respond to events. If set to `False`, events are ignored.

✒ Height As Int
Gets or sets the view's height.

🔧 Initialize (EventName As String)
Initializes the view and sets the subs that will handle the events.
Views added with the designer should NOT be initialized. These views are initialized when the layout is loaded.

⬡ *Invalidate*

Invalidates the whole view forcing the view to redraw itself. Redrawing will only happen when the program can process messages, usually when it finishes running the current code. If you only need to redraw part of the view, it is usually quicker to use `Invalidate2` or `Invalidate3`.

⬡ *Invalidate2 (Rect1 As Rect)*

Invalidates anything inside the given rectangle that is part of this view. Redrawing will only happen when the program can process messages, usually when it finishes running the current code.

⬡ *Invalidate3 (Left As Int, Top As Int, Right As Int, Bottom As Int)*

Invalidates anything inside the given rectangle that is part of this view. Redrawing will only happen when the program can process messages, usually when it finishes running the current code.

⬡ *IsInitialized As Boolean*

Whether this object has been initialized by calling `Initialize`.

⚒ *Left As Int*

Gets or sets the view's left position.

⬡ *RemoveView*

Removes this view from its parent. If this view has child views, then they are also removed.

⬡ *RequestFocus As Boolean*

Tries to set the focus to this view. Returns `True` if the focus was set.

⬡ *SendToBack*

Changes the Z order of this view and sends it to the back.

⬡ *SetBackgroundImage (Bitmap1 As Bitmap)*

⬡ *SetColorAnimated (Duration As Int, FromColor As Int, ToColor As Int)*

Changes the background color (page 345) with an animated transition from the `FromColor` to `ToColor`, during a period of `Duration` milliseconds. The transition is based on the hue-saturation-value (HSV (http://bit.ly/1Owhw6Y)) color space.

Note: the animation will only work on devices running Android 3 or later. On earlier devices, the color changes suddenly.

Example:

```
Activity.SetColorAnimated(1000, Colors.White, Colors.Red)
```

⬡ *SetLayout (Left As Int, Top As Int, Width As Int, Height As Int)*

Changes the view position and size.

⬡ *SetLayoutAnimated (Duration As Int, Left As Int, Top As Int, Width As Int, Height As Int)*

Changes the view's position and size from its current position to that specified by `Left,` `Top,` `Width` and `Height`, animated during a period of `Duration` milliseconds.

Note: the animation will only work on devices running Android 3 or later. On earlier devices, the view moves suddenly.

🔷 SetTextColorAnimated (Duration As Int, ToColor As Int)

Changes the text color from the current color to the **ToColor** color, with a transition animated during a period of **Duration** milliseconds. The transition is based on the hue-saturation-value (HSV (http://bit.ly/1Owhw6Y)) color space.
Note: the animation will only work on devices running Android 3 or later. On earlier devices, the color changes suddenly.

🔷 SetTextSizeAnimated (Duration As Int, TextSize As Int)

Changes the text size (page 163) to **TextSize** (in pixels), with a transition animated during a period of **Duration** milliseconds.
Note: the animation will only work on devices running Android 3 or later. On earlier devices, the text size changes suddenly.

🔷 SetVisibleAnimated (Duration As Int, Visible As Boolean)

Changes the visibility of the view to that specified by **Visible** during a period of **Duration** milliseconds.
Note: the animation will only work on devices running Android 3 or later. On earlier devices, the visibility changes suddenly.

🔑 Tag As Object

Gets or sets the Tag value. This is a place holder which can be used to store additional data.

🔑 Top As Int

Gets or sets the view's top position.

🔑 Visible As Boolean

Whether the user can see the object.

🔑 Width As Int

Gets or sets the view's width.

WebView

The WebView view uses the internal WebKit engine to display HTML pages. The page displayed can be an on-line page loaded with **LoadUrl** or an HTML string loaded with **LoadHtml**. This is an **Activity** object; it cannot be declared under **Sub Process_Globals**.

Permissions:

android.permission.INTERNET

Events:

PageFinished (Url As String)

The PageFinished event is raised after the page loads.

OverrideUrl (Url As String) As Boolean

OverrideUrl is called before loading any URL. If this method returns **True**, then the given **Url** will not be loaded. You can use this event as a way to handle click events in your code.

UserAndPasswordRequired (Host As String, Realm As String) As String()

This event is raised when accessing a site that requires basic authentication. You should return an array of strings with the username as the first element and password as the second element. For example:

```
Return Array As String("someuser", "password123")
```
Returning `Null` will cancel the request. Sending incorrect credentials will cause this event to be raised again.

Members:

🜲 Back
Goes back to the previous URL.

⚡ Background As Drawable
Gets or sets the background drawable.

🜲 BringToFront
Changes the Z order of this view and brings it to the front.

🜲 CaptureBitmap As Bitmap
Returns the complete HTML page as a bitmap.

⚡ Color As Int [write only]
Sets the background of the view to be a `ColorDrawable` with the given color. If the current background is of type `GradientDrawable` or `ColorDrawable`, the round corners will be kept.

⚡ Enabled As Boolean
If set to `True` then the `WebView` will respond to events. If set to `False`, events are ignored.

🜲 Forward
Goes forward to the next URL.

⚡ Height As Int
Gets or sets the view's height.

🜲 Initialize (EventName As String)
Initializes the view and sets the subs that will handle the events.
Views added with the designer should NOT be initialized. These views are initialized when the layout is loaded.

🜲 Invalidate
Invalidates the whole view forcing the view to redraw itself. Redrawing will only happen when the program can process messages, usually when it finishes running the current code. If you only need to redraw part of the view, it is usually quicker to use `Invalidate2` or `Invalidate3`.

🜲 Invalidate2 (Rect1 As Rect)
Invalidates anything inside the given rectangle that is part of this view. Redrawing will only happen when the program can process messages, usually when it finishes running the current code.

🜲 Invalidate3 (Left As Int, Top As Int, Right As Int, Bottom As Int)
Invalidates anything inside the given rectangle that is part of this view. Redrawing will only happen when the program can process messages, usually when it finishes running the current code.

✪ *IsInitialized As Boolean*
Whether this object has been initialized by calling `Initialize`.

✦ *JavaScriptEnabled As Boolean*
Gets or sets whether JavaScript is enabled.
JavaScript is enabled by default.

✦ *Left As Int*
Gets or sets the view's left position.

✪ *LoadHtml (HTML As String)*
Loads the given HTML. Example:
```
WebView1.LoadHtml("<html><body>Hello world!</body></html>")
```
You can use "file:///android_asset" to access files added with the file manager:
```
WebView1.LoadHtml("<html><body><img
src='file:///android_asset/someimage.jpg'/></body></html>")
```
Note that files added with the file manager should be accessed with a lower cased name.

✪ *LoadUrl (Url As String)*
Loads the given **Url**. Example:
```
WebView1.LoadUrl("http://www.google.com")
```

✪ *RemoveView*
Removes this view from its parent.

✪ *RequestFocus As Boolean*
Tries to set the focus to this view.
Returns **True** if the focus was set.

✪ *SendToBack*
Changes the Z order of this view and sends it to the back.

✪ *SetBackgroundImage (Bitmap1 As Bitmap)*

✪ *SetLayout (Left As Int, Top As Int, Width As Int, Height As Int)*
Changes the view position and size.

✪ *StopLoading*
Stops the current load.

✦ *Tag As Object*
Gets or sets the Tag value. This is a place holder which can be used to store additional data.

✦ *Top As Int*
Gets or sets the view's top position.

✦ *Url As String [read only]*
Returns the current URL.

✦ *Visible As Boolean*
Whether the user can see the object.

✦ *Width As Int*
Gets or sets the view's width.

⬡ Zoom (In As Boolean) As Boolean

Zooms in or out according to the value of **In**.
Returns **True** if zoom has changed.

🔑 ZoomEnabled As Boolean

Gets or sets whether the internal zoom feature is enabled.
The zoom feature is enabled by default.

3.4 Inline Code

B4A converts the BASIC code you write into Java. Although in most cases BASIC is easier to write, sometimes it is useful to be able to write directly in Java.

To do this, you need to include the JavaObject library (page 492) in your project, then write code such as:

```
Sub Process_Globals
 Private nativeMe As JavaObject
End Sub

Sub Activity_Create(FirstTime As Boolean)
 If FirstTime Then
  nativeMe.InitializeContext
 End If
 nativeMe.RunMethod("SetTitle", Null)
End Sub

#If JAVA
 public void SetTitle() {
  BA.Log("Main SetTitle");
  setTitle("Title has changed");
 }
#End IF
```

Note that BA is a special object that you can use to write to the log, raise events and to get access to the user activity, application context and other resources.

It is recommended using inline code to write only small amounts of Java code, or to access libraries (page 454).

More details about writing and using inline code here (http://bit.ly/1JQNpse). You will need to know how to write Java. If you want to access Android functionality within your inline code, you might find it useful to refer to the Android documentation here (http://bit.ly/1JQRDA5).

You will probably need to use some of the functionality used when creating B4A Libraries. The main reference is this online introduction (http://bit.ly/1HFLZtW).

Returning Data to B4A

If your inline code generates some data which you wish to make available within the B4A code, you will need to create a Sub and send the data to it by raising an event. For example:

```
Sub processData (data As Byte, message As String)
 ...
End Sub
#If JAVA
 ...
 processBA.raiseEvent(null, "processdata"), myData, myMessage);
```

Note: within Java, the name of the Sub **must** be in lower case.

The objects BA and processBA are created automatically.

Part 4: Libraries

In this reference section, we discuss libraries (only available if you have upgraded to the Full Version of B4A), and explain how to create your own libraries and share them with others (should you wish to).

We give full details of the Standard Libraries included in the Full Version installation. We also discuss some of the many Additional Libraries and Modules, including all the "Official" ones created by Anywhere Software, which you can download from the B4A website.

4.1 Libraries

Introduction

Libraries are key to gaining the full benefit of B4A. Note that, apart from the Core Library, they are only available in the Full Version.

What is a library?

A B4A library is an encapsulation of part or all of a project into a jar and an XML file which can easily be reused and shared with others. You can create your own, as described below.

Types of Libraries

There are several types of libraries in B4A: The Core Library, Standard Libraries, Additional Official Libraries and Additional User Libraries.

Core Library

This is included in both the Trial and the Full versions of B4A, and defines the Core Objects (page 336). Follow the link for more information.

Standard Libraries

When you upgrade from the Trial to the Full version, you get the Standard Libraries (page 457) which are saved in the Libraries folder in the B4A program folder. They are normally found in: C:\Program Files\Anywhere Software\Basic4Android\Libraries or C:\Program Files (x86)\Anywhere Software\Basic4android\Libraries

Additional Official Libraries

Additional Official Libraries (page 564) are produced by Anywhere Software (the makers of B4A) but are not included with the IDE. For a list of these, with links to the source for download, see the Additional Official Libraries (page 564) section.

Additional User Libraries

Additional User Libraries (page 569) have been produced by enthusiastic and generous users of B4A who have published their own libraries for the benefit of others. These add significantly to the capabilities of the product.

Additional libraries folder

It is required that you set up a special folder to save additional libraries, for example: C:\B4A\AddLibraries.

When you install a new version of B4A, all standard libraries are automatically updated, but the additional libraries are not included. The advantage of the special folder is that this folder is not affected when you install the new version of B4A.

Subscribing to Additional Library Updates

Because additional libraries are not systematically updated with new versions of B4A, you might want to subscribe here (http://bit.ly/18WJsgk) to be notified about updates.

Telling the IDE where to find Additional Libraries

When the IDE starts, it looks first for the available libraries in the Libraries folder of B4A and then in the folder for the additional libraries.

If you setup a special additional libraries folder, you must specify it in the IDE menu [Tools > Configure Paths]. The dialog allows you to specify the Additional Libraries folder.

Error message "Are you missing a library reference?"

If you get this message in the Compile & Debug dialog, it means that you either forgot to check the specified library in the Libraries Manager (page 87) window, or the library is missing from the folder.

Referencing Libraries

Before you can use the types and functions within a library, you need to add a reference to it in your project. Use the Libraries Manager (page 87) within the IDE.

If it's an additional library (page 564), you might have to download and install it first. Note that it is worth checking periodically if you have the latest versions of additional libraries, or subscribing to notifications about updates, as explained above.

Using Libraries

If you do not have full documentation for a library, you can discover the objects and methods contained in a library by reading the xml file. For example, the **phone.xml** file begins

```
<?xml version="1.0" encoding="UTF-8"?>
<root>
    <doclet-version-NOT-library-version>1.04</doclet-version-NOT-
library-version>
    <class>
        <name>anywheresoftware.b4a.phone.SmsWrapper</name>
        <shortname>SmsMessages</shortname>
```

This tells you there is an object (class) called SmsMessages, so in your code you can then declare:

```
Dim mgs As SmsMessages
```

Using Inline Code to access Libraries

You can also access the objects and methods of libraries by using inline code (page 450). For example:

```
Sub Process_Globals
  Private nativeMe As JavaObject
End Sub

Sub Globals
  Dim ID As PhoneId
End Sub

Sub Activity_Create(FirstTime As Boolean)
  If FirstTime Then
   nativeMe.InitializeContext
  End If

  Dim strPhoneNumber As String
  strPhoneNumber = nativeMe.RunMethod("GetNumber", Array (ID))
  Log ("strPhoneNumber=" & strPhoneNumber)
End Sub

#If JAVA
  public String GetNumber(anywheresoftware.b4a.phone.Phone.PhoneId x) {
   return x.GetLine1Number();
  }
#End If
```

To make this work, you need not only to check the Phone library but also the JavaObject library (page 492).

Creating Libraries

You can create your own libraries within B4A and, if you wish, you can share them with other developers via the B4A website. Or perhaps you have found some Java code which you wish to compile into a library so you can re-use it within your B4A projects.

There are two ways to build libraries: the easy way and the hard way.

The easy way is to write your code in B4A and compile modules from your project into a library. We describe this below.

The hard way is to write and debug the code in Java, perhaps using Eclipse (http://www.eclipse.org/). Although more difficult than B4A, writing in Java allows you to add features not possible using the easy method.

You then need to compile your library so B4A can use it, either by following the instructions here (http://bit.ly/1DpMoBg) if you want to use Eclipse or here (http://bit.ly/1DpIhoR) if you want to use Anywhere Software's Simple Library Compiler (SLC).

Benefits of creating Libraries

There are several benefits from compiling your own library:

Modular code: If your project is large, it will be easier to create and maintain if you can break it into several smaller projects.

Reusable components: You can reuse modules in several projects.

Share components: You can share your work with other developers.

Protect your code: Once compiled, the library can be distributed to others without revealing the source code.

Create different versions: You can have various versions of an app, for example, "Free" and "Paid for", by reusing the same core library.

Preparing Your Library

Main Activity Excluded

Except for the Project Attributes region, the Main Activity is not included in your library. This is necessary because the projects in which your library will be reused already contain a Main Activity.

The Main Activity in your development copy of the library can therefore be used to add code to test the library. You should add modules to contain the code of your library.

For details of what should be entered into the Project Attributes, see below.

Library specific attributes

The following attributes are specific for library compilation:

Project attributes

These are placed in the Project Attributes region of the main activity:

#LibraryAuthor: The library author. This value is added to the library XML file.

#LibraryName: The compiled library name. Sets the library name instead of showing the save dialog.

#LibraryVersion: A number that represents the library version. This number will appear next to the library name in the libraries list.

Module Attributes

#ExcludeFromLibrary: Whether to exclude this module during library compilation. Values: `True` or `False`.

Note that the Main activity is always excluded.

Classes Attributes

Event: Adds an event to the list of events. This attribute can be used multiple times. Note that the events list only affects the IDE events Autocomplete (page 83) feature.

How to Compile a Library

– First select the compilation mode (page 172) you wish to use: Release or Release Obfuscated (page 173). (Note that Strings will not be obfuscated.)

– Select menu [Project > Compile To Library] or type Alt+5. When you choose this option, all the modules except the main activity are compiled into a library. You can exclude other modules with the ExcludeFromLibrary attribute.

– The main activity (and the other excluded modules) can now be used to test the library. You can reference the library from other projects and access the same functionality as in the original project. There is more information on creating your own libraries on the web here (http://bit.ly/1DpMoBg).

Output

When you select menu [Project > Compile To Library], two files are created, both with the same name as the project:

– a jar (Java) file with the compiled code

– an XML file that includes the metadata that is required by the IDE.

These two files will be saved in the Additional Libraries folder specified in the [Tools > Configure Paths] menu dialog.

No Home Screen Widget Libraries

Services that host home screen widgets cannot be compiled into a library. See here for more information (page 130) about Widgets.

How to publish your library

Developers should edit the list of libraries here (http://bit.ly/16H9C7s) and add their libraries. (Contact support@basic4ppc.com if you do not have write permission.) For information about the impact of using libraries, see this (http://bit.ly/1OwhEU8) thread.

4.2 Standard Libraries included with Full Version

Introduction

Libraries and official updates are only available for users who have purchased B4A. If you have bought B4A but cannot download files, then please contact support@basic4ppc.com and send the User name and Email address used when purchasing B4A. See Libraries (page 452) for more information.

The following libraries are included in the Full version installation package. They are saved in the Libraries folder in the B4A program folder and are normally found in:
C:\Program Files\Anywhere Software\Basic4Android\Libraries or
C:\Program Files (x86)\Anywhere Software\Basic4android\Libraries
In order to use an object in one of these libraries, you need to reference its library in the Libraries Manager (page 87) window of the IDE.
In fact, the Core library is also included in the installation, but since you do not need to reference it, we deal with its objects in the Core Objects Chapter (page 336).

List of Standard Libraries

Accessibility
Administrator
Animation (page 460)
Audio (page 462)
B4XEncryption (page 471)
Camera (page 472)
ContentResolver (page 473)
Core (page 336)
DateUtils (page 476)
Daydream (page 477)
GameView (page 478)
GPS (page 480)
HTTP (page 483)
HttpUtils2 (page 487)
IME (page 490)
JavaObject (page 491)
JSON (page 493)
LiveWallpaper (page 495)
Network (page 496)
NFC (page 502)
NotificationListener (page 500)
Phone (page 503)
PreferenceActivity (page 529)
RandomAccessFile (page 532)
Serial (page 539)
Sip (page 543)

Accessibility Library

This library is included in the IDE installation package. It includes several accessibility related methods.

List of types:

Accessiblity (note the spelling).

Accessiblity

This library includes several accessibility related methods. The `SetNextFocus` methods allow you to explicitly set the focus order. This order is important when the user navigates your application with a directional controller (such as D-Pad). `SetContentDescription` sets the content that will be used by accessibility services such as TalkBack to describe the interface.

Members:

🕸 GetUserFontScale As Float

Returns the user-set font scale. The user can adjust this scale in the device Settings. This scale is applied automatically to all text based views.

🕸 SetContentDescription (View1 As View, Content As CharSequence)

Sets the view's description. This text will be used by accessibility services to describe the view.

🕸 SetNextFocusDown (ThisView As View, NextView As View)

Sets the next view that will get the focus when the user presses on the down key (when this view is focused). Example:

```
Dim Access As Accessibility
Access.SetNextFocusDown(Button1, Button2) 'When the focus is on
Button1 and the user presses on the down key,
'the focus will move to Button2.
```

🕸 SetNextFocusLeft (ThisView As View, NextView As View)

Sets the next view that will get the focus when the user presses on the left key (when this view is focused).

🕸 SetNextFocusRight (ThisView As View, NextView As View)

Sets the next view that will get the focus when the user presses on the right key (when this view is focused).

✪ SetNextFocusUp (ThisView As View, NextView As View)

Sets the next view that will get the focus when the user presses on the up key (when this view is focused).

Administrator Library

This library is included in the IDE installation package. Starting from Android 2.2 (api level 8), Android allows an application to be registered as an administrator. Administrator apps have the following special features
– Manually lock the screen
– Set the minimum password length and quality
– Wipe the entire device
– Set the maximum allowed time before the device locks
– Request the user to change password
– Manually set a new password
– Disable the camera
– Track password changes
– Some other security features as described here.
Note that the password is the screen lock password. Other passwords are not affected. The user needs to enable the admin app before it can have any special privileges. This is done either by calling Manager.Enable or from the Security settings page.

On-line Link

For more details about using the Administrator Library, and an example program, see here (http://bit.ly/15k06pn).

List of types:

AdminManager

AdminManager

Members:

✪ *Disable*

Disables the admin policy.

✪ *Enable (Explanation As String)*

Enables the admin policy. The user will be shown a dialog with the requested features. This method can only be called from an Activity context.
Explanation - A message shown at the top of the dialog.

🔩 *Enabled As Boolean [read only]*

Returns `True` if the admin policy is active.

✪ *LockScreen*

Immediately locks the screen. Requires the force-lock tag in the policies file.

🔩 *MaximumTimeToLock As Long [write only]*

Sets the maximum time (measured in milliseconds) before the device locks. This limits the maximum length of time that the user can set in the Security menu:

[Settings > Security > Automatically Lock]. This is not available on early versions of Android. Requires the force-lock tag in the policies file.

● *PASSWORD_QUALITY_ALPHABETIC As Int*

● *PASSWORD_QUALITY_ALPHANUMERIC As Int*

● *PASSWORD_QUALITY_NUMERIC As Int*

● *PASSWORD_QUALITY_UNSPECIFIED As Int*

● *PasswordSufficient As Boolean [read only]*

Returns TRUE if the current password meets the requirements. Requires the limit-password tag in the policies file.

● *RequestNewPassword*

Shows the new password activity. Note that the user might cancel the change.

● *ResetPassword (NewPassword As String) As Boolean*

Sets the given password as the device password. Requires the reset-password tag in the policies file.

● *SetPasswordQuality (QualityFlag As Int, MinimumLength As Int)*

Sets the minimum allowed length and quality for device passwords. These settings will affect new passwords. Requires the limit-password tag in the policies file.

QualityFlag - One of the password quality flags shown above.
MinimumLength - Password minimum length.
Example:

```
manager.SetPasswordQuality(manager.PASSWORD_QUALITY_ALPHANUMERIC, 4)
```

Animation Library

This library is one of several ways you can achieve animation (page 125). It is included in the IDE installation package.

Animation

The Animation object allows you to animate views (controls). These small animations can improve the user overall impression of your application. There are several types of animations. The `Initialize` methods determine the animation type.

This is an `Activity` object; it cannot be declared under `Sub Process_Globals`.

For a sample program demonstrating animations, see here (http://bit.ly/1dcOZ6u).

List of types:

Animation

Event: AnimationEnd

You can use this event to fire off another animation when the current one ends. Example:

```
Dim a6, a7, a8 As Animation

a6.InitializeTranslate("Animation", 0, 0, 0dip, 200dip)

Sub Animation_AnimationEnd
  If Sender = a6 Then
   a7.Start(Button6)
  Else If Sender = a7 Then
   a8.Start(Button6)
  End If
End Sub
```

Members:

✦ Duration As Long
Gets or sets the animation duration. Value is measured in milliseconds.
Example: `Animation1.Duration = 1000`

✦ InitializeAlpha (EventName As String, FromAlpha As Float, ToAlpha As Float)
Initializes an alpha animation. This animation affects the view's transparency (fading effect).
The **alpha** values are from 0 to 1, where 0 is fully transparent and 1 is fully opaque.
FromAlpha - The first frame value.
ToAlpha - The last frame value.

✦ InitializeRotate (EventName As String, FromDegrees As Float, ToDegrees As Float)
Initializes a rotation animation. The view will rotate between the given values. Rotation
pivot is set to the top left corner.
FromDegrees - The first frame rotation value.
ToDegrees - The last frame rotation value.

✦ InitializeRotateCenter (EventName As String, FromDegrees As Float, ToDegrees As Float, View1 As View)
Similar to `InitializeRotate`, with the pivot set to the given view's center.

✦ InitializeScale (EventName As String, FromX As Float, FromY As Float, ToX As Float, ToY As Float)
Initializes a scale animation. The view will be scaled (resized) during the animation. The
scaling centre will be set to the view's top left corner.
FromX - The first frame horizontal scale.
FromY - The first frame vertical scale.
ToX - The last frame horizontal scale.
ToY - The last frame vertical scale.

✦ InitializeScaleCenter (EventName As String, FromX As Float, FromY As Float, ToX As Float, ToY As Float, View1 As View)
Similar to `InitializeScale` with the scaling center set to the given view's center.

⬡ *InitializeTranslate (EventName As String, FromDX As Float, FromDY As Float, ToDX As Float, ToDY As Float)*

Initializes a translation animation. The view will move according to the given values.

FromDX - First frame horizontal position relative to the original position.

FromDY - First frame vertical position relative to the original position.

ToDX - Last frame horizontal position relative to the original position.

ToDY - Last frame vertical position relative to the original position.

⬡ *IsInitialized As Boolean*

Whether this object has been initialized by calling one of the `Initialize` methods.

⬢ *REPEAT_RESTART As Int*

A constant used by `RepeatMode`.

⬢ *REPEAT_REVERSE As Int*

A constant used by `RepeatMode`.

🔑 *RepeatCount As Int*

Gets or sets the number of times the animation will repeat after the first play. A value of 0 means that it will play once. A value of 1 means that it will play and then repeat once. Set to -1 for a non-stopping animation.

Example: `Animation1.RepeatCount = 1`

🔑 *RepeatMode As Int*

Gets or sets the repeat mode. Relevant only when RepeatCount is not 0. The default is REPEAT_RESTART, which means that the animation will restart each time. REPEAT_REVERSE causes the animation to repeat in reverse each time.

For example, if the animation moves the view to the right 100 pixels, in the next repeat it will move to the left. Example:

```
Animation1.RepeatMode = Animation1.REPEAT_REVERSE
```

⬡ *Start (View1 As View)*

Starts animating the given view. Note that a single animation should not be applied to more than one view at a time. Example:

```
Animation1.Start(Button1)
```

⬡ *Stop (View1 As View)*

Stops animating the given view.

Audio Library

This library is included in the IDE installation package.

List of types:

AudioRecordApp
Beeper
JetPlayer
MediaPlayerStream (page 466)
SoundPool (page 467)
VideoRecordApp (page 468)
VideoView (page 469)

AudioRecordApp

AudioRecordApp lets you use the default audio recorder application to record audio. After initializing the object, you should call **Record** to start recording. Example:

```
Sub Process_Globals
  Dim audioRecorder As AudioRecordApp
  Dim videoRecorder As VideoRecordApp
End Sub
Sub Globals
  Dim vv As VideoView
End Sub
Sub Activity_Create(FirstTime As Boolean)
  If FirstTime Then
   audioRecorder.Initialize("audioRecorder")
   videoRecorder.Initialize("videoRecorder")
  End If
  vv.Initialize("vv")
  Activity.AddView(vv, 0, 0, 100%x, 100%y)
  Activity.AddMenuItem("Record Video", "RecordVideo")
  Activity.AddMenuItem("Record Audio", "RecordAudio")
  ToastMessageShow("Press on Menu button...", True)
End Sub
Sub RecordVideo_Click
  videoRecorder.Record(File.DirRootExternal, "1.mp4")
End Sub
Sub RecordAudio_Click
  audioRecorder.Record(File.DirRootExternal, "1.3gpp")
End Sub
Sub videoRecorder_RecordComplete (Success As Boolean)
  Log(Success)
  If Success Then
   vv.LoadVideo(File.DirRootExternal, "1.mp4")
   vv.Play
  End If
End Sub
Sub audioRecorder_RecordComplete (Success As Boolean)
  Log(Success)
  If Success Then
   vv.LoadVideo(File.DirRootExternal, "1.3gpp")
   vv.Play
  End If
End Sub
```

Event:

RecordComplete (Success As Boolean)

The RecordComplete event will be raised when recording completes.

Members:

Initialize (EventName As String)

Initializes the object and sets the sub that will handle the event.

❖ Record (Dir As String, FileName As String)

Calls the recording application. **Dir** and **FileName** set the output file location.

Beeper

Plays a "beep" sound with the given duration and frequency. Example:
```
Dim b As Beeper
b.Initialize(300, 500)
b.Beep
```

Members:

❖ Beep

Plays the sound.

❖ Initialize (Duration As Int, Frequency As Int)

Initializes the object with the given duration, measured in milliseconds, and the given frequency, measured in Hertz. The music volume channel will be used.

❖ Initialize2 (Duration As Int, Frequency As Int, VoiceChannel As Int)

Similar to Initialize. Allows you to set the volume channel.

❖ Release

Releases the resources used by this beeper.

⬤ VOLUME_ALARM As Int

Alarms channel.

⬤ VOLUME_MUSIC As Int

Music channel.

⬤ VOLUME_NOTIFICATION As Int

Notifications channel.

⬤ VOLUME_RING As Int

Phone ring channel.

⬤ VOLUME_SYSTEM As Int

System sounds channel.

⬤ VOLUME_VOICE_CALL As Int

Voice calls channel.

JetPlayer

JET is an interactive music player for small embedded devices. It works in conjunction with SONiVOX's Embedded Audio Synthesizer (EAS) which is the MIDI playback device for Android. Both the JET and EAS engines are integrated into the Android embedded platform through the JetPlayer class, as well as inherent in the JET Creator application. As such, the JET content author can be sure that the playback will sound exactly the same in both the JET Creator and the final Android application playing back on Android mobile devices. More details here (http://bit.ly/1OwhHiM).

Events:

QueuedSegmentsCountChanged (Count As Int)

CurrentUserIdChanged (UserId As Int, RepeatCount As Int)

Members:

ClearQueue

Clears the segments queue.

CloseFile

Closes the resources related to the loaded file.

Initialize (EventName As String)

Initializes the object and sets the Subs that will handle the JetPlayer events.

IsInitialized As Boolean

Whether this object has been initialized by calling `Initialize`.

LoadFile (Dir As String, File As String)

Loads a JET file.

MaxTracks As Int [read only]

Returns the maximum number of simultaneous tracks.

Pause

Pauses playback.

Play

Starts playing the segments queue.

QueueSegment (SegmentNum As Int, LibNum As Int, RepeatCount As Int, Transpose As Int, MuteArray() As Boolean, UserId As Byte)

Adds a segment to the queue. No more than 3 segments are allowed.

SegmentNum - The segment identifier.

LibNum - The index of the sound bank associated with this segment. Pass -1 if there is no sound bank.

RepeatCount - Number of times the segment will be repeated. 0 means that it will be played once. Pass -1 to repeat indefinitely.

Transpose - The pitch transition. Should be from -12 to 12.

MuteArray - An array of booleans that sets the mute value of each track. The array length must be equal to MaxTracks value.

UserId - An id given to this segment. When the current segment changes, the `CurrentUserIdChanged` event is raised with this id (assuming that the id of the previous segment was different).

Release

Releases all resources allocated for the JetPlayer.

SetMute (MuteArray() As Boolean, Sync As Boolean)

Sets the tracks' mute state.

MuteArray - An array of booleans that sets the mute state of each track. The array length must be equal to MaxTracks value.

Sync - If `False`, the change will be applied as soon as possible, otherwise the change will be applied at the start of the next segment or next repeat.

🔖 *SetTrackMute (Track As Int, Mute As Boolean, Sync As Boolean)*

Similar to SetMute but only changes the state of a single track.

MediaPlayerStream

MediaPlayerStream is similar to MediaPlayer. Unlike MediaPlayer, which plays local files, MediaPlayerStream plays audio streams which are available on-line. Another difference between the objects is that, in this case, the `Load` method is asynchronous. Only when the file is ready, the `StreamReady` event will be fired and you can start playing. According to the Android documentation, the on-line resource must support progressive download.
Example:

```
Sub Process_Globals
   Dim mp As MediaPlayerStream
End Sub
Sub Globals
End Sub
Sub Activity_Create(FirstTime As Boolean)
   If FirstTime Then
      mp.Initialize("mp")
   End If
   mp.Load("http://www...")
End Sub
Sub mp_StreamReady
   Log("starts playing")
   mp.Play
End Sub
Sub mp_StreamError (ErrorCode As String, ExtraData As Int)
   Log("Error: " & ErrorCode & ", " & ExtraData)
   ToastMessageShow("Error: " & ErrorCode & ", " & ExtraData, True)
End Sub
Sub mp_StreamBuffer(Percentage As Int)
   Log(Percentage)
End Sub
```

Permissions:
android.permission.INTERNET

Events:

StreamReady
Fired when the file is ready to play. Once this event has fired, call `Play` to start playing the stream.

StreamError (ErrorCode As String, ExtraData As Int)
This event is fired when there is an error with the stream. For example, if the target URL does not exist, you would get an error with ErrorCode= MEDIA_ERROR_UNKNOWN and

ExtraData= -1004. For more about MediaPlayer errors, and lists of ErrorCodes and EstraData Constants, see here (http://bit.ly/GVziCW).

StreamBuffer(Percentage As Int)
Percentage of a stream which has been downloaded.

Complete
This event fires when the stream has finished playing.

Members:

⚐Duration As Int [read only]

⬡Initialize (EventName As String)
Initializes the object.
EventName - Name of Subs that will handle the events.

⬡IsPlaying As Boolean

⬡Load (Url As String)
Starts loading the resource from the given **Url**. `StreamReady` event will be raised when the stream is ready.

⚐Looping As Boolean

⬡Pause

⬡Play

⬡Release

⬡SetVolume (Right As Float, Left As Float)
Sets the playing volume for each channel. The value should be from 0 to 1.

⬡Stop

SoundPool
SoundPool holds a collection of short sounds which can be played with low latency. Each sound has two Id values which you should work with. The first is the `LoadId`, which is returned when loading the sound with `Load`. The second is the `PlayId`, which is returned when you call `Play`. When working with `SoundPool`, it is useful to watch the unfiltered (page 182) LogCat for messages (for example when the sound is too long).

Members:

⬡Initialize (MaxStreams As Int)
Initializes the SoundPool and sets the maximum number of simultaneous streams.

⬡IsInitialized As Boolean
Whether this object has been initialized by calling `Initialize`.

⬡Load (Dir As String, File As String) As Int
Loads a sound file and returns the sound LoadId. Example:

```
Dim LoadId As Int
LoadId = SP.Load(File.DirAssets, "sound.wav")
```

❖ Pause (PlayId As Int)

Pauses the stream with the given PlayId.

❖ Play (LoadId As Int, LeftVolume As Float, RightVolume As Float, Priority As Int, Loop As Int, Rate As Float) As Int

Plays the sound with the matching LoadId and returns the PlayId. Returns 0 if there was an error.

LoadId - The value returned when loading the file.

LeftVolume / RightVolume - The volume value (0 - 1)

Priority - A priority value which you assign to this sound. The higher the value, the higher the priority. When the number of simultaneous streams is higher than the value set in `Initialize`, the lowest priority stream will be stopped.

Loop - Number of times to repeat. Pass **-1** to repeat indefinitely.

Rate - Playback rate (0 - 2).

❖ Release

Releases all resources allocated to this object.

❖ Resume (PlayId As Int)

Resumes the stream with the given PlayId.

❖ SetRate (PlayId As Int, Rate As Float)

Sets the rate of the stream with the given PlayId. **Rate** is from 0 to 2.

❖ SetVolume (PlayId As Int, Left As Float, Right As Float)

Sets the volume of the stream with the given PlayId. **Left** and **Right** are from 0 to 1.

❖ Stop (PlayId As Int)

Stops the stream with the given PlayId.

❖ Unload (LoadId As Int)

Unloads the stream with the given LoadId.

VideoRecordApp

VideoRecordApp lets you use the default video recorder application to record video.
After initializing the object, you should call **Record** to start recording. Example:

```
Sub Process_Globals
   Dim audioRecorder As AudioRecordApp
   Dim videoRecorder As VideoRecordApp
End Sub
Sub Globals
   Dim vv As VideoView
End Sub
Sub Activity_Create(FirstTime As Boolean)
   If FirstTime Then
        audioRecorder.Initialize("audioRecorder")
      videoRecorder.Initialize("videoRecorder")
   End If
   vv.Initialize("vv")
```

```
    Activity.AddView(vv, 0, 0, 100%x, 100%y)
    Activity.AddMenuItem("Record Video", "RecordVideo")
    Activity.AddMenuItem("Record Audio", "RecordAudio")
    ToastMessageShow("Press on Menu button...", True)
End Sub
Sub RecordVideo_Click
    videoRecorder.Record(File.DirRootExternal, "1.mp4")
End Sub
Sub RecordAudio_Click
    audioRecorder.Record(File.DirRootExternal, "1.3gpp")
End Sub
Sub videoRecorder_RecordComplete (Success As Boolean)
    Log(Success)
    If Success Then
        vv.LoadVideo(File.DirRootExternal, "1.mp4")
        vv.Play
    End If
End Sub
Sub audioRecorder_RecordComplete (Success As Boolean)
    Log(Success)
    If Success Then
        vv.LoadVideo(File.DirRootExternal, "1.3gpp")
        vv.Play
    End If
End Sub
Sub Activity_Resume
End Sub
Sub Activity_Pause (UserClosed As Boolean)
End Sub
```

Event RecordComplete (Success As Boolean)

The `RecordComplete` event will be raised when record completes.

Members:

🔧 Initialize (EventName As String)

Initializes the object and sets the sub that will handle the event.

🔧 Record (Dir As String, FileName As String)

Calls the recording application. **Dir** and **FileName** set the output file location.

VideoView

VideoView is a view that allows you to play video media inside your application. The VideoView optionally shows a media controller when the user touches the view. The `Complete` event is raised when playback is completed. A simple example of using VideoView:

```
Sub Globals
   Dim vv As VideoView
End Sub
Sub Activity_Create(FirstTime As Boolean)
   vv.Initialize("vv")
   Activity.AddView(vv, 10dip, 10dip, 250dip, 250dip)
   vv.LoadVideo(File.DirRootExternal, "somefile.mp4")
   vv.Play
End Sub
Sub vv_Complete
   Log("Playing completed")
End Sub
```

This is an **Activity** object; it cannot be declared under **Sub Process_Globals**.

Event: Complete
The Complete event is raised when playback is completed.

Members:

🔧 *Background As Drawable*

⚙ *BringToFront*

🔧 *Color As Int [write only]*

🔧 *Duration As Int [read only]*
Gets the video duration (in milliseconds).

🔧 *Enabled As Boolean*
If set to **True** then the **VideoView** will respond to events. If set to **False**, events are ignored.

🔧 *Height As Int*

⚙ *Initialize (EventName As String)*
Initialize the object and sets the name of the subs that will handle the events.

⚙ *Invalidate*
Invalidates the whole view forcing the view to redraw itself. Redrawing will only happen when the program can process messages, usually when it finishes running the current code. If you only need to redraw part of the view, it is usually quicker to use **Invalidate2** or **Invalidate3**.

⚙ *Invalidate2 (Rect1 As Rect)*
Invalidates anything inside the given rectangle that is part of this view. Redrawing will only happen when the program can process messages, usually when it finishes running the current code.

⚙ *Invalidate3 (Left As Int, Top As Int, Right As Int, Bottom As Int)*
Invalidates anything inside the given rectangle that is part of this view. Redrawing will only happen when the program can process messages, usually when it finishes running the current code.

⚙ *IsInitialized As Boolean*
Whether this object has been initialized by calling **Initialize**.

IsPlaying As Boolean
Returns TRUE if the video is currently playing.

Left As Int

LoadVideo (Dir As String, FileName As String)
Loads a video file and prepares it for playing. It is not possible to load files from the assets folder.

Advanced: you can pass "http" to the Dir parameter and then a full URL (including http) to the FileName. In this case, the on-line video will be streamed. Note that you need to add the INTERNET permission (page 131) for this to work.

MediaControllerEnabled As Boolean [write only]
Sets whether the media controller is enabled. It is enabled by default. **Note** that the media player gets attached to the VideoView parent.

Pause
Pauses the playback.

Play
Starts or resumes playing.

Position As Int
Gets or sets the playing position (in milliseconds).

RemoveView

RequestFocus As Boolean

SendToBack

SetBackgroundImage (arg0 As Bitmap)

SetLayout (arg0 As Int, arg1 As Int, arg2 As Int, arg3 As Int)

Stop
Stops the playback.

Tag As Object

Top As Int

toString As String

Visible As Boolean
Whether the user can see the object.

Width As Int

B4XEncryption Library

This library is included in the IDE installation package.
It includes one type: B4XCipher.

B4XCipher

B4XCipher uses the Advanced Encryption Standard (AES (http://bit.ly/1OwhKuQ)) with a random salt and random initialization vector to encrypt the data. The methods are compatible with B4J jB4XEncryption and B4i Encryption libraries, which means that you can encrypt the data on one platform and decrypt it on another.

Events:

None

Members:

⬡ *Decrypt (Data() As Byte, Password As String) As Byte()*

Decrypts the given data with the given password.
Note: on Android 4.3 and below, the password should only include ASCII characters.
The salt and initialization vector are stored in the returned data.

⬡ *Encrypt (Data() As Byte, Password As String) As Byte()*

Encrypts the given data with the given password.
Note: on Android 4.3 and below, the password should only include ASCII characters.
The salt and initialization vector are stored in the returned data.

Camera Library

This library is included in the IDE installation package.

List of types:

Camera

Camera

The camera object allows you to access the device cameras. This library is supported by Android 1.6+. **Note**: if possible, it is recommended to work with the CameraEx (page 565) class that wraps this object and adds many features. The CameraEx class requires Android 2.3+.
Camera is an `Activity` object; it cannot be declared under `Sub Process_Globals`.

Permissions:

android.permission.CAMERA

Events:

Ready (Success As Boolean)

The Ready event will be raised when the Initialize action has finished opening the camera.

PictureTaken (Data() As Byte)

The PictureTaken event will be raised when the TakePicture action finishes and the picture is ready.

Preview (Data() As Byte)

Once the StartPreview action has been taken on a Camera, the Preview event is raised automatically whenever an image is ready.

FocusDone (Success As Boolean)

The FocusDone event will be raised when AutoFocus completes.

Members:
🔷 *AutoFocus*
Starts auto-focus function. The FocusDone event will be raised when the operation completes. You can check whether the "auto" focus mode is supported with CameraEx class.

🔷 *CancelAutoFocus*
Cancels the auto-focus operation. Does nothing if no such operation is in progress.

🔷 *Initialize (Panel As ViewGroup, EventName As String)*
Initializes the rear-facing camera. If the device only has one camera which is front-facing, use `Initialize2`.
Panel - The preview images will be displayed on the panel.
EventName - Events subs prefix.
The Ready event will be raised when the camera has finished opening.

🔷 *Initialize2 (Panel As ViewGroup, EventName As String, CameraId As Int)*
Same as `Initialize`, but you can specify which camera to use.
CameraId - the Id of the hardware camera. If there is only one camera on the device, its Id is 0. If there are two cameras, use 0 for the rear-facing camera, 1 for the front-facing one.
The Ready event will be raised when the camera has finished opening.
This method is only available from Android 2.3+.

🔷 *Release*
Releases the camera object and allows other processes to access the camera.

🔷 *StartPreview*
Starts displaying the preview images. Once the StartPreview action has been taken on a Camera, the Preview event is raised automatically whenever an image is ready.

🔷 *StopPreview*
Stops displaying the preview images.

🔷 *TakePicture*
Takes a picture. When the picture is ready, the `PictureTaken` event will be raised. You should not call `TakePicture` while another picture is currently being taken. The preview images are stopped after calling this method. You can call StartPreview to restart the preview images.
The image will be stored in the folder: /mnt/sdcard/DCIM/Camera.

ContentResolver Library

ContentResolver library allows you to access "content providers" applications.
This functionality is already available with objects such as: CallLog, Contacts, Contacts2 and others. With this library you have more flexibility as you can implement it completely in B4A.
The classes in this library are similar to the Java classes. The purpose it to make it easier to convert Java code. Note that most of the constants are not available in this wrapper. This means that you need to replace them with the actual values.

The features of ContentResolver are similar to SQL features. The main operations are: Query, Insert, Update and Delete. For each feature there is a synchronous method and an asynchronous method (QueryAsync, InsertAsync...). The asynchronous methods raise events when the operation completes.

Note that you usually need the SQL library together with this library.

See online examples (http://bit.ly/1LKJb0l).

List of types:
ContentResolver
ContentValues
Uri

ContentResolver
ContentResolver allows you to interact with other content providers.

Events:
QueryCompleted (Success As Boolean, Crsr As Cursor)
InsertCompleted (Success As Boolean, Uri As Uri)
UpdateCompleted (Success As Boolean, RowsAffected As Int)
DeleteCompleted (Success As Boolean, RowsAffected As Int)

Members:

✪ Delete (Uri As android.net.Uri, Where As String, SelectionArgs() As String) As Int
Deletes rows based on the given criteria.
Uri - Content Uri.
Where - The selection criteria. Can include question marks.
SelectionArgs - An array of strings that replace the question marks in the Where clause.

✪ Initialize (EventName As String)
Initializes the object and sets the subs that will handle the asynchronous operations.

✪ Insert (Uri As Uri, Values As android.content.ContentValues) As Uri
Inserts a row.
Uri - The content Uri.
Values - The values to insert.

✪ InsertAsync (Uri As Uri, Values As android.content.ContentValues)
Starts an asynchronous insert. The InsertCompleted event will be raised when operation completes.

✪ Query (Uri As Uri, Projection() As String, Selection As String, SelectionArgs() As String, SortOrder As String) As CursorWrapper
Queries the content provider.
Uri - Content Uri.
Project - An array of strings. The columns to return.
Selection - The criteria.
SelectionArgs - An array of strings that replace question marks in the selection string.
SortOrder - The sorting column (or empty string if sorting is not required).

◆QueryAsync (Uri As Uri, Projection() As String, Selection As String, SelectionArgs() As String, SortOrder As String)

◆Update (Uri As android.net.Uri, Values As android.content.ContentValues, Where As String, SelectionArgs() As String) As Int

Updates rows with the given values.

Uri - Content Uri.

Values - Values to update.

Where - Selection criteria.

SelectionArgs - An array of strings that replaces questions marks in the Where clause.

◆UpdateAsync (Uri As android.net.Uri, Values As android.content.ContentValues, Where As String, SelectionArgs() As String)

Starts an asynchronous update. The UpdateCompleted event will be raised when operation completes.

◆UpdateDelete (Uri As android.net.Uri, Where As String, SelectionArgs() As String)

Starts an asynchronous delete. The DeleteCompleted event will be raised when operation completes.

ContentValues

Holds pairs of keys and values.

Events:

None

Members:

🔹*Initialize*

🔹*IsInitialized As Boolean*

🔹*PutBoolean (Key As String, Value As Boolean)*

🔹*PutByte (Key As String, Value As Byte)*

🔹*PutBytes (Key As String, Value() As Byte)*

🔹*PutDouble (Key As String, Value As Double)*

🔹*PutFloat (Key As String, Value As Float)*

🔹*PutInteger (Key As String, Value As Int)*

🔹*PutLong (Key As String, Value As Long)*

🔹*PutNull (Key As String)*

🔹*PutShort (Key As String, Value As Short)*

🔹*PutString (Key As String, Value As String)*

🔹*Remove (Key As String)*

Uri

Events:

None

Members:

🔹*FromParts (Scheme As String, SSP As String, Fragment As String)*

Creates a new Uri from the given parts.

🔹*IsInitialized As Boolean*

🔹*Parse (UriString As String)*

Creates a new Uri from the given string.

🔹*ParseId As Long*

Returns the Id part of the current Uri.

🔹*WithAppendedId (BaseUri As android.net.Uri, Id As Long)*

Creates a new Uri by appending the Id to the given Uri.

🔹*WithAppendedPath (BaseUri As android.net.Uri, PathSegment As String)*

Creates a new Uri by appending the path to the given Uri.

DateUtils Library

This library is included in the IDE installation package.

Period

Events:
None

Members:

Days As Int

Hours As Int

Initialize
Initializes the fields to their default value.

IsInitialized As Boolean
Tests whether the object has been initialized.

Minutes As Int

Months As Int

Seconds As Int

Years As Int

Daydream Library

This library is included in the IDE installation package.

List of types:
Daydream

Daydream

Daydream is a new "screen saver" feature introduced in Android 4.2. See the Daydream tutorial (http://bit.ly/15mgqWA) for more information.

Events:

DreamStarted

SizeChanged

DreamStopped

Members:

Canvas As CanvasWrapper [read only]
A placeholder for Canvas.

Finish
Manually finishes the dream.

FullScreen As Boolean
Gets or sets whether the system bar appears.

Initialize (EventName As String)
Initializes the object and sets the subs that will handle the events.

✒ *Interactive As Boolean*

Gets or sets whether user interactions will be handled instead of finishing the dream.

✒ *Panel As PanelWrapper [read only]*

Returns the main panel.

✒ *ScreenBright As Boolean*

Gets or sets whether the screen should stay bright.

GameView Library

This library is included in the IDE installation package. GameView is a view that allows you to draw hardware accelerated graphics. Compared to software accelerated graphics, hardware accelerated graphics are many times faster. Using hardware accelerated graphics, it is possible to create smooth, real-time games.

Note: the acceleration method used by GameView is only available from Android 3.0 and above. This also means that, under [Tools > Configure paths], you need to reference android.jar on Android platform 11 or above.

Tutorial

For a tutorial on creating a 2D game using GameView see this (http://bit.ly/1Owi4tr) web page.

List of types:

BitmapData
GameView

BitmapData

Members:

● *Bitmap As BitmapWrapper*

The bitmap that will be drawn.

● *Delete As Boolean*

If Delete is **True**, then the BitmapData will be removed from the list when GameView is redrawn.

● *DestRect As RectWrapper*

The target rectangle. Determines the location and size of the drawn bitmap.

● *Flip As Int*

Flips the bitmap based on one of the FLIP constants.

● *FLIP_BOTH As Int*

● *FLIP_HORIZONTALLY As Int*

● *FLIP_NONE As Int*

● *FLIP_VERTICALLY As Int*

● *Rotate As Int*

Number of degrees to rotate the bitmap.

SrcRect As RectWrapper

The source rectangle. Determines the bitmap's region that will be drawn. The complete bitmap will be drawn if the rectangle is uninitialized.

GameView

A view that draws itself with hardware accelerated graphics. Suitable for 2d games. See this (http://bit.ly/1Owi4tr) tutorial. The hardware acceleration method used is only available in Android 3.0 and above (API level 11 and above).

This is an `Activity` object; it cannot be declared under `Sub Process_Globals`.

Events:

Touch (Action As Int, X As Float, Y As Float)

Members:

Background As Drawable

BitmapsData As List [read only]

Returns the list of BitmapData objects.

BringToFront

Color As Int [write only]

Enabled As Boolean

If set to `True` then the `GameView` will respond to events. If set to `False`, events are ignored.

Height As Int

Initialize (arg1 As String)

Invalidate

Invalidates the whole view forcing the view to redraw itself. Redrawing will only happen when the program can process messages, usually when it finishes running the current code. If you only need to redraw part of the view, it is usually quicker to use `Invalidate2` or `Invalidate3`.

Invalidate2 (Rect1 As Rect)

Invalidates anything inside the given rectangle that is part of this view. Redrawing will only happen when the program can process messages, usually when it finishes running the current code.

Invalidate3 (Left As Int, Top As Int, Right As Int, Bottom As Int)

Invalidates anything inside the given rectangle that is part of this view. Redrawing will only happen when the program can process messages, usually when it finishes running the current code.

IsHardwareAccelerated As Boolean [read only]

Returns `TRUE` if hardware acceleration is supported.

IsInitialized As Boolean

Whether this object has been initialized by calling `Initialize`.

Left As Int

⚙ *RemoveView*

⚙ *RequestFocus As Boolean*

⚙ *SendToBack*

⚙ *SetBackgroundImage (arg0 As Bitmap)*

⚙ *SetLayout (arg0 As Int, arg1 As Int, arg2 As Int, arg3 As Int)*

🔧 *Tag As Object*

🔧 *Top As Int*

🔧 *Visible As Boolean*
Whether the user can see the object.

🔧 *Width As Int*

GPS Library

This library is included in the IDE installation package. The GPS library allows you to get information from the phone's GPS device. There are three types of relevant objects:
– The main one is GPS. The GPS manages the connection and events.
– The second is Location. A Location is a structure that holds the data available regarding a specific "fix". The data includes the latitude and longitude coordinates, the time (expressed as ticks) of this fix and other information like bearing, altitude and so on. It may happen that not all information is available (due to poor reception for example). The Location also includes other functionalities like calculating the distance and bearing to another location and methods to convert the coordinates string formats. Usually you will work with Location objects passed to you in the LocationChanged events. However, you can also initialize such objects yourself (this is useful for calculating distance and bearing between locations).
– The third relevant object is GPSSatellite. This is a structure that holds various information regarding the currently known satellites. It is passed to you in the `GPSStatus` event.
See the GPS tutorial (http://bit.ly/18OcTkc) for more information about this library.

List of types:
GPS
GPSSatellite
Location

GPS
The main object that raises GPS events.
Note that this library requires Android 2.0 or above.

Permissions:
android.permission.ACCESS_FINE_LOCATION

Events:

GpsStatus (Satellites As List)
This event, which returns a list of GPSSatellite objects, is raised once per second, regardless of the **MinimumTime** parameter of the `Start` command.

LocationChanged (Location1 As Location)

This event is generated when the GPS detects that the device has moved. Its frequency depends upon the **MinimumDistance** of the `Start` command.

Location1 – The new location of the device.

NMEA (TimeStamp As Long, Sentence As String)

This event contains **Sentences** (lines of data) in NMEA format (as specified by the National Marine Electronics Association) containing details about the GPS sensor. These events are raised every few seconds.

UserEnabled (Enabled As Boolean)

This event is generated when the user changes the status of the GPS sensor.

Members:

GPSEnabled As Boolean [read only]

Returns TRUE if the user has enabled the GPS.

Initialize (EventName As String)

IsInitialized As Boolean

Whether this object has been initialized by calling `Initialize`.

LocationSettingsIntent As Intent [read only]

Returns the intent that is used to show the global locations settings.
Example:
```
If GPS1.GPSEnabled = False Then
  StartActivity(GPS1.LocationSettingsIntent)
```

Start (MinimumTime As Long, MinimumDistance As Float)

Starts listening for events.

MinimumTime - The shortest period (measured in milliseconds) between events (other than `GpsStatus`). Pass 0 for highest frequency.

MinimumDistance - The shortest change in distance (measured in meters) for which the `LocationChanged` event is raised. Pass 0 for highest frequency.

Stop

Stops listening to the GPS. You will usually want to call Stop inside `Sub Activity_Pause`.

GPSSatellite

The GPSSatellite object holds various information about a GPS satellite. A List with the available satellites is passed to the GpsStatus event.

Members:

Azimuth As Float [read only]

Returns the satellite azimuth in degrees (0 - 360).

Elevation As Float [read only]

Returns the satellite elevation in degrees (0 - 90).

IsInitialized As Boolean

Whether this object has been initialized by calling `Initialize`.

✦ Prn As Int [read only]

Returns the PRN (pseudo-random number) for the satellite.

✦ Snr As Float [read only]

Returns the signal to noise ratio for the satellite.

✦ UsedInFix As Boolean [read only]

Returns TRUE if this satellite was used to calculate the most recent fix.

Location

A Location object holds various information about a specific GPS fix. In most cases, you will work with locations that are passed to the GPS LocationChanged event. The Location object can also be used to calculate distance and bearing to other locations.

Members:

✦ Accuracy As Float

Gets or sets the fix accuracy (meters).

✦ AccuracyValid As Boolean [read only]

Returns True if the fix includes accuracy value.

✦ Altitude As Double

Gets or sets the fix altitude (meters).

✦ AltitudeValid As Boolean [read only]

Returns True if the fix includes altitude value.

✦ Bearing As Float

Gets or sets the bearing of the current location relative to the previous location. The value is given in degrees measured clockwise from true North. Check the value of BearingValid before using this value.

✿ BearingTo (TargetLocation As Location) As Float

Calculates the bearing to **TargetLocation** from the current location, measured clockwise in degrees, starting from North.

✦ BearingValid As Boolean [read only]

Returns True if the location includes bearing value.

✿ ConvertToMinutes (Coordinate As Double) As String

Converts the given **Coordinate** to a string formatted with the following format:
[+-]DDD:MM.MMMMM (Minute = 1 / 60 of a degree)

✿ ConvertToSeconds (Coordinate As Double) As String

Converts the given **Coordinate** to a string formatted with the following format:
[+-]DDD:MM:SS.SSSSS (Minute = 1 / 60 of a degree, Second = 1 / 3600 of a degree)

✿ DistanceTo (TargetLocation As Location) As Float

Returns the distance from the current location to the given **TargetLocation**, measured in meters.

✿ Initialize

Initializes an empty Location object.

⬡ Initialize2 (Latitude As String, Longitude As String)
Initializes the Location object with the given **Latitude** and **Longitude**.
Values can be formatted in any of the three formats:
Degrees: [+-]DDD.DDDDD
Minutes: [+-]DDD:MM.MMMMM (Minute = 1 / 60 of a degree)
Seconds: [+-]DDD:MM:SS.SSSSS (Second = 1 / 3600 of a degree)
Example:
```
Dim L1 As Location
L1.Initialize2("45:30:30", "45:20:15")
```

⬡ IsInitialized As Boolean
Whether this object has been initialized by calling one of the `Initialize` methods.

⚡ Latitude As Double
Gets or sets the fix latitude (degrees from -90 (South Pole) to 90 (North Pole)).

⚡ Longitude As Double
Gets or sets the fix longitude (degrees from -180 to 180, positive values represent the eastern hemisphere).

⚡ Speed As Float
Gets or sets the fix speed (meters / second).

⚡ SpeedValid As Boolean [read only]
Returns `True` if the fix includes speed value.

⚡ Time As Long
Gets or sets the time of the GPS fix, given in ticks (page 350).

HTTP Library

This library is included in the IDE installation package. It allows you to communicate with web services and to download resources from the web. Because network communication can be slow and fragile, this library handles the requests and responses in the background and raises events when a task is ready.
Note that HttpUtils2 (page 487) extends the functionality of this library and make it easier to access web services.

List of types:
HttpClient
HttpRequest
HttpResponse

HttpClient
HttpClient allows you to make HTTP requests. Instead of using HttpClient directly, it is recommended to use HttpUtil2 (http://bit.ly/19SbQnA) modules which are much simpler to use.

Permissions:
android.permission.INTERNET

Events:

ResponseSuccess (Response As HttpResponse, TaskId As Int)

ResponseError (Response As HttpResponse, Reason As String, StatusCode As Int, TaskId As Int)

Members:

Execute (HttpRequest As HttpRequest, TaskId As Int) As Boolean

Executes the HttpRequest asynchronously. `ResponseSuccess` or `ResponseError` events will be fired later. Note that in many cases the Response object passed in the `ResponseError` event will be `Null`. If there is a request with the same **TaskId** already running, then this method will return `False` and the new request will not be submitted.

ExecuteCredentials (HttpRequest As HttpRequest, TaskId As Int, UserName As String, Password As String) As Boolean

Same behavior as **Execute**. The **UserName** and **Password** will be used for Basic or Digest authentication. Digest authentication is only supported for GET requests.

Initialize (EventName As String)

Initializes this object. **IMPORTANT**: this object should be declared in `Sub Process_Globals`.

EventName - The prefix that will be used for ResponseSuccess and ResponseError events.

InitializeAcceptAll (EventName As String)

Similar to Initialize, with one important difference. All SSL certificates will be automatically accepted.

This method should only be used when trying to connect to a server located in a secured network.

IsInitialized As Boolean

Whether this object has been initialized by calling `Initialize`.

SetHttpParameter (Name As String, Value As Object)

Sets the value of the parameter with the given name.

SetProxy (Host As String, Port As Int, Scheme As String)

Sets the proxy to use for the connections.

Host - Proxy host name or IP.

Port - Proxy port.

Scheme - Scheme name. Usually "http".

SetProxy2 (Host As String, Port As Int, Scheme As String, Username As String, Password As String)

Sets the proxy to use for the connections, with the required credentials.

HttpRequest

Holds the target URL and other data sent to the web server.

The initial time-out is to 30000 milliseconds (30 seconds).

Members:

🔹InitializeDelete (Url As String)
Initializes the request and sets it to be an HTTP Delete method.

🔹InitializeGet (Url As String)
Initializes the request and sets it to be an HTTP Get method.

🔹InitializeHead (Url As String)
Initializes the request and sets it to be an HTTP Head method.

🔹InitializePost (Url As String, InputStream As java.io.InputStream, Length As Int)
Initializes the request and sets it to be an HTTP Post method. The specified **InputStream** will be read and added to the request.

🔹InitializePost2 (Url As String, Data() As Byte)
Initializes the request and sets it to be an HTTP Post method. The specified **Data** array will be added to the request. Unlike `InitializePost`, this method will enable the request to retry and send the data several times in case of IO errors.

🔹InitializePut (Url As String, InputStream As java.io.InputStream, Length As Int)
Initializes the request and sets it to be an HTTP Put method. The specified **InputStream** will be read and added to the request.

🔹InitializePut2 (Url As String, Data() As Byte)
Initializes the request and sets it to be an HTTP Put method. The specified **Data** array will be added to the request.

🔹RemoveHeaders (Name As String)
Removes all headers with the given name.

🔹SetContentEncoding (Encoding As String)
Sets the encoding header of the request.
This method should only be used with Post or Put requests.

🔹SetContentType (ContentType As String)
Sets the Mime header of the request. This method should only be used with Post or Put requests.

🔹SetHeader (Name As String, Value As String)
Sets the value of the first header with the given name. If no such header exists, then a new header will be added.

🔥Timeout As Int [write only]
Sets the request timeout (measured in milliseconds).

HttpResponse
An object that holds the response returned from the server. The object is passed in the ResponseSuccess event. You can choose to read the response synchronously or

asynchronously. **It is important** to release this object when it is not used anymore by calling `Release`.

Events:
StreamFinish (Success As Boolean, TaskId As Int)

Members:

☞ *ContentEncoding As String [read only]*
Returns the content encoding header.

☞ *ContentLength As Long [read only]*
Returns the content length header.

☞ *ContentType As String [read only]*
Returns the content type header.

✪ *GetAsynchronously (EventName As String, Output As java.io.OutputStream, CloseOutput As Boolean, TaskId As Int) As Boolean*
Asynchronously reads the response and writes it to the given **OutputStream**. If there is a request with the same **TaskId** already running, then this method will return **False**, and the response object will be released. The **StreamFinish** event will be raised after the response has been fully read.

EventName - The sub that will handle the StreamFinish event.
Output - The stream from the server will be written to this stream.
CloseOutput - Whether to close the specified output stream when done.
TaskId - The task id given to this task.
Example:
```
Sub Http_ResponseSuccess (Response As HttpResponse, TaskId As Int)
  Response.GetAsynchronously("ImageResponse", _
     File.OpenOutput(File.DirInternalCache, "image.jpg", False), True, _
TaskId)
End Sub
Sub ImageResponse_StreamFinish (Success As Boolean, TaskId As Int)
  If Success = False Then
     Msgbox(LastException.Message, "Error")
     Return
  End If
  ImageView1.Bitmap = LoadBitmap(File.DirInternalCache, "image.jpg")
End Sub
```

✪ *GetHeaders As Map*
Returns a Map object with the response headers. Each element is made of a key which is the header name and a value which is a list containing the values (one or more). Example:
```
Dim list1 As List
list1 = response.GetHeaders.Get("Set-Cookie")
For i = 0 To list1.Size - 1
  Log(list1.Get(i))
Next
```

✪ *GetInputStream As InputStreamWrapper*
This method is deprecated and will not work properly on Android 4+ device.

Use GetAsynchronously instead.

⊕ *GetString (DefaultCharset As String) As String*
This method is deprecated and will not work properly on Android 4+ device.
Use GetAsynchronously instead.

⊕ *Release*
Frees resources allocated for this object.

⚐ *StatusCode As Int [read only]*
Returns the response HTTP code.

HttpUtils2 Library

This library is included in the IDE installation package.
It allows you to use POST and GET to retrieve data from a web server, and then handle the data when it eventually arrives. Example of usage:

```
Sub Activity_Create(FirstTime As Boolean)
    Dim job1, job2, job3 As HttpJob
    job1.Initialize("Job1", Me)

    'Send a GET request
    job1.Download2("http://www.basic4ppc.com/print.php", _
         Array As String("first key", "first value :)", "second
key", "value 2"))

    'Send a POST request
    job2.Initialize("Job2", Me)
    job2.PostString("http://www.basic4ppc.com/print.php", "first
key=first value&key2=value2")

    'Send a GET request
    job3.Initialize("Job3", Me)
    job3.Download("http://www.basic4ppc.com/forum/images/categories/a
ndroid.png")
End Sub

Sub JobDone (Job As HttpJob)
    Log("JobName = " & Job.JobName & ", Success = " & Job.Success)
    If Job.Success = True Then
        Select Job.JobName
            Case "Job1", "Job2"
                'print the result to the logs
                Log(Job.GetString)
            Case "Job3"
                'show the downloaded image
                Activity.SetBackgroundImage(Job.GetBitmap)
        End Select
    Else
        Log("Error: " & Job.ErrorMessage)
        ToastMessageShow("Error: " & Job.ErrorMessage, True)
    End If
    Job.Release
End Sub
```

HttpJob

Events:

None

Members:

Class_Globals As String

Class module

Complete (id As Int) As String

Called by the service when job completes

🔷 Download (Link As String) As String

Submits a HTTP GET request.
Consider using Download2 if the parameters should be escaped.

🔷 Download2 (Link As String, Parameters() As String) As String

Submits a HTTP GET request.
Encodes illegal parameter characters.
Example:
job.Download2("http://www.example.com", _
 Array As String("key1", "value1", "key2", "value2"))

🔶 ErrorMessage As String

🔷 GetBitmap As BitmapWrapper

Returns the response as a bitmap

🔷 GetInputStream As InputStreamWrapper

🔷 GetRequest As HttpUriRequestWrapper

Called by the service to get the request

🔷 GetString As String

Returns the response as a string encoded with UTF8.

🔷 GetString2 (Encoding As String) As String

Returns the response as a string.

🔷 Initialize (Name As String, TargetModule As Object) As String

Initializes the Job.
Name - The job's name. Note that the name doesn't need to be unique.
TargetModule - The activity or service that will handle the JobDone event.

🔷 IsInitialized As Boolean

Tests whether the object has been initialized.

🔶 JobName As String

🔶 Password As String

🔷 PostBytes (Link As String, Data() As Byte) As String

Sends a POST request with the given string as the post data

🔷 PostFile (Link As String, Dir As String, FileName As String) As String

Sends a POST request with the given file as the post data.
This method doesn't work with assets files.

🔷 PostString (Link As String, Text As String) As String

Sends a POST request with the given data as the post data.

🔷 Release As String

Should be called to free resources held by this job.

⬢ *Success As Boolean*

⬢ *Tag As Object*

⬢ *Username As String*

IME Library

Android has very good support for custom input method editors (IMEs). The downside for this powerful feature is that interacting with the soft keyboard can be sometimes quite complicated. This library, which is included in the IDE installation package, includes several utilities that will help you better handle the soft keyboard. A tutorial with a working example is available here (http://bit.ly/14hx2OB).

Example
```
Sub Globals
  Dim IME1 As IME
End Sub

Sub Activity_Create(FirstTime As Boolean)
  IME1.Initialize("IME")
End Sub
```

List of types:
IME

IME
This is an `Activity` object; it cannot be declared under `Sub Process_Globals`.

Events:

HeightChanged (NewHeight As Int, OldHeight As Int)
This event is raised when the height of the keyboard changes.

HandleAction As Boolean
This event is raised by the EditText which is specified by the member AddHandleActionEvent when the user clicks the action button (the button that shows Next or Done) on the keyboard. For an example, see below. The return value specifies whether to keep the keyboard visible. Returning `True` will keep it visible, returning `False` will close the keyboard.

Members:

⬢ AddHandleActionEvent (EditText1 As EditText)
Adds the HandleAction event to the given EditText. Example:
```
Sub Activity_Create(FirstTime As Boolean)
  IME1.Initialize("IME1")
  IME1.AddHandleActionEvent(edtTextToSpeak)
End Sub
```

```
Sub IME1_HandleAction As Boolean
 Dim edtTxt As EditText
 edtTxt = Sender
 If edtTxt.Text.StartsWith("a") = False Then
  ToastMessageShow("Text must start with 'a'", True)
  'Consume the event.
  'The keyboard will not be closed
  Return True
 Else
  Return False 'will close the keyboard
 End If
End Sub
```

♦ AddHeightChangedEvent

Enables the HeightChanged event. This event is raised when the soft keyboard state changes. You can use this event to resize other views to fit the new screen size.
Note that this event will not be raised in full screen activities (an Android limitation).

♦ HideKeyboard

Hides the soft keyboard if it is visible.

♦ Initialize (EventName As String)

Initializes the object and sets the subs that will handle the events.

♦ SetCustomFilter (EditText1 As EditText, DefaultInputType As Int, AcceptedCharacters As String)

Sets a custom filter.
EditText - The target EditText.
DefaultInputType - Sets the keyboard mode.
AcceptedCharacters - The accepted characters.
Example: Create a filter that will accept IP addresses (numbers with multiple dots)
```
IME.SetCustomFilter(EditText1, EditText1.INPUT_TYPE_NUMBERS,
"0123456789.")
```

♦ ShowKeyboard (View1 As View)

Sets the focus to the given view and opens the soft keyboard.
The keyboard will only show if the view has received the focus.

JavaObject Library

This library is included in the IDE installation package.
The JavaObject library is similar to the Reflection library (page 581) in that it allows you to call Java APIs based on reflection features, but in most cases JavaObject is simpler to use. However, JavaObject does not replace the Reflection library as it does not support all of the same features. Note that you can use both libraries together. Both are lightweight libraries. See here (http://bit.ly/18xHPub) for more details.
JavaObject is also needed when using Inline code (page 450).

JavaObject

Events:

Event (MethodName As String, Args() As Object) As Object.
See member **CreateEvent** for an example.

Members:

◈ *CreateEvent (Interface As String, EventName As String, DefaultReturnValue As Object) As Object*

Creates an instance of the interface and binds it to the object.

Interface - The full interface name. You can find these within the Android Developer website, for example here (http://bit.ly/1IIPMHD).

EventName - The prefix of the event sub.

DefaultReturnValue - This value will be returned if no value was returned from the event sub. This can happen if the Activity is paused for example.

For example:

```
Sub Activity_Create(FirstTime As Boolean)
 Dim b As Button
 b.Initialize("")
 Activity.AddView(b, 0, 0, 200dip, 200dip)
 Dim jo As JavaObject = b
 Dim e As Object = jo.CreateEvent("android.view.View.OnTouchListener",
"btouch", False)
 jo.RunMethod("setOnTouchListener", Array As Object(e))
End Sub

Sub btouch_Event (MethodName As String, Args() As Object) As Object
 Dim motion As JavaObject = Args(1) 'args(0) is View
 Dim x As Float = motion.RunMethod("getX", Null)
 Dim y As Float = motion.RunMethod("getY", Null)
 Log(x & ", " & y)
 Return True
End Sub
```

◈ *CreateEventFromUI (Interface As String, EventName As String, ReturnValue As Object) As Object*

Similar to CreateEvent. The event will be sent to the message queue and then be processed (similar to CallSubDelayed).

◈ *GetField (Field As String) As Object*

Gets the value of the given field.

◈ *GetFieldJO (Field As String) As JavaObject*

Similar to GetField. Returns a JavaObject instead of Object.

◈ *InitializeArray (ClassName As String, Values() As Object) As JavaObject*

Creates an array with the given class and values.

◈ *InitializeContext As JavaObject*

B4A only method.

Initializes the object with the current context (current Activity or Service).

✪ *InitializeNewInstance (ClassName As String, Params() As Object) As JavaObject*

Creates a new instance of the given class.
ClassName - The full class name.
Params - An array of objects to pass to the constructor (or Null).

✪ *InitializeStatic (ClassName As String) As JavaObject*

Initializes the object. The object will wrap the given class (for static access).
ClassName - The full class name.

✪ *IsInitialized As Boolean*

✪ *RunMethod (MethodName As String, Params() As Object) As Object*

Runs the given method and returns the method return value.
MethodName - The case-sensitive method name.
Params - Method paramters (or Null).

✪ *RunMethodJO (MethodName As String, Params() As Object) As JavaObject*

Similar to RunMethod. Returns a JavaObject instead of Object.

✪ *SetField (FieldName As String, Value As Object)*

Sets the value of the given field.

JSON Library

This library is included in the IDE installation package.

About JSON

JSON (JavaScript Object Notation) is a lightweight data-interchange alternative to XML intended to be easy for both humans and computers to generate and parse. See here (http://www.json.org/) and here (http://bit.ly/1DyrmyK) for descriptions of JSON.
JSON might represent a person as:

```
{
  "firstName": "John",
  "lastName": "Smith",
  "address": {
    "streetAddress": "21 2nd Street",
    "city": "New York",
    "state": "NY",
    "postalCode": "10021-3100"
  }
}
```

JSON is built on two structures:
- A collection of name/value pairs such as `"firstName": "John"`. These pairs could be stored in an object or a map.
- An ordered list of values such as those in an array or list.

JsonTree (http://bit.ly/1Dysh2f) is a B4A tool to help you when working with JSON.
See also the ExecuteJSON (page 221) method in the DBUtils library for a method of
generating a map from an SQLite database which you can pass to JSONGenerator to create
JSON text.

List of types:
JSONGenerator
JSONParser

JSONGenerator
This object generates JSON strings. It can be initialized with a Map, an Array or a List. They
can contain other Maps, Arrays or Lists. See the B4A JSON tutorial (http://bit.ly/18clue0).

Members:

⊕ *Initialize (Map As Map)*
Initializes the object with the given Map.

⊕ *Initialize2 (List As List)*
Initializes the object with the given List or Array.

⊕ *ToPrettyString (Indent As Int) As String*
Creates a JSON string from the initialized object. The string will be indented and easier for
reading. **Note** that the string created is a valid JSON string.
Indent - Number of spaces to add to each level.

⊕ *ToString As String*
Creates a JSON string from the initialized object. This string does not include any extra
whitespace.

JSONParser
Parses JSON formatted strings. JSON objects are converted to Maps and JSON arrays are
converted to Lists. After initializing the object, you will usually call NextObject to get a
single Map object. If the JSON string top level value is an array, you should call NextArray.
Afterward, you should work with the Map or List and fetch the required data. See the JSON
tutorial (http://bit.ly/18clue0) for more information. Typical code:
```
Dim JSON As JSONParser
Dim Map1 As Map
JSON.Initialize(File.ReadString(File.DirAssets, "example.json")) 'Read
the text from a file.
Map1 = JSON.NextObject
```

Members:

⊕ *Initialize (Text As String)*
Initializes the object and sets the text that will be parsed.

⊕ *IsInitialized As Boolean*
Whether this object has been initialized by calling `Initialize`.

⊕ *NextArray As List*
Parses the text assuming that the top level value is an array.

🔹 NextObject As Map

Parses the text assuming that the top level value is an object.

🔹 NextValue As Object

Parses the text assuming that the top level value is a simple value.

LiveWallpaper Library

This library is included in the IDE installation package.

List of types:

LWEngine
LWManager

LWEngine

Represents a wallpaper instance.
A tutorial is available here (http://bit.ly/1Owi7pk).

Members:

🔥 Canvas As CanvasWrapper [read only]

Returns the canvas which is used to draw on the wallpaper.
Changes will not be visible till you call Refresh or RefreshAll.

🔥 CurrentOffsetX As Int [read only]

Returns the current horizontal offset related to the full wallpaper width.

🔥 CurrentOffsetY As Int [read only]

Returns the current vertical offset related to the full wallpaper height.

🔥 FullWallpaperHeight As Int [read only]

Returns the full wallpaper height.

🔥 FullWallpaperWidth As Int [read only]

Returns the full wallpaper width. A wallpaper can be made of several screens.

🔹 IsInitialized As Boolean

Returns TRUE if this object is initialized.

🔥 IsPreview As Boolean [read only]

Returns TRUE if this wallpaper is running in "preview mode".

🔥 IsVisible As Boolean [read only]

Returns TRUE if this wallpaper is visible.

🔸 Rect As RectWrapper

A convenient Rect object which you can use. This object is not used internally.

🔹 Refresh (DirtyRect As Rect)

Refreshes the given region.

🔹 RefreshAll

Refreshes the complete screen.

🏷 *ScreenHeight As Int [read only]*
Returns the screen height.

🏷 *ScreenWidth As Int [read only]*
Returns the screen width.

⬛ *Tag As Object*
Gets or sets the Tag value. This is a place holder which can be used to store additional data.

LWManager
Manages the wallpaper events and the timer. A tutorial is available here
(http://bit.ly/17dre8v).

Events:

SizeChanged (Engine As LWEngine)

Touch (Engine As LWEngine, Action As Int, X As Float, Y As Float)

VisibilityChanged (Engine As LWEngine, Visible As Boolean)

EngineDestroyed (Engine As LWEngine)

Tick (Engine As LWEngine)

OffsetChanged (Engine As LWEngine)

Members:

⬡ *Initialize (EventName As String, TouchEventsEnabled As Boolean)*
Initializes the object.
EventName - Sets the Subs that will handle the events.
TouchEventsEnabled - Whether the wallpaper should raise the Touch event when the user
touches the screen.

⬡ *StartTicking (IntervalMs As Int)*
Starts the internal timer.
IntervalMs - Interval (in milliseconds).

⬡ *StopTicking*
Stops the internal timer.

Network Library

This library, which is included in the IDE installation package, includes two objects for
working with TCP (`Socket` and `ServerSocket`) and two objects for working with UDP
(`UDPSocket` and `UDPPacket`).
Using a `Socket`, you can communicate with other devices and computers over TCP/IP.
`ServerSocket` allows you to listen for incoming connections. Once a connection is
established, you will receive a `Socket` object that will be used for handling this specific
connection. See the Network tutorial (http://bit.ly/17c4yY7) for more information.
A `UDPSocket` supports sending and receiving `UDPPackets`.

List of types:
ServerSocket

Socket
UDPPacket
UDPSocket

ServerSocket

The ServerSocket object allows other machines to connect to this machine.

The ServerSocket listens to a specific port. Once a connection arrives, the NewConnection event is raised with a Socket object. This Socket object should be used to communicate with this client. You may call Listen again and receive more connections. A single ServerSocket can handle many connections. For each connection, there should be one Socket object.

Permissions:

android.permission.INTERNET
android.permission.ACCESS_WIFI_STATE

Event: NewConnection (Successful As Boolean, NewSocket As Socket)

Members:

Close

Closes the ServerSocket. This will not close any other sockets.
You should call Initialize if you want to use this object again.

GetMyIP As String

Returns the server's IP. Will return "127.0.0.1" (localhost) if no other IP is found. This method will return the wifi network IP if it is available.

GetMyWifiIP As String

Returns the IP address of the wifi network. Returns "127.0.0.1" (localhost) if not connected.

Initialize (Port As Int, EventName As String)

Initializes the ServerSocket.
Port - The port that the server will listen to. Note that you should call Listen to start listening. Port numbers lower than 1024 are restricted by the system.
EventName - The event Sub prefix name.

IsInitialized As Boolean

Returns TRUE if the object is initialized.

Listen

Starts listening in the background for incoming connections. When a connection is established, the `NewConnection` event is raised. If the connection is successful, a Socket object will be passed in the event. Calling `Listen` while the ServerSocket is listening will not do anything.

Socket

The Socket object is an endpoint for network communication. If you are connecting to a server, then you should initialize a Socket object and call `Connect` with the server address. The `Connected` event will be raised when the connection is ready or if the connection has failed.

Sockets are also used by the server. Once a new incoming connection is established, the `NewConnection` event will be raised and an initialized Socket object will be passed as a parameter.

Once a socket is connected, you should use its `InputStream` and `OutputStream` to communicate with the other machine.

Permissions:
android.permission.INTERNET

Event: Connected (Successful As Boolean)

Members:

🔧 Close
Closes the socket and the streams. It is safe to call this method multiple times.

🔧 Connect (Host As String, Port As Int, TimeOut As Int)
Tries to connect to the given address. The connection is done in the background. The Connected event will be raised when the connection is ready or if it has failed.
Host - The host name or IP.
Port - Port number.
TimeOut - Connection timeout. Value is specified in milliseconds. Pass 0 to disable the timeout.

🔧 Connected As Boolean [read only]
Returns TRUE if the socket is connected.

🔧 Initialize (EventName As String)
Initializes a new socket.

🔧 InputStream As java.io.InputStream [read only]
Returns the socket's InputStream which is used to read data.

🔧 IsInitialized As Boolean
Returns TRUE if the object was initialized.

🔧 OutputStream As java.io.OutputStream [read only]
Returns the socket's OutputStream which is used to write data.

🔧 ResolveHost (Host As String) As String
Resolves the host name and returns the IP address.
This method is deprecated and will not work properly on Android 4+ devices.

🔧 TimeOut As Int
Gets or sets the timeout of the socket's InputStream. Value is specified in milliseconds. By default there is no timeout.

UDPPacket
A packet of data that is being sent or received. To send a packet, call one of the Initialize methods and then send the packet by passing it to `UDPSocket.Send`. When a packet arrives, you can get the data in the packet from the available properties.

Members:

⚡ Data() As Byte [read only]
Gets the data array received.

⚡ Host As String [read only]
This method is deprecated and will not work properly on Android 4+ device.
Use HostAddress instead.

⚡ HostAddress As String [read only]
Gets the IP address of the sending machine.

🔷 Initialize (Data() As Byte, Host As String, Port As Int)
Initializes the packet and makes it ready for sending.
Data - The data that will be sent.
Host - The target host name or IP address.
Port - The target port.

🔷 Initialize2 (Data() As Byte, Offset As Int, Length As Int, Host As String, Port As Int)
Similar to Initialize. The data sent is based on the Offset and Length values.

🔷 IsInitialized As Boolean
Whether this object has been initialized by calling one of the `Initialize` methods.

⚡ Length As Int [read only]
Gets the length of available bytes in the data. This can be shorter than the array length.

⚡ Offset As Int [read only]
Gets the offset in the data array where the available data starts.

⚡ Port As Int [read only]
Gets the port of the sending machine.

🔷 toString As String

UDPSocket

UDPSocket supports sending and receiving UDPPackets. Sending packets is done by calling the `Send` method. When a packet arrives, the `PacketArrived` event is raised with the packet.
This example sends a string message to some other machine. When a packet arrives, it converts it to string and shows it:

```
Sub Process_Globals
  Dim UDPSocket1 As UDPSocket
End Sub
Sub Globals
End Sub
Sub Activity_Create(FirstTime As Boolean)
  If FirstTime Then
    UDPSocket1.Initialize("UDP", 0, 8000)
  End If
  Dim Packet As UDPPacket
```

```
    Dim data() As Byte
    data = "Hello from Android".GetBytes("UTF8")
    Packet.Initialize(data, "10.0.0.1", 5000)
    UDPSocket1.Send(Packet)
End Sub
Sub UDP_PacketArrived (Packet As UDPPacket)
    Dim msg As String
    msg = BytesToString(Packet.Data, Packet.Offset, Packet.Length,
"UTF8")
    Msgbox("Message received: " & msg, "")
End Sub
```

Permission: android.permission.INTERNET

Event: PacketArrived (Packet As UDPPacket)

Members:

Close
Closes the socket.

Initialize (EventName As String, Port As Int, ReceiveBufferSize As Int)
Initializes the socket and starts listening for packets.
EventName - The name of the Sub that will handle the events.
Port - Local port to listen on. Passing 0 will cause Android to choose an available port automatically.
ReceiveBufferSize - The size of the receiving packet. Packets larger than this value will be truncated. Pass 0 if you do not want to receive any packets.

IsInitialized As Boolean
Returns TRUE if this object is initialized.

Port As Int [read only]
Gets the local port that this socket listens to.

Send (Packet As UDPPacket)
Sends a Packet. The packet will be sent in the background (asynchronously).

toString As String

NotificationListener Library

This library is included in the IDE installation package.
NotificationListener allows you to access the device notifications.
This is only supported by Android 4.3+ (api 18+).
You need to add a Service module named NotificationService (the name must be exact) and add the following code to the manifest editor:

```
AddApplicationText(
<service
 android:name =
  "anywheresoftware.b4a.objects.NotificationListenerWrapper"
 android:label = "Notification Listener"
 android:permission =
  "android.permission.BIND_NOTIFICATION_LISTENER_SERVICE"
>
  <intent-filter>
   <action
    android:name =
     "android.service.notification.NotificationListenerService"
   />
  </intent-filter>
</service>)
```

You can change the value of android:label

For full details of how to use this library see this tutorial (http://bit.ly/1g5aMkZ).

Events:

NotificationPosted (SBN As StatusBarNotification)
NotificationRemoved (SBN As StatusBarNotification)

Members:

ClearAll

Clears all non-ongoing notifications.

ClearNotification (SBN As StatusBarNotification)

Clears the given notification (if it is not an ongoing notification).

GetActiveNotifications

Causes the listener to repost all the active notifications.

HandleIntent (StartingIntent As IntentWrapper) As Boolean

Handles the intent with the notifications information.
Returns true if the intent was handled.

Initialize (EventName As String)

Initializes the object and sets the subs that will handle the events.

StatusBarNotification

Events:

None

Members:

Id As Int [read only]

Returns the notification id.

IsInitialized As Boolean

Notification As NotificationWrapper [read only]

Returns the internal notification object.

🔧 *PackageName As String [read only]*
Returns the notification package name.

🔧 *TickerText As String [read only]*
Returns the notification ticker text field.

NFC Library

About NFC
Near field communication (NFC) is the set of protocols that enables smartphones and other devices to talk to each other by bringing them closer than about 10 cm (3.9 in). See here (http://bit.ly/1DyxZ4a) more about NFC.

The NFC library, which is included in the IDE installation package, requires Android version 2.3.3 or above (API level 10 or above). It lets you read NFC tags formatted in NDEF form (NFC Data Exchange Format). You can find more about the internal process here (http://bit.ly/1Owid05).

List of types:
NdefRecord
NFC

NdefRecord
Members:

🔹*GetAsTextType As String*
Reads the payload and returns the stored text.

🔹*GetAsUriType As String*
Reads the payload and returns the stored URI ("Uniform Resource Identifier" identifying the resource to get).

🔹*GetPayload As Byte()*
Returns the whole payload.

🔹*IsInitialized As Boolean*
Whether this object has been initialized.

NFC
Supports reading NDEF (NFC Data Exchange Format) tags.
See this (http://bit.ly/1Owii3Q) tutorial for more information.

Permissions:
android.permission.NFC

Members:

🔹*GetNdefRecords (Intent1 As Intent) As List*
Retrieves the NdefRecords stored in the Intent object.

🔹*IsNdefIntent (Intent1 As Intent) As Boolean*
Returns TRUE if the Intent contains data read from an NDef tag.

Phone Library

The Phone library gives you access to many features of an Android device. It contains the following objects:

CallLog and **CallItem** give access to the phone calls log.

Contacts2 (page 507) (or the legacy **Contacts (page 506)**) give access to the stored contacts, retrieved as a **Contact**.

ContentChooser (page 508) allows the user to choose content from other applications. For example, the user can choose an image from the Gallery application.

Email (page 509) helps with building an Intent that sends an email.

LogCat (page 510) tracks the internal phone logs.

PackageManager (page 510) allows you to retrieve information about the installed applications.

Phone (page 511) object includes information about the device and also other general features.

PhoneAccelerometer (page 514) and **PhoneOrientation (page 518)** objects are legacy objects, now replaced with **PhoneSensors (page 518)**.

PhoneEvents (page 515) allows you to handle all kinds of system events.

PhoneId (page 517) gives access to the the specific phone values.

PhoneIntents (page 517) and **PhoneCalls (page 514)** include several useful intents.

PhoneSensors (page 518) support many sensors such as accelerometer and orientation.

PhoneSms (page 521) supports sending Sms messages.

PhoneVibrate (page 522) vibrates the phone.

PhoneWakeState (page 522) allows you to force the screen and power to remain switched on.

RingtoneManager (page 523) allows you to control the ringtone.

SmsInterceptor (page 526) intercepts incoming Sms messages.

SmsMessages (page 527) together with **Sms (page 525)** support fetching messages from the phone database.

VoiceRecognition (page 528) converts speech to text.

See also the user-generated Toggle Library (page 589) which contains many useful routines for controlling the device's features.

CallItem

Represents a single call in the call logs. See CallLog for more information.

Members:

⬡ *CachedName As String*

Returns the cached name assigned to this call number at the time of call.
Returns an empty string if no name was assigned.

⬡ *CallType As Int*

The call type. This value matches one of the TYPE constants.

🔶 *Date As Long*
The call date measured as ticks.

🔶 *Duration As Long*
The call duration in seconds.

🔶 *Id As Int*
The call internal id.

🔶 *Number As String*
The call phone number.

🔶 *TYPE_INCOMING As Int*
CallType for incoming calls.

🔶 *TYPE_MISSED As Int*
CallType for missed calls.

🔶 *TYPE_OUTGOING As Int*
CallType for calls made from this device.

CallLog

CallLog allows you to browse the call logs.
Retrieved calls are always ordered by descending date.
Usage example:

```
Dim Calls As List
Dim CallLog1 As CallLog
Calls = CallLog1.GetAll(10) 'Get the last 10 calls
For i = 0 To Calls.Size - 1
  Dim c As CallItem
  c = Calls.Get(i)
  Dim callType, name As String
  Select c.CallType
     Case c.TYPE_INCOMING
         callType="Incoming"
     Case c.TYPE_MISSED
         callType = "Missed"
     Case c.TYPE_OUTGOING
         callType = "Outgoing"
  End Select
  name = c.CachedName
  If name = "" Then name = "N/A"
  Log("Number=" & c.Number & ", Name=" & name _
     & ", Type=" & callType & ", Date=" & DateTime.Date(c.Date))
Next
```

Permissions:
android.permission.READ_CONTACTS

Members:

🔷 *GetAll (Limit As Int) As List*
Returns all calls, ordered by date (descending), as a List of CallItems.

Limit - Maximum number of `CallItems` to return. Pass 0 to return all items.

⬡ *GetById (Id As Int) As CallItem*

Returns the `CallItem` with the specified **Id**.

Returns `Null` if no matching `CallItem` found.

⬡ *GetSince (Date As Long, Limit As Int) As List*

Returns all `CallItems` with a date value on or after the specified **Date**.

Limit - Maximum number of items to return. Pass 0 to return all items.

Example:
```
Dim cl As CallLog
Dim logList As List
Dim startDate As Long
startDate = DateTime.DateParse("01/16/2013")
logList.Initialize2(cl.GetSince(startDate,0))
For Each call As CallItem In logList
 Log(DateTime.Date(call.Date))
Next
```

Contact

Represents a single contact. The Contacts or Contacts2 objects should be used to get lists of Contact objects.

The available email types are identified by constants named EMAIL_x.

The available phone types are identified by constants named PHONE_x.

Members:

⬡ *DisplayName As String*

The displayed name. Equal to the Contact Name if the Name is not empty; otherwise equal to the contact's first email address.

⬡ *EMAIL_CUSTOM As Int*

⬡ *EMAIL_HOME As Int*

⬡ *EMAIL_MOBILE As Int*

⬡ *EMAIL_OTHER As Int*

⬡ *EMAIL_WORK As Int*

⬡ *GetEmails As Map*

Returns a Map with the email addresses of the Contact as keys and the email types as values. This will send a query to the device's contacts service, so it might be slow.

⬡ *GetPhones As Map*

Returns a Map with all the contact's phone numbers as keys and the phone types as values. This will send a query to the device's contacts service, so it might be slow.

⬡ *GetPhoto As BitmapWrapper*

Returns the contact photo or Null if there is no attached photo. This will send a query to the device's contacts service, so it might be slow.

⬡ *Id As Int*
Internal Id.

⬡ *LastTimeContacted As Long*
Last time that this contact was contacted. Value is given in ticks (page 350).

⬡ *Name As String*
Contact name.

⬡ *Notes As String*

⬡ *PHONE_CUSTOM As Int*

⬡ *PHONE_FAX_HOME As Int*

⬡ *PHONE_FAX_WORK As Int*

⬡ *PHONE_HOME As Int*

⬡ *PHONE_MOBILE As Int*

⬡ *PHONE_OTHER As Int*

⬡ *PHONE_PAGER As Int*

⬡ *PHONE_WORK As Int*

⬡ *PhoneNumber As String*
Primary phone number.

⬡ *Starred As Boolean*
Whether this contact is a "favorite" contact.

⬡ *TimesContacted As Int*
Number of times that this contact was contacted.

Contacts
This is a legacy object and has been replaced by Contacts2. For new projects, it might be better to consider using the ContactsUtils (http://bit.ly/180A35y) module with the ContentResolver Library (http://bit.ly/1djfesb) instead of Contacts or Contacts2.
The Contacts object allows you to access contacts stored on the device.

Permissions:
android.permission.READ_CONTACTS

Members:

⬡ *FindByMail (Email As String, Exact As Boolean) As List*
Returns a List of Contact objects with all contacts matching the given email.
Email - The email to search for.
Exact - If True, then only contacts with the exact **Email** address (case sensitive) will be returned, otherwise all contacts' email addresses that include the **Email** string (case insensitive) will be returned.

⬡ *FindByName (Name As String, Exact As Boolean) As List*
Returns a List of Contact objects with all contacts matching the given name.

Name - The name to search for.

Exact - If `True`, then only contacts with the exact **Name** value (case sensitive) will be returned, otherwise all contacts' names that include the **Name** string (case insensitive) will be returned.

GetAll As List

Returns a List of Contact objects with all the contacts. This list can be very large.

GetById (Id As Int) As Contact

Returns the Contact with the specified Id. Returns `Null` if no matching contact found.

Contacts2

The Contacts2 object allows you to access contacts stored on the device. **This type is based on a new API supported by Android 2.0 and above and supersedes the legacy Contacts type.** For new projects, it might be better to consider using the ContactsUtils (http://bit.ly/180A35y) module with the ContentResolver Library (http://bit.ly/1djfesb) instead of Contacts2.

The following example finds all contacts whose name contains the string "john", and print their fields to the Log. It will also fetch the contact photo and other details, if they exist:

```
Dim allContacts As Contacts2
Dim listOfContacts As List
listOfContacts = allContacts.FindByName("John", False, True, True)
For i = 0 To listOfContacts.Size - 1
  Dim Contact1 As Contact
  Contact1 = listOfContacts.Get(i)
  Log(Contact1) 'will print the fields to the LogCat
  Dim photo As Bitmap
  photo = Contact1.GetPhoto
  If photo <> Null Then Activity.SetBackgroundImage(photo)
  Dim emails As Map
  emails = Contact1.GetEmails
  If emails.Size > 0 Then Log("Email addresses: " & emails)
  Dim phones As Map
  phones = Contact1.GetPhones
  If phones.Size > 0 Then Log("Phone numbers: " & phones)
Next
```

Permissions:

android.permission.READ_CONTACTS

Events:

Complete (ListOfContacts As List)

Members:

FindByMail (Email As String, Exact As Boolean, IncludePhoneNumber As Boolean, IncludeNotes As Boolean) As List

Returns a List of Contact objects with all contacts matching the given **Email**.

Email - The email to search for.

Exact - If `True`, then only contacts with the exact **Email** address (case sensitive) will be returned, otherwise all contacts' email addresses that include the **Email** string (case insensitive) will be returned.

IncludePhoneNumber - Whether to fetch the default phone number.
IncludeNotes - Whether to fetch the notes field.

⬡ *FindByName (Name As String, Exact As Boolean, IncludePhoneNumber As Boolean, IncludeNotes As Boolean) As List*

Returns a List of Contact objects with all contacts matching the given name.
Name - The name to search for.
Exact - If `True`, then only contacts with the exact **Name** value (case sensitive) will be returned, otherwise all contacts' names that include the **Name** string (case insensitive) will be returned.
IncludePhoneNumber - Whether to fetch the default phone number.
IncludeNotes - Whether to fetch the notes field.

⬡ *GetAll (IncludePhoneNumber As Boolean, IncludeNotes As Boolean) As List*

Returns a List of Contact objects with all the contacts. This list can be very large.

⬡ *GetById (Id As Int, IncludePhoneNumber As Boolean, IncludeNotes As Boolean) As Contact*

Returns the Contact with the specified Id. Returns `Null` if no matching contact found.
IncludePhoneNumber - Whether to fetch the default phone number.
IncludeNotes - Whether to fetch the notes field.

⬡ *GetContactsAsync (EventName As String, Query As String, Arguments() As String, IncludePhoneNumber As Boolean, IncludeNotes As Boolean)*

This method is an asynchronous version of GetContactsByQuery. Once the list is ready, the `Complete` event will be raised. The **EventName** parameter sets the sub that will handle this event.

⬡ *GetContactsByQuery (Query As String, Arguments() As String, IncludePhoneNumber As Boolean, IncludeNotes As Boolean) As List*

Returns a list of contacts based on the specified query and arguments.
Query - The SQL query. Pass an empty string to return all contacts.
Arguments - An array of strings used for parameterized queries. Pass `Null` if not needed.
IncludePhoneNumber - Whether to fetch the phone number for each contact.
IncludeNotes - Whether to fetch the notes field for each contact.

ContentChooser

The ContentChooser object allows the user to select a specific type of content using other installed applications. For example, the user can use the internal Gallery application to select an image. If the user has installed a file manager, then the ContentChooser can be used to select general files. This object should usually be declared as a `Sub Process_Globals` object. After initializing the object, you can let the user select content by calling Show with the required MIME types.
The `Result` event will be raised with a `Success` flag and with the content `Dir` and `FileName`. Note that these values may point to resources other than regular files. Still, you can pass them to methods that expect `Dir` and `FileName`.
Only content types that can be opened with an `InputStream` are supported.

Event: Result (Success As Boolean, Dir As String, FileName As String)
Members:

Initialize (EventName As String)
Initializes the object and sets the Sub that will handle the Result event.
Example:
```
Dim CC As ContentChooser
CC.Initialize("CC")
```

IsInitialized As Boolean
Whether this object has been initialized by calling `Initialize`.

Show (Mime As String, Title As String)
Sends the request to the system. If there is more than one application that supports the given Mime, then a list with the applications will be displayed to the user. The Result event will be raised after the user chooses an item or cancels the dialog.
Mime - The content MIME type.
Title - The title of the chooser dialog (when there is more than one application).
Examples:
```
CC.Show("image/*", "Choose image")
CC.Show("audio/*", "Choose audio file")
```

Email
Using an Email object, you can create an intent that holds a complete email message. You can then launch the email application by calling StartActivity. Note that the email will not be sent automatically. The user will need to press on the "Send" button. Example:
```
Dim Message As Email
Message.To.Add("SomeEmail@example.com")
Message.Attachments.Add(File.Combine(File.DirRootExternal,
"SomeFile.txt"))
StartActivity(Message.GetIntent)
```

Members:

Attachments As List

BCC As List

Body As String

CC As List

GetHtmlIntent As Intent
Returns the Intent that should be sent with StartActivity. The email message will be an HTML message.

GetIntent As Intent
Returns the Intent that should be sent with StartActivity.

● *Subject As String*

● *To As List*

LogCat

LogCat allows you to read the internal phone logs. Refer to the LogCat documentation (http://bit.ly/1OwixvZ) for more information about the optional arguments. The LogCatData event is raised when there is new data available. You should use BytesToString to convert the raw bytes to string.

Note that the LogCatData event is raised in a different thread. This means that you can only log the messages.

You can also use the Threading library to delegate the data to the main thread.

Permissions:

android.permission.READ_LOGS

Event: LogCatData (Buffer() As Byte, Length As Int)

The LogCatData event is raised when there is new data available.

Members:

● *LogCatStart (Args() As String, EventName As String)*

Starts tracking the logs.

Args - Optional arguments (http://bit.ly/1OwixvZ) passed to the internal LogCat command.

EventName - The Sub that will handle the LogCatData event.

● *LogCatStop*

Stops tracking the logs.

PackageManager

The PackageManager allows you to find information about installed applications. Applications are referenced using their package name. You can get a list of all the packages by calling `GetInstalledPackages`.

Members:

● *GetApplicationIcon (Package As String) As Drawable*

Returns the application icon. Example:

```
Dim pm As PackageManager
Activity.Background = pm.GetApplicationIcon(
"com.google.android.youtube")
```

● *GetApplicationIntent (Package As String) As IntentWrapper*

Returns an Intent object that can be used to start the given application. Example:

```
Dim In As Intent
Dim pm As PackageManager
In = pm.GetApplicationIntent("com.google.android.youtube")
If In.IsInitialized Then StartActivity(In)
```

● *GetApplicationLabel (Package As String) As String*

Returns the application label.

● *GetInstalledPackages As List*

Returns a list of the installed packages. Example:

```
Dim pm As PackageManager
Dim packages As List
packages = pm.GetInstalledPackages
For i = 0 To packages.Size - 1
  Log(packages.Get(i))
Next
```

🎛 *GetVersionCode (Package As String) As Int*
Returns the application version code.

🎛 *GetVersionName (Package As String) As String*
Returns the application version name.

🎛 *QueryIntentActivities (Intent1 As Intent) As List*
Returns a list of the installed activities that can handle the given intent. Each item in the list is the "component name" of an activity. You can use `Intent.SetComponent` to explicitly choose the activity. The first item is considered the best match. For example, the following code lists all the activities that can "view" a text file:

```
Dim pm As PackageManager
Dim Intent1 As Intent
Intent1.Initialize(Intent1.ACTION_VIEW, "file://")
Intent1.SetType("text/*")
For Each cn As String In pm.QueryIntentActivities(Intent1)
  Log(cn)
Next
```

Phone

Members:

🎛 *GetDataState As String*
Returns the current cellular data connection state.
Possible values: DISCONNECTED, CONNECTING, CONNECTED, SUSPENDED.

🎛 *GetMaxVolume (Channel As Int) As Int*
Gets the maximum volume index (value) for the given channel.
Channel - One of the VOLUME constants given above.

🎛 *GetNetworkOperatorName As String*
Returns the name of the current registered operator. Returns an empty string if it is not available.

🎛 *GetNetworkType As String*
Returns the currently used cellular network type. Possible values:
1xRTT, CDMA, EDGE, EHRPD, EVDO_0, EVDO_A, EVDO_B, GPRS, HSDPA, HSPA, HSPAP, HSUPA, IDEN, LTE, UMTS, UNKNOWN.

🎛 *GetPhoneType As String*
Returns the phone radio type. Possible values: CDMA, GSM, NONE.

❂ GetResourceDrawable (ResourceId As Int) As Drawable

Returns an internal drawable object. See this page (http://bit.ly/1OwiMam) for a list of available resources.
Example:
```
Dim p As Phone
Dim bd As BitmapDrawable
bd = p.GetResourceDrawable(17301618)
Activity.AddMenuItem2("Menu1", "Menu1", bd.Bitmap)
```

❂ GetRingerMode As Int

Returns the phone ringer mode. Value will be one of the RINGER constants.

❂ GetSettings (Settings As String) As String

Returns the value of the phone settings based on the given key. The possible keys are listed here (http://bit.ly/1OwiUGK). The keys are lower cased. Example:
```
Dim p As Phone
Log(GetSettings("android_id"))
```

❂ GetSimOperator As String

Returns the code of the SIM provider. Returns an empty string if it is not available.

❂ GetVolume (Channel As Int) As Int

Returns the volume of the specified channel.
Channel - One of the VOLUME constants.

❂ HideKeyboard (Activity As ActivityWrapper)

Hides the soft keyboard if it is displayed. Example:
```
Dim p As Phone
p.HideKeyboard(Activity)
```

❂ IsAirplaneModeOn As Boolean

Returns TRUE if the phone "airplane mode" is on.

❂ IsNetworkRoaming As Boolean

Returns True if the device is considered roaming on the current network.

⚑ Manufacturer As String [read only]

⚑ Model As String [read only]

⚑ Product As String [read only]

⬤ RINGER_NORMAL As Int

Normal phone ringer mode.

⬤ RINGER_SILENT As Int

Phone ringer will be silent and the device will NOT vibrate.

⬤ RINGER_VIBRATE As Int

Phone ringer will be silent and the device will vibrate.

⚑ SdkVersion As Int [read only]

Returns an integer describing the SDK version.

❖ *SendBroadcastIntent (Intent1 As Intent)*

Sends an intent to all BroadcastReceivers that listen to this type of intent. Example of asking the media scanner to rescan a file:

```
Dim i As Intent
i.Initialize("android.intent.action.MEDIA_SCANNER_SCAN_FILE", _
  "file://" & File.Combine(File.DirRootExternal, "pictures/1.jpg"))
Dim p As Phone
p.SendBroadcastIntent(i)
```

❖ *SetMute (Channel As Int, Mute As Boolean)*

Mutes or unmutes the given channel.

Channel - One of the VOLUME constants.

Mute - Whether to mute or unmute the channel.

❖ *SetRingerMode (Mode As Int)*

Sets the phone ringer mode.

Mode - One of the RINGER constants.

Example:

```
Dim p As Phone
p.SetRingerMode(p.RINGER_VIBRATE)
```

❖ *SetScreenBrightness (Value As Float)*

Sets the brightness of the current activity. This method cannot be called from a service module.

Value - A float from 0 to 1. Set -1 for automatic brightness.

Example:

```
Sub Process_Globals
  Dim phone1 As Phone
End Sub
Sub Globals
  Dim sb As SeekBar
End Sub
Sub Activity_Create(FirstTime As Boolean)
  sb.Initialize("sb")
  sb.Max = 100
  sb.Value = 50
  Activity.AddView(sb, 10dip, 10dip, 90%x, 30dip)
End Sub
Sub sb_ValueChanged (Value As Int, UserChanged As Boolean)
  phone1.SetScreenBrightness(Max(Value, 5) / 100)
End Sub
```

❖ *SetScreenOrientation (Orientation As Int)*

Changes the current activity orientation. This method cannot be called from a service module.

Orientation - -1 (minus 1) for unspecified, 0 for landscape and 1 for portrait.

❖ *SetVolume (Channel As Int, VolumeIndex As Int, ShowUI As Boolean)*

Sets the volume of the specified channel.

Channel - One of the VOLUME constants.

VolumeIndex - The volume index. GetMaxVolume can be used to find the largest possible value.

ShowUI - Whether to show the volume UI windows.

Example:
```
Dim p As Phone
p.SetVolume(p.VOLUME_MUSIC, 3, True)
```

Shell (Command As String, Args() As String, StdOut As StringBuilder, StdErr As StringBuilder) As Int

Runs a native shell command. Many commands are inaccessible because of OS security restrictions. Returns the process exit value.

Command - Command to run.

Args - Additional arguments. Can be **Null** if not needed.

StdOut - A StringBuilder that will hold the standard output value. Can be **Null** if not needed.

StdErr - A StringBuilder that will hold the standard error value. Can be **Null** if not needed.

Example:
```
Dim p As Phone
Dim sb As StringBuilder
sb.Initialize
p.Shell("df", Null, sb, Null)
Msgbox(sb.ToString, "Free space:")
```

VOLUME_ALARM As Int

Alarms channel.

VOLUME_MUSIC As Int

Music channel.

VOLUME_NOTIFICATION As Int

Notifications channel.

VOLUME_RING As Int

Phone ring channel.

VOLUME_SYSTEM As Int

System sounds channel.

VOLUME_VOICE_CALL As Int

Voice calls channel.

PhoneAccelerometer

This is a legacy object and should not be used. The PhoneSensors (page 518) object provides greater functionality, supports all existing sensors and will be expanded to support future ones. That should be used instead.

PhoneCalls

This object creates an intent that launches the phone application. The reason that it is not part of the PhoneIntents library is that it requires an additional permission (page 131).

Permissions:

android.permission.CALL_PHONE

Member:

🔷 *Call (PhoneNumber As String) As Intent*

Creates an intent that will call a phone number.
Example:

```
Dim p As PhoneCalls
StartActivity(p.Call("1234567890"))
```

PhoneEvents

The Android OS sends all kinds of messages to notify applications of changes in the system. The PhoneEvents object allows you to catch such messages and handle those events in your program.

Usually, you will want to add this object to a **Service** module instead of an **Activity** module in order not to miss events that happen while your activity is paused. You should declare this object in **Sub Process_Globals** and initialize it in **Sub Service_Create**. For example, to monitor the level of the battery you could use:

```
Sub Process_Globals
  Dim phoneEvent As PhoneEvents
End Sub

Sub Activity_Create(FirstTime As Boolean)
  phoneEvent.Initialize("phoneEvent")
End Sub

Sub phoneEvent_BatteryChanged (Level As Int, Scale As Int, _
    Plugged As Boolean, Intent As Intent)
  Log(Intent.GetExtra("level"))
End Sub
```

Events:

Note that each event has an Intent (page 378), sent by Android, carrying extra information.

AirplaneModeChanged (State As Boolean, Intent As Intent)

Raised when the "airplane mode" state changes.
State - `True` when airplane mode is active.
Intent - this object is sent by Android.

BatteryChanged (Level As Int, Scale As Int, Plugged As Boolean, Intent As Intent)

Raised when the battery status changes.
Level - The current level.
Scale - The maximum level.
Plugged - Whether the device is plugged to an electricity source.
Intent - this object is sent by Android.

ConnectivityChanged (NetworkType As String, State As String, Intent As Intent)

There was a change in the state of the WIFI network or the MOBILE network (other network).
NetworkType - WIFI or MOBILE.

State - One of the following values: CONNECTING, CONNECTED, SUSPENDED, DISCONNECTING, DISCONNECTED, UNKNOWN.
Intent - this object is sent by Android.

DeviceStorageLow (Intent As Intent)

Raised when the device internal memory condition is low.
Intent - this object is sent by Android.

DeviceStorageOk (Intent As Intent)

Raised when the device internal low memory condition no longer exists.
Intent - this object is sent by Android.

PackageAdded (Package As String, Intent As Intent)

An application was installed.
Package - The application package name.
Intent - this object is sent by Android.

PackageRemoved (Package As String, Intent As Intent)

An application was uninstalled.
Package - The application package name.
Intent - this object is sent by Android.

PhoneStateChanged (State As String, IncomingNumber As String, Intent As Intent)

The phone state has changed.
State - One of the three values: IDLE, OFFHOOK, RINGING. OFFHOOK means that there is a call or that the phone is dialing.
IncomingCall - Available when the State value is RINGING.
Intent - this object is sent by Android.

ScreenOff (Intent As Intent)

The screen has turned off.
Intent - this object is sent by Android.

ScreenOn (Intent As Intent)

The screen has turned on.
Intent - this object is sent by Android.

SmsDelivered (PhoneNumber As String, Intent As Intent)

An Sms message sent by your application was delivered to the recipient.
PhoneNumber - The target phone number.
Intent - this object is sent by Android.

SmsSentStatus (Success As Boolean, ErrorMessage As String, PhoneNumber As String, Intent As Intent)

Raised after your application sends an Sms message.
Success - Whether the message was sent successfully.
ErrorMessage - One of the following values: GENERIC_FAILURE, NO_SERVICE, RADIO_OFF, NULL_PDU or OK.
PhoneNumber - The target phone number.
Intent - this object is sent by Android.

Shutdown (Intent As Intent)
The phone is shutting down (turned off, not just sleeping).
Intent - this object is sent by Android.

TextToSpeechFinish (Intent As Intent)
The Text-To-Speech engine has finished processing the messages in the queue.
Intent - this object is sent by Android.

UserPresent (Intent As Intent)
The user has unlocked the keyguard screen.
Intent - this object is sent by Android.

Members:

Initialize (EventName As String)
Initializes the object and starts listening for events.
The PhoneStateEvent will not be raised. Use InitializeWithPhoneState instead if it is needed.

InitializeWithPhoneState (EventName As String, PhoneId As PhoneId)
Initializes the object and starts listening for events. The PhoneStateEvent will also be handled. Example:
```
Dim PhoneId1 As PhoneId
Dim PE As PhoneEvents
PE.InitializeWithPhoneState("PE", PhoneId1)
```

StopListening
Stops listening for events. You can later call **Initialize** to start listening for events again.

PhoneId

Permissions:
android.permission.READ_PHONE_STATE

Members:

GetDeviceId As String
Returns a unique device Id. Returns an empty string if the device Id is not available (usually on wifi only devices).

GetLine1Number As String
Returns the phone number string for line 1 as configured in the SIM card. Returns an empty string if it is not available.

GetSimSerialNumber As String
Returns the serial number of the SIM card. Returns an empty string if it is not available.

GetSubscriberId As String
Returns the unique subscriber Id. Returns an empty string if it is not available.

PhoneIntents
This object contains methods that create intents objects. An intent does nothing until you call StartActivity with the intent. Calling StartActivity sends the intent to Android.

Members:

🔹 *OpenBrowser (URI As String) As Intent*

Creates an intent that will open the specified URI.

URI – a "Uniform Resource Identifier" identifying the web address of the page to open.
Example:

```
StartActivity (PhoneIntents.OpenBrowser("http://www.google.com"))
```

🔹 *PlayAudio (Dir As String, File As String) As Intent*

Creates an intent that will start playing the given audio file with the default player.
This method cannot work with internal files.

🔹 *PlayVideo (Dir As String, File As String) As Intent*

Creates an intent that will start playing the given video file with the default player.
This method cannot work with internal files.

PhoneOrientation

This is a legacy object and should not be used. The PhoneSensors object provides greater
functionality, supports all existing sensors and will be expanded to support future ones. It
should be used instead.

PhoneSensors

Most Android-powered devices have built-in sensors that measure motion, orientation, and
various environmental conditions. See the Members list below for the possible sensor types.
Bear in mind that most devices do not support all possible sensors. The **StartListening**
method returns **False** if the requested sensor is not supported.

Sensors are capable of providing raw data with high precision and accuracy, and are useful if
you want to monitor three-dimensional device movement or positioning, or you want to
monitor changes in the ambient environment near a device.

The PhoneSensors object allows you to listen for changes in one of the device sensors.
Example to check accelerometer and show values:

```
Sub Process_Globals
  Dim accel As PhoneSensors
End Sub

Sub Globals
  Dim lbl As Label
End Sub

Sub Activity_Create(FirstTime As Boolean)
  If FirstTime Then
    ' Initialize accelerometer
    accel.Initialize(accel.TYPE_ACCELEROMETER)
  End If

  ' Prepare label to receive data
  lbl.Initialize("")
  lbl.TextColor = Colors.White
  Activity.AddView(lbl, 10dip, 10dip, 100%x - 10dip, 45dip)
```

```
End Sub

Sub Activity_Resume
  'Here we start listening for SensorChanged events.
  'By checking the return value we know if the sensor is supported.

  If accel.StartListening("accel") = False Then
    lbl.Text = "Accelerometer is not supported."
    Log("Accelerometer is not supported.")
  End If

End Sub

Sub Activity_Pause (UserClosed As Boolean)
  'Stop listening for events.
  accel.StopListening
End Sub

Sub accel_SensorChanged (Values() As Float)
  Dim ps As PhoneSensors
  'Get the PhoneSensors object that raised this event.
  ps = Sender
  If Sender = accel Then
    lbl.Text = "Accelerometer data: " _
      & " X=" & NumberFormat(Values(0), 0, 3) _
      & ", Y=" & NumberFormat(Values(1), 0, 3) _
      & ", Z=" & NumberFormat(Values(2), 0, 3)
  Else
    Log ("xxx")
  End If
End Sub
```

See here (http://bit.ly/16oqRsm) for a more detailed example.

Event: SensorChanged (Values() As Float)

After initializing the object and calling **StartListening**, the **SensorChanged** event will be raised each time the sensor value changes. The value is passed as an array of Floats. Some sensors pass a single value and some pass three values. Example:

```
Sub Sensor_SensorChanged (Values() As Float)
 Dim ps As PhoneSensors
 Dim sd As SensorData
 Dim lbl As Label
 'Get the PhoneSensors object that raised this event.
 ps = Sender
 sd = SensorsMap.Get(ps) 'Get the associated SensorData object
 lbl = SensorsLabels.Get(ps) 'Get the associated Label
 If sd.ThreeValues Then
   lbl.Text = sd.Name & " X=" _
    & NumberFormat(Values(0), 0, 3) & ", Y=" & NumberFormat(Values(1),
 0, 3) _
    & ", Z=" & NumberFormat(Values(2), 0, 3)
 Else
   lbl.Text = sd.Name & " = " & NumberFormat(Values(0), 0, 3)
 End If
End Sub
```

Members:

Initialize (SensorType As Int)

Initializes the object and sets the sensor type (one of the **TYPE** constants).

Initialize2 (SensorType As Int, SensorDelay As Int)

Initializes the object and sets the sensor type and sensor events rate.
SensorType - One of the **TYPE** constants.
SensorDelay - A value from 0 (fastest rate) to 3 (slowest rate). This is only a hint to the system.

MaxValue As Float [read only]

Returns the maximum value for this sensor.
Returns **-1** if this sensor is not supported.

StartListening (EventName As String) As Boolean

Starts listening for sensor events. Returns **True** if the sensor is supported. Usually, you will want to start listening in **Sub Activity_Resume** and stop listening in **Sub Activity_Pause**.

StopListening

Stops listening for events.

TYPE_ACCELEROMETER As Int

A constant identifying the Accelerometer sensor.
```
 Dim accel As PhoneSensors
 accel.Initialize(accel.TYPE_ACCELEROMETER)
```
The SensorChanged event receives an array of three values when this type of sensor changes. See example above. The values give the acceleration measured in Meters / Second ^ 2 for each axis (X, Y and Z).

⬡ *TYPE_GYROSCOPE As Int*
A constant identifying the Gyroscope sensor. The SensorChanged event receives an array of three values when this type of sensor changes. See example above. The values give the angular velocity measured in Radians / Second around each of the three axis.

⬡ *TYPE_LIGHT As Int*
A constant identifying the Light sensor. The SensorChanged event receives a single value when this type of sensor changes. See example above. The values give the ambient light level measured in SI lux units.

⬡ *TYPE_MAGNETIC_FIELD As Int*
A constant identifying the Magnetic field sensor. The SensorChanged event receives an array of three values when this type of sensor changes. See example above. The values give the ambient magnetic field measured in micro-Tesla for the X, Y and Z axis.

⬡ *TYPE_ORIENTATION As Int*
A constant identifying the Orientation sensor. The SensorChanged event receives an array of three values when this type of sensor changes. See example above. The values give the orientation measured in degrees for azimuth, pitch and roll.

⬡ *TYPE_PRESSURE As Int*
A constant identifying the Pressure sensor. The SensorChanged event receives a single value when this type of sensor changes. See example above. The values give the atmospheric pressure in units of hectoPascals (hPa) or, equivalently, millibars (mbar).

⬡ *TYPE_PROXIMITY As Int*
A constant identifying the Proximity sensor. The SensorChanged event receives a single value when this type of sensor changes. See example above. The values give the proximity measured in centimeters. Most devices will return only two possible values representing "near" and "far".
"far" should match MaxRange and "near" should be a value smaller than MaxRange.

⬡ *TYPE_TEMPERATURE As Int*
A constant identifying the Temperature sensor. The SensorChanged event receives a single value when this type of sensor changes. See example above. The values give the ambient temperature in degrees Celsius.

PhoneSms
Permissions:
android.permission.SEND_SMS
Members:
⬡ *Send (PhoneNumber As String, Text As String)*
Sends an Sms message. Note that this method actually sends the message (unlike most other methods that create an intent object). You can use `PhoneEvents` to handle the `SmsSentStatus` and `SmsDelivered` events. This method is equivalent to calling `PhoneSms.Send2(PhoneNumber, Text, True, True)`

❦ *Send2 (PhoneNumber As String, Text As String, ReceiveSentNotification As Boolean, ReceiveDeliveredNotification As Boolean)*

Sends an Sms message without notification. Note that this method actually sends the message (unlike most other methods that create an intent object). You can use **PhoneEvents** to handle the **SmsSentStatus** and **SmsDelivered** events.

ReceiveSentNotification - If True then the SmsSentStatus PhoneEvent will be raised when the message is sent.

ReceiveDeliveredNotification - If True then the PhoneEvent SmsDelivered will be raised when the message is delivered.

Example:

```
Sub Globals
  Dim Sms As PhoneSms
  Dim PE As PhoneEvents
  Dim btnTest As Button
  Dim strPhoneNumber As String = "01234567890"
End Sub


Sub Activity_Create(FirstTime As Boolean)
  PE.Initialize("PE")
  Sms.Send2(strPhoneNumber, "This sms was sent from B4A",  True, True)
End Sub


Sub PE_SmsDelivered (PhoneNumber As String, Intent As Intent)
  Log ("SMS delivered to " & PhoneNumber)
End Sub


Sub PE_SmsSentStatus (Success As Boolean, ErrorMessage As String,
PhoneNumber As String, Intent As Intent)
  If Success = True Then
    Log ("SMS Sent to " & PhoneNumber)
  Else
    Log ("Failed to send SMS to " & PhoneNumber & ". Error = " &
ErrorMessage)
  End If
End Sub
```

PhoneVibrate

Permissions:

android.permission.VIBRATE

Members:

❦ *Vibrate (TimeMs As Long)*

Vibrates the phone for the specified duration.

PhoneWakeState

The PhoneWakeState object allows you to prevent the device from turning off the screen. Once you call **KeepAlive**, the phone screen will stay on until you call **ReleaseKeepAlive**.

It is important to eventually release it. A **recommended usage** is to call KeepAlive in `Activity_Resume` and call **ReleaseKeepAlive** in `Activity_Pause`.

Note that the user can still turn off the screen by pressing on the power button. Calling **PartialLock** will prevent the CPU from going to sleep even if the user presses on the power button. It will not, however, affect the screen.

Permissions:

android.permission.WAKE_LOCK

Members:

❧ KeepAlive (BrightScreen As Boolean)

Prevents the device from going to sleep. Call ReleaseKeepAlive to release the power lock. **BrightScreen** - Whether to keep the screen bright or dimmed.

❧ PartialLock

Acquires a partial lock. This will prevent the CPU from going to sleep, even if the user presses on the power button. **Make sure** to call ReleasePartialLock eventually to release this lock.

❧ ReleaseKeepAlive

Releases the power lock and allows the device to go to sleep.

❧ ReleasePartialLock

Releases a partial lock that was previously acquired by calling **PartialLock**.

RingtoneManager

The RingtoneManager object allows you to set or get the default ringtone. It also provides access to the default ringtone picker. The **PickerResult** event will be raised when the picker is closed with the URI ("Uniform Resource Identifier", ie the address) of the selected ringtone. **Note** that an empty string will be returned if the "Silence" option was selected. Example of playing the selected ringtone with MediaPlayer:

```
Sub Globals
  Private btnPlay As Button
  Dim rm As RingtoneManager
  Dim strUri As String
End Sub

Sub Activity_Create(FirstTime As Boolean)
  rm.ShowRingtonePicker("rm", rm.TYPE_RINGTONE, True, "")
End Sub

Sub rm_PickerResult (Success As Boolean, URI As String)
  If Success Then
    If URI = "" Then
        ToastMessageShow("Silent was chosen", True)
    Else
      strUri = uri
    End If
  Else
      ToastMessageShow("Error loading ringtone.", True)
  End If
End Sub

Sub btnPlay_Click
    rtm.Play(strUri)
End Sub
```

Permissions:
android.permission.WRITE_SETTINGS

Event: PickerResult (Success As Boolean, URI As String)
URI – the "Uniform Resource Identifier" specifying the address of the selected ringtone.

Members:

AddToMediaStore (Dir As String, FileName As String, Title As String, IsAlarm As Boolean, IsNotification As Boolean, IsRingtone As Boolean, IsMusic As Boolean) As String

Adds a sound file to the internal media store and returns the URI (address) to the new entry.

Dir - The file folder. Should be a folder under the storage card (public folder).
FileName - The file name.
Title - The entry title.
IsAlarm - Whether this entry should be added to the alarms sound list.
IsNotification - Whether this entry should be added to the notifications sound list.
IsRingtone - Whether this entry should be added to the ringtones sound list.
IsMusic - Whether this entry should be added to the music list.
Example:

```
Dim r As RingtoneManager
Dim u As String
u = r.AddToMediaStore(File.DirRootExternal, "bounce.mp3", "Bounce!",
True, True, True, True)
r.SetDefault(r.TYPE_RINGTONE, u)
```

♥ DeleteRingtone (URI As String)

Deletes the given entry.

URI – the "Uniform Resource Identifier" (the address) of the ringtone to delete.

♥GetContentDir As String

Returns a string that represents the virtual content folder. This can be used to play a Ringtone with MediaPlayer.

♥ GetDefault (Type As Int) As String

Returns the URI (address) of the default ringtone of a specific type, or an empty string if no default is available. Example:

```
Dim mp As MediaPlayer
mp.Initialize
Dim r As RingtoneManager
mp.Load(r.GetContentDir, r.GetDefault(r.TYPE_NOTIFICATION))
mp.Play
```

♥ Play (URI As String)

Plays the ringtone with the given URI. The URI can be found using `ShowRingtonePicker`, as in the example given above.

♥ SetDefault (Type As Int, URI As String)

Sets the default ringtone for the given type.

URI – the "Uniform Resource Identifier" (the address) of the new ringtone default. In order to get the URI, you should use `AddToMediaStore` (for new sounds) or `ShowRingtonePicker` (for existing sounds).

♥ ShowRingtonePicker (EventName As String, Type As Int, IncludeSilence As Boolean, ChosenRingtone As String)

Shows the ringtone picker activity. The PickerResult will be raised after the user selects a ringtone.

EventName - Sets the sub that will handle the PickerResult event.

Type - Defines the type(s) of sounds that will be listed. Multiple types can be set using Bit.Or.

IncludeSilence - Whether to include the Silence option in the list.

ChosenRingtone - The URI (address) of the ringtone that will be selected when the dialog opens. Pass an empty string if not needed.

⬢ TYPE_ALARM As Int

⬢ TYPE_NOTIFICATION As Int

⬢ TYPE_RINGTONE As Int

Sms

Represents an SMS message. SMS messages are retrieved using an SmsMessages object.

Members:

🔹 Address As String
The message address.

🔹 Body As String
Message body.

🔹 Date As Long
The date of this message.

🔹 Id As Int
Message internal Id.

🔹 PersonId As Int
The Id of the person who sent the message. It will be **-1** if this data is missing.
You can find more information about this person by calling `Contacts.GetById`.

🔹 Read As Boolean
Whether this message has been read.

🔹 ThreadId As Int
Thread Id.

🔹 Type As Int
The message type. One of the SmsMessages constant values.

SmsInterceptor

Listens for incoming SMS messages. The MessageReceived event is raised when a new message arrives. Returning **True** from the MessageReceived event will cause the broadcasted message to be aborted.

This can be used to prevent the message from reaching the standard SMS application. However, in order for your application to receive the message before other applications, you should use Initialize2 and set the priority value to a value larger than 0. It should be 999 according to the Android documentation.

Permissions:
android.permission.RECEIVE_SMS

Event: MessageReceived (From As String, Body As String) As Boolean

Members:

🔹 Initialize (EventName As String)
Initializes the object and starts listening for new messages.

🔹 Initialize2 (EventName As String, Priority As Int)
Initializes the object and starts listening for new messages. **Priority** defines the application priority compared to other applications that listen to incoming messages.

According to the official Android documentation, in order to receive the message first, you should set **Priority** to 999. However, it is possible that a third party application has used a higher value. The highest possible value is the maximum value of an Int, 2147483647.

✿ *StopListening*

Stops listening for events. You can later call Initialize to start listening again.

SmsMessages

Provides access to the stored SMS messages. **Note** that you can use PhoneSms to send SMS messages. Example of printing all messages from the last week:

```
Dim SmsMessages1 As SmsMessages
Dim List1 As List
List1 = SmsMessages1.GetAllSince(DateTime.Add(DateTime.Now, 0, 0, -7))
For i = 0 To List1.Size - 1
  Dim Sms1 As Sms
  Sms1 = List1.Get(i)
  Log(Sms1)
Next
```

Permissions:

android.permission.READ_SMS

Members:

✿ *GetAll As List*

Returns all stored messages.

✿ *GetAllSince (Date As Long) As List*

Returns all messages with a date value on or after the given date.

✿ *GetBetweenDates (StartDate As Long, EndDate As Long) As List*

Returns all messages between the given dates. Start value is inclusive and end value is exclusive.

✿ *GetByPersonId (PersonId As Int) As List*

Returns a list with all messages received from the person with the given Id.

✿ *GetByThreadId (ThreadId As Int) As List*

Returns a list with all messages with the given ThreadId.

✿ *GetByType (Type As Int) As List*

Returns a list with all messages of the given type. The type should be one of the **TYPE** constants.

✿ *GetUnreadMessages As List*

Returns all unread messages.

● *TYPE_DRAFT As Int*

● *TYPE_FAILED As Int*

● *TYPE_INBOX As Int*

● *TYPE_OUTBOX As Int*

● *TYPE_QUEUED As Int*

● *TYPE_SENT As Int*

● *TYPE_UNKNOWN As Int*

VoiceRecognition

Most Android devices support voice recognition (speech to text). Usually, the service works by sending the audio stream to some external server which analyzes the stream and returns the possible results. Therefore, a data connection is required.

You should declare a VoiceRecognition object as a `Sub Process_Globals` object and initialize it in `Activity_Create` when `FirstTime` is `True`. Later, when you call `Listen`, a dialog will be displayed, asking the user to speak.

Event: Result (Success As Boolean, Texts As List)

The `Result` event will be raised with a **Success** flag and a list with the possible results (usually one result). You will need a Sub to process the result:

```
Sub VR_Result (Success As Boolean, Texts As List)
  If Success = True Then
   ToastMessageShow(Texts.Get(0), True)
  End If
End Sub
```

Members:

● *Initialize (EventName As String)*

Initializes the object and sets the Sub that will catch the Ready event. Example:

```
Dim VR As VoiceRecognition
VR.Initialize("VR")
```

● *IsSupported As Boolean*

Returns **TRUE** if voice recognition is supported on this device.

● *Language As String [write only]*

Sets the language used. By default, the device default language is used. Example:

```
VR.Language = "en"
```

● *Listen*

Starts listening. The Ready event will be raised when the result arrives.

● *Prompt As String [write only]*

Sets the prompt that is displayed in the "Speak now" dialog in addition to the "Speak now" message.

PreferenceActivity Library

The PreferenceActivity library (included in the IDE installation package) allows you to show the standard settings interface and provides an easy way to handle applications settings.

In order to use this library, you need to edit the manifest file (using the Manifest Editor (page 115)) and add the line:

```
AddApplicationText(<activity
android:name="anywheresoftware.b4a.objects.preferenceactivity"/>)
```

See the tutorial (http://bit.ly/11jIyFd) (and the example project which it contains) for more information about how to use this library. **Note**: although the modification to the manifest is not visible in the example project (because the manifest is read-only), it is still required in any projects you create that use this library.

PreferenceActivity Limitations

Note that the actual values of items (such as EditText1 or List1 in the above example) cannot be seen until you click on the arrow. Also you cannot specify the format of text, such as requiring it to be a number. Nor can you set the width of the view which is shown. It always fills the full screen.

List of types:

PreferenceCategory
PreferenceManager
PreferenceScreen

PreferenceCategory

PreferenceCategory holds a group of other preferences.

Members:

AddCheckBox (Key As String, Title As String, Summary As String, DefaultValue As Boolean)

Adds a preference entry with a check box. The entry values can be either **True** or **False**.
Key - The preference key associated with the value.
Title - Entry title.
Summary - Entry summary (second row).
DefaultValue - The default value of this preference entry if the key does not already exist.

AddEditText (Key As String, Title As String, Summary As String, DefaultValue As String)

Adds a preference entry which allows the user to enter free text.
Key - The preference key associated with the value.
Title - Entry title.
Summary - Entry summary (second row).
DefaultValue - The default value of this preference entry if the key does not already exist.

AddList (Key As String, Title As String, Summary As String, DefaultValue As String, Values As List)

Adds a preference entry which allows the user to choose a single item out of a list.
Key - The preference key associated with the value.
Title - Entry title.
Summary - Entry summary (second row).
DefaultValue - The default value of this preference entry, if the key does not already exist. Should match one of the strings in **Values**.
Values - A list of strings with the possible values.

AddPreferenceCategory (PreferenceCategory As PreferenceCategory)

Adds a PreferenceCategory. A preference category is made of a title and a group of entries. **Note** that a PreferenceCategory cannot hold other PreferenceCategories.

AddPreferenceScreen (PreferenceScreen As PreferenceScreen)

Adds a secondary PreferenceScreen. When the user presses on this entry, the second screen will appear.

CreateIntent As Intent

Creates the Intent object that is required for showing the PreferencesActivity. Example:
  `StartActivity(PreferenceScreen1.CreateIntent)`

Initialize (Title As String)

Initializes the object and sets the category title.

PreferenceManager

Provides access to the saved settings. Using PreferenceManager, you can get the stored values and modify them.

Members:

ClearAll

Clears all stored entries.

⬢ *GetAll As Map*

Returns a Map with all the Keys and Values. Note that changes to this map will not affect the stored values.

⬢ *GetBoolean (Key As String) As Boolean*

Returns the Boolean value mapped to the given key. Returns **False** if the key is not found.

⬢ *GetString (Key As String) As String*

Returns the String value mapped to the given key. Returns an empty string if the key is not found.

⬢ *GetUpdatedKeys As List*

Returns a list with the keys that were updated since the last call to GetUpdatedKeys. Note that the updated keys may include keys with unchanged values. If, for example, the user changed the value of an item, and then restored it to the original value, this item would still be returned in the list of updated keys.

⬢ *SetBoolean (Key As String, Value As Boolean)*

Maps the given key to the given Boolean value.

⬢ *SetString (Key As String, Value As String)*

Maps the given key to the given String value.

PreferenceScreen

Members:

⬢ *AddCheckBox (Key As String, Title As String, Summary As String, DefaultValue As Boolean)*

Adds a preference entry with a check box. The entry values can be either **True** or **False**.
Key - The preference key associated with the value.
Title - Entry title.
Summary - Entry summary (second row).
DefaultValue - The default value of this preference entry if the key does not already exist.

⬢ *AddEditText (Key As String, Title As String, Summary As String, DefaultValue As String)*

Adds a preference entry which allows the user to enter free text.
Key - The preference key associated with the value.
Title - Entry title.
Summary - Entry summary (second row).
DefaultValue - The default value of this preference entry if the key does not already exist.

⬢ *AddList (Key As String, Title As String, Summary As String, DefaultValue As String, Values As List)*

Adds a preference entry which allows the user to choose a single item out of a list.
Key - The preference key associated with the value.
Title - Entry title.
Summary - Entry summary (second row).

DefaultValue - The default value of this preference entry if the key does not already exist. Should match one of the strings in **Values**.

Values - A list of strings with the possible values.

AddPreferenceCategory (PreferenceCategory As PreferenceCategory)

Adds a PreferenceCategory. A preference category is made of a title and a group of entries. Note that a PreferenceCategory cannot hold other PreferenceCategories.

AddPreferenceScreen (PreferenceScreen As PreferenceScreen)

Adds a secondary PreferenceScreen. When the user presses on this entry, the second screen will appear.

CreateIntent As Intent

Creates the Intent object that is required for showing the PreferencesActivity. Example:
```
StartActivity(PreferenceScreen1.CreateIntent)
```

Initialize (Title As String, Summary As String)

Initializes the object and sets the title that will show. The summary will show for secondary PreferenceScreens.

RandomAccessFile Library

This library is included in the IDE installation package.

List of types:

AsyncStreams

The AsyncStreams object allows you to read from an InputStream and write to an OutputStream in the background without blocking the main thread.
See the AsyncStreams Tutorial here (http://bit.ly/1Owj5BS).

Events:

NewData (Buffer() As Byte)

NewData event is raised only with full messages (not including the 4-bytes length value).

Error

Error event is raised when an error is encountered. You should check LastException to find the error.

Terminated

The Terminated event is raised when the other side has terminated the connection.

Members:

Close

Closes the associated streams.

Initialize (In As java.io.InputStream, Out As java.io.OutputStream, EventName As String)

Initializes the object. Unlike in prefix mode, the NewData event will be raised with new data as soon as it is available.

In - The InputStream that will be read. Pass `Null` if you only want to write with this object.

Out - The OutputStream that is used for writing the data. Pass `Null` if you only want to read with this object.

EventName - Determines the Subs that handle the NewData and Error events.

⚙ *InitializePrefix (In As java.io.InputStream, BigEndian As Boolean, Out As java.io.OutputStream, EventName As String)*

Initializes the object and sets it in "prefix" mode. In this mode, incoming data should adhere to the following protocol: every message should begin with the message length as an Int value (4 bytes). This length should not include the additional 4 bytes.

The NewData event will be raised only with full messages (not including the 4 bytes length value). The prefix Int value will be added to the output messages automatically. This makes it easier as you do not need to deal with broken messages.

In - The InputStream that will be read. Pass `Null` if you only want to write with this object.

BigEndian - Whether the length value is encoded in BigEndian or LittleEndian.

Out - The OutputStream that is used for writing the data. Pass `Null` if you only want to read with this object.

EventName - Determines the Subs that handle the NewData and Error events.

⚙ *IsInitialized As Boolean*

Returns `TRUE` if this object has been initialized.

⚙ *OutputQueueSize As Int [read only]*

Returns the number of messages waiting in the output queue.

⚙ *Write (Buffer() As Byte) As Boolean*

Adds the given byte-array to the output stream queue. If the object was initialized with `InitializePrefix`, then the array length will be added before the array. Returns `False` if the queue is full and it is not possible to queue the data.

⚙ *Write2 (Buffer() As Byte, Start As Int, Length As Int) As Boolean*

Adds the given byte-array to the output stream queue. If the object was initialized with `InitializePrefix`, then the array length will be added before the array. Returns `False` if the queue is full and it is not possible to queue the data.

CompressedStreams

The CompressedStreams object allows you to compress and decompress data using the **gzip** or the **zlib** compression methods. For more information about these, see here (http://bit.ly/1Owj94L) and here (http://bit.ly/1OwjdRS).

There are two options for working with CompressedStreams:

– Wrapping another stream by calling WrapInputStream or WrapOutputStream.

– Compressing or decompressing the data in memory.

The following example demonstrates the use of this object:

```
Sub Activity_Create(FirstTime As Boolean)
   Dim sb As StringBuilder
   sb.Initialize
   'Concatenation operations are much faster with StringBuilder than
with String.
   For i = 1 To 10000
      sb.Append("Playing with compressed streams.").Append(CRLF)
```

```
  Next
  Dim out As OutputStream
  Dim s As String
  Dim compress As CompressedStreams
  s = sb.ToString
  'Write the string without compressing it (we could have used
File.WriteString instead).
  out = File.OpenOutput(File.DirRootExternal, "test.txt", False)
  WriteStringToStream(out, s)

  'Write the string with gzip compression.
  out = File.OpenOutput(File.DirRootExternal, "test.gz", False)
  out = compress.WrapOutputStream(out, "gzip")
  WriteStringToStream(out, s)

  'Write the string with zlib compression
  out = File.OpenOutput(File.DirRootExternal, "test.zlib", False)
  out = compress.WrapOutputStream(out, "zlib")
  WriteStringToStream(out, s)

  'Show the files sizes
  Msgbox("No compression: " & File.Size(File.DirRootExternal,
"test.txt") & CRLF _
      & "Gzip: " & File.Size(File.DirRootExternal, "test.gz") & CRLF _
      & "zlib: " & File.Size(File.DirRootExternal, "test.zlib"), "Files
sizes")
  'Read data from a compressed file
  Dim in As InputStream
  in = File.OpenInput(File.DirRootExternal, "test.zlib")
  in = compress.WrapInputStream(in, "zlib")
  Dim reader As TextReader
  reader.Initialize(in)
  Dim line As String
  line = reader.ReadLine
  Msgbox(line, "First line")
  reader.Close

  'In memory compression / decompression
  Dim data() As Byte
  data = "Playing with in-memory compression.".GetBytes("UTF8")
  Dim compressed(), decompressed() As Byte
  compressed = compress.CompressBytes(data, "gzip")
  decompressed = compress.DecompressBytes(compressed, "gzip")
  'In this case the compressed data is longer than the decompressed
data.
  'The data is too short for the compression to be useful.
  Log("Compressed: " & compressed.Length)
  Log("Decompressed: " & decompressed.Length)
  Msgbox(BytesToString(decompressed,0, decompressed.Length, "UTF8"),
"")
```

```
  End Sub
  Sub WriteStringToStream(Out As OutputStream, s As String)
    Dim t As TextWriter
    t.Initialize(Out)
    t.Write(s)
    t.Close 'Closes the internal stream as well
  End Sub
```

Members:

🔷 *CompressBytes (Data() As Byte, CompressMethod As String) As Byte()*
Returns a byte array with the compressed data.
Data - Data to compress.
CompressMethod - The name of the compression method (gzip or zlib).

🔷 *DecompressBytes (CompressedData() As Byte, CompressMethod As String) As Byte()*
Returns a byte array with the decompressed data.
CompressedData - The compressed data that should be decompressed.
CompressMethod - The name of the compression method (gzip or zlib).

🔷 *WrapInputStream (In As java.io.InputStream, CompressMethod As String) As InputStreamWrapper*
Wraps an input stream and returns an input stream that automatically decompresses the stream when it is read.
In - The original input stream.
CompressMethod - The name of the compression method (gzip or zlib).

🔷 *WrapOutputStream (Out As java.io.OutputStream, CompressMethod As String) As OutputStreamWrapper*
Wraps an output stream and returns an output stream that automatically compresses the data when it is written to the stream.
Out - The original output stream.
CompressMethod - The name of the compression method (gzip or zlib).

CountingInputStream

`CountingInputStream` and `CountingOutputStream` allow you to monitor the reading or writing progress. Counting streams wrap the actual stream and provide a `Count` property which allows you to get the number of bytes read or written. Counting streams are useful when the reading or writing operations are done in the background. You can then use a timer to monitor the progress. This example logs the downloading progress:

```
  Sub Process_Globals
    Dim hc As HttpClient
    Dim cout As CountingOutputStream
    Dim length As Int
    Dim timer1 As Timer
  End Sub
  Sub Globals
  End Sub
  Sub Activity_Create(FirstTime As Boolean)
```

```
  If FirstTime Then
    hc.Initialize("hc")
    timer1.Initialize("Timer1", 500)
  End If
  Dim req As HttpRequest
  req.InitializeGet("http://www.basic4ppc.com/android/files/b4a-
trial.zip")
  hc.Execute(req, 1)
End Sub
Sub hc_ResponseSuccess (Response As HttpResponse, TaskId As Int)
  cout.Initialize(File.OpenOutput(File.DirRootExternal, "1.zip",
False))
  Timer1.Enabled = True
  length = Response.ContentLength
  Response.GetAsynchronously("response", cOut, True, TaskId)
End Sub
Sub hc_ResponseError (Response As HttpResponse, Reason As String,
StatusCode As Int, TaskId As Int)
  Log("Error: " & Reason)
  If Response <> Null Then
    Log(Response.GetString("UTF8"))
    Response.Release
  End If
End Sub
Sub Response_StreamFinish (Success As Boolean, TaskId As Int)
  timer1.Enabled = False
  If Success Then
    Timer1_Tick 'Show the current counter status
    Log("Success!")
  Else
    Log("Error: " & LastException.Message)
  End If
End Sub
Sub Timer1_Tick
  Log(cout.Count & " out of " & length)
End Sub
```

Members:

🍲 BytesAvailable As Int

🍲 Close

🎣 Count As Long
Gets or sets the number of bytes read.

🍲 Initialize (InputStream As java.io.InputStream)
Initializes the counting stream by wrapping the given input stream.

🍲 IsInitialized As Boolean
Whether this object has been initialized by calling `Initialize`.

⬢ **ReadBytes (arg0() As Byte, arg1 As Int, arg2 As Int) As Int**

CountingOutputStream
See CountingInputStream for more information.

Members:

⬢ **Close**

🔧 **Count As Long**
Gets or sets the number of bytes written.

⬢ **Flush**

⬢ **Initialize (OutputStream As java.io.OutputStream)**
Initializes the counting stream by wrapping the given output stream.

⬢ **IsInitialized As Boolean**
Whether this object has been initialized by calling `Initialize`.

⬢ **ToBytesArray As Byte()**

⬢ **WriteBytes (arg0() As Byte, arg1 As Int, arg2 As Int)**

RandomAccessFile
This object allows you to non-sequentially access files and byte-arrays. You can also use it to encode numbers to bytes (and vice versa). **Note** that assets files (files added with the file manager) cannot be opened with this object as those files are actually packed inside the APK file. A short tutorial about the encryption methods is available here (http://bit.ly/159hDmT).

Members:

⬢ **Close**
Closes the stream.

⬢ **CurrentPosition As Long**
Holds the current file position. This value is updated automatically after each read or write operation.

⬢ **Flush**
Flushes any cached data.

⬢ **Initialize (Dir As String, File As String, ReadOnly As Boolean)**
Opens the specified file. **Note** that it is not possible to open a file saved in the assets folder with this object. If needed, you can copy the file to another location and then open it.
ReadOnly - Whether to open the file in read-only mode (otherwise, it will be readable and writable).
Example:

```
Dim raf As RandomAccessFile
raf.Initialize(File.DirInternal, "1.dat", false)
```

Initialize2 (Dir As String, File As String, ReadOnly As Boolean, LittleEndian As Boolean)

Same as Initialize with the option to set the byte order to Little Endian instead of the default Big Endian. This can be useful when sharing files with Windows computers.

Initialize3 (Buffer() As Byte, LittleEndian As Boolean)

Treats the given buffer as a random access file with a constant size. This allows you to read and write values to an array of bytes.

ReadBytes (Buffer() As Byte, StartOffset As Int, Length As Int, Position As Long) As Int

Reads bytes from the stream and into to the given array. Returns the number of bytes read (which is equal or smaller than Length).

Buffer - Array of bytes where the data will be written to.
StartOffset - The first byte read will be written to Buffer(StartOffset).
Length - Number of bytes to read.
Position - The position of the first byte to read.

ReadDouble (Position As Long) As Double

Reads a Double value stored at the specified position. Reads 8 bytes.

ReadEncryptedObject (Password As String, Position As Long) As Object

Reads an encrypted object from the stream.
Password - The password used when the object was written.
Position - Stream position.

ReadFloat (Position As Long) As Float

Reads a Float value stored at the specified position. Reads 4 bytes.

ReadInt (Position As Long) As Int

Reads an Int value stored at the specified position. Reads 4 bytes.

ReadLong (Position As Long) As Long

Reads a Long value stored at the specified position. Reads 8 bytes.

ReadObject (Position As Long) As Object

Reads an object from the stream. See `WriteObject` for supported types.

ReadShort (Position As Long) As Short

Reads a Short value stored at the specified position. Reads 2 bytes.

ReadSignedByte (Position As Long) As Byte

Reads a signed byte (-128 to 127) stored at the specified position.

ReadUnsignedByte (Position As Long) As Int

Reads an unsigned byte (0 to 255) stored at the specified position. The value returned is of type `Int` (because a `Byte` can only store values from -128 to 127).

Size As Long [read only]

Returns the file size.

❖WriteByte (Byte As Byte, Position As Long)
Writes a Byte value at the specified position. Writes 1 byte.

❖WriteBytes (Buffer() As Byte, StartOffset As Int, Length As Int, Position As Long) As Int
Writes the given buffer to the stream. The first byte written is Buffer(StartOffset) and the last is Buffer(StartOffset + Length - 1). Returns the numbers of bytes written.

❖WriteDouble (Value As Double, Position As Long)
Writes a Double value at the specified position. Writes 8 bytes.

❖WriteEncryptedObject (Object As Object, Password As String, Position As Long)
Similar to WriteObject. The object is encrypted with AES-256 and then written to the stream. **Note** that it is faster to write a single large object compared to many smaller objects.
Object - The object that will be written.
Password - The password that protects the object.
Position - The position in the file that this object will be written to.

❖WriteFloat (Value As Float, Position As Long)
Writes a Float value at the specified position. Writes 4 bytes.

❖WriteInt (Value As Int, Position As Long)
Writes an Int value at the specified position. Writes 4 bytes.

❖WriteLong (Value As Long, Position As Long)
Writes a Long value at the specified position. Writes 8 bytes.

❖WriteObject (Object As Object, Compress As Boolean, Position As Long)
Writes the given object to the stream. This method is capable of writing the following types of objects: Lists, Arrays, Maps, Strings, primitive types and user defined types. Combinations of these types are also supported. For example, a map with several lists of arrays can be written. The element type inside a collection must be a String or primitive type. Note that changing your package name may make older object files unusable (requiring you to write them again).
Object - The object that will be written.
Compress - Whether to compress the data before writing it. Should be **True** in most cases.
Position - The position in the file that this object will be written to.

❖WriteShort (Value As Short, Position As Long)
Writes a Short value (2 bytes) at the specified position.

Serial Library
This library is included in the IDE installation package.

List of types:
BluetoothAdmin
Serial

BluetoothAdmin

BluetoothAdmin allows you to administrate the Bluetooth adapter. Using this object, you can enable or disable the adapter, monitor its state and discover devices in range.

Permissions:

android.permission.BLUETOOTH
android.permission.BLUETOOTH_ADMIN

Events:

StateChanged (NewState As Int, OldState As Int)

The StateChanged event is raised whenever the adapter state changes. The new state and the previous state are passed. The values correspond to the STATE_xxxx constants.

DiscoveryStarted / DiscoveryFinished

The DiscoveryStarted and DiscoveryFinished events are raised when a discovery process starts or finishes.

DeviceFound (Name As String, MacAddress As String)

The DeviceFound event is raised when a device is discovered. The device name and MAC address are passed.

Members:

CancelDiscovery As Boolean

Cancels a discovery process.
Returns `False` if the operation has failed.

Disable As Boolean

Turns off the Bluetooth adpater. The adapter will not be immediately disabled. You should use the StateChanged event to monitor the adapter.
This method returns `False` if the adapter cannot be disabled or is already disabled.

Enable As Boolean

Turns on the Bluetooth adapter. The adapter will not be immediately ready. You should use the StateChanged event to find when it is enabled. This method returns `False` if the adapter cannot be enabled or is already enabled.

Initialize (EventName As String)

Initializes the object and sets the subs that will handle the events.

IsEnabled As Boolean

Returns TRUE if the Bluetooth adapter is enabled.

IsInitialized As Boolean

Returns TRUE if the object is initialized.

StartDiscovery As Boolean

Starts a discovery process. You should handle DiscoveryStarted, DiscoveryFinished and DeviceFound events to get more information about the process. Returns `False` if the operation has failed.

● *STATE_OFF As Int*

● *STATE_ON As Int*

● *STATE_TURNING_OFF As Int*

● *STATE_TURNING_ON As Int*

Serial

The Serial library allows you to connect with other Bluetooth devices using the Radio Frequency Communication protocol RFCOMM (http://bit.ly/1dgYl19), which emulates serial ports.

This library requires Android 2.0 (API level 5) or above.

The Serial object should be declared as a `Sub Process_Globals` object. After initializing the object you can connect to other devices by calling Connect with the target device MAC address. This can be done by first getting the paired devices map. This map contains the friendly name and address of each paired device.

To allow other devices to connect to your device, you should call `Listen`.

When a connection is established, the `Connected` event will be raised. There is no problem with both listening to connections and trying to connect to a different device (this allows you to use the same application on two devices without defining a server and client).

One Serial object can handle a single connection. If a new connection is established, it will replace the previous one. See this tutorial (http://bit.ly/19FCUCS) for more information.

Permissions:

android.permission.BLUETOOTH

Event: Connected (Success As Boolean)

The Connected event will be raised after the `Connect, Connect2, Listen` or `Listen2` command is issued, when the connection is ready (or fails).

Members:

♪ *Address As String [read only]*

Returns the current device MAC address.

♦ *Connect (MacAddress As String)*

Tries to connect to a device with the given address. The connection is done in the background. The Connected event will be raised when the connection is ready (or fails). The UUID used for the connection is the default UUID: 00001101-0000-1000-8000-00805F9B34FB.

♦ *Connect2 (MacAddress As String, UUID As String)*

Tries to connect to a device with the given address and UUID. The connection is done in the background. The Connected event will be raised when the connection is ready (or fails).

♦ *Connect3 (MacAddress As String, Port As Int)*

This method is a workaround for hardware devices that do not connect with Connect or Connect2. See this issue (http://bit.ly/1Owjm7T) for more information.

ConnectInsecure (Admin As BluetoothAdmin, MacAddress As String, Port As Int)

Tries to connect to a device over an unencrypted connection.
Admin - Object of type BluetoothAdmin.
MacAddress - The address of the remote device.
Port - RFCOMM (http://bit.ly/1dgYl19) channel.

Disconnect

Disconnects the connection (if such exists) and stops listening for new connections.

GetPairedDevices As Map

Returns a map with the paired devices' friendly names as keys and their addresses as values.
The following code shows a list of available devices and allows the user to connect to one:

```
Dim PairedDevices As Map
PairedDevices = Serial1.GetPairedDevices
Dim l As List
l.Initialize
For i = 0 To PairedDevices.Size - 1
  l.Add(PairedDevices.GetKeyAt(i))
Next
Dim res As Int
res = InputList(l, "Choose device", -1) 'show list with paired devices
If res <> DialogResponse.CANCEL Then
  Serial1.Connect(PairedDevices.Get(l.Get(res))) 'convert the name to
MAC address and connect
End If
```

Initialize (EventName As String)

Initialized the object. You may want to call IsEnabled before trying to work with the object.

InputStream As java.io.InputStream [read only]

Returns the InputStream that is used to read data from the other device. Should be called after a connection is established.

IsEnabled As Boolean

Returns TRUE if the Bluetooth is enabled.

IsInitialized As Boolean

Whether this object has been initialized by calling `Initialize`.

Listen

Starts listening for incoming connections using the default UUID. The Connected event will be raised when the connection is established. Nothing happens if the device is already listening for connections.

Listen2 (Name As String, UUID As String)

Starts listening for incoming connections. The Connected event will be raised when the connection is established. Nothing happens if the device is already listening for connections.
Name - An arbitrary string that will be used for internal registration.
UUID - The UUID defined for this record.

⬡ ListenInsecure (Admin As BluetoothAdmin, Port As Int)

Starts listening for incoming unencrypted connections.
Admin - An object of type BluetoothAdmin.
Port - The RFCOMM channel.

🔑 Name As String [read only]

Returns the current device friendly name.

🔑 OutputStream As java.io.OutputStream [read only]

Returns the OutputStream that is used to write data to the other device. Should be called after a connection is established.

⬡ StopListening

Stops listening for incoming connections. This will not disconnect any active connection.

Sip Library

The Sip library lets you make audio calls using Voice over Internet Protocol (Voip) services. Sip features were added in Android 2.3 (API level 9). Note that not all devices above Android 2.3 support Sip features. In order to use this library, you will need to set android.jar in [Tools > Configure Paths] to platform-9 or above.

This library is included in the IDE installation package. A tutorial is available here (http://bit.ly/14tU0mz).

List of types:

Sip
SipAudioCall

Sip

Sip is the main object which manages the Sip services. Once you make a call or receive an incoming call, you will get a **SipAudioCall** object, which represents the call.

Permissions:

android.permission.USE_SIP
android.permission.INTERNET
android.permission.RECORD_AUDIO
android.permission.ACCESS_WIFI_STATE
android.permission.WAKE_LOCK
android.permission.MODIFY_AUDIO_SETTINGS

Events:

Registering

RegistrationDone (ExpiryTime As Long)

RegistrationFailed (ErrorCode As Int, ErrorMessage As String)

CallEstablished

CallEnded

Calling

CallError (ErrorCode As Int, ErrorMessage As String)

CallRinging (IncomingCall As SipAudioCall)

Members:

🔧*AutoRegistration As Boolean [write only]*
Sets whether the Sip manager will register automatically if needed.

🌐*Close*
Closes the connection.

🔧*DisplayName As String [write only]*
Sets the user display name.

🌐*Initialize (EventName As String, User As String, Host As String, Password As String)*
Initializes the object.
EventName - Sets the subs that will handle the events.
User - User name.
Host - Host name or IP address.
Password - Account password.

🌐*Initialize2 (EventName As String, URI As String, Password As String)*
Initializes the object.
EventName - Sets the subs that will handle the events.
URI – the "Uniform Resource Identifier" (address) of the profile resource, for example: "sip:zzz@iptel.org"
Password - Account password.

🔧*IsInitialized As Boolean [read only]*
Returns TRUE if the object was initialized.

🔧*IsSipSupported As Boolean [read only]*
Returns TRUE if Sip API is supported on the device.

🔧*IsVoipSupported As Boolean [read only]*
Returns TRUE if Voip is supported on this device.

🌐*MakeCall (TargetUri As String, TimeoutSeconds As Int) As SipAudioCall*
Makes an audio call. This method should only be called after registering.
TargetUri - The address of the target.
TimeoutSeconds - The timeout (measured in seconds).

✦ OutboundProxy As String [write only]
Sets the outbound proxy address.

✦ Port As Int [write only]
Sets the connection port.

✦ ProfileName As String [write only]
Sets the user-defined profile name.

✦ Protocol As String [write only]
Sets the protocol. Either "TCP" or "UDP".

✿ Register
Sends a registration request to the server. The following events will be raised: either `Registering` and `RegistrationDone`, or `RegistrationFail`.

✦ SendKeepAlive As Boolean [write only]
Sets whether keep-alive messages will be sent automatically.

SipAudioCall
Represents an audio call. This object is created by calling `Sip.MakeCall` or from the `CallRinging` event.

Members:

✿ AnswerCall (TimeoutSeconds As Int)
Answers an incoming call.
TimeoutSeconds - Allowed time for the call to be established.

✿ EndCall
Ends the current call.

✦ IsInCall As Boolean [read only]
Returns TRUE if the call was established.

✿ IsInitialized As Boolean
Whether this object has been initialized.

✦ IsMuted As Boolean [read only]
Returns TRUE if the microphone is muted.

✦ PeerUri As String [read only]
Gets the address of the peer.

✿ SendDtmf (Code As Int)
Sends a Dtmf tone. Values can be 0-15, where 0-9 are the digits, 10 is '*', 11 is '#' and 12-15 are 'A'-'D'.

✦ SpeakerMode As Boolean [write only]
Sets the speaker mode.

✿ StartAudio
Starts the audio for the call. Should be called in CallEstablished event.

🗘 *ToggleMute*

Toggles the microphone mute.

SQL Library

This library (included in the IDE installation package) allows you to create and manage SQLite databases. See the Databases Chapter (page 215) for more information.

List of types:

Cursor
SQL

Cursor

A cursor is the object returned from a database query. It consists of a set of records and a pointer to the current record.

It is similar to a **recordset** in Visual Basic.

Members:

🗘 *Close*

Closes the cursor and frees resources.

🖋 *ColumnCount As Int [read only]*

Gets the number of fields available in the result set.

🗘 *GetBlob (ColumnName As String) As Byte()*

Returns the blob stored in the given column. Example:
```
Dim Buffer() As Byte
Buffer = Cursor.GetBlob("col1")
```

🗘 *GetBlob2 (Index As Int) As Byte()*

Returns the blob stored in the column at the given ordinal. Example:
```
Dim Buffer() As Byte
Buffer = Cursor.GetBlob2(0)
```

🗘 *GetColumnName (Index As Int) As String*

Returns the name of the column at the specified index. The first column index is 0.

🗘 *GetDouble (ColumnName As String) As Double*

Returns the Double value stored in the given column. The value will be converted to Double if it is of different type. Example:
```
Log(Cursor.GetDouble("col2"))
```

🗘 *GetDouble2 (Index As Int) As Double*

Returns the Double value stored in the column at the given ordinal. The value will be converted to Double if it is of different type. Example:
```
Log(Cursor.GetDouble2(0))
```

🗘 *GetInt (ColumnName As String) As Int*

Returns the Int value stored in the given column. The value will be converted to Int if it is of different type. Example:

```
Log(Cursor.GetInt("col2"))
```

GetInt2 (Index As Int) As Int

Returns the Int value stored in the column at the given ordinal. The value will be converted to Int if it is of different type. Example:

```
Log(Cursor.GetInt2(0))
```

GetLong (ColumnName As String) As Long

Returns the Long value stored in the given column. The value will be converted to Long if it is of different type. Example:

```
Log(Cursor.GetLong("col2"))
```

GetLong2 (Index As Int) As Long

Returns the Long value stored in the column at the given ordinal. The value will be converted to Long if it is of different type. Example:

```
Log(Cursor.GetLong2(0))
```

GetString (ColumnName As String) As String

Returns the String value stored in the given column. The value will be converted to String if it is of different type. Example:

```
Log(Cursor.GetString("col2"))
```

GetString2 (Index As Int) As String

Returns the String value stored in the column at the given ordinal. The value will be converted to String if it is of different type. Example:

```
Log(Cursor.GetString2(0))
```

IsInitialized As Boolean

Whether this object has been initialized.

Position As Int

Gets or sets the current position (row). Note that the starting position of a cursor returned from a query is `-1`. The first valid position is 0. Example:

```
Dim SQL1 As SQL
Dim Cursor1 As Cursor
Cursor1 = SQL1.ExecQuery("SELECT col1, col2 FROM table1")
For i = 0 To Cursor1.RowCount - 1
  Cursor1.Position = i
  Log(Cursor1.GetString("col1"))
  Log(Cursor1.GetInt("col2"))
Next
Cursor1.Close
```

RowCount As Int [read only]

Gets the numbers of rows available in the result set.

SQL

The main object that accesses the SQLite database built-into Android. See the Databases Chapter (page 215) for more information.

Events:

QueryComplete (Success As Boolean, Crsr As Cursor)

NonQueryComplete (Success As Boolean)

Members:

⬢ AddNonQueryToBatch (Statement As String, Args As List)

Adds a non-query statement to the batch of statements. The statements are (asynchronously) executed when you call ExecNonQueryBatch. **Args** can be Null if it is not needed. Example:

```
For i = 1 To 10000
     sql1.AddNonQueryToBatch("INSERT INTO table1 VALUES (?)", Array As
Object(Rnd(0, 100000)))
Next
sql1.ExecNonQueryBatch("SQL")
...
Sub SQL_NonQueryComplete (Success As Boolean)
  Log("NonQuery: " & Success)
  If Success = False Then Log(LastException)
End Sub
```

⬢ BeginTransaction

Begins a transaction (page 227). A transaction is a set of multiple "writing" statements for which either all or no changes will be saved to the database. Changes are held in a temporary form and, if there is an error, all changes are reversed so the database is restored to its original state. **It is very important** to handle transactions carefully and close them. The transaction is considered successful only if **TransactionSuccessful** is called. Otherwise, no changes will be saved.

⬢ Close

Closes the database. Does not do anything if the database was never opened or has already been closed.

⬢ EndTransaction

Ends the transaction.

⬢ ExecNonQuery (Statement As String)

Executes a single non query SQL statement. Example:

```
SQL1.ExecNonQuery("CREATE TABLE table1 (col1 TEXT , col2 INTEGER, col3
INTEGER)")
```

If you plan to do many "writing" queries one after another, then you should consider using **BeginTransaction** and **EndTransaction**, which will execute significantly faster.

⬢ ExecNonQuery2 (Statement As String, Args As List)

Executes a single non query SQL statement. The statement can include question marks which will be replaced by the items in the given list. Note that B4A converts arrays to lists implicitly. The values in the list should be strings, numbers or byte-arrays. Example:

```
SQL1.ExecNonQuery2("INSERT INTO table1 VALUES (?, ?, 0)", Array As
Object("some text", 2))
```

⬢ ExecNonQueryBatch (EventName As String)

Asynchronously executes a batch of non-query statements (such as INSERT).

The NonQueryComplete event is raised after the statements are completed.
You should call AddNonQueryToBatch one or more times before calling this method to add statements to the batch. **Note** that this method internally begins and ends a transaction.

♘*ExecQuery (Query As String) As Cursor*
Executes the query and returns a cursor which is used to go over the results. Example:
```
Dim SQL1 As SQL
Dim Cursor1 As Cursor
Cursor1 = SQL1.ExecQuery("SELECT col1, col2 FROM table1")
For i = 0 To Cursor1.RowCount - 1
  Cursor1.Position = i
  Log(Cursor1.GetString("col1"))
  Log(Cursor1.GetInt("col2"))
Next
```

♘*ExecQuery2 (Query As String, StringArgs() As String) As Cursor*
Executes the query and returns a cursor which is used to go over the results. The query can include question marks which will be replaced with the values in the array. Example:
```
Dim SQL1 As SQL
Dim Cursor1 As Cursor
Cursor1 = SQL1.ExecQuery2("SELECT col1 FROM table1 WHERE col3 = ?",
Array As String(22))
```
SQLite will try to convert the string values based on the column types.

♘*ExecQueryAsync (EventName As String, Query As String, StringArgs() As String)*
Asynchronously executes the given query. The QueryComplete event will be raised when the results are ready. Example:
```
sql1.ExecQueryAsync("SQL", "SELECT * FROM table1", Null)
...
Sub SQL_QueryComplete (Success As Boolean, Crsr As Cursor)
  If Success Then
     For i = 0 To Crsr.RowCount - 1
         Crsr.Position = i
         Log(Crsr.GetInt2(0))
     Next
  Else
     Log(LastException)
  End If
End Sub
```

♘*ExecQuerySingleResult (Query As String) As String*
Executes the query and returns the value in the first column and the first row (in the result set). Returns Null if no results were found. Example:

```
Dim NumberOfMatches As Int
NumberOfMatches = SQL1.ExecQuerySingleResult("SELECT count(*) FROM
table1 WHERE col2 > 300")
```

❦ ExecQuerySingleResult2 (Query As String, StringArgs() As String) As String

Executes the query and returns the value in the first column and the first row (in the result set). Returns Null if no results were found. Example:

```
Dim NumberOfMatches As Int
NumberOfMatches = SQL1.ExecQuerySingleResult2("SELECT count(*) FROM
table1 WHERE col2 > ?", Array As String(300))
```

❦ Initialize (Dir As String, FileName As String, CreateIfNecessary As Boolean)

Opens the database file. A new database will be created if it does not exist and CreateIfNecessary is True. Example:

```
Sub Process_Globals
  Dim SQL1 As SQL
End Sub

Sub Activity_Create(FirstTime As Boolean)
  If FirstTime Then
  SQL1.Initialize(File.DirRootExternal, "1.db", True)
  End If
End Sub
```

❦ IsInitialized As Boolean

Returns TRUE if the database is initialized and opened.

❦ TransactionSuccessful

Marks the transaction as a successful transaction. No further statements should be executed till calling EndTransaction.

StringUtils Library

This library is included in the IDE installation package.

List of types:
StringUtils

StringUtils
Collection of string-related functions.

❦ DecodeBase64 (Data As String) As Byte()
Decodes data from Base64 notation.

❦ DecodeUrl (Url As String, CharSet As String) As String
Decodes an application/x-www-form-urlencoded string. See Text Encoding (page 368) for details of character sets.

❦ EncodeBase64 (Data() As Byte) As String
Encodes the given byte-array into Base64 notation. Example:

```
Dim su As StringUtils
Dim encoded As String
encoded = su.EncodeBase64(data) 'data is a byte-array
```

❖EncodeUrl (Url As String, CharSet As String) As String

Encodes a string into application/x-www-form-urlencoded format.

Url - String to encode.

CharSet - The character encoding name. See Text Encoding (page 368) for details of character sets. Example:

```
Dim su As StringUtils
Dim url, encodedUrl As String
encodedUrl = su.EncodeUrl(url, "UTF8")
```

❖LoadCSV (Dir As String, FileName As String, SeparatorChar As Char) As List

Loads a CSV file and stores it in a list of string arrays.

Dir - CSV file folder.

FileName - CSV file name.

SeparatorChar - The character used in the original file to separate fields. For the tab character, use `Chr(9)`.

Example:

```
Dim lvTest As ListView
Dim lstCSV As List
Dim StrUtil As StringUtils
Dim strRow(), strOneLine As String
Dim iRowCount As Int

' prepare ListView to show data
lvTest.Initialize("")
Activity.AddView(lvTest, 0,0,100%x, 100%y)

 ' Read the csv file
lstCSV.Initialize
lstCSV = StrUtil.LoadCSV(File.DirAssets, "book2.csv", ",")

For iRowCount = 0 To lstCSV.Size - 1
 strRow = lstCSV.Get(iRowCount)
 strOneLine = ""
 For i = 0 To strRow.Length - 1
  strOneLine = strOneLine & strRow(i)
  If i < strRow.Length - 1 Then
   strOneLine = strOneLine & ", "
  End If
 Next
 lvTest.AddSingleLine(strOneLine)
Next
```

⬙ LoadCSV2 (Dir As String, FileName As String, SeparatorChar As Char, Headers As List) As List

Similar to LoadCSV, except that it loads the first row into the Headers list of strings.

⬙ MeasureMultilineTextHeight (TextView1 As TextView, Text As String) As Int

Returns the required height in order to show the given text in a label. This can be used to show dynamic text in a label. Note that the label must first be added to its parent and only then its height can be set. Example:

```
Dim Label1 As Label
Label1.Initialize("")
Label1.Text = "this is a long sentence, and we need to " _
   & "know the height required in order To show it completely."
Label1.TextSize = 20
Activity.AddView(Label1, 10dip, 10dip, 200dip, 30dip)
Dim su As StringUtils
Label1.Height = su.MeasureMultilineTextHeight(Label1, Label1.Text)
```

⬙ SaveCSV (Dir As String, FileName As String, SeparatorChar As Char, Table As List)

Saves the table as a CSV file.

Dir - Output file folder.

FileName - Output file name.

SeparatorChar - Separator character. The character that will separate the fields in the output file.

Table - A List with arrays of strings as items. Each array represents a row. All arrays should be of the same length.

Example to create a CSV file:

```
Dim lstCSV As List
Dim StrUtil As StringUtils
Dim iRowCount As Int = 10
Dim iColCount As Int = 5

lstCSV.Initialize
```

```
' create a list of string arrays containing the data
For iRowCount = 0 To 9
 Dim strRow(iColCount) As String
 For iColCount = 0 To 4
  strRow(iColCount) = "Row " & iRowCount & ", Col " & iColCount
 Next
 lstCSV.Add(strRow)
Next

StrUtil.SaveCSV(File.DirDefaultExternal,"book2_output.csv", ",",
lstCSV)
```

⚙ SaveCSV2 (Dir As String, FileName As String, SeparatorChar As Char, Table As List, Headers As List)

Similar to SaveCSV, except the first row will come from the Headers list, which should be a list (or array) of strings.

TTS Library

This library (included in the IDE installation package) provides for text to speech (TTS). For an example program which performs both TTS and Voice Recognition, see this web page (http://bit.ly/14kXKG4).

TTS

Synthesizes text to speech and plays it. After initializing the object you should wait for the Ready event. We give an example below of how to do this using a timer.

Event: Ready (Success As Boolean)

Example:

```
Sub Globals
 Dim tmr As Timer
End Sub

Sub Globals
 Dim tts1 As TTS
 Dim ttsOK As Boolean
 Dim strTextToSpeak As String
 Private btnSpeak As Button
End Sub
```

```
Sub Activity_Create(FirstTime As Boolean)
 btnSpeak.Initialize("btnSpeak")
 Activity.AddView(btnSpeak, 20dip, 20dip, 100dip, 60dip)
 btnSpeak.Text = "Speak"
 tmr.Initialize("tmr", 1000)
End Sub


Sub Activity_Resume
 tmr.Initialize("tmr", 1000)
 If tts1.IsInitialized = False Then
  ttsOK = False
  tts1.Initialize("TTS1")
  ' set text to speak once engine is ready
  strTextToSpeak = "We are ready to do some work!"
  ' start timer to wait until TTS is ready
  ProgressDialogShow2("Waiting for Text To Speech Engine", False)
  tmr.Enabled = True
End Sub


Sub Activity_Pause (UserClosed As Boolean)
 tts1.Stop
 tts1.Release
 tmr.Enabled = False
End Sub


Sub TTS1_Ready (Success As Boolean)
 ' come here once tts1 is ready to speak
 If Success Then
  Log("TTS1_Ready success")
  ttsOK = True
 Else
  ttsOK = False
  Log("TTS1_Ready failure")
  Msgbox("Error initializing TTS engine.", "")
 End If
End Sub


Sub tmr_Tick
 If ttsOK = True Then
  tts1.speak(strTextToSpeak, False)
  tmr.Enabled = False
  ProgressDialogHide
 Else
  ' wait for timer to finish next time
 End If
End Sub
```

```
Sub btnSpeak_Click
  If ttsOK = True Then
    tts1.speak("Button Speak is working", False)
  End If
End Sub
```

For another example of using TTS, see this example (http://bit.ly/11lo8KN).

Members:

🔹 Initialize (EventName As String)

Initializes the object. The `Ready` event will be raised when the text to speech engine is ready.
EventName - The Sub that will handle the Ready event.

🔹 IsInitialized As Boolean

Whether this object has been initialized by calling `Initialize`.

🔧 Pitch As Float [write only]

Sets the pitch value. Default is 1. Example:
```
TTS1.Pitch = 1.5
```

🔹 Release

Releases any resources related to this object. You will then need to initialize the object again before use. **Note** that it is safe to call this method with an uninitialized object.

🔹 SetLanguage (Language As String, Country As String) As Boolean

Sets the spoken language.
Language - Language code. Two lowercase letters.
Country - Country code. Two uppercase letters. Pass an empty string if not needed.
Returns `True` if a matching language is available. The country value will be ignored if the language code matches and the country code does not match.

🔹 Speak (Text As String, ClearQueue As Boolean)

Speaks the given text.
ClearQueue - If `True`, then all waiting texts are dismissed and the new text is spoken. Otherwise, the new text is added to the queue.

🔧 SpeechRate As Float [write only]

Sets the speech rate. Default is 1. Example:
```
TTS1.SpeechRate = 0.5
```

🔹 Stop

Stops speaking any currently-playing text (and dismisses texts in the queue).

USB Library

This library is included in the IDE installation package.
Universal Serial Bus (USB) is a standard which defines both hardware and software involved in connecting computers to peripherals. For details see here (http://bit.ly/1DyKpcf). Note that detailed explanation of this library is outside the scope of this book. A complete working example with a tutorial is available here (http://bit.ly/1deHpbH).

List of types:

MtpDevice
UsbAccessory
UsbDevice
UsbDeviceConnection
UsbEndpoint

MtpDevice

Members:

🎲 *Close*

🎲 *Initialize (EventName As String, UsbDevice1 As UsbDevice)*

🎲 *IsInitialized As Boolean*

Whether this object has been initialized by calling `Initialize`.

🎲 *Open (Connection As UsbDeviceConnection)*

🎲 *test*

UsbAccessory

Represents a Usb accessory.

Members:

🎲 *Close*

Closes the accessory. The accessory input and output streams should be individually closed first.

🔖 *Description As String [read only]*

Gets the description of the accessory.

🔖 *InputStream As InputStreamWrapper [read only]*

Gets the input stream for the accessory. When reading data from an accessory, ensure that the buffer that you use is big enough to store the USB packet data. The Android accessory protocol supports packet buffers up to 16384 bytes, so you can choose to always declare your buffer to be of this size for simplicity.

🔖 *Manufacturer As String [read only]*

Gets the manufacturer of the accessory.

🔖 *Model As String [read only]*

Gets the model name of the accessory.

🔖 *OutputStream As OutputStreamWrapper [read only]*

Gets the output stream for the accessory.

🔖 *Serial As String [read only]*

Gets the unique serial number for the accessory.

🪶 URI As String [read only]
Gets the URI (Internet address) for the website of the accessory.

🪶 Version As String [read only]
Gets the version of the accessory.

UsbDevice
Represents a Usb device.

Members:

🪶 DeviceClass As Int [read only]
Gets the device class.

🪶 DeviceId As Int [read only]
Gets the device Id.

🪶 DeviceName As String [read only]
Gets the device name.

🪶 DeviceSubclass As Int [read only]
Gets the device subclass.

🌐 GetInterface (Index As Int) As UsbInterface
Gets the interface at the given index.

🪶 InterfaceCount As Int [read only]
Gets the number of interfaces.

🌐 IsInitialized As Boolean
Whether this object has been initialized.

🪶 ProductId As Int [read only]
Gets the product Id.

🪶 VendorId As Int [read only]
Gets the vendor Id.

UsbDeviceConnection
Represents a connection between the host and a client. UsbDeviceConnection is created by calling `UsbManager.OpenDevice`. Once connected, you should call `StartListening` to start listening for completed requests. Sending requests is done with `UsbRequest.Queue`. You should call `ContinueListening` to allow the listener to listen to the next completed request (after another IN request is sent).
Calling `StopListening` will close the connection. `ControlTransfer` method sends requests to endpoint zero which is the control endpoint. `ControlTransfer` is a blocking method (it waits for the transaction to finish, unlike `UsbRequest.Queue` which is asynchronous).

Event: NewData (Request As UsbRequest, InDirection As Boolean)
The NewData event is raised when a request completes. The request is passed as a parameter.

Members:

⬡ *BulkTransfer (Endpoint As UsbEndpoint, Buffer() As Byte, Length As Int, Timeout As Int) As Int*

Sends a synchronous request.

Endpoint - The endpoint for this transaction. The transfer direction is determined by this endpoint.

Buffer - Buffer for data to send or receive.

Length - The length of the data.

Timeout - Request timeout (in milliseconds).

⬡ *CloseSynchronous*

Like `StopListening`, `CloseSynchronous` closes the connection.

Note: this method should only be used when the asynchronous listener was not started.

⬡ *ContinueListening*

Notifies the listener to continue listening for completed requests.

⬡ *ControlTransfer (RequestType As Int, Request As Int, Value As Int, Index As Int, Buffer() As Byte, Length As Int, Timeout As Int) As Int*

Performs a control transaction on endpoint zero. Returns the number of bytes transferred.

RequestType - The request type. It should be either UsbManager.USB_DIR_IN or UsbManager.USB_DIR_OUT to set the request direction.

Request - Request Id.

Value - Value field.

Index - Index field.

Buffer - Buffer for data portion. Pass `Null` if not needed.

Length - The length of the data to send or receive.

Timeout - Timeout (in milliseconds).

⬡ *GetRawDescriptors As Byte()*

Returns the raw descriptors as an array of bytes.

This method is only available in Android 3.2 or above. It will return an empty array in Android 3.1 and earlier versions.

⬡ *IsInitialized As Boolean*

Returns `TRUE` if the object was initialized.

⚒ *Serial As String [read only]*

Returns the connected device serial number.

⬡ *StartListening (EventName As String)*

Starts listening for completed requests. When such are available, the `NewData` event will be raised.

EventName - The name of the sub that will handle the events.

⬡ *StopListening*

Stops listening to requests and closes the connection.

UsbEndpoint

Represents an endpoint in a specific interface.

Members:

Address As Int [read only]
Gets the endpoint address.

Attributes As Int [read only]
Gets the endpoint attributes.

Direction As Int [read only]
Gets the endpoint direction. Can be UsbManager.USB_DIR_IN or UsbManager.USB_DIR_OUT.

EndpointNumber As Int [read only]
Gets the endpoint number.

Interval As Int [read only]
Gets the interval field.

IsInitialized As Boolean
Whether this object has been initialized.

MaxPacketSize As Int [read only]
Gets the maximum packet size.

Type As Int [read only]
Gets the endpoint type.

UsbInterface
Represents a USB interface on a specific device.

Members:

EndpointCount As Int [read only]
Gets the number of endpoints available in this interface.

GetEndpoint (Index As Int) As UsbEndpoint
Gets the endpoint at the given index.

InterfaceClass As Int [read only]
Gets the interface class.

InterfaceProtocol As Int [read only]
Gets the interface protocol.

InterfaceSubclass As Int [read only]
Gets the interface subclass.

IsInitialized As Boolean
Whether this object has been initialized.

UsbManager
UsbManager gives access to the connected USB devices. It also holds the related constants. This library requires Android SDK 12 or above (Android 3.1 or above). You should configure B4A to use android.jar from android-12 or above.

Members:

❖ GetAccessories As UsbAccessory()
Returns an array of UsbAccessories with all the connected USB accessories.

❖ GetDevices As UsbDevice()
Returns an array of UsbDevices with all the connected USB devices.

❖ HasAccessoryPermission (Accessory As UsbAccessory) As Boolean
Returns TRUE if your application has permission (page 131) to access this accessory. Call
`RequestAccessoryPermission` to receive such permission.

❖ HasPermission (Device As UsbDevice) As Boolean
Returns TRUE if your application has permission (page 131) to access this device. Call
`RequestPermission` to receive such permission.

❖ Initialize
Initializes the object.

❖ OpenAccessory (Accessory As UsbAccessory)
Connects to the given accessory

❖ OpenDevice (Device As UsbDevice, Interface As UsbInterface, ForceClaim As Boolean) As UsbDeviceConnection
Connects to the given device and claims exclusive access to the given interface.
ForceClaim - Whether the system should disconnect kernel drivers if necessary.

❖ RequestAccessoryPermission (Accessory As UsbAccessory)
Shows a dialog that asks the user to allow your application to access the USB accessory.

❖ RequestPermission (Device As UsbDevice)
Shows a dialog that asks the user to allow your application to access the USB device.

❖ USB_CLASS_APP_SPEC As Int

❖ USB_CLASS_AUDIO As Int

❖ USB_CLASS_CDC_DATA As Int

❖ USB_CLASS_COMM As Int

❖ USB_CLASS_CONTENT_SEC As Int

❖ USB_CLASS_CSCID As Int

❖ USB_CLASS_HID As Int

❖ USB_CLASS_HUB As Int

❖ USB_CLASS_MASS_STORAGE As Int

❖ USB_CLASS_MISC As Int

❖ USB_CLASS_PER_INTERFACE As Int

❖ USB_CLASS_PHYSICA As Int

❖ USB_CLASS_PRINTER As Int

⬡ *USB_CLASS_STILL_IMAGE As Int*

⬡ *USB_CLASS_VENDOR_SPEC As Int*

⬡ *USB_CLASS_VIDEO As Int*

⬡ *USB_CLASS_WIRELESS_CONTROLLER As Int*

⬡ *USB_DIR_IN As Int*

⬡ *USB_DIR_OUT As Int*

⬡ *USB_ENDPOINT_DIR_MASK As Int*

⬡ *USB_ENDPOINT_NUMBER_MASK As Int*

⬡ *USB_ENDPOINT_XFER_BULK As Int*

⬡ *USB_ENDPOINT_XFER_CONTROL As Int*

⬡ *USB_ENDPOINT_XFER_INT As Int*

⬡ *USB_ENDPOINT_XFER_ISOC As Int*

⬡ *USB_ENDPOINT_XFERTYPE_MASK As Int*

⬡ *USB_INTERFACE_SUBCLASS_BOOT As Int*

⬡ *USB_SUBCLASS_VENDOR_SPEC As Int*

⬡ *USB_TYPE_CLASS As Int*

⬡ *USB_TYPE_MASK As Int*

⬡ *USB_TYPE_RESERVED As Int*

⬡ *USB_TYPE_STANDARD As Int*

⬡ *USB_TYPE_VENDOR As Int*

UsbRequest

This object represents a USB request packet. The `Queue` method sends the request.

Members:

⚑ *Buffer() As Byte [read only]*
Returns the buffer associated with the request.

⬡ *Initialize (Connection As UsbDeviceConnection, Endpoint As UsbEndpoint)*
Initializes the request. The request will be binded to the given connection and endpoint. **Note** that for control transactions you should use: `UsbDeviceConnection.ControlTransfer`.

⬡ *IsInitialized As Boolean*
Whether this object has been initialized by calling `Initialize`.

⚑ *Name As String*
Gets or sets an arbitrary string that can be used to identify the request.

⬡ *Queue (Buffer() As Byte, Length As Int)*

Queues the request for sending. The `UsbDeviceConnection_NewData` event will be raised when the transaction completes.

🗡 *UsbEndpoint As UsbEndpoint [read only]*

XmlSax Library

This library (included in the IDE installation package) provides an XML Sax Parser.

XML

XML (Extensible Markup Language) is a way of encoding data into a document which can be read both by humans and computers. It is widely used to send structured data over the Internet. More information here (http://bit.ly/1OwjqVb).

Sax

SAX (Simple API for XML) is a standard method of parsing (processing the elements of) an XML document. It is event-based (page 297). See this tutorial (http://bit.ly/143HXuY) for a working example.

List of types:

Attributes
SaxParser

Attributes

This object is passed in the `StartElement` event.

Members:

⬡ *GetName (Index As Int) As String*

Returns the name of the attribute at the specified index. **Note** that the order of elements can change.

⬡ *GetValue (Index As Int) As String*

Returns the value of the attribute at the specified index. **Note** that the order of elements can change.

⬡ *GetValue2 (URI As String, Name As String) As String*

Returns the value of the attribute in the namespace specified by the given **URI** (an empty string if no namespace is used) and **Name**. Returns an empty string if no such attribute was found.

⬡ *IsInitialized As Boolean*

Whether this object has been initialized.

🗡 *Size As Int [read only]*

Returns the number of attributes in this element.

SaxParser

A parser that sequentially reads a stream and raises events at the beginning and end of each element.

Events:

StartElement (URI As String, Name As String, Attributes As Attributes)

URI - Uniform Resource Identifier (address) of namespace, or an empty string if there is no namespace.

Name - The element name.

Attributes - An Attributes object holding the element's attributes.

EndElement (URI As String, Name As String, Text As StringBuilder)

URI - Uniform Resource Identifier (address) of namespace, or empty string if there is no namespace.

Name - The element name.

Text - The element text (if such exists).

Members:

Initialize

Initializes the object. Usually this object should be a `Sub Process_Globals` object.

Parents As List

A list that holds the names of the parent elements. During parsing you can use this list to recognize the current element.

Parse (InputStream As java.io.InputStream, EventName As String)

Parses the given InputStream.

EventName - The prefix of event subs.

Parse2 (TextReader As java.io.Reader, EventName As String)

Parses the given TextReader.

EventName - The prefix of event subs.

4.3 Additional Libraries and Modules

Introduction

Additional libraries are libraries which you either create yourself or download from the B4A website or receive from somebody else. It is necessary to use a specific folder for Additional libraries. You need to specify this location within [Tools > Configure Paths]. In the following, we divide libraries into:
– Additional Official Libraries: libraries created by Anywhere Software (the makers of B4A)
– Additional User Libraries (page 569): libraries which users have created and published on the B4A website.
Note: some of the following are not actually libraries but code modules (classes or services) which you include directly in your project.

Additional libraries folder

You need to set up a special folder to save additional libraries, for example: C:\B4A\AddLibraries. When you install a new version of B4A, all standard libraries are automatically updated, but the additional libraries are not included. The advantage of the special folder is that this folder is not affected when you install the new version of B4A. **Note** the additional libraries are not systematically updated with each new version of B4A. You might want to periodically check for updates.

Telling the IDE where to find additional libraries

When the IDE starts, it looks first for the available libraries in the Libraries folder of B4A and then in the folder for the additional libraries. You must specify your additional libraries folder in the IDE menu [Tools > Configure Paths]. The dialog allows you to specify the Additional Libraries folder.

List of Additional Libraries

The latest list of additional libraries is available here (http://bit.ly/16H9C7s).

Additional Official Libraries

These libraries (only available if you have the Full version) were created by Anywhere Software, the makers of B4A. We do not have the space to describe them all here. The links below will take you to the B4A website where you can learn more about each library. Follow the first links to download the library.

Adiquity

(For more information see http://bit.ly/19UgZbZ)
this library adds support for AdiQuity (http://adiquity.com/) advertising.

AdMob

(For more information see http://bit.ly/11PfPuO)
this library lets you display Google ads in your applications.

AnotherDatePicker class
(For more information see http://bit.ly/GMbTE6)
a class module which provides a "web style" date picker.

AsyncStreamsText
(For more information see http://bit.ly/16FcRfw)
a class module which allows you to read a text stream over a network.

Analytics
(For more information see http://bit.ly/16FcTUT)
a library which adds the power of Google Analytics V2 to your application and track its usage.

Audio
(For more information see http://bit.ly/1DyG7BH)
a library which includes objects which let you record audio and video, play video, play beeps and choose short sounds from a pool, use the JetPlayer (http://bit.ly/1HQyRTs) and stream audio over the Internet. Formal specification here (http://bit.ly/1HQzEUq).

Bluetooth Low Energy
(For more information see http://bit.ly/1DyEaoZ)
Bluetooth Low Energy (BLE) support was added with Android 4.3. The way Android has implemented this is less robust than Apple, but it can be made to work with some effort and by using this library. In addition there is a user-generated library which contains some useful extensions to this library, available here (http://bit.ly/1DyGQ5O). The user-generated Toggle (http://bit.ly/1DyHyQC) library contains useful methods for turning Bluetooth on and off.

Camera
(For more information see http://bit.ly/15ymkoe)
A library which allows access to the device's camera(s) and lets the user take and preview pictures. It is supported by Android 1.6+. If possible, it is recommended to work with the CameraEx class that wraps this object and adds many features. Formal specification here (http://bit.ly/1HQzKeZ).

CameraEx
(For more information see http://bit.ly/16XWdKt)
This library extends the Camera library functionality. The CameraEx class requires Android 2.3+. It allows you to easily open the back or front camera, preview and save images, and includes methods to convert preview images to JPEG, to save the pictures taken, etc.

CustomeListView
(For more information see http://bit.ly/Zoo9Rv)
A class module providing a flexible list based on ScrollView (page 432). It is suited for lists of up to 2000 items. Each item is made of a Panel that can hold any views. Each item can have a different height and the height can be set automatically based on the text.

DBUtils
(For more information see http://bit.ly/1eihJc5)
A code module providing database utilities which help you integrate SQLite databases in your program. We discuss this in the DBUtils (page 219) section of this book.

DropBox Sync
(For more information see http://bit.ly/11PhQap)
This library wraps the Dropbox Sync API. Using this API, it is quite simple to store (and retrieve) data in a folder inside the user's Dropbox account.
But note: Dropbox has deprecated (http://bit.ly/1LCOcf7) the Sync API and it will stop working in 2016. It is being replaced by API v2 (http://bit.ly/1LCObIf). At the time of writing, no alternative library had been developed. See here (http://bit.ly/1LCO4fz) for a discussion of the future of this library.

Excel
(For more information see http://bit.ly/1cK2gDC)
This library wraps the open source jexcel (http://bit.ly/1LCI46P) project and allows you to read or write Excel workbooks. This library supports only XLS files; XSLX is not supported. Formal specification here (http://bit.ly/1HQzQ6d).

GamePad
(For more information see http://bit.ly/GXt2ud)
This class module implements a multitouch gamepad made of two "joysticks".

Google Maps
(For more information see http://bit.ly/GXt3yj)
A library which allows you to add Google maps to your application. This library requires Android 3+ and will only work on devices with Google Play services. There is an on-line tutorial (http://bit.ly/10koqra) to support this library. Formal specification here (http://bit.ly/1LCHVjB). See also the following discussion on Google Play Services.

Google Play Services
(For more information see http://bit.ly/1FyM2ss)
This library is installed using the SDK Manager (page 103) and is found under Extras. Several libraries depend on it, such as AdMob, GoogleMap, Google Play Game Services, Google Analytics and others. Once it is downloaded to your android sdk library, you should copy the google-play-services.jar from <android sdk>\extras\google\google_play_services\libproject\google-play-services_lib\libs to your Additional Libraries folder. Always repeat this step whenever you update Google Play Services.
Some libraries, such as Google Maps (see previous item) depend on resources within Google Play Services. In this case, you need to add the following attribute to the Main module:
```
#AdditionalRes: <android
sdk>\extras\google\google_play_services\libproject\google-play-
services_lib\res, com.google.android.gms
```
where <android sdk> is the location of your android sdk folder.
For further discussion see here (http://bit.ly/1FyObnV).

HttpServer

(For more information see http://bit.ly/16XWCg2)
A library which allows you to easily embed an HTTP server in your application. Formal specification here (http://bit.ly/1HQzVa9).
InAppBilling (http://bit.ly/19UidUJ)
This library is described elsewhere in this book (page 267).

JSch

(For more information see http://bit.ly/17ndfMr)
A library supporting SFTP (SSH File Transfer Protocol, also called Secured File Transfer Protocol). Formal specification here (http://bit.ly/1HQzXPd).

JTidy

(For more information see http://bit.ly/16FdINo)
A library which allows you to convert an HTML page to XHTML. This can then be parsed with an XML parser, which can be more efficient than parsing the HTML using regular expressions (page 288). Formal specification here (http://bit.ly/1HQA4u5).

KeyValueStore

(For more information see http://bit.ly/1fu3UdE)
A class which uses an SQLite database to store and retrieve any kind of values you need to store persistently, such as user parameters, where each value is mapped to a key. A Keystore is very similar to a Map except that the data are stored in the file system. It can be used to store user preferences before Android calls **Activity_Pause**, then restore them on **Activity_Resume**. However, you might want to consider using StateManager for this purpose. See below.
To use KeyValueStore, you need to include the KeyValueStore module in your project. Then declare it in your main module:

```
Sub Process_Globals
    Private kvs As KeyValueStore
End Sub
```

And use it:

```
Sub Activity_Create(FirstTime As Boolean)
    If FirstTime Then
     kvs.Initialize(File.DirInternal, "datastore")
    End If
    'put a simple value
    kvs.PutSimple("time", DateTime.Now)
```

Note
KeyValueStore will create the file to hold the data if it does not already exist, using the code SQL.Initialize(). Note that you need to specify a folder which is writeable (page 366) when you call this sub.

Licensing

This library is described elsewhere in this book (page 267).

Net

(For more information see http://bit.ly/123LkwZ)

This library supports FTP, SMTP and POP3 protocols. Both regular connections and SSL connections are supported. Formal specification here (http://bit.ly/1HQA9On).

OAuth

(For more information see http://bit.ly/ZRSPuG)

A library which implements the OAuth protocol to allow you to sign HTTP requests (as required by some servers). Formal specification here (http://bit.ly/1LCG7Hw).

PayPal

(For more information see http://bit.ly/11PgPPN)

This library is a wrapper for the PayPal Mobile Payments Libraries (MPL) SDK. It allows users to pay for something using their PayPal account. Note that, as this book goes to press, PayPal is in the process of migrating to a new SDK named Mobile SDK (http://bit.ly/GXuDAq).

SearchView

(For more information see http://bit.ly/ZRU0Kz)

A class providing a more powerful alternative to AutoCompleteEditText (page 403). SearchView is quicker than AutoCompleteEditText and shows items that contain the input text anywhere, not just at the start of the item.

SMB

(For more information see http://bit.ly/165Yoqn)

This library provides access to a Microsoft Windows Network. There is a tutorial here (http://bit.ly/165YEWk) on how to use it. Formal specification here (http://bit.ly/1LCGa65).

Speak Button

(For more information see http://bit.ly/11Pf1X2)

This class makes it easy to add a button which allows users to input data into an EditText field by speaking.

SQLCipher

(For more information see http://bit.ly/165Z6Uq)

This library allows you to encrypt an SQLite database.

StateManager

(For more information see http://bit.ly/10mRVZv)

A code module which takes care of handling the application UI state and settings including saving them to a file. It is available within the StateManagerExample which can be found here (http://bit.ly/10mRVZv), where documentation can also be found.

StdActionBar Library

(For more information see http://bit.ly/1McS4DG)

This library was introduced to support tabs and dropdown lists to the action bar for Android 4. See the discussion of the Action Bar (page 121).

Typically you might use a StdActionBar to give the user tabs or icons on which to click, and a StdViewPager to scroll through the pages available in your app. The user can also swipe the pages left and right. You can use the StdTab object to modify the tabs during the execution of your app.

Note: in Android 5, the `ButtonClicked` event no longer fires when the user clicks the action bar icon (page 123). Instead you should use the `activity_ActionBarHomeClick` (page 338) event.

Note also that if you are using the StdActionBar library (http://bit.ly/1McS4DG) and handling the `ButtonClicked` event (when the user clicks the Up Button (page 122)) then you need to update the library to v1.52, otherwise the app will crash. Note that the `ButtonClicked` event will not be raised on Android 5 devices. Instead you need to handle the Activity.ActionBarHomeClick.

TableView

(For more information see http://bit.ly/165ZUIM)

This class makes it easy to add to your project and instantiate any number of tables in a layout. It is possible for tables to contain 500,000 cells. This is far easier than implementing a table using a ScrollView (page 432).

Tap for Tap

Tap for Tap offers a way to promote your app and a way of generating ad revenue, or perhaps to do both. It is described elsewhere in this book (page 266).

USB Host

(For more information see http://bit.ly/11Pjzwu)

This library allows you to connect your device (Android 3.1 and above) to support USB host mode. With this feature you can connect to regular client usb devices. A tutorial is available here (http://bit.ly/11Pj3hZ). Formal specification here (http://bit.ly/1LCGf9K).

USBSerial

(For more information see http://bit.ly/11PiqoA)

This library supports various popular chips that support serial emulation over a USB connection and provides a common API to communicate with them all. Formal specification here (http://bit.ly/1LCGhi1).

XMLBuilder

(For more information see http://bit.ly/1663zXh)

This library allow you to create simple XML documents quickly and painlessly. Formal specification here (http://bit.ly/1LCGnGo).

YouTube

(For more information see http://bit.ly/16648QF)

This library allows you to play YouTube videos inside your application. Formal specification here (http://bit.ly/1LCGth7).

Additional User Libraries

Introduction
There are many superb user-created libraries because the B4A community is very fortunate to have some great library developers who love B4A and want to share their work freely with others.

There are too many libraries for us to describe them all, and new ones are being added all the time. We provide links to lists of them and give details below of several of them to give a flavor of the types of libraries available.

To obtain or update a user library
– Follow the links given below
– Download the library zip file somewhere.
– Unzip it.
– Copy the xxx.jar and xxx.xml files to either the
– Copy the rest of the folder into your Projects folder
    · B4A Library folder for a standard B4A library or
    · Additional libraries folder for an additional library.
– In the IDE, right-click in the Libraries Manager window and select Refresh.

Which ones does a project need?
If you want to open an existing project which requires libraries, you need to ensure you have these libraries To discover which additional libraries a project needs, you can open the B4A (.b4a) file with a text editor. The libraries are listed in the file headers.

When you add libraries, you do not need to restart the IDE. You can just right-click on the list of libraries and select Refresh.

How to use a library
Most user-generated libraries include an example.b4a file demonstrating how to use the components of the library.

List of libraries

Additional User Libraries
We give some examples of user-created libraries below. For a list of other user libraries with links to their documentation, see here (http://bit.ly/1LCI9ay).

Downloading User Libraries
For a list sorted by the user who created the library with links to the download page, see here (http://bit.ly/16H9C7s). Note that this list is not being maintained. You need to search the forum to find libraries, for example http://www.basic4ppc.com/search?query=Dialogs Library

How to create a library
For details on how to create your own library, see here (page 455).

How to Share your Library

License
Unless otherwise stated, user-created libraries (jar files) which are uploaded to the B4A website are licensed with the creative commons CC BY 3.0 license (http://bit.ly/1LCISbG). Only B4A licensed users can use the JAR files and XML files to create apps, and distribute apps that have these libraries included, but the individual jar and XML files should not be distributed separately.

Dialogs Library

This library (written by Andrew Graham) contains several modal, that is blocking, dialogs by which the user can enter data. Presently, they are an InputDialog for text, a TimeDialog for times, a DateDialog for dates, both a ColorDialog and a ColorPickerDialog for colors, a NumberDialog for numbers, a FileDialog for folders and file names, and a CustomDialog.

Source
Download the library here (http://bit.ly/168SKTs).

Notes
Android does not provide modal dialogs, but B4A has a special mechanism to permit them. The Android Activity lifetime system makes this support complicated because Activities can be created and destroyed at will by Android. To avoid stack runaway on the GUI thread when an Activity is destroyed, the stack must be unwound to the lowest level.

The B4A modal mechanism does this by closing any modal dialog being shown and exiting the Sub that called the dialog, plus exiting any Sub that called that Sub, and so on, in order to return the main thread to the message loop. This means that the application does not necessarily receive a return value from the dialog and has its expected flow of execution interrupted. This will probably most often happen if the device is rotated while a modal dialog is displayed, so the Activity is destroyed and rebuilt with a new layout.

Because this may happen unexpectedly, applications (depending upon their logical structure) may need code in the **Pause** and **Resume** Subs to deal with the fact that modal dialog closure may not always be detected. For example, when a modal dialog is shown, you could set a Boolean as **True**. This variable would have to be declared within **Sub Process_Globals**. When the modal dialog returns you could clear the Boolean with some checking code in the **Resume** Sub.

The above discussion also applies to the B4A modal dialogs **InputList**, **InputMultiList**, **Msgbox** and **Msgbox2**.

Response Codes
The value returned from the dialogs, called the "dialog return value" is:
-1 if the user clicks the right button (called "Positive" in the documentation below)
-2 if the user clicks the left button (called "Negative" in the documentation below)
-3 if the user clicks the center button (called "Cancel" in the documentation below)

So the commands
```
Dim nd As NumberDialog
...

ret = nd.Show("Button Sequence", "Positive", "Cancel", "Negative",
Bmp)
```
Would produce the dialog

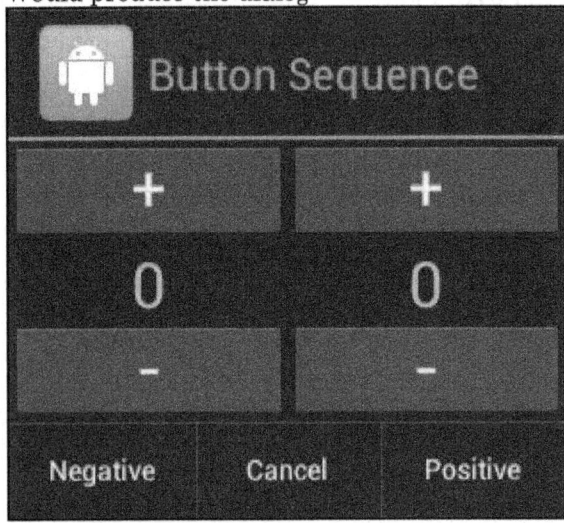

List of types:
ColorDialog
ColorDialogHSV
ColorPickerDialog
CustomDialog (page 575)
CustomDialog2 (page 576)
DateDialog (page 576)
FileDialog (page 577)
InputDialog (page 579)
NumberDialog (page 580)
TimeDialog (page 581)

ColorDialog
This modal dialog allows the user to define a color by its Red, Green and Blue components.
This is an **Activity** object; it cannot be declared under **Sub Process_Globals**.

Members:

ARGB (Alpha As Int) As Int
Returns an integer value representing the color built from the three components and with
the specified alpha value.
Alpha - A value from 0 to 255, where 0 is fully transparent and 255 is fully opaque.

Blue As Int
Sets the value of the blue component of the dialog when it is initially shown. Returns the
value of the blue component of the dialog when it was closed.

🔥 Green As Int
Sets the value of the green component of the dialog when it is initially shown. Returns the value of the green component of the dialog when it was closed.

🔥 Red As Int
Sets the value of the red component of the dialog when it is initially shown. Returns the value of the red component of the dialog when it was closed.

🔥 Response As Int [read only]
Returns the response code that the dialog returned when it last closed.

🔥 RGB As Int
Sets the value of the red, green and blue components of the dialog when it is initially shown. Returns the color of the red, green and blue components of the dialog when it was closed. Alpha of the provided color is ignored; the alpha of the dialog is set to 255 (opaque).

⚙ Show (title As String, Positive As String, Cancel As String, Negative As String, icon As Bitmap) As Int
Shows a modal color dialog with the specified title.
Title - The dialog title.
Positive - The text to show for the "positive" button. Pass "" if you don't want to show the button.
Cancel - The text to show for the "cancel" button. Pass "" if you don't want to show the button.
Negative - The text to show for the "negative" button. Pass "" if you don't want to show the button.
Icon - A bitmap that will be drawn near the title. Pass `Null` if you don't want to show an icon.
Returns one of the DialogResponse values.

🔥 Version As Double [read only]
Returns the version of the library.

ColorDialogHSV
This modal dialog allows the user to define a color by its Hue, Saturation and Value components. This is an `Activity` object; it cannot be declared under `Sub Process_Globals`.

Members:

⚙ ARGB (Alpha As Int) As Int
Returns an integer value representing the color built from the three components and with the specified alpha value.
Alpha - A value from 0 to 255, where 0 is fully transparent and 255 is fully opaque.

🔥 Hue As Float
Sets the value of the hue component of the dialog when it is initially shown. Returns the value of the hue component of the dialog when it was closed. The range of valid numbers for hue is 0.0 to 360.0.

⚡ Response As Int [read only]

Returns the response code that the dialog returned when it last closed.

⚡ RGB As Int

Sets the value of the red, green and blue components of the dialog when it is initially shown. Returns the color of the red, green and blue components of the dialog when it was closed. Alpha of the provided color is ignored and the alpha of the dialog is set to 255 (opaque).

⚡ Saturation As Float

Sets the value of the saturation component of the dialog when it is initially shown. Returns the value of the saturation component of the dialog when it was closed. The range of valid numbers for saturation is 0.0 to 1.0.

⬡ Show (title As String, Positive As String, Cancel As String, Negative As String, icon As Bitmap) As Int

Shows a modal color dialog with the specified title.

Title - The dialog title.

Positive - The text to show for the "positive" button. Pass "" if you don't want to show the button. **Cancel** - The text to show for the "cancel" button. Pass "" if you don't want to show the button.

Negative - The text to show for the "negative" button. Pass "" if you don't want to show the button.

Icon - A bitmap that will be drawn near the title. Pass `Null` if you don't want to show an icon.

Returns one of the DialogResponse values.

⚡ Value As Float

Sets the value component of the dialog when it is initially shown. Returns the value of the dialog when it was closed. The range of valid numbers for Value is from 0.0 to 1.0.

⚡ Version As Double [read only]

Returns the version of the library.

ColorPickerDialog

This modal dialog allows the user to select a color from a palette of colors. The color may be from a standard palette in the dialog or a custom programmed palette. This is an `Activity` object; it cannot be declared under `Sub Process_Globals`.

Members:

⬡ ARGB (Alpha As Int) As Int

Returns an integer value representing the color built from the chosen color and with the specified alpha value.

Alpha - A value from 0 to 255 where 0 is fully transparent and 255 is fully opaque.

⬡ GetPaletteAt (index As Int) As Int

Gets the value of the color at the specified index in the current palette.

⚡ Palette() As Int

Copies the colors in the array provided to the palette of colors in the dialog. The provided array should contain 15 colors. Returns an integer array that is a copy of the present palette.

☸ *ResetPalette*

Reset the palette of colors to the standard palette of the dialog.

☛ *Response As Int [read only]*

Returns the response code that the dialog returned when it last closed.

☛ *RGB As Int*

Sets the value of the chosen color of the dialog when it is initially shown. Returns the value of the chosen color of the dialog when it was closed.

☸ *SetPaletteAt (index As Int, color As Int)*

Sets the value of the color at the specified index in the current palette. This allows replacing just one or two colors without defining an entire palette.

☸ *Show (title As String, Positive As String, Cancel As String, Negative As String, icon As Bitmap) As Int*

Shows a modal color picker dialog with the specified title.
Title - The dialog title.
Positive - The text to show for the "positive" button. Pass "" if you don't want to show the button.
Cancel - The text to show for the "cancel" button. Pass "" if you don't want to show the button.
Negative - The text to show for the "negative" button. Pass "" if you don't want to show the button.
Icon - A bitmap that will be drawn near the title. Pass `Null` if you don't want to show an icon.
Returns one of the DialogResponse values.

☛ *Version As Double [read only]*

Returns the version of the library.

CustomDialog

This modal dialog displays a custom set of controls laid out on a B4A Panel. The Panel is displayed at an abolute position and size within the dialog. This is an `Activity` object; it cannot be declared under `Sub Process_Globals`.

Members:

☸ *AddView (view1 As View, left As Int, top As Int, width As Int, height As Int)*

Adds the custom layout view, most probably a Panel, to the custom dialog. Although named AddView to match B4A syntax, only one view can be added. Adding a view replaces any existing view previously added to the dialog.

☛ *Response As Int [read only]*

Returns the response code that the dialog returned when it last closed.

☸ *Show (Title As String, Positive As String, Cancel As String, Negative As String, icon As Bitmap) As Int*

Shows a modal custom dialog with the specified title.

Title - The dialog title.

Positive - The text to show for the "positive" button. Pass "" if you don't want to show the button.

Cancel - The text to show for the "cancel" button. Pass "" if you don't want to show the button.

Negative - The text to show for the "negative" button. Pass "" if you don't want to show the button.

Icon - A bitmap that will be drawn near the title. Pass `Null` if you don't want to show an icon. Returns one of the DialogResponse values.

Version As Double [read only]

Returns the version of the library.

CustomDialog2

This modal dialog displays a custom set of controls laid out on a B4A Panel. The Panel will be automatically centred in the displayed dialog. This is an `Activity` object; it cannot be declared under `Sub Process_Globals`.

Members:

AddView (view1 As View, width As Int, height As Int)

Adds the custom layout view, most probably a Panel, to the custom dialog. Although named AddView to match B4A syntax, only one view can be added. Adding a view replaces any existing view previously added to the dialog.

Response As Int [read only]

Returns the response code that the dialog returned when it last closed.

Show (Title As String, Positive As String, Cancel As String, Negative As String, icon As Bitmap) As Int

Shows a modal custom dialog with the specified title.

Title - The dialog title.

Positive - The text to show for the "positive" button. Pass "" if you don't want to show the button.

Cancel - The text to show for the "cancel" button. Pass "" if you don't want to show the button.

Negative - The text to show for the "negative" button. Pass "" if you don't want to show the button.

Icon - A bitmap that will be drawn near the title. Pass `Null` if you don't want to show an icon.

Returns one of the DialogResponse values.

Version As Double [read only]

Returns the version of the library.

DateDialog

This modal dialog allows the collection of user-entered data in the form of a date. This is an `Activity` object; it cannot be declared under `Sub Process_Globals`.

Members:

🪶 DateTicks As Long

Sets the date value of the dialog when it is initially shown. Returns the date value in ticks of the dialog when it is closed.

🪶 DayOfMonth As Int

Sets the day of month value of the dialog when it is initially shown. Returns the day of month value of the dialog when it is closed.

🪶 Month As Int

Sets the month value of the dialog when it is initially shown. Returns the month value of the dialog when it is closed.

🪶 Response As Int [read only]

Returns the response code that the dialog returned when it last closed.

🔹 SetDate (dayofmonth As Int, month As Int, year As Int)

Sets the date values of the dialog when it is initially shown.

🔹 Show (Message As String, Title As String, Positive As String, Cancel As String, Negative As String, icon As Bitmap) As Int

Shows a modal date input dialog with the specified message and title.
Message - The dialog message.
Title - The dialog title.
Positive - The text to show for the "positive" button. Pass "" if you don't want to show the button.
Cancel - The text to show for the "cancel" button. Pass "" if you don't want to show the button.
Negative - The text to show for the "negative" button. Pass "" if you don't want to show the button.
Icon - A bitmap that will be drawn near the title. Pass `Null` if you don't want to show an icon.
Returns one of the DialogResponse values.

🪶 ShowCalendar As Boolean

Gets or sets a flag indicating whether to show the Calendar part of the DateDialog. This only works on devices supporting API 11 (Honeycomb 3.0.x) or later

🪶 Version As Double [read only]

Returns the version of the library.

🪶 Year As Int

Sets the year value of the dialog when it is initially shown. Returns the year value of the dialog when it is closed.

FileDialog

This modal dialog allows the user to choose a folder and choose or enter a filename. This is an `Activity` object; it cannot be declared under `Sub Process_Globals`.

Members:

ChosenName As String

Sets the filename initially shown to the user. Returns the filename entered or chosen by the user.

FastScroll As Boolean

Gets or sets whether the fast scroll thumb (an indicator that can be dragged to quickly scroll through the list) is displayed by the dialog.

FileFilter As String

Gets or sets the filter values of the dialog. The filter can be a single value ".txt". The filter can also be a comma-separated list of values ".jpg,.png". Note that spaces in filter values are significant and are not ignored. If a filename contains the text of a filter value, the file will be displayed. A value of an empty string, the default, will show all files.

FilePath As String

Sets the file path of the dialog when it is initially shown. Returns the file path of the dialog when it is closed. Note that setting the file path also sets ChosenName to an empty string.

KeyboardPopUp As Boolean

Gets or sets whether the keyboard only pops up when the EditText is clicked.

Response As Int [read only]

Returns the response code that the dialog returned when it last closed.

ScrollingBackgroundColor As Int

Gets or sets the background color that will be used while scrolling the list. This is an optimization done to make the scrolling smoother. Set to Colors.Transparent if the background behind the list is not a solid color. The default is whatever is the default for the particular device.

Show (Title As String, Positive As String, Cancel As String, Negative As String, icon As Bitmap) As Int

Shows a modal file dialog with the specified title.
Title - The dialog title.
Positive - The text to show for the "positive" button. Pass "" if you don't want to show the button.
Cancel - The text to show for the "cancel" button. Pass "" if you don't want to show the button.
Negative - The text to show for the "negative" button. Pass "" if you don't want to show the button.
Icon - A bitmap that will be drawn near the title. Pass `Null` if you don't want to show an icon. Returns one of the DialogResponse values.

ShowOnlyFolders As Boolean

Gets or sets whether to show only folders and not files in the dialog.

Version As Double [read only]

Returns the version of the library.

InputDialog

This modal dialog allows the collection of user-entered data in the form of text. The default is free text, but the input can be restricted to numeric characters only or to signed numbers, including a decimal point. This is an `Activity` object; it cannot be declared under `Sub Process_Globals`.

Members:

🔥 Hint As String

Gets or sets the text that will appear when the dialog is empty.

🔥 HintColor As Int

Gets or sets the hint text color.

🔥 Input As String

Sets the initial text when the dialog is shown and returns the text entered by the user.

🔷 INPUT_TYPE_DECIMAL_NUMBERS As Int

🔷 INPUT_TYPE_NONE As Int

This can be useful, for example, if you use a read-only `InputDialog` for which you do not want a keyboard to be displayed.

🔷 INPUT_TYPE_NUMBERS As Int

🔷 INPUT_TYPE_PHONE As Int

🔷 INPUT_TYPE_TEXT As Int

🔥 InputType As Int

Sets or returns the input type accepted by the input box. Possible values are:
– ThisDialogName.INPUT_TYPE_NUMBERS for integer numbers.
– ThisDialogName.INPUT_TYPE_DECIMAL_NUMBER for signed decimal numbers.
– ThisDialogName.INPUT_TYPE_TEXT for free text.
– ThisDialogName.INPUT_TYPE_PHONE for telephone numbers.

🔥 PasswordMode As Boolean

Sets or returns whether this dialog hides the actual characters entered by the user.

🔥 Response As Int [read only]

Returns the response code that the dialog returned when it last closed.

🌐 Show (message As String, title As String, Positive As String, Cancel As String, Negative As String, icon As Bitmap) As Int

Shows a modal text input dialog with the specified message and title.
Message - The dialog message. Title - The dialog title.
Positive - The text to show for the "positive" button. Pass "" if you don't want to show the button.
Cancel - The text to show for the "cancel" button. Pass "" if you don't want to show the button.
Negative - The text to show for the "negative" button. Pass "" if you don't want to show the button.

Icon - A bitmap that will be drawn near the title. Pass **Null** if you don't want to show an icon. Returns one of the DialogResponse values.

🎵 *Version As Double [read only]*
Returns the version of the library.

NumberDialog
This configurable modal dialog allows the user to enter a number. The dialog is configurable to show any number of digits between a minimum of one and a maximum of nine The display of a decimal point is optional and the character displayed as the decimal indicator is configurable. Note that the number accepted and returned by the dialog is an integer value and so may need scaling appropriately. This is an **Activity** object; it cannot be declared under **Sub Process_Globals**.

Members:

🎵 *Decimal As Int*
Gets or sets the position of a displayed decimal point in the dialog. Zero (the default) displays no decimals, one indicates a single decimal, and so on.

🎵 *DecimalChar As Char*
Gets or sets the displayed decimal character in the dialog. The default is ".".

🎵 *Digits As Int*
Gets or sets the number of digits displayed in the dialog when it is open. One is the minimum, nine is the maximum. The default is five. If ShowSign is **True**, then the leftmost digit will display a "+" or "-" and only eight digits will be shown.

🎵 *Number As Int*
Sets the number initially displayed in the dialog when it is shown. If the number is negative and ShowSign is **False**, then the absolute value is displayed. Gets the number entered by the user after the dialog is closed. If ShowSign is **True**, the sign of the number corresponds to the sign entered by the user.

🎵 *Response As Int [read only]*
Returns the response code that the dialog returned when it last closed.

🌀 *Show (title As String, Positive As String, Cancel As String, Negative As String, icon As Bitmap) As Int*
Shows a modal number picker dialog with the specified title.
Title - The dialog title.
Positive - The text to show for the "positive" button. Pass "" if you don't want to show the button.
Cancel - The text to show for the "cancel" button. Pass "" if you don't want to show the button.
Negative - The text to show for the "negative" button. Pass "" if you don't want to show the button.
Icon - A bitmap that will be drawn near the title. Pass **Null** if you don't want to show an icon.
Returns one of the DialogResponse values.

ShowSign As Boolean

Gets or sets whether the displayed number includes a sign character. The default is **False**, so no minus sign is displayed if the number is negative.

Version As Double [read only]

Returns the version of the library.

TimeDialog

This modal dialog allows the collection of user entered data in the form of a time. The time may be entered in 12 or 24 hour format as determined by the programmer. This is an **Activity** object; it cannot be declared under **Sub Process_Globals**.

Members:

Hour As Int

Sets the hour value of the dialog when it is initially shown. Returns the hour value of the dialog when it is closed.

Is24Hours As Boolean

Sets or returns whether the dialog shows the time in 24 hour format.

Minute As Int

Sets the minute value of the dialog when it is initially shown. Returns the minute value of the dialog when it is closed.

Response As Int [read only]

Returns the response code that the dialog returned when it last closed.

SetTime (hour As Int, minutes As Int, hours24 As Boolean)

Sets the time values of the dialog when it is initially shown.

Show (Message As String, Title As String, Positive As String, Cancel As String, Negative As String, icon As Bitmap) As Int

Shows a modal time input dialog with the specified message and title.
Message - The dialog message.
Title - The dialog title.
Positive - The text to show for the "positive" button. Pass "" if you don't want to show the button.
Cancel - The text to show for the "cancel" button. Pass "" if you don't want to show the button.
Negative - The text to show for the "negative" button. Pass "" if you don't want to show the button.
Icon - A bitmap that will be drawn near the title. Pass **Null** if you don't want to show an icon.
Returns one of the DialogResponse values.

TimeTicks As Long

Sets the time value of the dialog when it is initially shown.
Returns the time value in ticks of the dialog when it is closed.

🔖 *Version As Double [read only]*
Returns the version of the library.

Reflection Library

This library (written by Andrew Graham) is perhaps one of the most useful user contributions. It contains the Reflector object which allows access to methods and fields of Android objects that are not exposed in the B4A language. It does this by means of a facility called "Reflection" that uses meta-data for objects that are included in the application package and allows dynamic access to fields and methods at runtime.

Source
Download the library here (http://bit.ly/11f1e7K).

Notes
For more information about this library see here (http://bit.ly/1LCIXfy).
The JavaObject library (page 492) provides similar functionality to the Reflection library, but is usually simpler to use, having an object-oriented approach, although it lacks some of the Reflection library features.

List of types:
Reflector

Reflector
This is the object that does the reflection. In order to use this successfully, you will need an understanding of the use of Java classes and their fields and methods.
Technical documentation (although often lacking useful explanatory details) is available on the Google Android website (http://bit.ly/1LCIYA5).
Java is case sensitive and, as used for Android, does not support properties. Properties, as implemented in B4A, are actually methods with lower-case prefixes 'set' and 'get'. 'set' methods take a single parameter and return void, 'get' methods take no parameters and return the requested values. Any other method signatures are exposed by B4A as normal methods. For example, the Left property of a View is actually implemented in Java code as two methods, `int getLeft()` and `void setLeft(int left)`. The B4A compiler makes them look like a single property to the programmer.

Events:
Click(ViewTag As Object); LongClick(ViewTag As Object) As Boolean; Focus(ViewTag As Object, Focus As Boolean); Key(ViewTag As Object, KeyCode As Int, KeyEvent As Object) As Boolean; Touch(ViewTag As Object, Action As Int, X As Float, Y As Float, MotionEvent As Object) As Boolean.

Example

```
Sub RegexReplace(Pattern As String, Text As String, Replacement As
String) As String
' example RegexReplace("abc(d)(e)", "abcde", "$2 $1")
 Dim m As Matcher
 m = Regex.Matcher(Pattern, Text)
 Dim r As Reflector
 r.Target = m
 Return r.RunMethod2("replaceAll", Replacement, "java.lang.String")
End Sub
```

Members:

💠 CreateObject (type As String) As Object

Creates and returns a new object of the specified type using the default constructor.

💠 CreateObject2 (type As String, args() As Object, types() As String) As Object

Creates and returns a new object of the specified type using the constructor that matches the array of type names given and passes it the arguments provided. The array of type names is needed in order to find the correct constructor because primitives passed in the Args array are boxed and so CreateNew cannot tell whether to look for a target constructor that accepts a primitive parameter type or a boxed primitive object type.

💠 GetActivity As Activity

Returns the current activity if any. To avoid memory leaks, this should not be used by a **Reflector** that is a **Sub Process_Globals** object. To use this requires a knowledge of the structure of a B4A application.

💠 GetActivityBA As BA

Returns the Activity BA of the current activity. To use this requires a knowledge of the structure of a B4A application and an explanation is beyond the scope of this book. To avoid memory leaks this should not be used by a Reflector that is a **Sub Process_Globals** object.

💠 GetArray (indices() As Int) As Object

Returns the Object at the position(s) in an array specified by the contents of **indices**. **indices** - must be an integer array of the same rank as the Target array or an error will occur.

💠 GetB4AClass (component As String) As Class

Returns the Java Class for the specified B4A Activity, Service or Code module. To use this requires a knowledge of the structure of a B4A application.

💠 GetContext As Context

Returns the Context of the Process to which the Reflection object belongs. This is the Application object returned from Activity.getApplicationContext().

💠 GetField (field As String) As Object

Returns the value of the field of the current target. Protected and private fields may be accessed if allowed by any security manager which may be present. Target must be an instance of a Class, not a Class object.

❖ *GetField2 (fieldinfo As Field) As Object*

Returns the value of the field of the current target. Target must be an instance of a Class, not a Class object.

❖ *GetFieldInfo (field As String) As Field*

Finding a field from its string representation is expensive, so this method can be used to get the Field information object and save it for multiple accesses of the same field. Protected and private fields may be accessed if allowed by any security manager which may be present.

❖ *GetMethod (method As String, types() As String) As Method*

Finding a method from its string representation is expensive, so this method can be used to get the Method information object and save it for multiple invocations of the same method. The String array of type names is needed in order to find the correct variant of the method.

❖ *GetMostCurrent (component As String) As Object*

Returns the current instance for the specified B4A Activity or Service module. This might return **Null** if the Activity or Service is not instantiated. Note that Code modules do not have a current instance. To use this requires a knowledge of the structure of a B4A application.

❖ *GetProcessBA (component As String) As BA*

Returns the processBA instance for the specified B4A Activity or Service module. To use this requires a knowledge of the structure of a B4A application.

❖ *GetProxy (interfacenames() As String, b4asubname As String) As Proxy*

In Java, you can generate an interface at runtime and have it run a pre-compiled method. Many events in Android are handled by an interface that typically has an "onXxxxx" method that is called with some parameters relevant to the event. The interface is typically set on an object using that object's "setOnXxxxxListener" method.

This GetProxy method dynamically creates a proxy instance that implements one or more specified interfaces and which contains the code to call a specified B4A Sub when any of the interface methods are called.

Typically, this instance will implement one or more listeners and will then be assigned to an object instance using RunMethod4 and its setOnXxxxxListener method.

When a method of one of the specified interfaces is called, the proxy will call the specified B4A Sub passing the method name as a string and any arguments in an object array.

Note that interfaces declared as internal to a class will need a "$" instead of a "." as their final separator and all interfaces need to be fully qualified. e.g android.view.View$OnTouchListener.

The B4A Sub called must have the signature Sub WhateverName(method As String, anyargs() As Object) As Object.

❖ *GetPublicField (field As String) As Object*

Returns the value of the public field of the current target. This is more efficient than GetField but can only access public fields. Target must be an instance of a Class, not a Class object.

❖ *GetStaticField (classname As String, field As String) As Object*

Returns the value of the specified static field of the specified class. Protected and private fields may be accessed if allowed by any security manager which may be present. Static fields may also be accessed with GetField and an instance of the class.

🔮 InvokeMethod (instance As Object, method As Method, args() As Object) As Object

Invoke the provided Method on the provided object instance and return the result.

🔧 IsNull As Boolean [read only]

Returns `True` if the present value of Target is `Null`.

🔮 RunMethod (method As String) As Object

Runs the specified method on the current target. Protected and private methods may be accessed if allowed by any security manager which may be present.

🔮 RunMethod2 (method As String, arg1 As String, type1 As String) As Object

Runs the specified method on the current target passing it the argument provided. Protected and private methods may be accessed if allowed by any security manager which may be present.

🔮 RunMethod3 (method As String, arg1 As String, type1 As String, arg2 As String, type2 As String) As Object

Runs the specified method on the current object passing it the arguments provided. Protected and private methods may be accessed if allowed by any security manager which may be present.

🔮 RunMethod4 (method As String, args() As Object, types() As String) As Object

Runs the specified method on the current target passing it the arguments provided. Protected and private methods may be accessed if allowed by any security manager which may be present.
The String array of type names is needed in order to find the correct method because primitives passed in the Args array are boxed and so RunMethod cannot tell whether to look for a target method that accepts a primitive parameter type or a boxed primitive object type.

🔮 RunPublicmethod (Method As String, Args() As Object, types() As String) As Object

Runs the specified method on the current target passing it the arguments provided. This is more efficient that RunMethod4 but the method must be public.
The String array of type names is needed in order to find the correct method because primitives passed in the Args array are boxed and so RunMethod cannot tell whether to look for a target method that accepts a primitive parameter type or a boxed primitive object type.

🔮 RunStaticMethod (classname As String, method As String, args() As Object, types() As String) As Object

Runs the specified static method of the specified class passing it the arguments provided. Protected and private methods may be accessed if allowed by any security manager which may be present.
The String array of type names is needed in order to find the correct method because primitives passed in the Args array are boxed and so RunMethod cannot tell whether to look for a target method that accepts a primitive parameter type or a boxed primitive object type. For methods that take no parameters, `Null` may passed for args and types.

⚙️*SetArray (indices() As Int, value As String, type As String)*

Set the position(s) in an array specified by the contents of indices to the specified value. indices must be an integer array of the same rank as the Target array or an error will occur.

⚙️*SetArray2 (indices() As Int, value As Object)*

Set the position(s) in an array specified by the contents of indices to the specified value. indices must be an integer array of the same rank as the Target array or an error will occur.

⚙️*SetField (field As String, value As String, type As String)*

Sets the specified field of the current target to the value provided. Protected and private fields may be accessed if allowed by any security manager which may be present. Target must be an instance of a Class, not a Class object.

⚙️*SetField2 (field As String, value As Object)*

Sets the specified field of the current target to the value provided. Protected and private fields may be accessed if allowed by any security manager which may be present. Target must be an instance of a Class, not a Class object.

⚙️*SetField3 (fieldinfo As Field, value As String, type As String)*

Sets the specified field of the current target to the value provided. Target must be an instance of a Class, not a Class object.

⚙️*SetField4 (fieldinfo As Field, value As Object)*

Sets the specified field of the current target to the value provided. Target must be an instance of a Class, not a Class object.

⚙️*SetOnClickListener (sub As String)*

Target must be a View of some sort. In most cases, B4A will have already exposed this as a Click event. Sets the OnClickListener of the view to a Sub that must have a signature of Sub Whatever(viewtag As Object).

⚙️*SetOnCreateContextMenuListener (sub As String)*

Target must be a View of some sort. This is included for completeness of all the Listeners that class View supports. Sets the OnCreateContextMenuListener of the view to a Sub that must have a signature of Sub Whatever(viewtag As Object, menu As Object, menuinfo As Object)

⚙️*SetOnFocusListener (sub As String)*

Target must be a View of some sort. Sets the onFocusChangeListener of the view to a Sub that must have a signature of Sub Whatever(viewtag As Object, focus As Boolean).
You should make sure not to call DoEvents, Msgbox or any modal Dialog inside this event as it will fail in Android 4.0.3 and above.
It may also fail if Debug is paused in the event in Android 4.0.3 and above.

⚙️*SetOnKeyListener (sub As String)*

Target must be a View of some sort. Sets the onKeyListener of the view to a Sub that must have a signature of Sub Whatever(viewtag As Object, keycode As Int, keyevent As Object) As Boolean.
This Sub must return `True` if it wants to consume the event or `False` otherwise.

❧*SetOnLongClickListener (sub As String)*

Target must be a View of some sort. In most cases B4A will have already exposed this as a LongClick event. Sets the OnLongClickListener of the view to a Sub that must have a signature of Sub Whatever(viewtag As Object) As Boolean. This Sub must return `True` if it wants to consume the event or `False` otherwise.

❧*SetOnTouchListener (sub As String)*

Target must be a View of some sort. Sets the onTouchListener of the view to a Sub that must have a signature of Sub Whatever (viewtag As Object, action As Int, X As Float, Y As Float, motionevent As Object) As Boolean.

This Sub must return `True` if it wants to consume the event or `False` otherwise.

You should make sure not to call DoEvents, Msgbox or any modal Dialog inside this event as it will fail in Android 4.0.3 and above. If you want to do so, put the code in another sub and call this sub with CallSubDelayed.

It may also fail if Debug is paused in the event in Android 4.0.3 and above.

❧*SetPublicField (field As String, value As String, type As String)*

Sets the specified field of the current target to the value provided. This is more efficient than SetField but can only access public fields. Target must be an instance of a Class, not a Class object.

❧*SetPublicField2 (field As String, value As Object)*

Sets the specified field of the current target to the value provided. This is more efficient than SetField but can only access public fields. Target must be an instance of a Class, not a Class object.

❧*SetStaticField (classname As String, field As String, value As String, type As String)*

Sets the specified static field of the specified class to the value provided. Protected and private fields may be accessed if allowed by any security manager which may be present. Static fields may also be accessed with SetField and an instance of the class.

❧*SetStaticField2 (classname As String, field As String, value As Object)*

Sets the specified static field of the specified class to the value provided. Protected and private fields may be accessed if allowed by any security manager which may be present. Static fields may also be accessed with SetField and an instance of the class.

❧*Target As Object*

This field holds the object that is being reflected upon. The target object is assigned to this field where it can then be manipulated as required.

❧*TargetRank As Int()*

Returns an int array whose length is the number of dimensions of the array and whose contents are the length of the first element of each array dimension. A zero length integer array is returned if Target is not an array.

❧*ToString As String*

Returns the result of running the "toString()" method of the current object.

🏮 *TypeName As String [read only]*
Returns the name of the class of the current object.

🏮 *Version As Double [read only]*
Returns the version number of the library.

TabHostExtras Library

This library, created by WarWound, adds functionality to the TabHost (page 439) view.
For the library and a sample project, see here (http://bit.ly/16Bb09a).

getTabContentViewPadding (tabHost1 As TabHost) As RectWrapper
Gets the layout padding of tabHost1 TabContentView. Returns a Rect object containing pixel values.

getTabEnabled (tabHost1 As TabHost, index As Int) As Boolean
Get the Enabled state of TabIndicator #index in tabHost1.

getTabHeight (tabHost1 As TabHost) As Int
Get the height (in pixels) of the TabIndicators in tabHost1.

getTabHostPadding (tabHost1 As TabHost) As RectWrapper
Get the layout padding of tabHost1 container View. Returns a Rect object containing pixel values.

getTabTextSize (tabHost1 As TabHost) As Float
Get the text size (page 163) (in pixels) of all TabIndicators.

getTabVisibility (tabHost1 As TabHost, index As Int) As Boolean
Get the visibility of TabIndicators #index in tabHost1.

setTabContentViewPadding (tabHost1 As TabHost, left As Int, top As Int, right As Int, bottom As Int)
Set the layout padding (in dip) of tabHost1 TabContentView.

setTabEnabled (tabHost1 As TabHost, enabled As Boolean)
Enable or disable all TabIndicators in tabHost1.

setTabEnabled2 (tabHost1 As TabHost, enabled As Boolean, index As Int)
Enable or disable TabIndicator #index in tabHost1.

setTabGradientDrawable (tabHost1 As TabHost, orientation As String, color1 As Int, color2 As Int, cornerRadius As Float)
Set a `GradientDrawable` as the background on all TabIndicators in tabHost1. All four corner radii of the `GradientDrawable` are set to the value of cornerRadius (in pixels).

setTabGradientDrawable2 (tabHost1 As TabHost, orientation As String, color1 As Int, color2 As Int, cornerRadius As Float())

Set a `GradientDrawable` as the background on all TabIndicators in tabHost1. Corner radii of the `GradientDrawable` are set individually (in pixels) based upon the number of elements in the array cornerRadius:
1 element defines all corner radii
2 elements define corner radii in order top left and right, bottom left and right
4 elements define corner radii in order top-left, top-right, bottom-right, bottom-left

setTabHeight (tabHost1 As TabHost, tabHeight As Int)

Set the height (in pixels) of all TabIndicators in tabHost1.

setTabHostPadding (tabHost1 As TabHost, left As Int, top As Int, right As Int, bottom As Int)

Set the layout padding (in dip) of tabHost1 container View.

setTabTextColor (tabHost1 As TabHost, Color As Int)

Set the color to be used for all tab indicators text.
This color will be used for all tab indicators regardless of their selected state.

setTabTextColorStateList (tabHost1 As TabHost, ColorStateListName As String)

Set a ColorStateList to be used for the text color of all tab indicators.
The ColorStateList must be defined in XML in your application Objects/res/drawable folder.
Color for selected and not-selected tab state can be defined.

setTabTextSize (tabHost1 As TabHost, TextSize As Float)

Set the text size of all TabIndicators. TextSize is assumed to be in units of dip.

setTabTitle (tabHost1 As TabHost, Title As String, TabIndex As Int)

Set the Title text of TabIndicator #TabIndex in tabHost1.

setTabVisibility (tabHost1 As TabHost, visible As Boolean)

Set the visibility of all TabIndicators in tabHost1.

setTabVisibility2 (tabHost1 As TabHost, visible As Boolean, index As Int)

Set the visibility of TabIndicator #index in tabHost1.

Toggle Library

This library created by user XverhelstX allows you to do many useful things:
- Bluetooth: Toggle, Enable, Disable, Check.
- Airplane Mode: Toggle, Enable, Disable, Check.
- WiFi: Toggle, Enable, Disable, Check.

- GPS: Toggle, Enable, Disable, Check.
- DataConnection** (GPRS,...): Toggle, Enable, Disable, Check.
- RingerMode: Toggle, Enable, Disable. (Vibrate, Silent or Normal)
- Change Brightness
- Change Mediavolume.
- Reboot, GotoSleep, UserActivity, isScreenOn

To download the library, see here (http://bit.ly/1DyHyQC).

Index

The page numbers in the index refer to the printed and the PDF versions of this book. Readers of the Kindle and EPUB versions should use their search facility to find the actual text.

Lightning Source UK Ltd.
Milton Keynes UK
UKOW05n0712030118
315439UK00003B/28/P

9 781871 281323